The Writer's Handbook

Edited by

SYLVIA K. BURACK
Editor, The Writer

Publishers　　　　THE WRITER, INC.　　　　Boston

CONTENTS
PART I—BACKGROUND FOR WRITERS

PART II—HOW TO WRITE: TECHNIQUES

General Fiction

SPECIALIZED FICTION

NONFICTION: ARTICLES AND BOOKS

PART IV—WHERE TO SELL

THE WRITER'S HANDBOOK

BACKGROUND FOR WRITERS

1

TO BE A WRITER: WHAT DOES IT TAKE?

BY JOHN JAKES

YOU CAN answer the question two ways.

If you're an aspiring fiction writer, you might say something like, "It takes the ability to sense, imagine, and tell a strong story. It also takes talent for writing efficient dialogue that gives the illusion of reality and carries a lot of plot or characterization freight at the same time. Besides that, it takes good powers of description. . . ." You could spin out your answer to cover all the basic tools and techniques of the fiction writer's craft, and you would be right.

If you're an aspiring poet, you might mention meter and form first. A dramatist would think of structure and exposition. Those answers, too, would be right.

There's a second answer, though, equally correct but more fundamental. An answer that actually precedes the learning of technique, no matter what sort of writing you prefer.

By way of illustration, think about golf. I think about it a lot, because I love it, and I play badly. Obviously, good golf calls for certain skills. Strong, straight drives based on a good swing. Dependable putting. A keen eye for reading greens. Expert chipping to rescue your ball from a trap. But you can achieve none of that without certain broader fundamentals. Excellent hand-eye coordination and muscle memory (I don't have either one). Ability to concentrate. A liking for the game itself. All these underlie technique.

So, too, do certain attitudes underlie all the skills a writer must have. I call those attitudes states of being. During a professional career that spans thirty-seven years, I've thought about these states of being a lot. Added some, subtracted others. Finally distilled and described seven. I believe a writer must "be" all seven, even before taking the first steps toward technical mastery. Indeed, so crucial are these seven states of

3

being, I believe that if you lack them, you will never be a professional, only an eternal novice.

Each of the seven is simple to describe, but profound in its impact on your life. Here they are, then . . . the seven "states of being" that support a writing career.

1. BE SURE. Do you really want to pay the price? It isn't small. Are you willing to isolate yourself day after day, session after session, year after year, in order to learn your craft the only way you can—by writing?

There are much easier, more pleasant ways to pass the time, though few so rewarding intellectually and spiritually. But it's no sin to be honest and admit it if you'd rather garden, fish, or socialize with friends than go it alone as a writer, with no guarantee of success. If you aren't sure you're up to all that writing demands of a person, go no further.

2. BE DETERMINED. This is a re-statement of one of my "three P's" of a writing career—practice. You must have guessed by now that I believe many parts of the writing process (though not all) can be learned, just as golf can be learned. It's true. You may never be a Fuzzy Zoeller or a Nancy Lopez—there are few out-and-out champions in any field—but, with determination and practice, you can probably become at least a part-time professional. To do it, however, you must write and keep on writing, trying to improve all the time.

3. BE PATIENT. This equates with the second of my "three P's," persistence. The writing profession is not, thank God, the record business. Idols are neither born nor made on the strength of a single three-minute album cut. A more substantial body of work is required. Nor do many stars emerge in the writing field at eighteen (only to be forgotten six months later). Except for a very few, a solid writing career usually arrives later in life.

Also, you must remember that publishing, like any other art that is part industry, changes constantly. Editorial people change jobs. A house or publication that rejects you this year may, under a new editor, say yes the next. Failure to realize this can increase your impatience to the danger point . . . the point at which you say, "What's the use?"

We live in an age of instant gratification. You won't get it writing . . . except for the joy in the work itself.

4

4. BE OPEN. This is the last of my "three P's"—professionalism. By being open, I mean being willing and eager to have all the flaws in your work exposed, so that you can fix them. I mean being anxious to have a working partnership with an editor who admires your strengths but won't spare you criticism of your weaknesses.

Don't let the editor do all the work, though. You must want to find the weak places for yourself, before the editor sees them. It is this rather cold-blooded attitude that sets most money-earning writers apart from dabblers and those who would rather talk about being a writer than do what it takes to be one. "No pain, no gain," runners say. It's the same with writing. Unless you're open to tough criticism and willing to do something about it, you'll never go the distance.

5. BE CURIOUS. Read everything you can read. Read widely, not merely in your chosen field of writing. Spend as much time as you can with your mouth shut and your eyes and ears open. Don't strive for attention . . . strive to go unseen in a crowd, on the beach, at a party. Watch people. Watch the sky. Watch a baby's repertoire of expressions. Watch the way sun puts shadow on a wrinkled garment. Nothing should escape your notice. Everything eventually contributes to what you write, even though the way it contributes is totally unknown to anyone, including you.

6. BE SERIOUS. Give unstintingly of yourself when you write. The kind of effort NFL players casually refer to as "110 percent." There's something to it.

Once again, if you dabble . . . withhold part of your energy . . . refuse to commit your whole mind and heart to the work . . . that will be reflected in a lackluster creative product. Give your work the best you have to offer at the moment you do it. Give it a clear head, and a body that's fit and rested.

On the other hand, while you're taking the work seriously, don't take yourself seriously. I abhor the kind of writer who can't laugh at himself . . . who can't avoid pretentious pronouncements (probably to cover a raging insecurity) . . . who carries "the gift" like a royal scepter and never stops waving it about for others to see.

Too many writers unwittingly play what I call Immortality Roulette. They get involved in worrying about their own reputations. How will they be remembered in a hundred years? They grow desperate, sometimes almost maniacal about it. They write nasty letters to harsh critics—or at least talk about doing it. They are happy or sad depending on a few words from a total unknown (most reviewers). The result of all this is often compensation in the form of overweening self-importance.

The saddest cases are the most marginal . . . those very competent popular writers who probably will be largely forgotten, except by a few trivia scholars or aficionados, as time goes by. Since most of us can't answer questions about posterity—a Hemingway, acknowledged a genius in his own lifetime, is a rarity—just do the best you can. No one can ask more, and what more can you logically ask of yourself? Posterity will take care of itself, with or without you.

7. BE YOURSELF. Above all, let who you are, what you are, what you believe shine through every sentence you write, every piece you finish. I don't mean preach. Just be natural. The originality and power of Tolstoy's *War and Peace* do not lie in the fact that he was the first to write a mammoth novel about Imperial Russia facing Napoleon. I don't know whether he was first or not. I suspect so; it doesn't matter. What matters is that he was unique, a singular person, and his great novel emerged from what *he* had to say about his homeland and its people in wartime. One of my favorite statements about writing, encountered so long ago I can't even acknowledge the source, is this:

"True originality lies not in saying what has never been said, but in saying what you have to say."

So there you are. Seven "states of being" you must achieve before you start your work in order to master the specific tools of your craft. Again, if you honestly feel these requirements are too tough—simply not for you—no one will blame or criticize you. But if you say, "Yes, I will be a writer because I can be all of those things . . . I am all of those things . . . or I'm willing to try to become them," then I predict eventual success for you.

Not enormous wealth, mind you. Not a best seller every year. Not immortality—just the solid satisfaction of being a *writer.* It's a proud and ancient profession . . . and it's a great feeling to achieve even a little success in the business of entertaining and enlightening millions with your own words. It's a calling very much worth the price.

2

Don't Think: Write!

By Madeleine L'Engle

WHEN we write, for whom do we write? Or, as we would be more likely to ask, whom do we write for?

It sounds like an easy question to answer, and in some ways it is. But when it is applied to the matter of fiction, the logical answer—that we write for a specific audience—does not work. At least not for me.

Each year I teach at one or more writers workshops. I enjoy them for many reasons, not the least of which is the opportunity to meet other workshop leaders, often writers whose work I have long admired. Writing is a solitary profession, and a writers conference gives us a chance to get together. Another reason I enjoy the workshops is that I am forced to articulate what I have learned about the techniques of the craft of fiction writing; it is easy to get forgetful and sloppy. Having to explain imagery, simile, metaphor, point of view, is a way to continue to teach myself as well as the people who have come to the workshop.

At one workshop, I talked, as usual, about all the hard work that precedes the writing of fiction. Often there is research to be done. For my Time Trilogy I had to immerse myself in the new physics: first, Einstein's theories of relativity and Planck's quantum theory for *A Wrinkle in Time;* then cellular biology and particle physics for *A Wind in the Door;* and astrophysics and non-linear theories of time for *A Swiftly Tilting Planet.* For *The Love Letters* I had to learn a great deal more about seventeenth-century Portuguese history than I needed or wanted to know, so that the small amount needed for the book would be accurate. Before, during, and after research, the writer needs to be thinking constantly about the characters, and the direction in which the novel seems to be moving.

Does the story have the Aristotelian beginning, middle, and end? How do the events of the novel relate to me, personally, in my own journey through life? What are my own particular concerns at the time of writing, and how should they affect—or not affect—the story? When I actually sit down to write, I stop thinking. While I am writing, I am listening to the story; I am not listening to myself.

"But," a young woman in the class said in a horrified tone of voice, "my creative writing teacher says that we must keep the audience in mind at all times."

That is undoubtedly true for the scientist writing an article that is expected to be understood by people who have little or no scientific background. The writer will have to keep simplifying scientific language, explaining technical terms. Keeping the audience in mind is probably valuable for reporting in newspapers and magazines. The reporter is writing for the average reader; language should be neither so bland as to be insulting, nor so technical as to demand special knowledge.

As for lawyers, I assume they have each other in mind at all times as they write. Certainly they don't have most of us in mind. Their grandiosity appalls me. In a movie contract, I was asked to grant the right to my book to the producers, in perpetuity, throughout the universe. When I wrote in, "With the exception of Sagittarius and the Andromeda galaxy," it was accepted. Evidently the lawyers, who are writing to avoid litigation in a litigious world, did not anticipate a lawsuit from Sagittarius.

Of course I am being grossly unfair to many lawyers; I come from a family of fine lawyers. But the language used in a will or a contract is indeed a special language, and it is not aimed at the reader who enjoys stories, the reader of fiction.

Whom, then, does the writer of fiction write for? It is only a partial truth to say that I write for myself, out of my own need, asking, whether I realize it or not, the questions I am asking in my own life.

A truer answer is that I write for the book.

"But why do you write for children?" I am often asked.

And I answer truthfully that I don't. I haven't been a child for a long time, and if what I write doesn't appeal to me, at my age, it isn't likely to appeal to a child. I hope I will never lose the child within me, who has not lost her sense of wonder, of awe, of laughter. But I am not a child; I am a grown woman, learning about maturity as I move on in chronology.

A teacher, in introducing me to a class of seventh graders, said,

"Miss L'Engle has made it in the children's field, and she is now trying to break into the adult market."

I felt that I had better not explain to this teacher that I had no desire to break into the adult market and see my fiction in "adult bookstores." I am not interested in writing pornography. I did explain that my first several books were regular trade novels, which means that they were marketed for a general audience, not for children. And I explained that when I have a book that I think will be too difficult for a general audience, then we will market it as a juvenile book. It is a great mistake to think that children are not capable of understanding difficult concepts in science or philosophy.

A book that has a young protagonist will likely be marketed as a children's book, regardless of content. Since adolescents are usually more willing than their elders to ask difficult questions, and to accept the fact that the questions don't have nice, tidy answers but lead on to more difficult questions, approximately half of my books have young protagonists. But while I am writing, I am not thinking of any audience at all. I am not even thinking about myself. I am thinking about the book.

This does not imply anything esoteric. I do not pick up the pen and expect it to guide my hand, or put my fingers on the keyboard of the typewriter and expect the work to be done automatically. It is work. But it is focused work, and the focus is on the story, not on anything else.

An example of the kind of focus I mean is a good doctor. The good doctor listens to the patient, truly listens, to what the patient says, does not say, is afraid to say, to body language, to everything that may give a clue as to what is wrong. The good doctor is so fully focused on the patient that personal self-consciousness has vanished. Such focused listening does not make the doctor—or any of the rest of us—less ourselves. In fact, such focused listening makes us more ourselves.

The same thing is true in listening to a story as we write it. It does not make us any less writers, this strange fact that we do not think about writing as we are writing; it makes us more writers.

Then, of course, there is all the revising to be done. We do not always listen well. We do not always have our full attention on the story. Some scenes will need to be written and rewritten a dozen or more times before they work. We do have to revise with attention to infelicities of rhythm, flaw of syntax; there is, indeed, a great deal of conscious work

9

to be done. But still, the writer is paying attention to the work itself, not the potential audience. I have, it is true, toned down scenes when the decision has been made to market a book as a "young adult" novel, because I know that young adult novels are read as often by nine- and ten-year-olds as by young adults. But such revisions are done long after the story has been listened to as attentively as possible, and cannot mutilate or betray the intent or integrity of the story.

It would be very inhibiting for me to have to keep an audience in mind. It would take a large piece of my mind off the story as it is unfolding, and I want all of my mind to be where it belongs: on the writing.

Have I had an audience in mind while I have been writing this piece? Not particularly. I'm telling myself things I need to remember. Nobody but someone interested in the writing of fiction is going to want to read this, so I am also writing for people who share my own concerns.

So, gentle reader (the Victorians seems to assume that all readers are gentle), give yourself the pleasure of forgetting earnestly to remember your audience at all times, and give yourself the fun of plunging deeply into your story, and having your mind focused on that, and nothing else. If the story that comes from this way of writing is a better story than the forcedly audience-centered story (and I am convinced it will be), it will have a wider audience. And isn't that what we hope for?—to reach as many people as possible, because we believe that what the story has to say is worth saying.

3

EVERYTHING YOU NEED TO KNOW ABOUT WRITING SUCCESSFULLY— IN TEN MINUTES

BY STEPHEN KING

I. *The First Introduction*

THAT'S RIGHT. I know it sounds like an ad for some sleazy writers' school, but I really am going to tell you everything you need to pursue a successful and financially rewarding career writing fiction, and I really am going to do it in ten minutes, which is exactly how long it took me to learn. It will actually take you twenty minutes or so to read this essay, however, because I have to tell you a story, and then I have to write a *second* introduction. But these, I argue, should not count in the ten minutes.

II. *The Story, or, How Stephen King Learned to Write*

When I was a sophomore in high school, I did a sophomoric thing which got me in a pot of fairly hot water, as sophomoric didoes often do. I wrote and published a small satiric newspaper called *The Village Vomit*. In this little paper I lampooned a number of teachers at Lisbon (Maine) High School, where I was under instruction. These were not very gentle lampoons; they ranged from the scatological to the downright cruel.

Eventually, a copy of this little newspaper found its way into the hands of a faculty member, and since I had been unwise enough to put my name on it (a fault, some critics would argue, of which I have still not been entirely cured), I was brought into the office. The sophisticated satirist had by that time reverted to what he really was: a fourteen-year-old kid who was shaking in his boots and wondering if he was going to get a suspension . . . what we called "a three-day vacation" in those dim days of 1964.

I wasn't suspended. I was forced to make a number of apologies— they were warranted, but they still tasted like dog-dirt in my mouth—

11

and spent a week in detention hall. And the guidance counselor arranged what he no doubt thought of as a more constructive channel for my talents. This was a job—contingent upon the editor's approval—writing sports for the Lisbon *Enterprise,* a twelve-page weekly of the sort with which any small-town resident will be familiar. This editor was the man who taught me everything I know about writing in ten minutes. His name was John Gould—not the famed New England humorist or the novelist who wrote *The Greenleaf Fires,* but a relative of both, I believe.

He told me he needed a sports writer and we could "try each other out," if I wanted.

I told him I knew more about advanced algebra than I did sports.

Gould nodded and said, "You'll learn."

I said I would at least try to learn. Gould gave me a huge roll of yellow paper and promised me a wage of ½¢ per word. The first two pieces I wrote had to do with a high school basketball game in which a member of my school team broke the Lisbon High scoring record. One of these pieces was straight reportage. The second was a feature article.

I brought them to Gould the day after the game, so he'd have them for the paper, which came out Fridays. He read the straight piece, made two minor corrections, and spiked it. Then he started in on the feature piece with a large black pen and taught me all I ever needed to know about my craft. I wish I still had the piece—it deserves to be framed, editorial corrections and all—but I can remember pretty well how it looked when he had finished with it. Here's an example:

Last night, in the ~~well-loved~~
~~gymnasium of~~ Lisbon High School, partisans
and Jay Hills fans alike were stunned by
an athletic performance unequalled in school
history: Bob Ransom, ~~known as "Bullet" Bob~~
~~for both his size and accuracy,~~ scored
thirty-seven points. He did it with grace
and speed...and he did it with an odd courtesy
as well, committing only two personal fouls
in his ~~knight-like~~ quest for a record which
has eluded Lisbon ~~thinclads~~ *is basketball team* since 1953...

12

When Gould finished marking up my copy in the manner I have indicated above, he looked up and must have seen something on my face. I think *he* must have thought it was horror, but it was not: it was revelation.

"I only took out the bad parts, you know," he said. "Most of it's pretty good."

"I know," I said, meaning both things: yes, most of it was good, and yes, he had only taken out the bad parts. "I won't do it again."

"If that's true," he said, "you'll never have to work again. You can do *this* for a living." Then he threw back his head and laughed.

And he was right: I *am* doing this for a living, and as long as I can keep on, I don't expect ever to have to work again.

III. *The Second Introduction*

All of what follows has been said before. If you are interested enough in writing to be a purchaser of this magazine, you will have either heard or read all (or almost all) of it before. Thousands of writing courses are taught across the United States each year; seminars are convened; guest lecturers talk, then answer questions, then drink as many gin and tonics as their expense-fees will allow, and it all boils down to what follows.

I am going to tell you these things again because often people will only listen—really *listen*—to someone who makes a lot of money doing the thing he's talking about. This is sad but true. And I told you the story above not to make myself sound like a character out of a Horatio Alger novel but to make a point: I saw, I listened, and *I learned*. Until that day in John Gould's little office, I had been writing first drafts of stories which might run 2,500 words. The second drafts were apt to run 3,300 words. Following that day, my 2,500-word first drafts became 2,200-word second drafts. And two years after that, I sold the first one.

So here it is, with all the bark stripped off. It'll take ten minutes to read, and you can apply it right away . . . if you *listen*.

IV. *Everything You Need to Know About Writing Successfully*
1. *Be talented*

This, of course, is the killer. What is talent? I can hear someone shouting, and here we are, ready to get into a discussion right up there with "What is the meaning of life?" for weighty pronouncements and total uselessness. For the purposes of the beginning writer, talent may as well be defined as eventual success—publication and money. If you wrote something for which someone sent you a check, if you cashed the check and it didn't bounce, and if you then paid the light bill with the money, I consider you talented.

Now some of you are really hollering. Some of you are calling me one crass money-fixated creep. And some of you are calling me *bad* names. *Are you calling Harold Robbins talented?* someone in one of the Great English Departments of America is screeching. *V. C. Andrews? Theodore Dreiser? Or what about you, you dyslexic moron?*

Nonsense. Worse than nonsense, off the subject. We're not talking about good or bad here. I'm interested in telling you how to get your stuff published, not in critical judgments of who's good or bad. As a rule the critical judgments come after the check's been spent, anyway. I have my own opinions, but most times I keep them to myself. People who are published steadily and are paid for what they are writing may be either saints or trollops, but they are clearly reaching a great many someones who want what they have. Ergo, they are communicating. Ergo, they are talented. The biggest part of writing successfully is being talented, and in the context of marketing, the only bad writer is one who doesn't get paid. If you're not talented, you won't succeed. And if you're not succeeding, you should know when to quit.

When is that? I don't know. It's different for each writer. Not after six rejection slips, certainly, nor after sixty. But after six hundred? Maybe. After six thousand? My friend, after six thousand pinks, it's time you tried painting or possibly computer programming.

Further, almost every aspiring writer knows when he is getting warmer—you start getting little jotted notes on your rejection slips, or personal letters . . . maybe a commiserating phone call. It's lonely out there in the cold, but there *are* encouraging voices . . . unless there is nothing in your words which warrants encouragement. I think you owe it to yourself to skip as much of the self-illusion as possible. If your eyes are open, you'll know which way to go . . . or when to turn back.

2. *Be neat.*

Type. Double-space. Use a nice heavy white paper, never that erasable onion-skin stuff. If you've marked up your manuscript a lot, do another draft.

14

3. *Be self-critical*

If you *haven't* marked up your manuscript a lot, you did a lazy job. Only God gets things right the first time. Don't be a slob.

4. *Remove every extraneous word*

You want to get up on a soapbox and preach? Fine. Get one and try your local park. You want to write for money? Get to the point. And if you remove all the excess garbage and discover you can't find the point, tear up what you wrote and start all over again . . . or try something new.

5. *Never look at a reference book while doing a first draft*

You want to write a story? Fine. Put away your dictionary, your encyclopedias, your World Almanac, and your thesaurus. Better yet, throw your thesaurus into the wastebasket. The only things creepier than a thesaurus are those little paperbacks college students too lazy to read the assigned novels buy around exam time. Any word you have to hunt for in a thesaurus is the wrong word. There are no exceptions to this rule. You think you might have misspelled a word? O.K., so here is your choice: either look it up in the dictionary, thereby making sure you have it right—and breaking your train of thought and the writer's trance in the bargain—or just spell it phonetically and correct it later. Why not? Did you think it was going to go somewhere? And if you need to know the largest city in Brazil and you find you don't have it in your head, why not write in Miami, or Cleveland? You can check it . . . but *later*. When you sit down to write, *write*. Don't do anything else except go to the bathroom, and only do that if it absolutely cannot be put off.

6. *Know the markets*

Only a dimwit would send a story about giant vampire bats surrounding a high school to *McCall's*. Only a dimwit would send a tender story about a mother and daughter making up their differences on Christmas Eve to *Playboy* . . . but people do it all the time. I'm not exaggerating; I have seen such stories in the slush piles of the actual magazines. If you write a good story, why send it out in an ignorant fashion? Would you send your kid out in a snowstorm dressed in Bermuda shorts and a tank top? If you like science fiction, read the magazines. If you want to write confessions stories, read the magazines. And so on. It isn't just a matter of knowing what's right for the present story; you can begin to catch on, after awhile, to overall rhythms, editorial likes and dislikes, a magazine's entire slant. Sometimes your reading can influence the *next story,* and create a sale.

7. *Write to entertain*
Does this mean you can't write "serious fiction"? It does not. Somewhere along the line pernicious critics have invested the American reading and writing public with the idea that entertaining fiction and serious ideas do not overlap. This would have surprised Charles Dickens, not to mention Jane Austen, John Steinbeck, William Faulkner, Bernard Malamud, and hundreds of others. But your serious ideas must always serve your story, not the other way around. I repeat: if you want to preach, get a soapbox.

8. *Ask yourself frequently, "Am I having fun?"*
The answer needn't always be yes. But if it's always no, it's time for a new project or a new career.

9. *How to evaluate criticism*
Show your piece to a number of people—ten, let us say. Listen carefully to what they tell you. Smile and nod a lot. Then review what was said very carefully. If your critics are all telling you the same thing about some facet of your story—a plot twist that doesn't work, a character who rings false, stilted narrative, or half a dozen other possibles—change that facet. It doesn't matter if you really liked that twist or that character; if a lot of people are telling you something is wrong with your piece, it *is.* If seven or eight of them are hitting on that same thing, I'd still suggest changing it. But if everyone—or even most everyone—is criticizing something different, you can safely disregard what all of them say.

10. *Observe all rules for proper submission*
Return postage, self-addressed envelope, all of that.

11. *An agent? Forget it. For now*
Agents get 10% of monies earned by their clients. 10% of nothing is nothing. Agents also have to pay the rent. Beginning writers do not

contribute to that or any other necessity of life. Flog your stories around yourself. If you've done a novel, send around query letters to publishers, one by one, and follow up with sample chapters and/or the manuscript complete. And remember Stephen King's First Rule of Writers and Agents, learned by bitter personal experience: You don't need one until you're making enough for someone to steal . . . and if you're making that much, you'll be able to take your pick of good agents.

12. *If it's bad, kill it*

When it comes to people, mercy killing is against the law. When it comes to fiction, it *is* the law.

That's everything you need to know. And if you listened, you can write everything and anything you want. Now I believe I will wish you a pleasant day and sign off.

My ten minutes are up.

4

WHEN YOU WRITE ABOUT PEOPLE YOU KNOW

BY WINIFRED MADISON

WHENEVER MY LONG-TIME FRIEND, Stephen, comes to town, once a year or so, we go to our favorite Greek restaurant and in a dimly lit corner catch up on each other's lives. Stephen—fiftyish, a physicist and pianist, a cosmopolitan man—is someone I treasure as a friend. The last time we met we began talking casually about what we had been doing since our previous meeting, but by the time the *moussaka* came, I sensed something was troubling him. After an uneasy pause, he leaned forward and in a low voice recounted some recent events in his life. I listened with compassion and disbelief at his appalling revelations, yet my wicked writer's mind was already projecting his dilemma into a novel. (This behavior may be regrettable, but that's how writers are much of the time.)

As we left the restaurant, Stephen said, "Of course, you must keep all this confidential. You will, won't you?"

"Of course, Stephen," I answered quickly, aware of how harmful it would be to him and his family if word about what he told me got around. "But you wouldn't mind if I wrote a novel about it, would you? Maybe a novella? Maybe a little short story?"

At this he looked so stricken, I had to reassure him at once.

"Just joking," I said.

And so another good story was lost.

This is the writer's dilemma. The standard advice is to WRITE WHAT YOU KNOW. How easy it sounds! What do you know better than your own life, that of your parents, your siblings, your friends, and even an enemy or two? How tempting it is to put these ready-made characters into fiction. But do you have the right to do so?

The obvious answer is to use the story but disguise the characters. So conceivably I could use Stephen's story, making him a beery truck driver. The events of his life might be as moving and tragic as Stephen's. But what makes Stephen's story memorable is his unique personality and the atmosphere in which he lives. Too much would be lost in transforming him into another personality. He is perfect for the role and nobody else will do.

Since first novels are frequently autobiographical, it is not surprising for a new writer to vent his frustrations on members of his family. Parents are particularly vulnerable targets, and there is little they can do about it. Parent-bashing is a shameful, immature sport, and it can boomerang, making readers dislike the writer. Friends and relatives of a writer deserve sympathy, for many of them live in fear that one day the brat-genius will reveal them, not only warts and all, but with a few extra blemishes they never had.

Yet exceptions occur. Countless writers have used members of their families, making remarkable characters of them, and somehow it is all right. A kind of truth shines through. Perhaps *right intention* is what counts.

Another hazard of writing is that sometimes a reader may accuse a writer he knows of describing him in a certain character when nothing of the sort was intended. Or he may fail to recognize himself even when described with acute accuracy. For example, a certain writer of juvenile fiction used her sister as the model for a disagreeable spinster librarian and then, feeling guilty about it, lovingly dedicated the book to her sister. To her amazement, her sister thanked her effusively, thinking she had been the model for the attractive young heroine!

Conclusion: You never know.

Writers can sometimes find practical solutions. For a long time I wanted to write about those two weeks each summer when, as a child, I went with my family to a beautiful Rhode Island beach where my aunts, uncles, and cousins gathered. But I could not write about my family. For one thing, there was no plot, and if I made one up, someone would surely say it couldn't have happened. Then I'd be criticized for not saying enough or putting too much in. So I made up another family for my children's book, *The Party That Lasted All Summer,* but in essence this story was a tribute to the pleasure of being with my family in a magic place in the sweetness of summer.

Still, the question has not yet been answered. What do you do when a perfect story is handed to you but is meant to be kept confidential? Here are some choices:

1. You are ethical and do not give away confidences, and that is that. You work on something else.

2. You decide to wait until the person who has revealed this remarkable story has died, but that might take a long, long time. Or the excitement of it may fizzle out in the waiting. Besides, this attitude is just too grim for most writers.

3. You can be tough, state a few platitudes about art and truth, and go ahead and write, no matter what happens. However, if you do, there is the possibility that you will never be able to go home again.

Perhaps the most shocking and celebrated case is that of Truman Capote, the brilliant and highly respected author, who became the darling of the social set. Prominent persons who had befriended him made the mistake of confiding in him, and he told all their secrets. For this unpardonable offense, he was dropped, cut off, and left sadly alone.

4. If you are haunted by a remarkable but confidential story, there may be one other way to handle it safely. Chances are that such a story contains a universal truth that appeals to you. It is also possible that you may feel you have been *chosen* to receive such a story, and you would be ungrateful to reject it outright. There you are, caught between opposing options.

What you can do is wait. Whether you think of your brain as a computer or a compost heap, it's a useful place to store information and then wait to see what happens. Possibly your impulse to write that particular story will disappear, in which case you can work on something else. Or in time that confidence may combine with your writer's imagination and, when it is ready, the story will rise to the surface of your consciousness, and you may then begin to write without fear or guilt.

5

THE WRITER'S COMPASS

BY WILLIAM STAFFORD

WE WRITERS try to help each other, sometimes. But there is a catch in this generosity: if you begin to rely only on what others say about your work, you may become like a compass that listens to the hunches of the pilot. You may be good company, but you are useless as a compass.

So, when we meet, say at a conference or workshop, we look each other in the eye with an estimate hovering between us. We know that our kind of activity has some complexities not evident to others, and we wonder if those complexities will be recognized in any interchanges about our craft.

For instance, we know that our work is insufficiently judged if much time is given over to assessing the topics of our work. We know that a critic who discusses whether we talk enough about Nicaragua or not, or human rights or not, or the general topic of enlightenment or not, is missing the mark.

We know that there is something supremely important in the creating of a story or poem that all too often will escape the attention of an outsider trying to assess it. And for those outsiders, general readers, even critics, it may not be devastating if they talk at large: the main point is that such readers be affected, no matter what they ascribe our influence to. But for us writers it would be fatal to be misled by superficial assessments; and in fact one of the main hazards for a "successful" writer may be the insidious intrusion of those outer assessments on the inner process that allows us writers to find our way.

We must have an inner guide that allows us to rove forward through the most immediate impulses that come our way. For us, our whole lives are our research; and caught up by our best subjects we become not just an expert, but the only expert there is. We have to be the sole authority for what comes toward us, where we are, with our unique angle of seeing.

21

Though this inner guide is difficult to talk about, it is supremely important; and it is different from that urge for money, publication, recognition, that is glibly identified as the bait for a writer. You can get lost, following the whims of the public. And the public can give you recognition, or withhold it; but afterward you must set forth again, alone.

If the most significant writing comes from this inner guidance, who will help you find it? Would it be someone who interposes the considerations of the marketplace while the delicate time of discovery is going on? Would it be the person who puts primary emphasis on your imitation of forms and strategies?

Let me plead, not for ignoring advice from wherever it comes, but for allowing in your own life the freedom to pay attention to your feelings while finding your way through language. Besides that audience out there in the world, there is some kind of ideal audience that you have accumulated within your individual consciousness—within your conscience!; and abiding guidance is your compass, one that constitutes what you have to contribute to discourse with others.

Moving back and forth from the inner to the outer world might be the way to your best writing.

Into the unknown you must plunge, carrying your compass. It points at something more distant than any local guidance. You must make "mistakes"; that is, you must explore what has not been mapped out for you. Those mistakes come from somewhere; they are disguised reports from a country so real that no one has found it. When you study that country, shivers run down your back—what a wilderness out there! What splendid stories flicker among those shadows! You could wander forever.

Odd words keep occurring to you—pauses, side glances—mysterious signals. What hidden prejudice brought that next word into your mind? If you hastily retreat to an expected progression, what shadowy terrain might you be neglecting? What revelations might you miss by any "expert" weaving of another well-crafted poem or story?

Like Don Quixote on his unorthodox steed you must loosen the reins and go blundering into adventures that await any traveler in this multi-level world that we too often make familiar by our careful threading of its marked routes between accustomed places.

And like Don Quixote you must expect some disasters. You must

22

write your bad poems and stories; for to write carefully as you rove forward is to guarantee that you will not find the unknown, the risky, the surprising.

Art is an activity in which the actual feel of doing it must be your guide; hence the need for confidence, courage, independence. And hence the need for guardedness about learning too well the craft of doing it.

By following after money, publication, and recognition, you might risk what happened to the John Cheever character who in like manner "damaged, you might say, the ear's innermost chamber where we hear the heavy noise of the dragon's tail moving over the dead leaves."

6

THE MAKER'S EYE: REVISING YOUR OWN MANUSCRIPTS

BY DONALD M. MURRAY

WHEN THE BEGINNING WRITER completes his first draft, he usually reads it through to correct typographical errors and considers the job of writing done. When the professional writer completes his first draft, he usually feels he is at the start of the writing process. Now that he has a draft he can begin writing.

That difference in attitude is the difference between amateur and professional, inexperience and experience, journeyman and craftsman. Most productive writers share the feeling that the first draft—and most of those which follow—is an opportunity to discover what they have to say and how they can best say it.

Detachment and caring

To produce a progression of drafts, each of which says more and says it better, the writer has to develop a special reading skill. In school we are taught to read what is on the page. We try to comprehend what the author has said, what he meant, and what are the implications of his words.

The writer of such drafts must be his own best enemy. He must accept the criticism of others and be suspicious of it; he must accept the praise of others and be even more suspicious of it. He cannot depend on others. He must detach himself from his own page so that he can apply both his caring and his craft to his own work.

Detachment is not easy. Science fiction writer Ray Bradbury supposedly puts each manuscript away for a year and then rereads it as a stranger. Not many writers can afford the time to do this. We must read when our judgment may be at its worst, when we are close to the euphoric moment of creation.

The writer must also learn to protect himself from his own ego, when it takes the form of uncritical pride or uncritical self-destruction.

Just as dangerous as the protective writer is the despairing one, who thinks everything he does is terrible, dreadful, awful. If he is to publish, he must save what is effective on his page while he cuts away what doesn't work. The writer must hear and respect his own voice.

Remember how each craftsman you have seen—the carpenter eyeing the level of a shelf, the mechanic listening to the motor—takes the instinctive step back. This is what the writer has to do when he reads his own work. "The writer must survey his work critically, coolly, and as though he were a stranger to it," says children's book writer Eleanor Estes. "He must be willing to prune, expertly and hard-heartedly. At the end of each revision, a manuscript may look like a battered old hive, worked over, torn apart, pinned together, added to, deleted from, words changed and words changed back. Yet the book must maintain its original freshness and spontaneity."

It is far easier for most beginning writers to understand the need for rereading and rewriting than it is to understand how to go about it. The publishing writer doesn't necessarily break down the various stages of rewriting and editing, he just goes ahead and does it. One of our most prolific fiction writers, Anthony Burgess, says, "I might revise a page twenty times." Short story and children's writer Roald Dahl states, "By the time I'm nearing the end of a story, the first part will have been reread and altered and corrected at least 150 times. . . . Good writing is essentially rewriting. I am positive of this."

There is nothing virtuous in the rewriting process. It is simply an essential condition of life for most writers. There are writers who do very little rewriting, mostly because they have the capacity and experience to create and review a large number of invisible drafts in their minds before they get to the page. And many writers perform all of the tasks of revision simultaneously, page by page, rather than draft by draft. But it is still possible to break down the process of rereading one's own work into the sequence most published writers follow and which the beginning writer should follow as he studies his own page.

Seven elements

Many writers at first just scan their manuscript, reading as quickly as possible for problems of subject and form. In this way, they stand back from the more technical details of language so they can spot any weaknesses in content or in organization. When the writer reads his manuscript, he is usually looking for seven elements.

25

The first is *subject*. Do you have anything to say? If you are lucky, you will find that indeed you do have something to say, perhaps a little more than you expected. If the subject is not clear, or if it is not yet limited or defined enough for you to handle, don't go on. What you have to say is always more important than how you say it.

The next point to check is *audience*. It is true that you should write primarily for yourself, in the sense that you should be true to yourself. But the aim of writing is communication, not just self-expression. You should, in reading your piece, ask yourself if there is an audience for what you have written, if anyone will need or enjoy what you have to say.

Form should then be considered after audience. Form, or genre, is the vehicle that will carry what you have to say to your audience, and it should grow out of your subject. If you have a character, your subject may grow into a short story, a magazine profile, a novel, a biography, or a play. It depends on what you have to say and to whom you wish to say it. When you reread your own manuscript, you must ask yourself if the form is suitable, if it works, and if it will carry your meaning to your reader.

Once you have the appropriate form, look at the *structure,* the order of what you have to say. Every good piece of writing is built on a solid framework of logic or argument or narrative or motivation; it is a line which runs through the entire piece of writing and holds it together. If you read your own manuscript and cannot spot this essential thread, stop writing until you have found something to hold your writing together.

The manuscript which has order must also have *development*. Each part of it must be built in a way that will prepare the reader for the next part. Description, documentation, action, dialogue, metaphor—these and many other devices flesh out the skeleton so that the reader will be able to understand what is written. How much development? That's like asking how much lipstick or how much garlic. It depends on the woman or on the casserole. This is the question that the writer will be answering as he reads his piece of writing through from beginning to end, and answering it will lead him to the sixth element.

The writer must be sure of his *dimensions*. This means that there should be something more than structure and development, that there should be a pleasing proportion among all of the parts. You cannot decide on a dimension without seeing all of the parts of writing together. You have to examine each section of the writing in its relationship to all of the other sections.

Finally, the writer has to listen for *tone*. Any piece of writing is held together by that invisible force, the writer's voice. Tone is his style, tone is all that is on the page and off the page, tone is grace, wit, anger—the spirit which drives a piece of writing forward. Look back to those manuscripts you most admire, and you will discover that there is a coherent tone, an authoritative voice holding the whole thing together.

Potentialities and alternatives

When the writer feels that he has a draft which has subject, audience, form, structure, development, dimension, and tone, then he is ready to begin the careful process of line-by-line editing. Each line, each word has to be right.

Now the writer reads his own copy with infinite care. He often reads aloud, calling on his ear's experience with language. Does this sound right—or this? He reads and listens and revises, back and forth from eye to page to ear to page. I find I must do this careful editing at short runs, fifteen or twenty minutes, or I become too kind with myself.

Slowly, the writer moves from word to word, looking through the word to see the subject. Good writing is, in a sense, invisible. It should enable the reader to see the subject, not the writer. Every word should be true—true to what the writer has to say. And each word must be precise in its relation to the words that have gone before and the words that will follow.

This sounds tedious, but it isn't. Making something right is immensely satisfying, and the writer who once was lost in a swamp of potentialities now has the chance to work with the most technical skills of language. And even in the process of the most careful editing, there is the joy of language. Words have double meanings, even triple and quadruple meanings. Each word has its own tone, its opportunity for connotation and denotation and nuance. And when you connect words, there is always the chance of the sudden insight, the unexpected clarification.

The maker's eye moves back and forth from word to phrase to sentence to paragraph to sentence to phrase to word. He looks at his sentences for variety and balance in form and structure, and at the interior of the paragraph for coherence, unity and emphasis. He plays with figurative language, decides to repeat or not, to create a parallelism for emphasis. He works over his copy until he achieves a manuscript which appears effortless to the reader.

27

I learned something about this process when I first wore bifocals. I thought that when I was editing I was working line by line. But I discovered that I had to order reading (or, in my case, editing) glasses, even though the bottom section of my bifocals have a greater expanse of glass than ordinary glasses. While I am editing, my eyes are unconsciously flicking back and forth across the whole page, or back to another page, or forward to another page. The limited bifocal view through the lower half of my glasses is not enough. Each line must be seen in its relationship to every other line.

When does this process end? Most writers agree with the great Russian novelist Tolstoy, who said, "I scarcely ever reread my published writings, but if by chance I come across a page, it always strikes me: all this must be rewritten; this is how I should have written it."

The maker's eye is never satisfied, for he knows that each word he writes is tentative. To the writer, writing is alive, something that is full of potential and alternative, something that can grow beyond its own dream. The writer reads to discover what he has said—and then to say it better.

A piece of writing is never finished. It is delivered to a deadline, torn out of the typewriter on demand, sent off with a sense of frustration and incompleteness. Just as the writer knows he must stop avoiding writing and write, he also knows he must send his manuscript off to be published, although it is not quite right yet—if only he had another couple of days, just another run at it, perhaps. . . .

7

A Time to Backburner

By Dorothy Warner Trebilcock

IT IS BORROWED from Ecclesiastes, though, of course, backburnering—relegating soups and stews to simmer on a back burner of the old wood stoves—is not mentioned there. But the idea is the same: "To everything there is a season and a time to every purpose under the heaven. A time to be born and a time to die. A time to keep and a time to cast away." And now a more mundane thought: *A time to backburner.*

It seems to me that this concept applies to the writing process even though writers live with a continuing admonition, a constant pressure to write every day. We are advised never to let the sun set on a single day when we have not written at least something. There is a sort of doctrine of perpetual motion applied to those whose calling is to the pen, the typewriter, and, more recently, to the word processor. But is this concept of an occupation treadmill completely realistic?

Are there not times when there is neither the time nor the inclination to put words on paper, to submit same, to keep one's self in a continuous soul-to-notebook realm of activity?

This is not the same as a writer's block. It is not the absence of ideas or being faced with a blank sheet of paper. It is not sitting down at the typewriter with a case of the blahs where formerly there was a delicious sense of anticipation to Start Writing. The former is a void in which nothing happens. It is not the same as a need to backburner *when something is not yet ready to happen.*

For example, a writer friend has just completed a book about a particular time in her childhood. The book did not come in a sudden rush of insight. She spent months—years, I suspect—sorting, remembering, contemplating, thinking about it. Her story could not have been written in a state of every day spontaneous combustion. Backburnering was an absolute requisite.

Another friend is fascinated with pre-fire London. She collects all kinds of material about it, and she has been to London to do first-hand research on the subject. But right now, she has a job that requires most of her time and all of her creative energies. She, too, is mulling and piecing together and putting it all on the you-know-what. At the present time, I am consciously backburnering at least two stories and several poems-in-progress. One story concerns a young man who has come to the end of his ability to function in society. I remember him as a solemn-faced little boy who never seemed to do anything right but who must have longed to be accepted for himself, right or wrong. I want so much to write about him, but first I have to grapple with how to approach the writing. From whose vantage point should the story be told? Can I take my personal bias out of the situation in order to make it a meaningful story with, as Thomas Wolfe said, "facts selected and arranged and charged with purpose." I really don't know. It will have to wait on the back burner.

On the brighter side, there are beavers. Quite unexpectedly one day at the car repair shop, I met a woman who proceeded to tell me about the beavers that were coming every night and chewing down young trees in her yard bordering a river. "We can hear them chewing," she said. "Sometimes they actually keep us awake!"

"But are you sure it's beavers?" I asked her incredulously, my mind already spinning from the back burner to a red hot burner at the front of the stove. "It would make a wonderful story for children. Or for any age, I suppose," I told her. "But we really need to know for sure that it's the beavers at work."

"Oh, it's the beavers all right," she said. "I'm planning to get pictures, and when I have them, I'll call you and you can come to see the whole thing for yourself."

Good idea, I agreed. And so the beaver story is on the back burner for lack of the actual facts to make it complete. Yet I can just hear those trees snapping as my informant and her husband are jolted awake. I can see the little tree-choppers making their way back to the river, a night's work done. While the story is simmering, I will do some research on beavers and continue to chuckle at the possibilities. As far as poetry is concerned, I would have to guess that most poets keep many of their poems on the back burner simply because they (the poems) refuse to be forced. Midnight oil does not produce the right word or phrase. Determination seems to scare off the muse. Then, suddenly, in the midst of pulling clothes from the dryer or while standing in front of a beautiful display of broccoli at the supermarket, it comes. And if you haven't forgotten a pencil, you can add your inspirational words to the grocery list.

We all know that we can't wait until the muse taps us on the shoulder and whispers ever so gently, "It's inspiration time." But I don't like the idea of being made to feel guilty if I don't chain myself to the typewriter for x number of hours per day until a specified number of pages have been written. Some things are simply not *writeable*. Yet. And it seems to me that we ought to accept this, not as evasive, but as a legitimate link in the creative process.

Do keep lists. Record experiences and feelings in a journal. But once in awhile, just *be*. Remember the sting of sand on a winter beach. Savor the sight of gold and scarlet hills etched on an October sky. Remember the look of summer stars over your boat moored on waves that are singing *a cappella* in the moonlight. Notice I didn't say, "with a notebook in hand." Backburner the memory, the thoughts that mariners of old studied those same stars and found their way to far-off lands never dreamed of by those who stayed at home and, dutifully, wrote every single day, no doubt.

Keep some of your moments apart without a need to catalogue them immediately and commit them to paper. They may well improve with time to simmer slowly on the back burners of your heart and mind.

8

How to Find Time to Write When You Don't Have Time to Write

By Sue Grafton

EARLY in my writing career, I managed to turn out three novels, one right after another, while I was married, raising two children, keeping house, and working full time as a medical secretary. Those novels were never published and netted me not one red cent, but the work was essential. Writing those three books prepared the way for the fourth book, which *was* published and got me launched as a professional writer. Ironically, now that I'm a "full-time" writer with the entire work day at my disposal, I'm often guilty of getting less work done. Even after twenty-five years at it, there are days when I find myself feeling overwhelmed . . . far less effective and efficient than I know I could be. Lately, I've been scrutinizing my own practices, trying to determine the techniques I use to help me produce more consistently. The underlying challenge, always, is finding the time to write and sticking to it.

Extracting writing time from the fabric of everyday life is a struggle for many of us. Even people who are technically free to write during an eight-hour day often can't "get around" to it. Each day seems to bring some crisis that requires our immediate attention. Always, there's the sense that tomorrow, for sure, we'll get down to work. We're uncomfortably aware that time is passing and the job isn't getting done, but it's hard to know where to start. How can you fit writing into a schedule that already *feels* as if it's filled to capacity? If you find yourself lamenting that you "never have time to write," here are some suggestions about how to view the problem and, better yet, how to go about solving it.

First of all, accept the fact that you may never have the "leisure" (real or imaginary) to sit down and complete your novel without interruption. Chances are you won't be able to quit your job, abandon your family, and retire to a writers' colony for six weeks of uninterrupted writing every year. And even if you could, that six weeks probably wouldn't get the job done. To be productive, we have to make writing part of our daily lives. The problem is that we view writing as a luxury, something special to allow ourselves as soon as we've taken care of the countless nagging duties that seem to come first. Well, I've got news for you. It really works the other way. Once you put writing first, the rest of your life will fall into place.

Successful writers disagree about how much time is needed per stint—ranging anywhere from one to ten hours. I feel that two hours is ideal and not impossible to find in your own busy day. One of the first tricks is to make sure you use precious writing time for *writing* and not for the myriad other chores associated with the work.

"Writing" is made up of a number of sub-categories, each of which needs tending to. A professional doesn't just sit down and magically begin to create prose. The process is more complex than that, and each phase requires our attention. Analyzing the process and breaking it down into its components will help you understand which jobs can be tucked into the corners and crevices of your day. In addition to actual composition, writing encompasses the following:

Planning—initiating projects and setting up a working strategy for each.

Research—which includes clipping and filing.

Outlining—once the material has been gathered.

Marketing—which includes query letters, manuscript typing, Xeroxing, trips to the post office.

And finally, *follow-up* for manuscripts in submission.

All of these things take time, but they won't take *all* of your time, and they shouldn't take your best time. These are clerical details that can be dispatched in odd moments during the day. Delegate as much as possible. Hire someone for these jobs if you can. Have a teen-ager come in one day a week to clip and file. Ask your spouse to drop off a manuscript at the post office on his or her way to work. Check research books out of the library while the kids are at story hour. Use time waiting for a dental appointment or dead time at the laundromat to jot down ideas and get them organized. Take index cards with you every place.

Now take a good look at your day. Feel as if you're already swamped from dawn to dark? Here are some options:

1. *Stay up an hour later each night.* At night, the phone doesn't ring and the family is asleep. You'll have fewer distractions and no excuses. You won't drop dead if you cut your sleep by an hour. The time spent creatively on projects important to you will *give* you energy. Eventually, you can think about stretching that one hour to two, but initially, stick to a manageable change and incorporate it thoroughly into your new schedule before tackling more. I used to write from ten at night until midnight or one a.m., and I still find those hours best for certain kinds of work.

2. *Get up an hour earlier,* before the family wakes. Again, shaving an hour from your sleep will do you no harm, and it will give you the necessary time to establish the habit of daily writing. Anthony Trollope, one of my favorite writers, worked for most of his adult life as a postal clerk, on the job from eight until five every day. His solution was to get up at five a.m. and write 250 words every fifteen minutes till eight—three hours. If he finished a book before the time to go to work, he started a new project at once. In his lifetime, he turned out forty-six full-length books, most of them while he earned a living in another capacity.

3. *If you're employed outside your home, try working en route.* British crime writer Michael Gilbert wrote 23 novels . . . all while riding the train to his work as a solicitor. He used the 50-minute transit time to produce 2 to 2½ pages a day, 12 to 15 pages a week. Buses, trains, commuter flights can all represent productive time for you. Use those periods for writing, while you're inaccessible to the rest of the world.

4. *What about your lunch hour?* Do you go out to lunch every day to "escape" the tensions and pressures of the job? Why not stay at your desk, creating a temporary haven in your own head? Pack a brown bag lunch. It's cheaper, among other things, and if you limit yourself to fruit and raw vegetables, you can get thin while you pile up the pages!

5. *Look at your week nights.* See if there's a way to snag one for yourself. You'd make the time if you decided to take an adult education class. Invent a course for yourself, called "Writing My Novel At Long Last" and spend three hours a week in the public library. I heard about a writer who finished a book just this way, working only on Tuesday nights.

6. *Weekends generally have free time tucked into them.* Try Saturday afternoons when the kids are off at the movies, or Sunday mornings when everyone else sleeps late.

7. *Revamp your current leisure time.* Your schedule probably contains hidden hours that you could easily convert to writing time. Television is the biggest time-waster, but I've also realized that reading the daily paper from front to back takes ninety minutes out of my day! For a while, I convinced myself that I needed to be informed on "current events," but the truth is that I was avoiding my desk, squandering an hour and a half that I desperately needed to complete a manuscript. I was feeling pressured, when all the while, the time was sitting right there in front of me . . . literally. Recently, too, I took a good look at my social calendar. I realized that a dinner party for six was requiring, in effect, two full days of activity . . . time I now devote to my work. I still have friends. I just cut my entertainment plans by a third.

Now.

Once you identify and set aside those newly found hours, it's a matter of tailoring the work to suit the time available. This can be done in four simple steps:

1. Make a list of everything you'd like to write . . . a novel, a short story, a film script, a book review for the local paper, that travel article you outlined during your last trip.

2. Choose three. If you only have one item on your agenda, how lucky you are! If you have more than three projects on your list, keep the remaining projects on a subsidiary list to draw on as you complete the items on your primary list and send them out into the marketplace. I generally like to have one book-length project (my long-term goal) and two smaller projects (an article, a short story . . . short-term goals) on my list.

3. Arrange items on the list in the order of their true priority. Be tough about this. For instance, you might have a short story possibility, an idea you've been toying with for years, but when you come right down to it, it might not seem important enough (or fully developed enough) to place among the top three on your list. My first priority is

always the detective novel I'm writing currently. I work on that when I'm at my freshest, saving the smaller projects for the period after my first energy peaks. Having several projects in the works simultaneously is good for you psychologically. If you get stuck on one, you can try the next. As you finish each project, the feeling of accomplishment will spur you to renewed effort on those that remain. In addition, by supplying yourself with a steady stream of new projects, you'll keep your interest level high.

4. Once you select the three projects you want to work on, break the writing down into small, manageable units. A novel isn't completed at one sitting. Mine are written two pages at a time over a period of six to eight months. Assign yourself a set number of pages . . . 1 or 2 . . . and then meet your own quota from day to day. Once you've completed two pages, you can let yourself off the hook, moving on to the next task. By doing a limited amount of work on a number of projects, you're more likely to keep all three moving forward. Don't burden yourself with more than you can really handle. Assigning yourself ten pages a day sounds good on the surface, but you'll soon feel so overwhelmed that you'll start avoiding the work and won't get *anything* done. Remember, it's persistence that counts, the steady hammering away at the writing from day to day, day *after* day, that produces the most consistent work and the greatest quantity of it.

Essentially, then, all you need to do is this:

> Analyze the task.
> Scrutinize your schedule.
> Tailor the work to fit.

I have one final suggestion, a practice that's boosted my productivity by 50%. Start each day with a brief meditation . . . five minutes of mental quiet in which you visualize yourself actually sitting at your desk, accomplishing the writing you've assigned yourself. Affirm to yourself that you'll have a good, productive day, that you'll have high energy, solid concentration, imagination, and enthusiasm for the work coming up. Use these positive messages to block out your anxieties, the self-doubt, the fear of failure that in fact comprise procrastination. Five minutes of quiet will reinforce your new determination and will help you make the dream of writing real.

9

THE WRITER'S EYE

BY RANDALL SILVIS

A PART of every successful writer is, and must be, amoral. Detached. Unfeeling. As nonjudgmental as a tape recorder or camera. It is this capacity to stare at pain or ugliness without flinching, at beauty without swooning, at flattery and truth without succumbing to the lure of either, which provides the mortar, the observable details, to strengthen a story and make it a cohesive unit. This capacity I call the writer's eye.

As a child, I was and still am fascinated by the peaks and valleys of people's lives. I was blessed—or cursed—with what was often referred to as "morbid curiosity." At the scene of a funeral, I would be the one trying to inch a bit closer to the coffin, one ear turned to the dry intonations droning from the minister; the other to the papery rustle of leaves overhead. I would take note of how the mourners were standing, where they held their hands, if there were any clouds in the sky, who wept and who did not even pretend to weep, which shoes were most brilliantly shined, the color of the casket, the scent of smoke from someone's backyard barbecue, a killdeer whistling in the distance.

This is how I would remember and record the day, the event. In the details themselves, unbiased, unvarnished and pure, was every nuance of emotion such a tragedy produced. The same held true for weddings and baptisms, for joyous moments as well as sad. Almost instinctively I seemed to know that every abstraction had an observable form: To remark that my neighbor, a tired and lonely man, was drunk again, said nothing; to say that he was standing by the side of the road, motionless but for his gentle, oblivious swaying even as the cars zipped by and blasted their horns at him, his head down, eyes half-closed, hands shoved deep in his pockets as he sang a mumbled "Meet Me Tonight in Dreamland," said it all.

The writer's eye discriminates. It does not and cannot record every detail in a particular scene, only the most telling ones. It is microscopic in focus, telescopic in intent. If, for example, you wish to depict a woman who is trying to look poised despite her nervousness, does it deepen the depiction to say that she wears a two-carat diamond ring on her left hand? Probably not. But if she is shown sitting very straight, knees and feet together, a pleasant smile on her lips as her right hand unconsciously and repeatedly pulls at and twists the diamond ring on her left? These details are in and of themselves emotionally pallid, but in sum, they add to a colorful, revealing whole. In such a description, the word *nervous* need never be uttered. Yet the conclusion is inescapable, and all the more acute because the reader has not been informed of the woman's uneasiness but has witnessed it for himself.

In my novel *Excelsior* (Henry Holt, October, 1987), one of the most important scenes is a moment of closeness between an inept father and his six-year-old son. The scene takes place in a YMCA locker room minutes after the father accidentally knocked the terrified boy, who cannot swim, into the pool. Bloomhardt, the father, despises himself for his own incompetence, and believes that his son does, too. But during a rare moment of openness, six-year-old Timmy admits *his* feelings of frustration and failure. At this point, it would have been quick and easy to state simply that Bloomhardt was relieved, grateful that his son did not despise him, and was filled with a fervent, though awkward, desire to reassure the boy. Instead, I chose to show his state of mind as evidenced in observable details:

> Bloomhardt blinked, his eyes warm with tears. He leaned sideways and kissed his son's damp head. . . . He faced his open locker again, reached for a sock and pulled it on. He smiled to himself.

Bloomhardt's actions are elemental and, on their own, nearly empty of emotional value. But in the context of this passage and in relation to the man's and boy's characters as defined prior to this scene, these details are all that are needed to show the beginnings of a mutual tenderness, trust, and love.

The writer's eye is not merely one sense, but every power of observation the writer possesses. It not only sees, but also smells, tastes, feels, and hears. It also senses which details will paint the brightest picture, which will hint at an unseen quality, which will allow the reader to see beneath the surface of a character to the ice and fire of emotion within.

Think of each phrase of description, each detail, as a dot of color on a Seurat landscape. Individually, each dot is meaningless, it reveals nothing, neither laughter nor sorrow. But if you choose your dots carefully and arrange them on the canvas in their proper places, you might, with luck and practice, compose a scene to take the breath away.

10

SHOULD YOU KEEP A DIARY?

BY MARYANNE RAPHAEL

AFTER KEEPING A JOURNAL almost constantly for twenty-five years, I'm convinced that a diary can benefit writers in any field. A diary helps you to begin writing. Write regularly in your journal, and you will write easily and naturally. Soon your diary will become a confidant to whom you can entrust intimate secrets without interruptions or criticism.

In a diary, you write about life as you live it, as if you were telling a story to a friend; in a notebook, you jot down notes for future reference. Like many other writers, I use one book for both purposes.

If you can, write every day, before you're too tired to make an entry. Describe your experience before your memory changes it. Let each entry reflect the immediacy of your life.

Make diary entries spontaneous and conversational. Describe a scene. Record events, travel notes, and dialogue. Once on a Greyhound bus, I overheard a fascinating conversation between two teen-age girls who had dated men in motorcycle gangs. I recorded it in my diary word for word and used it in a novel with almost no editing.

A journal must be small enough to fit into your purse, pocket, or briefcase. Take it everywhere—the doctor's office, the bank, on a plane. Keep it next to your bed at night. You never know when inspiration will strike; a forgotten insight can be a lost opportunity. Record dreams as soon as you wake up; they can teach you about yourself and enrich your writing.

The journal helps you learn to use facts, quotes, anecdotes, and impressions. Make lists of characters, titles, themes, plots, people you've loved, your worst fears, places you have lived or visited, books you hope to read or write.

Read published journals for glimpses of ordinary moments in the lives of famous people and extraordinary moments in the lives of ordinary people. Experiment with various writing styles, and choose what works best. Don't worry about grammar, punctuation, or spelling. Let your writing reflect *you*.

Include letters, stories from family members, descriptions of your children, and other items of interest. Immortalize your love affairs in your diary.

Diary writing is the most private of all writing. Include your innermost thoughts, no matter how silly, selfish, or strange. Each time you write about an experience, examine your emotions. Explore and declare who you are and what you believe. Once you understand yourself, you will be better able to create believable characters and plots.

Your diary helps you understand life. You can experience angers, fears, and depressions as you reread your writing.

A diary aids memory. When I reread journals I wrote twenty years ago, I feel as if another person had written them. I read about old friends, and places that were once home for me, and often must read five or six pages before I can recall them clearly. Often there is little similarity between what I remember and what actually happened. But both versions have meaning for me as a writer.

Sharpen all your senses. In a restaurant, describe sensually in writing what you eat, including the aromas, textures, ambiance, and your reactions. One day when you need a restaurant scene, you can draw on this entry in your diary.

The journal is a key to the past and offers a glimpse into the meaning of life. Make your diary entries so real that when you read them over, you feel as if you've stepped into a time machine. Experience again those passionate goodbyes, hear that orchestra play, feel the ocean breeze on your face. These sensations will help you make your characters come to life. Pack enough meaningful details onto your pages to create realistic characters and plots.

You'll learn to enjoy the process of creating and not just the end product. You'll begin to love writing as much as you love having written. Your journal will become an invaluable resource for each new writing project. It will furnish ideas and inspiration for both fiction and nonfiction, and cure or prevent writer's block. Just writing in your diary can get your creative juices flowing. And the diary helps you remember what it was like to be you at different stages in your life. The theme is always personal, but you also describe your significant relationships as well as casual acquaintances. If you look deep enough into yourself, using all your senses to describe your world, your writing will become universal, touching everybody's truth.

Your diary can be a work of art in itself. You may even decide to publish it. Anaïs Nin published diaries that she had written between the ages of 11 and 73. In one journal, she wrote, "We write to create a world in which we can live, to heighten our awareness of life, to lure and enchant and console others, to serenade our loves . . . and to transcend our life."

She advised writers, "Don't generalize in your diary. Don't intellectualize. Write what you see, what you hear, what you feel."

Keeping a diary can be a powerful course in writing, and you may produce a tool that will help you all your life.

11

Notes on Carpentry and Craft

By Joanna Higgins

CARPENTRY—a magical craft akin to alchemy. At least it has seemed so to me, but then I'm someone who can drive a nail in straight maybe fifty percent of the time. When something in the house needs doing, my first thought is to call a carpenter friend who just might be between jobs. As a writer, though, I've learned the next best thing is to offer to help.

What I get in return—besides a fine new window, say—is the kind of soul-strengthening exercise writers seek at writers conferences. And each time I look at that window, I know that craft—any craft—is not a matter of arcane magic but quite mundane know-how combined with perseverance and humility.

This happened recently when our neighbor, an excellent carpenter, came over to replace a sliding glass door no longer weather-worthy.

Ninety degrees at noon and the treeline underwater-green in the humidity, but Clyde, in work boots, heavy jeans, and workshirt, didn't comment on the heat as he set out his tools, nor on the fact that our work area faced south, and it would soon be much hotter. And there was no transition, it seemed, from the preparatory stage to the next—taking out the glass panels of the old door and then ripping out the old jambs, rotting top, and aluminum sill. He didn't pause until the first problem surfaced. A rotting sill board. We looked at it. Conferred. Part of it could be salvaged, but part of it had to go. He measured. Decided. Go. All of it.

"See if there's something in the barn," he said. "Or I might have something down at the house." The nearest lumber yard is twenty miles away. Apart from that, it's country practice to make do with what you've tucked away somewhere.

I found a length of 4×6, left over from another job, that would work just fine. A sense of small triumph, then, but it took until three to get it in place. The sky in the west was storm-blue; the wind had picked up,

43

but Clyde, concentrating on confusing instructions, grumbling a bit yet superbly intent, ignored the murky light; the gnats; the possibility of a rain-soaked living room. What isn't here yet, isn't here. Keep going! Keep working! And he did—neither rushing, nor throwing down tools when things went against him; but, at the worst moments, whistling. When the new frame was finally in after a lot of shimming, he held his level against a jamb and said, "Boy. That's so close it's not even funny."

But it was—to me, lightheaded with fatigue. And so was the way he ignored the heat. And refused to get mad, though at four in the afternoon we were still just beginning. Analogies to the writing process came to mind—all at once, it seemed, but I suspect the unconscious must have been engaged in its own carpentry while the usually noisy conscious mind was lulled by the rhythms of physical effort.

1. A job will always take much longer than you think.

2. Unanticipated problems will always come up, especially when working on an older house. (Revisions!)

3. Always save stuff. You never know when it'll come in handy—and it always will. (Your journal as storage barn for things seen, felt, tasted, smelled, touched, heard.)

4. A good craftsman isn't afraid to improvise, in fact, he may have more fun improvising than rigidly following directions and plans. Don't be afraid to use those memory scraps. Try things. They might not work, but then again they might—really well.

5. The mess isn't important in the beginning. Let the sawdust lie. Let the flies zoom around the open living room for now. Kick bits of wood to the side, and *just keep working*. Don't be a fuss-budget on first drafts. Revel in the rough-draft mess. It means that important, necessary work is getting done, with the pleasures of leisurely fussing and polishing and finishing still ahead.

6. The buzzing gnats are an insignificant nuisance. When one of them gets in your eye, well, you have to stop a minute and get it out the best you can. Clyde used a blue farmer's handkerchief. Then he got back to work. Just expect them to be there—those tiny furies of doubt and anxiety and whining self-judgment.

7. Problems have solutions; some just take longer to find. It's a matter of having faith in your skills. What is faith but perseverance? And perseverance?—humility. That ability to come back again and again, often after periods of "rest," to a piece of work. Only inex-

perienced and probably not-very-good carpenters get mad and throw tools, expecting something to "fall into place" right away. In a writer, such self-defeating arrogance can only lead to erratic work habits, mental tool-tossing, brooding self-pity, and—worst of all—giving up.

The word "journeyman"—a skilled worker who practices a trade—has bearing here. The word derives from an early definition of *journey,* which meant the distance traveled in a day, as well as the work accomplished in a day—the latter usage still found in certain crafts. I like the word for its implications: skilled work, *and* movement toward completion through daily, incremental and cumulative stages, or "journeys." A carpenter measures, cuts, pounds in nails, drills, inserts, chisels, caulks, plumbs—small actions creating, over time, a fine whole. So, too, a writer fastens words one to another day after day. And good craftsmen, I suspect, love each day's "journey" as much as the arrival—if not more so.

When we broke off work that day, the job was far from finished; the window far from the glossy ideal portrayed in the brochure, but Clyde had the next day's starting point all lined up and sounded eager to begin. Oh, more problems to come, I knew, and snags, and the inevitable imperfections and lapses we might have to accept finally, but it was good to stand there in the twilight and just look at what we'd done so far. Happy enough to be *on the way.*

12

CONSISTENT VERSUS
VENTURESOME WRITERS

BY JOANNE GREENBERG

DOES A WRITER deliberately decide to be consistent or venturesome in his work, or is the decision part of his personality that reflects itself in his writing? I would like to explore both sides.

A consistent writer stakes out a subject or approach and stays with it from book to book. Readers know what they are getting when they pick up one of his works. There is comfort in this for readers; near surprises will come in plot twist but not in subject matter or approach. Louis Auchincloss is consistent; so is Louis L'Amour, although he has written books on other subjects in other styles. Kurt Vonnegut is consistent. So is Flannery O'Connor. Since *The Drifters,* so is Michener. Hemingway for all his changes in background was more consistent than Steinbeck, who wrote historical novels, comedies, romances, epics, in many different emotional climates and on different intellectual planes.

Like Steinbeck, venturesome writers become restless when faced with limits. They won't or can't stay on subject or style or point of vantage, consistent in pace or stance. John Williams has written a classic "western" *(Butcher's Crossing),* an academic novel in traditional style, but he won the National Book Award for a historical novel in the form of letters to and from Octavius, Augustus Caesar. Ray Bradbury is venturesome. So are Gore Vidal and Norman Mailer and Truman Capote. So am I.

You can see by the writers I listed in both categories that I am not comparing talent or style. My favorite writers come from both camps. There are advantages to each and drawbacks, strengths with each and weaknesses, glory and besetting sin.

For consistent writers, the commercial questions are easier. There is a readership, a "market," to which they address themselves and with which, from book to book, they can become more comfortable. Classification may limit them somewhat, but it is greatly to their advantage because they become associated with a mood, a flavor, which is identifiable. Readers will go to those writers when they want that mood. [This, of course, occasionally backfires. I was once very ill, and my husband, thinking to give me the healing laughter of a fine comic writer, got me one of Peter DeVries' books. Unfortunately, it was *Blood of the Lamb*, a shattering account of his child's death from leukemia. It nearly did me in.] Publishers and agents are comfortable with consistent writers. Their own competence in marketing can be displayed and readers respond with increased sales. Sure things.

The besetting sin for the consistent writer is, of course, repetition. Zane Grey, the ultimate in consistency, ended by writing the same book again and again. His Swedish translator, whom I met in 1976, spoke feelingly of *Riders of the Purple Sage*. Having read this book on his own, he was so enthusiastic that he contracted to do Grey's complete corpus. "It was two books later when I realized what I had done— twenty-six more translations, and all of them minute variations on *Riders of the Purple Sage!* I suffered for the next three years for my mistake."

But study Grey: He endures as few of us will. Lasting fame seems more likely to be granted to the consistent than the venturesome writer. There seems to be a need for a critical mass, a certain volume of work to assure reputation, even if only one or two books continue to be read. The books that are read only by scholars need to be neatly classifiable—in a word, consistent.

Venturesome writers pay for their courage (perhaps it is only restlessness), but they have more fun. "I never know what you are going to come up with next!" my agent complains. "I never know what you are going to come up with next!" a reader exults.

Relatively few readers do exult, however, and critics often seem to be comparing any new work with the one before, to its detriment. "If only she'd write another book like *I Never Promised You a Rose Garden,* or *In This Sign,* or *The King's Persons.*" Sometimes readers feel a sense of betrayal because the writer's switch in subject or approach has been into an area they cannot follow. "I liked you until all of a sudden you went religious on me." Two of my cousins protested that about my story collection *High Crimes and Misdemeanors.* My religious subject matter did not come all of a sudden; the writing about it did. They felt deceived in some way; I let them down. Except out of personal love, I

47

suspect they would not read my work thereafter. Once bitten . . . I have often felt the same way. I love Mary Renault, but only as a historical novelist. I read her World War II novel yearning for the first person account of high adventure in Homeric Greece or in Alexander's Macedonia.

Venturesome writers seem less likely to endure over time, and we are a present drag to our agents and publishers. Our besetting sin is that in covering all the bases, we may be sacrificing depth for novelty. Our strength is that we keep our careers interesting longer. I think we also provide something valuable to literature in general. Avant-garde writers are usually consistent—radical in style, but consistent. So, venturesome writers provide a link between what is avant-garde and what is seen as conventional. Their work bridges what few people presently read and what many will read in ten or fifteen years. They also test and extend the limits of the forms they work in. Because they are not wedded to one form or approach, they are often the ones whose work readies the public for the avant-garde writer. More people saw and loved Thornton Wilder's *The Skin of Our Teeth* than read James Joyce's *Ulysses*. Wilder was venturesome, Joyce avant-garde and consistent (after his more conventional warm-up—*Dubliners* and *Portrait of the Artist*). I believe that Wilder helped people to approach Joyce and appreciate him.

If a writer looks at his style—his way of approaching a story, his stance (the distance he stands from the characters and events he is portraying), and his subject (who and what he cares about) as part of himself, he is more likely to be consistent: My style is me, my writing is me. If a writer looks at himself as the teller of the story, and his style as being at the service of the characters or the plot, he is more likely to be venturesome. Each of these ways is valid, but if you are a consistent writer who is in trouble with a piece of work, perhaps your character or plot is calling for a change, a night out, some new approach. If you are venturesome and your work seems to have lost some of its flavor, you may need to go back and deepen the mine a little.

How To Write: Techniques

Fiction

13

WRITE THE STORY YOU WANT TO TELL

BY SUSAN ISAACS

SO THERE I WAS, at a "Meet the Author" luncheon in Detroit, my speech about how I became a writer finished, the question-and-answer segment concluded, when this ferociously determined woman with shoulder pads bulldozed a couple of innocent bystanders, came up beside me and announced: "Susan, you give me *such* confidence!" I smiled and began work on a modest thank you, but she cut me off: "If *you* can do it, anybody can."

Condescending? Sure. But also correct. If I could do it, so could she . . . or, if not, her neighbor . . . or you.

Of course, any literate person can write, but writing that *lives* is a gift; the earth is not teeming with billions of potential novelists, waiting only for time and a typewriter. Writing is a talent you're either born with or have acquired by the time you're eight or nine years old. Where does the gift come from? I don't know. How do you know if you have it? Only one way: you write.

This takes enormous courage. We all have successful writer dreams: exchanging bon mots with Johnny Carson, delivering our Nobel address. You will always be great in these dreams, but let me tell you: The reality of actually writing will wake you up. Nothing I've written is as clever, brilliant (or as well received) as my original conception of it. Deep down I think we all sense this disparity, this abyss between our dreams and our talents, so actually sitting down and writing an entire novel takes guts.

I used to think: Who am *I* to be a writer? Writers don't wear makeup. And they're gaunt, haunted-looking, like Virginia Woolf or Joyce Carol Oates or Joan Didion. Or else, writers are incessantly witty, urbane— even glamorous. Well, all that is nonsense, pure stereotype. A writer can look like Christie Brinkley or a troll. As for sophistication, a writer is not necessarily someone who can get a good table at Elaine's. In fact,

49

life in the fast lane probably does more to destroy talent than nurture it; look at F. Scott Fitzgerald, Truman Capote. Further, a writer is not someone who touts his or her genius or vulnerability. Nor is he or she someone who goes from writer's conference to writer's conference, year after year, working over the same fifteen pages of exquisitely refined prose.

A writer can be *anyone*—pretty or not, a sophisticate or a creep. As for writing, like making chicken soup or making love, it is an idiosyncratic act. There is no one right way to do it. I can only tell you how I do it.

Writing is a job, and I go to work every morning: nine o'clock, five days a week. I quit about noon when I'm working on a novel (creating a universe being somewhat fatiguing), although I might edit the two or three pages I've written the rest of the day, or go to the library: What did most women do about birth control in 1940? How did the OSS screen potential agents?

(Writing a screenplay is less taxing, and by the time production rolls around I am so familiar with my characters that I can, on occasion, write whole scenes on the set while electricians drag cables over my sneakers and the grips look over my shoulder and critique my dialogue.)

But back to the beginning writer. When I decided to start my first novel, which was to be *Compromising Positions,* I thought about taking a fiction workshop. Lucky for me, I couldn't get a baby-sitter at the time the New School's best course was being offered. So instead I bought a copy of John Braine's *Writing A Novel.*

Like the Montessori method of tying a shoelace, the book broke a complicated task into a lot of idiot steps, so that the job didn't seem overwhelming. *Make an outline of no more than four pages*: When I began all I knew was I had a housewife-detective who lived on Long Island. When I finished, I not only knew who'd done it, I knew where, how, and why. In writing those few pages, putting down ideas that had probably been whizzing around my unconscious for months or years, I discovered that my heroine, Judith Singer, and the homicide lieutenant were soulmates, while her husband . . . Well, you get the point. *Draw up a list of characters*: I did, and suddenly Judith's best friend, an ex-Southern belle with an earthy sense of humor, jumped up and winked at me. The victim? I considered who most deserved to die: a periodontist.

You know that old platitude: *write about what you know.* Well, it's not a bad idea. You can use what you know—computers, mahjongg, Harlem, or parakeets—either as the core of the novel or as a background. And write about what you care about. I care about people, character. For me, writing a novel is fashioning an intimate biography.

In *Compromising Positions,* I used my home, suburban Long Island, as the setting, and bestowed my then-job, housewife, on my heroine. In *Close Relations,* I drew on Brooklyn and Queens, the world I grew up in, the world of New York City ethnics. I also took my (brief) experience as a political speech-writer, as well as my passion for New York Democratic politics and gave them to Marcia Green. In *Almost Paradise,* I wrote about show business (this was before I became a screenwriter) and celebrity. Wasn't that writing about what I didn't know? Well, in America show business *is* everybody's business. And celebrity? I took my own minor exposure to it, my twelve-city book tour for *Close Relations,* and puffed it up: being on a TV talk show; being recognized by an effusive reader in the ladies' room; having mere acquaintances feel my sex life—to say nothing of my tax return—is their property.

By the time it came to writing *Shining Through,* I was secure enough in my proficiency as a novelist, in my imaginative ability, to write about what I didn't know: speaking German, being a spy in World War II. But what I *did* know was what it's like to look at the rich and powerful through the eyes of someone who was neither. Linda Voss, my heroine, like me, started as an outsider. Like Linda, I worked as a secretary and knew what it was like to be thought of as something more than a typewriter—but less than a human being. (Later when Linda became a spy, her "cover" was a cook. Listen, I was still writing about what I know. I was a housewife. I know from pot roast. I just transferred it to Germany and made it sauerbraten.)

In other words, in *Shining Through,* I was writing about *people.* I was writing about love—real and unrequited—and passion, honor, deceit, friendship, patriotism, courage, terror. In other words, having lived for over forty years, I *was* writing about what I knew.

Another suggestion: *write for yourself.* I was among the blessed. I never went to a writers' conference, never took a fiction workshop. I learned to write for *me,* not for a teacher, a critic, an editor or even that amorphous, intimidating mass, the "audience." I never allowed myself to worry: What will my mother think? The minute you write to please someone, or not to offend someone, or to take big bucks, or to be taken seriously, you're gazing outward, not inward, and you're doomed to lose sight of what is unique and true in you.

So then, what does it take to be a novelist? Well, a gift for writing. A willingness to sit alone in a room for one or three or ten years, telling yourself a story. Then you must be able to *become your toughest critic*. Ask yourself the blunt questions: What is there about this protagonist that would make someone else besides me, the creator, care about his or her fate? What propels the novel, what will drive the reader to turn the page? This may be the most difficult task of all. With all four of my novels, there were days I was embarrassed—no, mortified—at the drivel I was passing off as fiction; and there were days that I was jolted by the force of my own brilliance. You will discover, after many readings, that the truth lies somewhere in that broad range in between.

If you want to write, expect criticism, some of it personal. If you write about sex, someone will inevitably tell you that you have a dirty mind. If you are a woman and you write about something other than glitz or, on the other hand, quiet, domestic lives, you run the risk of being criticized for *chutzpah* or naiveté. ("Serious" American female novelists are almost all experts at literary petit point; the big canvas is left to the men with their broad strokes.) Don't be afraid of what They say. *Write*. Don't write the story you think they want to listen to. Write the story you want to tell.

I know, it seems overwhelming. But then again maybe that nagging thought—if *she* can do it, I can too—is really a good, honest gut feeling about your own talent. Do you think it's worth taking the chance to discover the truth?

❙ 14

THE READER AS PARTNER

BY TONY HILLERMAN

SOMETIME VERY EARLY in my efforts to make a living as a writer, I noticed an odd little fact, trivial but useful: People just back from seeing the Rocky Mountains didn't describe the Front Range. They told me about the clump of mountain iris they'd seen blooming through the edge of a dwindling snowbank. Witnesses of a train wreck I interviewed when I was a reporter would describe the women's clothing scattered along the right-of-way and ignore the big picture. The fellow drinking beer after watching the rodeo would talk about the sounds the bulls made coming out the gate—not the derring-do of the champion rider.

I noticed my own brain worked that way, too: It would store a scattering of details in full color and with every stitch showing, but the general scene would be vague and ill-defined. I presumed that this was the way run-of-the-mill men and women remembered things, and thus, it would be useful for writers in the process of converting a scene that exists in our minds into words that would recreate it in the imagination of those who read what we write.

I doubt if there is anything new or original about this thinking or this tactic. Selecting significant details to cause the reader to focus attention exactly where it's wanted was being done with quill pen on papyrus and probably before. Except for those dilettantes of the "art for art's sake" school, every writer is engaged in a joint venture every time he writes. He looks at what's behind his own forehead and translates it into words. At the other end of the crosscut saw, the reader drinks in those words and tries to transmute them back into images.

It's a partnership. We work at it. So does the reader.

But we're getting paid for it, in money, fame (if we're lucky), and in the fun of controlling the process. The reader expects a different reward for the cash and time he or she invests. Even so, that reader is a working member of the team.

53

I always write with some clear notions about those for whom I write. They are, for example, a little more intelligent than I am and have a bit better education. They have good imaginations. They enjoy suspense. They are impatient. They are middle-aged. They are busy. They know very little about the specific subject I'm writing about. They are interested in it only if I can provoke that interest.

Given that, how should I go about my business? For example, how should I describe in physical terms this benign character I am about to introduce in chapter three? Not much, probably, if that character is to be important to the plot, and the reader is to come to know him from repeated meetings. But quite a bit if said character takes the stage only briefly.

Why this odd inversion? Because my intelligent, well-educated, middle-aged, imaginative reader knows from personal experience what various sorts of people look like. Therefore, if you use a character a lot, the reader paints his own portrait. For example, as far as I can remember, I have never given more than the vaguest descriptions of either Joe Leaphorn or Jim Chee, the two Navajo tribal policemen who are often the protagonists in my mystery novels. Yet scores of readers have described them to me. Tall and short, big and little, plump and lean, handsome and homely. The reader's imagination creates the character from his or her own experience, making the policeman look exactly the way he should look. Why should the writer argue with that? Why should the person who is investing money and time in reading my story be denied his role in the creative process?

Minor characters, I think, need more description. The reader is likely to see them only briefly through the eyes of the protagonist. He should be as curious about minor characters as is the viewpoint character— looking for the spot of gravy on the necktie, the nervous twitch at the corner of the eye, the dark roots of the bleached blonde hair, the scar tissue on the left cheek. Our reader won't see this minor actor enough to fit him into any personal mold.

Sometimes, of course, the writer must exercise more control over the image the reader would create. The story line may demand that the reader know the character is burly, has an artificial hand, and that his eyes tend to water if he stands too long reading the sympathy cards in the Hallmark shop. Otherwise, I count on the reader to perform his half of the task with no interference from me. I think he enjoys it more.

This notion of the reader as partner in a game of imagination affects how I write in many other ways. For example, there's that hard-to-define something that I think of as "mood." It exists in my mind as I write a scene. Sometimes it is merely the mental state of the viewpoint character through whose eyes whatever is happening is seen. But it can be more than that, or even different from that. For example, I may need to send signals to the reader that it is time for nervous anxiety, while the protagonist is still happily remembering that there's nothing left to worry about.

I tend to take on the mood of the scene—writing with lower lip gripped between my teeth when doom is impending, writing with a grin when all is well in chapter nine. I want the reader to join me in this mood. And here I'm on shaky ground. I simply have no way of knowing if my tactics work.

They involve engaging the reader's senses. I interrupt the dialogue or the action to show the reader through the eyes of the protagonist the dust on the windowsill, the grime on the windowpane, the tumbleweeds blowing across the yard, the broken gate creaking in the wind, the spider scurrying toward the center of its web, the stuffed weasel in its frozen leap toward the cowering quail in the taxidermy display. I have the reader notice the odors of old age, of decay, and of air breathed too often in a closed and claustrophobic room. I have him hear the sort of vague sounds that intrude into tired, tense silences. These are the sorts of signals my senses are open to when I am in this certain mood. If they don't contribute to causing it, at least they reflect it. Perhaps the same will be true for the reader.

Another mood. Another set of sensory signals. Take satisfaction-contentment-happiness (what my Navajo characters might call "hozro"). There's the smell of rain in the air (remember, I write mostly about a landscape where rain is all rare and a joyful blessing), the aroma of brewing coffee, the promising voice of distant thunder, the sound of birds, the long view through slanting sunlight of sage and buffalo grass, and the mountains on the horizon, a sense of beauty with room enough and time enough to enjoy it, and the good feeling of fresh-baked bread under the fingertips.

Unless some psychologist can come up with a universal catalogue of which objects/smells/sounds are connected in the mind of Average

Human with which mood, neither you nor I will ever know how effective this technique is. My conversations with those who have read my work suggest that sometimes I can make it work, and sometimes I fail. But I am working at it, using my only laboratory animal—myself—as guinea pig.

Someone I meet pleases me. I think I would like them. Why? Well, you know . . . there was just something about him. But specifically, exactly what was it? Go back, you sluggard, and remember. What was it, specifically and exactly, that first caused you to start looking at and listening to this stranger? It was the body language, the expression, that told you he was really and intently listening when you talked to him. Interested in you and in what you were saying. So how can that be described most effectively? And what else was there? The way he said things? The turn of phrase. To defer. Not to interrupt. The tendency not to overdescribe, to presume his listener was intelligent and informed. Whatever it was, isolate it. Remember it. Have it handy the next time you want to introduce this sort of person to the reader.

A scene depresses me, leaves me out of sorts and angry. Why? The coldness of the room, the dim, yellow light, the tarnish on the gold tassel on the rope, the arrogant stare of the hostess, the slick, clammy coolness of the surface of this table. . . . What else?

I awake at night from a bad dream, tense and anxious. Quick. Dissect the mood before it evaporates. Nightmares are rare these days for me. For a man who deals in suspense, fear, and tension, they are too valuable to waste. What was in it and in the darkness around the bed that provokes this uneasiness and anxiety? Specifically, what do you hear, or smell, or feel or see that causes this painful tension?

I have been doing this for years: stripping down people and places, dissecting their looks and their mannerisms, filling the storage bins of imagination with useful parts; doing the same with street scenes, with landscapes, with the weather. When I wrote only nonfiction, such stuff was jotted in my notebook—the telltale details I trained my mind to isolate and collect. The anthropologist squatted on a grassy slope beside an anthill, his callused fingers sifting through those tiny grains ants bring to the surface, frowning in his fierce hope of finding a chip from a Stone Age artifact. The same fingers sorting through the residue left on the sifter-frame over his wheelbarrow, eliminating the gravel, roots, and rabbit droppings, saving the tiny chips flaked from a flint lance point; finding a twig to fish out the angry scorpion and return him to the grass. And that final detail, I hope my reader will agree, does more than put him on the scene with me. It gives him insight into the character of the man who owns the callused fingers.

15

A MATTER OF LIFE OR DEATH

By Phyllis A. Whitney

In beginning writers' fiction, we find too often that the story problem is static, giving rise to no immediate action. This can happen with the experienced writer as well, and we all need to be on guard.

Though a problem important to the main character may sit quietly offstage, generating little on-scene action because the writer knows that such action is coming later and believes that will save the day, that will be too late! The writer must be inventive enough to develop complications that will keep *some* problem alive from the first chapter on.

There are two methods by which we can introduce a novel's central problem. It can be gradually revealed through lesser problems until we are well into the story but before all is made clear to the reader. The second method is to disclose the prime direction at once—sometimes in the first scene. Either way will work, but each brings its own difficulties in procedure.

In my Maui novel, *Silversword,* problems arise at once, so that the main character is forced quickly into action. The reader, however, is not sure of the true course of the book for several chapters. In the beginning, Caroline, the viewpoint character, has just discovered that her mother, who she believed had died in Hawaii when Caroline was a child, is still alive. At the time, Caroline is living in San Francisco where she was brought by her father's mother when she was too young to understand the accident that killed her parents. The details of that tragedy have always been kept from her.

Immediate problems come up, even though the core of the novel won't be clear until later. The danger here would be to wait for important coming action, instead of bringing in urgent difficulties to carry the story along in the meantime. Caroline's first move is to return to Maui to find her mother. Each new scene involves problems she must act on or raises important questions she must find answers to. The emphasis is on the action she must take in solving these lesser issues—so the reader won't feel the story is sitting still.

In contrast, I used the second method in *Feather on the Moon*. Jenny is a young mother whose three-year-old daughter was kidnapped before the novel begins. She learns seven years later that a child of ten living in Victoria, British Columbia, may be her lost daughter. The main problem of the book is revealed at once: to recover the daughter who was taken from her years earlier. This basic problem will remain constant throughout, but I must bring in new questions and obstacles so the story won't become repetitive and tiresome.

When Jenny arrives in Victoria, she isn't sure whether Alice, the child, is really her daughter. Even when, several chapters later, she becomes convinced of Alice's identity, there is no easy way to prove this and take her back legally. Complications and conflicts (with various characters) multiply—and these are what keep any story alive.

The main problem in both these novels is a matter of life or death to the leading character. No writer can afford to deal with insignificant problems.

There should be immediate urgency, even though the life-or-death aspects may not appear until later. Happiness is always at stake, since that's what most fiction is about. We must ask ourselves if early problems are of sufficient importance to drive the main character into action.

Here are a few life-or-death problems I have used in past novels:

• Main character's brother is in jail with threat of a murder charge. She must prove him innocent.
• Main character is fleeing with her child to escape a brutal husband.
• Heroine's father, from whom she is estranged, is dying—she must go to him, though still unforgiving for the past.
• Heroine must save a brain-injured child from being institutionalized.

All these problems become much more complicated as a story develops and other characters enter and conflicts arise. Some problems need a good deal of explanation; others can be developed quickly. While we're explaining, we need to hold the reader's interest. It's a good idea to study the work of skilled writers and learn how they handle this.

In every instance, the main character *must* be emotionally involved or you will lose the reader. It cannot be said too often that you cannot allow the story problem to wait indefinitely for the right moment before it is faced by the main character. That moment (for *some* problem) is now, in *every scene*. We can never comfort ourselves because we know the main character will take exciting action five chapters ahead. *This* chapter, *this* scene is what matters. I must ask what my main character is doing, or planning to do *now*. The reader won't wait. If we allow the central character to become passive, and only a spectator who watches others act, there will be little suspense.

In order to keep our fiction ingredients dynamic, we must be clear ourselves about plot questions.

These must never be vague, general questions, such as, "How can my heroine succeed?" We must be specific, and I find that it helps if I write my questions down—really confront them. Then I can test their strength and weakness. Such questions come to mind quickly in my plotting stages—there's so much I don't know! And they keep on adding up as I move into the writing. Reading these over from time to time as I work helps keep my imagination creative.

While we stir and muddy the waters in order to puzzle our readers, we find quickly that not all scenes can carry high action. Nevertheless, there can be strong conflict in a scene where characters merely sit in a room talking. Dialogue can be used as a dueling with words, and tension can run high, even without physical action. Surprises often emerge from information given in a dialogue scene, so that more complications and conflicts can arise. Of course we break this up by small movements of our characters. Perhaps one walks over to a window and notes something happening outside, or she picks up some object of importance that helps keep interest alive. Even such small movements shouldn't be meaningless.

Whatever happens, we should stay inside the viewpoint character in each scene. It's all too easy to write objectively, letting the main character remain passive, and the reader uninvolved—only watching and listening. I must remind myself at such times that my reader wants to know what my main character is feeling and thinking (and perhaps planning)—which leads to action ahead.

When I write a novel, I choose to stay in the viewpoint of one character throughout the book, whether in first person or third. For me, there is an immediacy and continuity in this method that compensates for the difficulties of the single viewpoint. My main character, it's true, can't appear on every scene where I'd like her to be, but this can be worked out in other ways than by breaking viewpoint—for instance, by having someone describe what has happened in a scene when my heroine couldn't be present.

However, if you prefer to use more than one viewpoint—and many writers do this skillfully—remember that there can be a drop in interest when readers are forced to leave a character with whom they've become involved, and have to switch to someone unknown. Interest must be built up again quickly before disconcerted readers decide to dislike this change of viewpoints. One definite rule: Just one viewpoint per chapter! The reader who skips around from mind to mind—sometimes on the same page—creates a trail of confusion and loses emotional impact. Suspense can be lost as well, since it is sometimes more tantalizing *not* to know what another character is thinking.

Above all, a fiction writer must be inventive. We must continue to surprise our readers—surprise ourselves! The more we use our imagination, the more we reject the obvious and push ourselves to create and venture, the more practiced we become in providing ingenious twists and turns of plot. We mustn't be in such a hurry to finish that we settle for the cliché. Or—if we know it's shopworn, then we should turn it around and find a way to make it fresh.

To keep our scenes dramatic and convincing, we must make sure that the characters we see so clearly in our minds are really transferred to paper, so that our readers can know them as well as we do. Since we've given the reader the details about our characters when they first came onstage, why must we keep repeating these descriptions? If we don't, the reader will forget, and the impact we intend will be lost. It's fatal to have the reader ask the identity of a character who hasn't appeared for chapters and about whom the writer hasn't bothered to remind us. (I am a reader, too, and I hate this to happen.)

The same applies to settings: To keep everything dynamic and alive, the immediate background, whether a room or a mountaintop, had better be touched on again when the scene is repeated. Stories do not happen in a vacuum.

A successful writer of mystery novels once suggested to me that there is a "rule of three." If you want your reader to remember something, repeat it three times in the course of the story. I don't count; I try to vary my descriptions, but all the way through I remind myself that I must never take for granted the reader's memory about my characters and places.

At the outset, in addition to listing questions about phases of plotting, I make a second list that helps me make sure that my main problem will be strong enough to carry a whole novel. To accomplish this, I set down what the *penalties* will be if my main character fails, and what rewards she will receive if her efforts succeed. Sometimes just putting these down in writing will show me weaknesses I need to correct.

Success won by hero or heroine at the end of a valiant struggle against odds will bring reader satisfaction. If you are writing to entertain, your reader will want a strong character who wins. So it's wise to be aware of the importance of those penalties and rewards.

Dynamic problems lead to dynamic events that may lift the spirits and bring inspiration into the lives of those who read our novels.

16

TWENTY QUESTIONS—AND ANSWERS— ON FICTION WRITING

BY SIDNEY SHELDON

Q. *When beginning a novel, do you find it's easiest just to start writing and see where your characters lead you? Do you organize the plot when you feel you've developed the characters and created a certain tension and theme?*

A. When I begin a novel, I start with a character. I have no idea what the plot is going to be. Incidentally, this method of working is not one that I would recommend to an inexperienced writer because there are too many traps along the way. I dictate the first drafts of my novels and as I talk, the characters come to life and the plot begins to take shape. When I have finished the first draft, which can run to 1,500 pages, I take the typed pages and begin to rewrite, to polish and cut and shape.

Q. *Has discipline played an important role in your success? Were there times when you wanted to give up, yet you continued to persevere?*

A. Without discipline, nothing can ever get finished. Writing a novel takes a great deal of discipline and a lot of lonely hours. Is it worth it? That is up to each writer to decide.

Q. *Setting plays a very important role in your novels. How do you choose new settings? Are you inspired by stories or people? Travel?*

A. I like to write about exotic places because I think the readers enjoy reading about them. I try not to repeat the same locales, although sometimes repetition is inevitable. I will not write about a city or country that I have not been in. If I write about a meal in a restaurant in Sardinia, I have had that meal in that restaurant. If a writer cannot afford to go to foreign countries to do research, public libraries are a wonderful source of information.

Q. *It is often said that personal revelation is an intrinsic part of storytelling and that beginning writers tend to produce either thinly veiled autobiographies or stories so far from the writer's reality that they don't ring true. How do you strike a balance between your own experiences and your invented world?*

A. Someone once said that a writer papers his walls with himself. True. We all use experiences—things seen, heard, or felt—in our stories. I don't consciously think about using my experiences when I write a novel, but there are certainly events that have happened to me that may color what I write.

Q. *Your protagonists are morally strong individuals, and likewise, the endings of your novels leave the reader with the sense of justice having been served. How essential to modern storytelling is the element of good vs. evil?*

A. I think the element of good vs. evil goes back to the most ancient storytellers. I believe that if evil triumphs, the reader is left with a feeling of disappointment. It's like a sonata where the last chord is dissonant.

Q. *What are your thoughts on the author/editor relationship? How can a writer get the most out of the relationship?*

A. The author/editor relationship depends almost entirely on the confidence and the ability of the author. If we're speaking of a beginning writer, very often he or she will welcome the assistance of the editor. As a writer becomes more sure of himself and more capable, I think that dependence lessens a great deal.

Q. *How is your scriptwriting experience reflected in your novels (i.e. dialogue? pacing?), if at all, and vice-versa?*

A. My scriptwriting experience has played an enormous part in my writing novels. My early training in motion pictures, television, and the Broadway theater was in writing scenes for actors to play and dialogue for actors to read. Because of my background, I think in visual terms. For this reason, it has been easy for all of my novels to be adapted to the screen.

Q. *When you began to write, did you ever try to emulate another author's style—out of admiration or just for fun? Would this be a helpful exercise for beginning writers?*

A. I think every writer should develop his or her own style, and not emulate any other author. As a beginning exercise, it might be interesting to read a story by a famous author and then try to retell the story in your own words as though you had created it. But it is very important to find your own voice.

Q. *In the past, which writers have you found most inspirational? Do you read other novels while you're working on your own, or do you read only between your novels and scripts?*

A. I grew up reading some of the world's greatest storytellers: Somerset Maugham, Ernest Hemingway, Sinclair Lewis, Thomas Wolfe, etc. I don't read other novels when I'm working, but I do a great deal of reading between books.

Q. *How aware are you of your audience as you write? Is there such a person as "the average reader"? Should an unpublished writer try to envision an audience as he/she writes, or is it too inhibiting?*

A. There is no "average reader." My readers are truck drivers, college professors, nurses, hookers, scientists, housewives. If I tried to keep a "reader" in mind when I write a book, I'd go crazy. How do you please a scientist and a truck driver? I get an idea that excites me, and I spend two and a half years developing it until it is as good as I know how to make it.

A. *What do you do to ensure that you won't run out of material or that your plot line won't stall?*

A. There is no way to insure that we won't run out of material. Talent is a gift that is given to us and it can disappear as quickly as it came. I wrote two movies with Irving Berlin and he told me that his greatest fear was that he would awaken some morning and never be able to write another song.

Q. *Do you have any superstitions about the writing process—for example, never divulge the plot, wear a lucky sweater when you write, etc.?*

A. I don't think I have any superstitions about the writing process. I never divulge a plot I'm working on, but that has nothing to do with superstition. Many writers talk about their books and very often that dissipates the energy and the books never get written.

Q. *Is it important for beginning novelists to watch and study other media (film, stage, television)? Or do you think they'll learn more by concentrating on reading other writers?*

A. I think it is important for beginning novelists to read as many novels as they can, both classical and popular. I do not believe it is important to watch a lot of films or TV shows.

Q. *Most successful writers have experienced failure early on and intermittently throughout their careers. Do you see early failures or successes as somehow detrimental to beginning writers? Is there any way to use these extremes to the writer's advantage?*

A. The effect of early failure or success depends on the person to whom it happens. Failure spurs some people on and discourages others. I think the saddest thing is when a writer has an enormous early success and is never able to achieve it again. I firmly believe that if a person has talent in any field, and perseveres, nothing can stop that person from succeeding.

Q. *Do you find that you must put yourself on the line and take risks when you write—that it's essential to good writing? Is one form of writing—film, TV, novel—riskier for you than another?*

A. Every time any artist creates something, he puts himself on the line. Whether you're an actor, painter, or writer, your critics and your audience are out there, waiting to judge you. No matter what form of writing you pursue, the only thing you should worry about is doing the best you can.

Q. *How do you handle endings? Are they among the last scenes you write (or rewrite), or are they decided beforehand?*

A. If an author arbitrarily decides on what the ending of his novel is going to be, that author is in big trouble. The ending has to be shaped by the story and by the characters. All the author has to do is get out of the way.

Q. *You have been able to use violent scenes to move the plot, and certainly to grab the reader's attention. How do you handle these scenes and prevent them from being gratuitous? How do readers respond to these scenes?*

A. I do not gratuitously use violence or sex or drama in any of my novels. Those things come from the characters, and they respond as anyone would given the circumstances.

Q. *You do several drafts of a novel before you are finished. How do you know when your work is completed—are you ever wholly satisfied, or do you want to revise* after *it's in print?*

A. I usually do a dozen complete drafts and spend two and one-half years on each novel before I turn it in. After it's turned in, I always want to revise it.

Q. *Do you sometimes make changes in a draft of a novel if a scene seems sentimental? How do you differentiate between sentiment and sentimentality?*

A. As far as sentimental scenes are concerned, if the characters are real, they, and not the author, will determine what their emotions are and how they react to them.

Q. *The threat of censorship—direct or indirect—weighs heavily on writers these days. Do you think we will see the effect of this on writers and their work within the next few years? Or, will the effect be less visible, say, if writers choose to avoid certain topics altogether or publishers refuse to print books on certain subjects?*

A. There is no such thing as a little bit of censorship. It's like being a little bit pregnant; it's going to get bigger. I abhor censorship and do everything I can to fight it. About ten years ago, I was invited by the South African Government to be a guest in their country. I agreed to go on condition that I could speak about censorship. I did shows on the South African Broadcasting television and radio network. On one radio call-in show, the majority of callers said that they wanted to be told what they could read and what movies they should be permitted to see. That's what happens when a population becomes brain-washed.

17

EMOTION IN FICTION

BY ROSAMUNDE PILCHER

I WAS, AS A CHILD, extremely emotional. Almost anything or anybody could make me cry. I wept copiously as I listened to Paul Robeson singing "Ol' Man River." Soggy with sentiment, I begged my Scottish mother to oblige me with a rendering of "Loch Lomond," swearing that I wouldn't blub. But when she got to the bit, "But me and my true love will never meet again," my good resolutions went with the wind and the tears poured down.

There were books as well. A dreadful Victorian drama for children called *A Peep Behind the Scenes.* I have no recollection of the plot, but I know that almost everybody, in some way or another, died. Mother had tuberculosis, and a saint-like child who crossed the road in order to pick buttercups in a field was squashed flat beneath the wheels of a passing cart. When I found myself with an empty afternoon and no one to play with, I would find myself drawn, with hideous inevitability, to the bookshelf, and the dismal book. Sitting on the floor, I would turn the pages, scarcely able to see the print for weeping.

In other words, I, like an awful lot of other people, enjoyed a good cry.

The poem, "The Raggle, Taggle Gypsies" had the same effect on me, and, oddly enough, so did Beatrix Potter's "Pigling Bland." I say "oddly enough," because Beatrix Potter was always marvelously un-sentimental and thoroughly practical about the seamy side of life. Jemima Puddleduck, laying her eggs in the wrong places, was deemed a simpleton. Squirrel Nutkin, teasing the owl, got his deserts and lost his tail. And right and proper, too. But Pigling Bland was different. He and his little girlfriend Pig Wig finally escaped the dreadful fate of being sent to market, and sent off on their own, running as fast as they could.

> They came to the river, they came to the stream,
> They crossed it, hand in hand,

Then over the hills and far away,
She danced with Pigling Bland.

It made me cry, not because it was sad, but because it was beautiful. I still think it is beautiful, and I still get a lump in my throat when I read it aloud to my grandchildren.

The most subtle form of arousing emotion is to slip the reader, with little or no warning, from laughter to tears. James Thurber wrote a piece entitled "The Dog That Bit People." It was about an Airedale called Muggs. He didn't simply bite people, but terrified the life out of deliverymen and was regularly reported to the police. Told in Thurber's laconic style, it was marvelously funny.

But in the last paragraph, Muggs dies, quite suddenly, in the night. He is duly buried, in a grave alongside a lonely road. Mother wants a marble headstone erected, but finally settles for a smooth board, on which Thurber wrote, with an indelible pencil, "Cave Canem," and his mother was pleased with the simple classic dignity of the old Latin epitaph.

All right; so the death of any faithful animal is a sure-fire tear-jerker, but it still gets to me, every time I read it.

Emotion, conveyed by the written word, is a delicate business. Like humor, it cannot be pushed, or it slips into sentimentality. Hemingway, that master of reported speech, could wring the heart by the bare bones of his painful dialogue. He never stressed the fact that he was telling you something that went beyond ordinary feelings, and yet you read the mundane, oft-used words, and hear his voices, and recognize the poignancy of the frailty of man, and there comes the lump in the throat and the sting of incipient tears.

Some years ago, I wrote a three-act play, with a single set; not a very accomplished piece of work, but it was produced by our local repertory theater, and for a few weeks I enjoyed a mild local fame. For the first time in my life, I was invited to open fetes, judge competitions, and hand out prizes for various contests. I found none of this too daunting. But then I was approached by a woman famous for her good works, and asked if I would make an appeal on radio to raise funds for her pet project—a training center for young mothers (scarcely more than schoolgirls) unfit to care for their unwanted babies. Touched by the plight of these little families, I agreed. Only then was I told that not only would I have to deliver the appeal, but would have to write the message myself.

It was the first time that I had been faced with a situation in which I deliberately had to drag emotion out of the bag. For without emotion, I should not touch hearts, and if I didn't touch hearts, I would not touch pockets. I engaged the help of a bright girl who was involved in the project, and for two days we sat at our typewriters, finally bashing out five minutes' worth of heartbreak, sentiment, and crying need. I duly read this out over the radio one Sunday morning, and by the end of the week the center was about a hundred and fifty pounds to the good. It wasn't much, and it wasn't enough. They struggled on for a month or two, and then closed down. We had tried, but it hadn't worked.

Much more recently, the very opposite occurred. In Dundee, Scotland, a small boy was desperately ill. Specialized neurosurgery was required, but the Dundee Royal Infirmary did not have the necessary equipment. In Boston, Massachusetts, however, the equipment was available, and this was flown, in some urgency, to Scotland. The two neurosurgeons had never used the device before, but they operated, with total skill, and the small boy's life was saved.

The story appeared the next day in our local paper, *The Dundee Courier and Advertiser*. A plain, factual account of what had taken place. We learned that the reason the equipment had had to be borrowed was that the Infirmary could not afford the £60,000 necessary to purchase it. With some idea of expressing my gratitude and admiration for the two doctors, I put five pounds in an envelope and posted it to the Infirmary. So did just about everyone else, who, that morning, took the paper. A fund had to be hastily set up, without an appeal ever having been launched, and within the next two weeks, the £60,000 target had been achieved. Which proves that if you've got a good story to tell, you don't need to play your sobbing violin at the same time.

Sadness, bravery, beauty, all touch our heart strings. Great happiness can be deeply touching, else why do we sometimes weep at weddings, or that moment when an old gentleman heaves himself to his feet at his Golden Wedding party and raises his champagne glass to his wife?

My novel *The Shell Seekers* covered a span of fifty years, and because of this, the varying ages of the characters, and the intrusion of two terrible wars, I found myself writing, more than once, about death. The demise of an elderly person I do not, in fact, find particularly sad. A shock and a loss, certainly, to be followed by a period of grieving, but death is part of life, and just about the only thing we can all be certain of.

However, the death of the young officer, Richard Lomax, killed on Omaha Beach, with all his life ahead of him, I found quite agonizing to set down. And worse was endeavoring to describe the reactions of Penelope Keeling, who when told of his tragic end, knew that their brief love was finished, and that the rest of her life would have to be lived without him. Struggling, as she struggled, for words, I gave her only the most banal of sentences to utter. And then cheated, and instead let her recall the final passage of the Louis MacNeice poem which they had both known and loved.

> . . . the die is cast
> There will be time to audit
> The accounts later, there will be sunlight later,
> And the equation will come out at last.

Cheating, perhaps. But it seemed to me to say it all.

To sum up, an analysis of what touches the writer is what will eventually get through to the reader. Understated, underplayed, unexaggerated, and yet totally sincere. There has to be rapport, a chime of instant recognition, clear as a bell. If you don't produce tears, you will at least kindle understanding, identification, and so forge a bond with the reader. And, at the end of the day, perhaps this is what writing is all about.

18

BEFORE THE BEGINNING

BY RICK DeMARINIS

HOW DO I BEGIN? Where do story ideas come from? What is the best way to proceed once I have my idea? These are among the most urgent questions beginning writers ask themselves, in one form or another, when faced with that awesomely vacant rectangle—the blank sheet of paper. If there is one unchanging constant in that never-routine enterprise, it has to be the frustrating inertia of imagination lurking in these questions.

Such questions may have no dependable answers. But maybe it would be helpful to think of the problem in another way. Let's for a moment assume that "the story" already exists in some recess of the mind, but, for some reason, our access to it is blocked. Maybe we contain thousands of stories, and all we need is the mechanism to draw them to the surface. For a moment, let's think of our energy, intelligence, passion, and perhaps our obsessive needs, as a kind of pump that should be able to raise these stories to the empty page. Yet, in spite of these worthy qualities, we often come up with nothing. What's wrong? Why does nothing at all occur to us in these desperate times? It could be that the pump needs priming. We know this much: when a writer is working well, the story flows out almost effortlessly. Sometimes it arrives with such abundance that the writer can hardly keep up with it.

Over the years I've developed some "pump-priming" exercises that occasionally work for me. (There is no guaranteed method.) Most people agree that the beginning of a story is the hardest part to write because the first paragraph or two must in some sense prefigure the entire story. This may sometimes lead the inexperienced writer to think that he must have the story completely thought out before he puts the first word of it down on paper. This is almost always self-defeating. Some writers can do it, but they are rare.

Exercise 1. Forget about writing a story. Instead, write the opening *paragraph* to a story whose outcome you are deliberately indifferent to. The requirements for this paragraph are twofold: It must contain an action of some kind, and it must suggest a mystery. (By "mystery" I simply mean that the action is not understandable from what we have been given in the paragraph.)

Example:

The man in the apple green suit started passing out candy bars to the group of grade school children at the crosswalk directly in front of Mrs. Freytag's living room window. "I *am* going to call the police this time," Mrs. Freytag said to her husband, Irv, who was lying on the couch balancing a Martini on his forehead.

These two sentences promise something to the reader. There is an action, and there is a mystery. The questions they raise are multiple: Who is the man in the apple green suit? Why does he give candy to children? Is he simply generous and kind, or is he a pervert? Why does Mrs. Freytag make it her business to spy on him? Why isn't Irv Freytag at work? Why is he lying on the couch balancing a Martini on his forehead? Is Mrs. Freytag really going to call the police this time or, as is suggested, fail once again?

Chances are good that a story is present in the answer to these questions. Chances are equally good that such a paragraph evokes no response in the writer, and it remains just what it is, an exercise. But what if the point of view is changed?

She's at the window again. Every time I look up she's opened the drape another inch. What the hell does she see? I know what she sees. She sees what she wants to see. Ugly doings. Crime. She says she's going to call the cops this time. Poor old Jensen, all he wants to do is make little kids happy. That's his crime. Hell, old Jensen's been passing out candy to kids every year since I can remember. He gave a candy bar to *me* thirty years ago! But she won't call. It's me she hates. It's me she wants to put away.

Sometimes an adjustment like this can alert the writer to possibilities he hadn't believed existed. He may not know what these possibilities are, but the sudden excitement he feels is the thing he must come to believe in. It's intuition, only intuition, but it's all he's got. I usually suggest to beginning writers that they write a number of such paragraphs, playing with the point of view, until something in the doing catches their interest. Is it necessary, at this point, to tell them to write

74

another paragraph that expands on this initially interesting effort? Hardly ever.

Exercise 2. Do the same sort of thing, but this time in dialogue. In this scene there will be two characters. One wants something from the other; the other doesn't want to give it. Do not use narrative to "explain" anything about these people. Let them act out their peculiar relationship. Use at least two "telling gestures."

Example:
   "So, what time do you want to go there?" Charles asked.
   Yvonne looked at him. Then, taking a deep breath, she said, "I told you. I'm not going."
   "If you get there early, they might have something for us."
   "I don't care what they have for us."
   Charles worked his toothpick between his top front teeth. "You'll be back here before seven if you leave now," he said. "Do you want to take the Ford, or do you want me to drive you?"
   Yvonne started to cry again. "Please," she said. "Please stop this."
   "All right," Charles said. "I'll drive you. We'll be there in less than an hour. It'll be good, you'll see."
   "It's never good!" she said. "It's always the same!"
   "Put on something a little sexier, will you? You know I hate that damned Girl Friday outfit."

The telling gestures—Charles picking his teeth, and Yvonne pausing to take a deep breath before she speaks—reveal economically states of mind that could take a paragraph of narrative. I have no idea what's going on between Charles and Yvonne, but I may be willing to write another few paragraphs in order to find out. (In this way we seduce ourselves into writing the story.) In such a scene, what one character wants could be any of a number of things, from the concrete to the abstract: money, drugs, property, love, cooperation, approval, respect, and so on. You could write this scene so that what is at stake may be the other character's spirit, as it evidently is in the above scene. The particular thing Charles wants from Yvonne is secondary to the fact that he is crushing her self-respect. He is dominating her cruelly, and *that* could be what he really wants.

Most of my beginning writers confuse the terms "plot" and "story." They are not exactly interchangeable. A story without plot is like a house without hallways or rooms. (There may be a lovely house somewhere in the world without hallways or rooms, but it would have to be an architectural tour de force.)

Example:
Story:
    I went to town yesterday afternoon. In J.C. Penney's I bought a new shirt. Then I had lunch. After lunch I went to Wilma's apartment.

Story & Plot:
    I decided to go to town after all. My first stop was J.C. Penney's where I bought the kind of shirt I used to wear when I was riding high. Alligators on the pockets. I left my old shirt in a trash basket in the dressing room. It looked like someone had been badly wounded in that beat-up shirt. It made me smile. In the full-length mirror my smile looked more like a snarl. I paid the clerk with my last twenty, and headed for the nearest McDonald's where I ordered three Quarter Pounders and coffee. Then I went to Wilma's place, knowing what a damn fool I was for thinking she'd welcome me with open arms.

    In the first paragraph, the events described have no antecedent events to give them significance. In the second paragraph, every event described clearly has some prior event of considerable significance, but at this point in the story, it is unknown to the reader. Some or all may be revealed eventually, thus providing the story events with causative factors. (Plot) *The expectation of these revelations is what makes the reader turn the page.*

    Admittedly, the second paragraph is heavily laced with dramatic bait. It isn't necessary to be so heavy-handed. What makes this paragraph heavy-handed is the number of significant events that lie behind it: I decided to go to town *after all.* (Our narrator obviously has been weighing the decision to go into town. Why? Is he a wanted criminal? Is he agoraphobic? Or is he simply bored with the town itself?) My first stop was J.C. Penney's where I bought *the kind of shirt I used to wear when I was riding high.* (O.K., he once was up, but now he's down. Why?) I left my old shirt in a trash basket in the dressing room. *It looked like someone had been badly wounded in that beat-up shirt. It made me smile.* (Has he been roughed up? Even wounded? What's so funny about it?) In the full-length mirror my smile *looked more like a snarl.* (It's not funny. But why this dissociation between his emotions and his facial expression? What has happened to him that he snarls when he wants to smile?) *Then I went to Wilma's place, knowing what a damn fool I was for thinking she'd welcome me with open arms.* (Ending the paragraph with this thunderclap lets the reader know that the story will unfold in a way that will be more or less determined by the history of the narrator's relationship with Wilma—the major event in his background.)

Exercise 3. Make a list of three or four significant, antecedent events (e.g., a car wreck, the alienation of a loved one, a prison term, a large inheritance, etc.). Write the opening paragraph for a story in which the influence of these events is strongly felt. This can be done subtly, or it can be laid on with a trowel, as in the above paragraph. Remember, don't tell the reader anything about the earlier events themselves. Keep him poking after answers. All stories, after all, should have some mystery in them.

Example:
  The Billetdoux front yard should have told me right away that the job wouldn't amount to much. The lawn was overgrown with spiky weeds, what grass there was had died a number of seasons ago, deep tire ruts oozy with muck grooved the front yard, and a rusty tub filled with crankcase oil sat on the warped porch. But I had just turned eighteen and was still untuned to the distress signals the world volunteers with unfailing reliability.

This is from a short story of mine called "Billy Ducks Among the Pharaohs"; it is admittedly a bit subtler than the previous example, as well as a trifle more complex. The young narrator is looking for a job, suggesting some degree of financial need. But there is a much subtler preexistent condition involved. He is naïve; *I had just turned eighteen and was still untuned to the distress signals the world volunteers with unfailing reliability.* But to have written such a sentence, the narrator is clearly no longer naïve (or eighteen). So, the readers' expectation here is to find a story about the progression from innocence to knowledge. Also, there is a secondary group of background events having to do with the Billetdoux family. Why is their yard so junky and uncared for? These events are given in the form of a series of images: weeds, dead grass, muck, a rusty tub filled with oil, a warped porch. The confrontation promises to be one between youthful ingenuousness and an apathy verging on despair.

You've probably noticed that all these exercises have something in common. They ask the writer to invent situations with no long-range strategies in mind. Strategic thinking thwarts the natural playfulness of the imagination. While working out one of these exercises, you are free from the adult responsibility of planning a serious story. And here's a confession: that is exactly how I go about writing serious stories. It always begins in play and in mystery. I try to write a "loaded" first paragraph. If I'm lucky, it starts something flowing. A story begins to spill out on the page. And I'm its first reader. If I'm eager to find out how it's going to turn out, chances are good that someone else will be, too.

19

CHARACTERIZATION

BY REX BURNS

THE IMPORTANCE OF CHARACTERIZATION is second only to an author's having something to say. In detective fiction, especially with a series, it takes on added importance because the reader must be convinced that the protagonist is capable of the physical or intellectual demands of capturing a challenging villain. Let me first discuss my selection of a central character and then go on to the topic of presenting characters convincingly. What I say here will be primarily for detective stories, but much of it can apply to other narrative fictions as well.

The old saw about imagining your character in full before you start telling the yarn may be a good one, but I've seldom followed it. For one thing, I have trouble knowing everything about myself let alone about someone else, fictional or real. For another, I don't have the patience to complete a detailed biography before I start a story's action. What I do find indispensable to start with is a sense, often vague, of the protagonist's personality. With Gabe Wager, the hard-nosed homicide cop who is the central figure in my series, I wanted a character with intense personal pride—at times to a fault—and the kind of leathery toughness designated by the Spanish word "duro." That was his nucleus.

The physical details followed—some more quickly than others—and were chosen to support this personality: a Spanish heritage (for the rigid pride) and short stature (for a bantam-rooster aggressiveness). He's also half-Chicano, half-Anglo. This was to heighten his isolation from both cultures and to emphasize the lone-wolf quality of his detection, a quality that so often puts him at odds with police bureaucracy. I'm not sure when I mixed his blood; it was before he had a name but after he had a soul, and somehow—given the soul—it seemed right that he be an "isolato." Gradually, but not until much later, I came to see him in much more physical detail: a small scar on his cheek, brown hair and eyes, sometimes a mustache. Usually, these characteristics would pop up as the story's development demanded. But the point is, these physical attributes (including his Spartan apartment and the Trans-Am he drives) are derived from his imagined core personality and from the requirements of the story's action.

I followed the same process in creating Devlin Kirk, a central character I recently launched in a new series. But this time I was more aware of something I had only half perceived when I began with Gabe Wager: The personality must somehow be interesting. With Wager, that was an unexplored given; I was—and still am—fascinated by the rigid personality surrounded by a fluid and at times chaotic world. But with Kirk, I actively searched my imagination for someone who could support a series of adventures and, one hopes, gather a following of readers. What would it take to provide such support? I'm embarrassed to admit how late in my writing career I discovered the simple answer: an intriguing personality. If the person interested me, I'd be more likely to hold the reader's attention.

Fundamental to this sustained interest is the question, "Will I be bored viewing the world through the protagonist's eyes?" If so, forget it; if not, go ahead and see what happens. The question has a lot of ramifications, entailing as it does the protagonist's quickness of eye, depth and agility of mind, and that ill-defined but vital thing called strength of character. Wager was primarily the result of a situation: What happens when a rigid figure tries to uphold the law in a world doing its best to be lawless. But that very rigidity narrowed considerably the spectrum of responses allowable. With Kirk, I purposefully chose a bright, well-read young man with a yearning for adventure and gave him just that quality. My hope, of course, is that throughout the series his mind will remain flexible so that I will not grow tired of seeing the world through his eyes. As with Wager, however, the nucleus of this protagonist wasn't physical appearance but a sense of his personality: quick-witted, self-confident, and daring, but with a strong element of reflective thought about the ultimate meaning of what he meets.

There's certainly nothing wrong in starting out with an image of a character's physical appearance—the only "rule" I've ever found in writing is "Do whatever works." But a protagonist usually requires some complexity of personality to sustain a reader's interest. Even with a severely one-dimensional protagonist such as James Bond, we can see

Ian Fleming and, later, John Gardner offering more and more facets to his character, facets that have little to do with the tumultuous action that is the series' mainstay.

Another, and to my mind lesser, means of attracting readers to a character might—in contrast to the above—be called external. It tends to make use of props of some kind. One detective might, for example, grow orchids and be a gourmet chef; another might be a suave connoisseur of labels and brands. Whatever the prop, it serves to make the reader care about something out of the ordinary in the person, something that makes him stand out against the rest of humanity and thereby gives a cachet of expertise that heightens the probability of solving baffling crimes. With a central figure, however, the prop is often only a temporary eye-catcher, and the real appeal is found in the character's personality.

The same external technique is often of help in quickly portraying villains and secondary figures. Think of the number of evil doers or sidekicks who are marked by an idiosyncratic quirk of behavior or a startling physical appearance. This verges on a caricature, but there's no problem there; Dickens raised it to a high art, and a writer could do worse than to emulate his economy and clarity in presenting memorable figures. Indeed, in a story that's primarily adventure, there's often too little room for more than one "rounded" or complex character, and the yarn's rapid movement demands the economy of characters whose personalities can be summed up in a single phrase—"tough but kind," or "oily and cowardly." The trick, of course, is to present such characters so that they don't come across as clichés. How this is done exactly, I'm not sure. I try to find a balance between such a figure's central motif and his probable human behavior in the novel's various situations. Perhaps with more time on stage, this kind of person could grow into complex roundness—the potential is there. And perhaps that's what I'm trying to say: A convincing "flat" character is one who has the clear potential of becoming "round," but is not given the opportunity in the flow of the story.

The use of props for external definition of a character is obviously a means of presenting character. But I don't think it's the primary one. To my mind, voice is character. By that I mean the narrative voice that tells the story as well as the dialogue spoken by the characters. If a story's in first-person point of view, this primacy of voice is self-evident; the reader is addressed directly by someone ("I") who saw the action and is telling about it in his own words.

Like the direct address to the reader, internal monologue or stream-of-consciousness can also serve to establish or advance our sense of who a character is. My Gabe Wager yarns are told in the restricted third-person point of view so that the reader knows only what Wager knows, and when occasion demands, the reader can also know what's going on in his skull. Here's an excerpt from a longer passage in *Ground Money;* it's intended to give not only a glimpse of Denver, but also of Wager's detached and even sarcastic assessment of his home town, an attitude that tells us something about Wager's personality:

. . .all over Denver Wager had seen a larger number of couples, many with children, setting up life in apartments and sharing houses with others. There was a touch of irony about that, for these were Anglos, the children of those who had taken their tax money out of the city to fill the surrounding suburbs with split-levels on lanes and drives and circles. Here their offspring were gradually developing the same kind of crowded and noisy neighborhoods Wager had grown up in. Now all they had to do was put in a corner grocery and a cantina and call it progress.

The clearest and often the most subtle means of presenting character is through dialogue between two or more speakers. In the following abbreviated passage from *Avenging Angel,* Wager and Axton are inter-viewing a man who discovered a body. I tried to let their voices reveal their states of mind as well as the orchestrated approach that Wager and Axton use on witnesses:

"You guys believe me, don't you?"
Wager looked at the witness. "Any reason we shouldn't?"
"No! But . . . I mean . . . all the questions. . . . Honest to God, Officer, I was just hitching along here!"
Axton nodded. "We understand that, Mr. Garfield. We just want to get everything down now so we don't have to call you up later."
Garfield sucked in a breath. "Yeah. It's just all of a sudden I thought, Jesus, what if you guys think I did it?"
"We don't know who did it," Wager said. "Yet."

A worried and nervous witness, phlegmatic Max, and an abrasive and aggressive Gabe—these are the character traits I tried to let the dialogue reveal directly to the reader.

Note the lack of adverbs in the above swatch of dialogue. Wager doesn't say "grimly"; Axton doesn't speak "kindly"; the witness doesn't stutter "nervously." The diction and syntax of the dialogue, in conjunction with the situation of the speakers, will—I hope—carry the very sound of the voices, so that the extra baggage of instructing the reader how to read isn't necessary. In fact, it's a good exercise for writers to strike out the adverbs and see if the dialogue can stand on its own. If it can't, then in most cases I would guess the writer doesn't have a clear sense of the voice—he doesn't hear the individual tones and word choices that make every person's language his own. And that's simply another way of saying he doesn't have a sense of his character.

In most fiction, character consistency is more effective than inconsistency, because the reader becomes oriented to a specific voice and behavior that have been given a name. But character consistency doesn't mean a lack of character change. For a long time, short fiction, especially, was built around the moment of character change; and many of the longer forms still trace a personality's journey from one condition to another. The so-called rounded characters are almost forced to undergo some kind of change because they're sensitive people who have faced some traumatic action. This is especially true in a series in which each volume is like a long chapter of an extended work. But the change in character generally should be consistent in order to be believable. This is another way of saying that, for me, character change comes from within and is based on the established personality. Sometimes, abrupt character change is explained as the result of an outside agent such as a demonic possession or chemical imbalance from a faulty experiment. But even in gothic fiction or SF, the reader is offered some explanation to make that change plausible within the world of the novel ("experimental" fiction is a different game with different rules). In realistic fiction, such outside agents of radical change are generally unconvincing unless they're couched in terms recognizable in the real world which that fiction mirrors—head trauma, dope addiction, degenerative disease, etc.

Most often, a character's change is more slowly paced and has a quality of inevitability about it. I've found that once a character is clearly established in the mind, then the probability of that character's actions can be projected. The result is the kind of change and development I'm talking about. This is also the root cause of that delightful surprise when characters "take over" and the author seems to become less a creator than a reporter of what the characters tell him.

The characters in fiction come from the world around us and from within. What is it we're interested in about ourselves? What is it about neighbors and acquaintances that attracts us? What's the most fascinating personality we've met? Who would we like to be? What evil or despicable aspect of our lives or the lives of others intrigues us? Out of these and other questions come the nucleus of character and the character's own voice. But just as our lives are modulated by the restrictions of social behavior, so the lives of fictional characters are modulated by the demands of fictional structures. The characters in novels who loom in my mind are those who somehow find the right balance between the thrusting, vital energy of their lives and their roles as contributing figures in a narrative tapestry.

20

So You Want to Write
A Bestseller?

By Barbara Taylor Bradford

WHEN I'm on tour to promote a new novel, I meet many people in bookstores, TV audiences, and lecture halls, who tell me they want to be a bestselling novelist. They seek my advice. Generally, I tell them to sit down and do it, because that is the only way a book is ever written. However, I usually make a point of asking each one the same question: Why do you want to be a novelist?

Invariably they tell me that they want to make a lot of money and become a famous celebrity.

These are the wrong reasons.

There is only one reason to write a novel and that is because writing fiction is absolutely essential to one's well-being. It is to mine and it always has been. In other words, it is the work that really counts, the sense of creation that is the important thing to me.

Don't misunderstand me. Of course I want readers, every author does. But I have never sat down at a typewriter and told myself that I'm about to write a great bestseller. I have no idea if a book of mine is going to sell in the millions when I actually start it. How could I know, since I don't have a secret recipe? All I have is a story to tell about a number of characters who are very real people to me. I knew I wanted to be a novelist when I was a child in Yorkshire. I had no brothers or sisters so I invented playmates and told them stories. When I was ten, my father bought me a second-hand typewriter and I typed out these little tales and stitched them in a folder with a hand-painted title.

When I was 12 I submitted one—about a little horse, I think—to something called *The Children's Magazine* and it was actually published. I got ten and six for it. I have never stopped writing since.

The first novel I attempted was about a ballet dancer named Vivienne Ramage who lived in a garret in Paris! By this time I had managed to get a job on the *Yorkshire Evening Post* and had been to the Paris fashion shows with the women's page editor.

Paris totally overwhelmed me. I came back, and began this story. My ballet dancer was desperately poor and it was all terribly dramatic and suspiciously reminiscent of Dumas' *La Dame aux Camélias*! Anyway, I got to about page ten and suddenly thought: I've a feeling I've read this somewhere before.

I kept experimenting like that all though my girlhood. Being on a newspaper, doing the police beat, covering the coroners' courts, exposed me to life in the raw and taught me that you can't just write about the landscape or a room setting—a story is only interesting if it's about people. Their tragedies, their dramas, their joys.

That's what I'm dealing in now, human emotions. The hope is that I can get them down on paper in such a way as to touch a nerve in the reader so that he or she identifies and is moved. At 17 I was very much in love with being a newspaperwoman—a newspaper*man* I should say—even down to wanting a dirty trench coat. My mother accused me of having dragged it round in the street to make it grubby.

But my newspaper career didn't begin as a reporter. The only job I could get at the start was in the typist pool. First day I was still typing away long after everybody had gone home. As I was leaving I saw the wastepaper basket overflowing with the company's crumpled, vellum-like notepaper and I thought, I'm going to get fired for wasting their stationery. So I took a handful into the ladies' room, lit a match to it and threw it down the toilet.

Well, the blaze was so enormous I then thought: this way I'll be fired for being an arsonist! So I collected up the rest, smoothed it out and hid it in the bottom drawer of my desk.

For a week after that I took one of my mother's shopping bags to work with me and brought the telltale paper home in batches. I think I eventually got a job as a cub reporter because I was such an awful typist.

But I worked at getting moved, too—I did little stories and handed them in to my editor, who finally put me in the newsroom.

At 18, I became women's editor. When I was 20 I left Upper Armley, Yorkshire, for London and a job on *Woman's Own* as a fashion editor, followed by a stint as a reporter and feature writer on the *Evening News*.

Naturally, that was a job in which I met actors, film stars, novelists, screenwriters, politicians—people who were "achievers"—but I never expected to find success or be rich and famous myself. However, when I look back, I realize my mother always instilled in me a desire to do my best. I wanted to please her. She loved the theatre, movies, music and art and she got me my first two library tickets when I was still very small. When she died in 1981—only 5 weeks after I lost my father—I found those tickets in her purse.

I continued writing after I moved to the United States, where I have lived since my marriage in 1963 to a Hollywood film producer, Robert Bradford. I wrote non-fiction books between 1963 and 1974, mostly on interior design, and two books for children.

Between 1968 and 1974, when I was writing a syndicated column for American newspapers, I started four novels but discarded them all after a few hundred pages. One was set in Paris and North Africa. It was called *Florabelle*. I liked strong heroines from the start. That one was an actress.

Yet another novel was set in North Africa—I was smitten with Morocco at that time—and that tale was about a woman photo-journalist. My next was sited in the South of France. But the one I was writing when I thought of *A Woman of Substance* was called *The Jasper Cypher*. It was a Helen MacInnes-type suspense novel starting in New York and moving to Spain.

But obviously I was wrong, wasn't I? I should have been writing about Yorkshire, not Morocco. I got to chapter four and I thought, this is boring. I asked myself a lot of questions that day. It was like a dialogue with myself. I said: Well, what *do* you want to write about? What *sort* of book do you want to write? Where do you want to set it? And of course I knew, suddenly, that I really wanted to set it in England, specifically Yorkshire. Then I said: And I want to write about a strong woman.

So, having decided to write about a Yorkshire girl who emancipates herself and creates a big business empire, I could see it would be more effective if she were born poor and in an age when women were not doing these things, and to have her working for a rich family who falls as she rises.

After a couple of hours of thinking along these lines I had the nucleus of my plot and started to jot down a few notes and I thought, yes, she becomes a woman of substance. And I looked at that on my pad and thought, that's a marvelous title.

At a point like this I put paper in typewriter and tap out a few details. I might take two days experimenting with a name for the character. It has to have just the right ring. Then I create the other protagonists, maybe draw a family tree, listing names and ages, their relationships.

All the time I'm asking myself questions and answering them on paper. When is it going to start, how old is she, what is her background, what motivates her, why did this woman do what she did, become what she became? All my characters are totally analyzed, as if I were a psychiatrist.

I then transpose these notes onto index cards, and I maintain these character cards as if I'm dealing with real people—and they become very real to me. As I develop them, somehow the plot falls into place almost automatically.

Once I have title, characters and story line in note form, I divide the book into parts. It's a way to organize the material. In *A Woman of Substance* I got titles for the sections from the land—the valley, the abyss, the plateau, the pinnacle, the slope. It was a method of tracing the rise and fall of a life. In *Voice of the Heart*, I used the stage—overture, wings, Act 1, downstage right and so on. In *Hold the Dream*, the phases are entitled "Matriarch"—that's Emma Harte in old age—and "Heiress and Tycoon," which is the ascent of her granddaughter, Paula.

At this stage I write a piece like the copy on a novel's dust jacket, the bare bones of the story. Then I finish the outline, which is ten to 20 pages. That takes me about a week to ten days.

Once I get going on a novel, a good day is when I've written five finished pages. I usually start in longhand, using a fine nibbed pen (Sanford's Expresso, if you like to know that sort of thing) and then move to the typewriter.

Someone once asked me what a novel is and I said: It's a monumental lie that has to have the absolute ring of truth if it is to succeed.

It's easy to know when something is good and, in a way, it's easy to know when something is bad. But to know *why* it's bad, that's the thing. And how do you change it?

I've gone back and looked at my first attempts at fiction, and there wasn't too much wrong with them, except that I wanted basically to write about Yorkshire and didn't know it. So I wouldn't say to the would-be novelist: press on with *anything* you start. You could be on the wrong subject matter, as I was.

However, I now realize that as I labored, I was in effect honing my craft, teaching myself how to write a novel. I truly believe that learning the craft of fiction writing is vital and that you can't do that at classes. You can perhaps learn techniques—I borrowed library books on journalism when I was trying to become a reporter—but no one can teach you to write a novel. You have to teach yourself.

Basic writing ability is still not enough. A would-be novelist must also observe what I call the five Ds:

D for desire—the desire to want to write that novel more than do anything else.

D for drive—the drive to get started.

D for determination—the will to continue whatever the stumbling blocks and difficulties encountered on the way.

D for discipline—the discipline to write every day, whatever your mood.

D for dedication to the project until the very last page is finished.

Finally, there is a sixth D—to avoid! This is for distractions—perhaps the most important D of all, the enemy of all writers, whether would-be or proven.

Writing novels is the hardest work I've ever done, the salt mines, really. I sit long hours at my desk, starting out at six in the morning and finishing around six or seven in the evening. And I do this six and a half days a week, till my neck and shoulders seize up. I make tremendous social and personal sacrifices for my writing, but after all, I chose to be a novelist. Nobody held a gun to my head.

But in all truth, it's not possible to be a full-time novelist and a social butterfly, living the so-called glamorous existence of the bestselling novelist.

There's nothing which faintly resembles glamour about the work I do. I spend all of my working hours alone, facing a blank sheet of paper, and myself. For I have to dredge through my soul and my memories every day of my life.

When a book is finished I have to go on promotion tours. This may sound exciting. But it isn't. Taking a different plane or train every day and heading for another city is hardly my idea of fun; neither are crowded airports, poor hotels or bad food eaten on the run.

Then there are the fairytales. When reporters come to interview me they sometimes have a preconception. It's nothing to do with what they've learned about me, it's what they've decided without knowing me. They want to make me into Emma Harte. They want a rags-to-riches story. Somebody asked me the other day about my enormous change of lifestyle since I wrote a bestseller. Well, I started off simply enough but, to be truthful, my lifestyle changed when I married 22 years ago and went to live in Manhattan and also had an apartment in Beverly Hills.

But whatever I say, they're determined to write the story they want to tell. So the only thing I can do when I read a misleading story is smile and say, well at least they spelled my name right! But I'm not Cinderella, and never was.

Still, I admit that a bit of fiction about oneself is not much to put up with. I've been accused of dressing my Bichon Frisé puppy, Gemmy, in a diamond-studded collar and of wearing a £25,000 dress. I was due to go and stay with an old friend in Ripon and she roared with laughter when she read that. "Do I have to get a burglar alarm installed?" she kidded me. She knew a Yorkshire girl would never spend £25,000 on a dress, that she'd be doing something extraordinary if she paid £250!

So why do I go on? The answer is easy. I can't *not* do it. Writing is a means of self-expression for me, and it gives me great gratification. Especially when I know that a novel I have striven over truly works, not only for me, but for readers all over the world . . . readers who have derived enjoyment from my work, who have seen life through my angle of vision . . . who have been touched, enlightened and entertained. That is the greatest satisfaction of all.

And if you are a would-be novelist, hellbent on pursuing this career, then what better inspiration is there?

Ten Questions for Would-Be Novelists

Let us assume that the would-be novelist has both ability and a talent for using words. What else is required in the writing of fiction? I think I would have to ask you these questions.

1. Are you imaginative?

If you create characters in your imagination that are interesting and different and yet with whom the reader can identify, then you have a good start. If you can picture scenes between characters you create and can also feel caught up in their emotions, that's what I call imagination.

2. Have you got insight?

A novelist must be able to understand what makes people tick. Insight is being able to weigh someone up, to understand why they do the things they do. You must have compassion, and be willing to understand all points of view.

3. Can you get under the skin of a character, express his or her nature?

You have to be able to put the feeling and thought processes of your characters on paper effectively. I think writing up character studies is helpful. It teaches you how to develop a *whole* person on paper, remembering that nobody is all good, nobody is all bad; we are all made up with many complexities in our nature.

4. Can you make readers care about your characters?

That depends on whether you can flesh them out so that the reader believes they truly exist. I've found reading biographies very useful since they are about real people.

5. Can you really tell a story?

If it's to be compelling, make the reader want to turn the page to find what happens next, a novel has to combine structure, plot and action in a way that produces narrative drive. I have what I call my "loving ears"—two girlfriends I can ring and say: May I read you these few pages? That's what I sometimes do if I'm trying to say something complex, and their reaction helps me know if I've refined it enough. Do they want to "hear on"? Some feedback is helpful if you're feeling unconfident.

Structure is very important. Studying favorite books is good homework here. The structure of *Tai Pan* by James Clavell, who also wrote *Shogun,* is marvelous. And Wilbur Smith did a trilogy, *Flight of the Falcon, Men of Men* and *The Angels Weep,* which are all well-constructed novels. And the classics of course. There's nothing better than studying Dickens. And Colette. Colette, by the way, said: Two things are important in life. Love and work. I like that. Yorkshire people have the work ethic. My mother was always polishing a chair or making a stew and I still feel I must work all day, every day, or God will strike me dead.

6. Have you a talent for plots?

Working out story lines and getting them down in, say, ten pages is the best way of finding out. For myself, an event will trigger a plot. For instance, a former friend who was dying and wanted to make peace with me and other friends she had once hurt led to my plot for *Voice of the Heart.* The story line may "unreel" in the bath or on a bus in anything from ten minutes to an hour.

I never use anything exactly as it has befallen me or my friends, but I've seen so much of what happens to people that I know my plots are not too far-fetched, not larger than life. Nothing is larger than life.

7. Can you create a sense of time and place, mood and atmosphere?

I rely on memory for scenes from nature but I have occasionally taken snapshots for interiors. For *Voice of the Heart*, I photographed a *schloss* in Germany, to help me keep the mood of the place in my mind. Note-taking is another helpful tool, and sensible for people who don't have photographic memories.

I can't explain how you create atmosphere. I mean, Stephen King, the "horror" writer who wrote *Carrie* and *The Shining*, among many others, is brilliant when he creates an atmosphere of horror, and I think he does it with his choice of words. Atmosphere is not something visual, it's a feeling, and it's conveyed by particular words, so I too feel I must find the *exact* word and I'll spend hours sometimes to arrive at it. But, having said that, it's hard for a writer to analyze how he or she writes: I always fear I might analyze it away!

8. Do you have the knack of writing dialogue?

Dialogue has to do several things. It has to move the plot along and provide information of some kind. It has to delineate the character of the person speaking—or somehow reflect his personality. It should add to the flavor of the book, convey emotion or feeling. So it has to be very structured, even though it must sound natural.

Ask yourself if the dialogue you have written does all of these things, and if in all honesty you have to answer "no" you will almost certainly find that you can throw it out without loss—indeed it will be an improvement—to your book.

Written dialogue is totally different from spoken dialogue—write down a taped conversation and you'll see it's unreadable.

9. Are you organized enough?

If you want your novel to have a feeling of authenticity, then you must write from strength, from knowledge—and that means research. But the important thing about research is to be able to throw it away! Put it all in and it slows down the narrative drive. I might do a day's research just for a few lines of dialogue but it has to be integrated so it's not apparent.

An efficient filing system is vital, as are good reference books and address books that record sources—or you will waste precious time and work in a muddle. I have a table next to my desk where I keep handy a large dictionary and the *Columbus Encyclopaedia*, along with a thesaurus, *Bartlett's Familiar Quotations*, a world atlas, and maps of England.

10. Do you have a sense of drama?

There's so much drama every day in the newspapers, surely everyone has. Reading plays, watching movies helps to sharpen a dramatic sense, teach you what makes a "story." A book I go back to time and again is *Wuthering Heights*. Every time I read it I find something I hadn't noticed before. It is extremely emotional to me, a very Yorkshire book—though structurally it's said *not* to be good.

21

"WHERE DO YOU GET YOUR IDEAS?"

BY ELIZABETH PETERS

ONE OF THE QUESTIONS most often asked of writers by readers and interviewers is, "Where do you get your ideas?" I used to sputter and roll my eyes when this query was put to me; there was in it the implication that ideas were physical objects, like avocados, and all one had to do was go to the proper store in order to pick up a supply.

However, my prejudice began to diminish when I started thinking seriously about the question. It is not a silly question. I thought it was silly only because I didn't know the answer. I still don't know the answer, but I have arrived at some answers—the sources from which I derive many of my ideas. I can't answer for other writers, but perhaps some of these will work for you.

First, let's define the term: An idea is not a plot. This distinction may seem so obvious that it isn't worth mentioning, but many of the earnest souls who offer me "plots" or "ideas" ("You write the book, and we'll split the royalties") don't know the difference. What I call an idea is not a plot. An idea is the germ from which a plot may one day develop if it is properly nurtured and tended. For me, the "idea" has two distinct stages.

It begins with a "one-liner"—a single sentence or a visual image, characterized by brevity and vividness. Since an idea is not an avocado, you can't simply go out and get one. In fact, the technique of finding a usable idea is more akin to birdwatching than to chasing butterflies: There are ideas all over the place, the trick is to recognize one of the elusive creatures when it flits past. I'm not being whimsical. It is certainly possible to search actively for an idea, but unless you know one when you see one, there is no point in looking.

The most obvious source of inspiration is your own hobby or profession or job specialty. My training is in archaeology and history, so I derive a good many plot ideas from those fields. The archaeology themes have been particularly prominent in my Elizabeth Peabody novels.

My hobbies—cats, needlework and gardening—have also provided me with ideas. Once when I was absorbed with collecting and embroidering samplers, I thought vaguely, "I wonder if I could use a sampler as a clue in a book?" This idea ended up as *House of Many Shadows*. I usually have an animal, or three or four, in my books, but cats have played seminal roles in the inspiration of ideas. "How about a ghost cat, who shows up in the nick of time to save the heroine?" That one turned out to be *Witch*.

Ideas don't always come from nonfiction reading. Sometimes irritation spawns a plot idea—when I read a book with a smashing twist that doesn't quite come off, prompting me to mutter, "I would have done that differently. . . ." And I do. Sometimes admiration of a particular book prompts not imitation so much as emulation. *Sons of the Wolf,* one of my early Gothics, was inspired by Wilkie Collins's *The Woman in White*. I took his two heroines, one dark and homely and competent, the other beautiful and blond and fragile. . . . Or so she seemed. It surprised me as much as it did some of my readers when the fragile blond came to the rescue in a moment of crisis, but her development was probably the result of my unconscious resentment of Victorian assumptions about women, which affected even so sensitive and gifted a writer as Collins. I turned his stereotype around to produce different characters and a different plot.

When you are looking for a plot idea, it is helpful, therefore, to read as widely as possible. I got one idea from the *Smithsonian Magazine,* not from an article but from a reader's letter that described a black rainbow. I had never heard of such a thing, but the image was so evocative I knew I had to use it.

Since I am by nature and by training a reader, I derive most of my ideas from books. However, visual images can also be useful. The most obvious visual image is physical—a handsome old house, a quaint village, a medieval town. The dark closes of old Edinburgh, the triple-layered church of San Clemente in Rome, a country inn in Western Maryland—these and other locations have inspired books of mine.

Other images from which I have derived ideas are also physical, but they are one step removed from reality. They are, in fact, misinterpretations of what I actually see. (Being absent-minded and/or nearsighted helps here.) The commonest misinterpretation, with which most of us are familiar, occurs when we wake in the night and see some familiar object in the room transformed by shadows and moonlight. A robe hanging on the bedpost becomes a dangling body or a looming spectre. A rocking chair appears to have an occupant, misshapen and frightening. My most recent stimulus of this nature came when I was driving alone a narrow country road and saw a bundle of trash lying in a ditch. (At least I hope it was a bundle of trash.) The shape suggested a human body, and all at once I had a mental image of a skeleton, dressed in a pair of overalls, sprawled by the road. The exigencies of the plot that I developed from this image demanded a female rather than a male skeleton, and the overalls turned into a calico dress.

Once you learn to spot ideas, you see them all over the place—remarks overheard on planes or buses, unusual signs in shop windows, street names, those one- or two-line fillers newspapers sometimes insert to fill out a column. Then there are satires and take-offs. Hundreds of ideas there! Having once attended a Romance Writers Convention, I knew I had to do a book about such a group. Nothing personal—I plan eventually to satirize cat shows, sci-fi conventions, and my own professional society meetings.

One purely mechanical technique you may want to develop is to write down or clip anything that seems to have potential, and file it away. I have a file bulging with cryptic notes. A few examples: a scribbled description of a mourning gown once worn by the Empress of Austria. It is a fantastic outfit, all black without a speck of color, featuring a face mask of black lace. What am I going to do with this? I don't know yet. But I have a hunch that one day a lady dressed in this fashion will make a marvelous ghost. In my file, there is also an eerie story told me by a local antique dealer about one of her customers; a notation on nuncupative wills; notes on an article on early American gravestones; and a list of terms for groups of animals (a kindle of kittens, a shrewdness of apes) from a book published in 1614. (Goodness, what a mess; I must clean this file out!)

Another file, labeled "miscellaneous," contains newspaper clippings. I keep separate files for clippings on archaeology, the supernatural, and crime. In the miscellaneous file I find, among many others, articles with the following headlines: "Twins May Have One Mind in Two Bodies"; "Switzerland's Dying Language (Romansh)"; and my personal favorite, "The Tree That Ate Roger Williams." Sooner or later I'll get a book out of one of these—maybe all of them.

But—I hear you, the reader, complain—it's a long way from your one-liner to a finished book. True, I told you that in the beginning, remember? An idea is not a plot. A "one-liner" may not even turn out to be an idea! For me, the second stage of the process loosely termed "getting an idea" is to encourage the initial image or brief sentence to develop into something a little more substantial. It's a difficult process to describe or define; perhaps an example will demonstrate what I mean.

Legend in Green Velvet started with a visual image—a view of a steep winding street in the Old Town of Edinburgh. The "idea" that popped into my mind was a single sentence: "What a super setting for a heroine to be chased in." (Grammar never concerns me at such moments.) But I was getting tired of reading and writing books about pursued heroines. Mulling this over, I thought, "How about having the heroine do the chasing for a change?"

Then I turned to my most useful source—books. I started reading about Edinburgh and its history. Before long I came across the old story of Mary, Queen of Scots' illegitimate baby, who was carried off and adopted by one of her ladies-in-waiting. If the story were true (I doubted it, but that wasn't important), Mary was not only an ancestress of the present British royal house, she was also an ancestress of a Scottish noble family. How about one of those close physical resemblances, between a young man (hero or villain, I hadn't decided which) and a Prominent Royal Personage?

I needed more. For one thing, if I decided to make my young man the hero, I needed villains. My reading turned up another intriguing story— that of the Scottish students who swiped the Stone of Scone from Westminster Abbey. The memory of a delightful conversation with an Edinburgh taxi driver who treated me to a fiery lecture on Scottish rights reinforced the idea of using a Scottish Nationalist group in my book. But I couldn't bring myself to make the Nationalists real villains. From what I knew of them, they were an amiable lot. They would, however, provide a useful red herring, and my heroine could safely pursue one of them, since he would not be inclined to harm her.

I still needed villians—genuine, wicked, evil villains. Back to the history books and eventually another piece of the plot. The ancient regalia of Scotland—vanished, during one of the periods of warfare.

By this time my original one-line idea of a heroine chasing a villain through the streets of Edinburgh had developed, not into a plot as yet, but into the skeleton of a plot. I had a heroine, a hero who bore an uncanny resemblance to a Royal Personage, and two sets of villains who were interested in the same treasure for different reasons. The Nationalists wanted the lost royal regalia for its symbolic importance; the genuine villains planned to steal it and sell it. I had strengthened and encouraged my original idea to a point where, or from which, it could be developed into a genuine plot.

There is another technique I often employ when engaged in this second stage of idea development. It is almost the exact antithesis of the active, reading-research method; one might call it a variety of free association. First, it is necessary to find an ambiance in which your mind is free to wander as it will. For me, the ideal situation is a form of mild physical activity (I never engage in strenuous physical activity) that requires minimal mental effort. Walking is ideal. Some types of housework, such as ironing, necessitate a blank mind. (If I thought about what I was doing, I wouldn't do it.) Total relaxation, flat on my back, doesn't work, because when I am relaxed I promptly go to sleep. But as I walk or push the iron across the fabric, a goodly portion of my mind takes off on a tack of its own. With a little encouragement I can turn that detached section down the track I want it to follow. "What about that girl chasing a man up a flight of stairs in Edinburgh? Why the dickens would she do that? Why do people chase people? Did she think he was someone she knew? Did she see him drop his wallet or his handkerchief?"

These methods work for me. They may not work for you, but something else will, if you experiment. And the most encouraging thing about writing is that, as with any other talent, your skill will improve with practice.

I still become irritated when people ask me where I get my ideas, not because it is a silly question, but because it is too complex to be answered in a few words. And also, perhaps, because to a writer getting an idea is the easy part. The hard part is turning that ephemeral one-liner into thousands of actual words on hundreds of actual pages in a connected, coherent manner.

22

STAYING WITH IT

BY MERRILL JOAN GERBER

The thing about the story, "Sorting Things Out," just finished, is that it enlarged like a yeast dough left to sit. Not that it's War and Peace, *of course, but having just finished and still being in the flush of satisfaction because the richness, such as it was, was found, I hasten to assure myself that perhaps this kind of discovery will also be possible, with a longer, deeper work that seems to start out shallow. Stay with it.*

I WROTE THE ABOVE WORDS in my journal one morning in the glow of having finished a story that I'd started six months earlier under the working title "Remodeling Story"—the first paragraph of the original story was as follows:

In twenty-five years of marriage, they had never had a fight like this—not the time Danny had taken home the new student-teacher to advise her on the grading system and stayed at her apartment for dinner . . . and then till midnight . . . without remembering to call Janet, not even the time Janet had given their daughter permission, against Danny's objections, to go to an orphanage in Mexico with some students and her sixth grade teacher, on a night that turned out to be stormy and treacherous.

The fight I envisioned was about a domestic disagreement: Danny wants to remodel the house, Janet doesn't. As I wrote page after page, I felt like a driver in a pelting rain whose windshield wipers weren't working. Where was the road? The subject, as it revealed itself to me, seemed to be—simply—anger. Anger of a wife at her good husband. Anger for no clear reason. The reason I finally settled on was that Danny wants to give his wife a "kitchen of her dreams" at just about the time of life she wants to be done with kitchens for good.

Was this enough of a basis for a story? (This is what you ask yourself about everything you begin to write; it's the common writer's disease known as "Smash yourself before the editors do it first.") Was this even a minor excuse for a story? Why bother to go on with it? What could possibly come of this situation I had taken such pains to set up? (These questions, regardless of how convincingly you attack yourself, have only one reply: You go on with it because that's what you do.)

So I went on, for at least another ten pages, and all I got in a great variety of scenes was more anger flowing in Janet's veins. And resentment. And sadness. (Could this wife's anger be entirely about her resistance to getting a new stove, a new sink, and a new refrigerator? I didn't think so. It didn't feel right to me. Clearly, the story wasn't working.)

I put the story in a folder and didn't open it for a few months, although I saw it daily on my desk and always managed to give myself a kick: another one of those failed stories, a story without a story in it.

Then, one day, I had an idea for a new story. I wrote the first six pages of it and realized (because I'm very good by now at recognizing failed stories) that it also had nowhere to go. It was, oddly enough, another story about a woman angry at her husband. It wasn't the old story, the remodeling story; it was a new story, but now the heroine was angry because her husband did crossword puzzles while she was cooking dinner, or she was angry because he tossed potato chips into his mouth when he was hungry, or because he read the first section of the newspaper every morning and automatically handed her the fashion and food sections. Here it was again. Anger—and lots of it.

But, as I wrote along, I observed that the heroine's target shifted. She was no longer angry at her husband, but was angry at bugs for invading her kitchen, angry at computers that called to sell her things at the dinner hour, angry at missionaries who knocked on her door to promise eternal salvation.

Well, as we all know, life can be very annoying, but since my character's main emotion (and in two separate stories I had started) seemed to be intense and constant anger, maybe something else was at work here, was trying to be expressed. Maybe this story, and the aborted story in the folder, were really about another project.

I continued to work on the story, which made reference to Janet's mother, who lived in a retirement home, from which, one day, two very old sisters go driving and are involved in a severe accident. Both women are killed. Janet's mother, in a fit of despair, confesses to Janet that it makes no difference what we do—"That's what it comes down to in the end. It's all a big nothing."

The anger in my story now gave way to unremitting sadness—Janet finds herself crying several times a day. Finally, she feels she must call her daughter at college to pass on the essential family wisdom which her mother has given her about life: "It's all a big nothing."

It was while writing the following scene that the true direction of the story was revealed to me:

"Myra," Janet said. "This is your mother."

"What's wrong, Mom? You sound funny."

"I'm not sure I should have had children," she said. "I'm not sure this world is such a good place, after all."

"What other world is there, Mom? What's going on? Is Daddy there?"

"He's just a man," Janet said. "Men don't have the main responsibility. They don't grow the babies."

"Mom, are you alone there? I think you better call someone to come over right away. . . ."

"I don't need company. That's the last thing I need. What I need to do is get into bed and stay there. I can't handle this stuff anymore."

"Mom, I think you need to see someone . . . a therapist."

This suggestion comes to Janet as a surprise, and yes, to me as the author. Janet protests: "I'm not crazy," and her daughter assures her she isn't, but that she does seem deeply stressed (as we all have a right to be at times) and a therapist may be able to help her sort out the "jumble" in her head.

Janet replies, "I'm not supposed to have a jumble. I'm a mother. I have three grown children. I am a mature woman. I have weathered many crises."

So: at last, as I later wrote in my journal, I had found my real intention. *This story is about the larger grief in Janet's life; disappointment, aging, mourning in advance the death of her mother.*

This suggestion that the heroine consider therapy, coming from her daughter, was what the story was leading me to discover all along: that the anger (the only emotion I could see at first as I wrote about this woman) was a symptom of much deeper stress, depression, and sadness. My own false leads in starting the story were exactly what the character's mind in depression would tend to focus on: reasons that

101

aren't the real reasons. (Or are only a very small part of the whole picture.)

If I'd known at the beginning that this story was going to be about a woman who finally decides to seek therapy, it might have been loaded, didactic, heavy-handed. But the illumination, which came suddenly in the story (and came to me just as suddenly), seems to make it right—into a story that works.

Those half-started, or half-finished, stories that plague every writer may just be the wedge into the deeper and richer story. It's best not to judge those false starts as worthless or barren. The creative mind has a way of working out solutions once the problem is set before it. We need not regard the process as mystical as much as one of patience and slow discovery.

Don't throw away those deeply felt but ambiguous starts: Wait a while. Try again. Try later—and try a new way. Try with a new voice, a new tense, a new place of physical entry into the story. See what emerges. If you stay at it, the breakthrough will come. Or at least we writers hope it will come. If we don't keep trying, though, there's no way to know.

23

EFFECTIVE TRANSITIONS

BY GEORGE R. HEMINGWAY

Jane got up early and made breakfast. She wasn't feeling well because she'd been out late the night before. She felt better now. She'd gone back to bed when things quieted down and had been able to sleep.

DID YOU NOTICE A MOMENTARY CONFUSION when you read this passage? It was due to a faulty transition.

The brain processes information a short time after the words have been read. By the time it was established that Jane was feeling rotten, you had already absorbed the information that she felt fine. So your brain sorted it out and said, "Oh, I get it now!—she was feeling bad earlier, but now it's later and she feels better." In the meantime, you have fed in the next sentence to be processed. All this gives rise to fog.

Much has been said about not revealing too much to readers—i.e., giving facts and descriptions, but letting them make of it what they will.

This is a sound principle; but what you *do* tell them, you must tell with utmost clarity!

A transition transfers the reader's attention smoothly from one situation to another. With a little careful thought, you can sometimes make several transitions in one statement.

There are four kinds of transitions:
- Space
- Time
- Emotion
- Viewpoint

Now, try this one:

When Alex left, Rosemary hurriedly fled up to her bedroom so no one would see the tears that achingly welled up in her eyes. She felt quite cheerful and full of optimism when she awoke next morning.

Below her, Aunt Nancy's flower garden shimmered unreal and fairylike in the early morning light. In the kitchen, she knew that preparations were already underway for the garden party that was to take place in the afternoon.

Here we have a problem involving a transition in time, a transition in emotion, and a couple of transitions in space.

You are in the bedroom with Rosemary and she is obviously distraught over something that Alex did or said. In the morning, she feels better—but you have to get her through the night! Suppose you simply insert something like this:

She tumbled exhausted into bed and soon lapsed into a dreamless sleep.

Now you've arrived at morning having made a transition in *emotion* as well as a transition in *time*.

But your reader is still in the bedroom with Rosemary. Somehow, you have to transport him/her to the flower garden and then to the kitchen.

Let's rewrite this:

When Alex left, Rosemary hurriedly fled up to her bedroom so no one would see the tears that achingly welled up in her eyes. *She tumbled exhausted into bed and soon lapsed into a dreamless sleep. When she awoke* she felt quite cheerful and full of optimism.

She moved to the window and opened the sash wide, inhaling the crisp morning air. As she gazed down at the colorful picture below her, Aunt Nancy's flower garden shimmered unreal and fairylike in the early morning light. *Noises through the open kitchen door rose to meet her.* Here, she knew that preparations were already underway for the garden party that was to take place in the afternoon.

If at all possible, don't make a reader engage in any secondary reasoning that would tend to becloud the written text. The ideal is to have your reader slide smoothly from one thought into the next, while being barely conscious that he/she is reading.

Let's go back to Jane at the introduction and concoct a brief fragment of life:

Jane got up early and made breakfast. She wasn't feeling well because she'd been out late the night before. She felt better now. She'd gone back to bed when things quieted down and had been able to sleep. It was hard to sleep in this weather because one stuck to everything.

Outside, the sun was boring down between the trees and the ground was steaming. Most of the year it steamed unless it was pouring rain and when it did there was a deluge.

Tarzan swung through the vines towards home. His last hurdle landed him on the front porch of the tree house.

"How come you're home before five o'clock?" Jane asked in surprise.

"Jane, mix me a martini," said Tarzan, not answering her question.

Jane shrugged. "We're out of olives," she said, "so you'll have to drink it the way it is."

Tarzan knocked it back in one gulp. Then he slammed the glass down heavily, his hand still on it.

"Jane, mix me a double," he barked.

"Say, what's getting into you?" stammered Jane. "You never drink doubles in the afternoon!"

"Jane, it's a jungle out there!" replied Tarzan.

This passage tends to be raggy and causes your reader to jump from one situation to another without warning, making it confusing, which if it goes on for very long, leads to reader fatigue.

By the judicious addition of a few well-placed transitions, you could smooth the passage right out.

As it stands, the reader would assume that Tarzan somehow came in from the porch and sat at a table. It is also implicit in the story that Jane got the mixings from somewhere and prepared his martini. In some situations, you might want to lead your reader into assuming certain things. But when this adds nothing to the story, but rather creates confusion, it is better to be explicit.

Let's redo the passage, adding some simple transitions:

When Jane had been up earlier and made breakfast, she hadn't felt well, having been out late the night before. She'd gone back to bed when things quieted down and had been able to sleep. *Now it was early afternoon,* and she felt better. It was hard to sleep in this weather because one stuck to everything.

She peered through the open window. The sun was boring down between the trees and the ground was steaming. Most of the year it steamed unless it was pouring rain, and when it did there was a deluge.

Her gaze focused on Tarzan, who was swinging through the vines towards home. His last hurdle landed him on the front porch of the tree house.

"How come you're home before five o'clock?" Jane stared at him in surprise.

Tarzan pushed past her without answer and seated himself at the small table in the breakfast nook.

"Jane, mix me a martini," said Tarzan, not answering the question.

Jane shrugged *and proceeded to take the gin and vermouth from the cabinet over the sink.*

"We're out of olives," she said, "so you'll have to drink it the way it is."

Tarzan seized the drink and knocked it back in one gulp. Then he slammed the glass heavily on the table, his hand still on it.

"Jane, mix me a double!" he barked.

"Say, what's getting into you?" stammered Jane. "You never drink doubles in the afternoon!"

"Jane, it's a jungle out there!"

A transition in viewpoint is a means of shifting the reader's attention from the viewpoint of one person to the viewpoint of another. This device may be a little more difficult to achieve than the others and not as widely used.

To effect a transition in viewpoint, a story has to enter the consciousness of more than one person, and is therefore used primarily in longer works, but even novelists don't use it extensively. They prefer to use the omniscient point of view—major character only—and switch the viewpoint chapter by chapter. However, in some instances, a transition in viewpoint is the only logical solution.

Here is another problem for Rosemary:

Rosemary gently lifted the new pearl necklace from the polished surface of her vanity table and fastened it around her neck. She glanced at the reflection of the tall figure in her mirror. His possessive, self-assured smile maddened her.

"So he thinks he can buy me," she thought, with fury. But she deemed it appropriate to play it low-key.

"They're lovely," she murmured, wondering what lay behind that smug demeanor.

Alex, seeing her assume a disarming role, experienced a vague feeling of confusion tinged with pity.

"But why feel sorry for her?" he chided himself. "She's never felt sorry for anybody in her life—least of all me. And she looks after herself very well."

Notice how the reader's attention traveled from her, through the mirror to Alex, and then into his consciousness.

Transition in time

Dr. Nixon delivers autopsy report to Sherlock Chauvin.

It was 4:00 p.m. but already dusk by the time I emerged from Westminster County Morgue. The Christmas Eve crowds were scurrying to-and-fro, intent upon their last minute errands.

"Taxi," I called, and dashed across the wet pavement as a cab drew up, its horse steaming and stamping on the cobblestones.

"Scotland Yard," I said as I entered the cab.

Comfortably settled in the cab, I had time to reflect. The minutes passed.

"Sometimes," I mused, "I regret going into pathology. My colleagues in ophthalmology have been idle for a week, their patients being reluctant to go for eye examinations in the Christmas season. But my patients have little regard for the season. On the other hand," I reasoned, "my patients seldom complain."

The cab *finally* drew up to Scotland Yard where I had arranged to meet Sherlock by appointment. I paid the driver and entered the building, only a few minutes late.

Transition in space

Janet peered through the window of the trim little cottage at the vast expanse of empty ocean before her. *She pictured the trawler "Josephine," her holds filled with fish—and Jim at her helm—as she plowed her way homeward.*

It transpired, however, that at that moment, Jim was not at the helm. Having broken an ankle in a freak squall the day before, he lay helpless in his berth.

Transition in emotion

When Keith got Barbara's letter breaking their engagement, he felt sick. He didn't go to work that day and plumbed the depths of despair; sprawled across his unmade bed, half grieving and half sulking. He slept some of the time and it was four o'clock when he finally woke up.

He stirred and blinked at the familiar surroundings. Then he decided that he felt hungry.

Reaching for the phone, he dialed.

"Hello! Cheryl? How have you been?"

"I'm O.K.—still upright anyway. . . . no, I haven't been going out much lately."

"I was just wondering, Cheryl, how about dinner tonight?"

"Great! I'll pick you up from your office at five."

Back to viewpoint

When Victoria entered his private office, David Sandover, the newly appointed President, was already at his desk.

"He's taller than his pictures—and younger," she thought, as she sat down and flipped open her steno pad.

Sandover was not given to publicly displaying his feelings, yet he seldom missed much. He feigned glancing at a report.

"Take a letter, Miss Brown," he said.

But as his steel blue eyes surveyed her, his thoughts were not on letters.

Acquiring the skill to handle transitions does not require genius. People may say of you, "I love to read her stories. She writes so smoothly and with such clarity."

This could be due, at least in part, to your ability to handle transitions effectively.

24

Developing a Specialty in Fiction

By Ellen Hunnicutt

The term "specialty writing" is usually associated with nonfiction. It makes us think immediately of food writers, medical writers, or baseball writers. But it can also be a useful and profitable avenue for fiction writers, especially beginners.

How does it work? I'm a music teacher, and one of my first published stories was about a violinist. That sounds simple enough. In fact, it was far from simple.

When I began trying to write fiction, I studied published stories intently. That was beneficial in some ways. Observing how other writers wrote dialogue, let stories build with rising action, or wrote effective endings taught me a lot about craft. But it was also detrimental because I attempted to use characters, subjects, and settings similar to those in published stories. Since I seldom, if ever, read stories about musicians in music settings, I assumed editors and readers had no interest in them, that my own personal experience had no value. I tried to write the fiction that seemed to be in vogue—stories about doctors, about people in New York, about writers living in Italy—even though I knew little about those subjects. After all, I reasoned, I could always research and "put in a little detail" to make a story "authentic." But those manuscripts were almost always rejected.

I wrote my first music story almost by chance, never expecting to have it published. One day I was looking at the shelves of music beside my piano, music I used for students, my own scores, the music I had inherited from my late violinist-father. I decided to write a story about a violinist. I think my purpose was to preserve some of the interesting and even funny childhood memories I had of violinists: how much time they spent practicing scales, how they were always searching for practice space without drapes because of the acoustics, how they always

108

wished they owned valuable violins but rarely did (contrary to romantic stories).

To my surprise, an editor accepted the story eagerly, saying he was pleased to have something "different," and that it was obvious I knew my subject because the story "rang true."

Both of the editor's comments are significant. An area of human experience that isn't often written about is an *excellent* subject for fiction. Editors are always looking for something fresh. The second point is that you can't write a convincing story if you don't know your subject.

When I read that first music story now, I blush. I'd write it differently today, with a firmer grasp of craft and more polish. But a story by a beginner, wobbly on craft, succeeded because the subject was fresh and the details authentic.

Many other stories with music backgrounds followed, and eventually a music novel. I don't think a writer's specialty is ever exhausted. But that doesn't mean the writer can continue working only from memory forever. Specialists find themselves out doing research as often as other writers. My research, however, is almost always interesting, and often pure joy. Through it, I keep gaining additional information about a subject I love. Once as a journalist, I had to research air conditioners for an assigned article. I am not mechanical, and that task was rock-splitting labor. Also, despite all the effort, my piece contained errors, because I'd had no body of general knowledge to begin with.

Here are a few things I've enjoyed learning: Has much music been written for solo viola? (Not much.) Can you use the nylon strings from a classical guitar on a folk guitar? (Yes, and they're much easier on the fingers than steel strings.) Do Suzuki violin classes really teach young children to play? (Sometimes yes, sometimes no, but observing the classes was fascinating.) My research is often in books I would select for recreational reading. My field work is usually an activity I'd eagerly choose for a day out.

Certainly, my most fascinating project was researching steam calliopes for my novel, *Suite for Calliope*. I read about them, attended circuses, examined and photographed several instruments, talked to players—in fact, I did virtually everything except play one. Each time I tried, I was told, "If anything went wrong, our insurance wouldn't cover you." That in itself was an interesting fact. (I was permitted to ride an elephant, but I was not allowed to go into the cage with a lion.)

I'm often asked by young writers if it's really necessary for details in fiction to be correct. Since in many cases readers aren't specialists, would they know the difference? The answer is *yes*. When the writer is "faking," readers are seldom fooled.

Here's a comparable situation. When reading a book translated from another language, we can sometimes tell the translation is poor, even if we don't know the original language. There's a clumsiness to it, the prose isn't fluent, details may be missing or may not make sense, or there are errors that are downright funny. That is typical of what can happen when writers undertake subjects they don't know.

I wrote the following examples for classroom use, patterning them after problems I see in student manuscripts.

The first is set in a research center:

Two scientists meet in their laboratory. The first asks, "Made any scientific breakthroughs lately?" The second replies, "No, but I expect to soon."

This is what I call "talking in headlines." Real people (and characters) usually talk about little things. We needn't be scientists to know this conversation doesn't "feel" authentic. Here's another:

He was a glass blower. He blew his glass every morning, a wide array of colorful trinkets and gadgets. [Then the subject of glass blowing is never again mentioned in the story.]

Again, the passage doesn't sound plausible. We are suspicious of "trinkets and gadgets." But there's a second problem. Simply labeling a character "glass blower" (stonemason, accountant, or whatever) isn't enough. When we introduce a subject to fiction, especially one as unusual as glass blowing, the reader expects to learn more about it. We'd want to know about the blower's pipe, his fire, and precisely what those "trinkets and gadgets" were. When the information does not appear, readers suspect they are being tricked. And one more:

She had a position high in city government, dealing with development. At parties, people always sought her out to press their special interests, and to get inside information about development.

In this sort of story, the writer doesn't quite talk in headlines, and does attempt to integrate the subject into the narrative, but manages only to produce ten or fifteen pages of generalities. Because specifics are missing, the reader of this story would assume (correctly) that the writer knew little about city development.

Another question often asked is, "What if I have no special knowledge?" The chances are very good that you do. Every human being is unique. Make an inventory of your experiences, your interests. Your subject should be one you enjoy and one that fits your talents. Remember, you needn't be the world's greatest authority at the beginning. You will add to your fund of knowledge as you go along.

Sometimes the best thing writers can do is stop taking writing classes. There are people who return to workshops semester after semester. Perhaps these people—and their writing—would benefit from courses in history or anthropology, from taking trips, or joining groups with interests other than writing.

And the final question: "Suppose I do have special knowledge. How do I integrate it into my fiction?" Background material needs, first of all, to be plausible and natural. Details are the best strategy. In *Suite for Calliope,* Ada, my heroine, is remembering from childhood how she was switched from piano lessons to violin lessons. She says:

Within a few weeks, I was playing adequately, with a fair vibrato and a strong bow arm.

Then, having introduced a subject, we have to stay with it, working it into the story. When Ada, now a teenager, runs away, she needs money to live on and earns it by playing music. In a strange city, she looks through a restaurant window and sees an organ sitting idle. She walks in boldly and invents a story, telling the hostess she has been sent to play. Ada knows that diners often tip musicians. Again, the passage works through details:

The organ stood behind the salad bar. To my surprise, it was a fine old Wurlitzer with draw bars. As I sat down, I looked directly into the face of a pink-cheeked elderly man with white hair. "Play 'Lady of Spain!' " he called out.

The information should not be too simplistic. It's boring to be told what we already know (that violins are played with bows, that people who lead orchestras are called conductors). D.H. Lawrence advised writers to "take the reader into secret places." Readers enjoy gaining new information, and it isn't necessary that they completely understand everything you write. Much later in *Suite,* Ada, now a composer, is sitting in a library, studying a music score:

[It was] a brief composition of only two pages, without key or time signature, without bar lines, and opening with a peculiar triplet formed from an eighth note and quarter note.

Perhaps only a trained musician would understand every word of the passage, but the average reader gets the point, that Ada has become a competent professional musician. It's important, of course, to keep the story on track, and not to lose it in a sea of technical information; but I think it's just as important to remember that readers enjoy entering the special world of a character.

Fiction writers find their specialties in the most amazing places. I wasn't surprised when one of my students, an attorney, began writing stories about lawyers; and it was predictable that a woman with a vast knowledge of birds would put birds in her stories. But in the last year I have seen two writers get off to grand starts with—of all things—Antarctica and gymnastics!

I hope, of course, that my fiction offers something worthwhile to readers; but I think my ultimate reason for writing it is the satisfaction it gives me. So often, we hear people say, "Work is eating up my life. I have no time left to pursue the things that really interest me." As a specialty writer, I pursue my own interests every day; my enthusiasm, in turn, drives the work. The best way to find your own specialty might be to ask yourself what you would rather be doing than what you're doing now.

25

THE MAJOR ROLE OF MINOR
CHARACTERS IN FICTION

BY HANS OSTROM

AFTER READING AN EARLY DRAFT of a novel I had submitted, my editor—as I expected—commented on several areas that needed improvement. One of her responses to the novel surprised me, however. She said that she had had some difficulty with several of the minor characters. In her view, I had not depicted these characters vividly enough, and when a significant amount of time had elapsed between appearances of some secondary characters, she found that her sense of those characters had become cloudy.

To be sure, the remarks about the novel's minor characters came toward the end of the editor's written evaluation, after she had commented on larger elements of the novel. I do not want to imply that a concern for minor characters should outweigh a concern for the plot, primary characters, threads of suspense, setting, and other crucial aspects of a novel.

Ironically, however, because novelists must focus so intently on these obvious concerns, minor characters may not receive the attention they deserve, especially in early drafts. And poorly conceived minor characters can weaken a novel substantially. As a newcomer to writing novels, I realized after reading my editor's letter that concentrating on the major areas of my novels did not mean that I could afford to neglect minor characters. I also realized that, perhaps unconsciously, I had made the mistake of equating "minor" with "incidental."

Revising the manuscript in response to my editor's concerns was not difficult, but my interest in the topic of minor characters did not stop there. I thought further about the essential ways in which minor characters contribute to novels in general, and I offer my observations here in hopes that they might help other new novelists.

Perhaps the most obvious function of minor characters is in advancing the plot. In basic terms, the plot consists of events in which the main character(s) take part. Nonetheless, minor characters can often play major roles in constructing the plot.

In mystery novels, they can provide a crucial bit of information to the sleuth, or they can become unwitting obstacles to the success of either a detective or a criminal, or they can trigger a memory on the part of a detective that will allow him or her to solve a puzzle or to take the right action. In mainstream novels, the contribution of minor characters to the plot can be just as important but in an even greater variety of ways. Virtually any element of crisis or resolution can be enhanced by a minor character.

Charles Dickens's novels remain an excellent example of this potential; even though ideas about "the novel" have evolved since his era, the range of ways in which he used minor characters to contribute to intricate plots still offers a model to novelists for what it is possible to do with minor characters. Compared with many contemporary novels, Dickens's works may sometimes seem crowded or "overpopulated" with minor characters, and yet the portraits and functions of those characters are always painstakingly precise. Dickens is beyond imitation, but he may be the best example of how seriously a novelist must take lesser characters. His works reinforce the platitude about a chain being as strong only as its weakest link: A minor character, even one with a bit part, can be the most important link in a chain of events that constitutes the plot of your novel.

A second major contribution minor characters can make to a novel is to enhance the development of the main character(s). We learn much about main characters *only* from main characters—from seeing them in action or from listening to their interior voices. However, we can learn as much about them from the way they behave in encounters with secondary characters. Even when such brief encounters are not crucial to the plot (and they often are), they show us how the main character functions in "ordinary life." Furthermore, the whole concept of "round" or "three-dimensional" characters depends on the existence of "flat," "two-dimensional" characters who allow primary characters to stand in relief. As in motion pictures, such characters literally "support" the major roles in novels.

Another way of describing this function of minor characters is to say that they add texture to a novel. In fact, one of the discoveries I made in my transition from writing short fiction to writing novels is that novel writing allows me more latitude to work to enrich the texture of my fiction. Generally speaking, one can employ a larger cast of characters in a novel than one can in a short story. This situation makes for more freedom, but it also asks the writer to think more extensively about what to *do* with the freedom and, more specifically, what to do with additional minor characters in the cast.

Minor characters can also contribute to the development of suspense, either in a scene or in a whole novel. Consider one example from a classic of the suspense genre, Dashiell Hammett's *The Maltese Falcon.* In Chapter 16, when "the black bird" suddenly falls into the hands of Sam Spade, it is delivered by a mysterious, dying stranger:

> The corridor door opened. Spade shut his mouth. Effie Perine jumped down from the desk, but a man opened the connecting door before she could reach it. . . . The tall man stood in the doorway and there was nothing to show that he saw Spade. He said, "You know—" and then the liquid bubbling came up in his throat and submerged whatever else he said. He put his other hand over the hand that held the ellipsoid. Holding himself stiffly straight, not putting his hands out to break his fall, he fell forward as a tree falls.

The scene itself is suspenseful, for as readers we sense the mixture of confusion and terror that Spade and his secretary feel when the dying man appears at their door. Moreover, in relation to the entire plot, the appearance of this minor character adds enormously to the suspense. Who is he? How did he get the Maltese Falcon? Who killed him? Will Spade be accused of killing him? What should Spade do now? To a great extent, suspense is uncertainty, and Hammett uses a minor character to dump a truck load of uncertainty on Sam Spade's doorstep.

Minor characters can contribute to suspense not just in mystery and action fiction but in virtually every kind. Rust Hills, in *Writing in General and Short Story in Particular,* applies the idea of suspense to all good fiction, saying that it "can function in literature as subtly and effectively as it does in music." Minor characters are one important source of such subtlety and effectiveness. In James Joyce's classic story "Araby," for example, the minor character of the uncle is an enormous problem for the main character, the boy who wants to go to the bazaar to buy something for the girl he worships. In coming home late and generally being difficult, the uncle delays the boy's departure, adding to the suspense of the story (will the boy make it to the bazaar or not?)

115

and to the sense of disillusionment and disappointed desire that Joyce creates.

Still another way minor characters can be useful to fiction writers is to help evoke a sense of place and atmosphere. Whether it's Conan Doyle's London, Raymond Chandler's Los Angeles, William Faulkner's Mississippi, or Ann Beattie's New York, our sense of place depends on the people in the place. Authors can use minor characters to help convey the flavor of a region or a city quickly and convincingly. Fog and gaslights add to our sense of Holmes's London, but Mrs. Hudson, cabbies, bobbies, and a legion of other minor characters contribute as much, if not more, to our mental picture of the fictional London Conan Doyle creates.

Finally, minor characters can be interesting in and of themselves. A quick sketch of a minor character can (and should) be vivid and entertaining—should stand on its own in some way. Moreover, like all characters, minor ones grow in surprising ways, demanding more attention from the author during revisions, competing for greater roles as novels or stories take shape. In my own novel, a bartender (of all people) who I thought would be almost incidental became more crucial to the plot and to the sleuth (a sheriff) than I had ever imagined. He became more of a confidante and a representative of sorts of the ordinary people in the rural county. Such "independence" on the part of minor characters may be even more likely to occur in novels than in short stories.

These, then, are several significant roles minor characters can play in fiction. In addition, there are some rules of thumb a writer should keep in mind during the revision process:

1. Beware of stereotyping. Because minor characters *are* minor, and because authors cannot afford to spend more than a few sentences describing them, a stereotype can be tempting. A waiter or a cop or a librarian need not be a stock character. Don't call Central Casting; instead, draw on your own experience and your notebook for a not-so-typical sketch.

2. Beware of the time lapses between appearances that minor characters make. If the interval between appearances is substantial (several chapters, for instance), it is even more necessary for the first appearance to be striking. As mystery novelist Lillian O'Donnell has remarked, "Clue: If I have to go back into the early pages of a first draft

to find out a character's name, that character is not real." O'Donnell's observation applies to mainstream fiction as well, of course, and one might add that if a reader's memory of a minor character's first appearance is fuzzy, how well is that character really functioning in the novel?

3. Give minor characters memorable but not outlandish names, and make sure the names and initials of your minor characters are sufficiently different to avoid confusing the reader. Don't make your reader wonder which character was Ron Ryan and which was Bryan Ray. Most of us are unconsciously attracted to a very narrow range of names, and we need to broaden that range in our fiction.

4. Don't be afraid to eliminate a minor character entirely. The fact that minor characters can themselves be interesting cuts both ways because a minor character can upstage a major one without contributing to plot, character development, suspense, or atmosphere. He or she may be engaging without being genuinely functional.

Ask yourself whether the character ought to appear at all. (If you are moving from short fiction to a novel, you may find that the comparative freedom of the novel creates a greater temptation to clutter the stage with characters; the clutter springs not so much from the number of characters as from the purposelessness of characters.) Such characters need not disappear forever. They may turn out to be useful in other stories and novels, and may even become main characters in other works.

Ultimately, the nature of minor characters in fiction is something of a paradox: although such characters are by definition secondary and often two-dimensional, they add depth to various elements of stories and novels.

26

CHOOSING AND USING TENSE IN FICTION

BY ANN HARLEMAN

TIME, EINSTEIN SHOWED US more than half a century ago, is relative. Our location in time, like our location in space, can change. Whether an action is in the past or the future, whether it lasts a long time or an instant, whether it happens once or over and over—all these matters depend on the position of the observer.

We fiction writers knew this all along. For Proust, the action of dipping a biscuit in tea and eating it lasts for seven volumes; for Jerzy Kosinski, in *The Painted Bird,* the destruction of an entire village along with the rape and murder of several dozen inhabitants takes only five pages. The relativity of time in fiction goes far beyond that of "real" time. Fictional time is as elastic as taffy.

In working with fictional time, the first rule to keep in mind is, *Choose your basic time frame to suit your story's needs.* Tense, the device language provides for expressing time, offers the choice of past, present or future. In choosing the base tense for your story, you are choosing more than just time. The tense you select affects the distance from which your reader views the action, the intensity of identification between your reader and your characters—even the voice in which you tell the story. Choice of tense—like choice of plot, setting, and characters—is a decision at the heart of your story's design.

Let's look closely at the three choices. The *past tense,* because it is the most natural, has traditionally been the tense of most fiction. It is the tense most readers expect to find when they open a novel. "It was the best of times; it was the worst of times," puts the reader securely in the position of hearing a tale unfold: events that have already occurred, a story whose ending the teller knows. The past tense puts readers at a distance from the story. The distance may vary—from the remote, "Once upon a time there lived a beautiful princess," to "Yesterday I finally realized what I had to do"—but the distance is there.

The advantage of the past tense is its flexibility; it works with any point of view. With a first-person narrator, past tense implies some development on the character's part. A narrator who doesn't develop, learn, or change comes across as blind or unreal—the "unreliable" narrator that Poe was so fond of. But how close your reader feels to your main character is up to you. How formal or colloquial your language is, whether your voice is lyrical or ironic—the past tense leaves these decisions open. And because it's the tense most commonly used, you run less risk of diverting your readers' attention from the story itself to your technique ("Look, Ma, I'm writing!").

The *present tense* lets you achieve special effects with distance, immediacy, and pace. It can plunge your reader right into the action, virtually eliminating the distance between reader and story—and, often, the distance between reader and character. In my story "Limbo," the point-of-view character is an eight-year-old girl whose fear of dying motivates the story's action. I wanted the reader to identify with her right away (the story is only 3,000 words long) and to feel the weight of her fear—otherwise the action wouldn't be believable. The story opens this way:

She's had the dream again. The dream that she can never remember once she wakes up, that leaves behind only its vinegar taste in her mouth. Her heart clatters heavily in her chest. The swell of her own breathing, raspy and tight, fills her ears.

Here, the readers are with the character from the first word, and her feelings have great immediacy even before the dream is described.

Bringing your reader close to action and character doesn't mean your story has to be fast-paced. If you want to create an effect of stopped time, the present tense can work as a "freeze-frame" device. In my story "Adam and Eve," told in the past tense by a young woman looking back to her fourteenth summer, I use the present tense for the moment when the narrator learns that her much-loved great-aunt, with whom she lives, has cancer—a moment that seemed to last forever at the time and that lives on, frozen, in her memory.

Or suppose you want another kind of timelessness—a sense of actions repeated over and over, forming a backdrop for the events of your story. The opening sentence of Toni Morrison's *The Bluest Eye* takes the reader right into the setting of the novel, a setting made up not of objects, but of endlessly repeated actions: "Nuns go by as quiet as lust, and drunken men and sober eyes sing in the lobby of the Greek hotel." Like her characters, readers are caught and held in an inescapable cycle.

The *present tense* works best with a first-person narrator—someone your readers feel so close to that it seems natural for them to experience each event as it occurs, without benefit of hindsight. If you use present tense with the third-person, shifting from outside your point-of-view character to inside can be awkward. "He walks up the path. He puts his hand on the gate. It swings open, and he steps into the yard." But suppose you want to convey your character's feelings. "He thinks, I don't like this" is too abrupt. "He is frightened" is telling rather than showing. All right, how about, "His hand is trembling"? Fine—but you're still *outside* the character. Your story is turning out to be imitation Hemingway.

What about the *future tense*? A stretch of future tense longer than a sentence or so tends to create an ominous voice. At its best, it is mysterious and prophetic. While the past tense conveys a solid sense of reality, describing events as if they had already happened, the future tense emphasizes the visionary, imaginative quality of events that haven't yet occurred. Mary Gordon uses the future tense for a narrator imagining the aftermath of nuclear war:

> I will have to kill her to keep her from entering our shelter. If she enters it, she will kill us with her knife or the broken glass in her pocket. Kill us for the food we hide, which may, even as we take it in, be killing us. Kill us for the life of her children.

The future tense pushes your storytelling voice toward the abstract and the general. Details like the knife and the broken glass ground your vision in the concrete and the specific, so that your readers can see it.

At some points in your story, you'll probably want to depart from your base tense to show events that take place before the story begins (flashback) or after it ends (flash-forward). This brings us to the second rule in working with fictional time: *When you depart from your basic time frame, make it logical.* Events earlier than the main action of your story need a tense more "in-the-past" than your base tense; events later than the main action need a tense more "in-the-future."

Flashbacks fill your reader in on your characters' pasts. When the base

120

tense of your story is the past, flashbacks have to be in the past perfect. This can involve you in a lot of syllable sludge:

That day at the beach two summers before, George had been swimming out beyond the breakers and had seemed to be in trouble. Martha had had to swim out to rescue him, and when she had reached him, he had been being pulled by the undertow, which had . . .

And so on, and so on. One way around this is to reduce the bulkiness of the verb forms by using contractions—"when she'd reached him, he'd been being pulled by the undertow." Another way is to enter and leave your flashback using the past perfect, but switch unobtrusively to simple past in between:

That day at the beach two summers before, George had been swimming out beyond the breakers and had seemed to be in trouble. Martha had to swim out to rescue him, and when she reached him, he was being pulled by the undertow . . . That was how they'd met. Now, thinking about it, Martha sighed.

When the base tense of your story is the present, the whole flashback can simply be in the past tense. Easing in and out of flashbacks is no problem:

That day at the beach two summers before, George was swimming . . . Now, thinking about it, Martha sighs.

If your story is going to have several flashbacks, you may want to choose the present as the base tense.

Flashbacks involve a trade-off. They enrich your narrative by providing your characters with a history and your events with a context. Your story gains depth and a greater sense of reality. But a flashback interrupts your story's momentum. It turns your reader's attention toward the past rather than pushing it in the direction your story is heading.

Flash-forwards describe something that happens *after* the main action. But future time has to be logical within your story's time frame. If the base tense of your story is the past, you'll cast your flash-forward in the subjunctive:

Mary, who in years to come would win the national rope-jumping competition and later go on to become world champion, had no time for play or idle chatter with the other little girls.

You'll use the future tense for glimpses of the future only if the base tense of your story is the present:

Mary, who in the years to come will win the national rope-jumping competition and later go on to become world champion, has no time for play or idle chatter with the other little girls.

Be even more sparing with flash-forwards than you are with flash-backs. Not only do they interrupt the flow of your narrative, they also cut down on suspense—the element that keeps your readers reading. If you can, make your flash-forward *ask* a question rather than answer it. Give just enough of a glimpse of future events to arouse your readers' curiosity. For example:

Years later, when I had a son of my own, I would finally understand why my father did what he did; but at the moment when I found him, I only knew that he hadn't cared enough about me to stick around.

Logic—replicating the "real"-time sequence of events—isn't the only reason to depart from the base tense of your story. Sometimes the story itself—because of subject matter, mood, distance—demands a shift in tense. The third and last rule in working with fictional time is: *Keep your time frame flexible.* This is where the relativity of fictional time can really work for you. Give yourself the freedom to shift tense, keeping it relative to your fictional effect—subject matter, action, mood, distance.

In my story "Someone Else" (runner-up in the *Chicago Tribune's* Nelson Algren Contest), I have the first-person narrator tell her story in the past tense. As the story opens, she's looking back on a series of events that span fifteen years. I wanted the story to begin with an opening sentence that would hook the reader right away. "Mary Lee Chase fell in love with my husband when she was twelve months old." That meant the story moved toward an outcome the reader already knew, so suspense would have to come from *how* it happened rather than from *what* happened. The final scene, in which the girl, on her sixteenth birthday, comes for the narrator's husband, was flat and anti-climactic. But how to avoid that, given the opening sentence? To see how it would sound, I shifted the final scene to future tense. It became the narrator's vision of what was going to happen three years after the moment that she's speaking—the *now* of the story.

122

The whole scene resonated; it came alive. But the new ending left the story's *now* too unclear. The entire story seemed to "float" in time. To anchor it, I added a sentence or two at the beginning of each scene (except the opening one), in the present tense, describing some aspect of the setting—the edge of a lake in Minnesota in early spring—where the narrator was walking as she told her story.

Play with tense the same way you play with setting, character, plot. Don't lock yourself into a set pattern. Don't decide that every section will open with the present and close with the past, for example. Or even that every flashback must be in the past. (Some flashbacks need to shift to the timeless present of frozen memories.)

Experiment. Change a section from past to present, from present to future, and see whether you like the result. And if you find yourself unintentionally writing a section in a tense that's not the one you started with, don't automatically go back and change it. Stop and look at how it works. Maybe your instincts are sounder than you think.

Your choice of tense is a way of locating your readers in time—giving them a position from which to view the characters and the action—just as setting is a way of locating your readers in space. Why not vary your temporal setting just as you do your spatial setting, to suit the needs of your story? By doing so, you can turn the relativity of fictional time to your advantage.

27

GREAT STORYTELLING

BY LINDA BARLOW

I WRITE POPULAR FICTION. When using that term I refer to the so-called good read—novels peopled with sympathetic characters who play their parts within the context of a well-plotted, well-paced, emotionally powerful story.

Think about some of the novelists whose books hit the bestseller lists every time. Some typical examples are Stephen King, Judith Krantz, Tom Clancy, Sidney Sheldon, and Danielle Steel. These writers differ greatly in their subject matter and style, but there is one attribute they all share: Once you start reading their books, it is unlikely that you will stop until you reach the end. They are terrific storytellers.

One reason such authors are so successful is that good storytellers have you at their mercy. While you are engaged in the act of reading one of their books, it briefly becomes the most important thing in your life—you empathize with the main characters, feeling their emotions as if they were your own; you stay up until two avidly turning the pages; and when you finally get to the end, you feel that odd combination of elation and sadness: elation because it's all worked out the way it ought to have worked out, and sadness because it's over.

Five years ago I was a suburban wife, mother, and part-time English teacher who had a dream: more than anything else I wanted to write a novel and get it published. Now I'm a successful author who's been fortunate enough to go from wondering how to make my fantasy come true to helping other writers who share the same dream.

How do writers inspire this total involvement on the part of their readers? There are several elements you must incorporate, but four that stand out: sympathetic characters, escalating conflicts, narrative drive, and narrative fulfillment.

1. *"I fell in love with the hero . . ."*
The first thing you, as a storyteller, must do is create a cast of characters whom your readers will care about and cheer for.

124

I've come to believe that sympathetic characters are the key to good storytelling. Why? There's an old adage that says "character is plot." In other words, what happens to your characters happens because of who they are. If they are interesting and likable, your readers' emotions will be engaged and they will begin to care about these people. If they care, they will keep reading.

You must make your readers want to keep reading—I mean *all* your readers, starting with the first agent or editor who sees the manuscript. They must become so intensely involved that they forget the world around them and lose themselves in your world. Few readers get emotionally involved with a plot or even with a string of beautiful metaphors. It is people—characters—who engage the emotions.

It is not necessary for every one of your characters to be likable; indeed, they should all have faults, and some will have more faults than others. Think in terms of heroes and villains when you are writing popular fiction. Realistic though your characters must be, they should also come across as slightly larger than life: Your protagonists might be slightly braver, more skillful, more honorable, more intelligent, even more physically attractive than the people you meet on the street. Similarly, their antagonists should be angrier, greedier, crueler, more obsessive.

The trick is to make your characters come alive, but I'm not suggesting that this is easy to accomplish. For me, character development is by far the hardest and most time-consuming thing about writing a novel. Eventually, my characters become just as real to me as many of the people I encounter in my daily life. But it is an agonizing process. I watch them develop in much the same way a mother watches her children grow and develop, learning new things about them every day.

One way to engage your readers' emotions is to show your protagonists doing something admirable early in the novel. In the beginning of *Leaves of Fortune*, for example, I introduce one of my main characters, Nick Templeton. We know very little about Nick at this point and will find out later that he has had to contend with a host of private demons. Not the macho type by any means, he's always been rather shy, and he's not quite confident enough to go after the things in life he still lacks. But since Nick is going to end up the hero of this novel, it's vital that my readers begin rooting for him in chapter one.

Nick is divorced and has a seven-year-old daughter who lives with her mother in another city. He keeps her picture beside him on his desk.

He interrupts his work to think about how much he misses his daughter. While remembering a recent conversation he's had with her, he takes a very simple action: reaching out, he brushes his finger against his daughter's hair in the photograph.

The result: instant sympathy for Nick. He's a sensitive, loving father. It will become apparent within a few more pages that he is caring and protective toward other people in his family, too. He may be anxious and insecure, but readers will forgive him his weaknesses because it's clear from the start that he has a great capacity for love. He has become real . . . yet he also has room to grow and develop, which is something your main characters must all do. The growth and development will become apparent in the next phase of your novel: the plot.

2. *"Something is rotten . . ."*

Once you have captured the interest of your readers, you must sustain it. You do this by means of your plot, which should involve your protagonists in a series of escalating conflicts that they must resolve as the narrative advances.

Dramatic conflict is an essential ingredient in any form of storytelling. When we learn early in Shakespeare's *Hamlet* that "something is rotten in the state of Denmark," this is an extremely significant statement because if something were not rotten, there wouldn't be a story to tell.

Popular novels are predicated on the idea that the proverbial apple cart has just been or is about to be upset. You have a cast of characters, you bring them together, and wham: something happens. Because of who these people are and how they relate to one another, strong conflicts arise—conflicts that will become more and more dramatic as the plot advances.

Your conflicts must be intense and believable. They must be serious enough to put doubt in the readers' minds as to whether your characters will prevail. Most important, the conflicts must escalate. As your protagonists grope their way through the various complications of your plot, they should find their situation becoming increasingly bleak. It isn't until they recognize their own mistakes and alter their methods of problem-solving that they are able, at the climactic point of the novel, to resolve their conflicts successfully enough to provide a satisfying ending.

At the beginning of *Leaves of Fortune,* Delilah, one of my heroines, returns to Boston to take over the tea empire run by Minerva Templeton, her grandmother. She has an unresolved conflict with Minerva that has lasted for sixteen years. She has contradictory feelings about Minerva's would-be heir, Travis, with whom she once had an intense love affair. Things are difficult even with her cousin Nick, who has always been Delilah's closest ally, because Nick sees Delilah as a threat to their grandmother's health and happiness.

While none of these conflicts may seem particularly dire, Delilah's return is the catalyst that brings on an agonizing soul-searching on Minerva's part and rakes up the banked coals of an inflammatory brother-brother conflict between Travis and Nick. Thus, Delilah's admirable attempts to resolve her old problems produce unanticipated new ones that finally lead to an explosive climax in which the lives of all four characters are on the line.

I doubt if anyone could stop reading *Leaves of Fortune* during the final section of the book; presumably, if the readers have gotten that far, they were hooked well toward the beginning. By the time they reach the last hundred pages of any novel, the narrative drive should have become so strong that they are helpless to do anything except to keep reading. Which brings me to my next point.

3. *"I couldn't put it down. . . ."*

When you submit your novel to an editor, there will be several things she'll ask herself, but this is by far the most important: "Is this manuscript so enthralling that I want to take my phone off the hook and read through lunch?" If the answer is yes, you're well on your way to making a sale.

In most respects, narrative drive is the *result* of sympathetic characters and mounting conflicts. As your readers see the people they care about plunged into trouble, the hope that your protagonists will solve their problems is coupled with the fear that they might not. This creates suspense, and your readers are compelled to keep turning the pages.

Although you might not be writing a novel that can be categorized as a suspense thriller, don't ever underestimate the importance of keeping your readers "hanging." Suspense is an element that should be a part of any "good read," whatever its genre.

Think of a novel as a series of questions that have to be answered:

Will the hero unmask the murderer before the murderer learns what he's up to and comes after him? Will the heroine stop falling in love with men whose selfishness recreates the same unsatisfying relationship she had with her father? What is the dark secret from the past that prevents one sister from acknowledging her deep love for the other?

A clever novelist will not give away the answers to these questions too soon. I believe it was Charles Dickens, one of the greatest storytellers of all time, who said, "Make 'em laugh, make 'em cry, make 'em *wait.*"

Besides suspense, there are several other elements that produce a strong narrative drive and are often areas in which an inexperienced writer runs into trouble:

• *Do* strike a good balance between action, description, and dialogue.

• *Don't* include scenes that are extraneous to the plot.

• *Do* make sure that your novel advances in a logical, coherent manner with clear transitions of time and place.

• *Don't* slow the pace with long paragraphs of irrelevant background detail.

You must be ruthless about expunging anything that does not develop your characters or your plot—that lovely description of the sunset, for example, or that bit of research you're so proud of and would like to show off. If your readers become confused about the significance of a particular scene or bogged down with too much detail, they will lose interest very quickly. Remember: A book that is impossible to put down is a book that *moves.*

4. *"Even though I didn't anticipate the ending, it was just right."*

Finally, great storytellers not only raise the readers' expectations, but satisfy them. The endings of their novels *work,* and this is what I call narrative fulfillment.

It has been said that a good opening chapter will sell your first novel to a reader, but that it takes a great final chapter to sell that reader your *next* novel. This makes sense, for while a customer browsing in a bookstore may pick up your book, read the first few paragraphs, and buy it if it sounds interesting, it's unlikely that he'll purchase another of your novels if your story disappoints him. As for the editor who took her phone off the hook and read through lunch, as she nears the end of your manuscript the primary thought in her mind is going to be, "So far, so good, but can this writer pull it off?"

How do you pull it off? You must both surprise and delight your readers. By this I mean that your ending should be in some way unexpected, yet, at the same time, it must be the only possible ending that fits everything you have revealed about the characters and their problems. All that is necessary to "figure out" the ending must be there in the text, but even so, your readers should not see it coming. A hackneyed, predictable ending will satisfy no one.

Of all the elements I've mentioned so far, this is perhaps the most difficult to give advice about. I've been complimented for my endings, but I don't really know how I write them. What usually happens is that I get to a point in the narrative at which it seems nothing will work out the way I want it to. Just as I feel most disgusted with this state of affairs, a mysterious creative force takes over, providing answers to questions that have mystified me, and suggesting solutions to seemingly unsolvable problems.

Clearly, not everything about the process of writing a novel can be objectively analyzed. One thing I can tell you, though, is that endings in popular fiction are much neater than endings in real life. In fiction, more often than not, justice does prevail: The good are rewarded and the evil punished. The murderer is captured, the romance is successful, and the protagonists gain the insight they need to change themselves for the better.

This is, in essence, the *raison d'être* of the storyteller—not only to imitate but to improve upon life. We read to gain respite from a world in which the murderer is not captured, the romance fades and dies, and most people go through life never changing at all.

Great storytelling gives us pleasure, hope, and belief in a world in which things work out for the best. Such novels might not change your life, but they will surely brighten up your day.

28

TOO GOOD TO BE TRUE: THE FLAWLESS CHARACTER

BY MARY TANNEN

MY MOTHER ONCE BOUGHT a new table that came with a card printed on buff-colored heavy stock explaining that the table had been "distressed" with artful gouges and well-placed worm holes to give it a patina of age. We (her four children) thought this was hilariously funny and said that if we had only known she wanted distressed furniture we would have been happy to oblige and that clearly we had misinterpreted her screams of anguish every time we left a soda bottle on the coffee table or ran a toy car up the leg of the Duncan Phyfe chair.

The very phrase "character flaw" makes me think of that distressed table, as if characters were naturally shiny new and perfect and needed only the addition of a flaw or two, artfully placed, to make them more realistic. To me, a personality, whether actual or fictional, is not solid but liquid, not liquid but airborne, as changeable as light. What looks like a flaw might turn out to be a virtue. Virtue might, under certain circumstances, prove to be a fault.

When my daughter was reading *Billy Budd* and having a hard time with it, she came storming into my room to protest, and seeing the book I was working on in galleys, took it into her room to read. She brought it back the next day and announced that it was "better than *Billy Budd*."

"Better than *Billy Budd*!" I could see it emblazoned across the book jacket. Actually, my novel isn't better than *Billy Budd*, but the style was a lot more congenial to my daughter. She was appalled by Melville's heavy symbolism, by the way Billy Budd was the representation of an idea, not an actual man.

Billy Budd had no flaws, physical or moral (except for his stutter). He was illiterate, of noble but unknown birth, untainted by the corrupting influence of either family or literature. He was a myth, "Apollo with his

130

portmanteau"! Melville never intended to create a realistic character. Billy Budd was Adam before the fall.

Sometimes when reading over a draft of a fiction piece I am working on, I realize that one of my major characters is suspiciously lacking in flaws. She is usually a person like me, but she is lacking in defects as well as in color and definition. When this happens in a piece of fiction I'm writing, it is a sign that I am identifying too closely with her. Just as I try to show my good and hide my bad, I am protecting this fictional person.

Recently I discovered a trick that helped me correct this. I was working with a character, Yolanda, a woman my age who ran a bookstore. Yolanda was nice. She was good. A nice good woman, and very bland. I couldn't get a grip on her or who she was. I went to my local swimming pool to do a few laps and take my mind off my troubles, when I saw a woman I'd seen many times before but don't know very well—a tall skinny woman with short elfin hair and wide-awake eyes. I decided to steal this woman's body and give it to Yolanda.

It worked miracles because now Yolanda was no longer me. She was this woman I didn't know very well. She began to exhibit all kinds of personality traits. She was allergic to almost everything and purchased her meals at the New Age Take-Out Kitchen. This explained why she was so thin. She spent lonely nights watching the families in the apartments across the street. The strange thing was that although Yolanda had many more weaknesses than she did before I discovered she wasn't me, I liked her better.

Another way to break the spell of the flawless character is to elicit the opinion of another character in the novel or story, one who dislikes, resents, or holds a grudge against the paragon of virtue. In *Second Sight,* I had a perfectly lovable older woman, Lavinia, who refused to believe that her philandering husband, Nestor, had left her for good. Instead of selling the house and investing the proceeds in order to live off the income, she managed on very little so that she could keep the house intact for Nestor's return.

Nestor (who had flaws to spare) had another version of the story. Lavinia's loyalty enraged him. He saw it as a ploy to make him feel guilty and remain tied to her. Indeed, at the end when Nestor asked Lavinia to take him back, Lavinia realized she no longer wanted to return to her old life with Nestor. She wondered if perhaps instead of being noble and true all those years, she hadn't actually been taking out a genteel and subtle revenge.

A character without flaws has nowhere to go. He can't change or grow. In Philip Roth's *The Counterlife,* the novelist Zuckerman, who used himself as a character in his books, was writing about his younger brother Henry. Because Zuckerman had given all the faults to himself-as-character, he had doomed his brother-as-character to a life of virtue. Henry had always been the good son, the good husband, father, dentist. Writing about Henry at thirty-nine, Zuckerman imagined him as the suffocating prisoner of his perfect but shallow life. The only way Henry could break the pattern was to escape altogether, leave his family and practice in New Jersey and begin anew in Israel. Zuckerman went to visit Henry in his kibbutz on the West Bank and found that his younger brother had simply exchanged one slavish system for another. He was still the good brother. He could change the scene, but he couldn't change himself because he was a character without flaws.

I realize I have been using the term "flaw" as if it could mean anything from nail-biting to one of the Seven Deadly Sins. I think of a flaw as a personality trait I wouldn't confess to, except on a dark and stormy night to a stranger passing through. And then there are the flaws we hide from ourselves, or lack the insight to see, but which help determine the course of our lives.

When I'm writing, the flaws that interest me are not the ones I assign ("Q kicks small dogs"), but those that emerge in the course of the story. Take Yolanda, who tries to be good, to be virtuous, to do no harm to others: I was amazed to discover, somewhere near the end of the first draft, that she had used someone, a man, a friend, to get over a wound suffered long ago, and in using him had hurt him. Yolanda didn't see how she could hurt this friend whom she considered much more powerful and attractive than she. The more I work on that novel, the more I see that Yolanda's major flaw is her modesty. She lets people down because she cannot conceive that she means as much to them as they do to her.

In *Second Sight,* the opposite was true: a character's flaw proved to be her saving grace. Delia, the widowed mother of a twelve-year-old son, lacked all marketable skills. She lived on welfare and whatever she could make telling fortunes over the phone. Everyone, but especially

Delia's career-minded sister Cass, faulted her for not taking her life in hand and finding a way out of the dead-end life of poverty she and her son had fallen into.

But Delia operated on another level from her more rational friends and relatives. She was watching for signs and portents, for signals that the time was right. She refused to force the unfolding of her life.

Delia did manage finally to bring about a change for herself and her son, to the amazement of the others, who began to see a glimmer of wisdom in her otherworldliness. Cass, however, could never accept that Delia's passivity had enabled her to recognize and receive love when it came her way. Cass would continue to take charge of her life, as Delia said, captaining it as if it were a ship, but never allowing for the influence of wind or tide or current.

People, fictional and real, are not perfect, like fresh-from-the-factory tables. They come with their faults built in, mingled and confused with their virtues. Whenever I find I am dealing with a character without flaws, and I am not intending a twentieth-century rewrite of *Billy Budd,* I take it as a sign that I have not done my work. I have not imagined my character fully, have not considered her through the eyes of the other characters. Finally, I have not cut the umbilical cord. I am protecting her, shielding her, and, at the same time, imprisoning her in her own virtue. It is time to let her go so she can fail and change and grow.

29

GETTING YOUR NOVEL STARTED IN TEN DAYS

BY GENNI GUNN

YOU'VE always wanted to write a novel but can find neither the time nor the starting point. You have unique experiences to record, hundreds of characters struggling to come out of your pen on to paper. What you need to do is make time to write and, perhaps most important, have a clear idea of *what* you are going to write.

A book is not written in one sitting. Even assuming you have a busy schedule, you need not wait to begin until you can afford to take a year's vacation from work. If your ideas are well organized, you can begin your novel now, by setting aside one hour a day in which to write.

Think of your novel as a jigsaw puzzle. Every day, you will examine one piece and put it in its proper place. The events, characters, and actions that first appear as a jumbled mass too big to tackle can be organized to make sense. You will need discipline and persistence.

Here's how to begin:

1) Set aside one hour a day for writing, if possible, the same time every day, so that eventually writing will become a habit.

2) Set up a place to write (preferably a desk where you can leave notes, typewriter, and necessary files) and return there every day to write.

Now you're ready to explore your novel idea. Where do you start? It is important to set realistic, achievable goals for each day. Here is a sample schedule for the first ten days:

Day 1. DEFINE YOUR IDEA. A novel begins as an idea. This can take the form of a character, an isolated event, or a lifetime struggle worth recording. Begin by asking yourself, "What is my novel about?" Write a one-sentence summary. If you can't do this right away, write down all the things you think your book is about. Read these over and condense them until you have *one sentence only*. Try to be as specific as possible.

134

At the end of your hour, type your finished sentence and tape it over your desk so it will always be visible as you write.

Day 2: LIST YOUR CHARACTERS under two headings: *Major Characters* and *Minor Characters*. Describe their relationship to one another. New characters may emerge as you write. Add them to your list. Fill in their descriptions later.

Day 3: LIST LOCATIONS AND SETTING in your novel: cities and towns (real or imaginary), houses, fields, roads, schools, etc., in which major events will take place. Fill in the detailed descriptions later.

Day 4: DEFINE YOUR CHARACTERS' GOALS. Your main characters must want something that they are unable to get. In one sentence, define *what* each of your main characters wants—tangible or intangible. As an example, here are three characters from an unwritten novel, and their three goals. At the end of Day 4, you should have a completed page that resembles the following:

GOALS

Paul wants: 1) money to settle pressing debts.
2) a means to live; a job.
3) a way to defend himself against his sister's accusations.
Alice wants: 1) to prove Paul's a swindler. She believes that before their aunt's death, Paul took money from their aunt that rightfully belonged to Alice.
2) her share of the money.
3) to keep Paul away from her adopted daughter, Judy.
Judy wants: 1) Paul.
2) her mother (Alice) to like Paul.
3) Paul to make a new start.

Day 5: LIST OBSTACLES that will prevent the main characters from getting what they want. These should be difficult for your characters to overcome; they can be other characters or physical or emotional impediments. Here, for example, are obstacles the characters described may have to surmount:

OBSTACLES

Paul: 1) Aunt Sophia, who was to leave him an inheritance, died penniless.
2) He has no skills with which to make a living. He is in his late thirties and feels he is too old to begin a trade.
3) His sister Alice.
Alice: 1) Paul won't divulge any information regarding his relationship with their Aunt Sophia prior to her death.

2) Paul is secretive about his financial affairs—she can't prove he has the money.

3) Her adopted daughter, Judy, is in love with Paul.

Judy: 1) Paul is not in love with her—he considers her his little niece.

2) Her mother distrusts Paul and won't let Judy see him.

3) Paul doesn't believe in his own ability to make a fresh start.

Day 6: PLAN THE CONCLUSION. Make up an ending for your novel. Write it in paragraph or point form and tape it over your desk. Characters often take on a life of their own and do things that are not what you had originally intended. Don't be afraid to rewrite the ending if your original version doesn't ring true.

Day 7: MAKE AN OUTLINE. The outline will serve as your guide while you're writing. (Update your outline if your story plot changes along the way.) When you are stuck in a chapter, choose something from the outline that interests you and begin writing about that event. It is not necessary to write chronologically. You may prefer to write separate sections of your novel and fill in the transitions later.

List the major events that will occur in your novel, not necessarily in detail.

Day 8: MAKE CHAPTER HEADINGS. Examine the events you listed yesterday. Separate them into chapters—with each chapter covering one major event. Now, write a one- or two-sentence summary description of what happens in each chapter. Tape the revised outline over your desk.

Day 9: SET UP FILES. Today will be an organizational day. Take blank file folders (either letter or legal size) and make a label for each one, using the following headings:

1) Characters
2) Locations
3) Chapters (one for each chapter heading)
4) Mannerisms
5) Speech patterns
6) General observations

These files will give you easy access to your information as well as suggest what to write about on those days when you lack inspiration. When you begin writing your novel, fill these files with the following information:

136

a) *Characters:* Write detailed descriptions—physical characteristics, emotional needs, family background, etc.—*know* your characters.

b) *Locations:* Where do your characters live? Where does the action take place in your novel? Think of writing as a visual art—write pictures for the reader.

c) *Individual chapters:* For your chapters in progress, notes, and ideas.

d) *Mannerisms:* Be observant. Record the way people show their emotions by body movements. To say, "He was angry" is vague and weak, but "He stamped his foot" *shows* the anger.

e) *Speech patterns:* Listen to people speak—the sound of their voices, the way they shape sentences, etc. This will be invaluable when writing dialogue, but remember that conversation is not dialogue. Give each of your characters distinct characteristics, perhaps a favorite phrase to repeat, short clipped sentences—whatever seems appropriate.

f) *General observations:* Keep a record of any thoughts you have about your novel or about human nature. You can always use these, even if not in your current project.

Make up you own file headings for other things that are important to your novel.

Day 10: WRITE YOUR OPENING PARAGRAPH. Begin your novel at that point at which your main character is faced with his or her major problem. Try to make your opening paragraph intriguing. Here is a possible opening for the novel example given earlier:

Paul had waited twenty years for his inheritance. He had squandered his time and what little money he'd earned with odd jobs on gambling and physical pleasures. After Aunt Sophia's funeral—a dull, dreary affair in which he'd been unable to feign sorrow—the will was read. Aunt Sophia died penniless.

This opening includes:
1) The main character
2) His predicament—therefore his problem
3) The necessary background to show the reader the gravity of his problem

If you're dissatisfied with your opening paragraph, put it aside and as you get new ideas, revise it.

From now on, each day, when you sit at your desk, you'll have a choice of things to write about. Look through your files for something that interests you. Describe characters, locations, mannerisms, or speech patterns and fit these into your novel later. Don't worry about the order. Get your story down on paper. You can fine-tune when you begin rewriting.

Set yourself realistic goals: One page a day for a year will yield 360 pages—a book-length manuscript. Half a page each day is even more realistic. Some days you'll write several pages; other days you'll struggle just to fill one. Most important, *stick with it*! Do nothing but write in the hour you've set aside, even if you only repeat a word to fill the page.

There are no easy ways to write a novel, no secrets, no shortcuts. It takes hard work, perseverance, and the belief that you have a story to tell.

30

How Do You Learn to Write?

By Ruth Rendell

POPULAR FICTION no more needs a formula than does the highest art in the mainstream novel. Indeed, I have always maintained that genre fiction, so-called, is better written as if it were mainstream fiction and that fitting it into a category is best forgotten. And one should write to please oneself. When I consider the number of readers who have written to me to ask why I bother about style and characters when all they need is the mystery, others who have written asking for more murders or fewer murders, those who have demanded only detective stories, and those who have asked for anything but detective stories, I wonder where I should be now if I had aimed to please a public rather than suited my own taste.

One myth I used to believe in has been thoroughly debunked. This is the illusion that writing cannot be taught. The truth of it is that the desire to write cannot be taught, and that desire, that longing, must be there. Perhaps it is all that must be there, for with care and awareness, and yes a certain humility, the rest may be learned. Innumerable books exist on the writing of fiction. There are more and more courses available. But I believe that the aspiring writer—come to that, the working writer—cannot do better than learn by reading other works of fiction. I read and read, more now than ever, and if my attitude to what I read has changed over the years, it is in that gradually I have brought to bear on my reading an analytical eye, a developing critical faculty, a hunger to learn more of the craft. Perhaps I have lost something thereby. Escape in fiction is less easy for me; identification with characters comes less readily; I no longer lose myself in the story. But I am first a writer. And I think these things well lost for my gain in knowledge of how to write, though I see how far I still have to go.

So what kind of fiction do I as a writer of crime novels read? Not crime fiction, not mysteries. Not any longer. I used to, and then I became afraid that I would come upon the plot I was currently writing or the twist in the tail I was so proud of. The best crime fiction anyway—always excepting the pure detective story—is simply fiction with crime in it. I read and reread the great Victorian classics that once afforded me sheer pleasure and now teach me how to evolve and develop a story and cliff-hang my protagonist at the end of a chapter. I read the best contemporary British and American masters of fiction, every novel that comes out and gets acclaimed by reviewers or wins a prize or gets itself talked about, everything we see adapted for television. My favorite novel used to be Samuel Butler's *The Way of All Flesh,* and I still love it and reread it, but its place in my top admiration stakes has for two or three years been occupied by *The Good Soldier,* by Ford Madox Ford. It has been called the finest novel in the English language, at least the best constructed. I read it once a year. Its structure, its author's skill in dealing with time, the smooth swift movements of its narrative through and in and out of the years, its curiously intimate, despairing, aghast creating of suspense—these are all marvels.

I recommend *The Good Soldier* to everyone who asks me how to write. I hope it has taught me something. It ought to have imparted some of its own subtlety, its wonderfully understated withholding from the reader—until nearly the end—of a chain of secrets, an interwoven carpet of mysteries. Victorian ghost stories also have a lot to teach us. M. R. James knew all about the power of reticence in building tension that is an essential element in my kind of fiction. And more than any modern master of horror, Perceval Landon teaches the writer all he needs to know about fear and how to create it in "Thurnley Abbey," the most frightening story I have ever read.

I am always a little dismayed by people who ask me where I get my ideas and go on to say that though they want to write, they don't know what to write about. Any aspiring writer of the sort of fiction that aims to entertain and be exciting should begin at any rate with more ideas than he or she knows what to do with. They want to tell a story, don't they? Isn't this what it's all about?

I never base my characters on real people. I mean this; I am being quite sincere. And yet, and yet . . . all we know of people is through the men and women we are close to or have met or those we have read of or seen on film. Heaven forbid that we should base our characters on those printed or celluloid personages others have created. So only

140

reality and living people remain. I suppose that we create amalgams, taking an appearance here, a quality there, and eccentricity from elsewhere. Increasingly, I look through books of pictures, the works of old or modern masters, for my characters' faces: to Rembrandt's "Juno," Greuze's "The Wool Winder," Picasso's "Acrobats," and Titian's dark sorrowful handsome man with the gloves. And for characters' names I go not to the telephone directory but to the street names in the back of a gazetteer.

It is interesting how a character begins to form itself as one gazes at some marvelously executed portrait. Slyness must lurk behind those eyes surely, cruelty in that thin-lipped mouth, subtlety and finesse revealed by those long thin fingers. I wish I had known of this method when I first began and struggled unwisely to make a character fit the plot instead of the plot growing naturally out of the behavior of the characters. I wish I had known then the abiding satisfaction of contemplating, say, Umberto Boccioni's self-portrait and seen there a young man's inner doubts, suspiciousness, intellect, hyper-nervousness, and begun to see my way to putting his counterpart into a book.

From the first, though, I listened to people talking. My friends tell me that my books are full of the things they have said. "We had that conversation in your house with such-and-such and so-and-so." It's true. I don't use my friends for my characters, but I use what they say for my dialogue. I listen in pubs to people talking and in restaurants and at airports, in trains, in shops. And when I write down what they say, I repeat it in my head, listening with that inner ear for the right cadence, the ring of authenticity. Is this how it really sounds? Is this the rhythm? Would my man with the thin body and sad face of Picasso's harlequin, the thin lips and the delicate upturned nose, would he use quite that word in quite that way? And if not, it won't do, must be changed and listened to all over again.

A publisher friend once said to me that the next time he received a manuscript that began with the protagonist waking up, feeling depressed, and going down to make himself a cup of tea, he wouldn't read on. All too many first books do begin like this. My experience of reading the manuscripts of unpublished writers is not that they are badly written or unreal or silly or badly constructed, but they are deadly boring. They are dull. The characters have no life and are undifferentiated; every piece of information is fed to the reader in the first chapter; no care has been taken over accuracy or authenticity. If they are not exactly plagiarisms of other more exciting works, they are deeply derivative. Originality is absent. There is no evidence of the writer's own experience being put to use.

Of course, few of us have first-hand knowledge of violence, even fewer of murder. How many of us have had a child kidnapped or know of anyone to whom this has happened? We should be thankful for our lack of experience. And the writer's imagination will supply what is needed here. We all know what it is like to walk alone along a dark road at night, be alone in a house and suspect the presence of a marauder outside, hear a footfall or a door close where there should be no footfall and no closing door, suffer the suspenseful anxiety of waiting for some loved person who is late home, long for the phone to ring yet dread it, miss a train and a date, fear flying, suffer jealousy, envy, love, and hate.

These are the raw materials the writer must use. Journalists ask me if I have known many murderers, visited courts and prisons. I have known none, and it is twenty-five years since I was in a court. But I can read the great psychiatrists, the newspapers, look at faces in pictures, and I can use my imagination. If a would-be writer doesn't have an imagination, he or she should find it out young and serve the world in perhaps a worthier way by making a career in a government office or a hospital. Newspapers as sources of stories and portraits of psychopathic perpetrators of violence have their value but to my mind have been overrated by teachers of mystery writing. Sociological case histories and transcripts of trials supply better models.

I have never been much interested in writing about heroes and villians, and I think the time for a blackness and whiteness of characters, a Dickensian perfect good and utter evil, has long gone by. We have all read novels in which our attention has flagged halfway through. Sometimes this is because the characters are all so unpleasant that we lost interest in their fate. For even the worst character in a novel should inspire in the reader some fellow-feeling. It is an intriguing fact that in order to make readers care about a character, however bad, however depraved, it is only necessary to make him love someone or even something. A dog will do, even a hamster will do. I once had a character called Finn in a novel, a psychopathic hit man, almost irredeemable, one would have said. My aunt read the book and told me that for all his vices and all his crimes, she couldn't help liking Finn because he loved his mother.

Structure and the movement of my characters I used to find hardest. Moving people about I still find hard. It was Graham Greene, I think, who in giving advice on how to write about violent or dramatic action, recommended the paring down of the prose into brief sentences without adjectives or adverbs. And nothing else must be allowed to intervene, no descriptions of the room or the terrain or the people or the weather. While X is killing Y, let him do it bare, in Anglo-Saxon nouns and verbs, in short brisk sentences. This way the action will come across swift and shocking.

I've never had problems moving my characters in time. The associative process takes care of this beautifully for the writer. We all understand it; it works for us in reality. The stray word, the seldom-heard name of person or place, the sight of something or the scent—all these can evoke the past, and in fiction at any rate carry the protagonist back in time days, months, or years to when that was last heard, smelt, mentioned. There are subtler ways, but these will be learnt along the way.

Writing begets writing. Successful writing—and I mean not only worldly success but that private satisfaction that comes from doing something well—inspires the writer to do better, to attempt the scaling of greater heights, hitherto daunting obstacles. So when a technique has been mastered, instead of sitting back to rest and preen himself or herself, the writer should investigate more subtle methods. Smoother transitions in the matter of flashbacks, for instance, subtler differentiations of character by means of dialogue alone, atmospheres created without violent words or hyperbole but on a lower, more fearful key. And how to make that which is very, very hard look easy.

31

CREATING SHORT FICTION FROM CHARACTER: FIVE RULES

BY LUCIA NEVAI

FEW OF TODAY'S GREAT SHORT STORIES achieve their power from strong plots. If you are at work on a story or want to try your hand at one, keep in mind the importance of fully conceived characters. Vladimir Nabokov in the chapter on Dickens in his *Lectures on Literature* says that every Dickens character has his attribute, *a kind of colored shadow that appears whenever the person appears.* To me, the important phrase is *whenever the person appears.* If you introduce your main character with an adjective-filled paragraph on page one, that may not be enough to bring him to life.

The reader has to smell his hair oil when he sweats on page two, worry about his excess weight when he trudges heavily up the fire escape on page four. A common exercise used to help writers get to know about characters that interest them is to have them write a brief biography of each one. Sounds easy, sounds obvious. Try it once, and you will see how little you know about your character at the outset. Even if you don't use the material discovered in your biography in the actual story, the reader will know how well you know whom you're writing about. It's O.K. to know more than you tell—in fact, it creates a pleasant suspense between you and the reader.

After you've written the biography (or -phies), revise your plot—it will need revision. If you don't have a plot, don't berate yourself for not being a real writer. Some writers do not conceive plots and characters in a single spontaneous stroke of inspiration. List events that might test, reveal, ruin, or redeem the major character. If you discover through writing, write first. Then reread and rethink the structure and purpose of the story. If you prefer to think first, fine. Try to extract the story—a sequence of deeds—from the character's essence. Then write. Your folders will be thinner. Both routes require you to think; both routes require you to rewrite. Short fiction today is extremely accomplished. Editors are used to reading tightly written, professionally edited material.

It goes without saying that you will have numerous drafts of almost any story. In order to keep in focus the purpose and the music of the story, I can recommend these five rules for rewriting and editing your drafts:

• **One.** *Always keep in mind the image that first led you to want to write about this character.* If a character has mystery, power, and subtlety, the reasons for this are in the sensory details of the image that has led you to want to write about him. Return to these details when you feel the story wobble off track. Remind yourself what time, what season, what mood are in the image. Where is the character? What has just happened, what is about to happen? This image probably appears in the story, but it doesn't have to. Whether or not it does, nothing emotional that happens in the story should contradict the gist of this image. This image remains greater than the sum of its parts and may function as an after-image, lingering with the reader when the story is over.

• **Two.** *Isolate one strong central action that symbolizes this character's resolution of a dilemma.* The only difficulty presented by this rule is that first you must know the character's dilemma; you must know how he or she would resolve it emotionally; and you must know the action options afforded by the plot. If you really know all that, it's usually easy to isolate an action that formally depicts or symbolizes the resolution. If isolating this action seems difficult or arbitrary, it's probably because you have either too much action or too little—a common problem among beginning writers. If you have too much, use restraint. Choose one gesture, one reaction, emphasize it and play down the others. If you have little or no action, go back to the biographies to see if there is an act or idea in the minds and histories of your characters. Do not force a deed on a character, or you'll end up with a stereotype or an inconsistency. The deed, remember, can be passive: a thought, a decision, a withholding of help or harm.

• **Three.** *Keep the tone of the story consistent throughout and reflective of the vision you offer.* This is not easy. From draft to draft, you have to become very adept at editing your work for consistency. The reason is that as a story finds its tone, language will have survived from previous

145

drafts (descriptions, dialogue, narration) that detracts from or contradicts the emerging tone. If you love your sad description of a lake in late afternoon, you may have to force yourself to eliminate it or adapt it when the scene turns out to be ironic. Conversely, if you discover your humorous sketch has a poignant underbelly, you may have to relinquish some of your broader jokes. Tone, remember, is tone of voice. Someone can ask you how you are, but the real meaning of the question is in the tone: sarcastic, sympathetic, habitual, romantic, wary, threatening. The second part of the rule, the relation between tone and vision, is also tricky. They don't have to match, but they have to be appropriate and consistent. A sarcastic portrayal of a girl's naïve fling with a self-help group is appropriate, but you would have to be very clever to depict with sarcasm a weighty event like an abortion.

• **Four.** *Is the emotional progress of the story satisfying to the reader?*
Now that you've had your fun, said what you had to say, take a look at the progress of emotion in the story to see if it works and makes sense. A short story should begin at one point emotionally and end at another. Your sad story should not read like the Book of Job; your happy story (much harder to write, by the way) should find its happiness. *Show, don't tell* is an important exercise in evoking emotion in a story. If, for example, a woman goes to work at the office even though she's grieving over the death of her mother, the reader should recognize her emotional state in the language you choose—and not by reading the sentence, "She felt sad." Imbue the woman's actions with her feelings, and the reader will come with you. Emotional progress is satisfying and the basis of much entertainment. This rule keeps you from jumping around too much, leaving scenes too quickly, jumbling up your story with episodes that derail the narrative.

• **Five.** *Could anyone but you have written this story in just this way?*
Depending on your weaknesses and strengths as a writer, you may have more faith in your ability to sound like other writers you've read than to sound like yourself. In this case, *yourself* is the feeling, observing person who is mystified or curious, impassioned or outraged, fascinated or mortified by life and wants to articulate something of the experience. You can always go back to your imagination, where both your experience and your love of language have their source. Look and listen one last time to make sure the characters and images have the

unique stamp of *your* character, and that your colored shadow, to use Nabokov's phrase, appears on every page.

Although it is difficult to separate the elements that contribute to the power of successful short fiction, the element of character is especially strong in the following twelve stories by very different authors, male and female, legendary and emerging. Go to the library and browse through the collections and anthologies that include stories like these. When you find two or three voices that please and excite you, read those authors.

Some questions to ask as you read include: How does the author use description and dialogue to set up contrasting characters? What is the social relationship of the characters—does it differ from the moral relationship? How does the relationship change during the story? What is the progress of emotion? And finally, whose story is this? Although the action may center on one character, the purpose of the story might be to reveal another character, or even the narrator who seems to stand outside the action.

Twelve Great Short Stories

"Alaska," Alice Adams
"The Privy Councilor," by Anton Chekhov
"Mr. Burdoff's Visit to Germany," by Lydia Davis
"Water Liars," by Barry Hannah
"Patriotic," by Janet Kaufman
"Labor Day Dinner," by Alice Munro
"The Artificial Nigger," by Flannery O'Connor
"How Can I Tell You?" by John O'Hara
"The Saint," by V. S. Pritchett
"Bad Characters," by Jean Stafford
"The Gift of the Prodigal," by Peter Taylor
"The Rich Brother," by Tobias Wolff

32

LET FICTION CHANGE YOUR LIFE

BY LYNNE SHARON SCHWARTZ

THE LURE OF USING our own experiences in fiction is almost irresistible—not only for beginners but for seasoned pros as well. What could be more natural, or more inevitable? To tell what has shaped us, to cast the incidents of our lives in the form of narrative, with ourselves as heroes and heroines, is instinctive: It shows itself as soon as children acquire language. And personal experience is a vital source of fiction, one might even say the only source: what else *can* we write of but what we have seen, felt, thought, done, and as a result, imagined? As readers, we're touched most deeply by stories that possess, in Henry James's phrase, the sense of "felt life," stories the author has cared about and lived with and presented in all their intensity; the others lie stone cold on the page. Indeed, a corollary to the old saw, "write what you know," could be, "write what you care about."

But if all of the above is true, then fiction might be no more than faintly disguised autobiography, an indulgent exercise in self-expression. Fiction would be a sorry, impoverished thing indeed, deprived of the rich and incomparable offerings of the imagination and the unconscious, with their enigmatic leaps and turns. Thankfully this isn't so.

How do we make use of the tremendous stores of material our lives provide, and at the same time avoid boring our readers by being that most tedious of companions—the kind we all know and dread—who talks only of himself, by himself, and for himself?

The lamest excuse beginning fiction writers give in response to criticism is, plaintively, "But that's what really happened." Who cares, I'm tempted to ask. To put it more tactfully: If you want to write fiction that others will love to read, you have to be willing to sacrifice parts of your life. Or if that sounds rather extreme, let's call it giving up "the way it really happened" in favor of a greater truth. For a story, in some unaccountable fashion, makes its own demands, like a child outgrowing the confines of the parental home. When you're willing to let the story's life take precedence over your own and go its way, you've taken the first step to becoming a successful writer.

Once you've embarked on that journey, the urge to tell what happened is slowly transformed into the desire to give events pattern and significance, to construct a *thing*, almost like a free-standing sculpture whose shape and contours are clear to all, with the power to delight, or amuse, or provoke, or disturb. Above all, to draw in an entrance. In its final form, while the construction may have been inspired by happenings in the writer's own life and may still contain their germ, it has taken on its own life. It has, sometimes in most surprising ways, gone beyond the writer's experience.

This doesn't mean you can't allow your deepest concerns into your fiction—quite the contrary. Look at the work of Jane Austen, who has left us the most witty, thorough, and painstaking account of nineteenth-century courtship and marriage rites in the middle classes; no sociological study could be more informative, not to mention enchanting. Little is known of Austen's personal life; we cannot say for certain who were her suitors or why she did not marry; we cannot point to episodes in her novels and trace their origins. What we do know is that she scrutinized the mating game in all its aspects, with a unique blend of irony, skepticism, and mellow acceptance. In other words, Austen managed to put her individual sensibility into her work in a far more profound way than by merely drawing on actual events.

As a humbler example, since it's what I know best, I'll use my own novel, *Rough Strife,* which also happens to be about a marriage. The story follows some twenty years in the life of a couple, Caroline and Ivan, who meet in Rome then return to the United States to live in Boston, Connecticut, and finally New York City—settings I chose because I knew them and felt on "safe" territory. During the time I was writing *Rough Strife,* a spate of novels appeared in which married women, weary and disgusted with the inequities of family life, were cutting loose to find independence and adventure. Something about the ease and abruptness of their flights from home bothered me; much as I sympathized with the problem of constraint, the solution seemed oversimplified. I was determined to write about a heroine who stayed to see it through, to learn where that route could lead. At the same time I, too, was determined not, fashionably, to abandon my marriage, a fact that surely influenced the book.

I suppose I planned, in some imprecise way, to have Caroline and Ivan face many of the issues my husband and I faced. But in the end the couple bypassed me to lead their own lives. Caroline, for example, surprised me by having a difficult time conceiving their first child. A mathematics professor, she has an affair with a graduate student, which leads to an abortion; later on, her second child with Ivan turns out to be hyperactive. Why, I wondered as I wrote, did I invent all that? Why did it invent itself, might be more accurate. Well, I wanted to illustrate the enormous effects that bearing and raising children have on a marriage, and those events heighten the illustration. They apply pressure and create tension. They arose from the imagination, wisely, I think, to serve the story.

At still another point the characters escaped me, quite against my will. I was writing a scene of a marital quarrel, with some rather acidic repartee. No one could have been more alarmed than I when Ivan suddenly turned violent, pushing Caroline to the floor. It was not at all what I had intended—not with these characters, anyway, civilized people, incapable of such behavior. In shock and horror, I watched a rape scene unfold. How much more shocking that it was coming from my own pen! And Caroline's reaction was equally horrifying. Instead of being indignant and repelled, she thinks she invited it in some way. She even feels sorry for Ivan in his guilt and remorse! The whole incident contradicted my beliefs as well as my experience—in real life I would have shaken them both to their senses. But this was not real life. This was the utter mystery and excitement of fiction, where characters rebel and demand their own errors and their own destiny, and we had best not stand in their way.

In the end, I had a novel about a couple whose story barely resembled my own. The only autobiographical elements left were a certain analytical turn of mind and a sense of the complex, ambiguous accommodations involved in living with another person. Whatever my original aims, I had written about the gradual process of accepting the results of one's uneducated choices. With the benefit of several years' hindsight, I can see that this notion of process, not the details of the plot, is what makes the book personal as well as, I hope, universal.

The same shifts occur in writing stories, only on a smaller scale. How well I remember lying awake one entire night with a gray spot jiggling before my eyes—something the doctors call a "floater," I later learned. It didn't let me sleep, and as the hours passed, I slipped into a miserable, unreasonable state of mind, berating myself for all the mistakes of my past, wondering what it all meant, if anything. . . . Anyone who's spent a sleepless night recently will know what I mean. The experience was so powerful and disturbing that naturally I wanted to write about it. The result was a story, "Acquainted With the Night," whose main character turned out to be a male architect ten years older than I. Why, I can't say. He too lies awake, victim of a floater, examining and agonizing over his past, which, needless to say, has nothing in common with my own. (I took the opportunity to give him a life full of moral crisis, without the straints I might have felt about detailing mine.) Again, the common and personal element, as well as the universal one, is simply the insomniac's painful and—in the light of day—distorted trip, a trip almost every reader has taken at one time or another.

The path leading to a newer story was more circuitous. Several years ago, a fire forced my husband and me out of the apartment building where we had lived for twenty years and raised our two daughters. Besides the shock and pain of losing our home, we and our fellow-tenants were outraged at the behavior of the landlord, Columbia University, in the aftermath of the fire. A lengthy court case ensued, with the tenants ranged against the power and willfulness of a large institution. Two years later I completed a book about the fire, the legal proceedings, and the social implications of institutions as landlords. Since I had written mainly fiction till then, I was prepared when friends asked why I hadn't turned my experience into a novel—what an ideal story it seemed, full of drama and conflict. My answer was, first, that the truth was topically urgent and needed to be told precisely as it happened; and second, that the story (plus the research it would entail) really didn't interest me as a novelist. I had been writing long enough to know that real estate practices, demographics, and the nature of bureaucracy were not my subjects.

Some time later, though, probably under the influence of many newspaper and magazine articles about homelessness in New York City, an imaginary family moved into my mind. Little by little their features became clear: they were newcomers from the Virgin Islands, the father was an electrician but temporarily working at a lunch counter, they were black, they were very proper and conventional, there were three young children. . . . They too had been forced out of their apartment by a fire, but unlike my family, they had had to accept the city's offer of a welfare hotel, a dismal and dangerous environment. The father, a proud man, found that intolerable, but with so little money what could he do? I became obsessed with the family until their story virtually wrote itself—"The Last Frontier," in which George and Louise Madison and their children move onto the stage set of a situation comedy, contrasting the whitewashed TV image of family life with their own reality.

None of the details about the Madisons corresponded to my own life—none, that is, except their condition of homelessness, and the resulting anger, frustration, and bewilderment. In those feelings that give the story its life, we were identical. One might say it is auto-biographical in the deepest sense.

The ability I've been discussing—giving up the facts for the broader reaches of the imagination—may sound daunting, but it comes with experience, and with the confidence and willingness to let the story take control. For almost always, at some point in the arduous process, the inner voice will whisper, "What if . . . instead of . . . ?" The secret is to listen, and to yield.

But that's not the only way. Some fiction gets written backwards, so to speak. In the case of *Balancing Acts* (my first novel, though it was published second), I was on the third draft and puzzled over why it wouldn't come right, when I finally grasped what the book was about and what its connection was to me.

I had begun it after a friend told me about her ten-year-old daughter's strong attachment to an elderly man, a volunteer teacher in her school. The man had just died, and the child was suffering the sort of grief—for the loss of a close friend—that most of us don't know till later in life. The story stayed with me—I didn't know why; one often doesn't—and I constructed a novel around it, with background and details far different from those of my own life. I couldn't help but notice, though, that the man in my novel had much in common with my father, and the thirteen-year-old heroine, with me. Not circumstantial matters in common, but affinities of temperament and attitude. Only on that third draft, when I realized that book was a particular emotional struggle on my part, connected with my aging father, could I rewrite it with coherence and conscious design. Plot, setting, and characters all remained the same, but I had found the autobiographical impulse at the core and could work outwards, using its energy.

Giving the imagination free reign, or conversely, locating the fertile source of a story, is exhilarating as well as productive. But it has its negative side (doesn't everything?). The upshot of letting fiction change the events of your life is losing parts of your past. It's not an overstatement to confess that looking over my work, I occasionally note bits that sound familiar, yet I can't quite remember whether they happened or whether I made them up. Did the neighbors down the street when I was nine years old really shout those awful things out the window, or did I imagine it? Or exaggerate it? Did that man in the boat really look at me in that seductive way? Was the path behind the country houses really as dark and lush with greenery as I wrote? And were my grandmother's glasses of tea with lumps of sugar as wonderful as I've made out? The line between memory and invention blurs; I can't say for sure what happened, and I have the sinking feeling that I've erased parts of my life in order to write stories over them. I may have given up more than I expected, becoming a writer. The only relief for such doubts is to go back and write some more. Because in the end, as the Roman poet said, life is short, but art is long.

33

WRITING THE SHORT STORY: THREE BASIC POINTS

BY MARYCLARE J. HEFFERNAN

LEARNING HOW TO WRITE FICTION that appeals not only to your husband and your sister in Connecticut, but also to the editors at *Ladies' Home Journal* or *Redbook,* is not a simple process.

There are no algebraic equations to apply to this craft. No easy answers as to what works and what doesn't. It is, rather, an unclear creative process complicated by each writer's individual experience, drive, and ability.

I wrote my first short story in 1982. It wasn't very good—although at the time I thought it was tremendous—but it was a story. The exhilaration of creating characters who talked to each other, acted out their emotions, and moved around on my pages had a startling effect on me. There was no doubt about what I wanted to do for the rest of my life. All I needed to know was how to write well enough for editors to like it, too.

Two years and a folder full of rejection slips later, I sold my first short story to *Ladies' Home Journal.* Not too bad, really. But that's the beginning, not the end of my story.

I haven't become famous. I haven't sold every piece I've written since then. I still don't always know what's going to work and what's not. Worst of all, the more I learn about this writing process the more elusive it becomes.

I do know that learning to write well is an unending effort—one filled with self-discovery and satisfaction, but also with crushingly frustrating moments and piles of polite but firm rejection slips.

Yet, despite an unplotted route toward that constantly moving goal of better writing, I've become one of the many who are hooked on the journey. While there are hundreds of helpful writing tips along the way, I've found three basic points to hang onto every time I roll a blank paper into my typewriter, hoping the next story will be my best.

1) Above all, *write about real people*. Flat, one-dimensional, paper doll characters won't make it. Mary Lou Mullen, Book and Fiction Editor at *Ladies' Home Journal*, recently told me she looks for stories that are realistic. "The stories that work the best for us are those that most clearly resemble nonfiction," she said. "We want characters the readers will relate to and care about. And we want them in realistic situations."

The only way to write about real-life situations convincingly is to write about real people—*fictitious* real people, but nevertheless people who speak and act like human beings we know.

When I begin a short story, I start with an idea of who the main characters will be. Rarely do I have a plot worked out ahead of time, although I may have a general sense of the story I want to tell. By giving the characters personalities, voices of their own, and allowing them to behave almost as they wish, I let their story develop.

In "Too Tired for Love" *(Redbook)*, I began with an image of a woman who's just had her second baby. The story opens with the narrator, Alice, setting the tone for the story:

Nothing fits me anymore. This morning I stood naked in front of the full length mirror on my closet door and sucked in my stomach with all my might. This made my figure look a tiny bit better but my face took on a contorted, unnatural look.

That short paragraph accomplished two things. It established the mood and grounded the story in reality. Not only could I see Alice and begin to develop a sense of her state of mind, but so could the reader. While not everyone has had a baby, most of us have had unhappy moments in front of a mirror.

2) Another technique I use is to *begin the dialogue early* in the story. It not only helps flesh out the characters by hearing their voices, but also sets the story in motion from the beginning.

In the first short paragraph of "Simple Celebrations" *(Ladies' Home Journal)*, Sally, the narrator, muses that she's always loved weddings. The dialogue begins in the second paragraph:

That's what Jenny reminded me of after she told me Jack was getting married again. "I thought you loved weddings, Mom," she said, leaning across the kitchen counter to get a better look at my face. "Daddy says you can go if you want."

I didn't look up at her but chopped carrots into smaller and smaller pieces. "He said I could go?" I asked, amazed at the suggestion. "Why in the world would I want to go to his second wedding?"

By allowing the characters to talk to each other I feel them take shape. Yet talking alone won't bring characters to life.

People are almost never completely still, especially when involved in conversation. We talk while we're tying our sneakers, diapering the baby, or washing out the coffeepot. We'll occasionally glance up to make eye contact, to reveal with our facial expressions or body language how we're feeling. Except when we're trapped somewhere, as in a dentist's chair, we don't sit still for very long. And even in the dentist's chair, we have definite ways of making our feelings known.

Give the reader glimpses of what your characters are doing. Be selective, but use their movements to reveal emotions, to hint at conflict or agreement. You'll give your work a feeling of reality, as well as energy and movement.

Look at the same paragraph with the body language removed:

That's what Jenny reminded me of after she told me Jack was getting married again. "I thought you loved weddings, Mom," she said. "Daddy says you can go if you want."

"He said I could go? I asked, amazed at the suggestion. "Why in the world would I want to go to his second wedding?"

As this paragraph comes early in the story, it remains in space without the kitchen descriptions to give it a setting. More important, without Jenny's leaning forward to get a better look at her mother's face, or Sally's chopping carrots into tiny bits, the tension is not established.

I must add that I use description sparingly, but by weaving just enough description into the dialogue a piece develops a natural feel. It plays much like reality. After all, in real life we don't separate our surroundings from other things that may be happening at the same time.

As we breathe life into our walking, talking characters, we're moving naturally toward another critical element: caring.

The reader has to care about our characters, or else when they drive off a cliff or despair over a broken heart, it won't matter. And if the reader doesn't care, then what's the point?

156

Some writers have greater instinct than others for hooking the reader on their characters. Basically, readers all respond to recognizable human emotions. When our characters behave in a way that strikes a chord of familiarity, when the reader says, "I know just how she feels," as writers we're eliciting a universal response.

An editor once wrote in a rejection note to me that she didn't care about those particular characters and therefore had no interest in their story. I was crushed. Yet once I was able to reread the piece with some objectivity, I found that my characters lacked depth, moved sluggishly around, and sort of whined all the time. They were spoiled creatures who spent too much time worrying about insignificant problems.

I have sold stories that were rejected half a dozen times before being accepted. Editors aren't always right. They're individuals with personal likes and dislikes. But I've never sold that story, and that editor was right.

The reader has to have a clear sense of who our characters are. Good writers know much more about their characters than they choose to reveal on paper, but we can't ever assume that because we know where our characters are coming from, the reader will, too.

Fiction has a hard fight for print space in today's magazines. Every word counts. But we must make sure that enough of those precious words are there to give a sense of history and depth to our characters.

When the reader knows where these fictitious people have come from, they'll more likely understand their motivations, their present frustrations, and their dreams for the future.

In "Sprung Traps" (*Ladies' Home Journal*), Callie, about to have her first baby, is worried about how her husband Neil will fill the role of father. I had to show the reader why she was worried. The story is set in the present tense, but Callie switches to the past tense as she describes a bit of Neil's background:

Neil is an only child. He was raised in one of those square houses fifteen minutes off the exit ramp in New Jersey. The walls of his parents' hallways hold a hundred little Neil faces in plastic frames. No one else, just him.

In having our characters glance backward to reveal a telling scene or replay a snatch of remembered conversation, we give purpose to the story.

3) Which brings me to the third, and for me, the most difficult point. *Be sure to tell a story.*

A collection of realistic characters engaged in true-to-life behavior is fine up to a point. But if all they manage to do is grope around saying lovely words to each other, we haven't done our work well.

The ultimate purpose of our craft is to move the readers somehow. Not necessarily to leave them weeping or laughing out loud, but to leave them satisfied.

Editor Mullen says she knows right away when a story is good. "It's hard to define what makes a story work, but it somehow carries you along. It tugs at your heartstrings. It leaves an emotional impact long after you've finished reading it."

That may sound pretty vague, but I think she's right. I don't believe the art of good storytelling can be taught. It's too individual, too complicated to pull apart and dissect. Once we begin to do that, a story becomes nothing more than unconnected phrases and bits of free-floating dialogue.

Sure, there are hundreds of tips on writing crisp dialogue, creating clear characters, painting vivid descriptions. But the actual storytelling is up to the writer alone.

The best learning comes from reading—listening to the rhythms, absorbing the tones and voices, enjoying the impact of a good piece—and then writing.

We test ourselves with each new story. Will it come together this time? Will our past experiences and those voices in our heads combine with just the right mix of magic to form a story that leaves the reader moved?

There are no easy answers, only reams of clean, blank paper, and us. Can we write well enough to please not only our next-door neighbor, but also the editors? There is, of course, only one way to find out.

34

AGAINST NOSTALGIA

BY SUMNER LOCKE ELLIOTT

HAVING BEEN born in Australia but having lived in the United States since 1948 and having written four-and-a-half novels with settings in Australia (the other half of one is set in California and New York), I am sometimes lauded, sometimes berated, for writing nostalgia. To both I object strenuously. *Webster's* defines nostalgia as "homesickness, a sentimental or morbid yearning for the past." In nearly forty years, I have never had a twinge of homesickness and most certainly no morbid yearning for the past, the past being generally the reason that I fled Australia. I am not prone to tears at "Waltzing Matilda" nor the smell of rain on eucalyptus leaves, and I am not bound to compare every harbor in the world to Sydney's. Possibly because I was born not unpatriotic, but un-nationalistic. I have never been easily aroused by the marching bands, the flags and confetti, or the insistence of mass enthusiasm. But I am moved more often by trivia, by hearing in my mind the raucous sound of thousands of green locusts (which is what they call cicadas there) in the quickening mornings of the marvelous Australian summers, which, unlike the summers of the east coast of America, are invigorating. I'm moved by the gift of a little mountain devil, which is a face of a small pointed elf with horns and which grows on a prickly bush in the Blue Mountains of New South Wales.

Of course there must be a trace of nostalgia in all memory. But even memory is fiction. The delineation of the past becomes the copyright of the individual and subject to his or her arrangement of the circumstances (as in Alan Jay Lerner's song, "Oh Yes, I Remember It Well"); what passes for the memory in my mind is not the same as in someone else's remembrance. Fiction, of course, frees us from the boundaries that confine us and undernourish the inherent drama in our work. It is the combination of memory and fiction that makes the work more readable in every way than the account even of some sensational event told with every facet of truth intact.

For me, at any rate, what memory does is impel the resolution of some action, and the memory is of no use without the resolution. Here, for instance, is the beginning of a short story that I have not yet written but the memory of the incident is vividly stored in my mind:

I am about seven years old. I am watching from a short distance two women in a lighted room. One is standing, the other seated in a chair. The one standing is my aunt. She is middle-aged and becoming stout; she has never been good-looking, and a heart condition has drawn little scarlet veins across her nose and cheeks. She wears her graying hair drawn back into a bun. She is dressed in a wool skirt and with a tweed cardigan covering a beige cashmere sweater or what Australians then called a "jumper." I have never liked her, and in some dim response out of starvation, she has poured gifts and protestations of love on me, which have only served to widen the gulf between us, because sometimes the responses of children are unmitigating. Her responses to my unrelenting disapproval have been expensive toy trains and riding boots of exquisite styling and leather, but she is wont not to risk exposure of herself in embraces or kisses. I watch her and the other woman deep in soft conversation. The other woman's back is turned to my aunt. Without warning, my aunt leans suddenly over the chair and kisses the top of the woman's head. I am appalled.

What could it mean? A simple demonstration of affection? Sublimated perversion? But the incident itself, the memory, is of no use unless it is projected into the scheme of a story, so that it becomes a link in the chain of emotional jousting that took place between aunt and nephew; it must be realized in the fuller context and resolved.

In my first novel, *Careful, He Might Hear You*, the same aunt is a major character, and in that book (the thought occurs to me more than occasionally that it was deliberate homicide), I contrived to have her die in a ferry accident. In real life (never as authentic to me as the fiction), she died as a result of the heart condition she had had for many years, and to my astonishment I wept inconsolably. She was in deadly fear of thunder and lightning, and when I visited her grave in 1974 on a trip back to Australia, as I alighted from the suburban train, a thunderstorm of such sudden ferocity broke that I thought, "Aha, she knows I am coming to her." But this is too pat for consideration in a book; it is the kind of trite metaphor that should be instantly rejected.

As I have said, memory is fiction. *Careful, He Might Hear You* was denounced by the only living person who could remember the event and who knew most of the participants. "Not the people *I* knew," she said. Naturally enough. I was disconcerted at first, foolishly believing she would have recognized every nuance of the time and of the characters that I had so carefully reproduced. It was through a different lens that she had looked at my world. This is part of the reason most people fail to recognize themselves as the original models of fictitious characters. How delightful it would be to know that the original Mr. and Miss Murdstone read *David Copperfield* in all innocence.

In a different sense the "I" character of the first-person novel is never really the author. Up to now I have avoided the use of the first person because I find it confining, and not being able to get into the minds of other characters is an irretrievable loss to me. This is especially so in the autobiographical novel, and in mine the principal character was myself as a child. I always felt completely disassociated from this child, never more so than when I first saw the film version of the book. It was not unlike looking at a photograph of one's self as a child.

I look at the photograph. It is in sepia. The upward-turned face with the carefully brushed clean hair is seraphic, trusting, virginal. I remember that at that age I was in love with a little girl named Beryl Garside. We were in Sunday school together. I recall the circle of baby chairs we sat in. In those days, little girls wore their best hats to Sunday school, and the hats were confections. Beryl had—to me—the most wonderful hats in the world, and many of them. Each Sunday she would be there resplendent in straw and ribbons that extended down her back. I loved to see Beryl's hats, I dreamed about them at night. Then one shocking rainy Sunday, Beryl appeared in a plain black felt hat, so unadorned and ugly that I could scarcely believe my eyes, and Beryl's pretty face mostly hidden under the wide brim seemed to have taken on an ugliness also. Without a second's thought, I leapt up, and snatching off the offending hat, slapped Beryl in the face, screaming, "I hate your hat, Beryl." Her consternation was more shock at my outrageous action than at the slap itself. Fancy dear little Putty Elliott doing such a thing, an angel like him! We are subject to the stranger in all of us.

Fifty years later, I was to write a scene in which a drunken bully

161

snatches the new hat off a frightened girl, yelling, "I hate that hat you're wearing," and throws it into a fountain. The bully's tipsy sycophants laugh loudly, and the wretched girl is forced into laughter also until the rich bully's fiancée says cuttingly to him, "Pay her. Pay her for the hat." The scene, which was in a book called *Signs of Life,* passed through my mind and onto the typewriter without the ghost of a memory of Beryl Garside until months later, when, reading the galleys, I almost tripped over the fact that I had resurrected my Sunday school disgrace.

It is easy to blame it all on the unconscious, which stores away everything that we would most like to forget. Often it is through our unconscious memory that we find the inspiration without knowing. But that fortunately is not nostalgia.

Occasionally, try as I may, I cannot fit the memory in. Or else it does not belong to the book. There is a little string of rather plaintive memories that I have considered for several books but which refused steadfastly to be included, or else were later wisely omitted. Again I see my plain aunt weeping to my good-looking male violin teacher, while I am told to wait outside in the corridor where somebody in the distance is practicing Kreisler's "Caprice Viennois."

The importance of balance can often be vital. For instance, I am usually opposed to scenes in which a major event or anything of a tragic or dramatic nature takes place during bad weather: In fiction writing, never have the storm outside when there is a storm within. At the picnic in ideal weather, the water rippling in sunlight, the drowsy hum of bees, the tablecloth laid out with the tempting food, the baby lamp chops grilling on the twig fire, wild flannel flowers and blue sky—then the child can be beckoned away behind a tree to be told of a terrible death in an accident.

Possibly this is a finnicky, old-maidish trickery. There are no rules to writing, and what is law to one writer can be anathema to another. I abhor descriptions of good-looking people, especially of beautiful women, often found in novels. Margaret Mitchell disposed of a leading character in American fiction in her opening sentence: "Scarlett O'Hara was not beautiful, but men seldom noticed it."

But the risk is that we do look back on the past with nostalgia. When I was growing up, I used to spend the long Christmas holidays with my cousins on a farm in another state. I had to travel overnight to Melbourne on the express. No more glamorous experience in memory could outdo the excitement of that train. I can still smell the musty odor of the compartments and see the sleeping cars with their softly lighted corridors over the dark red carpeting with the words "NSW Railways" woven into them, and the dark green leather seats, half of which let down out of the wall and became the upper berth, reached by a small ladder with velvet-covered steps, and I can feel the rhythm and sway of the train and the thick brown blanket that smelled faintly of smoke. In a moment, in a word or two, if I am not careful, I will be on a journey of such nostalgia as to make Dickens's Little Nell seem brittle. Nostalgia must be used only as background (and not go on for too long), the sounds of the rushing train must be there only to conceal partially the sounds of weeping in the next compartment, and then . . .

But I cannot write about the past and not mention the trams. Sydney used to be a tram city (Melbourne still is), and it was the most generally used public transport to and from the city to the suburbs. The trams were big, gray and dirty cream-colored, lumbering but capable of fairly high speed, attached by long poles to the overhead electric wires. They were not dinky and pretty like the San Francisco trolleys, and they were not trolleys; they were *trams*. Shirley Hazzard has described them as "toast racks," which is accurate—the open compartments at either end, the rows of seats, doors with windows that opened in the middle, and the narrow wooden running-boards on which the conductors with their heavy bags of change clung perilously to the sides of the rocking vehicle in all weather. Wedging his shoulder firmly into the door against the swaying of the tram, the conductor gave out the tickets and made change, walking along the little footboards not more than eight inches wide. I can still hear the snap of the leather strap he pulled and the tinkle of the bell in the driver's cabin when the last people had gotten off and others got on. I can see the names of the suburbs on the roller in front: BALMORAL, THE SPIT, TARONGA PARK ZOO, CROW'S NEST.

It is six in the evening. I am in a big two-storied white house overlooking the harbor, and I can hear the Dover Road tram climbing the upward curve of the hill outside with a grinding noise. I am in bed having bread and milk off a tray. I am four, and I am filled with delight.

That is nostalgia.

163

‖ 35

GRILLING ED MCBAIN

BY EVAN HUNTER

Evan Hunter: I'm often asked why I chose to use the name Ed McBain on my crime fiction. I always respond that when I first started writing the 87th Precinct novels . . .

Ed McBain: I thought *I* was the one who wrote the 87th Precinct novels.

EH: The point is . . .
McB: The point is, *we* chose the McBain pseudonym because we didn't want to mislead people.

EH: Mislead them how?
McB: Into believing they were buying a mainstream novel, and then opening the book to find a man with an ax sticking out of his head.

EH: Yes. But in addition to that, mysteries back then were considered the stepchildren of literature, and . . .
McB: They still are, in many respects.

EH: You surely don't believe that.
McB: I believe that a grudging amount of respect is given to a good mystery writer. But if you want to win either the Pulitzer Prize or the National Book Award, stay far away from corpses among the petunias.

EH: You've been writing about corpses among the petunias . . .
McB: Other places, too. Not only in flower beds.

EH: For thirty-three years now. You've remarked that you begin work at nine in the morning and quit at five in the . . .
McB: Don't you?

EH: Exactly.

McB: Just like an *honest* job.

EH: But I wonder if you can share with us how you manage such a regimen. It must require a great deal of discipline.

McB: No. Discipline has nothing whatever to do with it. Discipline implies someone standing over you with a whip, *forcing* you to do the job. If you have to be *forced* to write, then it's time to look for another job. If you don't *love* every minute of it, even the donkey work of endless revisions, then quit.

EH: Do you make endless revisions?

McB: Not endless, no. One of the most important things about writing is to know when something is finished.

EH: When is it finished?

McB: When it works.

EH: But how many revisions *do* you make?

McB: As many as are required to make the thing *work*. A good piece of fiction *works*. You can read it backward and forward, or from the middle toward both ends, and it will *work*. If a scene isn't working, if a passage of dialogue isn't working . . .

EH: What do you mean by working?

McB: Serving the purpose for which it was intended. Is it supposed to make my hair stand on end? If my hair isn't standing on end, the scene isn't working. Is it supposed to make me cry? Then there had better be tears on my cheeks when I finish it.

EH: Do you make these revisions as you go along, or do you save them all up for the end?

McB: I usually spend the first few hours each morning rewriting what I wrote the day before. Then, every five chapters or so, I'll reread from the beginning and rewrite where necessary. Happily, nothing is engraved in stone until the book is published. You can go back over it again and again until it works.

EH: There's that word again.

McB: It's a word I like.

EH: How do you start a mystery novel?

McB: How do *you* start a mainstream novel?

EH: With a theme, usually.

McB: I start with a corpse, usually. Or with someone about to become a corpse.

EH: Actually, though, that's starting with a theme, isn't it?

McB: Yes, in that murder is the theme of most mysteries. Even mysteries that start out with blackmail as the theme, or kidnapping, or arson, eventually get around to murder.

EH: How do you mean?

McB: Well, take a Private Eye novel, for example. When you're writing this sort of book, it's not necessary to discover a body on page one. In fact, most private eyes—in fiction *and* in real life—aren't hired to investigate murders.

EH: Why are they hired?

McB: Oh, for any number of reasons. Someone is missing, someone is unfaithful, someone is stealing, someone is preparing a will, or inheriting money, or settling his son's gambling debts, or what-have-you. But hardly any of these reasons for employment have anything to do with murder. In fact, the odd thing about private-eye fiction is that the presence of the p.i. on the scene is usually what *causes* a murder. Had the p.i. not been hired, there'd have been no body.

EH: What about other categories of mystery fiction?

McB: Such as?

EH: Well, Man on the Run, for example. Is it necessary to start with a body in this type of story?

McB: That depends on why the guy is running, doesn't it?

EH: Why *would* he be running?

McB: Because he did something.

EH: Like what?

McB: Anything but murder. If he's done murder, you can hardly ever recover this guy; he's already beyond the pale, so forget him as a hero. I would also forget rape, kidnapping, terrorism, child abuse, and arson as crimes to consider for your hero. But if he's committed a less serious crime—such as running off with a few thousand dollars of the bank's money—then the police are after him, and he must run. And running, he meets a lot of different people, one of whom he usually falls in love with, and experiences a great many things that influence his life and cause him to change—for the better, we hope.

EH: That's what fiction is all about, isn't it? Change?

McB: I like to think so.

EH: But surely there are dead bodies in a Man-on-the-Run novel.

McB: Oh, sure. Along the way. I'm merely saying that in this sub-genre of Man on the Run, it isn't essential to *start* with a corpse.

EH: Are there other sub-genres?

McB: Of Man on the Run? Sure. We were talking about a man who'd actually *done* something. But we can also have a man who'd done absolutely *nothing*.

EH: Then why would he be running?

McB: Because the something he didn't do is usually murder. And that's where we *do* need a corpse. Immediately. For the police to find. So that they can accuse our man and come looking for him, which prompts him to flee, fly, *flew* in order to solve the murder and clear his name while of course falling in love with someone along the way.

EH: A Man on the Run can also be a person who *knows* something, isn't that so?

McB: Yes. Where the body is buried, or who caused the body to become a body, or even who's about to *become* a body. Dangerous knowledge of this sort can cause a person to become a man who knows too much and who must flee north by northwest in order to escape becoming a body himself.

EH: On the other hand, it isn't necessary that he *really* be in possession of dangerous knowledge, is it?

McB: No. As a matter of fact, he can know absolutely nothing. In which case, he merely *appears* to know something which the bad guys think he actually *does* know.

EH: And this semblance of knowledge becomes even more dangerous to him than the knowledge itself would have been because he doesn't even know *why* someone wants him dead.

McB: In either case, a body is the essential element that sets the plot spinning.

EH: A body, or a substitute for one. The body doesn't have to be an *actual* stiff, does it?

McB: No, it can be what Alfred Hitchcock called the MacGuffin. I prefer the real thing, but there are many successful thrillers that utilize to great effect a substitute corpse.

EH: Can you give us some examples?

McB: Well, the classic Woman-in-Jeopardy story, for example, may very well be *Wait Until Dark,* where a *blind* woman unknowingly carries through customs a doll in which the bad guys have planted dope. They want the dope back. So they come after her.

EH: That's a woman in jeopardy, all right.

McB: In spades.

EH: A gender reversal of Man on the Run.

McB: Which all Woman-in-Jeopardy stories are. In this case, the substitute corpse is a doll—a graven lifeless image of a human being. The woman doesn't *know* where the body is buried, but they think she does. Without the doll—that is, without the corpse—there'd be no reason to stalk and terrify this woman, and there'd be no thriller.

EH: And in much the same way that our Man on the Run learns and changes from *his* hair-raising escapes, so does our Woman in Jeopardy become stronger and wiser by the end of *her* ordeal.

McB: Leaving the reader or the viewer feeling immensely satisfied.

EH: Let's get back to the way you begin one of your mysteries.

McB: With a corpse, yes. Well, actually, before the corpse, there's a title.

EH: I find titles difficult.

McB: I find them easy. I look for resonance. A title that suggests many different things. For example, the title *Ice* seemed to offer limitless possibilities for development. Ice, of course, is what water becomes when it freezes. So the title dictated that the novel be set during the wintertime, when there is ice and snow . . . ah. Snow. Snow is another name for cocaine. So, all right, there'll be cocaine in the plot. But in underworld jargon, to ice someone means to kill him. And ice also means diamonds. And, further, ice is the name for a box-office scam in which tickets to hit shows are sold for exorbitant prices. The title had resonance.

EH: A lot of people had trouble with one of my titles.

McB: Which one?

EH: *Love, Dad.*

McB: That's because it's a terrible title, very difficult to say. You have to say "My new book is called Love Comma Dad." Otherwise, no one will know what you're talking about.

EH: Most people thought the title was *Dear Dad.*

McB: Why?

EH: I don't know why. Actually, I thought *Love, Dad* was a wonderful title.

McB: You should have called it *No Drums, No Bugles.*

EH: Why?

McB: Were there any drums or bugles in it?

EH: No.

McB: There you go.

EH: Tell me where *you* go after you've got your title and your corpse.

McB: I write the first chapter. Or the first two or three chapters. As far as my imagination will carry me until it gives out.

EH: Then what?

McB: I'll outline the next few chapters ahead.

EH: Not the whole book?

McB: No.

EH: Why not?

McB: Because in mystery fiction, the reader never knows what's going to happen next. It helps if the *writer* doesn't quite know, either. If what happens is as much a surprise to him as it is to the reader.

EH: Isn't that dangerous?

McB: *If it doesn't work, you can always go back and change it.*

EH: As I understand it, then, you keep outlining as you go along.

McB: Yes. Whenever I feel a need to move things along in a certain direction. Which, by the way, may change the moment the characters *get* there and discover things I didn't know they'd discover.

EH: I always love the moment.

McB: Which moment?

EH: When the characters do just what the hell they *want* to do.

McB: When they come alive, yes.

EH: That's when you know you've got a book. That's when you know these aren't just words on paper.

McB: A lot of writers talk about how *awful* it is to be a writer. All the suffering, all the pain. Doesn't anyone find *joy* in it?

EH: I do.

McB: So do I.

EH: You once said . . . or *we* once said . . .

McB: *We* once said . . .

EH: . . . when asked which qualities we considered essential for a writer of fiction today . . .

McB: Yes, I remember.

EH: We said . . . a head and a heart.

McB: Yes. The head to give the work direction, the heart to give it feeling.

EH: Would you change that in any way now?

McB: I would say only please, please, please don't forget the heart.

36

THINK OF THE READER

BY PIERS ANTHONY

I AM KNOWN AS A WRITER of popular fantasy and science fiction, though my output is not limited to that. Thus my view is that of a genre writer who is trying to understand more general principles.

Back when I was struggling to break into print, I took a correspondence course in writing. The instructors knew a great deal about writing, but little about science fiction. No matter, they said; the fundamentals of good writing apply to all genres, and they could help me. They were only half right: the fundamentals do apply, but you do have to know the genre—any genre—in order to write successfully for it. I studied my market on my own, and in the end I made it on my own. From this I derive a principle: There is virtue in being ornery. I continue to be ornery and continue to score in ways the critics seem unable to fathom.

A writer *should* study his market, and study general principles; both are essential. He should also forge his own way, contributing such limited originality as the market will tolerate. There is plenty of excellent instruction elsewhere on such things. I am concerned here with a more subtle yet vital aspect of writing than most: the writer's liaison with the reader. This can make or break a piece of writing, yet few seem to grasp its significance. This is one of my many differences with critics, so I will use them as a straw man to help make my point.

I picture a gathering of the elite of the genre, who are there to determine the critic's choice of the best works of science fiction and fantasy of all time. That is, the List that will be graven on granite for the edification of the lesser aspirants. In the genre these would be Samuel Delany's *Dhalgren,* Brian Aldiss' *Report on Probability A,* and Russell Hoban's *Riddley Walker,* and the finest writer of all time would be J. G. Ballard, despite his one failure with *Empire of the Sun.*

Have you read any of these? Have you even heard of them? No, except that you did like the motion picture based on the last? Well, the critics have an answer for you: You are an ignorant lout whose library card and book store privileges should be suspended until your tastes improve.

Yet any ordinary person who tries to read such books will wonder just what world such critics live in. The answer is, of course, a different world. They are like the poet Shelley's Ozymandias, whose colossal ruin lies in the barren sand. "Look on my works, ye mighty, and despair." Yet his works are completely forgotten.

I am in the world of commercial writing, which means it is readable and enjoyable, and the only accolade it is likely to receive from critics is a mock award for WHO KILLED SCIENCE FICTION? (I was in a five-way tie for runner-up on that one last year, but there's hope for the future.)

But I maintain that the essence of literature lies in its assimilation by the ordinary folk, and that readability is the first, not the last criterion for its merit. Therefore I address the subject of writing, regardless of genre, from this perspective. What makes it readable? To hell with formal rules of writing; they are guidelines in the absence of talent and should be honored only so long as they do not interfere. If it's clear and interesting and relates to the needs of the reader, it will score. I like to tell audiences that they may love or hate what I write, but they will be moved by it. Then I prove it. The only person to fall asleep during one of my recent readings was a senior editor. Well, there are limits, and even I can't squeeze much blood from a stone. I am successful in part because I make connections with my readers that bypass the editors as well as the critics.

How do I do it? Well, there are little tricks, and one big secret. All of them are so simple that it's a wonder they aren't practiced by every writer. But they are not, and indeed critics condemn them, and editors try to excise them from my manuscripts. I have had many an internecine battle with editors, and finally left a major publisher because of this. I understand I am known as a difficult writer to work with, though no editor says it to my face. I can't imagine why!

All the tricks can be subsumed under one guideline: *Think of the reader.* Do it at every stage. Every paragraph, every word. If you are writing fantasy, don't use a word like "subsumed" because the reader won't understand it. It's a lovely word, but unless your readership consists of intellectuals or folk interested in precise usage—such as those who are presumed to read a book like this one—forgo your private pleasure, and speak more plainly. "All the tricks add up to this." I can with ease overreach the horizons of my readers, but I do my damnedest not to. Any writer who thinks he's smart when he baffles his readers, whether by using foreign phrases or obscure terminology, is the opposite.

When you refer to a character or situation that has not been mentioned for some pages, refresh the matter for the reader, so that he won't have to leaf back interminably to find out what you're talking about. Don't say, "The List is foolish." Huh? What list? Say "The List of the critics' top genre novels I parodied above is foolish." Editors seem to hate this; they blue-pencil it out as redundancy. But it enables the reader to check in with your concept without pausing, and that's what counts. Never let your reader stumble; lead him by the hand—and do it without patronizing him.

When you introduce a new character, don't just throw him at the reader unprepared. Have him introduced by a familiar character, if you possibly can. In my forthcoming mainstream novel *Firefly,* I start with one character, who later meets another, and then I follow the other character. That one meets a third, and I follow the third. In the course of 150,000 words, the only character the reader meets cold is the first one. Thus the reader can proceed smoothly throughout, never tripping. It was a job to arrange some of the handoffs, but that *is* my job as a writer: to do the busy-work for the reader. Some of the concepts in this novel are mind-stretching, but the little tricks smooth the way.

When I do a series—and I've done ten so far—I try to make each novel stand by itself, so that the reader who comes to it new does not have to struggle with an ongoing and confusing situation. Yes, this means repeating and summarizing some material, and it is a challenge to do that without boring those who have read the prior novels. But it means, for example, that a reader can start with my tenth Xanth novel and read backwards toward the first, and enjoy them all. Xanth has many readers, and this is part of the reason: It is easy to get into, and it does not demand more than the reader cares to give. Perhaps no other series shows a greater dichotomy between the contempt of critics and the devotion of readers. I do know my market, and it is not the critics. I suspect the same is true for most commercial writers.

Science fiction is fantastic stuff. Little of it is truly believable, and less is meant to be. It represents a flight of fancy for the mind, far removed from the dullness of mundane affairs. Yet even there, human values are paramount. There needs to be respect for every situation and every character, no matter how far out. Every thing is real on its own terms, and every one is alive, even when the thing is as outrageous as a night mare who is a female horse carrying bad dreams and the one is the Incarnation of Death itself, complete with scythe. Can a robot have feelings? Yes, and they are similar to those of a human being. For in the tacit symbolism of the genre as I practice it, a humanoid robot may be a man whose color, religion, or language differs from those of the culture into which he is thrust, and his feelings are those any of us would experience if similarly thrust. The essence of the genre is human, even when it is alien.

I am in an ongoing situation that illustrates the way that even the most fantastic and/or humorous fiction can relate to serious life. A twelve-year-old girl walking home from school was struck by a drunk driver and spent three months in a coma, barely responsive to any outside stimulus. At her mother's behest, I wrote her a letter, for she was one of my readers. I talked about the magic land of Xanth, and the sister realm of Elfquest by another author, and the value of children to those who love them, and I joked about the loathsome shot the nurse would give the Monster Under the Bed if she saw him. I spoke of the character with her name who would be in a future Xanth novel, an elf girl or maybe an ogre girl.

The child's mother read the letter to her, and it brought a great widening of her eyes, and her first smile since the accident. She became responsive, though able to move only her eyes, one big toe, and her fingers. She started to indicate YES or NO to verbal questions by looking to placards with those words printed on them. She made her preference emphatically clear: an elf girl, not an ogre girl!

It is my hope that she is now on the way to recovery, though there is of course a long way to go. It was fantasy that made the connection to reality, her response to my interest and my teasing. I think that fantasy needs no more justification than this. I, as writer, was able to relate to her, my reader, and she responded to me. The rest will be mostly in the province of medicine, but the human spark was vital to the turning point.

And here is the secret I am working toward: Writing and reading are one on one, writer to reader and back again, and the rest of the universe doesn't matter. The writer must know his readers, not the details of their lives, which are myriad, but their hearts and dreams. He must relate. He must care.

When I write to you, it is as if we are in a privacy booth, and we are sharing things that neither of us would confess elsewhere. We love, we hurt, we laugh, we fear, we cry, we wonder, we are embarrassed—together. We *feel,* linked. We share our joy and our shame, and yes, I feel your tears on my face as you feel mine on yours. We may be of different sexes and other generations, or we may match—but we relate to each other more intimately than any two others, dream to dream, our emotions mixed and tangled—for that time while the book that is our connection is open. When it closes we are cut off from each other, and we are strangers again, and we regret that, but we remember our sharing, and we cherish it. We were true friends, for a while. How precious was that while!

37

ALWAYS A STORYTELLER

BY MARY HIGGINS CLARK

THERE'S A THEORY that our lives are set in seven-year cycles. Vaguely, I remember that the basis for that belief is that in seven years every cell in our bodies has replaced itself. In case that's mountain-folk legend, I hasten to apologize to the more learned in the scientific fields. Recently I reread an article on suspense writing that I wrote just seven years ago to see what I've learned since.

My conclusion is that the more you know, the more you don't know. I've written four books, short stories, a novella, and film treatments since then, and I'm not sure I've gained any greater insight into this wondrous, complex and tantalizing field we call writing.

However, we must start somewhere, so let's go with the basics. How do you know that you are supposed to be a writer? The first necessity is that utter yearning to communicate, that sense that "I have something to say"; reading a book and knowing, *knowing* that you can write one like it; the sense that no matter how well ordered your life is, how thoroughly you delight in your family and friends and home and job, something is missing. Something so absolutely necessary that you are constantly swallowing ashes. You want to write. You must write.

These are the people who just might make it. That yearning is usually accompanied by talent, real talent, often native, undisciplined, unfocused talent, but certainly it's there. The degree of yearning separates the *real* potential writer from the truism that everyone has one story in them. How many times are professional writers approached at seminars or parties with the suggestion, "I've got a great story to tell. You jot it down for me, and we'll split the royalties."

Face the yearning. At some point, you'll have to or else eventually go to that great beyond unfulfilled. My mother always told me that my grandmother, struggling to raise her nine children and an orphaned

177

niece, used to say, "Oh, how I'd love to write a book." On her deathbed, she was still regretting that she'd never tried.

Now you've acknowledged that you've simply got to try. Where do you begin? Most of us have a sense of what we want to write. If you don't, a terrific clue is to analyze what you like to *read*. I hadn't the faintest idea that I could write suspense, but after my first book was published, a biographical novel about George Washington that was read by the favored few, I knew that if I tried again, I'd really want to look forward to that lovely mailing from the publisher known as a royalty statement. I cast about for a story idea and looked at the bookshelf. I was astonished to realize that ninety percent of the books I'd read in the last couple of years had been mysteries. I did further soul-digging and began naming my favorite authors: Mary Roberts Rinehart, Josephine Tey, Agatha Christie, Charlotte Armstrong, and on and on. That was the clue that helped me decide to try a suspense novel. The one I launched was *Where Are the Children?* It's in its forty-second printing right now.

Footnote, just so I don't forget. Judith Guest's first novel was turned down by two publishers. She then looked at her bookshelf and realized that many of the books she read were published by Viking Press. She sent her manuscript to them. Months later she received a telegram. "Viking Press is honored to publish *Ordinary People*." The point is that the books you like to read give you a clue to what you may write best. The publisher of the books you read may turn out to be the best potential publisher for you.

Back to the beginning. Having determined whether you want to begin the writing adventure in the field of suspense or romance or science fiction; mainstream novels or books for children or adolescents; or poetry or articles, the next step is to treat yourself to several subscriptions. *The Writer* is the best at-home companion for the aspiring and/or achieving writer I can suggest.

I sold my first short story on my own. It went to forty magazines over the course of six years before it found a home. Which leads to the next question the new writer invariably asks. "How do I get an agent?" It's the chicken-and-egg query. In my case, in 1956 a young agent read the story and phoned me, saying, "I'd like to represent you." We were together thirty years until she retired two years ago. I'm still with her agency and the terrific people she put in her place. The point is, I

think it's a lot easier to get an agent after you've proven yourself, even if your success is a modest one. That story brought me one hundred dollars. But remember. No story or book should ever sit in your drawer. If you get it back from one editor, send it out to the next. And don't sit in never-never land waiting for that one to sell. Start on the next project.

O.K. You have the determination; you know what you want to write; you're gathering the tools. I think it's fundamental to set aside time every day. Even one hour a day creates a habit. When my children were young, I used to get up at five and work from five until seven. I have the whole day to write now and don't get up that early, but I'm tempted to start setting the alarm again. There is something exhilarating about the world being quiet and you're somehow alone in it knowing that the phone won't ring or someone won't stop by. On the other hand, maybe you work best at night. Take that extra hour after everyone else in the family has been tucked in and use it to work on the story or poem or novel. No matter how tired you are when you start, I promise you that the sense of accomplishment of seeing even a page or two completed will make your dreams blissful.

I urge you to join some kind of writing group. Writing is one of the most isolated professions in the world. Your family can be marvelously supportive, but it's not the same. One of two things happen. They see the rejection slips and urge you not to keep banging your head against a wall. "Give it up, dear. It's just too tough to break into that field." Or they think that every word you write is gospel and expect a massive best seller any minute. Your local college or library may have writing courses available. Sign up for one of them. Don't worry about the fact that you'll inevitably miss three or four classes during the semester. You'll make the other ten or twelve. Listening to a professional, getting to know people who are in the field or aspiring to it is balm to the soul. When you begin having contact with others who share your need, you'll experience the feeling Stanley must have had when he said, "Dr. Livingston, I presume."

Be aware that there is probably an organization in your general area you should join: mystery writers, science writers, poets, among others. They're waiting for you. After that first story sold, I joined the Mystery Writers of America. I still remember my first meeting. I didn't know a soul. I was in awe of the name writers around me. Many of my best friends today I met at MWA meetings. And oh the joy of talking shop! Besides that, at these professional organizations you get to meet editors and agents who otherwise would be behind closed doors.

That's how it should be in the beginning. The determination. The quest to know what to write. The studying of the craft. The fellowship of other writers. And then in the quiet of that study or the space you cleared for yourself in the corner of the kitchen or bedroom, begin to write. Always remember that what you are is a storyteller. No matter how elegant your prose, how descriptive your passages, how insightful your eye, unless you tell a story people want to hear, you're not going to make it. A story has a beginning and a middle and an end. It tells about people we all know and identify with. It tells of their hopes and dreams and failures and triumphs. It tells of the twists of fate that bestow fortune on one person and rob another who is equally deserving. It makes us laugh and mourn and hope for the people whose lives we are sharing. It leaves us with a sense of catharsis, of emotion well spent. Isaac Bashevis Singer is a dedicated mystery reader. Several years ago at the Mystery Writers annual banquet, he received the award as Mystery Reader of the Year. This great writer offered simple yet profound advice. It was that the writer must think of himself or herself primarily as a storyteller. Every book or story should figuratively begin with the words "Once upon a time." Because it is as true now as it was in the long ago days of wandering minstrels, that when these words are uttered, the room becomes quiet, everyone draws closer to the fire, and the magic begins.

38

THE SCIENCE FICTION VIRUS

BY JOHN SLADEK

WHEN I WAS A KID, what I really wanted to do was to waste my time hanging around the town pool hall. But since they wouldn't let me in, I had to waste my time hanging around the town library. Now that I think of it, the library was a lot like a pool hall; they both had the same kind of lamps with green glass shades, casting little cones of light over the broad tables. While there, I managed to read everything that came to hand, including the Oz books, the Hardy Boys mysteries, and a lot of O. Henry stories. Finally I picked up *From Earth to Moon,* by someone called Jules Verne. I opened the book. A science fiction virus leapt straight from its pages to the center of my brain, where it took root. I've never been the same since.

Actually, I'd already run across science fiction, but only on the radio. There was a terrifically frightening radio program called "Dimension X," which I never missed. Radio really is a superior medium for stimulating the infantile imagination. Someone only has to gasp, or whisper "What's that over there—in the corner—*my God, it's alive!*" and the listener's heart starts pounding. I remember one eerie program which began "The last man on Earth sat alone in a room. *(Pause)* There was a knock at the door." It never occurred to me, as I sat there covered with goose bumps, that this science fiction stuff could be found in books, too.

After Verne, I spent a couple of years reading all the SF I could get my hands on: mostly anthologies from the library and an occasional pulp magazine. Then some other interest came along—girls or model airplanes—and I stopped reading science fiction and forgot all about it.

Or so I thought. I continued reading other things and, somewhere in high school, I decided to become a writer. Naturally, I would only write Good Stuff. Or if not Good, at least Avantgarde Stuff. I scribbled my way through high school and college. There was my F. Scott Fitzgerald phase, my Dostoyevsky phase, and my unfortunate Kerouac phase. There was almost everything but a science fiction phase. I had already dismissed science fiction as a frivolous comic book genre, not for serious adults like me.

After college, I began a novel that was going to be high art indeed: a long, pretentious work-in-progress in the manner of Samuel Beckett (so I imagined). I might still be in progress with it, if a merciful fate had not permitted me take the manuscript to Europe with me and lose it on a train. What a tragedy! And hey, what a relief!

While recovering from this ordeal in New York, I stayed with a friend who was already writing and selling science fiction. By my incredibly high standards, this didn't make sense. Here was a literate, well-read guy, writing for pulp magazines with titles like *Amazing*. I grew curious enough about science fiction to start reading it again. The writing was uneven—pulp-magazine writers are not Samuel Becketts—but the ideas were mind-shattering.

For example, I was brought up short by an episode in one novel by Philip K. Dick. He describes perfectly ordinary surroundings—a beach where a man approaches a soft-drink stand to buy a drink. Suddenly, the stand, with all its wares and even its attendant, shimmers and disappears, leaving only a typewritten slip of paper. The man picks up the slip. It reads SOFT-DRINK STAND.

That did it. The goose bumps were back, and I was reinfected. Here was a popular fiction that could tackle big themes like the nature of reality, *and get away with it*. This had to be worth trying.

Not everyone catches the science fiction virus in just this way. There are probably a million ways to catch it. For some, it's a childhood disease that lingers. They keep on reading SF as they grow up. They join fan clubs, go to conventions, and eventually timidly try out their own stories in one of the thousands of small amateur SF publications, the "fanzines." (SF is deeply rooted in amateurism, with all the good or ill that amateurism implies.) A surprising number of big names in SF—including nearly all of the very biggest ones—began this way. Robert Silverberg was a fan before he published his first story at age eighteen. Frederik Pohl was a fan before he became an editor at twenty. Arthur C. Clarke was well-known in fan circles before he began to publish. In no other industry do fan clubs provide the stars.

The virus also hits grownups, sometimes without warning. This may explain why some established "straight" writers have suddenly, for obscure reasons, discovered the uses of SF. Even major literary figures have occasionally dipped into SF to handle themes too difficult for "straight" fiction. For instance, E. M. Forster wrote "The Machine Stops" to satirize our mechanistic, labor-saving world. (In his story, machines have saved us from even the labor of human relations.) Others who have taken the plunge include Saul Bellow, John Updike, Doris Lessing, Don DeLillo, and Gore Vidal.

Reading up

If you've been hit by the SF virus, you'll have already taken the first step to writing, which is to read constantly. Immerse yourself in the stuff you admire: magazines, anthologies, novels. You no doubt already have a favorite author or two. If you're like most of us, you'll probably begin writing by modeling your work on one of those favorites.

My own early favorites included Alfred Bester, Ray Bradbury, Brian Aldiss, and Frederik Pohl, among others.

But please don't stick exclusively to SF. Remember that SF is a little parish in a big forest. Read plenty of good fiction by good writers of every kind. Never rule anything out as too remote from science fiction concerns. Science fiction, like the Inquisition, concerns itself with everything.

Those "crazy ideas"

As in any profession, you have to be prepared to answer one question a thousand times. People will continually ask artists what their paintings "mean." Everyone wants to know how a prostitute got started in her business. If a man merely digs a hole in the street, someone is bound to come along and ask, "Digging it up, eh?" For science fiction writers, the question is always: "Where do you get all your crazy ideas?"

There's no good answer to this. Harlan Ellison used to reply: "From a crazy idea factory in Schenectady, dummy!" The truth is, getting ideas is seldom a problem.

First of all, there's science itself. Hardly a week goes by that I don't read or hear something astonishing. Scientific notions can come from the daily paper, or from magazines like *Scientific American*. A few recent examples (with my jotted notes in parentheses):

- Manic-depressive syndrome turns out to be genetic; in fact they've found the chromosomal location of the gene for it. (What about other mental states? Is there a gene for normality? For criminality? Is there a gene that compels people to sign their names with little smiling faces?)

- Killer bees are now in Mexico, heading north. (What other insect horrors might be on the way?)

- The Greenhouse Effect could change the shape of human society. (Would it be canceled by a nuclear winter?)

- Nanotechnology—the building of incredibly tiny machines that could sail the human bloodstream, repairing damage and maintaining health—offers a world of possibilities. (What if the tiny machines formed unions and threatened strikes?)

Not only the hard sciences come into play. SF writers use whatever interests them: Kate Wilhelm has used psychology; Ursula Le Guin, anthropology; Damon Knight, linguistics. But almost anything is grist to science fiction's mill:

- **History.** Orson Scott Card sets a series in an 1811 "alternate world." John Brunner describes a world where the Armada won, and America is a Spanish colony.

- **Crime fiction.** Isaac Asimov's robot detective is well-known, but SF detectives are common.

- **Literature.** Anthony Burgess developed an unusual theory of Shakespeare's authorship in a SF story

- **Politics.** I've recently seen SF novels advocating pacifism, militarism, technocracy, the Green Party, and the global electronic village. SF embraces all viewpoints: conservative, liberal, right-wing libertarian, and Marxist—and everyone in between.

- **Religion.** Robert Heinlein proposed exciting and disturbing societies based on new religions. There's plenty of New Age mysticism, too: Ian Watson, for one, has explored UFOs and whale telepathy.

- **War.** Lucius Shepard and Jerry Pournelle write war fiction from very different perspectives.

- **Social Theory.** Brian Aldiss created a congeries of interacting societies across a world in his *Helliconia* series, where periodic ice ages bring inexorable change.

Although scientific ideas can be important in science fiction, they're by no means primary. Good SF stories must first and last be good stories. One of the most brilliant SF stories ever is Avram Davidson's "And All the Seas with Oysters." It contains no science at all, unless you count the technology of bicycle repair, but it's unforgettable.

While I'm listing crazy ideas, let me put in a word for SF humor, especially satire. The premise of satire, like that of much SF, is that today's world is itself crazy, or at least badly made. The SF utopian may try to present an ideal world with the flaws removed. The SF satirist, by contrast, shows a world in which the flaw has grown huge and grotesque. Science fiction satire is a noble tradition, enfolding Jonathan Swift, Nathaniel Hawthorne, Samuel Butler, Mark Twain, H. G. Wells, and George Orwell.

If you're serious about writing SF, try not to become so involved in the trappings—conventions, workshops, fanzines—that you lose track of writing itself. Conventions can be fun, and they're a good way of meeting your fellow writers, prominent editors, and even your readers.

But conventions can be too much of a good thing. Indeed, there are one or two writers who engage in a continual round of public appearances, but never get around to writing anything. Remember that, though there are at least eighty conventions each year, they are primarily social occasions that have little to do with writing. No one gets any writing done during any of them. Writing is a solitary activity that, alas, has nothing to do with social life.

What about SF writer's workshops? These range from instant workshops at conventions to more serious ones set up by science fiction societies. Join one if you wish, but don't hope for magical results. At its best, a workshop can make you concentrate and put pen to paper, it can show you that other people have problems similar to yours, and it can give you a certain amount of confidence. But don't expect too much.

At its worst, a workshop can be destructive. Merciless criticism, often by the unqualified, can destroy self-confidence and make a shy person wish he or she had never thought of writing.

Finally, pay no attention whatsoever to reviews of your work. I speak as a reviewer. Remember that a review expresses only one person's opinion, shared with his readers. The best and worst that a review can do is to call the readers' attention to a book they might otherwise miss (among the 100–200 published each month).

On the other hand, it's important to keep track of the market, both magazines and book publishers. The magazines range in payment from

Omni and *Playboy,* who pay thousands for a story, down to fanzines, who pay in copies. No false modesty—send your stuff to the best market you honestly think you can sell it in.

Book publishers of science fiction abound. A new one seems to pop up (or vanish) every month, and their requirements change rapidly too, so it pays to keep close tabs on them. One good source for monthly info for the SF professional is the magazine *Locus* (copies are available in SF bookstores, subscriptions from *Locus* Publications, 34 P.O. Box 13305, Oakland, CA 94661).

The nature of the virus

I swore I wouldn't get involved in defining science fiction, but. . . . There are so many popular misconceptions about it. It isn't necessarily about space travel, or the future. Nor is it usually just a catalogue of brilliant inventions. (This answers another common question: "Aren't you worried that technology will overtake your stories and make them obsolete?" No, because I'm not writing user guides for new gadgets.)

Ideally, science fiction is fiction about humans dealing with science or technology (in the broadest sense). Some stories can be oddly unbalanced. At one extreme is the dreary high-tech novel that gives you the mass of the spaceship in kilograms, the mean temperature in degrees Kelvin, and the solar radiation in microwatts per square meter. No human beings in sight.

The other extreme eschews technology by proposing (say) an alternate universe where magic works. Alas, this quickly degenerates into a tedious tale of dragons, dwarfs, and sorcerers, remaining science fiction only by association. Neither extreme really has much to do with real human beings, and consequently neither is worth reading.

Between the extremes, there's room for plenty of vital innovation. And here I must stop defining SF. Real science fiction is undefinable—but you'll know it when you catch the virus.

39

WRITING A SUCCESSFUL SUSPENSE THRILLER

BY WILLO DAVIS ROBERTS

I ASSUME THAT IF YOU WANT TO WRITE a syspense novel or thriller, you like reading them. Don't attempt to write one unless you do. You must have the *feel* for this kind of writing, a genuine sense of what it takes to send prickles down a reader's spine, or make his adrenaline level shoot up.

So how do you go about writing a suspenseful book that will lure an editor into offering a contract and induce readers to buy it?

It is possible to start writing a book with only a character and a situation firmly in mind, as opposed to making a detailed outline, but it's difficult to do a mystery/suspense novel that way unless you've had lots of experience; in that case, your unconscious is doing a lot of the work for you.

I have never done a detailed written outline (though all the basic elements are in my head), but there are advantages in being able to do this. For beginners, making an outline assures their being able to follow through and finish the book, rather than getting lost in the middle of it. It may enable you also, when you've a few published books to your credit, to sell a novel on a proposal or several chapters and outline.

A prospective writer in any genre should analyze other books in the field and figure out how the writer put the book together, what makes it succeed. When you do this, you'll find similarities in how the authors handle basic techniques. Note particularly how the writer begins and ends the book; chances are, in a suspense novel, both will be chilling and/or thrilling.

Some years ago, in a writer's workshop to which I belonged, a talented newcomer read the beginning of a Gothic novel she was working on. It had chains rattling in the attic, a terrified heroine in a strange place, all kinds of mysterious goings-on. The author had bogged down, however, not knowing where to go next, and when we asked who was rattling the chains and why, we found out: The author didn't know!

It read like a Gothic, but she hadn't figured out ahead of time exactly who was the villain or why he was threatening the heroine. She had no idea when she sat down and began to type, where the story was going. (Once she worked it out, she finished and sold the book.)

Where is the story going?

There are few rules that can never be broken under any circumstances. But here is one: Never, *never,* begin a mystery novel without knowing where you're going with it. By that I mean that you should know who the villain is, what his motivations are, and what he does to threaten someone else. These things can be a mystery to the reader as well as to the characters, but it should never be a mystery to the writer. You don't have to know exactly how the novel is going to end, but you should decide ahead of time the general direction the action will take. I almost never know the details of the climax until I get there; it's more fun for me to write if the action develops out of the characters, when I say "What would I do if I were confronted by this problem?"

What I would actually do would be to get hysterical and call the cops, but one's protagonist must have more fortitude than that. What I want is for the characters to develop to the stage where they are "real" people, and then act as sensibly or courageously as they can. If the characters are sufficiently well developed, they will be obliging enough to do this.

Once in a while I do work myself into a trap by not figuring out enough ahead of time. Having cut off all escape—because in order not to appear moronic, the protagonist has to be *unable* to walk away from the dangers—it sometimes takes considerable ingenuity to extricate the poor soul.

Knowing you'll have to do that, prepare for the ending. Don't forget that the villain needs to be just as strongly motivated as the protagonist: He's greedy, he's insane, he's protecting himself against the consequences of prior actions, he hates, he loves, etc. *All* characters, major and minor, must have credible reasons for whatever they do. The heroine who walks into the dark alley may do it, believably, to rescue someone else; she'd be stupid to do it for a less compelling reason. A hero might attempt a risky jump between roof-tops or off a bridge to escape a pursuer, but don't have him do it for a lesser reason that to save his own or someone else's life.

Don't write dramatic scenes that are suspenseful but don't make sense in the overall context of the story. Unless the character is literally insane, give him logical motivation. That goes for all the characters. The reader will suspend his disbelief in order to be entertained, but only to a point.

Before I begin a story, I make a list of characters. Their names, their physical descriptions, their likes and dislikes, their habits—whether they smoke, what they drink, what they eat, their backgrounds, etc. I leave space on my master list to add things that occur to me as I go along, so there will be no discrepancies. I once wrote a novel in which a character disguised himself with a full beard; he was eventually recognized without my saying that the beard had been shaved off. The editor, the copy-editor, and I all read and re-read that manuscript and didn't catch that, but a reader did!

I begin to write when I have the characters sketched out—a file card or a couple of typed pages for each one—and when I know the basic situation. Though I don't at that point have the specifics worked out, I know the general direction the novel will take: people dying under mysterious circumstances at a rest home, and a girl who goes to work there will join forces with an ex-cop whose uncle was one of the victims, to ferret out the truth about the deaths.

Beginnings

The opening is the most important part of the novel. This applies to almost every work of fiction, but particularly to suspense novels. These days many so-called mysteries are not mysteries at all, in the sense that you have a puzzle to solve. Often a story is told from the viewpoint of the perpetrator; the reader knows all along who is doing what and why, but he is kept holding his breath to see if the villain gets away with it, or when and how he'll be caught.

The opening has to have that narrative hook, that grabber that makes a reader turn the page and become immediately absorbed in the story. My favorite from my own novels reads:

The mercury stood at 98 degrees on the thermometer next to the kitchen door. I wondered afterward why that should have registered with me; one thin red line, when there was red all over the kitchen itself. Fresh blood. Her blood. Alison's.

189

Some of the manuscripts I've been asked to read and criticize purport to be mysteries, but the action doesn't start until page 10, or even chapter five. More than once I've suggested throwing away the first chapters, retaining some essential minor bits to be inserted later, and beginning the novel 30 to 50 pages into the manuscript, because that's where the action starts.

Begin the action, the suspense, on page 1, paragraph 1.

That's the hard part. Resist the temptation to foreshadow. The old Gothics sometimes began "If I had only known what awaited me at Castle Craig—" Today, foreshadowing is done subtly or, better yet, dispensed with altogether. The old saw about starting a book as close to the end as possible is still valid. Start with action, then work in the background as you go, or do a flashback, as I did in *Didn't Anybody Know My Wife?* After I'd set the stage for the murder of Dr. Scott's wife, I went back to the morning of the same day and then carried through on the story chronologically.

Sometimes you need go back for only a scene or two; sometimes you start with an exciting part and flash back for years, if necessary, to get in everything the reader must know that led up to the murder or whatever your opening ploy is. The important thing to remember about flashbacks is that the reader must never be confused about whether it's "now" or "then."

Usually I lead into a flashback by the use of "had." As in, *Scotty had expected her to be on time, but she'd never shown up.* Once you've established that you're *in* a flashback, drop the "hads" and tell it in simple past tense. And then when you come back to the present, be sure it's clear that you've done so. As in, *Now here he was, looking at the body of the woman who had been his wife.*

The climax is the next most important part of the novel, and that should be smashing, too. One way to kill an otherwise acceptable story is to wind up with a chapter or two of explanation after the excitement is over. To avoid that, get the explaining in before the final confrontation between protagonist and villain. Keep something exciting for the very last pages.

Dialogue that speaks for you

I've mentioned letting the characters take over the action and determine the course of the story. This can work only if the characters are truly individuals. You have to know how they will think and act in various circumstances, so that they'll be different from one another.

Ideally, the reader should be able to tell who is speaking by what he or she is saying. For instance, imagine that you are a woman who has just wrecked the family car. You come home and relate your tale of woe. Now, write down what the response would be from your mother ("Oh, Grace, were you hurt?"), your children ("Oh, gosh, Dad'll kill you!"), your best friend ("Your insurance will take care of it, won't it?" or maybe "Do you think you can get it fixed before George sees it?"), and your husband ("You did what? #$%$@!"). They would not all have the same point of view nor the same concerns—and neither would your characters—about the things that happen in your story. Some of them may express *your* opinions on capital punishment, or abortion, or other controversial subjects. There should, however, be convincing alternate viewpoints. This is not the place to overpower the reader with personal opinions.

A character with a hot temper speaks in an explosive manner, with exclamation points and possibly profanity. Show aggression, or tenderness, or timidity, in the dialogue; don't be content with letting adverbs to do it for you, or *telling* the reader a character is tough or gentle.

A note of caution on "realistic" dialogue: Leave out the small, irritating things that many people say, such as, "you know," unless this is essential to the character. If a scene takes place at a dining table, by all means mention the food, but don't put in every "please pass the salt." It's boring and it adds nothing to the story.

"Show, don't tell," also applies to action. Instead of telling us the girl is timid, have her be hesitant to act, or her lips tremble, or tears fill her eyes. Don't tell us a husband is a wife-beater. Have him hit the wife, swear at her, lose control of his temper. Every character, even the minor ones, will have some definite traits that can be conveyed both in speech and action.

Shared emotion

Create emotion. One way to hold your readers is to make them *care* what happens to the protagonist. Make them fear for her, laugh with her, cry for her. Make the reader *identify* with your characters, feel the sorrow, the pain, the fear, the thumping heart and the labored breathing.

A character not only can, but should, have flaws that make him human. There are editors who want all the women to be gorgeous, all the men handsome, everyone sexy and romantic. My own belief is that someone with warts, even figurative ones, is more interesting. Everyone can identify with the person who has a weight problem, or is trying to quit smoking, or is self-conscious about a big nose or an overbite or an inability to think of a retort in time to use it. Don't overdo this, but small defects can be engaging.

Thrillers should move along at a brisk pace. They should not be travelogues, with endless pages of description of an exotic setting, yet *brief* insertions of such color can add authenticity and needed atmosphere. Having mastered beginnings and endings—still a struggle for many of us, even after many years of working with them—all you have left to do is the middle. The long, long middle.

Keep it moving. Make every word count. If it doesn't move the story forward or add to our understanding of the character, cut it out. If it begins to drag, throw another problem or predicament at your protagonist. Eventually, he or she will solve or overcome all. Remember: it's O.K. to complicate the plot with coincidence—the earthquake, the accident, the bad luck—but don't *solve* it except through the actions of the protagonist. Make him or her figure out the answers and solutions, and keep them logical. It's all right to go back and add clues that you didn't think of in your first draft. If possible, set the finished manuscript aside for a time to let it "cool," and then read it again before you type the final draft. That will help you spot the places that need fixing, sometimes hard to see during the passion of writing it.

If you can do all this, chances are you'll find a publisher, and that's what it's all about.

40

No Gore, Please—They're British
An Interview with P. D. James

By Marilyn Stasio

Q. *Would you care to present your series detectives and tell us how they operate?*

P.D.J.: Adam Dalgliesh is Commander of the [London] Metropolitan Police Force. I know that makes it sound as if he had a naval rank; but it is, in fact, a rank peculiar to the Metropolitan Police Force. He is a professional policeman and head of the Murder Squad, which makes him lucky in the sense that he has the entire resources of the police behind him. He has access to police computers and to the assistance of police inspectors, constables, scene-of-crime officers and, of course, to forensic pathologists at the Metropolitan Police forensic science laboratory. I hope he's a good, realistic professional cop; I certainly intend that he shall be.

Q. *You have another detective, though, who is not affiliated with the police.*

P.D.J.: Cordelia Gray, whom I introduced in *An Unsuitable Job for a Woman.* Cordelia is a private eye who inherited her very rundown, seedy agency from a man who was formerly a detective with the Metropolitan Police. He trained her in the trade and she hopes she goes about it in a very professional way. She is not licensed, however, because we have no system here for licensing our private eyes. It's one of the differences between England and the United States.

Since it isn't at all realistic for private detectives to get involved in murder, we have to involve them in cases where it *does* seem natural and logical, either because the police have written off a particular case—as a suicide, for example—or because the detective somehow has a personal interest.

Q. *Aside from the technical challenge, doesn't having a detective who works outside the law also give the hero a chance to operate beyond the law?*

P.D.J.: Cordelia respects the methods of the professional police. But they certainly don't welcome her with open arms, as they used to do the private detective in English fiction of the 1930's. In Dorothy Sayers's Lord Peter Wimsey novels, the chief constable was always saying: "Well, my Lord, how *thankful* we are that you're here!"

In the early books of Dashiell Hammett and Raymond Chandler—which I so much admire because they were very, very fine writers who influenced the novel generally, not only their own genre—the police were commonly regarded by the heroes as brutal or corrupt or incompetent. The detective was essentially a lonely man, a crusader striding the mean streets. The private war that those heroes waged was as much against the official police force and society itself as it was against the ostensible villains.

Even Hammett's hard-boiled detective Sam Spade had his own morality. He always tried to give his clients good value for their money.

Q. *What about Raymond Chandler's Philip Marlowe?*

P.D.J.: "A man who is neither tarnished nor afraid. He must be a *complete* man in his own world and a *good* enough man for any world." Chandler says at the end of that passage, I believe, that if there were enough men like Philip Marlowe, the world would be a very safe place to live in, and yet not too dull to be *worth* living in. I believe it was that same brilliant essay, *The Simple Art of Murder,* in which Chandler also attempted to demolish the genre of the English detective mystery. He said it should be taken away from the vicarage and handed over to those who understood it. He wrote that the English may not be the best writers in the world, but they are the best *dull* writers in the world.

Q. *You hear that charge of "dull" writing from readers who prefer the pace and action of hard-boiled mysteries.*

P.D.J.: Actually, Chandler was not saying that the *writing* was dull. Only that that *kind* of crime writing was dull, in the sense that it was *unrealistic,* prettifying and romanticizing murder, but having little to do with real blood-and-guts tragedy. This was very true of many books written in the so-called Golden Age of the English mystery. One simply cannot take these as realistic books about murder, about the horror of murder, the tragedy of murder, the harm that murder does.

Q. *And yet, Agatha Christie is very popular here in the United States—along with such traditionalist British writers as Ngaio Marsh, Margery Allingham, Edmund Crispin, Michael Innes.*

P.D.J.: There's been a huge resurgence of interest here in England, too. Many of the old favorites, which have been out of print, are now being reissued. They were wonderfully ingenious, all those red herrings and false clues. But in that period, readers expected the murderer to be *diabolically* clever, and everything else became subordinate to the ingenuity of the puzzle, including character and motivation. That is the real criticism made of those writers; and for many of them, it certainly is a valid criticism.

Q. *Since you admire the moral integrity of certain hard-boiled heroes, how do you account for readers' strong genre preferences?*

P.D.J.: The separate traditions, of course, are quite distinctive in their appeal. The American crime novel seems to be very much in the hard-boiled tradition that emerged in the aftermath of the First World War—the end of puritanism, the Depression, Prohibition, gangsterism and so on. Your heroes tend to be tough and sensational, reacting very instinctively to danger and absorbing more punishment. Your stories are also generally set in a more violent society.

The British detective story is gentler, more pastoral. Because it is firmly rooted in the soil of British literary tradition, it shares assumptions that are strong in our literature; for example, the assumption that we live in an intelligible and benevolent universe; the assumption that law and order, peace and tranquility are the norm; that crime and violence are the aberration; and that the proper preoccupation of man is to bring order out of chaos. Our stories are also more likely to have happy endings.

Also in English fiction they don't believe the system to be corrupt, certainly. I think that the American private eye sees the police force more as the enemy than as an ally. I think that the English private eye sees the police force more as an ally.

The old psychological and moral certainties have changed although in one respect that has had a positive effect on genre fiction, by moving it closer to the so-called straight novel. There's a greater emphasis on stylistic realism, and a *far* greater emphasis on the psychological realism of character.

Q. *Does that realism extend to the depiction of violence?*

P.D.J.: Well, I would hope so, speaking for my own novels, in which I use the formula of the detective story in a realistic manner in order to try to say something that is true about men and women and, in particular, about society. But although it is true that we are a very, very much more violent society than we used to be, murder is still a very uncommon crime in England. I think the total homicide figure is well below 1,000 a year.

Q. *Are there any crimes, then that you—or, more properly speaking, your characters—are unlikely to deal with?*

P.D.J.: Yes. I don't think I would feel very happy writing a book about the torture and murder of a child. I think that would be extremely painful to do.

Even in a lawless society, fictional crime need not escalate. Of more interest than the event is what is going on in the mind of your character, who does not need a whole series of increasingly horrific murders in order to react in a believable manner.

Q. *In an age of increasing social turmoil, why are people turning more and more for both pleasure and reassurance to crime genre forms that, however realistic in execution, still adhere to conventions established in other, less turbulent ages?*

P.D.J.: Because they do affirm the intelligibility of the universe; the moral norm; the sanctity of life. And because, at the end, there is a *solution*. I think I'm very frightened of violence. I hate it. I'm very worried by the fact that the world is a much more violent place than when I was a girl. And it may be that by writing mysteries I am able, as it were, to exorcize this fear, which may very well be the same reason why so many people enjoy reading a mystery. It seems to me that the more we live in a society in which we feel our problems—be they

196

international problems of war and peace, racial problems, problems of drugs, problems of violence—to be literally beyond our ability to solve, it seems to me very reassuring to read a popular form of fiction which itself has a problem at the heart of it. One which the reader knows will be solved by the end of the book; and not by supernatural means or good luck, but by human intelligence, human courage, and human perseverance. That seems to me one of the reasons why the crime novel, in all its forms and varieties, does hold its place in the affections of its readers.

41

WHICH VIEWPOINT—AND WHY

BY MAX BYRD

THE MOST IMPORTANT DECISION a novelist makes is whether to write in the first or third person.

When I began *Target of Opportunity,* it was to be the fourth novel in my series about Mike Haller, the hard-boiled, egg-headed private detective I had described to myself as "the grandson of Philip Marlowe," a character I had grown fond of, a comfortable old shoe of a voice.

My editor said no.

She read a few chapters of the new manuscript, then called me to say that by now the voice was *too* comfortable, the private-eye formula routine. She wanted me to break out of the detective genre and try to write a bigger, more ambitious book. And, unlike my earlier novels, she wanted this one to be written in the third person.

For a month or so I attempted to cooperate and still stay comfortable. I rewrote all of my new chapters, seventy pages or so, simply altering Mike Haller's conventional first person to an objective, neutral third-person narrative: "He said" for "I said." But it didn't need another phone call from the editor to convince me that this approach wasn't working. What was gained by my substituting neutrality and objectivity for a characteristic human voice? Who would want to read it? I was rearranging my formula, but I wasn't creating something new. To write in the third person, I had to admit, meant writing in a completely different way, with completely different characters. As things turned out, it also meant solving a problem of plotting that up until then had seemed to me unsolvable.

The advantages of first person are easy to see—directness, intensity, ease, naturalness. It was no accident, I told myself, that the very first English novelist, Daniel Defoe, had turned instinctively to first-person narration: All of his characters tell their stories in distinctive, confessional voices. Robinson Crusoe recounts his own "life and surprising adventures"; Moll Flanders tallies up husbands, lovers, thefts, and bankruptcies on her own nimble fingers. Even the eighteenth-century novelists who had come immediately after Defoe followed his example. The epistolary novels of Samuel Richardson, for example, including his great tragic masterpiece *Clarissa,* were all variations of the first-person technique Defoe had pioneered. Through his device of conflicting letters from many different characters, Richardson achieved a wider scale and point of view than Defoe, each letter writer telling his story in the first person. Richardson himself peeps up occasionally as "editor" of the letters, a mild voice from the prompter's box, barely audible against the actors on the stage.

When I looked at my shelf of detective novels, I saw that a disproportionate number of those I admire were in autobiographical first person: Dick Francis, Raymond Chandler, Ross MacDonald, Robert B. Parker. None of them had apparently even tried third person. And understandably enough: In the classic detective story, the detective is always a kind of surrogate novelist; his job, like the novelist's, is to understand the characters perfectly and to tell and retell the plot until it comes out right. His voice is the voice of the writer himself, projected onto the screen of the blank page.

This, when I thought about it, was the greatest advantage of first-person narration, the reason beginning writers are urged (rightly) to use it. There is no quicker, surer way to your own feelings. The person who writes: "I said . . ." "I did . . ." "I wanted . . ." for three hundred pages is unavoidably writing about himself, drawing consciously or unconsciously on his own personality for material, then recreating that personality, however distorted by plot, in the story he writes. First-person writing is ventriloquism. It's no surprise that steeplechase jockey Dick Francis, who was thrown violently from so many horses, writes so often and so powerfully about physical pain; or that Lew Archer expresses in every dark metaphor the wise *tristesse* that Ross MacDonald always communicated in real life; or that Philip Marlowe turns so often to the bottle that Raymond Chandler kept in his desk drawer.

But with all this in mind I still remembered my editor's admonition that Henry James—she had rolled out the big guns—believed no writer achieved the level of *art* as opposed to autobiography until he mastered the third person. And so I set out to write *Target of Opportunity* as a brand-new story.

Two things I gave up at once: the character of Mike Haller and nearly the same thing—Mike Haller's *style,* his wise-cracking, Marlowesque, conventionally ironic way of talking.

Three things I saw I had gained:

1. Scale. Third-person narration permitted a grand expansion of geographic scale. The book was to be set in many distant places: London, the English countryside, the Dordogne Valley of southwestern France in 1944, San Francisco, Lake Tahoe, Boston today. With a cinematic flick of the eye, while Mike Haller was still slowly boarding a plane, third person could change cities or even continents. For a moment, I felt like a lordly Ludlum or Forsyth, studying my novel as if it were a huge map of the world, moving my characters effortlessly across it like plastic models.

2. I had gained flexibility of subplot. In first-person narration, any subplot necessarily has to involve the narrator, sometimes as observer, more frequently as participant: He must be on the spot when the subplot starts rolling. In most cases, this limitation means that the subplot of an action novel has to be a romance: When not busy solving the crime, the hero or heroine has to be falling in or out of love (this works to perfection in such novels as Dick Francis's *Whip Hand* or Chandler's *Long Goodbye*). But a larger, more complete effect comes about when the subplot *independently* reflects the themes of the main action, as Gloucester's tribulations with his sons reflect King Lears' with his daughters. For the first time my plot and subplot could hold mirrors up to each other: The secondary theme I had chosen of fathers and sons at war in present-day America would reflect fathers and sons at war in 1944.

3. I had also gained a wider cast of characters. Elmore Leonard has noted that in every book he writes some minor character unexpectedly grows to importance or even threatens to take over the whole story. But of course a writer needs to be free to let these characters perform. In *Target of Opportunity,* I suddenly found that I could wheel the spotlight wherever I wanted. To give only one example, nothing makes a

character seem more realistic than giving him or her strong, habitual likes and dislikes, especially in small things; they push the character back in time, forward into the future, they give him depth. In first person, it is easy enough for the narrator to reveal that from childhood on he has hated the smell of coffee or loved women with freckled noses, but it is frequently awkward for other characters to say such things to the narrator. By contrast, the third-person voice can swoop in and out of any character's mind, like a bird through an open window, observing everything, bringing everything back. Here is John LeCarré building two characters at once in *The Little Drummer Girl*, letting Kurtz's habitual impatience with detail play against Lenny's goodness:

Lenny was big-hearted and kind, but a little shy of people he was not observing. He had wide ears and an ugly, over-featured face, and perhaps that was why he kept if from the hard gaze of the world. . . . In other circumstances Kurtz could tire of detail very quickly, but he respected Lenny and paid the closest attention to everything he said, nodding, congratulating, making all the right expressions for him.

With these "gains," I had, however, also raised an unexpected question: In third person, how loud is the narrator's voice to be? In first-person narration, there is never a difficulty about point of view or voice: It is always the narrator speaking, even if he tells somebody else's story. But in third-person narration, do you look over every character's shoulder? or only one?

Most writers decide on multiple points of view, either alternating them in chapters or larger sections (as I chose to do), or darting back and forth on the same page as Elmore Leonard does. Curiously, Martin Cruz Smith's marvelous novel *Gorky Park* takes the point of view of only one person—the Moscow policeman Arkady—yet sticks to the third person. The advantages Smith gains are subtle but strong: Typically he begins a chapter with no more than a sentence or two of capsule biography/description ("She had a broad, child's face, innocent blue eyes, a narrow waist and small breasts with nipples as tiny as vaccination marks.") More frequently, he begins with a paragraph of setting:

Almost all Russia is old, graded by glaciers that left a landscape of low hills, lakes and rivers that wander like the trails of worms in soft wood. North of the city, Silver Lake was frozen, and all the summer dachas on the lake were deserted, except Iamskoy's.

At which point he smoothly moves his protagonist in front of the picture ("Arkady parked behind a Chaika limousine"), so that the effect is of seeing these things through Arkady's mind, though they are rarely things he would have thought or known. And this is all the more important because a major strength of Smith's book is the knowledge it gives us of an exotic land, the encyclopedic, wide-screen effect of scale it creates, even while its focus stays tightly on Arkady's actions.

For *Target of Opportunity* I lacked (among many other talents) Smith's gift for linking geographic scale and individual character. But I noticed that many of his preliminary settings did what my notion of habitual likes and dislikes did: They established a depth of time, geological and historical, that lent still more realism to his fictional world. A third-person narrative, I realized, was free to manipulate *time* as well as place. And with that realization my unsolvable problem of plot was solved.

My original plan had been to have a plot in which, as I pictured it, two parallels meet. That is, I wanted to draw on the detective story premise as old as at least Sophocles: *There is always an earlier crime.* The present crime is always explained by discovering the crime that has provoked it, so my protagonist was to solve a present crime in Boston by uncovering an earlier crime in the French Resistance, some forty years before. When writing a first-person Mike Haller novel, I saw no easy way to describe those events of 1944. Haller obviously couldn't be there. I might have someone *tell* him about it, or he might find an incriminating diary or letter, but these seemed very mechanical devices and likely to work only with a good deal of creaking. Third-person narration, however, would allow me to set my two story lines down independently. I could simply start with the enigmatic scenes of 1944— write what amounted to fifty pages of historical fiction, something I had never done before—and then let those scenes collide in the reader's imagination with contemporary events in Boston. The past was a bullet aimed at the present. Past and present would intersect explosively. Individual lives would gain scale and depth because their courses had been set long ago, fatally, by the great war. History was destiny.

To my surprise, third-person narration had not only solved my technical problem, it had also revealed my basic theme.

42

PLOT AND CHARACTER IN SUSPENSE FICTION

BY JOAN AIKEN

WHICH CAME FIRST, the chicken or the egg? Does plot arise from character, or character from plot? The question is in many ways an artificial one; most writers have felt, at one time or another, the heady excitement of knowing that a whole story, or at least its basic elements—plot, character, and development all tangled together—is struggling to emerge from the dark.

But if this does not happen?

"What is character," says Henry James in *The Art of Fiction* (1884), "but the determination of incident? What is incident but the illustration of character?" And the Old Master goes on to add (several pages later), "The story and the novel, the idea and the form, are the needle and the thread, and I never heard of a guild of tailors who recommended the use of the thread without the needle, or the needle without the thread."

Perfectly true, and you have to have both before you can begin. But, suppose you have only half of the combination?

Characters are generally the problem. *Plots* come a dime a dozen, they are easy to pick up. We read them every day in the papers. A mother, even after several years, remains positive that the death of her teenage son, classified as suicide, was not so; but whenever she pushes her inquiries about it, other unexplained deaths take place. The pet poodle of a notorious Chicago mobster is stolen. The CIA sets up a spurious marine engineering firm in an effort to salvage a sunken Soviet submarine. A middle-aged woman demands a daily love poem from her browbeaten husband. A descendant of one of the twenty-one victims of the Boston Molasses Disaster is still seeking compensation. A convention of magicians plans to meet in an Indian town, but the citizens raise strong objections. . . .

Any of these incidents, all culled from the daily press, might trigger a story, might produce that wonderful effervescent sensation, familiar to every writer (it really is like the working of yeast in one's mind), when different elements begin to ferment together and create something new. The best plots, of course, instantly create their own characters. That wife, that domineering wife, compelling her husband to produce a new love lyric every evening: we know at once what she would be like. And the cowardly put-upon husband, submitting to this tyranny, trudging off to the library for new rhymes and new verse forms, until the climactic moment when he rebels, and supplies you with the start of your story. Or the grieving, brooding mother, worrying on and on about her son's death, gradually acquiring little bits of information. It would be very easy to tell her story.

But if you have the plot without the characters?

There's nothing so frustrating for the reader as a potentially interesting, intricate story, full of turns and twists, in which the characters are so flat, machine-made, and lifeless that they form a total barrier to following the course of the narrative, because it is impossible to remember who is who. Is Miranda the actress or the secretary? Was it Wilmost whose car was stolen, or Harris? Is Casavecchia the gangster or the millionaire? Why *does* Kate hate Henry?

In murder mysteries and procedural detective novels, character portrayal is not so important. The reader won't expect great depth among the victims and suspects, while the detective probably has a number of well-established peculiarities, built up over a series of books: he is Spanish, wears elegant grey silk suits, and carries his exclamation point upside down; or he is very fat and drinks a pint of beer on every page; or he is a rabbi; or she is female, karate-trained, and has a huge wardrobe, which is just as well, since the vicissitudes of her job frequently reduce her clothes to tatters. We know all these and love them as old friends.

The problem of character arises most particularly—and can be a real handicap—in suspense novels.

Suspense novels are deservedly popular, but very hard to define. They are not murder mysteries. They are not just straight novels, because something nasty and frightening is bound to happen. That is the promise to the reader. They are not spy stories, and they are certainly not procedurals. One of the very best suspense novels ever written, *A Dram of Poison,* by Charlotte Armstrong, had no murder in it at all, not even any death (except a natural one in the first chapter, setting off the whole course of events), but it possesses more riveting tension than any other story I can recall.

In a suspense novel, the element of character matters very much indeed. The hero/heroine is pitted, not against organized crime or international terrorism, but against a personal enemy, a personal problem; the conflict is on an individual, adversarial level. And so, if either hero or hero's enemy is not a flesh-and-blood, fully rounded, recognizable entity, the tension slackens, the credulity drops.

In *A Dram of Poison,* all the mischief is caused in the first place by the arrival of the hero's sister, one of those terrible, self-satisfied, know-it-all characters (plainly Charlotte Armstrong wrote the story in the white heat of having recently encountered one of them) who can always interpret other people's motives and give them some disagreeable psychological twist. By her confident assertions, she soon has the heroine paralyzed with self-distrust and the hero downright suicidal. Then, in between the breathless excitement of trying to find what he did with that wretched little bottle of poison he had meant to swallow, the reader has the fearful pleasure of knowing that, in the end, odious Sister Ethel is bound to receive her comeuppance.

Charlotte Armstrong was particularly skilled at villains; the frightful parasitical pair of sisters who, in *Mask of Evil,* (originally published as *The Albatross*) come and prey on the two central characters are particularly memorable, with their sweet saintly selfishness. The sense of being *invaded,* taken over, in their own home, by repulsive aliens, was particularly well conveyed in that story.

The suspense novel is often a closed-world plot. The hero/heroine must battle it out against the adversary in a situation that, for some reason, allows for no appeal to outside help. There must be valid reasons for this. If not a snowstorm, with all phone lines down, then the villain has bruited it around that the hero is hysterical, unbalanced, alcoholic, a drug abuser, or just traumatized by recent grief so no call for help will be heeded or believed.

Ursula Curtiss had a particular gift for these enclosed-world situations, and she had a masterly touch with villains as well. It is an interesting exercise to compare some of her stories with others, for she was a very fertile creator of creepy domestic-suspense plots. Many of her ideas were brilliant, but some of them succeeded far better than others. Why? Because of the characters with which they were animated. *Voice Out of Darkness*, which has a fine snowy Connecticut setting and an excellent basic idea—harking back to the long-ago question of whether the heroine did or did not push her very unpleasant adoptive sister under the ice when they were both eleven—yet somehow fails to come off because it is peopled with rather stock characters: two handsome young men, two pretty girls, and some recognizable small-town citizens, the drunk writer, the gossipy lady. Her novel, *The Stairway*, however, is pure gold from the first page to the last. Why? Because of its villainness, the repulsive Cora. Judged dispassionately, the plot is simple and only just credible. Madeline, the heroine, is married to Stephen, an intolerable man whom she is about to divorce, a monster of tyranny who terrifies her small son. But Stephen falls downstairs and breaks his neck. Cora, the humble cousin, the poor relation, by pretending to believe that Madeline pushed him, gradually assumes more and more dominance over the household and seems all set to stay for the rest of her life. Madeline, in a bind because *she* believes that *Cora* pushed Stephen, feels that she can't betray her and is helpless. All this, given a moment's cool thought, seems hard to swallow. Why had Madeline married the horrendous Stephen in the first place? Why should she submit to Cora for a single moment? But Cora is made so *real*, with her greediness, her anxious, reproachful air, her dreadful clothes, her fondness for eating candy out of a paper bag and rustling the sheets of the newspaper, that all she does and says is instantly, completely credible.

Playwright Edward Albee once observed that the test he had for the solidity of his characters was to imagine them in some situation other than the play he had in mind and see if they would continue to behave in a real manner. The character of Cora would be credible and recognizable whether we saw her in a hospital ward, a supermarket, or a graveyard.

The Stairway was an early Curtiss novel, but one of her later ones, *The Poisoned Orchard*, contains the same terrifying claustrophobic, inturned quality, again because of its hateful and convincing villainness, the heroine's cousin Fen, and her accomplice, the cleaning lady, Mrs. List. This sinister pair have Sarah the heroine hog-tied, especially clowning, ugly, self-assured Fen, who continually manages to force her much nicer, much better-looking cousin into the unenviable role of straight man refusing to laugh at Fen's jokes. The relationship between the two is beautifully and most credibly realized, so that the reader is prepared to swallow the fact that Fen and her evil ally seem to be omniscient and omnipresent, able to anticipate Sarah's efforts to combat their plots almost before she can make a move. And what is it all about? We hardly know. A wicked deed, way back in Fen's past, that is catching up with her. And anyway, what can they *do* to Sarah? It hardly matters. The point is that they are menacing, and that she is more and more at their mercy. Fen is a wholly convincing monster, the more so because she is quick-witted and amusing, as well as being unprincipled. *Fear* is the essential ingredient of a suspense novel, and fear can be achieved only if the reader thoroughly sympathizes with the main character and thoroughly believes in the villain.

If the villain is less convincing, then the main character must be made more so.

Dick Francis, the English writer of deservedly best-selling mysteries with horse-racing backgrounds, wrote an interesting early novel, *Nerve*, in which all the jockeys on the turf were being persecuted by a well-known TV personality who secretly spread malicious gossip about them, prevented their getting to races on time, and had their horses doped. Why does he do this? Because he, son of a famous racehorse owner, is terrified of horses, and therefore psychotically jealous of all who succeed in the horsey world.

What a preposterous theme it sounds, set down in cold blood. And the villainous TV star, Maurice Kemp-Lore, somewhat sketchily depicted, only just makes his murderous obsession credible to the reader. What does give the book immediate life, great energy and plausibility, so that it moves at a rattling pace and carries the reader along, completely hooked by the story, is the treatment of the hero. As always in Dick Francis novels, the hero tells the story in the first person; in common with other Francis heroes he is an odd man out, who has fallen into the racing world by a series of accidents. Descended from a family of professional musicians, he is the only non-musical one; despised by his kin, he has had to justify himself in some other direction. The contrast between the hero's elegant relations conducting Beethoven at the London Festival Hall, while he gallops through the mud at Ascot, is bizarre enough to be convincing, so that we are passionately on the hero's side as he struggles to combat what he begins to recognize as a sinister plot against his whole *raison d'être*. The villain remains shadowy, but the hero, in this case, carries enough weight to sustain the story.

Given a satisfactory plot, it should not be too hard to equip it with characters. But what if the boot is on the other foot?

Some writers are compulsive character collectors. Wherever they go, they watch, listen, record, jot down notes and descriptions: the fat woman in the black-striped dress at the rail station with two elegant little pig-tailed girls, also in black-and white striped outfits, hanging on her arms. The lanky, unshaven six-foot male in the subway, with a shock of red hair and gold rings in his ears. The professional portrait painter, met at a party, who has produced a portrait every two months for the last twenty years, and has a photographic eye for a face. The woman who, though courteous and well-mannered, is an obsessive corrector, so that she can never hear a sentence spoken without chipping in to put the speaker right—politely, but *oh, so* firmly. . .

Character collecting is an excellent habit, because sooner or later some of these characters will start to move.

You have a whole cast of characters, but no plot. So: Make extensive notes about them—their preferences, dislikes, habits, childhood history. Like Edward Albee, set them in different environments, confront them with crises. What would the woman in the black-striped dress do if she were in charge of forty school children on a sinking cruise liner? Make them encounter each other. Suppose the portrait painter were sitting in a subway train, drawing lightning sketches, and the man with red hair and gold earrings, unaccountably angry at being drawn, grabs the sketchbook and gets out at the next stop? A character may suddenly get up and walk away, pulling a skein of plot behind him. Suppose they then meet by chance, somewhere else?

Imagine Jane Austen saying to herself, "Now, let's tell a story about a sensible practical sister and a self-indulgent, overemotional sister. What sort of men shall they fall in love with?"

Suppose in writing *Sense and Sensibility,* she turned her story the other way round. Suppose sensible Elinor had fallen in love with handsome, romantic Willoughby, and susceptible Marianne had been bowled over by reliable, prosaic Edward? But, no, it won't work. Marianne could never have fallen for Edward, not in a thousand years. Jane Austen, even at a young age (she was twenty-two), had her characters and plot inextricably twined together, one growing out of the other; there is no separating them. But it is fun to probe and investigate and reconsider; fun, after all, is what writing is all about. Jane Austen took huge pleasure in writing *Sense and Sensibility.* The fact is evident; she knew these characters entirely before she put pen to paper.

What is the best way of displaying your characters?

There are, of course, hundreds, but the worst way is to describe them flatly.

My recent novel, *Blackground,* has the theme of two characters who marry in romantic haste, and then, on a winter honeymoon in Venice where they are, as it were, suspended together in a vacuum, they discover that they had in fact met long ago and aren't at all the people each thinks the other to be. To make this as much of a shock as I intended, both of them and, hopefully, for the reader, I had to be familiar with their life stories right back to childhood. In order not to a) begin too early or b) bore the reader with too much flashback, I make Character A tell his story to Character B on the honeymoon, while hers is disclosed to the reader in snatches throughout the narrative.

Michael Gilbert, a writer of several different kinds of mysteries, whose characters are always remarkably individual and three-dimensional, adopts a very swift and vivid method of displaying his quite large cast of characters in his suspense novel *The Night of the Twelfth* (about sadistic murders in a boys' school). Sometimes a whole chapter is divided into blocks of conversation, often only about half a page— between A and B, between B and C, between C and A, between A and D—these fast-moving dialogues equally convey character and advance the action.

Sometimes you know your character *too* well; you could write volumes about his quirks and complications. But how do you get all this across to the reader without being pompous, or overexplicit?

How about portraying this person as seen through the eyes of another narrator, quite a simple soul (like Nelly Dean, the housekeeper in *Wuthering Heights,* who tells much of the story), or even a child? *What Maisie Knew,* by Henry James, can be an example to us all.

"Try to be one of those people on whom nothing is lost," said Henry James.

Perfect advice for a writer!

209

43

SERIAL RITES

BY REGINALD HILL

AS A LARGE PART of whatever reputation I enjoy rests on my Mid-Yorkshire police novels, I thought it might be interesting to set down my ideas on series writing. It seems to me that the trio to get right are *setting, character,* and *chronology,* and like a good classicist, I'll start in the middle.

I'm very much against test tube characters; let them come naturally or not at all. This may seem like retrospective wisdom when I admit that I never set out to create a series. Having written my first Pascoe and Dalziel novel, I felt like writing a sequel, and it was only then that I realized that Dalziel and Pascoe were likely to be with me forever. Now I wondered if I wouldn't have done better to start them off with even more distinctive features. Perhaps Dalziel could have worn an eyepatch and carried a pet vulture on his shoulder. Perhaps Pascoe could have been an expert on Old Norse sagas and developed a terrible stutter at the sight of blood. But the multiplication of absurdities proves nothing except how much easier it is to make a character distinctive than to give him life.

Not that life itself is a guarantee of success. We all meet plenty of people who are fine as fellow dinner guests or even shipmates on a holiday cruise but we don't particularly want to meet again. The reasoning may be different in books (I can't imagine anyone wanting to dine with a real-life Dalziel *twice*), but the principle is constant. If, unlike me, you are planning ahead from the start, ask yourself: Why on earth should anyone want to meet these characters again?

The answer should be simple but twofold: because of what they are; because of what may become of them.

Different writers emphasize different parts of this answer. Take Ian Fleming. Though a truly serial element did develop in the later Bond books, on the whole we can read them (or avoid them) in any order

because of what Bond is—a steel-nerved, sexually promiscuous, cold-blooded killer. Only a very naïve reader would believe that Bond was drawn from life. He is not "real" in that sense, but what he does have in abundance is that other quality of life that we mean when we say someone is "full of it." He is alive; he may be two-dimensional, but both dimensions crackle with energy. Sherlock Holmes is like that, and Sam Spade; Tarzan and Allan Quartermain. Other equally famous series characters seem to me to fail in both respects, but clearly that doesn't matter as long as they work for enough other readers. You won't find many minority taste series in the publishers' lists!

The rounder and more detailed your characters are, the more your readers are likely to be concerned with what is going to happen to them beyond the confines of the present story. Real life isn't neatly episodic with each adventure a self-standing unit. Once a character has that third dimension of actuality, you will find you have to put him in a context that is equally three-dimensional, which means that the whole sweep of your series has to exist, develop, and be logical within the fourth dimension of time.

Chronology

Chronology is the great enemy of the series writer. The author foolish enough to locate his characters too precisely in time by using public or even private events may soon find himself in trouble as he develops the series. Every time I start a new Dalziel/Pascoe novel, I find myself kneading away at time like a piece of dough, here compressing it into a lump, there rolling it out into a wafer, here corrugating it, there teasing it into tiny threads, and all the while feeling increasingly tempted to say, to hell! and stick it in the oven. After all, if the filling's good, who cares about the shape?

Well, I do, of course. And so, I hope, will you. Art is the perfection of nature, and though time to the series writer is the most intractable natural element of all, the writer must never give up the effort to get it right in both big and little things. The more contemporaneous and the more complex the work, the greater the problem. Study any of the great novel series—Trollope's Barsetshire Chronicles, for instance—and it is easy to find a variety of inconsistencies. No doubt Trollope would look you straight in the eye and say firmly: "Sometimes accuracy of detail must be sacrificed to integrity of plot." Or perhaps, because Trollope never put on airs about his art, he might have admitted rather sheep-ishly, "Sorry. I simply forgot!"

For it is easy to forget. From the start it is wise to keep careful record of such things as personal descriptions, likes, dislikes, family back-grounds and birthdays, domestic circumstances, house decoration, type of toothpaste, make of car—in fact, *everything.* This will save many frustrating hours thumbing through your own works to check your own facts. I speak again from experience.

Setting

The main rule about choice of setting is that you have to feel at home in it. The SF writer may create a futuristic world, and the historical writer may recreate a past one, but the degree to which these worlds persuade will be the degree to which their authors are at home in them. I've never seen any merit in not stating the obvious when silence may sound like scorn, so let me say at once that the place where most of us feel most at home is at home. I wrote my first Dalziel novel twenty years ago just after I'd moved into Yorkshire; that's where I set it, because that's where I was. As my knowledge of the county has developed over twenty years of experience and exploration, I feel that the settings of my books have become more and more important. In writing, famil-iarity often breeds freshness. And even if your reader should happen to know the area as well as you do, remember that the pleasure of novelty is often surpassed by the delight of recognition.

Just how particular you decide to be depends on where you are. If you live in a small town of a couple of thousand souls, it might be advisable to change its name to protect the guilty—and to protect yourself from lawsuits! A big city gives more scope, especially if it's big enough to have international resonances. Otherwise, anonymity or pseudonymity may still make sense. The city that houses Mid-York-shire's finest has no name. It is an amalgam of various Yorkshire towns. I saw no reason why I should not perfect, if not nature, at least urban geography, and pick the layout, architecture, industry, and social mix that suited me best. Mid-Yorkshire itself, a nonexistent area in local administration terms, partakes of various elements of North, South, and West Yorkshire, which do exist. Thus I hope I have combined authen-ticity with flexibility and also avoided the wrath and reprisals of CID chiefs fearful of being taken for Andy Dalziel's original.

212

So to all aspiring series writers the sum of my advice is, pay attention to detail and take more forethought than I did, but don't plan out of sight. You, too, have to be surprised, for large among the many pleasures of series writing is the delight of returning to your characters and finding out what they've been up to since last you visited them. If that delight ever fades, then push them over the Reichenbach Falls as soon as you can!

44

HISTORICAL DETECTION, UNLIMITED

BY ALLISON THOMPSON

YOU WAKE UP ONE MORNING with a terrific idea for an historical novel. Your heroine will be called Jennifer (Stormy? Shana?), and she will always wear her waist-length red hair loose and flowing. Your hero—Blaze? Colt? Randy?— will defy the conventions of the time and . . .

But what were the conventions of the time they lived in? And are those names really appropriate for the period? Are you in command of your facts, or will your intelligent reader groan at the historical anachronisms you use? It's time you engage in some historical detective work to keep your novel from being illogical, inconsistent, and contrary to the easily obtained historical facts.

Engaging in historical detection has two important benefits. First, increased accuracy will save you from receiving *un*-fan mail, letters that begin: "Dear Sir or Madam, It has obviously escaped your attention that . . ." Second, your work will take on a new richness. Readers won't simply skim your prose to discover exactly when the hero and heroine fall into bed together; instead, they will be transported to a different era. They'll gag when the maggots writhe in the bread that the sailors must choke down in the ship's dark hold; they'll gasp when the heroine feels faint from the tight lacing of the corset stays that squeeze her waist into a fourteen-inch circle; they'll marvel at the gaslights that so miraculously illumine the London streets already disappearing under the first smog of the early days of the Industrial Revolution. Your characters will live with all the passions and prejudices of the period. You will produce a greater richness of plot twists and developments.

So how do you begin? How and where do you start your research, and how do you organize all that information?

Begin your research with some general sources, such as the encyclopedia or one of the many well-written, illustrated books that encapsulate the social history of a given period. Skim these to set the basic facts of the period in your mind. Also helpful are the "timeline" books available in most libraries that list concurrent events in politics, science, art, music, literature, and world affairs. These sources give you a sense of continuity and can also be a useful source of plot developments.

Once you've done your basic research on the period, try to avoid "secondary" sources, as they tend to be too general for the historical detective; instead, look for works that focus on a particular aspect of the period in which you are interested, such as Dorothy Hartley's study of rural life in fifteenth-century England, *Lost Country Life*. Best of all, listen to the people of the time themselves, as they speak through their letters, diaries, and journals. Reading through this material will improve your feel for the language and sentiments of the time. They may also give you useful plot developments, character motivation, and background lore on household expenses, servant problems, and social or political gossip of the day.

Period paintings, fashion plates, illustrations, photographs, and maps

Visual aids are invaluable to the historical detective. Use as many of them as you can. You might, for instance, examine any of the typical family portraits of a wealthy English family of the 1760s: the father, the mother, and two or three children. What are the people doing? Is their pose formal? Imperious? What do their gestures and facial expressions tell you? Do they carry implements such as a sketch pad, a bow and arrows, or a riding crop to indicate that they engage in certain activities? What is the background like? A great house? A gloomy mountain? A rich interior? Do you think you would like these people? Could you see your characters in this setting?

What conventions of physical beauty do the people exhibit? In the highly romantic 1830s, both men and women are portrayed with small heads, huge eyes, and tiny hands and feet, all characteristics thought at the time to exhibit refinement and gentility. By contrast, the "Gibson Girls" of the 1890s are tall, robust and almost Amazonian. Think about how the conventions of beauty affect character and action and vice versa: The droopy, romantic female of the idealistic 1830s would be ill at ease in the ebullient, athletic 1890s.

Don't forget to look for such items as political cartoons; fashion plates; amateur sketches of people, or watercolors of the interiors of houses; period illustrations in books or popular magazine articles; photographs and *cartes des visites*; craftsmen's drawings of furniture, guns or inventions; architects' renditions of houses and public buildings; and merchants' catalogues like those produced by Sears and Roebuck or Montgomery Ward.

Finally, don't forget resources such as atlases and maps, dictionaries (to verify usages of slang terms), and reference works such as *Bartlett's Quotations.*

What did they read?

Immerse yourself in the literature of the period for an appreciation of the social customs of the time and an instinctive ear for the use of the language. Take, for example, Samuel Richardson's *Pamela,* written in the restrained, rational language of 1740. In it, the servant girl heroine, who is so hotly pursued for immoral purposes by her wicked employer, expresses herself in a very different fashion from the impassioned, romantic hero Heathcliffe in Emily Brontë's *Wuthering Heights* (1847). While you might not choose to write in either style, your knowledge of the real sensibilities, speaking styles, and attitudes of the period will add flavor to your work.

For those researching the nineteenth century, periodicals such as *Harper's Magazine* or *Godeys Ladies' Book* are invaluable sources. Read them carefully for the tone of the period, the advertisements and the prices for unusual products, recipes, advice for the care of the ill; views on how to educate children, and the editor's opinions on deportment, education for women, and various political topics.

Read fiction of the periods before and after as well as during the specific period you are researching. Fashions and custom changed more slowly in the past than they do now. Read critically, asking yourself what social conventions a particular book or character exhibits. What does it say about the culture of the time? What are the standards of good and bad conduct? Would your hero or villain speak that way?

Art and music

Get records or tapes from the library and listen to some music of the period. Is it the rational, intellectual, and restrained music of J.S. Bach (1685–1750)? The passionate and romantic preludes of Chopin (1809–1849)? A lively galliard of the 16th and 17th century, or a perky polka of the late Victorian period? The skirl of the bagpipe or the scrape of the fiddle? What kind of music would your characters listen to? Some writers even like to have the music of the period playing while they write.

Look at paintings and sculpture of your period. The orderly interiors of the Dutch Renaissance painters represent a culture and perception of man and nature that is entirely different from the paintings of the French Impressionists.

Read etiquette books, cookery books

Etiquette manuals, beginning with Castiglione's *The Book of the Courtier* (1528) and moving through the precepts of Lord Chesterfield (1774), give an invaluable glimpse not only of what was considered proper behavior, but of the more common *improper* behavior the reader is exhorted to shun. You can learn from them what separated a gentleman from a commoner, and how a wise mistress managed servants, taught her children, and maintained the affections of her husband. Historical detectives of the nineteenth century will in particular want to read Isabella Beeton's book on cookery and domestic economy, published in 1861, and Catherine Beecher's *Treatise On The Domestic Economy* of 1846.

Historical Societies, Lecture Series, and Specialty Publications

Many cities and states have historical societies that can provide the historical detective with unusual local source materials. In addition to their research function, these organizations often sponsor special historical exhibits and lecture series. Your local art museum or gallery may also run lecture series to accompany traveling exhibits of historical works. Take advantage of these resources.

Visit antiquarian or used-book stores. In addition to old fiction, biographies, and histories, many also carry sheet music, cookbooks, children's books, and home furnishing books. You will also want to get on the mailing lists of specialty book dealers, such as those dealing in the Civil War or in Celtic lore.

Several publishing houses (in particular Dover Publications, 31 East 2nd Street, Mineola NY 11501) specialize in reprints of old books. Dover's list is particularly rich in nineteenth-century works, and carries books on architecture, plumbing, agricultural implements, and methods of transportation, as well as collections of photographs from the nineteenth century.

Make your research specific. Ask yourself difficult but important questions. Exactly how much can fit into a Conestoga wagon, and what beloved belongings will the heroine have to abandon? How long does it take to reload a muzzle-loader, and how many different steps does it entail? If the hero clasps his corseted mistress to him, will she really feel soft and yielding in his arms? Enlist your local librarian for help in finding answers to questions like these.

What about character and motivation? Could your gently born Regency heroine *really* deny her twenty-one years of strict upbringing to dress up as a highwayman, ride astride, and brandish a pistol?

The process

Taking a little extra time to conduct your research thoroughly will pay off, particularly if you plan to write more than one book set in the same period.

Start a bibliography file. On a separate index card for each book or source examined, write down the author, title, publisher, publication date, and your library's call number. If you use more than one library, note its name as well. You might also include the date you read the source, and what pages were particularly helpful.

Make your research notes on large file cards with only one topic point or quotation or fact per card. You can color-coordinate if you like (pink = fashion; green = political history; blue = domestic tips). Later, you'll be able to shuffle the cards around as you write. Note the source of the information by an abbreviated title or a code (also noted on the bibliography card) and include the pages cited. Careful organization and attention to detail at this stage will pay off as you begin to write.

Photocopy everything! It's more practical than having to go back to look at that crucial fashion plate or political cartoon. Remember to write a complete bibliographic citation on each photocopy that you make.

When you finally begin to write, keep in mind that you're not producing a scholarly thesis. The richness of the information that colors but does not dominate your work will make your writing live and will keep your readers coming back for more.

45

How to Write the Supernatural Novel of Suspense

By Barbara Michaels

SEVERAL YEARS AGO, I was invited to be guest of honor at a science fiction-fantasy convention. I accepted with pleasure, since I love being a guest of honor, but I was a trifle puzzled as to why I should have been selected. When I got around to asking, my genial hosts informed me that some of my novels are considered to be "occult" or "supernatural"—hence, legitimately, a form of fantasy.

I had never thought about it in those terms, since all my books can and should be classified as novels of suspense—specifically, romantic suspense. However, a good many of them do fall into a sub-sub-category of that genre, one which we might, somewhat laboriously, call supernatural romantic suspense.

To some degree this is a matter of the eerie atmosphere that prevails even in books where a rational explanation of seemingly uncanny events is provided. But the creation of such an atmosphere is a subject in itself, and one I won't go into at the present time. A true supernatural novel is not defined in terms of atmosphere alone; in such a book the suspense results from the activities, not of human villians, but of ghostly or non-material entities. In *Ammie Come Home,* the danger—a very real, life-threatening danger—comes from a malevolent spirit. In *Wait for What Will Come,* the heroine's life and sanity are endangered by a spiritual force as ancient as it is perilous.

The supernatural novels I most enjoy writing, because they present such a challenge of plot construction, offer the reader a choice of explanations. In *Be Buried in the Rain,* how did those pathetic skeletons get out of their graves? The county sheriff is satisfied with his solution of the case, which is, of course, pragmatic and nonsupernatural. But in the mind of the heroine and, one hopes, the reader, a doubt lingers. I used the same device in *Witch,* by exposing a human villain as the main source of the heroine's difficulties; yet one or two small details remain inexplicable in rational terms.

A common error committed by writers of supernatural fiction is to assume that the rules governing thrillers of other types don't apply to these. After all, they are not describing the real world; ghosts, vampires, and black magicians don't exist. Since these figures of fantasy are not limited by normal, human behavior patterns, they can be made to do anything the writer wants them to do. Right?

Wrong, wrong, wrong! Every novel of suspense must make the reader believe, if only temporarily, in the world the writer has created—a world that is, by definition, fictitious. The operative word here is verisimilitude—the appearance of truth—and Pooh Bah's statement in *The Mikado* puts the matter neatly: "Corroborative detail, intended to give artistic verisimilitude to an otherwise bald and unconvincing narrative." Details, precise and accurate, flesh out the skeleton of the narrative and give it a convincing appearance of life. This procedure is even more important when you are writing about vampires than about Soviet agents or psychopathic killers; in fact, the basic rule of suspense fiction ought to be: The more fantastic your basic premise, the more meticulously accurate your background must be.

But how can you create an accurate background when you are writing about imaginary creatures like vampires? Fortunately for you, the writer, the supernatural world does exist, in tradition, legends, and folklore. The tradition is centuries old, and the rules are as strictly defined as those of the "real" world. Furthermore, they are familiar to most readers because of those long centuries of common belief. For example: Suppose one of your characters is a psychic investigator who attempts to defend himself against a vampire by firing a silver bullet at it. The poor chap would end up dead and bloodless, because as you and I and most of the human race know, vampires aren't particularly bothered by silver bullets. They work well with werewolves, but if your hero wants to put an end to a vampire, he'll have to drive a stake through its heart.

In my library there are two shelves of books dealing with folklore and the supernatural. Your first task as a writer of eerie tales is to familiarize yourself with this research material. If the exigencies of your plot require that you violate a long-accepted rule, you must do it with care and with a detailed explanation as to why the rule does not apply in that case. In *Ammie Come Home,* one of the crucial scenes described a confrontation between the evil spirit and a Catholic priest armed with the conventional weapons of the faith. In the traditions of the supernatural, holy water, crucifixes, and prayer are effective against the powers of evil. In this case they failed, and the unfortunate cleric fled the house, leaving the inhabitants worse off than before, because they had counted on his success. This failure increased the suspense, so it was an effective device; but it was incumbent on me as a writer to explain why the conventional methods did not succeed—just as it would have been necessary to explain why a gun fired at point-blank range failed to stop a homicidal maniac. (Bullet-proof vest? Poor aim? Something, at any rate.)

By making use of the traditional literature of the occult you have achieved the first goal of successful thriller writing—sticking to recorded, accepted facts in order to give verisimilitude to your fictitious world. The same body of tradition gives you another useful tool, for the more closely you follow the "facts," the more successful you will be in conjuring up the proper blood-curdling, spine-chilling atmosphere. Your predecessors, whether they be novelists or students of folklore, have done half the work for you. Bram Stoker did such an effective job with his famous vampire that you need only mention some of this character's attributes to raise the hackles of your readers.

Let's say your heroine is attending a cocktail party. People are talking, drinking, milling around. Glancing into a mirror, the heroine decides she must have had one too many; she sees herself reflected, but where is the reflection of the tall dark handsome man who is gazing into her eyes with such intense ardor?

If the girl has an ounce of sense, and any familiarity with occult literature, she will refuse further invitations from this gentleman. Of course if she does that, your plot comes to an abrupt halt, unless you can think of a sensible reason for her to overlook this damning clue. There are ways out of the dilemma; here are a few do's and don'ts.

Don't make the girl so stupid she fails to understand the clue. That was, for me, one of the major flaws in a very popular and successful supernatural novel of several years ago. The author planted his clues so successfully that everybody except the heroine knew she was intimately involved with a group of devil worshippers, and my sympathy for her extraordinary plight was considerably dampened by my exasperation at her unbelievable naïveté.

Don't explain that your heroine is so madly in love that she doesn't care whether her inamorata is planning to drink her blood. That's worse than stupid, that's demented.

One way out of the difficulty is the one I have suggested. She's had a few drinks, there are a lot of people moving around. She was mistaken. And perhaps she is also nearsighted, and too vain to wear her glasses to a party. (Why not contacts? Work it out; I can think of several explanations, and if you can't, you shouldn't be writing thrillers.)

A supernatural menace, as opposed to one that is a material and realistic one, relieves you of one of the most pervasive problems facing a writer of romantic suspense. Why, when the heroine realizes she is in danger, doesn't she go to the police? It would be exceedingly difficult to convince a police officer, or anyone else, that she is threatened by a vampire. She can't believe it herself.

But the reader must believe it, or at least be willing to concede that it is possible. You have already taken the first step in convincing said reader by sticking to the rules that govern the habits and behavior of vampires. One way to maintain the willing suspension of disbelief is to let the hero and heroine share the reader's skepticism. Strip away their rational defenses slowly, one by one, eliminating all possible alternatives. Let your protagonists produce the arguments a skeptic would marshal, and then destroy them. Or let one protagonist be a believer, the other a doubter; let them argue and debate and invent tests to check their hypothesis. Use the methods of scientific investigation insofar as that is possible, for that adds another strand of cold reason to the framework of common sense in which your supernatural menace functions most effectively.

Another trick I use to strengthen the appearance of reality is to describe the prosaic, familiar details of daily living. To quote one of the characters in *House of Many Shadows:* "The kids get measles, the puppy chews up the carpet, guests drop in, meals have to be prepared. . . ." Not only do such homely details give the reader an impression of normalcy with which he can readily identify, but they provide an effective contrast to the shocking and inherently unbelievable menace threatening the protagonists. My characters are always cooking and consuming food. Many of my readers appreciate this touch, because they themselves are apt to nibble when they are nervous—and having a vampire or an evil spirit on his trail would make anyone nervous. Furthermore, the commonplace reality of pizza baking or spaghetti sauce bubbling on the stove makes the accompanying discussion of black magic seem almost reasonable.

I have always found humor to be not only compatible with but an enhancement of suspense. Since I insist that supernatural fiction demands an even closer attention to the rules governing other forms of suspense writing. I use humor in my supernatural novels, but sparingly and with caution. It will not do to make fun of evil spirits; that makes them less threatening and less believable. But your characters can make fun of themselves, wryly and with a touch of black humor, for their reluctant belief in the unbelievable.

Humor serves another useful purpose in controlling a scene that might otherwise topple over into unvarnished melodrama. Werewolves and Satanists are stock characters in books that today's sophisticated readership tends to dismiss as corny and old-fashioned; one cannot use such characters without risking a smile of contempt from the reader unless one leavens the drama with something less clichéd. Make the reader smile, not at the hero but with him, as he comments sardonically on his situation. The hero of *Prince of Darkness,* forced to confront a mob of maniacal Satanists in order to save one of their victims, is injured and weaponless. "What are you going to do?" one of the characters asks him. His response is, "What the hell can I do? Dance, sing, do card tricks. Anything to attract their attention."

Another of my heroes, besieged in a cottage by one of the most preposterous figures of evil I have ever invented, finds himself distracted by a cat who has been trying to eat off his plate. (As usual, he and the heroine are eating.) He scoops the cat up. "The animal . . . hung complacently from his hands with a full moon smirk on its fat face. The contrast between its furry blandness and Michael's drawn features turned Linda's cry of alarm into a semi-hysterical gasp of laughter."

Cats figure prominently in my supernatural novels, not only because I am addicted to cats, but because they serve a number of useful purposes. I am particularly proud of the above-mentioned feline because, with an economy toward which I constantly strive but seldom attain, it serves not one but four distinct functions in its brief appearance. First, it provides the required touch of mild humor. Second, it is a symbol of cozy domesticity and a reminder of the real world. Third, like the canary in the coal mine, it serves to warn the humans of the approach of their enemy. (The sensitivity of animals to supernatural entities is well documented.) And, fourth, the way Michael handles the cat tells the heroine, and the reader, what sort of person he is.

In his classic essay, "Supernatural Horror in Literature," H. P. Lovecraft says, "The appeal of the spectrally macabre . . . demands from the reader a certain degree of imagination and a capacity of detachment from everyday life." Perhaps so; but it is up to the writer to lessen the effort of detachment by making his fictitious and fantastic world as close to everyday life as possible.

46

SOME PROBLEMS FOR THE HISTORICAL NOVELIST

BY LAURIE MCBAIN

THE KEY TO A SUCCESSFUL NOVEL is to capture and hold the interest of the reader till the last page, whether you want to write contemporary, historical, fantasy-adventure, or science fiction. Each of these types of novel presents its own special problems for a writer.

Since I write historical novels, I can discuss only the problems I have faced in setting my stories in the past rather than in the present.

How do you work historical facts into a novel so that the reader absorbs the history while primarily enjoying the story?

How do you know when to work historical facts into the story?

How do you get the reader to identify with and feel for a character living in another century?

How do you overcome these obstacles while keeping the action moving forward, the characters interesting, and the plot intriguing and credible?

Prologues, epilogues, and the beginnings of chapters offer the writer the best opportunity for descriptive narrative, including passages full of historical detail to help create the right atmosphere. But, all too often, just when you think you have to insert some details, you find yourself right in the middle of a chapter, in the heart of an exciting action sequence, or a vital exchange of dialogue. You can't stop the momentum to describe some event or object, even though it may affect your plot or add necessary historical color.

What you can do is let your characters do some of the work for you. To convince the reader that these people of your imagination might actually have lived, you must have them experience real-life experiences, react to and be affected by the conditions prevalent at the time the novel takes place. By doing so, you will make your readers feel they know and can understand them.

In one of my novels, I had an English country-woman tell how to make mead, but did not list the ingredients and measurements and give step-by-step directions. In her own words, Mrs. Taylor explains how she'll go about making mead:

"I'll mix honey and ginger and a couple of handfuls of elder flowers in this pot of water and let it boil for an hour. Then, after it's been skimmed, I'll pour it into a tub and let it cool off so I can add the yeast . . . best thing around on a warm afternoon when you're bone-weary and parched with thirst . . ."

Thus, the reader knows exactly what mead is and what a person living in 18th-century England might drink on a warm afternoon.

To reveal attributes of an Elizabethan gentlewoman as well as set up a scene of confrontation between two women in my novel *Wild Bells to the Wild Sky,* I had a meddlesome, snobbish woman declare grandly:

". . . a woman must be well accomplished in all of the skills and graces of being a lady and a gentleman's wife. . . . Her reputation must be beyond question, her deportment never faulted. She would, of course, be an accomplished needle-woman, well versed in the art of lace-making, silk-spinning, and fine embroidery. For entertaining, she would indeed have to be a competent singer and musician, well skilled with lute, and virginal. But, most important, she should have a working knowledge of the household, for she would be required to handle the affairs of the family and staff at all times. . . ."

The reader now understands some of the demands made on a woman of "good family" in 16th-century England. However, the information was conveyed to the reader in the form of dialogue filled with undercurrents directed at the heroine by her rival.

In *When The Splendor Falls,* a novel set during the American Civil War, I had a scene in which the heroine, Leigh Travers, is looking through a blanket chest. Touching various items belonging to family members—a pair of gauntlet gloves and slouch hat, a packet of letters, a sketch book—she remembers the long years of the war and its devastating effect on her family. Until this point in the novel, the reader has not known what fate has befallen members of the Travers family. All of these characters were introduced earlier in the novel when the family lived an idyllic life at Travers Hill, their Virginia farm. Leigh holds a fringed officer's sash and the reader now learns of her brother's death, and also about one of the many battles of the war—a skirmish in the Shenandoah Valley, during the Romney Campaign when the brother rode with Stonewall Jackson. Leigh glances at a letter, and the reader remembers the laughter-loving sister who wrote it and the halcyon days that are no more, and also learns about life in the Confederate capital of Richmond during the war.

In another scene in *When The Splendor Falls,* I had a group of Union raiders become trapped behind Confederate lines. It is winter, and they are holed up in the stables at Travers Hill. Cold, tired, and frightened, these Yankees face almost insurmountable odds as Rebel troops close in around them. How do you bring this scene to life so the reader will feel the tension of their predicament and care what happens to them?

As these men sit huddled together in the stables, I have them going through their haversacks and finding comfort in personal belongings. One soldier looks at a treasured daguerreotype of a loved one; another thumbs through his New England *Almanac,* wondering if he'll be home in time for the spring planting; a couple of others play poker with a set of Miss Liberty playing cards, while another soldier stares down at the theater tickets for a performance he'll never attend. Then I have the reader see these men through Leigh Travers' eyes. She has discovered them in the stables. Although embittered, she tends to their wounds. Listening to them talk and joke, seeing the pain and suffering on youthful faces, she is reminded of her own brothers, and she cannot betray them.

Not only has this provided historical color and atmosphere, but this approach has now fleshed out the characters and advanced the story. The reader will respond and identify with these fictional people, who have become more than cardboard cut-outs. Their triumphs and tragedies become the readers', who will laugh with them and cry with them, and wait anxiously to find out what will happen next in their lives.

In *Tears of Gold,* my novel about Gold Rush California, I wanted the reader to appreciate fully the dangers and difficulties encountered in reaching those golden shores. I had to show the three routes the adventurers, prospectors, and settlers chose to reach California. To work that information into the story without making it sound like a history textbook, I had each of the three main characters travel by a different one of the perilous routes. The heroine and her family sailed around Cape Horn by clipper; the hero crossed the Isthmus of Panama, traveling up the Chagres River through mosquito-infested jungle, before catching a coastal steamer to San Francisco; a third character came by wagon train across the plains, mountains, and deserts of the continental United States. Each route was described through the experiences of the characters. The reader shared these experiences and gained a keener insight into the lives of these people.

When is the proper time to insert historical detail? To guide you in deciding when you need historical description, ask yourself exactly *what* the reader needs to know. What is the focal point of the scene?

At the beginning of *Tears of Gold,* when my heroine, Mara O'Flynn, was traveling to California, I described the voyage around Cape Horn this way:

It had taken them two weeks to round the Horn, their sails furled as they struggled against the head winds and through the cross seas, the ocean surging into the ship as heavy swells broke over the bow . . .

Later in the story, however, when the heroine sails from San Francisco, en route to New Orleans, I did not need to describe the voyage back around Cape Horn in detail. This time I wrote, ". . . they sailed southward toward the tip of South America and the passage around Cape Horn that Mara dreaded even worse than the first time, for now she knew what she could expect. . . ." So does the reader.

At a point like this in your story, you might want to make use of a condensed description, or one more poetic than detailed. The reader already knows about close-reefed sails and the lee lurch of a ship in heavy seas. Once again, ask yourself, what is the focus of the scene? What is the importance of it? What purpose does it serve?

In *Wild Bells to the Wild Sky,* I described a sea voyage this way:

The *Madrigal's* sails had seemed to sing, catching the wind and billowing with a thundering song. The curving sheets of canvas had been burnished by the sun from dawn till dusk, while shimmering sea had stretched as far as the eye could see.

The focal point of this scene is not the voyage, but what will happen to the characters at the end of it. The scene serves merely to bring the characters safely back to England and to give the reader a feeling of the triumphant destiny that awaited some—and the deadly reckoning that awaited others.

Wild Bells to the Wild Sky begins when the heroine, Lily Christian, is only six years old. The ship she is sailing on is sunk during a battle at sea, and she is stranded, along with members of her family, on an uninhabited island in the Caribbean. The focal point of the story, however, is Lily's life a decade later, after she has been rescued and returned to England. And yet, the reader will want to know something about the heroine's life on the island. But does the reader need a day-to-day account of what took place in that ten-year period?

The reader learns about Lily's life on the island when I bring her back into the story at the age of thirteen. Sitting beneath a scrubby pine, Lily remembers:

> . . . Basil kept a careful record of the passing days. He always knew exactly how long they had been on the island. He had even set up a sun dial to tell them the time of the day. Although stranded in the wilderness, they could continue to live as civilized human beings, he declared, causing them to giggle because he was standing barefoot before them as he said it . . . Up at dawn, hunting and fishing for the day's food, lessons, then a few hours to do as one pleased, then sunset. . . .

So, through Lily's recollections, the reader learns the fate of the castaways and how they managed to survive. The reader's curiosity has been satisfied and the momentum of the story has not been slowed.

Why will readers care what happens in your novel? You have to establish a bond of understanding and sympathy between the reader and your characters. This bond of sharing is how the characters become real, and why the reader will care about those characters and what happens on the final page.

But how does a writer make them real? Your characters are reacting to a period in history. They are living it. By working the historical details into the very fabric of their lives, by having the characters aware of what is happening around them and influencing their lives, you are making them real. These characters respond to what concerns them, whether in Elizabethan England, Gold Rush California, or Civil War Virginia, in the same manner in which readers today react to what concerns them—emotionally.

The characters are also responding to each other. You have taken a period of history and filled it with people, most of them from your imagination. The hero and heroine don't exist alone; they respond and react to the other characters that you have created. That is why I try to fill my fictional worlds with an assortment of characters from every walk of life: the innocent bystander, the best friend, the serving maid,

229

the hot-headed young brother, the garrulous innkeeper, the inquisitive neighbor, and countless others. These secondary characters watch and listen and become involved in the exciting lives of the heroes and heroines. Readers, who can't always relate to the hero and the heroine, or understand what they are feeling or the emotions we as writers wish them to experience, do so through the eyes of these other characters. In this way, they can recall and relive similar incidents in their own lives.

Secondary characters also provide an excellent opportunity for integrating historical detail into the story in a credible manner. The unperturbable butler knows far more about the household affairs on an English estate than the grand duchess or fashionable lord he serves, and the reader, following in the butler's footsteps as he goes about his duties, will, too. An old soldier's reminiscences to a group of impressionable young military officers allows for a colorful and exciting firsthand account of a significant battle in which historical information is related to the reader.

The problems encountered in trying to bring another period of history to life are what I find intriguing and challenging in writing the historical novel, which, according to Webster's, is ". . . based on or suggested by people or events of the past. . . ." Those are the factors that should be influencing the characters, plot, and atmosphere of your novel. How successful you are in recreating history and in capturing the imagination of your readers—to the extent that they believe they are part of another century and share the experiences of the characters— will ultimately determine the credibility and readability of your novel.

47

Techniques That Terrify

By John Edward Ames

If it sends a cold shiver down one's spine," Edith Wharton said of the horror tale, "it has done its job and done it well." For centuries savvy horror writers have passed this visceral test by relying on proven techniques that elicit shuddering, bristling, and terror. But horror writers do not claim eminent domain over the realm of fear, an emotion integral to every genre. Some conventions of dark fantasy offer a rich mother lode of fear-inducing techniques valuable to *all* fiction writers.

Exploit the power of suggestion. Subtle doesn't always sell. Nonetheless, discerning writers often evoke the fear response through the power of suggestion rather than with graphic descriptions. Granted, modern authors have broken new ground in the art of vivid, cinematic imagery, and this modern, aggressive style has often enriched their genres. But reader interest can be blunted by any stylistic overkill. H. P. Lovecraft made his horrors convincing simply by pretending they were too horrible to describe. Used judiciously, such deliberate restraint by the writer can be more chilling than explicit realism.

Instead of docudrama-style description of a mad slasher at work, for example, skip the "slice-and-dice" approach by shifting reader attention away from the violent act itself; suggest the savagery indirectly through the spontaneous reaction of a character who happens upon the aftermath of the attack. Remember that shock is initially an intensely physical experience—"a flash of ice, a flash of fire, a bursting gush of blood," as Robert Louis Stevenson described it. Use vivid sensory images that let inner intensity suggest outer atrocities.

Another effective technique is to use a jarringly inappropriate response—hysterical laughter, say, at the moment of terror—to suggest fear or grief so powerful it challenges the character's sanity. Sixteen-year-old Johnny is being dismembered by a group of rabid playmates who are under the spell of an evil mojo fetish. His dying thought is not focused on the terror at what's happening to him or the diorama of his life passing before his eyes. Instead, he dies in mortal shame, wondering what his mother will say about his dirty underwear.

Forestall the moment of terrifying revelation. The subtle touch can also improve your plot when you use it to slow down narrative time and thus heighten suspense. "The most chilling moment of any horror film," notes director Roger Corman, "usually relates to a scene in which some character is seen in a long corridor, running away from or approaching some unspecified object of unparalleled horror. The moment *before* this revelation of the nature of that 'thing' holds the fear." Stephen King echoes this advice in *Danse Macabre,* noting that a closed door is a continuous source of fearful suspense only so long as it remains closed. Once it's opened, and the Unknown Thing—no matter how horrible—confronted, suspense is resolved.

One key to forestalling the critical moment of revelation is cinematic pacing: delaying or freezing narrative time by backpedaling point of view to another character. Unlike the flashback, which can clumsily *interrupt* narrative time, backpedaling is merely retelling the same scene or sequence of events from another character's point of view, thus attenuating or repeatedly "freeze-framing" narrative time.

John Fowles used this strategy effectively to structure his psycho-thriller *The Collector.* The first half is narrated by a deranged kidnapper; the second half covers the exact same sequence of events from his victim's point of view. Only then is the denouement finally reached. Not only does this twice-told technique extend suspense, it allows the reader to consider frightening new perspectives and possibilities missed the first time around.

Use ongoing hooks. Fear is "a feeling of anxiety and agitation caused by the presence or nearness of danger, evil, or pain." It is thus inextricably linked to the broader feeling of suspense, "a state of usually anxious uncertainty." And another way to heighten suspense, that important prerequisite of fear, is through timely placing of hooks.

Most aspiring writers dutifully provide opening or closing chapter hooks. But they should also pay attention to subtly telegraphed teasers throughout chapters and scenes—less dramatic ongoing hooks intended to answer that nagging question that plagues most professional writers during composition: *Why* should my readers want to keep

232

reading? One answer is to supply irrestible minihooks between the mega-grabbers. These minihooks should unobtrusively promise more to come just around the narrative corner.

One of my all-time favorites is not found in the horror genre but in Owen Wister's classic western *The Virginian:* "They strolled into the saloon of a friend, where, unfortunately, sat some foolish people." This understated teaser occurs in the middle of a long scene and hardly produces *frissons* down the spine. Contrast its reduced intensity to the taut opening sentence of Robert Bloch's "The Closer of the Way": "To this day I don't know how they got me to the asylum." Yet both hooks serve the same basic narrative function: They contribute to a sense of menace and promise more to come, compelling the reader forward to find out what that "more" is.

Appeal to universal fears. Clinical psychology is replete with verbal labels for almost any conceivable fear. If, for example, you're diagnosed as triskaidekaphobic, you're badly frightened by the number 13. Some people are deathly afraid of certain colors or days of the week or foods; others have sought help because they irrationally believe their knees will suddenly collapse. While such real but relatively rare phobias may be fascinating to ponder, they don't usually underpin the most gripping fiction. But successful writers understand that archetypal fears, because of their universality, help ensure more reader identification with the characters.

Exploit traditional fears rooted in the "blood consciousness" of most of us: fear of someone or something lurking under the bed, closed (or partially opened) doors, hallways or tunnels that lead to two or more unknown fates, cramped spaces, basements, attics, heights, crowds, darkness, disease, doomsday, death. Don't neglect what may be man's most potent and ancient bête noire: fear of ostracism from society, a "phobic pressure point" that Stephen King touches so well in best sellers such as *The Dead Zone* and *Firestarter,* featuring heroes too weirdly different to fit in.

Modern writers may substitute shopping malls and high-rise apartment buildings for moors and Gothic castles. But they are still most effective when they appeal to traditional, universal fears.

Tease your readers. Dyed-in-the-wool horror fans—whose loyalty accounts for the steady sales—present a challenging paradox for writers: Such readers expect certain conventions, yet they rightly scorn too much predictability. Thus writers, especially in the horror, mystery, and private-eye fields, have learned to "tease" their readers, to *disrupt* expectations without disappointing them. One venerable technique for accomplishing this delicate balancing act is the strategic combination of the "fake scare" and the "fake release."

The fake scare can be any scene in which a character is startled, surprised, or shocked through a mistaken interpretation of a harmless event. Your heroine, stalked at night by a psychotic killer, is frantically rummaging through her purse for her house key; suddenly she cries out in fright at an abrupt skittering noise on the sidewalk behind her. It turns out to be only a discarded Milky Way wrapper propelled by a vagrant breeze.

But such a fake scare is in fact only the writer's equivalent of the set-shot in volleyball: a nasty "spike" may soon follow. The subsequent emotional relief experienced by character *and* reader is sometimes also a "fake release" of dramatic tension: The writer chooses this moment or one soon after, when the readers' psychological guards are down, to let the killer fling the door open from inside and leap at the heroine, his Sheffield boning knife glinting cruelly in a stray shaft of moonlight.

Readers expect these little tricks, so writers have to tease them a bit: Sometimes the harmless scare really *is* harmless, throwing readers off and providing the character (but not the uneasy reader, who *loves* this stuff) a genuine release of tension. And sometimes the skittering noise is neither harmless nor just a setup for a later zinger—the Horrible Thing really *is* there when the heroine spins around. Good writers somehow stay one step ahead of their readers, coming up with new and effective twists on the combination of fake scare and fake release. The pros know it's *technique* that delivers the scares required for almost every story.

48

WRITING REALISTIC WESTERN FICTION

BY ELMER KELTON

IDEALLY, the only major difference between a Western and any other good, serious novel should be the subject matter, the setting. A good story is a good story, and a bad story a loser whether the setting is Paris or London, Cape Cod or Dodge City. The same general principles of characterization, plot and movement apply.

Being set in the West automatically bestows upon a story certain advantages and certain limitations. The main advantage is a loyal if sometimes-too-small readership receptive to the Western scene. The principal limitation is that it is unlikely to be taken seriously by most of the critical establishment, making it a stepchild in the literary family.

Because of this old prejudice—call it snobbery if you wish—much fine writing has been accorded the "averted gaze," ignored in favor of "relevant" material not half so well written.

The cliché view of the classic Western is a story built around a strong, unsmiling hero who stands seven feet tall and invincible against the worst of villainy, unselfishly sets all wrongs right, and then rides away into the sunset.

Certainly, such Westerns exist. They started in the days of Ned Buntline a century ago, and they continue to appear. There is an audience for the "utility Western," typical of the Saturday-matinee "B" Western film, in which the same frontier-town set and the same outdoor scenery are interchangeable, whether the story is set in Texas or Oregon.

But I am convinced there is a larger audience for a Western novel firmly and accurately grounded in history, the story growing out of conditions inherent in and peculiar to a specific time and place, its conflicts not falling neatly into black and white.

I made my first Western short story sale, to *Ranch Romances,* in 1947. Even so, after some fifty magazine stories and twenty-six published novels, I still consider myself a learner. I continually read and watch for a good story idea, for an interesting character I can interpolate into a novel.

Most of the rules that apply to other fiction apply to the Western. A writer who approaches the Western with a down-the-nose attitude is unlikely to get far in the field. Like any other form, the Western deserves the respect of its writer—respect for the rules of good storytelling and for the realities of history around which the story revolves.

Nothing turns me off faster than to get into a story and find anachronisms and inaccuracies about the time, the place and the people. Any serious writer of historical fiction studies the history that will be the foundation of his novel. The Western deserves no less. This study does not have to be drudgery. Doing the historical research is often the most pleasurable aspect of writing fiction. A writer who does not love history has no business writing about it.

A majority of my novels have been strongly grounded in history. Before I start to write, I study the setting of the story, the historical situations that will form the framework, and the people of the time and place, their problems, their beliefs. Old newspapers, diaries, and written reminiscences are invaluable.

Intricate plots have never been my long suit, though I admire writers who can bring them off. Rather, I rely upon characters and the historical situation to set the pattern. I like the story to grow out of the history to such an extent that the plot could not be transferred to some other time and place without radical surgery.

An example is an early novel of mine, *Massacre at Goliad,* still reprinted periodically in paperback. Two brothers emigrate to Texas from Tennessee some years before the Texas revolution against Mexico. They live through the situations and events that gradually build the atmosphere for revolution. In modern terms, one is a hawk, the other a dove. They become estranged because of their political differences. However, once the fighting begins, they are brought back together by their concern for one another.

My biggest historical novel has been *The Wolf and the Buffalo,* about the lives of a black cavalryman on the Texas plains in the 1870s and a Comanche warrior against whom he is pitted, the black man fighting the red man so the white man can have the land. This novel gave me an opportunity to dramatize the daily life of both the buffalo soldier and his enemy. Gideon Ledbetter, the former slave now in uniform, is on a gradual ascent, while Gray Horse, the Comanche, is witnessing the twilight of his people's way of life.

It struck me that the two characters had a great deal in common. It was a temptation to have them realize it and perhaps come together in some way, but in real life it did not happen. The fact that it should have but did not is one of the ironies of history. I *did* let one black trooper in the story see the parallel and try to act upon it, deserting the army and riding out into Indian country with the idea of proposing an alliance against the white man. What happens to him is what would have happened in real life, more likely than not. The first Indians he encounters shoot him out of the saddle. They see him as an enemy, simply a white man with a black face.

At the end of the story the two characters come together in the only way they would in real life: in combat to the death.

This brings me to what I consider the most important element in a Western, or in almost any other type of fiction: characters.

I wrote the final scene of *The Wolf and the Buffalo* with tears in my eyes. Working with those characters for two years, I had come to care about them as real people. I gloried in their triumphs and felt deeply their personal tragedies.

Well-developed characters have a way of taking charge of a story and leading the writer in directions not anticipated. Often they change details, and sometimes they cause major alterations to the intended plot line. Usually I let them go their own way, for my unconscious is quietly telling me this is the natural and spontaneous thing for them to do.

In a recent question-and-answer session, a reader said she did not understand why I should let characters take over. "They are your creation," she declared. "You can make them do what you want them to."

But to force them into my preconceived plan makes the story seem mechanical and contrived. When in doubt, I follow the character. He knows himself.

In *Stand Proud*, I started with a young Texan forced into frontier service for the Confederacy late in the Civil War, carried against his will into an ill-considered Indian fight (a real one, incidentally) that gave him a wound he would have the rest of his life. Wherever other men led him, he invariably suffered. As the years passed, he increasingly resisted

237

advice; he ignored any judgment not his own. His stubbornness caused him to make mistakes, a few with dreadful consequences. Not until almost too late in his life did he begin to acknowledge his dependence upon others.

Sound like a typical shoot-'em-up plot? I hope not.

These are not men seven feet tall and invincible. These are men five-feet-eight and nervous. They are vulnerable; they can lose, and the reader knows it.

What is more, their opponents, by and large, are not the dog-kicking villains of the old "B" Western. Often they can evoke a certain sympathy and understanding. Sometimes the reader is not sure how he wants the story to come out because he can feel empathy for both sides.

This brings up the question of conflict. The traditional image of the Western is a simple white-hat vs. black-hat yarn, a tall, strong, silent hero against a dyed-in-the-wool villain. It is an old war-horse plot, though one that a gifted writer can still make seem fresh and alive. I am not that gifted. When I have tried to use it, the old horse has shown all his ribs.

Somebody once suggested looking for plots at periods of traumatic change, when an old order is being pushed aside by something new. You can find these anywhere in history. We see them all around us today.

I like to use these periods of change as the basis for historical Westerns, for they set up a natural and understandable human conflict, often between honorable people, each side convinced that it stands for God and the right.

This type of conflict may be cataclysmic, like the clash of the Union and Confederate armies at Gettysburg. Or it may be small and intimate, like the conflict between a modern elderly couple who want to hang onto the family farm or ranch despite all of today's rural economic misery, and their grown children who want them to sell the homestead and retire to town.

At either extreme, the conflict is the same: change vs. resistance to change. It is the oldest plot in the world, and yet it is always fresh.

The conflict may be intensified when it is within the character himself as much as or more than between him and others.

There is a built-in hazard in doing a historical Western, or a historical novel of any kind: the possibility of losing the characters and the story amid all the spectacle. A few years ago we had a rash of 100th anniversary celebrations of towns and counties in Texas. Many paid tribute to their past by staging historical pageants, parading costumed people, wagons, coaches, horses, mules, even Longhorn cattle and buffalo past the audience. The spectacle was grand, but with rare exceptions it was only that: a spectacle. The audience came away with little feeling for what it would have meant to be one of the historic personages represented. We saw them only from afar.

History provides the stage. The writer must provide the characters and make them walk and talk and breathe, feel joy and anger, exhilaration and despair. If he does not, he has simply a historical pageant, not a story.

A lot of myth surrounds the West, but the truth is there for the writer who wants to seek it out. The Western story does not deserve to be locked into any set pattern, any formula. It can be as varied as the land from which it springs.

It must be, if it is to survive in its second hundred years.

49

PLOTTING ADVENTURE FICTION

BY JOHN KEEBLE

FIRST THE TRUTH—the demands of writing good adventure fiction are mainly the same as those for writing any kind of fiction. When one moves from one genre to another, though, certain elements seem to receive more emphasis. In the case of the adventure novel, the emphasis is upon a vigorously paced plot, and as a part of this, upon a test or series of tests that the protagonist must endure.

Adventure fiction is often set outdoors. Manifestations of the natural world—sandstorms, typhoons, precipitous mountain slopes, etc.—may cause some of the protagonist's hardship, but a warehouse, a city street, even an apartment, and certainly a war zone could serve equally well as the setting for an adventure tale. The important thing to remember here is that setting will become inextricably tied up with the story, that it will become an adversary, in a way, and that at some stage the writer will need to think of it as a part of plot.

There are three things—or principles, perhaps—that I've come to consider important about plot: plot is thought; it is rhythmical; and it will call the characters into action. Stated this way, the principles might seem a little abstract, but I'll take them up in order and try to explain what I mean by each.

I've listed first the notion that plot is thought because I don't think a book truly gets underway until the writer begins to think systematically about action. I will have begun to write the novel before reaching that point, working out of a rough sense of who a few of my main characters are, what the book is to be about, what problems I want to spend a long time exploring.

In the case of my novel, *Yellowfish,* a book about the transportation of illegal aliens to the United States via Canada, I began with an interest in national boundaries. Like most good subjects, this one probably found me, since I am Canadian by birth and continue to live near the

240

border. I was aware, of course, of several things about that border: that it was the longest ungarrisoned border in the world, that it was easy to cross—surreptitiously or otherwise—and that, like many borders, there was a certain arbitrariness to it. Vancouver and Seattle, for example, have more in common with each other than either has with Montreal or New York. It seemed to me that there was an intriguing historical irony here, one that placed nationality at odds with culture, and that this had resonances that went beyond the immediate subject. That is how I always start, with some such inviting rumination, and with a sense of character.

But of course once the writing begins, one must move on to concrete detail. Before I can get very far with that, I have to formulate at least one good question. With *Yellowfish,* it came to be this: So you're going to use the border. In fiction what does one do with a border? The answer to that was easy: Bring something across it. The next question was, what? This took some hard thought because the decision would affect my book in all of its detail. I discarded various types of contraband until I finally hit upon an idea that clicked—people, illegal aliens—far more interesting than a load of drugs or military hardware, and a great deal more likely to enrich the book.

I decided that the people would come from Hong Kong, which I knew in fact to be a source of illegal immigration, and which—happily— extended my initial preoccupation with national boundaries still farther. I decided that my protagonist, who was the "escort," would pick the people up in Vancouver. From there I was able to take the first really important step toward constructing the novel: to imagine an ending, a target toward which the book would be aimed.

My protagonist would have to deliver his passengers to San Francisco. There were details attached to this, of course, certain vivid images I held in my mind as I worked, and which changed form several times. There came to be many more twists on the initial situation than I had first thought possible, especially as the adversaries—those who did not wish my characters to reach San Francisco—began to emerge. Even the ending I'd imagined turned out instead to be the penultimate scene. The point, however, is that once I had set up a target for ending the book, I could structure the book by imagining a series of events that would lead to that end. I could attend to the causality and order that is required by any plot.

This involved thinking, which may sound patently obvious. I feel, though, that writers, including me, sometimes neglect the need to think systematically (or strategically) about their novels. Plot construction, especially, requires the writer to pull back periodically from the page-by-page work and carefully think through what happens in the book, how one thing leads to the next. But I do not outline. My opinion is that anything as mechanical as an outline, with its headings and sub-headings, is too much needless work in the first place and ultimately antithetical to good writing. Good writing is fluid and best left to seek its own directions.

I do make lists, though, and some time ago I was thunderstruck to hear novelist Diane Johnson say she also kept lists, that lists were actually a form of outline. Just so. By the time I've finished a book, I'll have lists everywhere—in my notebook, on scraps of paper, in the margins of the manuscript. What I like about lists is that they also are fluid, and tentative, even easily destroyed, lost, or neglected, and that they act as triggers rather than as prescriptions. The making of lists about what should happen, where, and when in the story, about facts I need to know, about causality and about things that connect, begins in earnest once I have an ending to the story. Such lists enter freely into the play of the writer's thinking, and a well-constructed plot, carefully attuned to its ending, is finally an intricate and complete system of thought.

In an adventure story, the ending not only defines all the events that precede it, but it should also exert a very strong pull on them. This is one source of pace, or of rhythm. The very best prose writers, I think, show a strong sense of rhythm in at least two ways—in the wording, the sentence and paragraph construction, and in the overall rhythm of the story. Much of a novel's impact upon the reader is felt by virtue of the rhythms of the writing.

Writers should listen to their sentences and feel the rhythms of the narrative as it moves forward on that level of detail. An adventure story, especially, needs to have a strong pulse. If the story is good to begin with, if it has been *thought through,* and if scenes are placed in a way that heightens suspense, much of this pulse will emerge as a matter of course. At certain points in the process of revision, however, I have found it useful to think of the book in terms of its basic units, which for me are usually chapters. For another writer, these units might be scenes. Or there may be several different types of units—scenes, chapters, groups of chapters.

What the writer wants, then, is for the units to rise like waves. Early in the novel each chapter will swell strongly, but terminate before the wave begins to show white. A wave that shows white is breaking its surface tension. For the sake of suspense, it's important in an adventure tale to hold the tension as long as possible. Later on, or in a particularly crucial early section, a line of white may appear, and then, of course, as the book moves to its conclusion, the wave will come nearer and nearer to breaking apart and crashing against the sand. This process—the sense of the large rhythm that runs through an adventure tale—is actually more complicated than I have described it here, because of subplots that may come to completion at various points in the novel. These are like smaller waves, rolling in more rapidly. These establish a counterpoint to the central, overriding pulse of the book.

The writer needs to feel the movement of the story, the rising pulse of each succeeding chapter. I know that I have a chapter (or scene, or dramatic unit) close to completion when I can work through it in one sitting without getting bogged down, and by bodily experiencing its movement. This is incidentally, one of the great pleasures of writing— the physical and emotional engagement. It is also one of the things that makes writing novels difficult—the toll that an extended project can take upon the body.

Since plot is so important to adventure fiction, it follows that the characters will be expressed in large part through action. They will be best understood in terms of what they do. I might insert here that I never considered myself a writer of adventure fiction until I was told so by my publisher and the reviewers, following the publication of *Yellowfish*. I have always been most concerned with ideas and politics, with the emotional life of the characters, and with language. But maybe I also knew that such concerns when overwrought could cause the reader to close the novel—the most dreaded of all effects.

An advantage of writing so-called adventure fiction is that as soon as the basic shape of the adventure is grasped, then the writer has the framework for creating a line of action. In *Yellowfish*, the characters travel from Vancouver to San Francisco by car. My subsequent novel, *Broken Ground*, which concerns the construction of a prison in the Oregon desert, had an equally inescapable (but more complicated) "process" built into it. Once the writer builds the framework, he must respond to the necessities posed by the material—the route of the journey, for example, where stops are made, how long the stops are, who dies or gets hurt, and in any case, what hardships, tests, and opportunities for suspense the journey presents.

In addition, since most adventure fiction is "realistic," particular attention needs to be paid to accuracy, especially when real places and things are used. Remember that setting is tied up with the story, and that it often joins forces with adversary characters to work against the protagonist. Research may be required. Such accuracy lends credibility to the story and connects the world of the story to the world of its readers.

Even more important, the writer must respond honestly and cleanly to the deeper aspects of character—those traits, quirks, principles, and emotional qualities for each of them that become increasingly defined as the novel develops. The characters have been drawn outward through interaction with other characters. Also—and this is most critical—they will be drawn out by the demands of the fictional world in which they discover themselves. They will be changed by this world, and yet at the same time, even as they emerge, they must remain themselves.

The plot, or line of action, that has caught up the main characters and compelled them to act fills the story with detail, with movement, drama, and, not insignificantly, with moral substance. Because of its emphasis on action and conflict, adventure fiction always has a moral dimension. As the writer is drawn more and more deeply into the novel, dealing with all these problems can be challenging. This is where the lists come in again. By this time, however, as the characters and story have increasingly asserted themselves, an interesting thing has happened to those lists: Where once they were wish-lists, so to speak, or projections, they've become lists of things the writer must deal with. This is a sign that at last the writer, like the characters, has also been forced outward.

When the adventure tale starts to work well, it and the characters, who are delineated through action, take over. What was set in motion so long ago, what demanded all that systematic thinking, now proceeds on its own power. But there's a danger here, too. It's as if one had added garlic to stew. Left in long enough, the flavor pervades everything. It's too late to make certain changes. The writer has to keep thinking, and be alert, and patient, but so far as I'm concerned, reaching this stage is the reason for writing—because of the sense of discovery, the exhilaration, and sometimes the strangeness of what those first ruminations have led to.

50

FREE-FORM PLOTTING THE MYSTERY NOVEL

BY MARCIA MULLER

PLOTTING THE MODERN MYSTERY NOVEL is a complex task that bears as little resemblance to so-called formula writing as Miss Jane Marple does to Lew Archer. One of the questions most often asked by aspiring mystery writers (frequently in tones of frustration, after being outfoxed by one of their favorite authors) is, "How on earth do you complicate your plots and still get them to hang together?"

Unhappily for those who seek instant solutions, there is no one sure-fire method of plotting. The techniques vary from writer to writer along a continuum that stretches from detailed, extensive outlining to what I call winging it (writing with no planning whatsoever). Writers adopt the type of plotting that best suits their working styles and personalities. Some hit on the appropriate type immediately, others gradually make their way toward it through experimentation—plus hard work and practice. There are no major shortcuts, but there are *little* shortcuts. Tiny ones, actually. What I'm about to tell you about plotting is only my highly individualized technique; all, some, or none of my suggestions may help.

I've learned my craft the hard way. In the past fifteen years I've made every attempt to "reinvent the wheel," especially where plotting is concerned. I began by making detailed character sketches, outlines, and time charts, a method distilled down to a lengthy storyline synopsis. I've tried winging it, with unsatisfying results. What I've finally settled into is a technique that I call "free-form plotting"; as the term implies, its key ingredient is flexibility.

Before we go on, however, let's discuss the concept of plot. If someone were to ask you what a novel's plot is, you'd probably say "the story." But if you examine a given *plot,* you'll see it's somewhat different from the *story.* The story is linear; it is the events that happen, both on and off scene. The plot is the *structure* you impose on those events. You select which to include, in what order, and how to tell each one. You shape your plot from the raw material—the story.

Here's an example of a crime story, simplified for our purposes:

1. Killer meets victim; they interact.
2. Killer murders victim.
3. Murder is discovered; detective enters case.
4. Detective investigates.
5. Detective solves murder; killer is apprehended.

Taking the raw material of this particular story, you could plot in a number of ways. You could tell it in a linear fashion, from step one to step five (although that's not likely to be surprising or dramatic). You could start with the discovery of the murder, continue through to the killer's apprehension, explaining in flashback or dialogue what went on in steps one and two. You could start with the actual murder, masking the identity of the killer. The steps may be ordered any whichway, depending on what kind of book you want to write. It is up to you to decide how this simple story is told; the question we are addressing here is how you make and follow through on your decision.

What I like about free-form plotting is that it allows me to defer the decision, feeling my way as I write. It saves me from becoming locked into an inflexible plot outline that may, in the end, not suit my purposes. I can start a novel with a minimal idea of where I'm going, develop some ideas and characters, experiment with them, keep what fits, discard what doesn't. An example of this is how I plotted my most recent Sharon McCone novel, *There's Something in a Sunday*.

When I started I had in mind a beginning situation, a few characters, a background, a theme, and a hazy idea of the ending. The situation has Sharon McCone being hired to follow a man who came to San Francisco every Saturday night and stayed through the early morning hours on Monday. The characters were the man, Frank Wilkonson; Sharon's client; a woman the man was looking for; and a married couple who were friends of the woman's. The background was dual: neighborhood activism and the plight of San Francisco's homeless people. The theme was the relationships between men and women, and how they go awry. And the ending—well, I won't reveal everything.

When I start a mystery novel, I like to set the situation in the first one or two chapters. In this case, it was Sharon following Wilkonson, observing his eccentric Sunday activities, and wondering if the client had told her the entire truth about his interest in Wilkonson. Because she observed Wilkonson's movements closely for nearly twenty-four hours, she feels that she knows him—and so did I, although he had not as yet uttered a single word of dialogue. In these two chapters, I had developed his character in some depth, and had begun to consider him a real person. As he developed, I began to think differently about Wilkonson and what I intended to do with him later on.

I employed the rule of flexibility very early. When I read my first two chapters, I found something was wrong: Taken together, they moved too slowly. So I broke them up, inserting a flashback chapter between them, in which I introduced the client, Rudy Goldring, and showed how Sharon had come to spend her Sunday tailing Wilkonson. By the time I finished the scene, both Goldring and the derelict who served as "doorman" at his office building had come alive for me, and I began to see new ways they could be used in the plot.

My next step was to introduce the supporting characters: the people at All Souls Legal Cooperative, where Sharon works. Again, something was wrong with the scene I'd planned. I was tired of writing about the co-op in the same old way. If I had to write the scene with Sharon sitting in her boss's office discussing the case one more time. . . . My solution was to introduce a new attorney and an assistant for Sharon, to give more prominence to an old character, the secretary, and to create personal problems for the boss, whose previous life had been placid. Now I had a situation that I was eager to write about, and a fast-developing personal subplot that (because the life of Sharon and the people at All Souls is an ongoing story from novel to novel) didn't necessarily have to be wrapped up at the end.

Of course, what happened in the scene at All Souls required going back and making minor adjustments in the first three chapters; the new attorney, for instance, was now the person who had handed Sharon the Goldring assignment, rather than her boss. This is a time-consuming necessity of free-form plotting but, as we'll see later, it has its advantages.

At this point I was ready to establish my other characters. And, while a lot had happened and a number of questions about Wilkonson and Goldring had been raised, I needed something more dramatic—the murder.

At the scene of the crime I was able to introduce another of the main characters, an unnamed woman who appeared suddenly and then vanished. In the next few chapters, as Sharon followed up on the case for reasons of personal satisfaction, I brought in the other characters who would figure prominently: the married couple, Wilkonson's wife, and his employer.

Most of these characters had turned out differently from what I'd first envisioned. A character "taking over" the story is a phenomenon that writers often discuss. No one knows exactly why or how this happens, but I suspect it has to do with the writer's being relaxed and "into" the story. As you sit at the keyboard, new ideas start to flow. Characters take on fuller identities as you allow them to speak and act and interact with one another. When this happens to me, I simply go along with whatever is developing; often I write pages and pages of dialogue or action, then pare them down or toss them out entirely. It's easier to cut or eliminate your prose than to go back and add material later. By setting down these free-flowing scenes on paper, you will avail yourself of the opportunity to create something that may vastly improve your novel. And (impossible in real life) you can always rip up the pages or hit the delete key.

One example of this phenomenon is the development of the married couple that I've mentioned—Vicky and Gerry Cushman. Originally, I'd seen them in a strictly functional sense, as friends of the woman who appears at the murder scene and then vanishes—the pivotal character in the plot. But, as Vicky began to take shape, what emerged was not the coolly efficient neighborhood activist I'd planned, but a woman with severe emotional problems. And in response to this development, her husband Gerry emerged as a selfish man who exacerbated her problems. I had created an unexpected conflict that wove nicely into the theme of the novel—and I was able to use it to further complicate my plot.

At this point—the end of your primary development stage—you can take full advantage of free-form plotting. You have your characters in all their individuality and richness; you have a situation that is ripe for additional complication; you have an idea of where you're going. Now is the time to find out exactly where that is—and how you're going to get there.

The way I accomplish this is to read what I have on paper. Then I play the game of "what if." The game is a question-and-answer process: "What if such-and-such happened? How would that work?"

In *Sunday,* I reached this point just as Frank Wilkonson disappeared. He had gone to an abandoned windmill in Golden Gate Park; Sharon was following him, but lost him in the darkness and fog; Wilkonson never returned to his car. This was an unplanned development; the setting of the windmill had occurred to me while driving by it one day, and it seemed a perfect place for an eerie, late-night scene. The scene wrote easily, but at its conclusion I had to admit I had no idea why Wilkonson had gone there or where he'd gone afterwards. Time for "what if. . . ."

Why did he? I asked myself. The obvious answer was that he planned to meet someone there. Sometimes the obvious choice is the best. But who? I could think of one character who would have reason to be there, but no reason to meet Wilkonson. But what if he was asked to contact Frank? By whom? I knew who that might be. But then, why hadn't Sharon seen Frank meet the other person? What if Wilkonson had. . .?

By the end of this question-and-answer session I found myself in possession of a new plot twist: an eventual second murder and a killer who hadn't even been on my list of primary suspects. Because of my accidental choice of a setting and the manner in which I wrote the scene, my plot had taken on greater complication—and greater mystery.

A few chapters later I was faced with another situation calling for "what if." Sharon had finally located the woman from the murder scene. The woman had ties to all the major characters, but they were as yet nebulous. In a few cases, they were nebulous even to *me.* So I considered the connections among all six of these people. What if the client was an old friend of the woman? What if they had once been lovers? No, friends was better. But what if she had had a lover? What if it was Frank? Or Gerry? Or Frank's boss? Or. . .? Because the characters were well established at this time, I was able to come up with a logical answer.

As I've said, free-form plotting requires constant readjustments of scenes and details to make them consistent with one another. This is laborious at times, often necessitating extensive rewriting. But I'm convinced that it is also extremely beneficial. As you rewrite, you are forced to pay great attention to detail, to polish your prose, to reexamine your logic.

Logic is crucial to a mystery novel. If it is flawed, the whole plot—no matter how original your premise, fascinating your characters, or vivid your settings—simply falls apart. I advise frequent rewriting and rereading. Check every detail; make sure every place is described properly, especially if the action depends on the lay of the land. As I was preparing the final draft of an earlier McCone novel, *Eye of the Storm*, I found that I'd handled a description of a boathouse in two different ways. In the early chapters, it had been a building on pilings over the water; later on, it had a concrete foundation and boat wells. Since near the end something happened in one of those wells, the initial description made no sense whatsoever!

This may sound like an incredible error, but, believe me, things like this happen to professionals, too. When I discovered it, I had read the manuscript numerous times. A friend and frequent collaborator had read it twice. Neither of us had caught the discrepancy. So check your copy. Recheck. Publishing houses have copyeditors to catch the little things, but the big things are your responsibility.

There you have the basics of free-form plotting. Develop a general situation, background, theme, characters, and ending. Set the situation. Allow your characters to act and interact with one another. When the primary development stage is complete, complicate by playing "what if." Write some more. Be flexible; play "what if" again and again. Rewrite, reread. Check, recheck. And as you write, take advantage of the surprising things that develop—they will often point the way to a truly baffling plot!

51

How to Put Suspense in Your Story

By Heidi Vanderbilt

FIVE YEARS AGO, I sold my first short story, "Locked Doors," to *Ellery Queen's Mystery Magazine*. It won the Robert L. Fish Award, a special Edgar from Mystery Writers of America for best first mystery short story of the year. Yet, as I wrote "Locked Doors" I had thought I was writing a woman's story. It wasn't until I finished that I realized I had unconsciously written what I most often read—suspense.

I realized I didn't know how I had written it. I didn't think I'd be able to do it again. Since I wanted to write more suspense fiction, I spent some time thinking about what I had done in "Locked Doors" that would help me repeat its success. I realized that suspense is created through situation and through action. I had to decide what sort of heroine and villain a suspense story needs, what emotions aroused in the reader make the story satisfying, and how to build tension and immediacy.

First, I considered the old saw "Write what you know." It wasn't enough, I decided. I know a lot of things that would make worthless stories—I've tried writing them, and they won't work. For me, writing comes not just out of experience, but out of my passionate involvement with that experience, and this was never more true than for my first story.

"Locked Doors" came out of my own fear.

I had been a foster parent for several years when I wrote it. I changed characters, facts and details, but I was writing about tensions I'd lived with for a long time. They were part of my dreams; they were my nightmares.

"Locked Doors," is about Marta, a single parent living on an isolated island with her young son, Ezra. Shortly after moving to the island, a little boy named Sammy who has met Ezra on the playground, begins making nightly calls to Marta, asking to come over. At first she says no, but when the calls continue, she gradually involves herself with Sammy and Christine, his abusive mother. Eventually, Marta calls in social workers and the police, and Sammy is removed from Christine and placed with Marta. This begins several years of custody hearings until Marta, Ezra, and Sammy face the final court battle and Christine's last, desperate attempt to get her son back.

Every story, whether suspense or not, asks the same question: Will the protagonist get what he or she needs? In mainstream fiction, the need may be to understand, to love, to grow. In suspense fiction, the need is to survive (though survival may be interpreted broadly). There must be a threat to the protagonist by something or someone at least his equal. The tension grows out of the struggle between the hero, representing the reader as he wants to be, and the anti-hero, representing what the reader fears in himself. The more complex and evenly matched these two characters are, the more effective the suspense, the less predictable the outcome.

Marta is a decent person. She does what we all would like to think we'd do in the same situation: She tries to help a hurt child. But she has a certain blindness about the consequences of her altruism to herself and her son. She doesn't know what she is getting into; once involved, she can't abandon the child she has saved. She is trapped.

Just as I needed a heroine who was not too good, I needed a villain who was not too bad, someone intelligent, with understandable human qualities. If Christine had been completely loathsome, she would have undermined the suspense, flattened the story. There would have been no struggle between equals. I wanted readers to feel a little sorry for her, to understand her, to feel that the bad things she did were not too far from what the reader might do in the same situation.

At first, Christine thinks Marta is her friend; Marta acts like a friend, visits her, helps her with Sammy. Then, from Christine's point of view, Marta betrays her: She calls in social workers and the police. Sammy is taken away and given to Marta, who repeatedly goes to court and accuses Christine of incompetence and abuse. Marta has stolen Sammy and is now living a cozy life with him and her own child, while Christine is alone. Of course Christine wants revenge. In a sense, she deserves it. Readers—and Marta—know this.

The anticipation of punishment creates dread, which deepens suspense. Remember when you were a child and had done something wrong, even though you meant to do something right? And you knew you were going to be punished for it, even though that wasn't fair? Remember that feeling of helplessness, of inevitability, of "deserving" the punishment, even if you didn't?

There are several levels of injustice operating, most important, Christine's toward Sammy and Marta, and Marta's toward Christine and Ezra. Moral complexity inevitably creates suspense, not structurally from the movement of the plot, but from challenging the reader's sense of right and wrong, fair and unfair.

Another way to create suspense through situation is by establishing early on in the story that the hero is—or yearns to be—a domestic being. (Mary Higgins Clark does this wonderfully, creating threats to nice families; so does Robert B. Parker—his villains threaten Spenser's "family" life with Susan Sullivan and Hawk, his domestic relationship with the people he knows, the city he lives in.) We all want to protect those we love and to preserve or better the way we live. Any threat to this immediately sounds chords of major concern. Marta has her own son and another, hurt child to protect. Christine in her fury is a threat to them all.

Once I had my two main characters in their complicated and stressful situation, I structured the plot so the reader would want to stay with it.

I started small, with a minor incident—Marta gets a late-night phone call from a child she doesn't know—and built the story from there. Marta takes the simplest step to deal with Sammy's request to come over: She says no. When that doesn't work, she takes the next simplest step, then the next, and so on, always expecting that each step will provide the solution. She is frustrated and surprised when it doesn't and she has to try something else, then something else, until she becomes his foster parent—and the target of his mother's rage.

Now, this is important: Every time the heroine doesn't get what she needs, the story moves forward. When one need is met, another, more serious need must present itself, or the story is over. When Marta gets Sammy away from his mother, her immediate need to help him has been met. But in doing that she endangers herself and Ezra; now she herself needs help.

I also alternated moments of claustrophobia with moments of release, building to the scene in Marta's car as she drives Christine to find an open bar, while Sammy whines and kicks in the back seat. Then the claustrophobia eases—Marta takes Christine back to her garbage-strewn house and Christine eventually leaves the island—only to tighten again at the end.

There is another truism that says that to make a story work the main character must undergo a change, have an epiphany. I want to add to that: Along the way, the heroine must undergo several lesser reversals. She does well, then poorly, then better, then has a disaster, recovers and so on. An unvarying slide in any direction is monotonous. Things change for characters just as they do for people. Good news-bad news, up-down. It's like life, and it's interesting.

Dick Francis does this in his recent best seller, *The Edge*. When the story opens, Tor Kelsey, the hero, is living a lonely but interesting life. He's got an unusual job spying out trouble at a race track in England. He's a traveler by nature, but for now seems content to stay put. Then he gets an offer of a dream job—to travel across Canada, trouble-shooting on a deluxe Mystery Race Train, which combines an acted mystery with a week of elite thoroughbred racing. In other words, in Tor Kelsey's life, things have gone from all right to wonderful. Once on the train, of course, he has a bumpy (in all senses of the word) and exciting ride.

These reversals keep the story moving along. And as it does, questions arise in the reader's mind. In the first scene of "Locked Doors," Marta is brittle, compulsively working, afraid. The reader wonders, is she O.K.? In the next section, she is upstairs reading to Ezra and Sammy. The reader sees she's still doing her job, still caring for those little boys, no matter how strung out she is. And so on, building toward the inevitable confrontation between Marta and Christine late the night before the court hearing.

Once I'd structured the plot, I thought I had finished the story. I had two interesting, evenly matched characters in a dangerous situation. I had a fairly intricate plot with plenty of ups and downs. But as I reread what I'd written, I found the story was still missing something. It lacked a way for the reader to experience Christine as Marta experienced her, to see what an enormous danger she was. The threat lacked immediacy. Christine wasn't scary enough.

So I added a middle section, in the form of a diary entry, describing the nature of Christine's relationship to Sammy:

"Christine called early this afternoon." (Marta writes)

" 'Sammy sleeps with me,' she said. 'What do you think of that?' "

The reader goes with Marta to Christine's house . . .

"I couldn't smell the ocean for the stench of rotting food."

The reader sees Christine with Sammy . . .

"Sammy was naked . . . He pushed his mother's hand away from him . . ."

. . . and hears her talk about her son in front of him!

" 'I'll give him to you. Marta,' Christine called from the bed. 'You can have him. For keeps. Who'd want him, anyway?' "

Readers, experiencing this side of Christine for themselves, empathize with Marta's need to get involved. Anyone would want to help Sammy.

To summarize, suspense grows out of situation and action. You need an empathetic hero or heroine who deals with problems by trying the simplest solutions first—just as you would. The villain should be an even match for the hero and should have qualities the reader can identify with and understand. The things that happen to the protagonist alternate in a general way between bad and good, raising questions about his or her ability to cope, and build toward a climax which poses the question: Will he or she survive? And you must let the reader really feel the threat to the hero—don't just tell about the danger, show it. Show the villain on his way. Let your readers hear the heavy footfall, the labored breathing, sense something odd and unpleasant, not quite right. Otherwise, readers won't care enough to read to the end.

I didn't consciously know any of this when I wrote "Locked Doors." I just fumbled around, draft after draft, until I got the story to feel right and sound right. I didn't even realize I was writing in this genre until I'd finished the story, and then I wasn't sure until payment showed up.

But after I figured out what I'd done and how I'd done it, I sold six more stories to *Ellery Queen's Mystery Magazine*.

52

WRITING SCIENCE FICTION

BY JACK WOMACK

TWENTY-FIRST CENTURY ROSES shall be known by their thorns. How might science-fiction writers enable their readers to hold them that they may savor the scent?

What's your takehome, Glorp? It's hard to identify with Glorp if Glorp has nothing in common with you. So often in science fiction, character is trampled over by a stampeding plot, and the protagonists are so perfunctorily drawn as to seem almost allegorical, coming across to the reader as alien even when the story is set on earth. Believable characters redeem unlikely plots, in this genre as in all others. Know these people about whom you write; try to understand why they do as they do, keep in mind an awareness of whom they respect, what they fear, how much they've won or lost in their lives. Without good characters, you may as well write an essay. Characters aren't merely the writer's mouthpieces; write of them as you would write of yourself.

Your people are products of the world in which they live and therefore must behave and react according to the precepts of that world. A thought to consider is that you have more in common with a baker who lived in ancient Babylonia than you would with any being from any other planet. While your SF characters must be in some way understandable to your readers in an empathetic manner, your people will generally not be late 20th-century Americans and may not necessarily respond or behave as we do.

If you use a first-person narrator, you must tell the tale in the appropriate style and with the limited understanding of the character speaking. What this loses in flexibility is made up for by the chance to make the reader—through the reactions and opinions of your narrator—know more directly the smell and taste of a time that hasn't yet happened. Depending upon how badly—by our standards—your narrator behaves, readers may ascribe unsavory attitudes and beliefs to you. But to be believable, as approximately real in print as in person, a character has to be consistent, and a fully rounded character may well be best brought out only in darker shadows and tones.

A 3-D world on a 2-D page. The world you create must as well be thought of as a character, in that it must have a history and behave, or not behave, in a consistent manner. In describing a world, the steady accretion of incidental detail is one of the best ways to give a concept flesh, but details should not be troweled on simply to disguise gaps in the action or the cracks of a plot.

A world that is ages distant and miles away from where we are may be described in any way your imagination sees fit; in tales of the near future, as in my novels, the most memorable images inextricably tying together our world with that of our children's are those in which something immediately familiar is seen without warning in an unfamiliar light—striking images thrust unexpectedly into mundane situations, nails poking through the bed's mattress.

Take a naturalistic approach to unnatural material. If your people live in a domed city, what does the air smell like? How thick is the glass? Is it glass, or is it another transparent substance? When the outside air is colder, does steam form on the inside of the bubble? Where did they get the mold for such a dome? Your readers will want to know some of these things.

Building a better microbioinoculator. Structure should underpin science fiction as it underpins science. Many of this genre's writers have been notorious for using silly plots, and this shouldn't be the case. A science fiction writer may do much that a mainstream writer will not do, these days: consider the nature of creation, the essence of language, the development of thought; make anew myths of the human condition, redraw the boundaries of time; serve as Cassandra to a populace not entirely deaf.

But who cares so long as Buck rescues Wilma from those big green octopi for the umpteenth time?

The plot of a book must make more sense than the plot of a movie. To tell your story so that you will not be misunderstood, you must understand what your intentions are in writing it. Construct your tale before you begin jotting it down, as you would construct a trellis for roses, knowing where it will begin and where it will end, then building the frame in between. As you write, the story will entwine around your structure, and you must know when and where to prune. There'd be no need for editors if writers knew when to shut up. Scenes or lines neither bearing on nor contributing to either the action or intent should be cut, cut, cut. You say something you've written is too good in itself to lose? Cut, cut, cut. To edit is to love; after awhile you'll know when something's wrong without having to ask.

As one whose work has been described as a mink coat draped over a parking meter, I understand how difficult it can be to construct a seamless plot in these visual days, where holes of logic may be so quickly tarred over with images.

Wear glasses, staring into the future. One day your TV will ask you what you want to watch. Yes, sooner than you think. Will it therefore have the capability to discuss ethics, or theology? Doubtful.

In writing science fiction, you can't help but make predictions. Your characters may have nothing to do with the laws of their society or of ours, but they cannot ignore the laws of science. If you're going to write of atoms, or of alien ecology, or of fusion power, know what you're talking about; understand what is and isn't possible. A certain leeway in scientific believability may be allowed for literary or satiric effect, though perhaps I ignored my own advice in my second novel *Terraplane,* in which my characters transfer into a parallel world with the aid of a VCR.

Make yourself familiar with any material from which you extrapolate. There was a time when this advice was generally better heeded, but computers seem to have made too many minds' hard disks grow soft. A *deus ex machina* is no more improved for arriving equipped with keyboard, and anything that emerges from a computer must first be entered by a human being, with all ensuing limitations.

If you deal with our immediate future, with a twenty-first century that no longer seems so safely far away, prepare yourself for what you conceive by reading newspapers and watching TV, keeping in mind that what you make up can rarely equal what reality offers. In dealing with our world as it may be a few years hence, exaggerate reality only enough to be most believable and therefore disquieting to the reader.

Speak, Gort, speak. People seldom admit their personal plots even to themselves and never to their acquaintances at work or to those who have, say, taken them hostage. Citizens make speeches about the challenges of their times, or of the purpose of the universe, only when

259

drunk or running for office. When a man asks a woman the name of New York's mayor, he doesn't expect to hear in reply an exposition of how the city's political system works.

In much science fiction, banter of this sort constantly occurs, resulting in a much drier future than any greenhouse effect might produce. This genre's dialogue too often sounds to have been translated, badly, from Martian. Listen to how people speak. Read your work aloud to yourself; do you still believe it when you hear it? People's words circumvent their thoughts often enough that what your characters don't say can hold much more than what they do. While the best conversation tends to be brisk, wisecracks and one-liners are conversational lagniappe, and not the stuff of which a chapter's conversation is made. Upon meeting one another people do not offer as small talk their own condensed autobiographies unless they are frighteningly egocentric. A verity of drama is that the bad guy always gets the best lines.

Your characters need their own voices to be able to improvise from your script; for your sake, and the plot's, always give them reason to gab.

Let me play first or I'll take my future home. The theory that science fiction enables both writer and reader to understand better and appreciate foreign cultures is but infrequently employed in practice. Prejudice will not be absent from the future but there should be no room for it in the science-fiction writer's soul.

It should also be pointed out here that women are not representatives of an alien species, something male writers working in any genre should bear in mind.

Do the nebulae laugh? Once we were certain of the future's blessings; no longer, and the problem for the science-fiction writer is how to capture this unease while making the reader want to read on. Wit is an element too rarely injected into an often portentous genre. Humor provides the reader with an additional dash of the human element while enabling the writer to obtain distance enough to see the characters and the situation more clearly, from a new angle, as if viewing through a different window. If our immediate future is involved, the humor will of necessity tend toward the dark.

A science-fiction writer is one who carves fog, discerning and uncovering the human soul beneath the future's cloud. The best work in the genre allows both writer and reader to understand concepts and see new visions that may not otherwise have occurred to them. In societies which have become more authoritarian, growing into their futures, both writer and reader may still, through science fiction, celebrate human sensibilities while living within political and cultural systems that find such sensibilities not merely alien but superfluous to their needs. In the writing of science fiction, you can never forget that much more than our world exists.

The best science fiction springs from a wild imagination wisely leashed. In your writing keep in mind the camper's dictum, that you try to leave the field in better shape than you found it.

53

WRITING THE UN-HISTORICAL NOVEL

BY GARY JENNINGS

I AM REGARDED as an author mainly of "historical novels," though I have never in my life sat down to write any such thing. I staunchly maintain—and in these very pages I have said so before—that there really *is* no such thing as an "historical novel."

Unless a writer chooses to write about some imagined future, he or she *has* to write about the past, even if only yesterday's. Consider: It is not just a matter of tradition or convention that most novels are told in the past tense. The most up-to-date, hip and trendy "contemporary novel," about to be published tomorrow, is already a story about the past. I myself have toyed with the notion of doing a novel based on my adventures on Madison Avenue in the late 1950's—when all of us bright young admen considered ourselves the last word in up-to-date, hip and trendy—and, with some chagrin, I realize that the times, our society, our culture, all have changed so much in thirty years, that *that* would now be regarded as an "historical novel," if not a prehistoric artifact.

However, the novels that I have so far written have been set in more distant pasts—*Aztec*, 500 years ago; *The Journeyer*, 700 years; *Spangle*, 100 years—but only because, like any other novelist, I have chosen subjects, events, or characters that I knew would make a good story. It just so happened that those subjects were best represented, or those events occurred, or those characters lived in the past. I did not choose them because they were "historical."

And neither do the characters in my novels regard *themselves* as "historical," which brings me to the main point I want to make here. My fictional characters, as well as those drawn from real life—the Aztec named Mixtli and the journeyer Marco Polo and the circus troupers of *Spangle*—all think of themselves as up-to-date, hip and trendy, never once as "partakers in history." I may seem to be stressing the obvious, but I believe the point cannot be overstressed: that a writer writing about the long-ago must constantly be aware that it was not *then* the long-ago. That deliberate and constant awareness may be the most important of all the factors that go into the writing of such a novel, and sometimes it can also be the most difficult factor to manage.

The author of a Napoleonic-era novel has remarked that the hardest thing she had to do, while writing it, was to bear in mind that on the night before the battle of Waterloo, nobody knew who would win it. No author is likely to have his Babylonian hero carrying a purse of coins dated "B.C.," or to have his Westphalian hero say to the heroine, "Well, goodbye, dear, I'm off to the Thirty Years' War." But the temptation is ever present to give our long-ago characters a foreknowledge they could not have possessed.

Even when an author copes adequately with that time-frame aspect, there is another horn to the dilemma. Write about Napoleon, and you expect nearly every reader to be familiar with the history. But write about even an obscure person or era, and you have to assume that *some* readers will be familiar with it. In other words, they already know, to some degree at least, "how the story comes out." That being so, how do you simultaneously stay true to history, keep your characters properly in their time frame, *and* still make the story grip a reader who has the advantage of 20/20 historical hindsight? Well, sometimes that can be done by playing the two horns of the dilemma against one another.

And that has never been better done than by Frederick Forsyth in his *The Day of the Jackal*. Every reader of that novel knew, from page one to the end, that that story never happened at all in real history; that Charles de Gaulle never got assassinated by a sniper; that he was, in fact, still alive and feisty when the novel was published. However, *none of the novel's characters knew that,* and that was what gave such a headlong urgency to the race to intercept the jackal sniper.

Still, that would not have been enough to rivet the interest of the reader already aware that de Gaulle never got shot. So Forsyth did more. He so persuasively took us through the sniper's preparations and made his modus operandi so likely to succeed, that the reader willingly suspended the disbelief of "this never happened," and came to believe that "by damn, this scheme *could* have worked," and voraciously read on to find out "how the hell did this *not* happen?"

Forsyth managed this so superbly because (1) he made his characters believable persons with believable motives and believable responses;

(2) he had done his homework, on everything from ballistics to the most minute details of the story's time and locale; and (3) by the accretion of those realistic details he achieved a verisimilitude that no reader could fault or resist, that convinced every reader to believe "this could have happened."

Now, on the art of delineating character, I will not expound; the subject is too vast to go into here. But the other two techniques—the accretion of details and the achievement of verisimilitude—are well within the capability of even the beginning writer, if he or she is willing to put in the labor they entail.

Reality cannot be flattened down onto a two-dimensional printed page, but verisimilitude can—the *illusion* of reality. It is done by (1) knowing every last detail of your story's time and place, from architecture to climate to customs, etc., (2) knowing every last thing about your characters, from birth to story-time: their upbringing and education, their trades and the tricks thereof, their look and dress, their individual traits and crotchets . . . and then (3) immersing yourself so thoroughly in them, their surroundings, and their story that you forget they are in any sense "historical" and you live their lives and adventures right along with them.

You do not, of course, shovel into your narrative every last detail you have unearthed in your research. It is fatal to let the reader see how hard you have worked—and it is unnecessary. If you know your characters, the period and the locale inside out, believe me, your own assurance will convey that to the reader—but *only* if you know all those things inside out. When you do throw in some detail of curiosa, try to do it offhandedly, not obtrusively, and please do make sure it's a detail that your reader would not also be likely to know. (For a simplistic example: everybody knows that Roman senators wore togas and Greek bacchantes wore chitons, but who knows what they wore *under* them?)

Here again, it is equally important to know what your characters could *not* have worn or used or mentioned in dialogue, lest they step out of their time frame and destroy the story's verisimilitude. A recent novel about England's William Rufus lamentably dispelled its 12th-century mood when the author (more than once) had this or that character remark of another that he was "as flighty as a hummingbird." (No Englishman ever saw a hummingbird until he got to the New World, four hundred years or so after King William's time.)

By the way—and not at all incidentally—be sure to double-check your sources of any information from times past. A reader of my *Aztec* wrote to castigate me because I had mentioned bees and honey in that novel, and, said she, the *Encyclopedia Britannica* avers that there *were* no bees in the New World. If any edition of the *Britannica* makes any such statement, it is dead wrong. (True, the Aztecs did not have domesticated honeybees, but it is likewise true that, if the New World had had no wild bees to do the job of pollinating, it would also have been a world almost nude of vegetation.)

If you can adroitly manage the accretion of enough realistic details, and thereby achieve verisimilitude—whether you are writing a novel or trying to placate an irate spouse by inventing an excuse for some misbehavior on your part—you stand a good chance of being believed, whatever lie you're embedding in the story. And, come right down to it, fiction is nothing but expert and believable lying.

In each of my novels set in the past, I have tried to employ that method—details = verisimilitude—but in the case of *Spangle,* it led me to use a system of organization that I had never used before, and some of you might also find it useful.

First, of course, as we all must do, I did my bookwork and legwork research. The bookwork was to bone up on the history, geography, dress, customs, etc., of a hundred years ago. The legwork meant visiting and traveling with actual circuses to learn from their experts the tricks of their trades—the details of everything from lion-taming to tightrope-walking. That took me to circuses all over the world, from Nashville to Leningrad, and I have to admit that it was fun. Or most of it was. Less glamorous aspects of the circus were also necessary to my story—things like the setup and teardown of the Big Top (sometimes in terrible weather); the logistics of supply, transport, scheduling; even details like the shoveling of menagerie manure.

On occasion, I found myself instructing the experts—and this illustrates what I have said about a novelist's having to know what his characters could *not* have known. An Italian trapeze artiste told me that he supposed his act would have been done no differently a hundred years ago. I had to correct him. At that time no trapezist had ever done any such feat as a triple or quadruple somersault; the trapezist Léotard had just then introduced the simple leap from one bar to the other. Also, not Léotard or any other circus performer of that time had glitzy chrome-plated rigs, amplified music, strobe lights, etc. ("Per Bacco," muttered the artiste. "That's right, they didn't.")

Finally, home again and possessing far more information than I could ever cram into one novel, I conceived a curious system of organizing it all—the most outlandish-ever outline for a novel. It consisted of a sheet of brown wrapping paper, five feet wide and twenty feet long, scribbled and scrawled and diagrammed all over in different-colored inks. It might have been mistaken for the tracklines and timetables of every railroad in creation. The notes and diagrams began at one end of one side of the paper, with April 1865, ran all the way along that side of the paper, around the far edge and to the end of the other side—forty feet, in all—to June 1871.

To explain that, I must tell something about the story of *Spangle*. The circus that is the novel's collective "chief protagonist," finding itself impoverished and stranded in Virginia after the American Civil War, makes its way to Baltimore, sails to Europe, and there—traveling all over the continent—gradually recoups its fortunes, until it winds up in Paris just in time to be trapped in that city's siege during the Franco-Prussian War. The circus comprises a varying but always numerous cast of performers and crewmen and hangers-on, and they naturally have dealings with even greater numbers of "outsiders," including many real-life characters of the time. The circus travels through every kind of country, from the Shenandoah Valley to the Hungarian puszta and the Russian northland, and to cities as various as Baltimore, Florence, Vienna, Budapest, and St. Petersburg, before arriving in Paris.

Not only did I have to keep track of the whereabouts of each of my multitude of characters, their doings and interrelationships, the whole circus's triumphs and disasters and so on, during 1800 pages of type-script—I also had to keep track of significant dates and events, land-scapes and locales in the world that the circus travels through. And in those days it was a world of infinitely shifting political situations, alliances, even national boundaries. In brief, that Bayeux-tapestry thing plotted *Spangle* from the first page to the last and enabled me to have the circus always authentically situated in real time and place.

The outline truly was woven, like a tapestry, of warp and weft and intricate design. The long sheet of wrapping paper was divided by vertical lines, according to date and locale, and in those vertical spaces I scribbled the notes from my research as to what was going on then and thereabouts (just telegraphic code reminders to refer me to my more copious notebooks and file cards). Horizontally across those vertical warp lines, I wove the weft—long lines representing every one of my major characters, fictional or real, with notations along each line as to what each was doing at each time and place (for example, the developing complexity of an artiste's circus act), plus all of those characters' adventures and misadventures. Additional lines—diagonal, wiggly, criss-crossing—connected characters, to keep straight their interactions, romances, rivalries, enmities, etc. The tapestry, I am sure, would have been totally incomprehensible to anybody but its creator.

However, that peculiar outline did more than help me remember where everybody was—and when—and what he or she was doing at any specific point. It also enabled me to "live with" my characters, wherever and whenever they found themselves, and I could keep *them* from ever disrupting the time frame and mood of the story by having any pre-vision of what was to occur in the future. Also, in the occasional place where the circus itself did not provide enough action, incident, perilous situation or whatever, to keep the story lively, I could jump from the "horizontal-weft" to the "vertical-warp" notes, and bring in either true or based-on-true incidents from "outside" the circus. That was not often necessary—a circus is a perpetual adventure—but there *were* spots where real-life history was being even more dramatic than anything fictional that was going on under my Big Top.

Most of my writing colleagues and friends consider me woefully old-fashioned. I still prefer to compose (and even to do the grueling finished-typing of 1800 pages) on a manual typewriter, while they—ever so much more up-to-date, hip and trendy—have graduated to sophisticated computer word processors. Nevertheless, some of them have expressed awed admiration of the precision and flexibility with which I could work, using that "cumbersome, archaic, handwritten" roll of wrapping paper. It gave me an overview of *Spangle* that would be beyond the scope of any computer screen. As I say, I've never before resorted to any such system, and I may never do so again. (My next novel has a far less numerous cast of characters and covers a lot less territory.) But the Bayeux-tapestry layout worked splendidly for *Spangle,* and I hold no patent on it. If it appeals to you, and seems applicable to whatever novel you have in mind, feel free to imitate it. I wish you all success, and I won't even ask an acknowledgment.

267

❘❘ 54

Writing the Romantic Novel You'd Like to Read

By Margaret Chittenden

I WRITE ABOUT A VERY SERIOUS SUBJECT—love. To my amazement, I've discovered there are people who look upon the writing of romance as frivolous. This is far from the truth. There is nothing frivolous about love. Love is important to every member of the human race—it is one of the most complex emotions there is, and one of the most fascinating to explore in fiction.

One advantage in writing romantic novels is that you can draw on your own experience. You can't always do that with murder mysteries or police procedurals, but most of us have had some romance in our lives, and we can at least depend on memory.

Today's romance novel is a far cry from the old style "You Tarzan, me Jane." Even though some publishing companies issue guidelines, there is no formula that guarantees success. Reading published romance novels will show you how other writers do it, but won't necessarily show you how to do it yourself. Ten years ago, when I began writing romantic novels, I read widely in this genre; it seemed to me there was no reason I shouldn't simply write the kind of book I'd like to read. Nor could I see any reason why I shouldn't use the same methods I had used in writing suspense. After all, my romance novels wouldn't be solely about love any more than my suspense novels were solely about murder. Novels are about people. At least they ought to be.

My first thought in writing a novel has always been, where is it going to take place? Although I now live in the suburbs, at heart I am a city person. I love art galleries, big book stores, luxury hotels, museums, historic buildings, gourmet food. So, since I write to please myself first, I usually set my novels in or near a major city.

Usually, I visit my chosen location. I walk every alley, visit every important landmark. I talk to the people and eat their *paté de foie gras* or their fish and chips or their *Oyako Dombori*. I read local newspapers and brochures and books and my husband operates a video camera to record interviews and the sights and sounds of the place. By the time I leave, I am familiar with all the characteristics and elements that make that city different from other cities.

You don't have to travel long distances. My novel *Close to Home* (Harlequin Superromance) was set in a mountainous region fifty miles from my house. I visited every place I used in the book several times, observing at each one with a writer's eyes.

The next step is easy. With the background clearly in mind, the characters begin to emerge. The mountainous region produced a male ex-ski racer and a female mechanical engineer who works in her family's ski factory. My heroine is always an American. She is going to the place I have chosen. Why? "Why?" is always my first question. The answer starts my plot moving and raises other "whys" that keep the plot building.

While plotting, I try to visualize my characters—though they are not yet fully realized—against their background and setting and watch what they do. Usually, they start talking to me, prodded by a "why" here and a "how" there. After a time, they start talking and reacting to each other and generating conflict as well as attraction. Conflict is as necessary in a romance as it is in any other kind of fiction; perhaps more so. The road to true love does not run smoothly.

As my story people move and talk, I write down what they say and do. As they develop, my plot builds; as my plot builds, my characters develop. It's a symbiotic relationship.

I try to avoid stock characters. I imagine almost anyone could give me a quick description of the old style romance hero. He was over 6′ tall, and lean and muscular, or lean and lithe. Probably dark-haired. Usually rich. Perhaps grim, or brooding. Nowadays the hero doesn't have to be a cliché. Here again, I go back to my own preferences. What kind of man attracts me? Not the macho type who grabs the heroine by the wrist or ankle and pins her down on a sofa or bed in every scene. He's outdated anyway. I like a man who has a sense of humor, compassion, even humility. He might want to seduce the heroine, but he would never, ever, use force. I give him some flaws, but I try to make him a real person.

I want my heroine to be a real person, too. Some of the heroines I

269

used to read about seemed so dim-witted and silly, I couldn't imagine why any man would fall in love with them. My heroine is the kind of woman I would like to be: usually tall and physically healthy, she jogs or skis, or works out with weights. She is a career woman, intelligent, with a mind of her own. She may tremble a little from time to time, but who among us does not?

I try to avoid trite situations as well as people. I've lost count of the times I've read a scene in which the heroine appears in front of the hero clad only in a diaphanous nightgown. She does not realize this until two or three pages of dialogue later, *then* she remembers but it's too late!

I will confess I've done variations on this theme, though. In my first romance novel, *This Dark Enchantment,* the heroine often practiced ballet exercises in the basement recreation room. She wore a leotard, of course, which is not the most concealing of garmets. And of course, the hero happened upon her. (Well, no, not *happened;* he had a reason for being there—I try to motivate *everything* in my novels.)

One problem I have in writing romantic novels is that I run out of words to describe a romantic scene. I certainly don't want to use "tumultuous" or "magnetic" or "electrical" all the time, though some writers do. I've found that it is possible to come up with original descriptions of emotions if I refer to the background. In *Close to Home,* for example, I used metaphors and similes that refer to snow and skiing. Here's an example:

Her blood was singing through her body and she was beginning to feel exhilarated, as though she were skiing in clear thin air on new powder, blasting straight down the fall line trailed by plumes of snow . . .

While I'm writing I try to bear in mind that one thing hasn't changed in the writing of a romantic novel: *There should still be tension between the hero and heroine at all times.* It must be there when the man and woman are in the midst of a crowd, or when they are alone; when they are quarreling and when they are making love.

I also try to create suspense, even in minor ways. The main suspense of course is will they or won't they? And after they do . . . will they again? One minor example of suspense: At one point in my Superromance, *Song Of Desire,* Jason invites Vicki to go out to dinner with him. "I want to talk to you about something," he says. He looks rather furtively around the room. "Away from here," he adds. Vicki is filled with curiosity and a certain amount of apprehension, wondering what he wants to talk about that can't be discussed on the spot. The reader, I hope, will then eagerly read the next ten pages to find out what Jason is up to. Remember that if you create this kind of suspense, you have to follow through and make it important to the resolution of the novel; you can't let the reader down.

Though there may be subplots, and the story may turn on more than the romance between the hero and heroione (business complications, for instance, or cultural differences), the rocky road they travel before promising to love happily ever after is still the most important part of the plot. However, few of today's romantic novels restrict themselves to "pure" love. There's no longer an iron law that says that young women must be virgins.

Obviously the hero and heroine are going to have love scenes of varying degrees of intensity—and these have to be set somewhere. Again, I use experiences I have enjoyed on research trips, changed considerably, of course. While doing my research in Japan, for example, I formed a strong attachment to the traditional Japanese bath. In *To Touch the Moon*, my Superromance set in Tokyo, my hero and heroine take a Japanese bath together. It's a humorous scene—I enjoy humor so I use it whenever I can. When I say humor, I mean witty and lively dialogue rather than slapstick situations. Even a humorous scene can have strong sexual overtones.

In *This Dark Enchantment*, I wrote about the fireworks on Dominion Day in Quebec City. I had watched the fireworks and parade of boats from the Plains of Abraham. In the novel, the heroine watches them from the deck of a yacht, with the hero. And incidentally suffers from a touch of *mal de mer*—more romantic than seasickness. The hero is a French-Canadian doctor, so it's believable to have him escort the heroine to one of the cabins to make her more "comfortable," which of course provides a good opportunity for dalliance. In *Song Of Desire*, I used my own experience of punting on an English river, which in reality was hair-raising as well as hilarious, but in the novel, it became another opportunity for romance.

Everyone's experiences and preferences are unique. If a writer makes use of them, he or she will always be able to create original scenes. It might seem unrealistic to present life in romantic terms, but I think most people read romantic novels because they want to feel that life *sometimes* works out the way it should—or the way they'd like it to.

It is very easy to write mediocre romantic novels, but it's not necessary for romances to be mediocre. I work very hard on my novels; I'm always afraid someone will read one and say, "Is this the *best* she can do?" But it is. I polish and revise and agonize over every book until it's as good as I can make it—until it pleases *me*. I especially check to see that the viewpoint is consistent, that I'm never guilty of writing something awful like, "Sonia's emerald eyes glittered in her exquisite face," when I'm writing from Sonia's viewpoint. Sentences like that often appear in romance novels, but in my opinion such a sentence would put the reader off Sonia for life.

Writing romance is fun—it's fantasy time every day—it's escape—it's entertainment. It's also very hard work. Or it should be. I encourage other writers to *respect* their craft, whatever they are writing, and give it their best. The results will please them. Surely, all writers should enjoy reading their own books. That's one of the major rewards of being a writer.

55

THE FIRST PERSON AT THE SCENE OF THE CRIME

BY WILLIAM G. TAPPLY

WHEN I BEGAN SCRIBBLING on my first mystery, I knew something wasn't working. I had all the scenes down: the beautiful girl discovers the corpse washed up on the beach, the salty detective arrives on the scene, the mild-mannered pathologist performs the autopsy to determine the cause and manner of death, the family lawyer investigates. But taken together, the scenes lacked coherence.

I was plagued, I finally realized, by a typical novice's problem—the wandering point of view. I hadn't decided whose story it was, and I hadn't settled on a voice with which to tell it.

When I created Brady Coyne, my Boston-based lawyer/sleuth, and allowed him to tell the story, it began to come to life. His first tale, *Death at Charity's Point,* became my first published novel. Three others have followed. Brady has served me well. He allows me to present and withhold clues at will, putting my readers into the position of participating in the story almost as if they were the sleuths. The focus is sharp and clear. Readers know only what Coyne tells them. They are encouraged to outguess him. They know whose story it is.

A magical sort of reader-narrator bonding occurs with the first-person storyteller that is generally absent with the more remote third-person narrator, provided the narrator/sleuth fulfills certain requirements.

He must wear well. Readers must like, trust, and respect him. They must care about him, root for him to succeed. He must have an appealing and unique voice, a voice that doesn't call attention to itself too blatantly, but is neither bland nor boring. At best, it will be conversational. The first-person narrator speaks to his readers as a friend, up close.

Readers should be able to identify with the narrator, who may be strong, admirable, even a hero—but never larger than life. He must be

273

fully drawn, multi-dimensional. He should have expertise, speak authoritatively. But nobody likes a know-it-all.

The narrator must have credible motivations. An occupation such as private investigator, policeman, or reporter easily places him in the center of mysteries, and for an immediately understood reason: It's his job, and he gets paid for it. At the same time, there ought to be a twist to that job. My Brady Coyne is a lawyer. Conventional enough, but he specializes in the legal affairs of the very rich. He is willing to do things for his clients that other lawyers might refuse, because he emphasizes personal service and discretion in his practice. As he says, "I spend very little of my time arguing interesting points of law in courtrooms. I work on retainer plus fees. Generous fees. Outrageous fees, really." For this, he does what his clients ask him to do, even if it isn't, strictly speaking, legal work.

It serves my purpose. It gives him stories to tell.

For all the appeal of the first-person narrator, the budding mystery writer should understand the peculiar plotting problems this approach creates.

The narrator must be present at the scene of the crime much of the time, and he must be there for believable reasons. He must observe events firsthand. Things must happen to him. The writer's task is to put his narrator on the scene without contrivance. Readers must know and accept the reasons he's there. Because the narrator is more than an observer. He is a participant in events.

Sometimes this is neither possible nor even desirable. Readers will not accept the likelihood of the sleuth always being where the action is, and for mystery to be sustained, important events must sometimes occur offstage. One way to solve this problem is to have the narrator reconstruct events as he imagines them to have happened. This is both straightforward and effective. For example, when Brady Coyne decides to tell readers about the suicide of a character years earlier, he says "I have imagined what Dud did then." To reinforce it, the next paragraph begins, "I can still see Dud in my mind's eye, striding down the hallway . . ." *The Dutch Blue Error* begins with a five-page prologue written in the third person. Then Brady's first-person voice informs the reader, "That is how I imagined it happened. Of course, I wasn't there." This technique allows the narrator to be absent from some scenes he describes. It also invites readers to read on and to challenge the narrator's version of things.

Because he can't be everywhere at once, the narrator will, of necessity, learn some things secondhand—typically, via conversation. Beware. The writer risks the twin disasters of boredom and contrivance. In an early chapter of *Death at Charity's Point,* Brady Coyne must learn a number of technical details about a dead body. He goes to the office of Dr. Clapp, the pathologist who performed the autopsy. Despite the inherent appeal of the gory details, the scene could easily founder on a routine question-and-answer format. In many ways, it's the sort of scene made for the third person, putting the reader at the shoulder of the doctor as he cuts open the corpse. In a first-person format, this immediacy is not possible. One way or the other, Coyne has to ask questions, and the doctor has to answer them.

The trick in sustaining reader interest in what amounted to a lengthy conversation between two men sitting in an office was to give Dr. Clapp an interesting and authoritative voice, to have Coyne ask the right questions (the very questions the reader would want to ask), and to interject some grisly wit and human dimensions into the scene. Readers must not view Dr. Clapp as simply a vehicle for conveying information, even if he never appears in the story again. Offbeat details can sustain readers through such scenes. For example, in this case Coyne, a heavy smoker, notices on the doctor's desk "a large glass jar. Inside it, a dark grayish mass swam in a yellowish solution. It looked like a big, dirty jellyfish. Dr. Clapp followed my gaze. 'A smoker's lung,' he said. 'I keep it as a reminder. Better than will power.'"

But too many telephone conversations, too many discussions over lunch (regardless of how appetizingly described), or too many meetings (no matter how colorful the locations) will quickly wear thin. Readers want action, and they want the storyteller in the middle of it.

The suspense of the story will be sustained as long as readers feel they know as much as—but not more than—the narrator. A mistake I made in the early versions of my first novel, in my misguided effort to "be fair" to my readers, was to leave too many obvious clues scattered across the landscape, which Coyne dutifully reported to his readers but stupidly failed to recognize as significant. Readers of these flawed drafts rightfully complained that they had the mystery solved long before

Coyne did, and had lost respect for my narrator/detective in the process—both unpardonable sins for suspense writing.

There comes a time in most mysteries when the narrator/sleuth holds in his hand the last piece to the puzzle. He thinks he's solved the mystery. It's time to confront the criminal. This is the one time in the mystery story when the narrator can legitimately manipulate his readers. He cannot spoil the climax for his readers by revealing what he knows. What does he do? In effect, he tells them, "Now I think I know. But I'm not going to tell you. Not yet. Just come along with me and watch what happens next."

In *The Dutch Blue Error,* Coyne gets that last puzzle piece over the phone. It would destroy all suspense for him to report that conversation verbatim to his readers. So instead, he says:

"As Schwartz talked I jotted notes onto a yellow legal pad. He talked for fifteen minutes or more in that precise diction of his. My mind swirled with possibilities. I underlined several words on my notepad, drew arrows from this point to that, punctuated some of Schwartz's bits of information with question marks and exclamation points."

Do readers object to being maneuvered this way by the narrator they have come to trust? Do they think it unfair that Coyne refuses to report immediately what Schwartz tells him? Not at all. Mystery readers want to guess, and then read on to see if they've guessed correctly. And they secretly hope they haven't. Readers want to be surprised. In surprise comes delight.

Because the burden of sustaining reader interest falls entirely on the shoulders of the narrator, he must grow and change, within a single book, and through a series. He continues to reveal new dimensions of himself. Subplots related to his personal life accomplish this. So does a setting richly populated with a variety of minor but interesting characters, who are foils for the narrator and who reappear in each of his adventures. Brady Coyne regularly falls in and out of love, to the bemusement of Julie, his secretary, whose challenge is to teach her boss a few things about women. Coyne has an ex-wife and two almost-grown sons whom he adores but resists getting close to. He goes fishing and plays golf with his Yale Law School chum Charlie McDevitt, who has a fondness for shaggy dog stories. He exchanges gibes, and tests his liberalism, with Xerxes Garrett, a young black lawyer.

It is Coyne's interactions with these permanent members of the cast, perhaps as much as the mystery he's trying to solve, that prompt readers to ask the question this writer hopes they will ask: "I wonder what's going to happen to Brady next?"

In the course of pursuing a mystery, the first-person narrator will get into scrapes. When he's at the center of the action, as he must often be, he will find himself in danger. Readers want this. Brady Coyne has been kicked in the (to put it euphemistically) groin. He's been drugged with chloroform, shot in the thigh ("There'd be an unsightly scar to mar the classic beauty of my leg"), smashed over the head with the barrel of a shotgun, and stabbed in the arm with a pickle spear.

That the narrator will escape from these brushes with death is never in doubt, of course, and it would be an error for him to tell his story as if it were otherwise. Readers know he has lived to tell it, and they will resent his efforts to create suspense where it cannot exist. The suspense for mystery readers lies in wondering how he's going to escape. This is quite enough.

If you want to write mystery fiction, start by creating your sleuth. Give him a unique voice and let him tell your story. Imagine his life fully. Populate it with minor characters, also fully imagined. Give him a job with built-in motivation to pursue mysteries. There's no better motivation than fat fees. Then give him a problem, and allow him to grapple with it.

And while you're at it, you might as well think big. Imagine a series of adventures. Editors and publishers think this way, so you should, too. Imagine a long shelf stacked with mystery books, all with your name on the spine. Because if your first one catches on, if your first-person narrator speaks beguilingly to your readers, they'll want more of him.

Just be sure to put him at the scene of the crime.

56

HORROR FICTION: EXPLORING THE DARK SIDE

BY WILLIAM F. NOLAN

OVER THE PAST DECADE, I have chosen to concentrate on writing short horror fiction. I've often been asked why. Simple. Horror fiction offers the serious writer a wonderful opportunity to explore a wide variety of characters under stress, characters faced with bizarre situations, within the commercial framework of terror-suspense.

I am challenged as a writer as I explore the dark side of the human animal. We are all capable, under pressure, of aberrant behavior, and the more strain our minds are subjected to, the more we revert to that darker self. The thing that has always frightened me most is a human mind out of control—and I often write about people who have slipped over an emotional edge.

In my "Saturday's Shadow," I move inside the head of a cop who has gone over that edge; he kills his own sister to save her from what he believes to be a deadly shadow, which is, of course, only in his mind. In "One of Those Days," my protagonist hears mice singing in the walls, watches a cat with a baby in its paws cross a busy street, and finally realizes that his psychiatrist has turned into a shaggy dog. But these are all in his mind. . . .

My story "Ceremony" deals with *group* madness. It concerns a professional hit man, a killer for hire, who is lured to a small village in Rhode Island and who himself becomes a victim—trapped by sweet-talking "normal" folk who are actually as mentally twisted as the killer himself. Yet they *seem* so nice.

Which brings us to characterization. As writer, it is my job to make certain that the readers *accept* these people, not as monsters, but as individuals who have adjusted their moral values to fit their own desperate needs. This makes them all the more frightening.

Many beginning horror writers make the mistake of thinking that if the scare elements are horrific enough, then the story will succeed. Put

278

in enough vampires and ghouls, they say, and you don't need to worry about creating real people. In truth, horror fiction cannot be separated from mainstream fiction in this regard. Solid characterization always serves as the core, or central pillar, of any really effective story. In order to frighten a reader, you must create people your readers can recognize and identify with. Once they are willing to accept your characters, once you have won their emotional rapport with characters they believe in, they'll go along with you as storyteller. They'll follow your characters from a sunny street into the darkest alley—from sanity to nightmare. You must, therefore, graft a muscled skin of reality over your skeleton of terror.

The more realistic the external elements of your story, the more effective it becomes when you let loose the horror. Stephen King's great success in the terror genre can be attributed, mainly, not to the horrors he creates, but to the *people* he creates. In his novel, *The Shining,* he did not take his characters into the nightmarish hotel until he had fully established them as three-dimensional human beings. It took him 100 printed pages to do this. Then, and *only* then, was he ready to engulf his characters in the real terrors of the book.

In my short story "Trust Not a Man," I spend 98% of the story in building my character—a lonely young girl searching for a man she can love and trust. The reader identifies with her troubled past, her sadness, her empty life. Then she discovers she has become involved with a man who is about to assault her—and she reacts by feeding him to a large, flesh-eating thing in her greenhouse. I devote only four paragraphs, at the end of the story, to the horror. The rest is all buildup to this moment. By then the reader is ready to accept the horror *emotionally.* My skeleton has been fleshed with reality.

Beyond character, mood is an all-important factor in effective horror fiction. Atmosphere. The stage must be set for the events that follow. Very early, most often on the first page, I try to establish a sense of disquiet, of something *wrong,* an aura of dread, however subtle. Let me cite some openings from my work to demonstrate this.

Here's how I begin "The Yard":

It was near the edge of town, just beyond the abandoned freight tracks. I used to pass it on the way to school in the mirror-bright Missouri mornings and again in the long-shadowed afternoons coming home with my books held tight against my chest, not wanting to look at it.

The key words here are: *abandoned . . . long-shadowed . . . not wanting to look at it . . .* These words convey an atmosphere of isolation, darkness, and fear. Or let's look at the opening of "Dead Call":

Len had been dead for a month when the phone rang. Midnight. Cold in the house and me dragged up from sleep to answer the call. Helen gone for the weekend. Me, alone in the house. And the phone ringing . . .

Again, the key words: *dead . . . midnight . . . cold . . . alone*. What I'm demonstrating here is that terror has to be constructed as carefully as an office skyscraper or a fine automobile. A terror tale must be layered, with one effect built over another; it must achieve a *cumulative* effect just as, with music, a good symphony builds in intensity. Terror, then, must be carefully orchestrated.

Consider what may well be one of the most terrifying scenes ever written—the "woman in the room" scene in King's *The Shining*. It's five pages long, and each paragraph builds toward the author's horrifying climax. King starts with the boy, Danny, standing outside the room he fears. He has a pass-key but doesn't want to use it. His body trembles. He hums to himself. A stream of thoughts and images races through his mind. He opens the door, and we get a description of the room. Dark. Turns on a dim light. The bathroom door is ajar. Danny is scared because he knows *something* awful is in there. Big white tub in there, with a shower curtain drawn around it. Danny goes in, draws back the curtain. A long-dead woman is in the tub. Bloated and purple. She *sits up*. Horrified, Danny bolts from the bathroom, runs to the outer door. But it's closed. He hammers on it, telling himself that this corpse can't really hurt him, that it isn't real. And just when he almost has himself convinced, a pair of fishy dead hands close on his neck. . . .

King has *layered* this scene to gain his impact. Each sentence takes us deeper into the boy's nightmarish encounter. By the time those dead hands touch him we have been emotionally prepared to react *with* him, to be frightened and shocked.

Another key element in effective horror fiction is what I call "the echo effect." A good horror tale must leave the reader with something to think about beyond what is obvious in the story on the surface. It must resonate within the reader's psyche. I often construct a subconscious "basement" beneath the main floor of my narrative, creating a double level.

Example: In "The Halloween Man," the *surface* narrative concerns the frantic efforts of a young girl to escape from what she believes to be a ghoulish creature who appears on Halloween night to collect children's souls. She ends up, at the story's climax, hiding in her room—and when her father attempts to calm her increasing fears, she is certain that *he* is the Halloween Man. The reader is left with the question of the ghoul's ultimate reality. Did he actually inhabit the father's body or did he exist *only* in the mind of this frightened girl? Thus, my echo effect.

In another of my terror tales, "Fair Trade," the narrator, under arrest for murder, describes a bizarre journey into town with an animated dead man who attacks and kills a citizen. The narrator *could* be telling the truth or he could be making up a lurid story to cover the fact that he is indeed the real killer. The reader is left to ponder both levels of reality. The tale leaves an echo behind in the reader's mind.

There are, of course, many ways to construct a plot, but a favorite method of mine is to begin with a very ordinary situation and allow it to become more and more offbeat. Take my story "The Partnership." I begin with a folksy fellow named Tad Miller, who's chatting idly with the waitress in a roadside café. Tad tells us all about himself, and we *like* the guy. He's a good ole boy. He tells us that Sally, who runs the place, likes him. ("Most folks do. And that's nice. Person wants to know he's liked, even if he keeps mostly to home.")

Tad also tells us about his partnership with Ed. All very homey and comfortable. Stranger comes in. He and Tad get to talking. Tad ends up taking the stranger out to show him through an abandoned funhouse near the lake, in an old, closed-down amusement park. That's where we meet Ed—who just happens to be a giant half-rat-half-water creature with a razor mouth and glowing red eyes. Ed gets the stranger for dinner, and Tad gets the guy's fancy wristwatch. A partnership. My plot has taken the reader from light into darkness, from the ordinary to the extraordinary. And our guide has been good ole Tad.

Try not to give the reader what the reader may expect. The more familiar the situation, the easier it will be to take your reader wherever you wish. In my "Dark Winner," a man takes his wife back to Kansas City to visit his old neighborhood. Ordinary, right? Not quite—because the man discovers that his evil childhood self is waiting inside the house of his youth, waiting to claim him, body and soul. Adult is absorbed by child, leaving the wife alone and powerless.

What about a party? We've been to countless parties in our lives. Why not start with a man invited to one late at night? I did just that in my tale "The Party," in which we meet David Ashland, a hard-drinking man with an unhappy past, who is attending what seems to be just another cocktail party but which quickly takes on a surreal aspect. The party builds to a feverish pitch, and Ashland flees but finds he cannot leave the building. To his horror, he finds that the *same* party, with the same people, is going on in every room of every floor—a party that will never end. And, final irony, all the booze is watered! David is trapped in his own special hell.

And, as author, I took the reader there by saying, hey, let's go to a party.

Stories such as these sneak up on the reader; they are, in a sense, almost playful. But they have hidden teeth. They bite.

Let me sum up with my feelings about art versus exploitation. I've been asked what I think about the "slice and dice" school of horror, the films and stories that drench the audience in blood and gore. I have strong feelings about them. They anger and nauseate me. They fail to examine the human condition; they simply exploit it. The true art of fear is achieved through a layered use of sensual effects as the writer (or filmmaker) manipulates mood, atmosphere, and character to his subtle purposes. And, for me, that's the operative word: subtle. I have found that with horror less is often more.

As writer, I prefer to allow my audience to fill in the graphic details of horror, since nothing on paper or on film can match the horrific images we can conjure up inside our own heads. And that's the prime target: the human mind.

Your audience is out there, waiting to be frightened. So go ahead, sneak up on 'em and scare their socks off.

They'll love you for it!

❙ 57

THE BIRTH OF A SERIES CHARACTER

BY GEORGE C. CHESBRO

FOR MOST WRITERS of so-called genre fiction the quest is for a successful series character—a man or woman who, already completely brought to life in the writer's and readers' minds, leaps into action at the drop of a plot to wend his or her perilous way cleverly through the twists and turns of the story to arrive finally, triumphantly at the solution. Great series characters from mystery and spy fiction immediately spring to mind; Sherlock Holmes, James Bond, Sam Spade, Lew Archer, Miss Marple, et al. These characters may simply step on stage to capture the audience's attention, with no need for the copious program notes of characterization that must usually accompany the debut of a new hero or heroine.

Almost two decades ago, when I was just beginning to enjoy some success in selling my short stories, I sat down one day to begin my search for a series character. Visions of great (and some not-so-great) detectives waltzed through my head; unfortunately, all of these dancers had already been brought to life by other people. The difficulty was compounded by the fact that I didn't want just any old character, some guy with the obligatory two fists and two guns who might end up no more than a two-dimensional plot device, a pedestrian problem solver who was but a pale imitation of the giants who had gone before and who were my inspiration. I wanted a *character,* a detective with modern sensibilities, whom readers might come to care about almost as much as they would the resolution of the mystery itself. Sitting at my desk, surrounded by a multitude of rejection slips, I quickly became not only frustrated, but intimidated. I mean, just who did I think I was?

It was a time when "handicapped" detectives were in vogue on television: Ironside solved cases from his wheelchair and van; another was Longstreet, a blind detective. Meditating on this, I suddenly found a most mischievous notion scratching, as it were, at the back door of my mind. I was a decidedly minor league manager looking to sign a player who might one day compete in the major leagues. What to do? The answer, of course, was obvious; if I couldn't hope to create a detective who could reasonably be expected to vie with the giants, then I would create a detective who was unique—a dwarf.

Believing, as I do, that it's good for the soul as well as the imagination, I always allow myself exactly one perverse notion a day (whether I need it or not). I'd had my perverse notion, and it was time to think on. What would my detective look like. What kind of gun would he carry, how big would it be, and how many bullets would it hold?

Scratch, scratch.

Would his trenchcoat be a London Fog or something bought off a pipe rack? What about women? How many pages would I have to devote in each story to descriptions of his sexual prowess?

Scratch, scratch.

The damn dwarf simply refused to go away, and his scratching was growing increasingly persistent. But what was I going to do with a dwarf private detective? Certainly not sell him, since it seemed to me well nigh impossible to make anybody (including me) believe in his existence. Who could take such a character seriously? Who, even in a time of dire need, would hire a dwarf detective? Where would his cases come from? He would *literally* be struggling to compete in a world of giants.

Scratch, scratch.

No longer able to ignore the noises in my head, I opened the door and let the Perverse Notion into the main parlor where I was trying to work. It seemed there was no way I was going to be able to exorcise this aberration, short of actually trying to write something about him.

Observing him, I saw that he was indeed a dwarf, but fairly large and powerfully built, as dwarfs go. That seemed to me a good sign. If this guy was going to be a private detective, he would have to be more than competent at his work; he would need extra dimensions, possess special talents that would at least partially compensate for his size.

Brains never hurt anyone, so he would have to be very smart. Fine. Indeed, I decided that he was not only very smart, but a veritable genius—a professor with a Ph.D. in Criminology; a psychological and spiritual outcast. His name is Dr. Robert Frederickson. Now, where could he live where people wouldn't be staring at him all the time? New York City, of course.

So far, so good. The exorcism was proceeding apace.

Fictional private eyes are always getting into trouble, and they have to be able to handle themselves physically. What would Dr. Robert Frederickson do when the two- and three-hundred-pound bad guys came at him? He had to be able to fight. So he'd need some kind of special physical talent.

Dwarfs. Circuses. Ah. Dr. Robert Frederickson had spent some time in the circus (in fact, that was how he had financed his education!). But he hadn't worked in any side show; he'd been a star, a headliner, a gymnast, a tumbler with a spectacular, death-defying act. Right. And he had parlayed his natural physical talents into a black belt in karate. If nothing else, he would certainly have the advantage of surprise. During his circus days he had been billed as "Mongo the Magnificent," and his friends still call him Mongo.

Mongo, naturally, tended to overcompensate, to say the least. He had a mind of a titan trapped in the body of a dwarf (I liked that), and that mind was constantly on the prowl, looking for new challenges. Not content with being a dwarf in a circus (albeit a famous one), he became a respected criminology professor; not content with being "just" a professor, he started moonlighting as a private detective.

But I was still left with the problem of where his cases were going to come from. I strongly doubted that any dwarf detective was going to get much walk-in business, so all of his cases were going to have to come from his associates, people who knew him and appreciated just how able he was, friends from his circus days, colleagues at the university where he teaches and, for good measure, from the New York Police Department, where, his *very* big brother, Garth, is a detective, a lieutenant.

I set about my task, and halfway through the novella that would become "The Drop," hamming it up, I discovered something that brought me up short: Dr. Frederickson was no joke. A major key to his character, to his drive to compete against all odds, was a quest for dignity and respect from others. He insisted on being taken seriously as a human being, and he was constantly willing to risk his life or suffer possible ridicule and humiliation in order to achieve that goal. Dr. Robert Frederickson, a.k.a. Mongo the Magnificent, was one tough cookie, psychologically and physically, and I found that I liked him very much.

And I knew then that, regardless of how he was treated by any incredulous editor, I, at least, would afford this most remarkable man the dignity and respect I felt he so richly deserved. I ended by writing "The Drop" as a straight (well, seriously skewed actually, but serious) detective story.

"The Drop" was rejected. The editor to whom I'd submitted it (he had published my short stories) wrote that sorry, Mongo was just too unbelievable. (Well, of course, he was unbelievable. What the hell did he expect of a dwarf private detective?)

That should have ended my act of exorcism of the Perverse Notion. Fat chance! On the same day "The Drop" was rejected, I sent it right out again to another editor (after all, Mongo would never have given up so easily), who eventually bought it.

The next day I sat down and started Mongo on his second adventure. Mongo was no longer the Perverse Notion; I had created a man who intrigued me enormously, a man I liked and respected, a most complex character about whom I wanted to know more, and who fired my imagination.

My Perverse Notion in that second story was to include a bit of dialogue in which Garth tells Mongo; after some particularly spectacular feat, that he's lucky he's not a fictional character, because no one would believe him. "High Wire" sold the first time out—to the first editor, and this time he never mentioned a word again about Mongo's believability. Four more Mongo novellas followed and were published. In the seventh, "Candala," it seemed I had sent Mongo out too far beyond the borders defining what a proper detective/mystery story should be, into the dank, murky realms of racial discrimination, self-hate and self-degradation. I couldn't place "Candala" anywhere, and it went into the darkness of my trunk.

But Mongo himself remained very much alive. I was still discovering all sorts of things about the Frederickson brothers, and the curious psychological and physical worlds they moved in; they needed larger quarters, which could be provided only in a novel.

Six Mongo novels later, Mongo and Garth continue to grow in my mind, and they continue to fire my imagination. In fact, that Perverse Notion proved to be an invaluable source of inspiration. Mongo has, both literally and figuratively, enriched my life, and he and Garth are the primary reasons that I was finally able to realize my own "impossible dream" of making my living as a writer.

"Candala" finally appeared in print, between hardcovers, in an anthology entitled, *An Eye for Justice*.

It is always risky business to try to extrapolate one's own feelings or experiences into the cheap currency of advice to others (especially in regard to that most painfully personal of pursuits, writing). However, the thought occurs to me that a belief in, and a respect for, even the most improbable of your characters in their delicate period of gestation is called for. That Perverse Notion you don't want to let in, because you fear you will waste time and energy feeding and nurturing it for no reward, may be the most important and helpful character, series or otherwise—you'll ever meet in your life.

Nonfiction: Articles and Books

58

THREE SUREFIRE WAYS TO WRITE AND SELL NONFICTION

BY SAMM SINCLAIR BAKER

THE FOLLOWING THREE TESTED AND PROVED PATHWAYS to write and sell articles and books have worked for me. They have paid off from my earliest beginnings as a striving writer when I gathered far more rejection slips than acceptance dollars. Finally, they helped me score with blockbuster best sellers in recent years.

You'll sell, too, when you take these roads that have led me—as a fellow struggling writer who never stops struggling—to repeated sales. Simply apply your unique creativity along these lines:

I. Use Winning Fiction Techniques to Write Nonfiction That Sells

Some years back I asked a friend who has since become one of the top figures in book publishing, "What makes a best-selling novel?" He said, "There are many components, but one point is absolutely essential—*it must be a page-turner.* When readers reach the bottom of each page, your narrative must force them to turn to the next page. That goes for anything you write."

He went on to discuss some of the ABC's of writing fiction, including "anecdotes, background, characters, dialogue." I decided to adapt those fiction essentials to produce nonfiction that would sell. Here's exactly how I did it in what many regard as the toughest challenge of all: writing a self-help diet book utilizing fiction techniques.

These excerpts from the best-selling diet book ever, *The Complete Scarsdale Medical Diet,* show specifically how you can do it:

ANECDOTES. My co-author, Dr. Herman Tarnower, related an amusing encounter with a patient. I used that anecdote to open the diet book this way, the doctor speaking . . .

I, personally, explain the Scarsdale Medical Diet's phenomenal popularity in two words: "It works." A slim, trim lady said to me recently, "Your diet is beautifully simple, and the results are simply beautiful." I just say, "It works."

That anecdote pulled people into the book instantly, as a dry exposition about diet would not.

BACKGROUND. What an author might write about the first-person hero in a novel functioned this way for nonfiction . . .

Perhaps my background of over forty years as an internist, cardiologist, and family doctor has made me especially diet conscious, counseling patients to eat and drink sensibly and stay trim. To save time, I had copies made of my diet suggestions. Those sheets traveled all over the country and the world.

Instead of just listing dull details about "experience," as in most nonfiction of this category, the narrative-style description involved readers with the drama of diet sheets circling the world. They found the image of overweight people everywhere being helped by the Scarsdale Diet far more interesting and convincing than a flat recitation of a doctor's background.

CHARACTERS. How can you as author interest prospective buyers of nonfiction in characters? It's simple when you apply your creativity. In this instance, individuals were brought to life in "case histories" and testimonials from a wide assortment of dieters. An example from the book:

"Immediately after the birth of my first child, I began to get headaches. These would occur at any time. Dr. T. suggested that the headaches might be related to what I ate. I followed his suggestions . . ."

The fiction technique worked here to get readers to care about an individual in trouble. Letters from dieters revealed their identification with the woman in the case history, asked what happened to her later, whether her headaches disappeared, and how. A dry recital of the diet recommendations in general wouldn't result in the same page-turning sense of reader participation with the new mother.

DIALOGUE. Just as dialogue catches the attention and heightened engagement of readers in short stories and novels, it can be used effectively in nonfiction. It's true even in books as instructional as a diet book, in this way:

A sportsman said to me, "There is an old expression in life—'you get what you pay for'—but there are exceptions to this rule. Two years ago, you gave me some gratuitous advice which not only saved my life, but made it possible to enjoy it and to enjoy eating."

"Yes," I said, "I remember, of course. I told you to try sulfadiazine, the only thing we had to work with during the war . . ."

Note how quotation marks catch the eye, just as in fiction. Another novelistic technique that is readily adaptable to nonfiction is the question-and-answer form—especially successful in courtroom scenes. Many readers responded enthusiastically and asked for more "Q & A" in a follow-up book. Here's an example of how it worked for the Scarsdale Diet, as well as in all my diet books:

Q. I've heard that sex exertion uses up more calories than anything else; is that true?
A. Enjoy yourself, but if you're overweight, don't expect to get thin through sex alone. Sex is fine, but afterward if you eat a small apple, all the calories are back!

In most nonfiction you can employ effective fiction elements throughout, from Anecdotes to Zest. You'll bring life and sparkle to otherwise prosaic nonfiction. You're more likely to gain acceptance and success rather than rejection and failure.

II. Make Sales Via the *Roundup* Route

What's the roundup route for you as a writer seeking to make sales? It's simple—you pick a provocative question, ask people for their answers, combine them in an article. Here's an example: A friend striving to sell her writing told me, "My neighbor is one of those crazies with a spending hangup. He drives a big luxury sedan that cost him over forty grand. But he detours six miles out of his way daily to avoid a 25-cent toll."

I suggested, "There's a roundup article idea. Make some phone calls, ask each person about spending blocks. Use the oddball answers for an article on the subject."

She called back a week later. "I had a ball writing the roundup piece. I found these kooks . . ."

. . . a woman who pays $65 each week to a fancy beauty salon, but does her own nails because, she said, "I won't spend more than five dollars for a manicure, as I did in the good old days."

291

. . . a man who spent a thousand dollars for a custom-tailored cashmere jacket but insisted, "I won't pay more than ten to fifteen dollars for a tie to go with it, that's my limit for a tie."

. . . a lady who laid out hundreds of dollars to serve a superlative dinner party, then admitted, "I wouldn't pay fifty cents for a lemon at the supermarket because that price is unconscionable. Guests who asked for martinis with a twist were peeved because I wouldn't supply a lemon."

The writer collected many more such amusing contradictions and sold the piece quickly. You can do the same: Imagine that you're the editor of a popular publication. Ask yourself as editor, "What provocative roundup question could produce answers that our readers would enjoy and talk about?" Make a list and go to work.

A hilarious roundup piece featured recently in a leading publication asked women, "What items do you carry in your handbag, and how much does the filled bag weigh?" Basic, isn't it?

Here are a few roundup thoughts off the top of my head:
- "Have you a recurring daydream as most people do? What is it?"
- "How did your first kiss happen?"
- "What was your worst cooking disaster?"

You can do better than that in taking time to fashion queries. Go to it. Think of subjects that would intrigue many people (editors are people). Make your calls. Chances are that there will be many roundup sales in your future.

III. Send a Questionnaire, Sell the Results

Employ the questionnaire to amass authoritative material to provide a further opportunity to sell your writing. Here's exactly how to go about it.

I was shaping a proposal for my next how-to book, *Your Key to Joy*. As I was sweating over the content, my partner-wife suggested, "Why don't you send out a questionnaire on the subject to potential readers? Their answers will prod your thinking, as has happened in the past." Great idea. We all need reminders.

You can do the same to help write articles and books that sell. Here's the questionnaire I sent to hundreds of names we gathered—friends, acquaintances, work contacts, and such others as a newspaper delivery man, plumber, and so on. Over 65 percent responded, a variety of ages and life styles. Their astonishingly thoughtful, intelligent answers produced valuable material for me, impressed my agent, and sharpened the appetites of publishers.

HOW TO GET THE GREATEST JOY EACH DAY— that's the theme of my new book, just started. I'm seeking brief answers to the following questions. *For your answers, you'll get a free inscribed book when published.*

1. How do you define "Joy"?
2. In your usual day, what percentage of time do you feel joy?
3. For you, what's the difference between JOY and HAPPINESS?
4. What gives you the most joy?
5. What would give *you* more joy than what's in your life now?
6. Do you think people can gain more joy if shown *how* step by step?

The answers clarified my thinking, gave me a running start on the proposal and manuscript. You can cash in similarly on your writing projects. Note these added vital tips: Keep the questionnaire to one sheet. (I left enough space for an answer under each question.) Offer a reward, such as an inscribed book. Include an addressed, stamped envelope. The replies will surprise and inspire you.

There's no question that you'll be on your way, better equipped to write a proposal and manuscript that will sell.

⦚ 59

WRITING TRUE-LIFE CRIME

BY WILLIAM K. BEAVER

THE TRUE-LIFE CRIME GENRE originated in the late 19th century and has grown in popularity ever since. After nearly forty true-life detective magazines were born and died, modern magazine and book publishers discovered that a solid audience exists for the true-life crime story. Books like *The Preppie Murder* or *The Stranger Beside Me* consistently find their way to the bestseller lists.

Writing about true-life crime is not for hack writers. Finding a fresh detective story inside a crime that has already been widely covered by the media requires the skills of a sleuth and the style of a novelist. Here are seven secrets for writing successful true-life crime articles.

1. **Find the perfect crime.** Recognizing the perfect crime for a true-life article eventually becomes an intuitive flash. Many of the detective magazines will accept a story about almost any crime, but to increase the chance of success, search for a crime with some notoriety and color to it.

Serial killings, mass murders, and terrorist-related murders are obvious choices, but smaller crimes can also provide excellent material. Consider the following:

I queried an editor concerning the murder of a bank teller during an armed robbery. The young woman's murder was of itself interesting enough for an article, but what gave it a special twist was the brutal way the crime was committed. The assailant had started for the door to make his escape when he suddenly turned, walked back to the desk under which the teller was hiding, pulled her out, and shot her.

In writing the true-life crime story, the writer must face the worst that human beings are capable of doing. Forgetting the article and its subject sometimes takes effort, especially when you must visualize the event as you write.

294

The perfect true-life crime article for any of the detective magazines and for most book publishers requires another element—superlative detective work on the part of investigators. The readers of true-life crime want to know how the police solved aspects of the case that had originally stumped them. Articles editorializing what the police did wrong are best left to investigative pieces.

The third aspect of the perfect crime involves knowing the conclusion of the story. Articles about unsolved crimes or ones in which the accused is found innocent usually do not satisfy or appeal to editors or readers. Most true-life crime buffs believe in law and order, so stories in which the accused were found guilty usually stand the best chance of being accepted.

2. **Develop the available information.** To begin research for an article, first unravel the basic facts of the story by finding all the information that is readily available. The best method is to photocopy newspaper or magazine articles about the particular crime and use them as your starting point.

If you failed to follow the story and keep newspaper clippings as it developed, you will need to visit libraries and possibly newspaper morgues. Depending on the library, indexes may be available in which the story is listed under the subject of homicides and murders, or under the name of the victim and/or assailant.

After you gather the available information, organize it into four categories: information about the victim; the suspects; information from the police and coroner; and details of the crime scene. Correlate all the information you have collected under one of the four columns, noting what information and details are missing.

3. **Interview other sources.** You now must find information that the press or the investigators did not reveal at the time of the crime. Start with the investigation team at the police department. Your task becomes difficult because you are trying to write about a crime on which the police have already been endlessly questioned.

You can gain the police's cooperation by emphasizing that you wish to write the article from their point of view: how did the investigators crack the case? Ask to speak with the police officer in charge of the original investigation, since he's the person with the most knowledge about the crime.

The key to a successful interview with the police, like any other interview, is to prepare carefully for it. Ask the officer to tell you about the case in his own words, recording the interview if he will permit it. As he speaks, listen for the facts you already have, and especially for new material not mentioned previously.

Don't be afraid to ask for any additional details the police have.

I have managed to obtain copies of police reports and been given access to a complete case file, which provided a wealth of information not usually given to the press.

Be sure to double-check the facts you obtained from newspaper and magazine articles. Ask the police officer about such important details as names, dates, and methods. One newspaper article about the murder of a young girl described the murder weapon as a nail file found lying on the bedroom floor, but the detective told me the actual weapon was a box-cutting knife found in the suspect's apartment.

4. **Search for "color."** Little details discovered during your research add immeasurably to the story. I will often go to the neighborhood of the crime scene to absorb the sights, the sounds, and the people.

If the police give you access to photographs of the crime scene, look for details like the time on the clock, the furnishings in the room, unusual photographs on the wall or table.

Ask the police if there was anything unusual about the investigation. In writing about one crime I discovered that the police tried using a psychic to find the murderer. The psychic described a scene that did not relate to the crime in question, but sounded like another crime that took place in another city.

Investigators called the police there and gave them the psychic's information. When I later wrote about the second murder, the investigators mentioned the psychic's tip (which I already knew about), and I was able to use the anecdote in my story.

The suspect is another source of color. Try to find small bits of information that show how the criminal was perceived by those around him who were unaware of his activities. These could be observations of strange behavior or awards for good behavior. In fact, once when I worked as a resumé and business writer, I found the resumé belonging to the first mass murderer I wrote about. The resumé listed four awards for exemplary performance at the hospital where he murdered seventeen patients.

5. Use fiction techniques to develop both suspense and the characters. Once you discover the color of the story and gather all the information, start to weave the elements into a tight, cohesive story. A good true-life crime article demands the same attention to setting, character, and pacing as a fictional story does.

As with all articles, the choice of the lead is vital. You must decide on the starting point from which to develop the story, and also how to work in all the details. The first true-life piece I tackled concerned a serial killer—a hospital orderly—who murdered more than fifty-four people. I had several options for the lead, but a thorough review of the material provided it for me. A coroner's office pathologist detected the smell of almonds while performing an autopsy on an accident victim who had died in the hospital. The smell of almonds sometimes indicates the presence of cyanide, but since the odor can be detected by only twenty per cent of the population, the pathologist ran a test for cyanide. The test came back positive, the pathologist had discovered a murder that later led to the arrest of the serial killer/orderly, and I had my lead.

Try to pace the piece by developing the setting so the reader can visualize as much as possible. Describe the scene of the crime, the actions of the investigators, and what is known about the victim. The most important detail, however, is to delay identification of the murderer until the last possible moment. Use suspense techniques, such as dead-end investigative leads, to build the story.

Use the same format as you would in writing fiction: the introduction, story buildup, the climax, and finally the resolution.

6. Know the required format. Most true-life crime articles use the same basic formats, but it's a good idea to write to the various magazines and request their writers' guidelines.

Ask about photographs. Does the magazine pay extra for the pictures or are they included—even expected—in the manuscript price?

Always submit the query and manuscript in professional form. Nothing will bring a rejection faster than sloppy presentation or obvious mistakes. Keep track of all source materials, including interviews and newspaper clippings. Most magazines will check your facts and will require copies of your material for their files. These will provide references in the event of a lawsuit.

7. **Be on the lookout for more sources and the perfect crime.** If you continue as a true-life crime writer, you must gain the confidence of your sources in the police department and the coroner's office, among others, in the same manner a newspaper journalist might. Respect their wishes.

I approached a police department for information about a crime I was writing about. Since I was unknown to them, their reception was guarded and aloof. But when they later saw how I treated the story, the next time I went back, they shared information with me that the newspaper did not have, including the film taken by a hidden camera during the bank robbery/murder.

If you are serious about writing true-life crime articles, join any legal groups in your area. I was invited to speak about the pursuit of Nazi war criminals for a discussion group that included two county coroners, several legal aides, and several investigators and attorneys, all of whom expressed a willingness to help me in the future.

The key to writing true-life crime centers on *information* and *presentation*. If you have enough information and polish your presentation, chances are you will be successful writing about the perfect crime.

60

SELL YOUR HIDDEN GOLD WITH A QUERY

BY TOM JENKINS

A ONE-PAGE QUERY LETTER is the first step in selling your article to a magazine or newspaper. No matter how well you write, you need to market your work; otherwise, it may remain hidden gold.

A written query shows you respect the editor's time—it can be answered at his or her convenience—and indicates your trust that the editor can judge your worth as a writer by reading your writing sample: the query letter.

A query letter should do the following: (1) grab interest; (2) summarize your idea; (3) show you can organize and write simply; (4) sketch your qualifications; and (5) make it easy for the editor to respond.

1. *Grab interest*

No one knows the magazine better than its editor, so in reading a query letter, how long does it take him to know if an article idea fits his publication? The first few words of your query, therefore, are crucial: You may not get another chance. It is obvious you need to grab his interest immediately and keep it throughout the letter. If you can do it in the query, the editor will know you can probably do it in the article you are proposing.

The opener should be brief, arouse a bit of curiosity, and at times suggest a point of view.

Bamboozlement. That was the cry of an English teacher recently as advertising copy writing, a favorite target of the ignorant, became the subject of attack.

This was the opener of my query for an article intending to show the effectiveness of written advertising copy. Acknowledging the flaws and gimmickry of "adblat," I went on to give examples of good advertising copy. The result was an article that appeared in a local newspaper.

Sometimes you can get attention with a single and accurate superlative: "The oldest living organism on earth is alive and well in California: the bristlecone pine." This query opener led to an article published in *Garden* magazine. That was ten years ago.

Since that time, horticulturists have learned that a drab and common shrub growing in the Southwest deserts is older: the creosote bush, one of which is believed to be 11,700 years old. I queried *Garden* again with an opener comparing the bristlecone with the creosote bush, and that led to an article that the magazine bought and published.

Sometimes you can arouse interest and give information at the same time, often in presenting a query about an unusual person. I came across a 52-year-old man whose past nervous condition had caused ulcerative colitis resulting in surgery to remove eight inches of his colon. My query to *Signs of the Times* opened with the following:

He rides a bicycle, bowls, flies an ultralight and skydives, but he also carries his own portable toilet with him everywhere. This is not a gag but the truth about a courageous man. Robert Kidwell is an ostomate.

The article was published under the title, "Faith Can Fly."

2. *Summarize your idea*

Your query letter should reflect your careful study of the readership, editorial needs, and style of the magazine to which you are writing. A query letter is specific; it is not a form letter sent to multiple publishers simultaneously, hoping for a lucky hit. You are not just proposing an article; you are proposing an article for a particular publication.

Your letter should give an overview of your topic and treatment with just enough details to show the editor you not only know your material but also how to present it.

In a query to *Desert* magazine, I wrote:

Misunderstood, maligned, and condemned throughout the West, the nation's cleverest wild animal is a needed predator: the coyote.

With hair-trigger reflexes and superbly sensitive senses, the coyote's ability to adjust and survive in the wilds is uncanny. It can sprint 40 mph and cover 200 miles in a single day in search of food.

A social animal, attached to family and clan, the coyote has been undaunted by the growth of communities, suburban sprawl and compound 1080. Once concentrated almost entirely in the West, the coyote has turned up as far east as Maine, replacing the larger but less intelligent wolf as a wildlife predator.

The response was favorable, asking for the manuscript on speculation. The article appeared under the title, "The Controversial Predator."

Occasionally, a brief listing (but not a separate or complicated outline) in the body of the one-page query letter can give a structured overview some editors prefer. In a query to *Computer Decisions,* I suggested an article about how computerizing geographic data can save money for public utilities that depend upon large numbers of cumbersome, manually controlled maps.

The query included the following list:

With your approval, the article could be organized as follows:

1. Identify the basic problems of costly, non-integrated and outdated maps that are manually controlled by a gas, electric, telephone or water utility company.
2. Explain how integrating and automating the maps can save money.
3. Give the details of a particular public utility, probably a telephone company, that saves money by using this kind of map management.

The associate editor responded with handwritten comments on the query letter itself, and I wrote the manuscript accordingly. "Big Savings in Computer Management of Maps" appeared in the magazine six months later.

Usually, your article idea is presented—in a kind of extended summary—in the opener and throughout the entire letter. When I read a newspaper item about a local college professor involved in an excavation project in downtown Mexico City, I perked up. I arranged an appointment with him and was impressed, both by him and the article possibilities. My query opened as follows:

Beneath the busy streets of downtown Mexico City, another city is buried. It is the sacred center of an entire empire, including the Great Temple of Tenochtitlan of the Aztec people (circa 1521), a 15-story architectural marvel incongruously devoted to human sacrifice.

I went on to summarize the quest of the University of Colorado's Dr. David Carrasco and his students to accumulate a priceless archive of ritual findings for the college. The managing editor of *Westways* liked

301

the idea, but gave me the assignment only if I collected better photos than those I had submitted with the query. I did so, got an O.K., and the resulting article, "Digging Up a Dynasty," appeared in *Westways*.

3. *Show you can organize and write simply*

Organize your query letter in discrete but related parts, all contributing to the unity of your idea. Then say it simply. Don't try to impress an editor with multisyllabic words and elaborate phrases. Occasionally, you can use a quote to get attention and stress your point. In one query letter, I began with a two-word quote:

"Money walks."
This was the caption of a full-page photo in a national magazine. It was an Easter Seals advertisement showing a small boy, a polio victim, resting on his crutches and looking down at his dog at his side as the dog looked up at him.

The boy's desire to walk was depicted by the photo; the reader's opportunity to give money for research to help make his walking possible was conveyed by the two simple words. The photo by itself was incomplete; the copywriter's words made it complete. I added:

A picture isn't always worth a thousand words. No photo can do what the two words, "Money walks," can do. Those words grab more than the eyes. They grip the mind.
Such use of language is copywriting at its best.

This part of the query became part of the published article, entitled, "In Defense of Advertising Copywriting."

You can use plain words and write a query about a common subject:

It's a simple thing, really. It happens every year. In the fall, aspen leaves turn from green to gold. But the spectacle is stunning no matter how many times you've seen it.

This opener to my query to *Travel & Leisure* became part of the first paragraph of the article as published. The piece described a one-day aspen-viewing trip in the high country of Colorado. After one of the editors made some helpful suggestions, I included side roads, places to eat, and practical advice on what to bring and wear.

4. *Sketch your qualifications*

An editor wants to know if you can handle the article you are proposing. Although you can demonstrate your control of language in the query letter, your past success in published articles, as well as your education and work experience, are reasonable indicators of your ability to deal with a chosen subject.

Indicate your qualifications in the query. You can list them or combine the information with your proposed topic in the same paragraph. In a query that proposed a piece about an unorthodox inventor, I wrote as follows:

Frederick Fisher has built a prototype for a solar-powered crematorium. Yes, a device to make after-the-fact use of the same sun that gave life.

This kind of irony fits in with other articles I have written about paradox and the oddities of human nature. They include an acre of coffins, an automobile with a 1937 license plate parked in a driveway, untouched for 32 years, and a freelance cartoonist who draws 60 cartoons a week for 60 different newspapers with no written contract for payment.

The article, entitled "Burn Me Up," was accepted and appeared in an alternative newsweekly, *Westword*.

If you have not published anything yet and therefore have no "official" publishing credentials, let your choice of an appropriate idea targeted to a particular magazine contribute to your credibility as a writer. Refer to whatever applicable background you have as a worker, researcher, traveler, collector, hobbyist, or adventurer. Remember that your credentials also encompass your imagination, creativity, and intuitive powers. Be alert and observe carefully. You will find article ideas everywhere. An example: An item on a televised news broadcast about a missing railroad train engine caught my interest. I drove to the search site and became even more interested. This led me to the library and an eventual query:

On a proverbial dark and stormy night in 1878, Kiowa Creek flooded, washing out bridges and sending a Kansas-Pacific railroad train into the raging waters. Afterward, train cars were found, some smashed and almost entirely buried in the sandy creekbed.

But the locomotive was never recovered.

Today, 100 years later, a search is taking place.

I went on to tell about the excited people behind the search, including novelist Clive Cussler *(Raise the Titanic)*. The query to *True West* brought a go-ahead. I sent in the article and two weeks later a check came in the mail.

5. *Make it easy for the editor to respond*

It's an old but valid story. Always include an SASE or a self-addressed postcard for the editor who may not want to send a letter back to you. What could be simpler than a self-addressed postcard? You can even type on the reverse of it: Yes _____ No _____ Deadline _____ Photos preferred _____. Or variations of this. All the editor needs to do is make a check mark or two and perhaps indicate a word count. Nothing to dictate or write, no letter or envelope to type, and no stamping or metering. The editor will appreciate your thoughtfulness and assume you are organized and considerate.

I am not without my share of rejections; who isn't? It is unlikely that any of us can be 100 percent efficient in free-lance letter queries, but with practice you can come close. If you can query successfully, you will become a published writer.

There is no shortcut. It isn't an easy process, but it is a workable one. You need to know as much as you can about the publication you are querying. You need to know what articles it has published during the past year; you need to study them. Then you can write a query letter that will reveal your hidden gold.

❚ 61

RESEARCH TIPS TO HELP YOU WRITE

BY ALDEN TODD

IT HARDLY NEEDS stating that research is essential to good writing, because our words must convey authenticity, accuracy, and precision if we want readers to give us their confidence. This is true both in fiction and in non-fiction. Carelessness in research can lead to all kinds of embarrassments—misplaced dates, incorrect names, impossible meetings, and so on. We must, therefore, lay a solid groundwork of carefully researched facts for your writing, and sometimes this process requires considerably more time than the writing itself. The following tips can be helpful in improving and speeding the research that underpins good writing.

1. *Thinking through a research plan.* In doing research for writing, the beginner often makes the mistake of rushing to the first possible source of information that comes to mind, instead of considering several possibilities and then choosing the best order to follow. This order can be written down as a research plan and revised as work progresses.

In researching history, biography, and events of the recent past, particularly when looking for material in written form, a writer can get good results by playing detective and asking these questions:

Who would know? Who could care? Who would care enough to have it in print? The answers can often lead directly to the printed matter or to the people you'll need to interview.

Thinking through your plan of research may save you an hour or day, or even longer. Too much time is often spent in hunting for the written materials that might be spent more productively in actually doing the research. An important element in research skills lies in getting one's hands on the right material fast. Therefore, the writer whose work is based on solid research and who wants to be most productive should learn everything possible about the available reference books and periodicals, the local libraries, and what specialists to ask for the necessary information.

2. *Finding the right library.* It is natural to turn to the town or city public library as the first source of resource material. Because it must serve the entire community, the public library generally holds a much larger collection of reference books and other materials than the ordinary card holder realizes. So it is always a first good step to find out what standard reference works your public library has. In many places, counties have organized interlibrary loan systems; the local staff can tell you which cooperating public library can supply the books you need.

Bear in mind that the biggest library in your community is not always the best for your purposes. If your subject is art, you care only about the depth of its art reference collection. In fact, the small, specialized library often has a far better collection for your specific purpose than the large public library does. It is usually less crowded and staff members are more likely to know the collection thoroughly. The same is true of a departmental library of a large university system.

To find out about special libraries near you, ask the reference librarians whether they have a local or regional directory of the Special Libraries Association (SLA). Such directories are compiled for many metropolitan regions of the country for interlibrary loans and job placement. Librarians usually keep their SLA Directory behind the desk and show it only on request. The local directory of special libraries in law firms, medical centers, social work agencies, businesses, clubs, and many other places can be of great help to the writer. If the local SLA Directory is not available, ask for the national library directory and look in it for all the libraries in your area.

Writers often ask whether a person not connected with a company, professional school, or organization that maintains its own library can gain admission to it. In every case, I have found that if one asks permission to use such a library for a special purpose, such as writing an article, the librarians have been friendly and cooperative. Do not be timid: Special libraries can give you more help per hour spent in research than the large general library.

In localities where there is a college library, it is worth exploring the possibility of using that collection—either through a friend with a college connection or perhaps under a program that permits local residents to use the library for a fee. And within many universities, one often finds subsidiary libraries on special subjects (e.g. medicine, law, business, astronomy) in different parts of the campus, each with its own admission policies.

3. *Finding reference books.* The best way to find if there are standard reference books on your subject is to consult an experienced professional librarian acquainted with your field, if possible in a special library devoted to that field. Do not waste time browsing through reference book shelves in the hope of finding what you want. It's much more efficient to find people who know their collections, then state precisely what you want to find out, and ask for reference books that will help you.

Of course, you can start out by looking in the library catalogue under various subject headings to see which books the library carries on your subject. You may find a dozen books that are useful, or you may draw a blank. It's a matter of how broad or narrow your subject is, and how detailed the subject categorizing is.

The standard directory of reference book titles is the *Guide to Reference Books,* issued by the American Library Association and revised regularly. This is a comprehensive, 1,000-page, two-column work containing brief descriptions of books on all kinds of subjects. An experienced librarian can help you find the headings and pages relevant to your topic. It is worth the time of any serious researcher/writer to become generally familiar with the contents and organization of this valuable sourcebook.

A particularly useful and inexpensive guide to reference books that writers would do well to acquire for themselves is the paperbound *Reference Books: a Brief Guide,* by Bell and Swidan, published by the Enoch Pratt Free Library (400 Cathedral Street, Baltimore, MD 21201). This is the best low-price guide to reference works that I know, and it has been kept up to date by dedicated editors who are professional librarians.

One fast method of making at least a preliminary choice of books to consult on much-explored subjects is to look at the brief bibliographies that are appended to articles in major encyclopedias, such as *Encyclopedia Britannica.* You might not otherwise know where to begin among the many books that have been written on such subjects as George Washington or heart disease. Also, the sources suggested in the encyclopedia articles have passed the scrutiny of specialists and are authoritative.

Another useful reference work for your research is *Subject Guide to Books in Print,* an annual that lists more than 600,000 book titles currently in print and available from U.S. publishers. They are indexed with cross references under 63,500 subject headings. Here you can find all U.S. books in print on a particular subject. A companion guide is *Paperbound Books in Print,* which lists current books by title, author, and subject. Subject headings are not as numerous as in the subject guide to hardcover books, so within the more than 100 listed subject-areas, you must search for suitable titles.

Finally, the *Guide to American Directories* will tell you whether there is a directory in your field that would help you in your research.

4. *Finding periodical articles.* Most libraries subscribe to the *Readers' Guide to Periodical Literature,* which indexes by author and subject the articles published in about 200 periodicals. But for a comprehensive index of subjects published in other periodicals, academic publications, and learned society journals, the *Readers' Guide* is not sufficient, because it mainly indexes articles in general circulation magazines and covers relatively few others. To find such specialized articles, the researcher/writer should consult one or more other indexes that cover specialized magazines and journals. Examples are *Applied Science & Technology Index, Art Index, Business Periodicals Index, Education Index, Index to Legal Periodicals,* and the like. Ask a professional reference librarian what specialized periodical indexes are available, and you will discover how much depth they add to your research.

Note: You may have to visit a special library to locate some of these indexes as well as the back issues of periodicals to which they refer.

5. *Finding specialists and people who know.* There is, of course, more to research than turning to what others have written. Much that the writer wants to find out has not been put on paper, so he must frequently locate experts who can be interviewed, whether in a face-to-face meeting, by telephone, or by letter. It all depends on how accessible the expert is. As a writer you should, however, always remain a bit

skeptical, remembering that what you learn from someone else may only be that person's version or opinion of a past event and should be subject to the same critical scrutiny as that with which you approach a book or article.

One very handy way to find experts and specialists in all parts of the country is to use the *Encyclopedia of Associations,* which can be found in good reference—and sometimes business—libraries. The 1987 edition contains information on more than 23,000 national and international organizations operating in the U.S., including hobby clubs, professional societies, trade associations, labor unions—in fact, every sort of association in which members have a common purpose. Each entry in this multi-volume encyclopedia includes an association's address, purpose, activities, executive officers, and the titles and frequencies of publications. By writing or calling the association headquarters, you can locate a chapter or individual members in your city or region, and call on them for information in their special field.

Another way to find people with a special knowledge in a different part of the country is to consult *Editor & Publisher International Yearbook,* an annual directory of the daily and weekly newspapers of North America. For daily newspapers, it lists the editors and specialized reporters in various departments—music, sports, gardening, theater, and others. There is also the newspaper library, which contains clippings and memos about important happenings in the locality. I have called on newspaper editors and reporters several times in the course of my research and have always found them cordial and helpful.

6. *Using public relations sources.* Public relations professionals can be of great help to the researcher and writer. Their offices go under various names—public relations, PR, publicity, public information (the term used in government), press relations, and, in embassies, press attaché. Whatever the title, these are people whose job it is to supply information to the press and public on behalf of an organization, institution, or individual.

In recent years, the PR function has become so important in the U.S. that the person best equipped to supply information about an institution is often the PR director—not the president or chief executive officer. But no one seeking information from a PR source should park his critical faculties at the door. Researchers should be as careful in accepting what PR professionals tell them as they would about statements read in a journal article or a book. Similarly, one must be cautious and critical dealing with the public information officer of a university, government agency, manufacturing company, or airline. It is the researcher's job to separate the factual and valid from what may be exaggerated or even untrue.

Writers may sometimes become so fascinated and engrossed in their research that they lose their sense of time and purpose. The writer must recognize that the final purpose is writing, and that research is a subsidiary though necessary means to reaching the final goal.

62

WRITING ABOUT SCIENCE

BY DON BANE

SCIENCE WRITING IS EXCITING, challenging, enjoyable, and profitable for freelance writers. Freelancers who are curious, who will do the necessary research, and have sharpened their skills will find rewards in many places, not just science magazines.

Scientists and engineers do wonderful, creative work—discover new sources of energy and aim for the planets, for example. And I am a science writer; I cover scientists and their work for an audience that is not science-oriented.

Science writers without Ph.D. degrees or specialized knowledge have an advantage: They don't know the lingo, so they cut it out of an article ruthlessly. What scientists do affects our lives every day. With developments in today's technology, we must know what is happening so we can make intelligent choices about our lives and our planet. A good science article will help readers understand the subject, speculate about the future, discuss the issues involved, and understand those issues.

But the prospect of writing a science piece may intimidate a writer who has never considered it before. How do you go about it?

First, *the idea:* Ideas for science articles can be found everywhere—in newspapers, on television, in the questions children ask: "Why don't clouds fall down?" "Why didn't the weatherman know it would rain today?"

News media report scientific advances in brief. A short article in a newspaper can be your springboard to an in-depth magazine article. It gives you the opportunity to bring all those daily accounts together, with the background and explanation that will put them in broader perspective. You tell not only *what* happened, but *why* and *how,* and what the consequences may be. The world is full of good science stories waiting to be told.

Now you have your idea. How do you begin your own research? The public library is a great place to start. An encyclopedia will provide a general description of the subject, the background against which to present your angle. Science books and journals may also prove useful.

Suppose you want to write an article about some aspect of space exploration. Do your basic research in the library, then turn to the people who explore space. NASA has public information offices within reach of your telephone or a 25-cent stamp. All their information is free, and in the public domain. If you can visit a NASA field center, you might arrange to interview people directly involved.

When you are interviewing and don't understand something your subject says, always ask for an explanation, and keep asking until you understand. It's better to ask and risk seeming dumb than to write something that's not accurate.

A note of caution: Scientists work hard. Most can't find enough hours in the day to do their research, solicit grants, write progress reports, attend meetings, etc. Don't waste their time or yours. Do your home- work. Be organized in advance. Have your questions ready so you can conduct your interview efficiently. Say thanks and leave. Always write a short thank-you note to the person you've interviewed.

Once you have done enough research to know where your story is headed, it's time to query an editor. You must be familiar with the magazine you want to write for. If one editor says, "No thanks," don't give up.

One of my good science markets was an airline inflight magazine. Many of its business travelers worked in the space industry; many who didn't would be interested enough, the editors believed, to read 2,000 words between New York and Los Angeles, or Boston and Chicago.

That's the foundation. Now, how do you build the walls?

The chapter about science writing in William Zinsser's book, *On Writing Well,* should be required reading. He lays out the structure of a good science article, with superb examples. He says you must start with the single fact your reader needs to know to understand everything else in your article. He compares the structure of the science article to an inverted pyramid. The initial absolutely necessary fact goes first, at the bottom. The second fact broadens the pyramid, and the third broadens it still further. The piece that builds upon one simple fact and progresses outward and upward will finally lead the reader to the main point: the significance of the discovery and speculation on what it holds for the future.

When you sit down to write, remember: Editors (and, I believe, readers) love anecdotes. Scientists are human and often humorous. A researcher's struggle to make a discovery, complete with false starts and wrong turns, will be a bigger hit than his chemical formula.

In one piece I wrote, I told the story of a group of scientists who worked in the hills near Malibu, California. A brush fire broke out and swept toward them. They kept working, and finally escaped with their equipment only yards ahead of the flames and deputy sheriffs who swore to jail them for disobeying the evacuation order. Write about people—readers understand people.

Editors and readers love analogies, metaphors and similes. Complex ideas *can* be expressed simply.

For example, astronomical distances boggle my mind: The nearest star, beyond the sun, is something like 26 trillion miles away.

An astronomer helped me this way: "Let's say the sun is a grapefruit in Los Angeles," he said. "At that scale, the Earth would be a grain of sand a few hundred feet away . . . The next star is another grapefruit— in Chicago." That seemed clear enough, something I could relate to.

Or consider this:

The sun is a huge, rotating dynamo. Like any electric motor, it has a magnetic field. Tiny bits of atoms escape from the sun, some slowly, others near the speed of light, and race along the magnetic field lines. As the sun turns, it tangles the lines and the particles jump from one to another and back. The motions are so complex, physicists have difficulty studying them or explaining the process, even to each other.

Here's where science writing gets to be fun: A drive on the freeway provides a good analogy for the complicated motions of those particles in space. Look carefully as you drive: One group of cars moves slowly. Soon others overtake them. Faster cars weave from one lane to another and back, between the slower ones. That's precisely how those particles from the sun behave.

That's an analogy that everyone can grasp, and that's what you must strive for when you write about science.

Science writers must always describe complex concepts in terms readers can understand. That calls for simile, metaphor, word pictures. Sometimes, even when you asked all the right questions and thought you understood, you'll hit a wall while you're writing: Ask youself, "Do I have the important points, or am I grasping at an irrelevant straw just because I understand it?" When you find that is so, retrench. Do more research. Go back to your source. "Is this correct?" Scientists are friendly and helpful. They want you to get it right so others will understand it.

Good writing techniques help: Use strong action verbs. The active voice will strengthen and clarify your sentences. Use it and avoid the passive. Scientists overuse the passive voice. They claim the active voice makes them seem conceited. (It doesn't, but that's the prevailing idea.) But don't follow their example. The passive voice uses unnecessary words, is hard to read, and leaves readers wondering who did what to whom. The active voice will help your piece gallop along.

Search for the precise word and phrase. Make punctuation and grammar work for you. Use every tool at your command to help your readers understand and to drive your story forward.

Try to breathe some life into inanimate objects. Give a computer, a spacecraft, a laboratory instrument character, and transmit those traits to the reader. Scientists do it all the time. They say, "The computer told me," or, "I think the data's trying to tell us something." You'll sweep a reader right along with you.

Science is a fascinating field and so vast that a writer can spend a career covering it and hardly touch the same topic twice.

Researching and writing science articles is demanding and exciting. An elegant description of how something works is enlightening to both reader and writer. You'll get tremendous satisfaction from writing a story that illuminates important scientific developments. You are an eyewitness to life's cutting edge and what makes the world work.

63

TRAVEL WRITING, ANYONE?

BY BOB O'SULLIVAN

TRAVEL WRITING is *not* fun, but getting paid for an article and being patted on the head and told what a clever person you are, now that *is* fun. And if you're going to write, the travel field has something going for it that's a real plus—traveling.

There are two basic markets for travel articles: newspapers and magazines. What follows is mostly about newspapers, which represent by far the larger market; however, the writing aspects apply to magazines, too.

Before you decide whether you want to try travel writing, it might be a good idea to consider just what it is.

1. Travel writing is the stuff in the travel sections of newspapers and magazines that keeps those big ads from smashing into each other.

2. Travel writing is what makes those travel sections attractive to the advertisers, offering them an almost pre-sold readership, people who are interested in travel.

3. Travel writing is what lets people write their travel expenses off their income taxes. However, some "travel writers" have been learning lately that the IRS expects them to make a sale once in a while.

4. Travel writing is any travel-related story an editor will accept. It could be about places, it could be humor, even a childhood reminiscence as long as it's bright enough to get an editor's attention.

I'm no expert in the field of travel—I'm just a writer who's currently specializing in travel—but I've been on enough trips and done enough writing about them to know that the concepts above are all correct.

Like every other kind of journalism, travel is a tough way to make a living. If you're writing professionally now, you probably know that; if you're not, consider yourself warned. "Writing for a living" is close to being an oxymoron, which, in case you don't know, is the combination of two words that tend to cancel each other out, like thunderous silence, English cuisine, bitter sweet, kindly editor, unbiased opinion. "Writing" and "making a living" just seem to argue with each other.

Thirty years ago I worked in the radio, television, and motion picture industries. Then, I married a lovely lady, and we had four children. Now, this is where the oxymoron comes in. The "living" I was making as a writer was slowly making it impossible for the six of us to keep on living.

I joined the Los Angeles County Sheriff's Department, and as I gradually moved up through the ranks, keeping bread on the table ceased to be a problem. After the kids were out of college, my wife and I started spending money on ourselves by doing what we'd wanted to do for years. We traveled.

As I approached the Department's mandatory retirement age, I started getting nervous. "Now what do we do?" I asked myself.

The question was answered by Dan Byrne, a boyhood friend, who had been both an editor for the *Los Angeles Times* and the boss of the Los Angeles Times Syndicate.

"You used to be a writer," he said. "Why don't you do some travel writing about some of your trips?"

"What's travel writing?" I asked. He told me and offered to edit my first few articles. I took him up on it.

"If you really want to succeed, you've got to find an area within the travel field that's not already crowded." Having been a dramatist 25 years earlier, I picked human interest and humor.

Thanks in no small part to his editorial tightening—that is, cutting out every word that didn't advance the story—my travel articles sold pretty well.

Travel is a multi-billion dollar, worldwide industry and there just might be a piece of all that money with your name on it. Either way, you'll increase the scope of your work, have more to write about, and a brand-new, world-sized market in which to sell what you write.

But, there are rules to the game, and there are a few things I've picked up that might help. Let me give you some of both.

1. First, you've got to travel, and you've pretty well got to like it.

2. Travel editors receive a lot of free-lance submissions, so you have to get the editor's attention quickly. If you haven't got it in your first five

lines, chances are you won't get it at all. If you start your piece on the Philippines with, "Imelda's shoes were burning . . ." you've probably got him for the next few lines, at least.

3. Be businesslike. Always send a brief letter with the article. Include your Social Security number. This assumes the editor's going to buy it and removes any doubt about whether you expect to be paid for it. (This is child psychology, but it's O.K. as long as the editors don't know we're using it on them.)

Though some writers' guides say the average editor will accept two mistakes per page, they really don't. They're just like the rest of the reading public: A mistake in the piece, factual or typographical, makes the reader doubt everything else in your article.

4. If you want unaccepted stories back, enclose a self-addressed, stamped envelope. But, I think the psychology that goes with the SASE is a bummer. I always send a Xerox copy, never an original manuscript, and a self-addressed postcard with, "Yes, I'll take it," "Not at this time," and "Comments" rubber stamped on it. Then, in the letter I say that I don't need the copy back but would appreciate the editor using the response card.

5. Never nag, argue with, go over the head of, or resubmit a story to an editor without his expressed permission.

6. Try to write tight. If your piece is fifteen hundred words, go through it again to see if you can chop a couple of hundred more words out.

My editor friend, Dan, on a good day, could edit *War and Peace* down to just *War.* In those beginning days, he also gave me a few tips that might be useful to you. I remember one conversation quite well.

"Forget about adjectives," he said. "I see you use 'very' a lot. Don't. 'Very' is a very, very weak adjective."

I was pretending that what he was telling me was old stuff, but I was sneaking a few notes.

"You taking notes?"

"Just doodling."

"Don't use 'cute' or unusual words. If you've got a narrative going and a word comes up that's cute or out of the ordinary, it'll yank the reader out of the story faster than a punch in the nose."

"Will you tell me something I don't know?" I pleaded, doodling "no

317

cute words." He ignored me and went on. "As Sam Johnson said, 'If you write a word or a phrase you particularly like, strike it out.' You have enough to fight without becoming a victim of your own ego."

"Does that about cover it, Dan?"

"No, it'll take you years to cover it." Then he told me about such things as "white space," "multiple submissions," "self-syndication," "collecting tear sheets," "keeping my sense of humor," "forgiving the mailman," and "not giving up." I'll try to make it brief.

What you leave out can be (you should pardon the expression) *very, very* important. Give the editor *white space*. Double-space your copy and make lots of paragraphs, use wide margins. If you're using a word processor, leave the right side ragged, that is, don't use the Right Justification key.

The first reader, the editor, needs all the help he can get, so try to make your pages easy to read and easy on the eyes.

When I first heard about multiple submissions I thought it meant not sending more than one article to the same editor at one time. What it really means is, some newspaper editors just don't want a piece that is also being sent elsewhere.

These days, most of them realize that multiple submissions are an absolute necessity if the writer is going to make a living. Hence, syndication. Bombeck, Baker, Royko, Dear Abby appear in hundreds of papers, here and abroad, and all the editors in their individual market areas know that they have an exclusive *only* in their particular market.

For the beginning travel writer, self-syndication is the answer. A former *Los Angeles Herald Examiner* travel editor advised me to send my work out in "flights of twenty-five to fifty." Advise each editor that you are offering only "first serial rights" in his or her area. To be on the safe side, figure a market area to be a hundred-and-fifty-mile radius. Be sure you don't submit it to more than one publication in that area. Breaking this rule is a mortal sin.

(Most magazines want rights for all of North America for one year. *The Washington Post, Wall Street Journal,* and *The New York Times* want national first publication rights and won't settle for anything less.)

Tear sheets, or the section of the paper containing your article, will be mailed to you almost automatically by most papers and magazines. Keep them. Xerox them. Work to get some, even if you have to sell a few of your first pieces to weekly newspapers for absolute minimum payment. Magazine travel editors will usually ask to see a few of your tear sheets before committing themselves on a projected story.

Magazine editors also prefer queries to finished stories. Writing an editor to ask how he or she would feel about reading a piece on a certain subject saves the magazine editor a lot of time, but *it's your time*.

If you find yourself hating the mailman or mail-lady (is that an oxymoron?), don't. Though they may dump a rejection slip or two on you in the beginning, they'll be your readers someday.

DON'T GIVE UP. If you're just expanding your options by travel writing, a lot of this is old stuff; you know how the world works. But if you're just starting out, don't be discouraged. If editors don't reply, or never send back your response cards, keep sending submissions until they get to feeling guilty about seeing your stationery so often and not reading your work.

Of course, it also helps if you can write.

64

PERSONALLY YOURS

BY SHIRLEY LUETH

WRITING PERSONAL-EXPERIENCE articles is an ideal way to see your work in print. No one can tell your story quite the way you can. Putting your experiences on paper for others to laugh at, cry over, react to, learn from, and enjoy is the way to success in this field. It requires no time-consuming research or ponderous plotting.

Topics for personal-experience articles are as varied as the people who write them. Many magazines are looking for interesting, unusual or unique first-person pieces. A fresh angle, and the use of dialogue, anecdotes and characterization are the necessary ingredients.

When you write a personal-experience article, total recall can be your best friend, as any idea, bit of dialogue, descriptive phrase, thought, smell, or feeling recorded can help bring your work to life. If you have been blessed with a photographic memory, you are way ahead of the game. For those of us who don't have this ability, keeping some type of journal to help us recall today what we thought and felt yesterday is essential.

The entries in my private journal are written spontaneously, without thought to spelling, grammar or punctuation. I think of it as a place where I can fumble and no one knows it. Often the entries are useless; at other times they are very valuable. My notation may be only one word, a sly turn of a familiar phrase, or it could be a single idea to be expanded upon later.

Many years ago, I wrote in my journal:

Why do children always get the chicken pox in November? Today I heard Amy wail as she stood by the window, looking out at the snow. . . . "Where is that Popsicle Man? Where is he? Doesn't he know I'm sick?"

When I read that entry fifteen years later, the memories of being caught up in a toddler twilight zone with an ill child came rushing back and resulted in the "The Popsicle Man Doesn't Come in November." One small paragraph sparked an entire chapter in my book *Bubble, Bubble, Toil and Trouble*. Without my journal, the chances of my ever writing that chapter would have been pretty slim.

I work with intimate family problems. This isn't easy and must be handled with the touch of a feather. I have to stop to wonder who might be hurt, and then back off if I feel I might offend someone. Unless you are willing to cause a rift in your family, don't make a relative the heavy in anything you write.

I try to follow these five rules:

1. Avoid being sarcastic, caustic, or downright mean. You can poke fun, but try to interject a believable and positive response at the same time. Suppose, for instance, you are writing about the sometimes atrocious table manners of a child. By describing your emotions when her head is bent in innocent prayer, you can take the edge off your irritation when she goes "aaack, aaack, aaack" every time someone passes her the green beans. In that way, you reveal two strong parental feelings— love and exasperation.

2. Be objective when writing about personal problems. If you use a "poor little me" attitude throughout the article, an editor will send it right back. However, a credible solution to the problem could guarantee a sale. Consider as a possible example an article written by a man who has just been passed over for a job as sales manager. The company has brought in an outsider, and to top it off, the new boss is a woman. The theme of the piece might go back into the man's childhood, when his mother was the controlling and dominant influence in the household. His determination never to let another woman dominate his life adds to his struggle in deciding whether he should quit his job or resign himself to the responsibilities of supporting his family. Changing jobs would add financial strain, possible relocation, and loss of substantial benefits. The writer could describe these conflicts and eventually the man's discovery that the new boss has brought some innovative ideas to the company. The article would end with an incident that triggers the man's decision to overcome his prejudice and stay.

3. If you have a personal grudge to settle, don't try to do it in print. It won't get by the first reader. Don't write a tirade against the local banker who wouldn't grant you a loan; it's better to show how you managed to survive in spite of him. Outlining the steps you took to

achieve this and showing how your life changed or didn't change will make a much more salable article. Lambasting the cold-hearted villain might be a good tension release for you, so go ahead and write it—but don't send it out for publication!

4. Never write only for your personal pleasure. It is virtually impossible to avoid using "I" in a personal-experience piece, but keep in mind that you are writing for readers who must be able to identify with your experience.

5. Don't allow anyone to censor what you have written before you send it off to a publisher. Trust your own judgment and professional integrity. If you consistently worry about the reactions of friends and family as you write, you'll be paralyzed with hang-ups. One negative bit of feedback from one of them could cause a manuscript that might have sold to end up back in the desk drawer. Nearly everyone is a literary critic, but not everyone is an editor. Friends and family don't buy articles; editors do.

With these guidelines in mind, I salt my books, columns, and lectures with real-life family situations, and pepper them with humor. When people ask if everything I write is the absolute truth, I simply smile and say "almost." I remember the day an editor called and said, "Who is this Auntie-dear you are writing about in *I Didn't Plan To Be a Witch*? Is she real?" I explained that Auntie-dear was actually a composite of every spinster aunt, condescending mother-in-law and nosey neighbor I had ever known or heard about. She had the characteristics of many but the soul of none, and rather than clutter up the book with a plethora of aunts, cousins, neighbors, and friends, I simply created Auntie-dear and gave her a fictitious place in our family. It is much easier for a reader to identify with one strong personality than several weak ones. And because Auntie-dear had never been and never would be "one" person, I could let her do anything she wanted without fear of retribution.

If you were to write an article about how shocked you were to discover that your son's roommate was Joan and not Joe, it might have developed into a harsh, judgmental piece. But if you face today's reality and give the article a light touch, it will be a piece readers can identify with. Or if, as soon as I reached home, I wrote the article about taking my teen-aged daughter shopping for the first formal, my tired feet and her seeming lack of appreciation would have been the focus of the whole piece. Instead, I let enough time elapse for me to relax and see the funny side, so when I wrote "How Important Is This Dance?" I was able to treat the incident in a lighthearted, humorous way. Mothers who read the piece identified with the experience I described, and felt better knowing they weren't alone in their confusion and exhaustion as a fifteen-year-old worked her way through ten stores for three solid hours trying on prom dresses. Not all personal-experience pieces are humorous. This is my style; yours could be much different.

Regional magazines make up one of the best markets for personal-experience writing. Editors at most of these publications welcome free lancers, but usually want a regional or local touch. For example, *Omaha Magazine of the Midlands* isn't likely to be too enthusiastic about the piece entitled "Sailing into the Bermuda Triangle" unless there's a Nebraska or Iowa sailor at the helm.

National magazines such as *Ladies' Home Journal, McCall's, Woman's Day, Redbook,* and *Capper's* are also receptive to personal-experience pieces. But a word of caution: If you are seeking national publication, don't get caught up in your own area and its colloquialisms. In one of my books, I used the word "Runza" to describe a favorite food and was surprised to get a phone call from my editor, who asked, "What in blazes is a Runza?" I hadn't done my homework and didn't realize that this was a Nebraska franchise and not available everywhere. We substituted pizza for Runza in the final draft.

Personal-experience writing is not for the timid. It is important to describe your own feelings with a frankness and candor that some people can't handle. Start your article with a blast. Show pain, frustration, fear, joy, triumph, or courage right from the beginning. If readers had a choice between an article that began, "Cancer is the greatest killer of mankind," or "I've never known such fear as I did the day my doctor told me I had cancer," most would choose the second, because they know they'll immediately get involved with the gut feelings of the writer.

Most editors prefer a proposal for an article—a query—to a completed manuscript. The article query should be limited to one or two pages; a lively, catchy title helps. In your proposal, list the questions you will answer, the problem you will solve; tell the editors exactly why your article would be significant, informative, or enjoyable to the readers of that magazine.

323

Editors want to satisfy their readers. If you are one of them, you know what you like to read; you know why you pick up a favorite magazine month after month, buy a book by a certain author, faithfully read a particular columnist: It is because the writer has taught you something, explored a problem, touched you emotionally, or made you laugh.

If you want to write personal-experience articles, speak up. Don't be afraid to admit that you are scared of failing; that you are vulnerable to a vice, or that you have a human frailty. Remember, there are thousands upon thousands of people who feel the way you do. But they aren't writers. You are. If you can put into words what those thousands are feeling, you have a good chance of seeing your name in print.

65

Having Fun Writing Humor

By Gene Perret

IRONICALLY, writing and selling humorous magazine pieces follows the classic "good news-bad news" joke form. The good news is that editors want good, funny pieces. "We need good humor," or "We're constantly searching for people who can write humor," editors say. The bad news is that humor is one of the most difficult things to sell to those same editors.

That contradiction may seem as if it were created by a humorist, but it is logical. It's because magazine editors are so selective in buying humor that they're constantly in need of it. If humor were easy to write and sell, they'd have plenty.

Why are the editors so selective? First of all, comedy is an elusive art form. It is to writing what jazz is to music. It's innovative, often rebellious and more often than not, will break tradition rather than follow it. The standard rules might not apply to a humorous piece. Therefore, it can confuse and frighten editors.

With a conventional article, the editor can analyze the form and structure and can grade each piece, calculating whether it will hold the reader's interest. With humor, those hard-and-fast rules become only guidelines. The editor can only guess how effective the article will be.

The basis of judgment changes, too. It's no longer whether the article is well written and well constructed. It's whether the article is entertaining or not. Most editors are less sure of themselves on that ground. Consequently, they're more hesitant about buying.

Secondly, comedy is very subjective. A joke or story is funny only to the person hearing it. That person forms a picture in the mind. If that picture is amusing, the reader laughs; if it isn't, he doesn't. One article can be funny to reader A and not funny to reader B. Since editors are first of all readers, you can see the confusion.

I asked one managing editor how she bought humor for her magazine.

She said, "We pass it around to the various editors. If they all laugh, we buy it." If they ALL laugh! That's formidable veto power for a humorist to face.

None of this should discourage the aspiring comedy writer, though. Rather, it should be encouraging for several reasons:

1) Since humor writing is admittedly difficult to sell, it automatically cuts down the competition. If it were easy, everybody would be doing it. Lighter pieces may be a way of reaching editors who have their favorite writers for the more conventional articles.

2) There is a demand for humor. Those magazines that use it often admit that it usually finishes very high in their reader surveys. People enjoy a chuckle. They like comedy in the movies, on TV, and in their reading. And good humor is not easy to find. The demand is high, and the supply is low—that's a situation that every free lancer dreams of.

3) There is probably less rewriting demanded on light pieces than any other type of writing. Why? Because, again, it's an area that is foreign to most editors. They can strengthen a traditional piece with suggestions for rewrites or restructuring, but can they make something funnier? They're writers or journalists and usually not humorists. They leave that fine tuning to the wits. Also, there is less rewriting requested because the piece was basically amusing. If it weren't, it would have been rejected sooner.

4) Comedy is a rewarding type of writing. It's cathartic for the writer as well as the reader. It helps you get many little peeves out of your system and onto the paper. Humor also forces you, by definition, to search out the fun in any topic. Any time I suggest a humor project to a fellow comedy writer, regardless of whether it's a touch project or not, whether it has an unmeetable deadline or not, I always say, "Have fun with it."

Earlier I noted that humor writing was like jazz. It has rules, as jazz does. Music has mathematical rules of scales and rhythms, but sometimes the creativity comes from violating or bending those precepts.

It's difficult to define rules for writing humor. There are almost as many different forms of the art as there are humorists. Erma Bombeck is different from Art Buchwald is different from Stephen Leacock is different from H. Allen Smith. To limit one's style of writing is to restrict the innovation that creates the fun.

One way to create a humorous style is to read and study those humorists you enjoy. Then try to duplicate their style. Within a short time you'll be adding a flair of your own because humor demands that . . . it needs spontaneity. Soon you'll see that their style combined with your variations has created a new and different style.

A humor writer needn't be afraid of experimentation. Comedy has to be unpredictable. If it weren't, it wouldn't be as funny. People don't laugh as hard at a story they've heard before. The surprise element is part of the humor. It's fun writing that says to you, "Try anything."

While there may be few if any rules about the writing of lighter pieces, there are some universal truths about comedy that may keep your humorous writing more salable.

1) The best humor is based on truth. I used to write funny lines for Phyllis Diller. It's hard to imagine anyone more outlandish or bizarre than Phyllis. Yet she would say to me often, "Honey, if the jokes aren't true, don't send them to me." She knew what she was talking about.

Any humor you attempt should be based on a truthful premise. Like Phyllis Diller, you may then distort that truth. You can bend it, twist it, exaggerate it, carry it to extremes—even unbelievable extremes. The basic truth on which it was based remains.

To illustrate, suppose we do a comedy piece on where all the socks go that we lose in the wash. That's basically a truthful premise. Every household has had one unmatched sock show up after the family wash is done. For some reason the other one never does return. From that basic truthful premise you might hypothesize in your article that it goes down through the earth to Australia. You might conjecture that creatures from outer space feed on single socks. You might even suppose that they run off to join some sort of "sock circus." These are all wild, preposterous fantasies, but based on a totally believable, relatively truthful premise.

That's much more effective comedically than any humor based on a false, manufactured premise. For instance, suppose you were to do a hilarious treatise based on the fact that all people who own black dogs as pets are grouches. You may have some funny, plausible stories about people who own black dogs, but the basic premise is flawed. You created the premise to support your funny stories. Whereas in the first instance, you created the outrageous tales based on a believable premise.

Your humor will generally be stronger if it's based on truth.

2) Recognizable humor is usually more fun for a reading audience. Earlier I said that humor is graphic. A joke or story generates a picture in each reader's or listener's mind. If the picture is amusing, they laugh. If they can see themselves in that picture, they laugh harder.

In my lectures I tell the audience that humor is already around them. For example, I say, "If you see a man open the car door for his wife, you know right away either the car is new or the wife is." That line gets a quick response because so many listeners recognize themselves in that scene. The wives see their husbands, and the husbands see themselves. It has a high recognizability factor.

I once read a statement attributed to some vaudeville comic. I don't remember his name, nor do I know if he was a successful comic. I hope he was, because he knew what he was talking about. He said, "A good joke is saying what everybody else is thinking, only you say it better."

The best humor writers look at commonplace, everyday events from a fresh, oblique angle. The topic may be commonplace; the humorist's view of it is original.

3) Remember your readers. Again, the humorist can only suggest. The humorist paints the picture in the reader's mind. The reader then passes judgment on whether that scene is funny or not. You'll score higher if you know what your readers want to see. You do that by knowing who your readers are. Editors admonish us time and time again to "read the magazine." It applies as much in writing humorous pieces as it does in any other writing.

Since humor writing is different from conventional article writing, it also has some slightly different rules for marketing.

"Query first" is almost an absolute in dealing with magazine editors. It's not in selling humor. Editors have told me that they don't want to see a query letter or a proposal for lighter pieces. Why? Because they tell the editor practically nothing about how funny the piece will be. One writer may do a piece about the socks missing from the family wash and make it a masterpiece. Another may use the same premise and never generate a snicker. The value of a humorous piece is the humor. Editors can't tell how funny it is until it's written. So, humor writing will have to be submitted on speculation. Do the piece and then send it to the editors. It's wise to select subjects that have wide appeal—premises that would be of interest to many magazines. As an example, a piece on some aspect of cooking could be sent to all of the family and women's magazines. Then one rejection isn't catastrophic. It just means typing up a new submission envelope.

Try writing humor. The editors claim they want it and need it. We all know the world certainly could use a few more chuckles.

66

How to Write a How-to That Sells

By Gail Luttman

ANY ACTIVITY THAT INTERESTS YOU—from canoeing to cooking to collecting Civil War relics to cutting your own hair—is a potential how-to article. And whether you are an expert or a novice, you are qualified to write about it.

Where to start

The most successful introductions to how-to pieces state a problem and then propose one or more possible solutions, perferably those relating to the seven basic human motivators.

Ego—Does your solution to the problem improve the way you look, the way you feel about yourself, your ability to relate to others?

Economy—Does it save money, protect the environment, improve quality without increasing cost?

Health—Does it give you more energy, promote safety practices, increase your psychological well-being?

Romance—Does it enhance sex appeal, create a cozy atmosphere, improve personal relationships?

Family—Does it entertain children, foster loyalty, help research family history?

Leisure—Does it enliven holiday activities, provide an engrossing hobby, help plan exciting vacations?

Individuality—Does the activity appeal to the universal desire for uniqueness by offering something new, different or better?

These motivators often overlap. A hobby may bring in income. Dieting may improve both health and self-image. An inexpensive bungalow of unusual construction may serve as a romantic retreat. The more motivators you appeal to, the greater interest you will generate in your how-to.

Moving on

After piquing the reader's interest, offer a brief explanation of what the activity involves, couched in enthusiastic words that inspire confidence. Can the skill be learned in five easy steps? Fifteen minutes a day? Does it require a special setting, or will a corner of the garage do? What special tools or materials are needed?

Rather than barrage readers at the beginning with a large number of tools or materials required, you may want to list them in a sidebar, a separate boxed-off article that accompanies the main story. Sidebars are a great way to include data or lengthy explanations without interrupting the narrative flow. Some editors favor articles with one, two, or even three sidebars if the article is very long or complex.

Definitions of unfamiliar terms might go into a vocabulary sidebar, especially when they are numerous; on the other hand, if special words are few or are easy to define, it is better to explain their meanings as you go along.

Whenever possible, describe new concepts by drawing a comparison with something familiar. In a piece about building stone walls, for example, a description of the proper consistency of mortar as "buttery" sparks instant recognition.

Complicated procedures don't seem quite as confusing when written up in short, uncomplicated sentences of the sort found in cookbooks. Explicitness also ensures clarity. Vague directions such as "measure out six to eight cups of water" or "cut two to three yards of string" leave the reader wondering which of the two stated amounts to use.

Clarity is also improved by separating general principles from specific procedures. If you are writing about how to build a chicken coop, for example, after the introductory remarks, explain how the layout and dimensions are established, then include some specific plans. In a how-to about cooking a Christmas goose, first describe how to roast the goose, then offer some favorite recipes. In that way you'll satisfy both the creative reader who likes to improvise and the less adventuresome reader who feels more comfortable with step-by-step instructions.

The final and best way to ensure clarity is with illustrations. The less commonplace the subject, the more important photographs and sketches become, and they are essential when dimensions are involved. In addition, the market is more receptive to illustrated how-tos. But don't despair if you are not an accomplished photographer or artist; many how-to magazines have illustrators who will enhance your article with clear, easy-to-follow illustrations.

Organization

The subject of a how-to usually dictates whether to organize the steps chronologically or to start with simple procedures and work toward difficult ones. If two steps are to be taken at the same time, it is important to make that clear. In bread baking, for instance, point out that yeast should be softening in warm water while the other ingredients are being measured.

Repetition can help or hinder reader understanding. Too much repetition causes readers to lose interest. In a short article, a brief reference to the original explanation is usually all that's needed. But if the article is very long or complex and the explanation is relatively short, repetition is better than asking readers to flip pages back to find the required information.

Include a timetable for each step to help readers gauge their progress. How long does concrete take to set? Eggs to hatch? Wine to ferment? Do varying conditions influence timing? Can or should any deliberate measures be taken to speed things up or slow them down? What specific signs might the reader watch for as the project nears completion?

Finally, what can go wrong? Think twice before including a separate how-not-to section or a trouble-shooting sidebar. Faced with a long list of things that can go wrong, a reader might understandably wonder whether the whole thing is worth the bother. But, in general, as long as a how-to is clearly written and well organized, it doesn't hurt to point out danger spots along the way.

Research, including interviews with appropriate experts, supplies background that adds depth and authority to how-tos, thereby increasing reader interest and credibility. It also helps a writer discover whether his experiences are typical or not. If not, avoid making sweeping or questionable generalizations.

When consulting authoritative sources, watch out for regional variations in the terms and methods you plan to describe, especially when you're writing for a national magazine. Mention chicken wire and a southerner is likely to picture what the westerner calls lifestock fencing. Talk about reupholstering a divan or davenport, and there are readers who won't realize you are discussing a couch or a sofa. Before you write your article, look up alternative terminology from other areas.

Voice

Of course, the target audience determines how to approach your subject. If you are describing a new weaving technique to experienced weavers, you may use standard terms freely without defining them. But you should define any words that are specific to the new technique and you should definitely explain why the new technique is worth learning.

It is your job as a how-to writer to make certain that all readers achieve the same level of information by the time they reach the heart of your piece, and to do it without talking down. You can manage this by pretending you are writing a detailed letter to an interested friend.

You will find your most effective how-to voice by writing your article as if you were addressing a particular person who engages you in especially lively conversation. If you can't think of anyone suitable, invent someone. By writing expressly for that single reader, real or fictitious, you will delight all your readers with the personal tone of your how-to.

67

BIG AS ALL OUTDOORS

BY CHARLES NICHOLSON

ARE YOU LOOKING FOR a market that publishes new and little-known writers every month and pays well? One with a constant demand for straight expository articles, personal essays, fiction, humor, and even poetry and cartoons? One where editors truly want you to succeed and often go out of their way to encourage a talented novice? If you are, the outdoor sports market might be for you.

Ask yourself these two questions first, and answer them honestly. One: Can you write clearly and concisely in one or more of the forms mentioned above? You don't have to be a Hemingway, but his sparse, action-packed prose is some of the best outdoor writing ever published. Two: Do you truly love the outdoors? You don't have to be a Daniel Boone, but you should have more than a passing interest in outdoor sports—fishing, camping, skiing, hiking, outdoor photography, boating, golf, tennis, or any one of the dozens of outdoor recreational activities. If you can answer yes to both these questions, however tentatively, then the outdoor sports market may be for you. Let's see how you go about breaking into it.

There is an irritating myth about outdoor writing that I want to debunk right now. An old friend with whom I've fished and camped since we were kids asked to read a piece I was working on for a national sports magazine. It was about fishing and had a humorous reference to Captain Ahab and Moby Dick.

"Nice story," he commented, "but do you think the kind of people who read that magazine will know who Moby Dick was?"

I could hardly believe that he would say that. It would be disastrous for a writer trying to break into the outdoors market to have such a misconception. Readers of sports magazines are educated, literate, affluent enough to indulge in one or more expensive hobbies—and they read! Big words and literary references won't confuse them (but may turn them off). Make your article easy to read; concentrate on big thoughts, not big words.

Before you sit down to write, you should take time to read Ernest Hemingway's *The Old Man and the Sea* and *Green Hills of Africa.* Then read "The Bear" and "Delta Autumn," from William Faulkner's *Go Down, Moses.* Get a good translation of Ivan Turgenev's *Sketches from a Hunter's Album,* and read all of it, paying special attention to the stories called "Kasyan from the Beautiful Lands" and "Forest and Steppe." Study the very different ways each of these master craftsmen evokes the beauty of nature. Then discover the common bonds that unite such diverse characters as Santiago and Kandisky and Sam Fathers and Kasyan. When you understand these things, you will have found the essence of all good outdoor writing.

Next, study the magazines. You can find a complete listing of those currently being published at any major library. Look in *IMS Directory of Publications* under the section headed "Outdoors" for a list of publications with addresses, editors' names, frequency of publication, and circulation. If the sheer volume of periodicals overwhelms you, or you want more detailed information about editorial requirements, look in the market section of this book under "Sports, Outdoors, Recreation" and "Fiction." Other outdoor writing opportunities can be found even in literary journals! One of my best outdoor stories was first published in a small journal, although I prefer to sell to magazines that pay more.

When you've found a few magazines that interest you, buy the current issues, if available on the newsstands, or write for sample issues, which you can usually get for a dollar or two, and sometimes free. Go to the library and read all the current and back issues of magazines you may not find for sale. Keep in mind that each outdoor magazine has its own distinctive personality. To get to know those you want to write for, read the editorials in such magazines as *Field & Stream, Sports Afield, Southern Outdoors,* and *Outdoor Life,* among others. Read the ads and the letters to the editors, too, to find out what's on readers' minds. I've come up with more than one good story idea from those sources.

Read the magazines from cover to cover. Compare the table of contents to the masthead so you will know which articles are staff written and which are free-lance. Generally, the larger magazines publish more staff-produced material than smaller ones, but I know of no outdoor sports magazine that does not use some free-lance material. Technical articles are most often done by staff writers, while the more general pieces (the most fun to write) are more open to free lancers. Also, be aware that most of these magazines have very strict taboos. Almost all of them will send you free writers' guidelines if you send an SASE.

Now you're ready to write. Choose a form—essay, fiction, etc.—you've already had some success with. If you're unpublished, choose the form you most enjoy reading. Pick a subject you know, and try to come up with a unique angle. At this point, it is probably best to write a clear, short query letter to the editor of your target magazine. Send a rough outline of your idea, your qualifications to do the piece, and clips of your published work. If you want an answer, don't forget the SASE.

An unpublished writer has little chance of getting the go-ahead on a query unless he has an extremely unusual idea and impressive credentials, but don't let that deter you.

I've sold unsolicited manuscripts to *Sports Afield* and *Southern Outdoors* in less time than it took me to sell one I had queried *Field & Stream* about. I find that my chances of making a sale are better now if I query, but if I have a piece I feel is right for a particular magazine, I don't hesitate to submit the completed manuscript without querying first. The key is to know the market, and the only way to do that is to read the magazines.

A well-written query or finished piece about a unique subject, or a common subject handled uniquely, is difficult for an editor to reject. You don't have to go fly fishing on the Nile; just think about what you like to do and how to tell about it in a way that will intrigue a jaded editor.

The how-to article is the mainstay of outdoors magazines, but many also devote space to fiction and humorous or thoughtful essays. Again the key is uniqueness and originality. Don't suggest a story about a weekend camping trip unless you were attacked by a bear or mountain lion while you were there. Go to a remote area and do something unusual—not necessarily exotic, just different. Shed new light on an old subject, and, if you can do it well, take pictures. Articles with quality photographs are always welcome, and magazines usually pay more for them than for straight text pieces.

Now that you have the idea, go ahead and write the article or story.

But remember two things: Make it timely, and keep it short. The outdoors field is seasonal, and most material is purchased six months to a year before publication. The outdoors magazines rarely publish anything over 2,500 words, and if it's a humorous piece, better keep it below 1,500 words or risk automatic rejection. The editors won't try to cut it and won't ask you to do it: It just doesn't work and will be rejected.

I cured my wordiness, and a few other problems, in an unusual way. I had received rejections for every conceivable reason but bad writing, when an editor at one of the top outdoor magazines suggested I find a local newspaper editor to write for. So I wrote our local weekly newspaper, included clips of my published work, and described an eclectic, outdoors-oriented column I wanted to write for them.

As a result, I now write that column, "Up the Creek," on a regular basis, and the experience has been invaluable. I am limited to 500 words, which is a darn short space to say anything worthwhile. You learn to choose your subject matter carefully and edit your work wisely. My writing has become tighter and is rejected much less frequently. It's the only writing course I've ever had, and they pay me for taking it.

The outdoor sports market isn't an easy one to write for, but outdoor sports magazines pay well—from 10¢ to $1 per word and up. They have a high turnover of writers, so they are always looking for new talent.

I was lucky enough to sell a story when I was sixteen, but after that, I didn't write anything for several years. Then I wrote a deer-hunting story, put it aside, and almost forgot about it. Over a year later, I took it out and rewrote it. From a market listing, I learned that *Sports Afield* sometimes buys fiction related to outdoor sports. I thought about the story for a while, rewrote the ending again, and finally typed a short cover letter and submitted my unsolicited manuscript to that magazine. And waited.

A month later, the business manager of *Sports Afield* called me. It seems I had not put my Social Security number on the manuscript, and they had to have it before they could issue my check! When I asked how much I would be paid, the figure quoted was so high I thought there had been a mistake. I couldn't believe my work could be worth that much, but they thought it was. Yours could be, too, in the outdoor sports market.

68

THE Q'S AND A'S OF INTERVIEWING

BY MARY CRESCENZO SIMONS

EVERY TIME YOU ASK a question, whether you are just chatting on the telephone, conversing at a party, or simply asking someone's opinion, you are conducting an interview. The key to successful interviewing is sincere interest and attentive listening, which encourage dialogue and elicit relevant responses. This attitude is an important part of your job as an interviewer, but your first task is preparation. Fortunately, interviewers have the opportunity to gather information, materials, and questions *before* they begin their interviews.

Although thorough preparation gives you a feeling of confidence, you must always expect the unexpected. Don't try to map out the exact direction of an interview; you can only *guide* the interviewee to some degree toward the answers you are looking for.

One of the first things to do is to research the interviewee and his area of expertise. If you do not know much about his field, resource material and knowledgeable individuals, friends, and associates can brief you on the vocabulary and basics. Evaluate the information and compare various perspectives.

At the library, you may find clippings and additional background data on the interviewee. Also, previously published articles or interviews by or about him or her often provide quotes you may wish to refer to, asking the interviewee to comment on an earlier statement in the context of the current situation. Such articles may also offer information about other aspects of a person's life to help you create a multi-faceted profile.

For an interview with wildlife artist Daniel Smith, I had material only on his artistic background, but in a hometown publication, I discovered that he was also a body builder. This led to my asking him during the interview how he balanced these two contrasting disciplines. He pointed out that they are actually similar: both require a strong sense of

338

individuality, ego, and a drive for perfection. Later, in writing the article, I was able to use this new insight to give me a distinctive angle.

As you acquire background information in the course of your research, you should begin to compile and organize your questions by topic or in chronological order, covering such areas as childhood, family life, work, achievements, associates, rivals, challenges, problems, leisure activities, and expectations.

Leave wide spaces on your paper between questions for on-the-spot notes. Writing down summarized versions of questions with key words underlined or highlighted will help you ask your questions in a spontaneous manner, producing a relaxed atmosphere and fuller responses. Allowing the interviewee to speak freely and informally will give you more information than you would otherwise elicit. Showing interest in and knowledge of the interviewee's field and being prepared to follow the direction the interviewee may pursue with extemporaneous questions will produce dividends for you.

If your questions are dull, predictable, and abstract, the answers will be, too. Ask questions that require more than yes-or-no answers. Investigative yet thoughtful questions will lead the interviewee to tell you what he really thinks and feels.

I like to begin an interview with a warm-up question, something general but imaginative, personal without being probing, a question that will trigger pleasant thoughts or memories and will put the interviewee in a reflective, responsive mood. In an interview I did with Tina Turner before her reemergence into the mainstream of the rock-and-roll scene, rather than asking her at the outset about her musical and personal breakup with Ike Turner, I asked her if she could remember how she felt the first time she saw Ike's band on stage, before she joined the group. Later, I asked about phases in her personal life, her current work on the road as a woman, alone and independent, and her future goals.

You can start an interview by asking how your subject got started in his career or profession. For an article called "Is There a Collector in the House?" I interviewed three art collectors and asked why and how they began collecting. What was the first object or item they collected? This led to a lively discussion (which I later drew on for my piece) on how a novice collector can begin, what to look for, and what cautions to take when making purchases.

Ask the interviewee what his or her typical day is like. Whether you are focusing on someone's career, personal experiences or a specific incident or event in his life, initial questions should not be threatening or too personal.

Sometimes the best bits of information surface when your pen—and the interviewee's guard—are down. Gems are often dropped in the course of informal conversation, while you are still settling down for your talk or after you've packed up your material and are about to leave. As I left the office of the president of a local junior college after a long interview, I noticed there was no name plate on his door, although his name as founder and president appeared on bronze plaques throughout the campus. When I mentioned this, he told me that when the school first opened, his then young son scribbled "President" on his father's nondescript door in a temporary building. He went on to say that he still had that scrawled sign, and just never had a permanent one made. I used the anecdote in the opening and ending of my article about him to illustrate the unpretentiousness of the man and his close family ties.

About halfway into an interview, you can introduce more probing questions, but remember, when moving into controversial areas ask your questions with confidence and genuine concern. This is the point at which you can ask the interviewee to explain something you've learned or heard about his work or personal life, something he may not have known had been disclosed, or something he may wish to refute. Going on to less sensitive matters, you can ask what is the most rewarding and most frustrating part of the interviewee's work.

While interviewing syndicated cartoonist Dave Simpson, I noted a great deal of marine paraphernalia decorating his office. He later told me that scuba diving and model shipbuilding were his hobbies. In the corner of the room, behind his desk, stood a whaling harpoon. I decided to use this visual clue as a theme in my title, "Dave Simpson: Political Angler," and in the opening and closing statements, relating them to his stinging cartoons.

The opening paragraph began:

In the corner of his cluttered office rests an old whaling harpoon, overlooking the drawing table behind his desk. He is outspoken, witty, younger than you'd imagine, and to the point.

The article ended with his quote and a last tie-in phrase:

340

"I've mellowed through the years. I don't like to hit them over the head anymore to make a point. I'd rather prick them with a pin." Or maybe a harpoon.

Well into this interview, I said, "Someone told me you can be difficult. As an artist myself, I can understand how people sometimes react to creative people. Why do you think this comment would be made about you?"

"Because I say what I think."

Because I shared a bit about myself, he was encouraged to elaborate on this point. Through this exchange, I learned of a hilarious run-in with his boss, his determination to follow his own convictions, and the complimentary as well as hateful mail he receives from readers.

As your interview draws to a close, you want to be sure you have asked all of your questions and that the interviewee feels you have covered what is important. Questions that look toward the future or reflect on an aspect of the person's work or life are good ways to conclude the interview. Two examples are: "Who influenced you most in your life?" and "If you weren't working in this profession, what do you think you might be doing?" That kind of question allows the interviewee to reveal his personality through his fears, hopes, mistakes, and achievements. Other good closing questions: "What is the most important thing in your life?" "What do you see yourself doing 20 years from now?" "Is there anything you wish I had asked you about?"

When and where you conduct your interviews can have an effect on the results. It should always be at a time and place convenient to the interviewee. My interview with the legendary, elderly blues singer John Lee Hooker took place, at his suggestion, at his hotel, the day *after* his concert, since he was obviously tired immediately after his show. After the interview, the band joined us, and I had the opportunity to chat with them about their road experiences with Hooker and to observe the group's interaction with their leader. Later, as I reorganized my notes, I was able to incorporate the band's perspectives and relationship in my profile.

If you cannot interview someone in person, a phone interview can provide adequate information for a full and detailed profile. One advantage of a phone interview is that you can take detailed notes without distracting the interviewee. Unfortunately, it is more difficult by phone to gauge when someone is finished speaking; without face-to-face contact, you miss out on body language and facial expressions.

In-person interviews add warmth and informality to a conversation. The interviewer can look the interviewee in the eye as well as watch for nonverbal cues. In the early stages of a well-known musician's career, he wore dark sunglasses (long before the style was remarketed as fashionable) during my interview with him. This guarded signal alerted me to tread lightly, at least at first, in order to make the artist feel more comfortable. He never removed the glasses, but he did respond with increasing ease as the interview progressed.

One of the disadvantages of an in-person interview is that you must rely less on your note reading and taking, in order to keep the interview conversational and the interviewee paying attention to you rather than to your materials.

Some simple do's and don'ts of interviewing may seem minor, but these hints will help to enhance your professionalism and manner of creating comfortable surroundings for both you and the interviewee.

- Bring a tape recorder to record quotes and conversation accurately. The tape will free you to note other informative details, like mannerisms and surroundings.

- If you make an incorrect statement, be confident enough to acknowledge the error, apologize, and go on.

- Be on time with the necessary materials (pens, pencils, tape recorders, extra tapes, batteries, extension cords, notes, etc.).

- Reword a question if it is not understood, or bring it up later, in a different manner.

- Don't chew gum, smoke, mumble, keep your eyes glued to your notes, talk too much about yourself, or go over your allotted time.

- Don't ask for information from the interviewee that you can find through research.

- In trying to contact a person for an interview, don't take no for an answer. "He doesn't do interviews" usually means you have to try another, more determined approach.

As a writer obtaining information, whether for research data, a personality profile, or a question-and-answer article/interview, mastering the art of interviewing will help you discover the desired information plus additional facts, opinions, and observations that will enhance your work.

POETRY

69

FINDING THE SUBJECT FOR YOUR POEM

BY JOYCE PESEROFF

POEMS EVOLVE IN MANY WAYS. Sometimes they spring from a striking image preserved in a notebook, sometimes from a bit of overheard conversation that teases and intrigues, or a story that demands to be told. A poem may arise, full of energy, driven by the propulsive rhythm of a sentence or a phrase. I have written from all of these possibilities, but most often I begin with the desire to write about a subject—spring, a Maine landscape, or a birthday party; or my aging uncle, or my aerobic exercise class. All of these subjects—whether ancient as a classic text or commonplace and contemporary—offer prospects for a poet writing today. Yet in half of these poems, the topic was not immediately obvious to me; in fact, I began by writing about some other subject entirely.

Because poetry involves unconscious as well as conscious processes—like an iceberg, nine-tenths of a poet's work may lie below the surface of the mind—a poem's true subject may not reveal itself at once. I begin a poem with real interest and excitement, only to bog down around the third stanza. Energy that first generated line after enjambed line packed with vivid language evaporates; the urgency with which I began the poem later eludes me. I file the drafts in a "wait" folder and, grumbling, turn to other work.

When this happens, I know that I need to give my psyche time, as well as space, to discover what the poem is really about. Rather than abandon such promising starts, I go back, willing to cut and rewrite. With patience and openness to new directions, I find the poem's true subject—perhaps a difficult or uncomfortable one, perhaps merely more complex than first imagined—revealed. Let me give three examples of how such rewriting—and rethinking—works.

The first problem is common to novice poets, but more experienced ones also need to recognize what I call the "runway" problem. These

343

poems start with a long, often expository, foreground before they really take off. Example: A baby, at six months, has her final DPT shot; she's furious with the nurse who administers the needle. I begin a poem about her infant rage and go on to write about the mass immunizations begun in the 1950s with Salk's discovery of the polio vaccine. As I continue, trying to link this bit of history to the baby, I realize that it is *my* childhood I want to write about: the mysteriousness of grownups invading that world of children; the second-grader who cried invisibly behind a screen set up by the public health nurse. Soon I realize that although the baby's response was the key to my memories, it doesn't belong in the poem. It was the "runway" for my own experiences to emerge, brought forward by images of shots and nurses common to both scenarios.

Perhaps I will use the discarded material somewhere else. Often enough, in order to preserve the integrity of a poem, a writer must cut the line or stanza that pleases her most, even—and sometimes especially—if it was the sentence that started her writing in the first place.

My second example involves a poem I had been thinking about for a long time. I wanted to describe an incident my mother had mentioned when we were both looking through a box of family photographs: When I was four years old, my friends' parents had threatened to boycott a birthday party because my mother had invited the son of our apartment building's only black family. After hearing a poet I esteem read new work about her upbringing in the old *de jure* segregated South, I was moved to write about this incident in New York City's *de facto* segregated housing projects.

I got stuck while describing the room full of children—the hats, the cake, the furniture too large for them. I decided to look more closely at the *characters* I had introduced, possibly adding some, while exploring their family relationships. Although I did use material about the black boy's sisters, this did not lead to a satisfying resolution to the poem.

After character, I examined the poem's *setting*. Was there more to say about the place where I grew up? I had written about that subject before and didn't want to repeat myself; images and the emotion arising from them must be freshly discovered, not ready-made. Otherwise, a poet finds what Yeats called "rhetoric" doing the work of the imagination.

Finally, I returned to the source of the poem—the box of photographs. When I *dramatized* this scene between me and my mother, I found I could use it to frame the poem. The party became a flashback, which I rewrote in the past tense.

What else was in that box of photographs? I developed a new series of *images:*

Julian

Halloween—a sulky gypsy pines
for her sister's store-bought costume,
disdaining yards of Mother's precious scarves
and clinking necklaces . . .
        two women

rigged in a tight suit and lacy tablecloth
(bridegroom and pregnant bride)
who knocked door to door for drinks,
    demanded bread,
upset our cupboard for two cans of soup . . .

The images forced me to recall my mother's fury at these begging women, the same vulgar parents who nearly ruined a child's party because they felt superior to blacks. More and more of the poem's emotion seemed to center not on the boy, Julian, but on my mother.

I added her presence to the poem's first lines and concluded with images of my mother alone, drinking coffee and working a crossword puzzle. The birthday party—original impulse for the poem—shrank from two stanzas to four lines. The theme of "Julian," I discovered through rewriting, was not segregation but isolation, and its subject not, after all, the title character.

This last example began as two separate poems, one about fall and the onset of winter, the other about my grandmother's death. A careful reader might immediately notice the affinity between these subjects, since the first is often used as a metaphor for the second:

October

September cooling to October
stops the throat with a doughy phlegm—
a hundred years ago "lung fever"
killed thousands, left the rest
to cabin fever—then, for whoever emerged
from that white chrysalis: spring.
Dying, my grandmother became a student
of migration, tallying species

345

at the hospital feeder. I almost believed
the evening grosbeak put on earth
to soothe her, and the V of geese a sign
of direction in adversity.

It was the image of "fever" in the first half of "October" that alerted me to its connection with the untitled poem about my grandmother. I cut all description from my "fall into winter" poem that didn't share references to disease. From the second poem, I eliminated all details of hospital routine except the ones that involved the natural world: the feeder and the flying birds. I linked these two poems through their shared imagery and in the process noticed that my subject had shifted subtly: Instead of an elegy, I had written a testament to a living woman's courage in the face of death.

These are three examples I was able to salvage from the "wait" file and place, when completed, in a manuscript. I have many more poems that still need work as I approach their true subject. It may take months for a poem's subject to become clear to me. Often, I have to distract my conscious mind so that the unconscious might do the work of association and identification. Here are some suggestions that may help both with their proper tasks:

1) Save all drafts; throw nothing out. The image you discarded ten pages ago may give you the one necessary clue to your subject. The way you broke a line may suggest new connections as it shifts the emphasis of your poem from one word to another. This is the reason word processors are not useful to poets, at least during composition: You'd have to stop and print each version as you write it, in order not to lose anything.

2) Don't hurry. A poem may take months, or years, to complete. And even then, you may have to put it aside for another month or year before you're sure it's finished.

3) Look carefully at any two poems you begin at the same time. They may hold themes in common and point to concerns below the surface of your words. Look for images that recur, or a turn of phrase you repeat. As in "October," sometimes what begins as two poems may end as one.

4) Be ruthless with cuts. The loveliest, vowel-filled line does a poem no good if it distracts from what playwrights call the "through-line"— the inevitable chain of action leading to a satisfying conclusion. Be sure

346

your poems begin at the beginning, and not several sentences before. Sacrifice your most cherished stanza if it is irrelevant to what your poem is about. Save it for the next poem—for, just as two poems may turn out to be halves of one long lyric, one draft may contain the impulse for two or more successful poems.

70

THE WRITER AS STARLING: ADVICE TO A YOUNG POET

BY ROBERT DANA

It is always a matter, my darling,
Of life or death, as I had forgotten. I wish
What I wished you before, but harder.

"The Writer," by Richard Wilbur

IN HIS POEM "The Writer," Richard Wilbur re-experiences, as he listens to his young daughter typing, the urgency we all felt as young writers to express our feelings toward experience. These feelings are, he suggests, "the great cargo" of our first poems. Wilbur also recalls the difficulty of trying to write well. Words, the poem goes on to say, come "Like a chain hauled over a gunwale." The image is that of drawing up by hand a heavy anchor from very deep water, a few iron links at a time, phrase by phrase, across a threshold.

But the images of the heavy cargo and hauled anchor in Wilbur's poem are very quickly replaced by the image of the writer as a bird, a common starling which has flown mistakenly into a room and must keep trying, failure after failure, until it finally makes a "smooth course for the right window/And . . . the world."

". . . I wish/What I wished you before, but harder," he says finally. What he's wished for his daughter earlier in the poem is "a lucky passage." A phrase that means, as I read it, both a stretch of writing so good it could not have been written without the cooperation of chance, and a writing life marked by fame and good fortune.

Most of the young poets I encounter around the country seem to have started out for a life of fame and good fortune pretty much like Wilbur's daughter, like most of us for that matter, equipped with little more than luck and a precious cargo of feelings. Many are genuinely talented. And most of them are in the process of finding out that the work of a

348

professional poet is both more difficult and more mysterious than they had supposed. Like the trapped starling in Wilbur's poem, they find themselves "humped and bloody" with battering the glass of the wrong windows, looking for a clear "passage."

There is, of course, a limit to what I, or anyone else, can do to help them. If you set up shop as a teacher of poetry writing, it does help to be a poet. Then you know firsthand what it is to batter against glass, to see a world you cannot reach, to grow desperate. You know that learning to write consistently well is, for most of us, a long process, marked by many failures. You know that talent is not enough.

Knowledge and skill are qualities young poets begin to acquire when luck falters and feelings prove common to everyone. Even our experiences prove, alas, to be not entirely unique—frost on the tall grass, the ride down the mountain, love in a burning building. A real knowledge of subject, and skill with the language, we come to see if we stick it out long enough, are exactly the qualities that create the "lucky passage," the poetry that stuns the reader into wakefulness.

In my experience as a teacher, I am always astonished by the fact that young poets don't seem to have read much, if any, poetry. They often seem to think, oddly enough, that being a writer means to be exempt from reading. But how can young writers become poets without knowing what poetry is? And how can they know what poetry is without experiencing, many times over, the work of the best poets in the language: Shakespeare, Keats, Wordsworth, Whitman, Dickinson, Yeats, and all the rest?

Poetry at its highest levels is an art akin to magic. But at its basic level it's a craft, skills passed on from master craftsman to journeyman to apprentice. From Whitman to Frost to Sylvia Plath and Gerald Stern and Robert Dana. I doubt that these same young poets think that being able to pound a nail in the wall so that they can hang up their coat makes them a carpenter, but they will try to write poetry without really knowing quite what it is.

On the other hand, those who generally know "a hawk from a handsaw" where poetry is concerned often don't know the names of the trees they walk under every day, or the names of birds, or the slightest thing about string-theory or cellular biology or Fabian socialism. They know a great deal about Chaucer and Whitman but nothing about solar winds or limestone or tender offers. The kind of knowledge they lack is not so much the knowledge of craft, as knowledge of a working world. Information.

In fact, the kind of information I'm talking about—precise, accurate, and concrete—is the basis of all good writing, whether poetry or prose. It's exactly the kind of information Robert Lowell refers to in his poem, "Epilogue": "Pray for the grace of accuracy/ . . . give/ to each figure in the photograph/ his living name." But, of course, to do this means to take the time to learn the names of the figures in the photograph, or the things of this world. And not only the names, but the nature of things, whether flowers or political movements, business deals or pathological states.

This means, probably, not only reading but studying. Studying not only those subjects we like, but those we think we dislike and avoid: sciences and mathematics; political science and history. It means collecting names and dates and stories. And when I speak of "study," I certainly don't mean to imply that school is the only place where these things can be learned. They can be learned anywhere. From a *National Geographic* magazine, or a book on nuclear war. As one of my favorite students used to say, "Hell, you can get an education free if you want one. It's called a library card." And much of what any writer knows, he or she learns from careful, repeated, firsthand observation.

The only thing perhaps more important to a writer than subject matter is language. "A poem is a machine made of words," William Carlos Williams liked to say. I think Williams knew that people would find the notion of the poem-as-machine not only unglamorous, but shocking and offensive. But he also knew that the act of writing poetry had to be de-frilled and demystified, had to be seen as an efficient and practical aspect of everyday life, if it were to have any place in modern, industrial America. Secondly, I think Williams is talking about language as a tool. Poems are machines; words, parts of the machine, each with its specific function; clutch, drive shaft, fan belt, air filter, turn signals. Some poems, like some machines, are poorly made. On its way to the final draft, the poem often breaks down. The poet's job is to fix it. Or build a better poem. For this he or she needs a vocabulary adequate to the needs of the poem, and command of grammar (in some cases even of *un*grammar).

It would be wonderful to be able to say, "Poems break down for the following three reasons: . . ." But poems, in fact, break down for every conceivable reason: The poet doesn't know and can't find out what his poem is about; his or her language is inadequate or inappropriate to the experience; the poet has failed to think through the necessary transitions from one part of the poem to another—one could go on almost endlessly. "A poem is never finished; it's just abandoned," Paul Valéry said. That's certainly been my experience. But the poem is revised many times before we call it finished or simply leave it behind.

"Revision is the name of the game," I tell young poets. "If you can't revise, you'll never become a good writer." James Dickey used to talk about revising a poem as many as 150 times, working on it sometimes just "to get that worked-on quality out of it," to get that feeling of inevitability into the language. For good poetry always bears that impress of "rightness" in its language, that sense that the words for this specific experience must be these words and no other.

Sometimes those words come to you freely in a moment of perfect and intense perception. I remember driving from Gainesville, Florida, to Saint Augustine one day in 1974, "a thin, viral mist fizzing the windshield." I suppose I'd been listening to this particular kind of rain making its particular kind of sound for several months by then. It was not the kind of rain you get in the Midwest or the Northeast or the West, and it did not beat on the windshield or even fog it. It "fizzed." And it was thin and raw, the kind that brings on sickness if you're exposed to it very long, the kind of rain common to the malarial tropics. And when the words came, I knew they were exactly right. What I did not know was that it would be seven years, and I would be far from Florida, before the poem would show up in which I would use them in a stanza in "Everything Else You Can Get You Take":

> No place we ever imagined
> we'd be. No sea's edge
> where a low wave sputters,
> ignites like a fuse, and races
> hissing along the shore.
> No thin, viral mist fizzing
> the windshield, gorges rising
> grey as China in the rain.

On the other hand, how many years had I been watching lightning before I saw that it wasn't all one color, that besides white and yellow, some of it cracked red, some green, and some violet, an observation I made use of in the opening lines of "Getting It Right":

> Lightning cracks its red
> and green and violet whips,
> or sets its white hooks
> deep into your soundest sleep,
> and you wake.

And I suppose there are many things and feelings for which I will never find the word that is the perfect match. But as a poet, as a writer, it is my job to keep searching for it.

In my experience, we rarely get many of the words right in a first draft or even the second. The machine coughs and sputters, and its turn signals don't work. It takes days, even weeks, and when we're young, sometimes months, maybe a year even, to get one poem right. For a while, maybe we just abandon poem after poem. But we either believe in the value of what we are doing enough to work, really work at it, acquiring all the necessary knowledge and skills, including the ability to revise, or we don't. If we do, we sometimes come through, finally, to the "lucky passage," the one Ezra Pound used to call a "vortex," the passage that draws into its center everything we know, and all our skill with the language and more, to produce a breathtaking, a dazzling literary moment. Perhaps something we didn't even know we knew.

This is the point at which poetry ceases to be an exercise of will and skill and approaches the condition of genuine magic, or what Wilbur in his poem calls luck. Teachers can teach, and students can learn subject matter and techniques of language. They can even invent them. And it's probably true that the more you know about something—sailing, daylilies, Nicaragua—the more authority your language will have. But no one can teach you how to transform a merely very good passage into an inspired one.

It's popular among writers and critics to say things like "this poet has earned his distinctive voice," or "her poem has not earned its difficult and brilliant conclusion." My quarrel is not with these statements as value judgments, necessarily, but with the word "earned." It has the effect of reducing the act of writing to a business transaction. As if by investing time and effort, the writer, like the banker or broker, were guaranteed the reward of profit or interest. As if writing a poem word by word, and line by line, were an act akin to saving coins in a piggy bank, and when you got enough of them you changed them into a five-dollar bill.

Do I need to say that good writing is not a matter of earnings in this sense even if it is a matter of work? Good writing is its own pleasure. And great writing stops our breath, perhaps precisely because it seems to leap effortlessly the boundaries marked by the sweaty hand, the chewed pencil, or the word processor. I'm with Wilbur, gentle reader. ". . . I wish/What I wished you before, but harder."

71

WHAT MAKES A POET? WHAT MAKES A POEM?

BY PHYLLIS HOGE THOMPSON

HOW CAN YOU TELL if you really are a poet? *Can* you tell?

I think there are three clear signs: One is that poets love poetry. They read a lot of it. When I open a magazine, I turn first to the poems. In my personal library, hundreds of slender volumes of poetry cram every other kind of book off the shelves.

The second sign is that the poet loves the sound, the *sounds,* of language—the "feel" of words on the tongue, the rhythms words fall into, and those pleasurable echoes called alliteration, assonance, consonance, and rhyme. (Not all poets agree that sound and meaning are equally important. I think they are.)

Love of the sound of language cannot be altogether separated from love of language itself. A poet delights in words, their meanings, and the ways the meanings of words have changed, and the bones of the language—grammar and syntax. A poet gets a kick out of syntax, is not put off by grammar, and is probably interested in the history of language, which is, after all, the poet's instrument, as the violin is the instrument of the violinist. I call the general love of language the third sign.

These identifying characteristics are not all there is to it, naturally, but I think that almost everyone who takes the game seriously has at least these three.

I am intentionally leaving out what the world in general quite probably thinks of as the poet's stock in trade, that is, an artistic and sensitive temperament. I don't believe in it.

Depth of feeling is what the poet shares with every human being. It is what makes poetry important in the lives of those who do not write it. But it is mastery of craftsmanship that distinguishes the poet. Achieving such mastery takes years. It's hard work, but it's not a burden. Poets need to know how poems are constructed. Otherwise the poet is not in control of the poem.

If a poet can figure out what's going on grammatically in his or her poem, he can figure out what's happening in another poet's work and what techniques are being used. Poets read poetry for pleasure, but also to discover new tools to help them with their own poetry writing.

Almost (*almost*) everything else the poet has to learn depends on practicing technique. I think poets should be so thoroughly versed in all forms and meters that they can easily use them in writing their poems. In this way, the poet can be "ready" whenever a poem turns up, ready to give it whatever form is right for it, able to feel what fits a particular idea—a rhymed quatrain or blank verse or free, unmetered lines. Though it is useful to learn the descriptive names and definitions for various poetic forms, it is not essential. Learning through practice to use all of the forms, traditional and contemporary, is hard but essential, and for me surpasses all other entertainments. For one thing, the more one practices writing poetry in various forms, the more the poet gets a very reliable feel for where a line should end.

By learning how to make a rhymed thought draw to a close, or move along naturally into the next line, a poet even learns how to end a line of free verse. Practicing poets confront hundreds of problems during practice, and what's more important, they learn how to solve them in their own individual, even idiosyncratic way, under the critical eye of the sternest of teachers—themselves.

When the poet has achieved a certain mastery of the craft, enough to have some control of it, the next critical step is to recognize a poem when it comes along. A peculiar excitement tells me when a poem is coming. Something breathes energy into me, gathers my emotions around a center. They come together, coalesce into a poem.

The excitement is started off by a particular experience or event or sound—say, a name, a word, a bowl of blue flowers, or even an old blanket. But the difference between simply noticing blanket or flowers and the poetic moment is that at the same time I am experiencing a significant feeling, a feeling that may have to do with someone else, say love or praise or sadness, and also with a whole range of similar moments in my past, a group of memories. My poetic response is to try

355

to recreate that present moment in a poem, and to gather into the moment whatever from the past illuminates that single feeling. The precise thing that initiated the feeling may disappear from the final poem; that doesn't matter. It has done its work. It has inspired the feeling.

Here is the instance I was reminded of by an old blanket, together with a print of a Madonna and Child. The print had disappeared from the poem by the time it was finished.

A Childhood

First snow had fallen.
Inside, cross-legged on the bare wood floor,
We faced one another.
Wrapped in warm blankets,
We talked all night.
There was no lamp. The moon
Filled the window and flooded the cold room
Moving slowly around the walls
And away by daybreak.

In half a century
I have been equally happy maybe five times.

You turned twelve in December.

I did not know why I wept all spring
Or what I longed for.

From *The Ghosts of Who We Were*, University of Illinois Press, 1986.

After you've convinced yourself that you're a poet, all you have to do for the rest of your life is to follow your natural bent: You write poems and you soak in everything you come across in the language you make poems from. Much of it comes easily—origins of words, for instance, or the way one word is related to a word in another language. And since poets are addicted to dictionaries, these fascinating discoveries are exciting and stimulating.

Writing poetry takes time. If life—business, family, illness, study—presses in, demanding all the time a person has, there may be no time then for the poems to get written. But that doesn't mean they're not still there, waiting. Years may pass before the time comes. It's never too late, if the poems are really there.

Afterword

I can't recommend practice too strongly. Through all the years I didn't have enough hours in a day to write real poems, but I did have time to practice, until rhythms and forms pulsed in my veins.

Ten suggestions for practice in iambic pentameter

1. Write ten lines of blank verse.
2. Write ten lines of end-stopped blank verse.
3. Write ten lines of runover blank verse.
4. Change the position of the caesura in each line.
5. Add one syllable to each line.
6. Add two syllables to each line in different feet.
7. Rhyme the lines *abba*.
8. Rhyme the lines *abab*.
9. Rhyme the lines *ababcdcdefefgg* (sonnet).
10. Go through the same processes for iambic tetrameter (to get a feel for how pentameter differs).

If you can't think of anything to write about, take any—and I mean *any*—prose your eye lights on and use it as a basis for the exercise. For example, I took this totally at random from a book ad and reworked it:

"These brief, radiant essays discuss sixty key books that are basic documents in the history of the imagination."

> These brief and shining essays now discuss
> The sixty basic books that are for us,
> And for the world, the documental key
> Of the imagination's history.

72

THE POET WITHIN YOU

BY DAVID KIRBY

I FIGURE POETRY is a way of beating the odds. The world is never going to give you everything you want, so why not look elsewhere? In a wonderful book called *The Crisis of Creativity* (now regrettably out of print) by George Seidel, it is stated that the artist will always have one thing no one else can have: a life within a life.

And that's only the start. If you have talent and luck and you work like a son of a gun, you might even end up, as the poet John Berryman says, adding to "the store of available reality."

But at least you can have a life within a life, no matter who you are. Not all of us can be great poets. If that were so, the Nobel Prize would be in every box of breakfast cereal—you'd get up, write your poem for the day, and collect your prize. But every literate person has it in him- or herself to be a good poet. Indeed, I have wonderful news for you— each of us is a poet already, or at least we used to be. It's just that most of us have gone into early retirement.

Seriously, when interviewers ask the marvelously gifted William Stafford when he started to write poetry, Stafford often replies, "When did you stop?" All children put words together imaginatively; just talk to one and you'll see what I mean. But then they grow up and enter the world of bills and backaches. They start chasing that dollar, and suddenly their time is limited. Poetry is usually the first thing to go. People get so busy with their lives that they forget to have a life within a life. But you have a life anyway, right? So forget about it for a minute—it'll still be there when you come back—and let's talk about the poet within you.

The first thing you need to do is forget that all poets are supposed to be erratic or unstable. Flaubert was quite clear on this point. He said, "Be regular and orderly in your life, like a bourgeois, so that you may be violent and original in your work." In other words, there's no point in sapping your resources by pursuing some phony "artistic" lifestyle. First, the outer person has to be calm and self-disciplined; only then can the inner one be truly spontaneous.

And that means getting organized. Here are a few rules I use to make my life as orderly and bourgeois as possible, so that the poet within me can be as wild as he wants to be.

1) *Start small.* Most beginning writers tackle the big themes: love, death, the meaning of life. But don't we already know everything there is to know about these subjects? Love is wonderful, death is terrible, life is mysterious. So start small and work your way up. Take a phrase you overheard, a snippet of memory, a dream fragment, and make a poem of that. Once the details are in place, the big theme (whatever it is) will follow, but the details have to come first.

2) *Write about what you remember.* It is a commonplace that you should write about what you know, but usually the present is too close for us to see it clearly. We have to move away from the events in our lives before we can see them in such a way that we can write about them engagingly. Don't waste time on the guy you saw talking to his dog this morning; take a few notes, if you like, but if he's memorable, he'll pop into your mind later, when you really need him. Instead, why not write a poem about the girl in your third-grade class who could throw a baseball better than any of the boys and all the problems that caused? By putting these memories down on paper and shaping them, you're enriching not only your own life but also the lives of others.

3) *Be a sponge.* Shakespeare was. His plays are based on historical accounts and on lesser plays by earlier playwrights. So what are you, better than Shakespeare? I once wrote a poem called "The Last Song on the Jukebox" that was published in a magazine and then in a collection of my poetry and now in an anthology that is widely used on college campuses; people seem to like it pretty well. Looking back at the poem, I can hear in it echoes of two country songs that I used to be able to sing in their entireties but have since forgotten. Somebody says something in my poem that is a variation on something a character says in a novel called *Ray,* by the talented Barry Hannah. And the overall tone of "The Last Song on the Jukebox" owes much to a poet I heard reading his own work one night. His voice was perfect—it had just the right twang to it—so I used it for the speaker in my poem. Now that I

think about it, I realize that I didn't like the guy's poetry that much. That didn't stop me from adapting his twang to my purpose.

4) *Play dumb.* Just about anything can be turned into a poem if you play dumb about it, because when you're smart, everything makes sense to you and you go about your business, whereas when you're dumb, you have to slow down, stop, figure things out. Recently, in Chicago, I saw a man being arrested. The police had cuffed him and were hauling him away while an elderly woman shook with rage and screamed after them as they all climbed into the paddywagon. "Liar!" she shouted, "liar!" You mean you can get arrested just for lying, I said to myself? Is that only in Chicago, or does the law apply everywhere? Now if I were a smart person, I might have figured out what really happened: Probably the guy grabbed her purse, and she called the cops, and he said he didn't do it, and she said he *did* do it, and so on. But by being dumb, I got a flying start on a poem. I haven't finished the poem yet, but as you can see, I have already given myself a lot to work with, thanks to my astonishingly low IQ.

5) *Reverse your field.* When you catch yourself on the verge of saying something obvious, don't just stop; instead, say the opposite of what you were going to say in the first place. Listen to the poet within you. If you want to eat a chocolate bar, that's not poetry; everybody likes chocolate. But suppose the chocolate bar wanted to eat you? Now that's a poem. Here's another example: I'm thinking of ending my liar-in-Chicago poem with something about husbands and wives and how they have to be truthful to each other, and I can see myself heading toward a stanza in which the speaker wonders what his wife really means when she says (and this would be the last line of the poem), "I love you." The problem is that that's too pat for a last line, too cloying, too sentimental, an easy out. Instead, since people who are really crazy about each other sometimes kid around in a mock-hostile way, why not have the speaker wonder whether the wife is telling the truth or not when she laughs and hits him on the arm and says, "I hate you, you big lug!" Such an unexpected statement would come as a surprise to the reader, although first it will have come as a surprise to me, who was heading in the opposite direction before I realized that I needed to reverse my field.

6) *Work on several poems at once.* For one thing, you won't end up giving too much attention to a poem that doesn't need it—like children, some poems do better if you don't breathe down their necks all the time. For another, if you're working on just one poem and it isn't going anywhere, you're likely to feel terribly frustrated, whereas if one poem is dying on the vine and three others are doing pretty well, you'll feel as though you are ahead of the game (because you will be). Also, sometimes our poems are smarter than we are, and a word or a line or a stanza that isn't right for one poem will often migrate to another and find a home for itself there. Poems are happiest in the company of other poems, so don't try to create them in a vacuum. You probably wouldn't try to write four novels at once, but there's no reason why you shouldn't take advantage of poetry's brevity and get several poems going simultaneously.

7) *Give yourself time.* This is actually related to the preceding rule, since you wouldn't tend to rush a poem if you were working on several of them at once. I have a friend whose daughter is learning how to cook. But she's a little impatient, so when she has a recipe that says you should bake the cake at 350 degrees for thirty minutes, she doesn't see why you can't cook it at 700 degrees for fifteen minutes. If you take this approach to poetry, your poems are going to end up like my friend's daughter's cakes, charred on the outside and raw in the middle. If you saw a stunningly handsome stranger walking down the street, would you run up to him and shout, "Marry me"? Of course not—he might say yes! Poems are the same way, and if you try to make them yours too soon, you won't be happy with the results, I promise you. Be coy, be flirtatious; draw the poem out a little and see what it's really about. There's no hurry, because you've got all those other poems you're working on, remember?

8) *Find a perfect reader.* A perfect reader is like a perfect tennis partner, someone who is a little better than you are (so you feel challenged), but not that much better (so you don't get demoralized). And like an ideal tennis partner, a good reader is going to be hard to find. You don't play tennis with your mother, so don't expect her to critique your writing.

Anyway, what kind of mother would tell her own child that his poetry is terrible? That's what friends are for. So no parents. And no room-mates, either: people are always saying to me, "You're going to love this poem; my roommate says it's the best thing I've ever written." What else would a roommate say? You can hardly go on living with someone after you've told him to throw his notebook away and take up basket-weaving. Just as you would play tennis with a couple of dozen people before you pick the one you want to play with every Saturday, so too should you pass your poems around until you find the one person who can show you their strengths and weaknesses without inflating or deflating your ego too much. If you're lucky, you'll then do what I did when I found my perfect reader—you'll marry her (or him).

If you have a knack for language and you follow these rules and you get a break from time to time and you look both ways whenever you cross the street, after a while you will find you have created for yourself a life within a life. You will have awakened—reawakened, actually—the poet within you. And even if this isn't your year to win the Nobel Prize, I have to say that I never met anybody who didn't break out into a big happy smile when I introduced myself as a poet. I don't know what it is; maybe people associate me with Homer or Milton. At any rate, every-one seems happy to know there is a poet in the neighborhood.

Well, not everybody. Once I was negotiating with a man to buy his house, and I was getting the better of him. So the man lost his temper and said I didn't know what I was doing, I *couldn't* know, because I was a poet and I ought to go back to my poems and leave business affairs to men like him, practical, level-headed men. For a couple of days, I felt pretty rotten, although the whole thing turned out spledidly for me, since I later found another house I liked even better than his. Mean-while, the practical level-headed fellow had lost a great buyer; like Flaubert, I believe in paying my bills on time.

And I got my revenge: I wrote a poem about him.

73

BUILDING CONFIDENCE IN YOURSELF AS A POET

BY JAMES APPLEWHITE

THE WRITING OF A POEM from first draft to publishable version tends to fall into several phases. Getting a first draft down on paper is, or ought to be, a pleasurable process. Poetry incorporates an element of play. Word-sounds that echo against each other (in internal and end-line rhyme, consonance, assonance, and alliteration) are a kind of technical signature of this play, which extends through image, metaphor and whole narrative contour. That is, the poet's mind in the process of composing allows itself the child-freedom of lip-and-tongue eroticism, of language indulged *as if* in nonsense syllables. The idea of a poem is itself a playful invention, a bending or troping away from the literal into the figurative. "God a mighty," I still hear the field hand saying, "this here morning is cold as blue blazes." I *saw* the cold—materialized, active—in those "blazes," in those flames.

I like to alter Coleridge's image of the poet as a charioteer driving onward with loosely held reins. Instead of a horse as representative of that bodily, kinetic, spontaneous source of sound, association, and undisclosed motive, I propose the more contemporary machine of the bingo parlor. It is a kind of glass-sided till, within which numbered ping pong balls are steadily blown upward, like bubbles in the muses' fountain. You, the conscious half of the writer, are standing above, receiving into your hands these syllables of an evolving riddle breathed from beneath. It is like a popcorn machine, sounds a bit like one, and maybe the smell of popcorn blows through the tent. You don't accept every proposal for a word in your poem, or every rhythmic impluse, that so "pops up." You select, take some but push some back, asking for better imagination, a fresher number. Language, after all, is generic, a possession in common, and every sound and sense has been used to death. Some of "what comes" is inevitably cliché.

This is my image for stage one of the writing, and a point for appreciating a delicate balance. Coleridge had his driver—my caller of numbers—hold the reins loosely. The horse must, to some extent, have its head. A kind of momentum, expressed most obviously in the rhythm and sound, needs to develop, If the caller waits for too long to pick out one of the balls, they may pile up in frustration and cause a blockage. What wants and needs to be said has to get itself in motion. Altering the image, the words that begin to come are like the knotted scarves pulled by the magician from his hat. One is linked to another, and pulling them into motion the first time is necessary for the whole strip to unfurl.

For this stage of composition, then, I advise a willing suspension of disbelief in the validity of what you are saying. I don't mean that you should be wholly uncritical, but I do mean that you should allow yourself the freedom and self-approval to write without inhibition. You can't hit a golf or tennis ball or skate or dive if you are so self-conscious that your movements are deliberate and forced. You learn how to do it by practice, then *do* it, in a movement that is whole, feels spontaneous, and causes a certain delight.

The times to put the harder pressure on yourself are *before* this first writing, and after. What is available to you as you write is in part dependent upon your preparation. Wide reading, study, and analysis of poetry, reading aloud, developing access to your deeper sources of subject matter, all help enrich the mix of what is bubbling up from "below." Discriminating insight into language—sound as well as sense—should have become habitual in you *before* this moment. Put pressure on yourself to read and to understand, to know yourself, to begin the extraction of insights that lead to the richer interior. But don't freeze up when you should be intuitive. Admit to yourself that you love this verbalization of the irrational, this bingo game in which you fill in for yourself the missing columns of self-knowledge.

Getting down the first draft is phase one. You may, for a lyric-length poem, write it in one sitting, or begin it in one session, in the morning, and then continue for a bit more that evening before going to bed. *Phase one* goes on for as long as conception is still glowing inside your head. At this point, the text is illuminated by what you intended.

Here is the first draft of my poem, "Clear Winter." The reader will note that the published version (see page 373) is a few lines shorter, and that changes have been made in word order, word choice, and above all, in the rhythmic momentum or "flow." The finished poem runs on more swiftly, as I had from the beginning intended. But in the first attempt, I was unable quite to capture in writing the seamless movement I had felt. Still all the elements of the final poem are present in this first draft. This is a remarkably complete first version, for me. Even so, the poem had to go through a series of versions, before I was able to bring back those spontaneous phrases and movements from the manuscript and give them a more finely tuned setting.

Clear Winter
(First draft, January 8, 1985)

Confusion of seasons is over.
Today was clear winter.
Light that on trunks was warm
Looked bare and bleak
On chill limbs against chill air.
I saw everywhere corpses of trees
Piled mercilessly by past
High water, crotch-chunk
Of one upon trunk of another.
I worry about my brother.
Angular cedars with crowns
Thinned of needles in death
Seem some desert tribe
Overtaken by an angel of death.
Finally I climbed clear
Of the river valley where memory
Surrounded with its proxy history
Tree-corpses. I saw air clear
In its isolation and pure
As a star. We are unable
to endure this light
The cold whets like a knife.
I stand above this used,
Abused river land and
Hypothesize the being
We cannot undertand, who
Begins springs with fire of a star,
Who is the clarity of air
And the far zero dark.
I sniff for the scent of some fire,
For coffee or leaf smoke or
cigarette scent. All are purely
Absent. I turn toward home,
Alone as a pane of ice
This keen sun shines through.
I will kiss my warm wife,

> And under the first star,
> Gather cedar for a fire.

Phase two begins when the first glow has faded, or has begun to. *Then* there is the shock of recognition, as you encounter the text you have produced. It is not necessarily disappointing. You may be happily surprised by the electricity in some phrases. You may also note lapses, stretches of dead language, redundancy. Now, with the text in hand, you apply maximum pressure. The poem won't be inhibited. It already exists. *Always* keep the first draft. You aren't a painter who loses the early version in revision. Be as self-critical as you can be. Call everything into question. Go from self-love to self-hate. But avoid extremes. A *balanced* appreciation, an objective appraisal of weaknesses and failings in your own writing is needed. It is essential for you to recognize excellence as well as to admit fault.

You want to see the poem clearly, as it is, and for many poets (including myself), this requires part of phase two to be a revision that questions everything, that entertains the possibility that the whole poem may be a failure. I tend to over-revise at this point, possibly to over-rationalize, and perhaps to make the poetic statement artificially complete, too explicit. Since I seem to need to do this, I allow it to happen, knowing that it is part of phase two: critically confronting the poem.

Phase three emphasizes the fact that the "real poem" knows more than "I" do, that ideally it combines the phase-one spontaneity and the phase-two appraisal. Thinking too much about it, trying all possible combinations of key words in troublesome phrases, is only another effort on your part to see the essence of the poem clearly. Thus, phase three involves a kind of "forgetting" of this highly conscious, trial-and-error revision. I let the text rest, like dough between kneadings. This may be for weeks or months. Then something will reawaken interest. I will recall the true poem, the real poem, from the confusion of various versions. Sometimes I literally recall the poem by writing it out afresh as I remember it at this point, perhaps with help from earlier drafts, especially the first. Often I find that the revision has helped pare away the nonessential, and to prepare a place for what in the first draft was really final. I cherish the sense that for each real poem there is some absolute, inevitable form toward which I have been fumbling through successive drafts. This is in part an illusion, for even "final" texts get revised. You should never turn down what you consider better insight. The real poem seems to gather up into itself the many competing glimpses scattered through various versions. I think of prose as linear, a link through time, but a poem is more a circle, which, when completed, does not end. It looks forward and backward, resisting the erosion of more revisions.

I am myself a runner, and *River Writing: An Eno Journal* was largely composed while I was running along the Eno River in all seasons, all weathers. It started accidentally, but once begun, my premise came to be that the poem would be founded on whatever I saw or thought during the run. The river is over the ridge behind my house, so I could go out and return without interruption. (By the way, *shield* yourself from interruption during the time you set aside to write. If writing is as important to you as you think it is, treat it as such. Give it that central importance in your life.)

The finished version of "Clear Winter" is four lines shorter than the first draft, and words have been cut or substituted in a number of lines that remain. These changes help allow the rhythm of lines to fuse one into the other, so that the whole seems a single movement. For example, "chill limbs against chill air" becomes "chill limbs high in chill air." The first draft let the word *death* appear twice at the ends of lines, and the word *star* appears twice. It also allows the word *corpses* to come in too soon. It was as if my first impulse had known generally what it wanted, but had had to move toward that goal by trial and error. But notice that except for a change in tense, the ending stands as first imagined and drafted.

Here is the published version of "Clear Winter":

Clear Winter
(Published in *River Writing: An Eno Journal,*
Princeton University Press, 1988)

Confusion of seasons is over.
Today was clear winter.
Light that on trunks seemed warm
Looked bleak and bare
On chill limbs high in chill air.
I saw bodies of trees
Piled mercilessly by past
High water, crotch-chunk

367

Of one upon trunk of another.
Angular cedars, their crowns
Thinned of needles by drought,
Seemed a desert tribe
Overtaken by an angel of death.
Finally I climbed clear
Of the valley which memory
Stocked with its proxy
Corpses. I saw air
In its isolation now pure.
We are unable to endure
This light the cold whets to steel.
I stood above river land
And hypothesized the being
We cannot understand, who
Begins things with flame of a star,
Who is the zero far dark.
I sniffed for scent of some smoke,
For coffee, leaf-smolder or
Cigarette odor. All unendurably
Absent. I turned toward home,
Alone as a pane of ice
The keen sun shines through.
I kissed my warm wife
And under the first star
Gathered cedar for a fire.

Here is the lesson I learned from the poems in *River Writing*. It is good sometimes to let the cadences and larger structures of your poetry and its emotional momentum build. Learn to write with ease, with relaxation. You can't really run faster or farther over the long haul simply by bearing down harder. You have to raise the level of your effort, then relax, and trust that preparation. Then perfect the draft later. With joy. As Fred Astaire said to a new partner, "Don't be nervous, but don't make a mistake." Learning not to be nervous, not to make yourself nervous, because of your relaxation and confidence in revision, will help you prevent making a mistake. And remember that the only real mistake in poetry is not ever to get the poem written.

But the key element for most poets who are learning the process is knowing when and how to apply the pressure. Writing poetry is like training for athletic competition. Performance in the event—the writing of the poem—is largely a product of conditioning, associated with analysis of form and technique. But you don't perform that analysis in the act of writing. You somewhat analyze the problem before you, but finally you have to get in there and perform. You don't sit there anxiously wondering whether the last word was really the right one. You don't sit there worrying whether the poem will finally be any good. Time will tell.

74

MAKING A NAME IN POETRY

BY X. J. KENNEDY

AS POETS KNOW only too well, trying to sell poetry to paying magazines and book publishers is a rough task, often impossible. Even giving away poems may be difficult: Some little magazines that pay in free copies can be choosey. And as John Ciardi once observed, it is hard for poets to prostitute their talents. There just aren't that many buyers around.

It would be hypocritical for me to claim that for a poet to see print shouldn't matter. Of course it matters. If you write poems, having them accepted helps convince you that you are right to believe in yourself. Disappointments notwithstanding, just being published once in a while encourages a poet to stick to what William Butler Yeats glumly called "this sedentary trade."

That poems are hard to peddle isn't terribly depressing—to poets who live for the pleasure of making poems. "Well, so Editor X has bounced my sublime ode," they'll tell themselves. "The benighted creep." But to writers who aren't yet widely published and who fiercely crave to be, writers who live not necessarily to write good poems but to see their names in print, this difficulty leads to chagrin.

Writing poetry is radically different from writing articles, stories, or fillers. Most moneymaking writers—that is, writers who aren't poets—scout for a likely market. Then, they often shrewdly adapt their product to suit that market's needs. Their lives make sense: They can supply a demand. Poets, however, if they are serious about writing good poems, have to think differently.

Poetry is probably the one field of writing in which it is a mistake to try to psych out editors. In fact, specific marketing advice can sometimes harm the novice poet by enticing him to pursue fashions. The poet's best hope is to sound like *nobody* else: The finest, most enduring poetry constructs a new marketplace of it own.

Excellent poems are like better mousetraps: Build one, said Emerson, and the world will beat a path to your door. It always amazes me how quickly a good, original book of poetry becomes known: W. D. Snodgrass's *Heart's Needle*, for instance, a book acclaimed soon after publication and laden with a Pulitzer, despite the fact that its author had published relatively little before.

Evidently, it is much simpler to chase after fashions than to transform yourself into a fine poet, the likes of whom the world hasn't seen before. It is easy to advise anyone whose poetic ambition goes no further than to achieve publication. To such a person, I'd suggest the following strategies:

1. Center your poem on your experience, your family, your everyday concerns—however drab. If you write a poem about your cousin's case of AIDS, you will surely find an editor who will accept it, no matter how bad it may be, for he fears that if he doesn't, you will think him a coarse, unfeeling swine who won't sympathize with your cousin. I'm serious!

2. Write in the first person, in the present tense. Not long ago, Peter Davison, poetry editor for *The Atlantic*, remarked that most of the poems he currently receives are like that. Some other, less discriminating editors mistakenly believe that the present tense lends everything a kind of immediacy.

3. Brainstorm, force your unconscious to yoke together disparate things. In the midst of a dull poem on your grandfather's old antimacassar, throw in a mention of something completely far-out and unexpected, such as a fur-lined frying pan.

4. Include a dash of violent realism, preferably straight out of current news. If you can relate your workaday world to, say, war-torn Nicaragua, you've got it made.

5. Give your poem a snappy title to catch an editor's eye. With a little more brainstorming, you can readily invent titles of poems for which many editors, the dolts, will be pushovers: "Contracting Chicken-pox in a First Kiss," "A Lesbian Mother Tells Her Daughter the Facts of Life." Titles like that either promise something interesting, or else reek of Significance with a capital S.

6. Don't, whatever you do, write in traditional forms. To do so will only slow your rate of production. Even worse, you might reveal your

lack of skill. Traditional forms, such as sonnets and blank verse, which held sway over English-speaking poetry for five centuries (up until about 1960), can still nourish wonderful poems—as witness recent work by Seamus Heaney, Derek Walcott, Gjertrud Schnackenberg, and Timothy Steele. But remember, I'm not talking about quality. If you write in traditional forms, you had better be good. In rhymed metrical stanzas, mediocre poetry tends to look shoddy in an obvious way, while bad poetry looks really horrible. On the other hand, bad poems in open forms (or "free verse") tend to seem passable. And—I hate to say this, but it's true—mediocre poems in open forms look like most poems appearing nowadays in respectable places.

7. Study an annual that lists poetry markets such as the *International Directory of Little Magazines and Small Presses* (found in the reference section of many libraries). Then zero in on the less competitive markets, like *Superintendent's Profile & Pocket Equipment Directory,* a monthly for highway superintendents and directors of departments of public works. Although it uses only poems about snowplowing and road repairing, the magazine prints two out of every three poems it receives.

If indeed all you care about is becoming a widely published poet, those hints may be as good as any. What I hope, of course, is that you will ignore all those suggestions.

For a poet who cares about the art of poetry, merely to be published isn't enough. The first time you see your name in print, it may seem to scintillate on the page like a Fourth of July sparkler. Karl Shapiro once recalled the joy of seeing rows of his own book on a shelf, "saying my golden name from end to end." But after you see it a few times, your own name may not prove especially interesting. At the moment, the problem for a poet in this country isn't to get published. A couple of thousand markets now publish poetry, some of whose editors have no taste. And anyone who can't get published can, for $200, start his own little magazine and generously heap his own work with acceptances. Unfortunately, the problem, in this time of dwindling attention spans, is to find attentive readers.

Poets whose work is widely published may still be widely ignored. The poetry star system that produced household names like Robert Frost, Dylan Thomas, and E.E. Cummings passed away twenty years ago, so there is no longer much point in a poet's trying for celebrity. The celebrity that a poet may attain isn't the tenth part of one percent of the celebrity that a rock songwriter can attain from a single video. If you are going into the poetry writing business, you might as well forget about fame and fortune and seek other rewards.

Some writers think that bringing out that first collection of poems will be an experience far superior to beholding the beatific vision. This view is distorted. Publishing a book can be a lot of fun, but it may not transform your life. Having published a volume of poetry, you, unlike Michael Jackson or Madonna, can walk the streets and not be overwhelmed by autograph-seekers. Moreover, you can publish a book of poems and continue to suffer from any ailment or lacks that afflicted you.

Poetic fame, like sea water, isn't worth thirsting for. Poets, if they are any good, compete for space in books not only with their peers but with the giants of the ages. They race not only with John Ashbery and Tess Gallagher, to name two deservedly admired contemporaries, but with John Milton and Emily Dickinson. Let them not imitate the plumage of any currently acclaimed poet. Let them discover their own natures, however disappointing the discovery, and stay faithful to whoever they may be.

At the risk of appearing to hold myself up as a sterling example, I shall recall that as a whitehat in the Navy back in the early fifties, just beginning to fool around writing poems, I made plenty of mistakes. (One mistake was trying to write like Dylan Thomas, an attempt that rendered my work thick, fruitcake-like, and impenetrable.) One mistake I didn't make was to crave premature publication. I resigned myself to just writing, piling up poems, not showing them to anybody. Pigheadedly, I believed that one day an editor would print my work, or some of it. At least that attitude kept up my morale: I didn't have to cope with the rejection slips I would certainly have received. And when I finally started licking stamps and getting poems rejected, I was a little (but not a whole lot) more competent.

For a poet, there can be no greater luxury than to work as a complete unknown. When you are an undiscovered gem, there isn't the least bit of pressure on you to publish, to become better and better and stun your critics, to win prizes, and all that debilitating responsibility. All you need care about is writing good poems. Too many college sophomores and also a few grandparents who have never read any poetry other than Hallmark greeting card verse assume that if their first stumbling efforts don't get published, they have failed miserably. But that Sylvia Plath won a noteworthy prize when she was a college student, that Amy Clampitt published her first book in middle age and won immediate accolades, doesn't mean that they should feel any grim duty to succeed. America is full of excellent poets who have had their poems published for years, despite the fact that they receive little notice. Luckily for our poetry, they persist.

Nowadays, lust for hasty fame takes root early. The other day I was talking with a bunch of fourth-graders in a public library in Quincy, Massachusetts, and a lad of ten asked me again and again—insistently rephrasing the question—how you get poems published. I wanted to tell him, Kid, forget it. I'll bet your stuff at the moment, while it may show flickers of something good, is not much good yet; you will be smart to shelve your ambition for another ten or fifteen years. But, too craven to hit him with the hard truth, I pointed out how rare it is to publish poems in nationwide places when you are ten. Myra Cohn Livingston in her wonderful book *The Child as Poet* tells some horror stories about fledgling poets whose parents goaded them into print at an early age.

All right, call me a sourpuss. I'm trying to dash a little cold water on the notion, so dear to many unpublished writers, that publication is the be-all and end-all of existence. This attitude makes such people push-overs for racketeers: for contests that charge forty-dollar entrance fees, accept everything, then try to sell the contestants a bound volume containing their supposedly winning work for $38.95, or $62.95 for the gold-edged edition. It makes them suckers for vanity publishers who, appealing to their pride and frustration, urge them to subsidize an edition of their own poems, which will sell to nobody, or to practically nobody, unless they themselves sell the copies, and which no reviewer in a national magazine would touch with a thirty-foot flagpole.

Letting oneself be the victim of such con games is all right if seeing your name in print is your one aim. And with any luck, sheer, tireless stamp-licking will result in *some* kind of publication. But sometimes, if viewed as fortresses to be stormed and overpowered, poetry magazines tend to resist. I can recall when, as poetry editor for the *Paris Review,* I kept getting a tide of manuscripts from a poet who had published little but whose name must have been known to every poetry editor. His manuscripts came in *daily* showing the wrinkles of many previous rejections. Always folded and refolded sixteen times, sometimes looking as if they'd been given a fresh press with a steam iron, always in envelopes saying Biltmore and Statler and Hilton (pilfered, it seemed, from writing desks in hotel lobbies). If only the contributor had devoted as much time to learning to write as he spent stuffing envelopes!

Why is it that hundreds of thousands of people want to be poets? I don't know, but I have a hunch. In this anonymous society in which we feel like zip codes or social security numbers, writing a poem and publishing it is one way to stand up on your hind legs and sass the universe. A printed poem proclaims, "I exist." There is something powerfully appealing in the thought that you can seize paper and pencil in an odd moment and scrawl a few lines that might make you immortal in anthologies. Immortality is all very well, but it is more interesting to think about the problems of writing good poetry. You don't need to publish a thousand poems in order to become immortal; you need publish only one poem, if it is good enough.

Literary history is full of cases of great poets who garnered no fame or praise or significant publication in their lifetimes. Gerard Manley Hopkins, whose strange masterpiece "The Wreck of the Deutschland" was rejected by a small Jesuit magazine, showed his poems to only a tiny handful of correspondents. Emily Dickinson, after local newspaper editors rewrote the few items she submitted to them, evidently said the hell with them and stitched her poems into little packets that she stashed away in her attic, as is well known. Hopkins and Dickinson, to be sure, were superb poets whose work refused to die. But my point is that they placed quality first and bravely turned their backs upon celebrity.

Sometimes, when I look at the current spate of forgettable poems, I think it would be a great idea if literary magazines were to declare a moratorium on by-lines for a few years. Just suppose every poem were printed anonymously. By and by, of course, the real original poets would be recognized by the character of their work, as surely as "The Pearl" poet of the Middle Ages. But the great mass of poems, undistinguished and forgettable, would slip into oblivion. And there would be fewer of them, since people who now publish poems in order to boost their egos would have no reason to.

I think it is a good idea for young poets to start having their poems published in the very smallest magazines, those read by few people. If in later years they should decide that their maiden works were poor, they can comfort themselves with the knowledge that practically nobody will have read them. Most poets I have known have come to regard their first works as pretty embarrassing. John Ciardi, who won a prize in a student writing contest at the University of Michigan, once told me he longed to burgle his found manuscript from the library and burn it.

Those poets willing to try the most onerous route of all—growing in depth and in skill—might cultivate an aloof coolness toward publication. No formula, no market tip, no advice from me or anybody else will help you write a great poem. But you can take action. You can try reading. Most poets do too little of that. Talk to any editor of a poetry magazine, and you will learn that the would-be contributors usually outnumber paying subscribers by at least five to one. Many poets want to heap their outpourings upon the world, expecting the world to take them gladly. Too impatient to read other poets, they never find out how poetry is written, and they keep repeating things that have already been done well, and so do not need redoing.

If you haven't been published and deserve to be, you might make a personal anthology of poems you admire—the dozen or twenty poems you'd swear by. This task will concentrate your attention, make you aware of your own standards, and reveal your nature to you. I made such a anthology once and learned to my surprise that the poems I most cherish in all of literature are religious ones. You might also try writing a lot—and throwing most of it away. Delmore Schwartz said that a poet is wise to write as much, and to publish as little, as possible.

Keats put it beautifully in a letter to a friend: "I should write for the mere yearning and fondness I have for the beautiful, even if my night's labors should be burnt every morning and no eye shine upon them." That is, I think, a noble attitude. Rejections—or critical attacks—could not thwart a Keats; they simply had no great power over him. For a poet, the only sure reward is the joy of making a poem. Any reward besides—fame, prizes, publication—is like money found in the street. If you see a silver dollar gleaming on the sidewalk, you pick it up. But you need not roam the streets desperately looking for that gleam.

75

WRITING SHORT HUMOROUS VERSE

BY ROSEMARIE WILLIAMSON

A FUNNY THING HAPPENED—well, actually it wasn't funny, it was the way I *perceived* it that is really the keystone in the comedic arch. Humor, after all, is a point of view that depends in large measure on the intellectual and emotional experience of the viewer.

Subject matter for humor exists all around us; we must be alert to the potential of everyday happenings. Doors that won't open, zippers that won't close, lawn chairs that collapse—all these have more than just nuisance value: they can be turned into marketable humor.

Popular with readers, seasonal humor can be an ongoing source of revenue for the canny writer. Remembering the backbreaking chores involved in the annual spring lawn and garden resuscitation, I produced the following, which was published in *Good Housekeeping:*

Ode To the Outdoors
When Nature features GREEN-UP time—
It's human creatures' CLEAN-UP time!

Presto, change-o! Outdoor tasks became indoor ones the following month:

A Melody for Mother's Day
They lovingly prepared French toast,
And squeezed the juice for me to drink—
Which should give me strength enough
To wash those dishes in the sink!

Apparently this struck a familiar note with *Good Housekeeping*'s editor.

Magazines like *McCall's, Good Housekeeping,* and *The Atlantic* are always on the lookout for brief, well-written humor. *Reader's Digest* has several departments that accept amusing anecdotes, and it pays very well.

Making the most of the current fitness fad, I sold the following verse to *McCall's:*

Contour-Control Class
"Let's get it all together,"
They urged me at the start;
Till then I hadn't realized
It was quite so far apart.

Newspapers, too, are a good market for humor. *The New York Times,* for example, has a regular Wednesday feature called "Metropolitan Diary," which is a showcase for general humor, as well as things seen and heard in the New York area. My "Spring Breakthrough" appeared there a few years ago:

Though the snow is finally melting
And with spring fever now I'm smitten,
Those aren't crocuses emerging
But a missing pull-toy and a mitten.

The prize? A bottle of French champagne. Budding humorists, however, might feel more comfortable submitting witticisms to their weekly hometown newspapers. Regional papers frequently welcome this kind of material, particularly if it has a local slant.

The following anecdote, which appeared in *The American Legion Magazine,* happened to me almost verbatim (for some reason the editor transformed me into a "rich dowager"—which is funny in itself!):

Silver Service
Admiring an unusual piece of costume jewelry in a department store recently, the rich dowager asked a nearby salesperson if the brooch was made of abalone and silver. "I really don't know," the salesgirl replied, "but I'll ask Miss Johnson." A few minutes later, the woman overheard the clerk dutifully asking her department head if the jewelry in question was "Abalonian."

The same magazine also bought the following:

Ode to a Guard Dog
Though your tail's in friendly motion,
I think I'll keep my place;

There's welcome in your wagging,
But no-no on your face!

Humor is humor—right? Unfortunately, it's not that simple. Both form and content vary from publication to publication. That is why it's essential to familiarize yourself with a specific magazine or newspaper before making submissions. If your work is not geared to the requirements of a particular publication, you are wasting your own time as well as that of the editor.

Appropriate subject matter, tone, and vocabulary must all be considered. What gets a knee-slapping reaction on the "Party Jokes" page of *Playboy* wouldn't be suitable for *Family Circle* or *Woman's Day*. What *The Saturday Evening Post* would find right for its readers might prove offensive to the editors of *New Directions for Women*, a successful New Jersey-based feminist newspaper. An example of opposites, the following two verses appeared in the last two publications:

Cheers
(The Saturday Evening Post)

With grin askew, complexion ruddy—
He orders one more Bleary Muddy.

and

Silent Signatory
(New Directions for Women)

In making out a will
There was no place for her name
Just her husband's surname—
She was called "et ux."
In taking out a loan
This self-same nameless homemaker
Is now described as "co-maker":
Nonentity deluxe.

Whimsical writing can take the form of short prose, poetry, or one-liners—all ideally suited to the light touch. A truly funny idea has many possibilities. After selling it from one angle or in one form, you can often rework it, with a new slant and some language changes, and sell it elsewhere.

379

Serendipity steps in—sometimes. A few years ago I sold the following verse to *Good Housekeeping*:

Fun With Figures

I bought a calorie guide
With an eye on my plumpish condition;
Though I haven't lost an ounce,
I sure have improved my addition.

Several months after this appeared, I received a call from an editor at Hallmark Cards, asking to buy reprint rights to "Fun With Figures" for its projected hardcover volume entitled *Dieter's Fun Book*. This meant I would be paid a second time for the same poem.

It might be helpful to examine the above quatrain. Form and content seem simple enough—*however,* quite a bit is going on there. Let's start with the title (your first opportunity to catch the editor's eye): It's suitably short, it includes wordplay (both two-dimensional and three-dimensional "figures"), and also alliteration (two words beginning with "f")—all of which set a playful mood. The theme was (and still is) current—isn't everyone dieting? The poem itself addresses several aspects of human behavior: the enthusiastic purchase of books, tapes, etc., for what are often short-lived self-improvement projects, the universal perplexity associated with simple arithmetic, and the inevitable rationalization of our failed efforts. It's worth noting here that humor about situations or traits people can easily identify with is most readily marketable.

For wordplay or quizzes with a humorous slant, *The Saturday Evening Post*'s "Post Scripts" is a good market page. Below is a wholly imaginary "fish story" I sold to the *Post*:

Something Fishy

The following specials were advertised recently in the window of Pier Group Seafood Market:

Oh my cod
My brother's kipper
Future shark
Trick or trout
O sole mio
What the hake
Just for the halibut
Porgy and bass
Unexpected fluke

Excedrin haddock
Down the pike
Our pickerel's a dilly
True bluefish
A lofty perch

Have you any special interests or expertise? Good! Whether your theme is sports or cooking, dogs or doctors, a few relevant terms correctly used give your work authenticity. There's really no excuse for inaccuracy: When in doubt, look it up! A small, personal reference library, by the way, is an invaluable asset for a writer.

Markets exist for humor on every imaginable subject; this edition of *The Writer's Handbook* offers hundreds of sources for your perusal. I have sold humor to such diverse publications as *Insect World Digest, Antiques, Cats, Editor and Publisher, Family Weekly, The Carpenter* and *Computer Decisions* (on computer dating!).

Writing humor is not the path to quick riches. National magazines like *Good Housekeeping* typically pay about twenty-five dollars for anecdotes and light verse. Train yourself to be alert for amusing incidents or remarks you hear at the office, at home, in the streetcar, at parties, in the supermarket—almost anywhere. Be sure to jot them down *at the time* you hear them, or as soon as possible. Always keep a small pad and pencil handy.

A real plus in writing short humor is that your overhead is practically zilch: stationery, stamps, and occasionally a new typewriter ribbon—that's about it. While some publications pay less than others, the important thing to remember is that there is *always* a market for humorous material. If you work hard to make your short humor marketable, then, considering the minimal amount of time involved from idea to submission, you should turn a tidy profit.

76

POETIC DEVICES

BY WILLIAM PACKARD

THERE is a good story about Walter Johnson, who had one of the most natural fast balls in the history of baseball. No one knows how "The Big Train" developed such speed on the mound, but there it was. From his first year of pitching in the majors, 1907, for Washington, Walter Johnson hurtled the ball like a flash of lightning across the plate. And as often as not, the opposing batter would be left watching empty air, as the catcher gloved the ball.

Well, the story goes that after a few seasons, almost all the opposing batters knew exactly what to expect from Walter Johnson—his famous fast ball. And even though the pitch was just as difficult to hit as ever, still, it can be a very dangerous thing for any pitcher to become that predictable. And besides, there were also some fears on the Washington bench that if he kept on hurtling only that famous fast ball over the plate, in a few more seasons Walter Johnson might burn his arm out entirely.

So, Walter Johnson set out to learn how to throw a curve ball. Now, one can just imagine the difficulty of doing this: here is a great pitcher in his mid-career in the major leagues, and he is trying to learn an entirely new pitch. One can imagine all the painful self-consciousness of the beginner, as Johnson tried to train his arm into some totally new reflexes—a new way of fingering the ball, a new arc of the elbow as he went into the wind-up, a new release of the wrist, and a completely new follow-through for the body.

But after awhile, the story goes, the curve ball became as natural for Walter Johnson as the famous fast-ball pitch, and as a consequence, Johnson became even more difficult to hit.

When Walter Johnson retired in 1927, he held the record for total strike-outs in a lifetime career (3409), and he held the record for total pitching of shut-out games in a lifetime career (110)—records which

382

have never been equaled in baseball. And Walter Johnson is second only to the mighty Cy Young for total games won in a lifetime career.

Any artist can identify with this story about Walter Johnson. The determination to persist in one's art or craft is a characteristic of a great artist and a great athlete. But one also realizes that this practice of one's craft is almost always painstakingly difficult, and usually entails periods of extreme self-consciousness, as one trains oneself into a pattern of totally new reflexes. It is what Robert Frost called "the pleasure of taking pains."

The odd thing is that this practice and mastery of a craft is sometimes seen as an infringement on one's own natural gifts. Poets will sometimes comment that they do not want to be bothered with all that stuff about metrics and assonance and craft, because it doesn't come "naturally." Of course it doesn't come naturally, if one hasn't worked to make it natural. But once one's craft becomes second nature, it is not an infringement on one's natural gifts—if anything, it is an enlargement of them, and an enhancement and a reinforcement of one's own intuitive talents.

In almost all the other arts, an artist has to learn the techniques of his craft as a matter of course.

The painter takes delight in exploring the possibilities of his palette, and perhaps he may even move through periods which are dominated by different color tones, such as viridian or Prussian blue or ochre. He will also be concerned, as a matter of course, with various textural considerations such as brushing and pigmentation and the surface virtue of his work.

The composer who wants to write orchestra music has to begin by learning how to score in the musical notation system—and he will play with the meaning of whole notes, half notes, quarter notes, eighth notes, and the significance of such tempo designations as *lento, andante, adagio,* and *prestissimo.* He will also want to explore the different possibilities of the instruments of the orchestra, to discover the totality of tone he wants to achieve in his own work.

Even so—I have heard student poets complain that they don't want to be held back by a lot of technical considerations in the craft of poetry.

That raises a very interesting question: Why do poets seem to resist learning the practice and mastery of their own craft? Why do they

383

protest that technique *per se* is an infringement on their own intuitive gifts, and a destructive self-consciousness that inhibits their natural and magical genius?

I think a part of the answer to these questions may lie in our own modern Romantic era of poetry, where poets as diverse as Walt Whitman and Dylan Thomas and Allen Ginsberg seem to achieve their best effects with little or no technical effort. Like Athena, the poem seems to spring full blown out of the forehead of Zeus, and that is a large part of its charm for us. Whitman pretends he is just "talking" to us, in the "Song of Myself." So does Dylan Thomas in "Fern Hill" and "Poem in October." So does Allen Ginsberg in "Howl" and "Kaddish."

But of course when we think about it, we realize it is no such thing. And we realize also, in admiration, that any poet who is so skillful in concealing his art from us may be achieving one of the highest technical feats of all.

What are the technical skills of poetry, that all poets have worked at who wanted to achieve the practice and mastery of their craft?

We could begin by saying that poetry itself is language which is used in a specific way to convey a specific effect. And the specific ways that language can be used are expressed through all of the various poetic devices. In "The ABC of Reading," Ezra Pound summarized these devices and divided them into three categories—phonopoeia (sight), melopoeia (sound), and logopoeia (voice).

SIGHT

The image is the heart and soul of poetry. In our own psychic lives, we dream in images, although there may be words superimposed onto these images. In our social communication, we indicate complete understanding of something when we say, "I get the picture"—indicating that imagistic understanding is the most basic and primal of all communications. In some languages, like Chinese and Japanese, words began as pictures, or ideograms, which embodied the image representation of what the word was indicating.

It is not accidental that our earliest record of human civilization is in the form of pure pictures—images of bison in the paleolithic caves at Altamira in Northern Spain, from the Magdalenian culture, some 16,000 years B.C. And there are other records of stone statues as pure

384

images of horses and deer and mammoths, in Czechoslovakia, from as far back as 30,000 years B.C.

Aristotle wrote in the "Poetics" that metaphor—the conjunction of one image with another image—is the soul of poetry, and is the surest sign of genius. He also said it was the one thing that could not be taught, since the genius for metaphor was unaccountable, being the ability to see similarities in dissimilar things.

Following are the principal poetic devices which use image, or the picture aspect of poetry:

image—a simple picture, a mental representation. "That which presents an intellectual and emotional complex in an instant of time." (Pound)

metaphor—a direct comparison. "A mighty fortress is our God." An equation, or an equivalence: $A = B$. "It is the east and Juliet is the sun."

simile—an indirect comparison, using "like" or "as." "Why, man, he doth bestride the narrow world/Like a Colossus..." "My love's like a red, red rose."

figure—an image and an idea. "Ship of state." "A sea of troubles." "This bud of love."

conceit—an extended figure, as in some metaphysical poetry of John Donne, or in the following lines of Shakespeare's Juliet:

> Sweet, good-night!
> This bud of love, by summer's ripening breath,
> May prove a beauteous flower when next we meet...

SOUND

Rhythm has its source and origin in our own bloodstream pulse. At a normal pace, the heart beats at a casual iambic beat. But when it is excited, it may trip and skip rhythm through extended anapests or hard dactyls or firm trochees. It may even pound with a relentless spondee beat.

In dance, rhythm is accented by a drumbeat, in parades, by the cadence of marching feet, and in the night air, by churchbell tolling.

These simple rhythms may be taken as figures of the other rhythms of the universe—the tidal ebb and flow, the rising and setting of the sun, the female menstrual cycles, the four seasons of the year.

Rhythm is notated as metrics, but may also be seen in such poetic devices as rhyme and assonance and alliteration. Following are the poetic devices for sound:

385

assonance—rhyme of vowel sounds. "O that this too too solid flesh would melt..."

alliteration—repetition of consonants. "We might have met them dareful, beard to beard, And beat them backward home."

rhyme—the sense of resonance that comes when a word echoes the sound of another word—in end rhyme, internal rhyme, perfect rhyme, slant or imperfect rhyme, masculine rhyme, or feminine rhyme.

metrics—the simplest notation system for scansion of rhythm. The most commonly used metrics in English are:

iamb $(\smile\,')$
trochee $('\,\smile)$
anapest $(\smile\smile\,')$
dactyl $('\,\smile\smile)$
spondee $('\,')$

VOICE

Voice is the sum total of cognitive content of the words in a poem. Voice can also be seen as the signature of the poet on his poem—his own unmistakable way of saying something. "Only Yeats could have said it that way," one feels, in reading a line like:

That is no country for old men...

Similarly, Frost was able to endow his poems with a "voice" in lines like:

Something there is that doesn't love a wall...

Following are the poetic devices for voice:

denotation—literal, dictionary meaning of a word.

connotation—indirect or associative meaning of a word. "Mother" means one thing denotatively, but may have a host of other connotative associations.

personification—humanizing an object.

diction—word choice, the peculiar combination of words used in any given poem.

syntax—the peculiar arrangement of words in their sentence structures.

rhetoric—"Any adornment or inflation of speech which is not done for a particular effect but for a general impressiveness..." (Eliot)

persona—a mask, an assumed voice, a speaker pretending to be someone other than who he really is.

So far these are only words on a page, like diagrams in a baseball book showing you how to throw a curve ball. The only way there can be any real learning of any of these devices is to do endless exercises in notebooks, trying to master the craft of assonance, of diction shifts, of persona effects, of successful conceits, of metrical variations.

Any practice of these craft devices may lead one into a period of extreme self-consciousness, as one explores totally new reflexes of language. But one can trust that with enough practice they can become "second nature," and an enhancement and reinforcement of one's own intuitive talents as a poet.

77

FORM AND EXPERIMENTATION
IN POETRY

BY LIZ ROSENBERG

THE WAR between poetic form and poetic license has been raging for a long time and continues to this day. In 1668 the poet John Milton threw down one gauntlet, in his blank verse poem *Paradise Lost:* "This neglect of Rhyme so little is to be taken for a defect, though it may seem so perhaps to vulgar Readers, that it rather is to be esteem'd an example set, the first in English, of ancient liberty recover'd to Heroic Poem from the troublesome and modern bondage of Rhyming."

Three hundred years later Robert Frost dropped the other glove in his now-famous scorn of unrhymed verse: "I'd as soon play tennis with the net down."

Rhyme has been the chief net over which the opposing sides slug it out, maybe because it is the most instantly noticeable musical aspect of English poetry and poetic form, though by no means the only formal element available to the poet. Anglo-Saxon poetry, which was highly regimented, depended upon a certain number of stressed beats per line, and alliteration. Chinese poetry uses pitch. Other formal elements have held precedence at various times—the controlled musicality of Sapphic verse, syllabics, cinquains, haikus, William Carlos Williams's "variable foot," and so on. Between structure and freedom the pendulum swings widely and regularly, one way, then another. We tend to think of our own time as the absolute reign of free verse: unrhymed, unmetered, personal, brief, as jumpy as a gesture by James Dean—yet there are already signs of a swing leading the other way, in poems one feels an urge to call "verse"—the formal, rhymed, structured and ornamented work of poets like Amy Clampitt, Philip Booth, Gertrude Schnackenberg, and others.

As we draw closer to the end of the twentieth century, I suspect that the tendency both to poetic structure and poetic freedom will grow more exaggerated. Ends of centuries produce extremes, as witness

388

Alfred, Lord Tennyson on the one hand and Walt Whitman on the other, at the end of the nineteenth century. That these two poets had a great interest in and admiration for one another's work should come as no surprise. It's at both ends of the spectrum—extreme formal control, extreme poetic freedom—that the poet is pushing at boundaries, struggling to discover the necessities of the craft. It is exactly this pitched battle, *in extremis,* that produces great art, this pushing against limits, exploration of what is possible. The poet must write only according to internal necessity. The danger lies with those caught in the middle, like Dante's souls forever caught in the ante-chambers of hell, following first one flag and then another. This is the only mistake one can make in regard to poetic form: to allow the form to choose you. And it is as easy, as we have all lately discovered, to be the stooge of free verse as of formal verse. The worst one can do is to write in a particular form out of habit, intimidation, or laziness. There is an equal slackness in the doggerel rhyme of greeting cards or the nebulous free-form of Rod McKuen and his imitators. What one feels lacking in both is the tension of discovery, of necessity. And these are achieved only by a continual questioning of the status quo, by relentless experimentation and invention.

By "experimentation" I don't necessarily mean those finger exercises that are the stock in trade of many creative writing workshops. I'm not sure it's a good idea to get in the habit of just fooling around with poetry this way. It encourages a small kind of achievement; it puts a great emphasis on competence and cleverness, whereas great poetry is more like an explosion, built up under great pressure over a long period. One might practice with some of the tools of poetry—to sharpen musical and linguistic skills—but the poem, the thing itself, is not much good diluted.

Poets who practice with exercises must have a deep, nearly inexhaustible well of vital material. In this case, it will be impossible for anything the poet writes not to turn to poetry. But there is a frigidity in most poetic exercise, a sense of withholding that is deadly to real art. Poets shouldn't write villanelles or sonnets the way we are told we "should" write bread-and-butter letters or thank-you notes to Aunt Claire. This again is an encouragement to fall into the trap of thinking about form as somehow prescribed and habitual, as something one "really ought to do," rather than something one must do, having exhausted all other possibilities. It is only when this internal combustion forces one into new forms that something strange and lovely takes place.

"New" forms proceed from an intuition of potentialities, of something lurking around the corner, a sense that what *is* is not enough. "Mine deeper, that's the ticket!" wrote Melville, and his remains the one true battle cry of all art. Experimentation is as natural to poetry as breathing is to life. If one were content with the old forms, with things-as-they-are, and with things-as-they-have-been-said, one could not write poetry at all.

Invention is the almost incidental by-product of this constant chafing against what is, an emergence into discovery. Invention need not be new to the world; it need only be genuinely new and fresh to the writer, who discovers his or her form alone, in solitude, after many failures and much self-doubt. It is absurd to imagine that Robert Frost did not grope his way toward the lyrical, rhyming, colloquially American language that evolved as his own. All of the so-called traditional or classical poets were wildly inventive and outrageous in their day. Milton, with his thundering blank verse, is only one example. Dante dropped from the "acceptable" elevated language of great poetry—Latin—to the mundane Italian spoken by street vendors, fishwives, soldiers, and farmers, and he did it against the advice and imprecations of his friends. Shakespeare careens from blank verse to formal sonnets to prose, all within a single play, and anyone who believes that his verse was written in strict iambic pentameter has a tin ear: "Howl, howl, howl, howl!" or "Bare ruined choirs, where late the sweet birds sang."

Invention is playful, but it is not merely play. My one objection to Frost's famous remark on free verse is that poetry seems to me an infinitely more important and complex "game" than tennis. Invention is the one true genius child of necessity, and it comes with the kind of passion and power that we may imagine first breathed life into the planets and spun them, the impulse that is always behind birth and creation. It is not strange, but familiar and fundamental to the very fact of our existence. Perhaps this is why great "new" poetry feels at the same time shocking and yet inevitable. There is nothing alien or rarefied about poetry, in whatever form. It is indeed at its best when it is closest to the mundane mysteries, when it is fresh with its own discoveries, with invention, and therefore brings us close to the common, creative wellspring of all being.

JUVENILE AND YOUNG ADULT

78

CALLING IT QUITS

BY LOIS LOWRY

"You put <u>what</u> in it?" my son asked, his fork halfway to his mouth.
"Ginger snaps," I repeated. "Crushed ginger snaps."

"I thought that's what you said." I watched while he put his fork back down on his plate and then pushed the plate away from him. It was clear to me that my son, normally a good sport, was not going to eat my innovative beef stew.

It was clear to me, after I tasted it myself, that he had made the right decision.

SOMETIMES IN THE PROCESS OF CREATING, it is very difficult to know when to quit adding things.

Some years back, I received in the mail the first foreign edition of my first young adult book, *A Summer to Die*. Fortunately it was French. Later I would receive, with a gulp of astonishment, the Finnish, the Afrikaans, the Catalan; but this first one was French. French I can read.

And so I leafed through the pages, savoring the odd, startling sense of recognition that I had, seeing my own words translated into another language.

On the last page, I read the line of dialogue with which I had concluded the book. " 'Meg,' he laughed, putting one arm over my shoulders, 'you were beautiful all along.' " There it was, in French.

But there was something else, as well. I blinked in surprise, seeing it. In French, the book concluded: "They walked on."

They walked on? Of course they *had* walked on, those two characters, Meg and Will. I knew they had, and I had trusted the reader to know that they had. But I hadn't written that line. The translator had.

I don't know why. I can only guess that the translator simply couldn't resist that urge that makes all of us throw a crushed ginger snap into the stew now and then.

Knowing when to stop is one of the toughest tasks a writer faces.

Is there a rule that one can follow? Probably not. But there is, I think, a test against which the writer can measure his ending, his stopping place.

When something more is going to take place, but the characters have been so fully drawn, and the preceding events so carefully shaped that the reader, on reflection, knows what more will happen, and is satisfied by it—then the book ends.

In essence, you, as writer, will have successfully taught the reader to continue writing the book in his mind.

What about the concept of resolution, then? Isn't the writer supposed to tie up the loose ends of the story neatly at the conclusion? And if everything is neatly packaged and tied, then how on earth can something more take place?

Your story—your plot—your theme— is only a portion of the lives of the characters you have created. Their lives, if you have made them real to the reader, are going to continue in the reader's mind.

Your role is only a part of that process. And you need to know when and how to get out when your role is finished. As author, you tie up and resolve the piece of a life you have chosen to examine. Then you leave, gracefully. The life continues, but you are no longer looking at it.

You have engaged and directed the imagination of the reader; and then you have turned the reader loose.

Writing this, I looked at the endings of some of my own books, to see if they followed any kind of pattern.

In one, *Anastasia on Her Own,* a mother and daughter are laughing and tap-dancing together up a flight of stairs.

In *Find a Stranger, Say Goodbye,* a young girl is packing to go away; she is deciding what to take and what to leave behind.

The narrator and her mother in *Rabble Starkey* are together in a car, heading into a somewhat uncertain future. (Not coincidentally, that book is published in Great Britain under the title *The Road Ahead.*)

The forms of these endings are different. Some are descriptive, some consist of dialogue. Some are lighthearted, others more introspective.

But they do seem to have a few elements in common:

They all include the main character—sometimes more than one—in the final scene.

Each of them, in various forms, reflects a sense of motion, of flow, of moving forward.

And each in its own way contains a kind of conclusive statement.

Anastasia fell in behind her mother and tried to follow the complicated hops, turns, and shuffles her mother was doing. Together they tap-danced down the hall and up the stairs. It was silly, she thought; but it was fun. And it sure felt good, having her mother back in charge.

—Anastasia on Her Own

It was the throwing away that was the hardest. But she did it, until the trunk was packed, the trash can was filled, and the room was bare of everything except the memories; those would always be there, Natalie knew.

—Find a Stranger, Say Goodbye

She sped up a little, driving real careful, and when we went around the curve I looked, and it was all a blur. But there was nothing there. There was only Sweet Hosanna and me, and outside the whole world, quiet in the early morning, green and strewn with brand new blossoms, like the ones on my very best dress.

—Rabble Starkey

The common elements that you can see and hear in those ending paragraphs are a little like the basics in a good stew; maybe you could equate them to a garlic clove, a bay leaf, and a dollop of wine.

As for the crushed ginger snap? The ingredient that qualifies as overkill and makes the whole thing just a little nauseating?

Well, I confess that those three passages have one more thing in common. Each one was tough to end. Like the translator who added another sentence to my book, I wanted to go on, too. I wanted to add crushed ginger snaps: more sentences, more images, embellishments, explanations, embroidery.

And if I had? Take a look:

She sped up a little, driving real careful, and when we went around the curve I looked, and it was all a blur. But there was nothing there. There was only Sweet Hosanna and me, and outside the whole world, quiet in the early morning, green and strewn with brand new blossoms, like the ones on my very best dress.

What would the future hold for us? I had no way of knowing. But I remembered how, in the past years, my mother had worked and saved to bring us this

393

far. I looked at her now, her eyes intent on the road, and I could see the determination . . .

Et cetera. You can't read it—I couldn't *write* it—without a feeling of wanting to push your plate away. It's too much. It's unnecessary. It is, in a word, sickening.

The letters I get so often from kids provide me, unintentionally, with a reminder of the impact of a good ending. Boy, if anyone in the world knows how to *end*, it's a kid writing a letter.

"Well," they say, "I have to quit now."

79

WRITING NONFICTION BOOKS FOR YOUNG READERS

BY JAMES CROSS GIBLIN

WHERE do you get the ideas for your nonfiction books?" is often the first thing I'm asked when I speak to writers. My usual reply is, "From anywhere and everywhere."

I've found a good place to start in the search for ideas is with your own interests and enthusiasms. It also helps if you can make use of personal experience. For example, the idea for my *The Skyscraper Book* (Crowell) really had its beginnings when I was a child, and loved to be taken up to the observation deck of the Terminal Tower, the tallest building in my home city of Cleveland.

Years later, after I moved to New York, I rented an apartment that was just a few blocks away from the Flatiron Building, one of the city's earliest and most striking skyscrapers. No matter how many times I passed the building, I always saw something new when I looked up at the carved decorations on its surface.

Although I had edited many books for children, I'd never thought of writing for a young audience until I was invited to contribute a 500-word essay to *The New York Kid's Book*. I chose the Flatiron Building as my topic because I wanted to find out more about it myself.

That piece led to an expanded magazine article (for *Cricket*) called "Buildings That Scrape the Sky," and then to *The Skyscraper Book*. In the latter I was finally able to tell the story behind Cleveland's Terminal Tower, the skyscraper that had fascinated me forty years earlier.

Besides looking first to your own interests and knowledge, you should also be open to ideas that may come your way by luck or chance. The idea of *Chimney Sweeps* (Crowell) literally came to me out of the blue when I was flying to Oklahoma City on business.

The plane stopped in Chicago and a tall, rangy young man carrying what I thought was a musical instrument case took the seat next to me. We started to talk, and I discovered that the man—whose name was Christopher Curtis—was a chimney sweep, and his case contained samples of the brushes he manufactured at his own small factory in Vermont. He was on his way to Oklahoma City to conduct a seminar for local sweeps on how to clean chimneys more efficiently.

Chris went on to tell me a little about the history of chimney sweeping and its revival as a profession in the last decade, because of the energy crisis. In turn, I told him I was a writer of children's books, and that he'd fired my interest in chimney sweeps as a possible subject.

We exchanged business cards, and a month or so later I wrote to tell him that I'd followed up on the idea and had started researching the book on chimney sweeps. I asked him if he'd be willing to read the manuscript for accuracy. He agreed to do so and volunteered to supply photographs of present-day sweeps that could be used (and were) as illustrations in the book.

According to an old English superstition, it's lucky to meet a chimney sweep. Well, meeting Christopher Curtis was certainly lucky for me!

Evaluating an idea

Once you have an idea for a book, the next step is to decide whether or not it's worth pursuing. The first thing I do is check R. R. Bowker's annual *Subject Guide to Children's Books in Print*, available in the reference department of most libraries, to see what else has been written on the subject. With *Chimney Sweeps*, there was nothing at all. In the case of *The Skyscraper Book*, I discovered that there were several books about *how* skyscrapers are constructed, but none with a focus on *why* and *by whom* they're constructed, which was the angle of the book I wanted to write. There may be many books on a given subject, but if you find a fresh or different slant, there'll probably be room in the market for yours, too.

Another thing to weigh when evaluating an idea is the matter of levels: A subject worth treating in a book usually has more than one. For instance, when I began researching *Chimney Sweeps*, I soon realized that besides the obvious human and social history, the subject also touched on economic and technological history. Weaving those different levels together made the book more interesting to write—and I believe it makes it more interesting for readers also.

A third important factor to consider is what age group to write the book for. That decision has to be based on two things: the nature of the subject and a knowledge of the market for children's books. I aimed *Chimney Sweeps* at an older audience, because I felt that the subject required more of a sense of history than younger readers would have. At the same time, I kept the text as simple and compact as possible, because I knew that there's a much greater demand today for children's nonfiction geared to the upper elementary grades than there is for Young Adult nonfiction.

After you've checked out your idea and decided what slant to take with it, and what age group to write for, it's time to begin the research. An entire article could be devoted to research methods alone. The one thing I feel it's safe to say after writing seven books is that each project requires its own approach, and you have to discover it as you go along.

When I was researching *The Scarecrow Book* (Crown, 1980), I came up against one stone wall after another. It seemed no one had ever bothered to write anything about scarecrows. Research became a matter of following up on the skimpiest of clues. For example, a brief mention in a magazine article that the Japanese had a scarecrow god led me to the Orientalia Division of the Library of Congress, where a staff member kindly translated a passage from a Japanese encyclopedia describing the god and its relation to Japanese scarecrows.

The Skyscraper Book presented the opposite problem. There was so much background material available on skyscrapers that I could easily have spent ten years researching the subject and never come to the end. Choices had to be made early on. I settled on the eight or ten New York skyscrapers I wanted to discuss and sought detailed information only on those. I did the same thing with skyscrapers in Chicago and other cities around the country.

Chimney Sweeps opened up the exciting area of primary source material. On a visit to the Economics Division of the New York Public Library, I discovered the yellowing transcripts of early 19th-century British investigations into the deplorable living and working conditions of child sweeps.

Fireworks, Picnics, and Flags: The Story of The Fourth of July Symbols (Clarion) introduced me to the pleasures of on-site research. I had spent two days at beautiful Independence National Historical Park in Philadelphia. I toured Independence Hall, visited the rented rooms nearby where Thomas Jefferson drafted the Declaration of Independence, and watched a group of third-grade youngsters touch the Liberty Bell in its pavilion. I won't soon forget the looks of awe on their faces.

Whenever I go out on a research expedition, I always take along a supply of 4 × 6-inch cards. At the top of each one, I write the subject for handy reference when I file the cards alphabetically in a metal box. I also write the title, author, publisher, and date of the book I'm reading so that I'll have all that information on hand when I compile the bibliography for my book. Then I go on to jot down the facts I think I might be able to use.

I try to check each fact against at least two other sources before including it in the text. Such double-checking can turn up myths that have long passed as truths. For instance, while researching *Fireworks, Picnics, and Flags,* I read two books that said an old bell-ringer sat in the tower of Independence Hall almost all day on July 4, 1776. He was waiting for word that independence had been declared so that he could ring the Liberty Bell.

At last, in late afternoon, a small boy ran up the steps of the tower and shouted, "Ring, Grandfather! Ring for Liberty!" The old man did so at once, letting all of Philadelphia know that America was no longer a British colony. It makes a fine story—but according to the third source I checked, it simply isn't true.

By no means will all of the facts I find appear in the finished book. Only a small part of any author's research shows up in the final manuscript. But I think a reader can feel the presence of the rest beneath the surface, lending substance and authority to the writing.

Picture research

With most of my books, I've gathered the illustrations as well as written the text, and this has led me into the fascinating area of picture research. On *The Scarecrow Book,* for example, I discovered the resources of the Prints and Photographs Division of the Library of Congress, where I located several stunning photographs of Southern scarecrows taken during the 1930s. Later, in a back issue of *Time* magazine, I came across a story about Senji Kataoka, a public relations officer with the Ministry of Agriculture in Tokyo, whose hobby was taking pictures of scarecrows. Over the years, the article said, Mr.

Kataoka had photographed more than 2000 examples in the countryside around Tokyo.

I decided to follow up on this lead, remote as it might prove to be. From the Japanese consulate in New York I obtained the address of the Ministry of Agriculture in Tokyo, and wrote Mr. Kataoka there. Six weeks later his answer arrived in neatly printed English, along with eight beautiful color snapshots of scarecrows. I wrote back saying I needed black-and-white photos for the book and Mr. Kataoka immediately mailed me a dozen, four of which were used in the chapter on Japanese scarecrows. Another appeared on the jacket. When I asked Mr. Kataoka how much he wanted for his photos, he said just a copy of the book.

Experiences such as these have taught me several important things about doing picture research. The first is: Never start with commercial photographic agencies. They charge high reproduction fees which are likely to put you in the red if your contract states that you are responsible for paying such costs.

Instead, try non-profit sources like U.S. government agencies, which provide photographs for just the cost of the prints; art and natural history museums, which charge modest fees; and national tourist offices, which will usually give you photographs free of charge, asking only that you credit them as the source.

Other good sources of free photos are the manufacturers of various products. Their public relations departments will be happy to send you high quality photographs of everything from tractors to inflatable vinyl scarecrows in return for an acknowledgment in your book.

Selling

Writers often ask me if they should complete all the research for a nonfiction book before trying to sell the idea to a publisher. That's usually not necessary. However, if you're a beginner you should do enough research to make sure there's sufficient material for a book. Then you'll need to write a full outline and draft one or two sample chapters. After that, you can send query letters to publishers and ask if they'd like to look at your material.

If a publisher is interested, you should be prepared to rewrite your sample chapters several times before being offered a contract. That happened to me with my first book, *The Scarecrow Book,* and looking back now I'm glad it did. For it helped me and my collaborator, Dale Ferguson, to sharpen the focus of that book.

Of course it's different after you become an established author. Then both you and your editors know what you can do, and generally a two- or three-page proposal describing your new book idea will be enough for the publisher to make a decision.

Once you have your contract for the book in hand, you can proceed with the writing of the manuscript. Some authors use electric typewriters, others have turned to word processors. I write longhand in a spiral notebook and mark in the margins the date each passage was drafted. That encourages me as I inch through the notebook, working mainly on Saturdays and Sundays and during vacations from my full-time editorial job.

Achieving a consistent personal voice in a nonfiction book takes me at least three drafts. In the first, I get down the basic material of the paragraph or section. In the second, I make certain the organization is logical and interesting, and I then begin to smooth out those spots where the style of the original research source may be too clearly in evidence. In the third draft, I polish the section until the tone and voice are entirely mine.

After I deliver to the editor the completed manuscript and the illustrations I've gathered, I may heave a sigh of relief. But chances are my work won't be over. The editor may feel that extensive revisions are necessary; sections of the manuscript may have to be reorganized, others rewritten. Perhaps the editor will want me to compile a bibliography, or a glossary of unfamiliar words used in the text.

At last everything is in place, and a year or so later—during which time the manuscript has been copyedited, designed, and set in type— the finished book arrives in the mail. That's an exciting moment, followed by a few anxious weeks as you wait for the first reviews to appear. The verdict of the critics isn't the final one, though. There's yet another stage in the life of any children's book: the reaction of young readers.

Perhaps a boy will come up to me after a library talk and tell me that he was inspired to find out more about the skyscrapers in his city after reading *The Skyscraper Book.* Or a girl will write to say that the chapter on a day in the life of a climbing boy in *Chimney Sweeps* made her cry. It's only then that I know I'm on the way toward achieving my goal—to write lively, accurate, and entertaining books for young people.

80

PEOPLE I HAVE KNOWN

BY KATHERINE PATERSON

How do you build your characters?" It's a familiar question to those of us who write fiction and, I suspect, one of the most uncomfortable. When someone asks me about "building characters," I'm tempted to remind him that characters are people, not models you put together with an erector set. You don't "build" people, you get to know them.

All human beings are born on a certain day in a particular place and from two parents. These are all givens. When I am beginning a book, the central character is little more than an uneasy feeling in the pit of my stomach. I spend a long time trying to understand who this person is—where he or she was born, when, and from whom.

When I was trying to start *Jacob Have I Loved*, I knew the protagonist was a girl of about fourteen, who was eaten up with jealousy for a brother or sister. That was all I had to go on in the beginning. When I discovered, quite by accident, that she lived on a tiny island in the middle of the Chesapeake Bay, I was well on my way to getting to know her.

(Incidentally, anyone who has written fiction knows that such revelatory accidents are a way of life for writers. This one involved a Christmas gift book about the Chesapeake Bay which I happened to read because I was desperate for reading material on the 29th of December. Time after time, writers stumble blindly upon the very secrets that will serve to unlock the story they are currently struggling with.)

Anyhow, as I discovered, life on a Chesapeake Bay island is different from life anywhere else in America. On Tangier and Smith (the islands upon which I modeled my imaginary island of Rass), there are families that have lived on the same narrow bits of land since well before the Revolutionary War. The men of the island earn their living crabbing in the warmer months and oystering in the colder. For island people, all of life is organized about the water that surrounds them and even today cuts them off from the rest of our country. The speech of the people is unlike that of those in nearby Maryland or Virginia. Scholars think it may resemble the Elizabethan speech of colonial America. The islands were converted to Methodism in the 18th century and remain strongly religious communities. I could go on, but you can see how being born and spending her formative years on such an island would affect the growth of Louise Bradshaw. She could be molded by her adaptation to her environment or by her rebellion against it. Either way, the place is of vital significance to the person she is and will become.

When a character is born is another revealing point. You can see this in life. My husband and I were born at the height of the depression. Our older boy was born soon after Kennedy was assassinated. Our younger daughter was born the year both Martin Luther King and Robert Kennedy were killed. When I am trying to get to know a character, I always ask what was happening in the world when this person was born and what effect these events might have had on his life.

Usually, I determine the date of birth of all of my central characters, not just the protagonist. This was crucial to the story in my novel *Come Sing, Jimmy Jo*. James was born in 1973, and his mother was born in 1959. "But that means . . !" Yes, it means that Keri Su was fourteen when James was born. If I know that, I can begin to understand some of the problems that have always existed between them—why almost from birth James has looked to his grandma for mothering rather than his mother.

This leads directly to the question of parentage. When I first began writing *Jimmy Jo,* I assumed that Keri Su was James's mother, and Jerry Lee was his father. The fact that Jerry Lee was ten years older than his wife explained to some extent why he was the more responsible parent of the two. After all, he was already a grownup when the boy was born.

But the better I got to know this family, the more I realized that there was something there that they weren't telling. Gradually, I got a picture of Keri Su, a thirteen-year-old girl from the West Virginia hills. The mountain boyfriend who has made her pregnant has run away and joined the navy to escape the wrath of the girl's hard-drinking father. Now all of the father's anger is directed toward his daughter. She runs away with nowhere to run and happens into a tiny mountain town where the Johnson Family Singers are performing at one of the local churches.

The girl loves music, and she hangs around until the Johnsons, especially Grandma and Jerry Lee, realize the extent of her desperation and take her under their wings. She is a good-looking, spunky kid with a powerful singing voice, and Jerry Lee, with a mixture of admiration and pity and affection, marries her. James, the child that is born so soon afterwards, is a Johnson heart and soul, made so by the love of Jerry Lee and Grandma, who share with him the special love they have for one another.

What happens, then, to the rest of the family members? There is brother Earl, who was a young adolescent when Keri Su joined the family. He has always resented Jerry Lee, who is older, wiser, nicer, and, as Earl sees it, much their mother's favorite. Now his brother has married a girl Earl's own age, a girl, who under different circumstances, he might have liked to take out himself. Earl is jealous of the position Keri Su immediately achieves in the family and at the same time is attracted to her despite himself.

And what about Grandpa? He seems to take his wife for granted, but perhaps he, too, feels a wistful twinge when he sees how she dotes on Jerry Lee and on the fatherless child that their son has totally accepted as his own. Doesn't blood count for something? Grandpa wonders. Like most mountain men, he puts a lot of stock in good blood. He likes the boy and all, but it's not as if James were really his grandson.

So far nothing I've said is actually in the book. It is all in the background to the story—the life these people lived before they entered the pages of this particular book. But I have to know all of these things about the characters or run the risk that my characters will be as separate and inanimate as Barbie and Ken. If you let *living* people into a story, they will move each other. If you put in *constructed* characters, you'll have to do the moving yourself. The reader won't be fooled. He'll be able to tell which is which.

When it comes to deciding what about these people will actually be revealed on the printed page, I am guided, of course, by the story I want to tell, but also, quite particularly, by point of view. *Jacob Have I Loved* is written in the first person. The only point of view the reader is given is that of Louise, who is so jealous of her sister that she is blind to the affection that her parents, Call, the Captain, and even her sister have for her. Now I am not Louise. I can see what she cannot, and it breaks my heart to realize how much her mother loves her and to know how little Louise can understand or trust that love.

A wise reader will be aware of the narrowness of Louise's vision, but since I write principally for children and young people, I know that many of my readers will assume that Louise's badly skewed view is the correct view. I suppose I could have written the book differently to give Louise's mother and even sister Caroline a sporting chance, but then the power of Louise's jealousy would have been diminished. It would have been a different, and, I believe, weaker story.

Again, in *Come Sing, Jimmy Jo,* the story is told wholly from James's viewpoint. He's never been told about his origins, but that doesn't mean he doesn't feel the uneasiness of the other family members when the past is referred to.

Often children will ask me about the parents in my books. "Why are they so mean?" is a question I've gotten more than a few times about Jesse Aarons's parents in the book, *Bridge to Terabithia.* I use the occasion to try to help young readers understand point of view. All the parents in my stories are seen from their children's point of view, and it has been my experience that children are very seldom fair in their judgments of their parents. I hope I've sent all my questioners home to take another, more objective look not only at my book, but at their own parents, most of whom, I dare say, are like the parents in *Bridge to Terabithia,* doing the best they can under trying circumstances.

Characters are like people in another way. Some of them are very easy to get to know, others more difficult. Maime Trotter, the foster mother in *The Great Gilly Hopkins,* simply arrived one day full grown. She was so powerfully herself that the other characters in the book came to life responding to her immense loving energy. Gilly, who had spent her time before the book began cynically manipulating the people about her, had to learn how to reckon with a force greater than her own anger.

The actual appearance of one of the most important characters in *The Great Gilly Hopkins* takes up less than two pages of the text. She is Gilly's mother—the unwed flower child who gave Gilly up to foster care years before the book opens. Yet what she actually is and what Gilly dreams she is (two different things, as you might suspect) combine to help shape the troubled and troubling child, whom we first meet in the back seat of the social worker's car on the way to yet another foster home.

There is, finally, something mysterious about the life of one's characters. In my secret heart, I almost believe that one of these days I'll meet Jesse Aarons walking toward me on a downtown street. I'll recognize him at once, although he will have grown to manhood, and I'll ask him what he's been doing in the years since he built that bridge across Lark Creek.

On the second thought, I probably won't ask. I'll smile and he'll nod, but I won't pry. Years ago he let me eavesdrop on his soul, but that time is past. He is entitled to his privacy now. Still, I can't help wondering.

81

WRITING THE HISTORICAL NOVEL FOR YOUNG READERS

BY PATRICIA BEATTY

WHEN I AM ASKED, as I frequently am, "Where do you get your ideas?" I have no one response that applies to every book I have written. Sometimes a conversation sparks a book—sometimes a magazine article. A single paragraph in a memoir can get my mind racing, as in *Charley Skedaddle* and *A Long Way to Whiskey Creek*. Peripheral as well as major figures in biographies of noted men and women of the past can stimulate a novel that features one of the figures as a character (for instance, *Campion Towers,* using Oliver Cromwell). Now and then the history of a particular locale—such as the section of London I lived in, and one that in the 18th century had Samuel Johnson, William Hogarth, and Alexander Pope as residents—leads to my writing a book like *At the Seven Stars*. The California city in which I now live does not have a long or particularly interesting history, but some past events there led to my writing *The Queen's Own Grove* and others. I've used the West Coast (the Washington State "Peninsula Beaches") as the site for four of my novels. (This is where my mother's family fled when cyclones drove them out of Kansas in the early 1890s.) Very recently in a plane to New York I looked out the window onto what I figured was Missouri and said to myself, "Aha, Jesse James, would you have been the age I want you to be in 1865?" He was. That famous outlaw will be in a book-to-be.

There is no accounting for my titles, either. They either arrive in a flash before I actually start the writing, or they never come at all. Two books were given titles by my editors. The others are swift serendipity. If they sound "right" to me, I use them. When I have a story line in mind, I tell myself to start dreaming up a title and hope for a thunderbolt inspiration.

I never have used reference books that supply "basic plots" or advise how to plot a novel. I go ahead on my own, making up my own tale. I outline each book in a five- to six-page synopsis, double-spaced. After that, on separate pages, I make a list of the names of characters. Under the names I write down ages, physical characteristics, education, social status, personality traits, religious attitudes, etc. If my character is a real historical person, I try to make my description of him or her as accurate as possible from biographies, painted portraits, and photographs. In this way, my characters become "real" to me before I set pen to paper, and here I am being *very literal*. I write *everything* in longhand. My first revisions are done as I type. (I hate typing as a mechanical process, and I do not anticipate ever getting a word processor. I suspect that if I did, I'd create 120-word sentences, something I'm told happens even to professional writers of long experience.) What I have laboriously typed, I read aloud to myself for smoothness.

The historical novel for adults often becomes dynastic, following a character or a family through generations. This cannot be done in a historical novel for children. Children want to read about other children, not about adults or even a "child character" growing into maturity and into old age. In general, children want to read above their age: a ten-year-old wants to read of the doings of a twelve-year-old and chiefly about his or her own sex. Two years is about the span of time in a historical novel for young readers. Actual historical events should not be tampered with. For instance, if a battle took place on April 1, 1864, and another involving the same character happened on June 1, 1864, those two months will *have to be* accounted for in the story. This 60-day accounting need not be long and involved, but it must be given due attention for the sake of accuracy. If a historical character, such as a famous general, was not really present at a particular battle, don't put him there.

In writing my novels, I go, if possible, to the locale I will use as a setting. Seeing the site helps me visualize what a place was like in the era I want to write about. Of course, over the centuries it will have changed, but if the century chosen isn't too far back, the geographical features will still be there, as well as some of the buildings (for instance, old Panama's ruined cathedral, which I used in my book *Pirate Royale*). I buy guidebooks and take photographs and keep them for future books.

While this traveling is important, it's the minutiae of the period that chiefly bring the past alive in historical fiction. I find the little things I research matter most of all; in fact, the research I do often gives me more pleasure than the actual process of writing.

I love libraries! I could not write my books without them, especially the university library in the town where I live. Public libraries rarely have the number of books needed except for "local history," and inter-library loans, though useful, can be very slow. I buy some books for my special interests, but I have yet to write a book that didn't require glorious hours in library stacks and long talks with reference librarians. I don't often ask for specific facts from either librarians or academic experts in any given historical field, however. I ask for "sources" and do my own "searching." (When a book is published, I include in my acknowledgments the names of the people who have told me where to hunt.)

I have a definite method for my research, one I have used for many years. I set up a permanent file for future books I may want to set in the same period or place. I use large, thin white cards or pieces of stiff paper cut to fit neatly into shoe boxes. On the outside of each box I label what period the material inside covers, with a separate box for each of the following: the English Civil War, the American Civil War, Elizabethan England and Ireland, Cromwellian England, Jamaica and Panama 1670s, and Colonial South Carolina. I have other boxes for each Western state I've written about and the time setting of the novel devoted to that particular state. I can use any one of these boxes at any future time for material for a new book. Following this method, you can set up boxes for any period you choose.

At the top of each card I write a subject category, such as Foods (children love to know what children of various classes of the past ate), Times of Meals, Table Implements and Manners, Entertainment and Toys, Employment, Cosmetics and Styles, Housing, Towns and Cities, Education, Furniture, Medicine, and so forth. I am very much aware as I take notes that people of the past were not as "homogenized" as people are today. Older societies were class structured—this was true even in America. Millhand children did not mix socially with mill-owners' children. (I use the unpleasant but realistic categories "Upper Class," "Middle Class," and "Lower Class" on each card in descending order, as "U.C.," "M.C.," "L.C.") My research often reveals differences that will surprise today's young readers who would not know, for instance, that only rich children in 16th-century England ever tasted white bread.

There are some taboos in historical novels for children: heavy cursing, public executions, bloody riots involving religious differences, gross cruelty to animals, gruesome medical procedures, scatology, sexual scenes, horrendously bloody events of war, and so forth. Hard realism is fine if not lingered over; brutal sensationalism is not.

The speech of a particular era won't present much of a problem to a writer with an ear for dialogue. The place to find it is in the literature of the period. In researching different books, I've steeped myself in Shakespeare's plays, 18th-century English novels, and Civil War diaries and memoirs. I often write in the first person, so I note on the cards particular phrases and words that give the flavor I seek. I aim at a smooth approximation of the actual speech of the time, not a total recap of it—that would lose the young reader's interest fast. If I use an antique word, I define it right away in my text.

Today's moral attitudes differ greatly from those of the past—even of the fairly recent past of this century. Many scholars say Americans have gone through a "moral revolution" since the 1960s. Religious, racial, gender, and governmental oppressions have all laid a heavy hand on many people in the last and earlier centuries. A personal note of morality, integrity, truthfulness, honesty, hard work, and self-reliance was very often drilled into young people, who were considered "miniature adults" and chattels of their harsh fathers. The various moral codes considered "proper" for young people of a particular era must be taken into account in historical fiction. Having my hero in *Charley Skedaddle* run away from battle, for instance, would have been a far more heinous act in 1864 than today, in a society that increasingly condemns war and macho behavior and can find almost no justification for any war. For books set in pre-19th century eras, I find out the moral attitudes of a particular period from adults' and children's books published at the time. For books set at a later time, I use old newspaper accounts and bound volumes of magazines. Though hard on the eyes, microfilmed materials are often gold mines of information.

Every single fact an author needs to know when writing a historical novel is not going to come to hand, not even from scholars of the period or reference librarians. The author must use his or her imagination. (For example, I had no idea how committees were chosen in the House of Lords in 17th-century England, though the members of the House of Commons "shouted out" their preferences. I hunted for this fact for over twenty years, then finally settled on the House of Commons "method" for use in one of my books.)

As I write I am always aware of my readers—adults as well as children, because not only reviewers but parents and teachers read children's historical fiction. I try to give them all an interesting story not overburdened with detail that obscures the plot, but real events and actual historical personages depicted as they were seen by their contemporaries. I want my Oliver Cromwell and Queen Elizabeth I to appear as they do in the history texts but "brought more to life" in my fiction. If a child goes away from one of my books with a mental portrait of a real person from history and never again reads of that person, I want to feel that what I wrote was the proper stuff for intellectual baggage for a lifetime.

82

THINK PICTURE BOOK

BY EVE BUNTING

THE BAD NEWS IS THAT NO, picture books are not easy to write. The good news is that there are some useful guidelines in picture book writing, and although they will never guarantee a sale, they will at least put you on course if writing a beautiful picture book is your heart's desire. So let's think picutre book.

Most obviously, *think pictures*. Perceive your story as a moving slide show, vivid, arresting, and dramatic. Give the illustrator something to work with. If you are both author and illustrator you will be doing yourself the same favor. Incidentally, it is not necessary for you to provide the pictures. The publisher will take care of that for you.

Remember, static scenes without variety do not make a good slide presentation.

I once had a friend show me a picture book manuscript she'd written.

"It's so cute," she said. "But I've sent it out and sent it out, and no one wants to buy it. Why?"

In the book, a cat stands before a mirror, trying on hats—a cowboy hat, a fireman's helmet, a baseball cap, etc. One character, one scene, one action, repeated over and over.

"He could be a very cute cat," I said. "But nothing happens."

My friend looked puzzled and a little irritated by my lack of perception.

"Something does happen," she said. "He changes hats."

I amended my words. "Not enough happens."

That cat in the mirror would make a dull slide show and a dull picture book.

An art director in a major publishing house once told me: "The words in a picture book should be a gift to the illustrator."

I had always believed that the illustrator's paintings were gifts to the writers, adding dimensions often undreamed of. And that is true. But it

411

has to work the other way around, too. What the art director meant was that if the scenes in the text are varied, imaginative, plentiful, the illustrator doesn't have to struggle and the book is what it should be, a happy collaboration. To achieve this, keep in mind that the scenes should roll forward in an ever-moving diversity of character and action. This does not always happen naturally for me. I have to work at it. You can, too.

When you've finished your manuscript, divide it by drawing lines across the text to mark what you see as the natural ending of a page. Or set up a dummy by taking eight sheets of blank paper and folding them horizontally to make a 32-page book (32 pages is the usual picture book length, less three or four for front matter: title page, copyright, and dedication). Write your text on each dummy page. Do you have enough pictures? Do you have too many words? Look for balance. Visualize your little reader, or listener, impatient to get on with it, to turn the page to find out what happens next.

If I see an ungainly chunk of text in my own work, I deliberately set out to "break" it up with picture possibilities.

For instance, in *The Mother's Day Mice,* there is a scene in which the three little mice are watching Honeysuckle Cottage, waiting and hoping that the cat on the porch will go away. It is important here that I give the impression of time passing, since Little Mouse needs to hear many repeats of the song being played on the piano inside the cottage. When I read what I'd written, I realized I had a static scene. So I added:

(Middle Mouse) set his strawberry on the ground and a beetle came on the run. Middle picked it up again and shooed the beetle away.
Little Mouse began creeping toward the cottage on his belly.
Biggest yanked him back by his tail.

These few lines add action and a little humor. They use all three mouse characters and a new peripheral character, the beetle, is placed on the scene. But better, better, better, they add two picture possibilities. And Jan Brett, the illustrator, used both charmingly.

Adding scenes is not that difficult. But it is harder because of the second unbreakable law of the picture book—*think short*. Think 1,000 words, or less. Think concise. Say what you need to say in the most economical way possible that makes sense and that sounds poetic, because a poetic telling is the essence of the picture book.

A few weeks ago I visited a school where examples of "pretty sentences from picture books" were pinned on the wall of the library.

"We talk about them," the librarian told me. "We ask: 'Why did the author say it this way instead of another way?' We listen to the sounds of the words and the cadence of the sentence and look for images."

So "pretty" sentences are a must, if we want to make it on the wall. Not overblown, though. Not gushy or sentimentally sweet.

Isn't it more breathtaking to read, "The air hissed to the beat of wings" *(The Man Who Could Call Down Owls)* than, "There was the sound of wings in the air"? Try to use the actual "sound" word. The air *hissed;* the bus *wheezed;* the leaves *flurried* in the wind.

Long passages of undiluted description are out in the picture book. But I believe short descriptions add immeasurably to the texture of the story and enhance the word awareness of even the youngest reader. A line or two can set the scene:

Milk bottles stood on front steps, waiting to be let in. The sky was the color of his mother's pearl brooch. The one she wore on Sundays. *(St. Patrick's Day in the Morning)*

Crows cawed in the white air. The arms of the trees scratched at the sky. *(The Valentine Bears)*

Our table seemed monstrously big. Chairs, hump-backed, clawed and crouched around it. *(Ghost's Hour, Spook's Hour)*

Enough description, but not too much.

A picture book, then, must be short, not abrupt. It must be pure, not sterile. There is room for a story and for a few beautiful word pictures, too.

There is also room to say something valuable. A picture book that does not has no value of itself. Heavy or deeply moralistic, no. Worthwhile, yes. The treasure is well hidden, but it's there for the child to feel and understand. In *Ghost's Hour, Spook's Hour,* I am saying: "No need to be afraid of the dark. The scary things can be explained away. See? No need to be afraid." Those actual words never appear in the text. They are self-evident as Jake and his trusty dog, Biff, search the dark house for Mom and Dad while in the hallway the big clock strikes midnight—ghost's hour, spook's hour.

On a trip to mainland China a few years ago, I spent some time browsing in a bookstore and brought back with me a picture book

413

entitled *A Boy and His Kitten* (for children from 4 to 8). The story is about Maomao who will not go to bed. He and his kitten play through the night hours, disturbing his good little sister.

"How troublesome are those children who do not go to bed," the text says.

In the morning, little sister, who presumably got some sleep, is up at dawn doing her morning exercises. Alas for Maomao and his kitten who are now sleeping the day away:

> For them, it is too late
> To breathe the fresh morning air,
> Or hear their teacher's interesting stories.
> Oh, what a great pity it is
> for Maomao and his kitten!
>
> Our little friends,
> Be not like these two.
> Early to bed,
> And early to rise,
> Keeps you fit and wise.

One has to hope that the story lost a little something in the translation!

You must try not to do this in the picture books you write. In fact, I venture to say, do this and you'll never have a picture book. So *think subtle*. The worthwhile thing you have to say will come across just as clearly and much more palatably.

The picture book writer, perhaps more than writers in any other genre, must *think original*. The field is overflowing with books about cats and dogs, horses and ponies, dinosaurs, rabbits, ducks, mice; boys who are having terrible, awful days, girls who can be anything they want to be; moms, dads, pesky little sisters—all subjects that interest little kids. But writers need to find the *new* angle. As in Carol and Donald Carrick's book: *What Happened to Patrick's Dinosaurs?* The dinosaurs, Patrick says, liked helping people to build houses and lay roads. But after a while the people were willing to sit back and let the dinosaurs do it. They didn't help themselves. So the dinosaurs, for the sake of the people and still helping them, took off in space ships. And *that's* what happened! A nice, original touch and a theme that is there without being belabored.

When I wrote *Scary, Scary Halloween,* I knew of the numerous picture books about this popular holiday. What was there to say that hadn't already been said? So I did trick or treating from a cat's point of view, a mama cat, hiding under the house with her baby kittens, waiting fearfully for the monsters, who are the children in costume, to leave. When they do—

> It's quiet now, the monsters gone
> The streets are ours until the dawn.
> We're out, we prowlers of the night
> Who snap and snarl and claw and bite.
> We stalk the shadows, dark, unseen . . .
> Goodbye 'til next year, Halloween.

A different angle? I think so, and the editor agreed.

When you think picture book, think lasting and forever, because that is what the best picture books are. How many children have been frightened and reassured by *Where the Wild Things Are* (Maurice Sendak)? How many have learned to read for pleasure through the good graces of Dr. Seuss and *The Cat in the Hat* or *Green Eggs and Ham*? How many have gone to sleep to the lullaby lull of *Goodnight Moon*? How many will? A picture book is not temporary, it is not ephemeral. It is as lasting as truth itself and should, said Arnold Lobel, "Rise out of the lives and passions of its creators." It should be unique and ageless and seemingly effortless in its smooth, easy flow.

For all the effort involved, the pruning and shaping and sculpting of words, you will be rewarded with joy as you hold in your hand this small polished jewel that is *your* picture book.

83

CREATING SUSPENSE IN THE YOUNG ADULT MYSTERY

BY JOAN LOWERY NIXON

CREATING SUSPENSE in the young adult mystery novel is not just a matter of keeping the reader guessing: Suspense calls for all the nail-biting emotional responses of anxiety, excitement, and fear, as readers live through the viewpoint of the main character.

Young adult readers are impatient. They'll often read the first few lines of a book, and if it doesn't intrigue them, they'll put the book down and reach for another; so suspense must begin in the first few paragraphs, as in my book *The Kidnapping of Christina Lattimore:*

> I don't like the way he's looking at me.
> It's a kind of creepy look as though the two of us shared some kind of secret, and it's making me uncomfortable.

The story might begin with an immediate, fully written scene of terror, as in *The Dark and Deadly Pool:*

> Moonlight drizzled down the wide glass wall that touched the surface of the hotel swimming pool, dividing it into two parts. The wind-flicked waters of the outer pool glittered with reflected pin-lights from the moon and stars, but the silent water in the indoor section had been sucked into the blackness of the room.
> I blinked, trying to adjust my eyes to the darkness, trying to see the edge of the pool that curved near my feet. I pressed my back against the wall and forced myself to breathe evenly. I whispered aloud, "Mary Elizabeth Rafferty, there is nothing to be afraid of here! Nothing!" But even the sound of my own wobbly words terrified me.

It's not enough just to capture the attention and interest of young adult readers; the author has to keep them in suspense throughout the entire story, and there are a number of ways in which this can be done.

416

1. *Challenge readers with a situation that is completely new and different.* Many of us fondly remember stories from our childhood that involved buried treasure, trunks in attics, and secret passages. But those stories are familiar to today's adolescent mystery fans, too, and unless you can come up with an original, unusual twist, you'd better develop a plot based on your own ideas. Ask yourself an intriguing question and challenge yourself to find the answer.

What if a thirteen-year-old girl, who has been shot during a robbery, wakes from a semi-comatose state four years later to find that she is the only eyewitness to the unsolved crime? (*The Other Side of Dark*)

What if a girl with a serious illness has given up hope and decides not to fight for her life? Suppose her life were in danger from an unexpected direction— wouldn't she instinctively, automatically fight to live? (*The Specter*)

2. *Take a sudden, unexpected turn, making good use of the element of surprise.* In *The Seance,* another of my mysteries, the girls' nervousness during the seance builds to terror, resulting in a scene of panic, in which the candles—the only light in the house—are extinguished. During those few minutes of darkness, before a lamp is plugged in and turned on, one of the girls—Sara—disappears. It's a "locked room mystery" until readers are led to suspect that one of the other girls present must have been involved in Sara's disappearance. When it's revealed that the main character, Lauren, is the one who is responsible, it comes as a total surprise. From this point, the story shifts, and Lauren becomes a potential murder victim.

3. *Throw suspicion on someone whom the main character has trusted.* In *The Ghost of Now,* Angie's brother has been struck by a hit-and-run driver. She tries to unravel the events of that night and comes to suspect that her brother's accident had really been attempted murder. As Angie uncovers information that may lead to the identity of the killer, she confides in Del, a boy she's begun to care for. Then one night Del says something that arouses Angie's suspicions, and she begins to be afraid that Del might be the one who tried to kill her brother.

4. *Let readers know something that the main character hasn't found out yet.* In the novel of detection, a crime has been committed, and the

identity of the criminal must be discovered by both the main character and the readers. In the novel of suspense, someone is out to do away with the main character—who may or may not know the identity of this person—but readers know what is planned and watch the main character head into danger, ignorant of what awaits.

I combined these two forms in *The Stalker.* Every odd-numbered chapter is written in the form of *detection,* from the viewpoint of Jennifer, whose best friend's mother has been murdered. Circumstantial evidence points to the friend, but Jennifer enlists the help of a retired police detective to help her prove Bobbie's innocence. Every even-numbered chapter is written in the form of *suspense,* in the mind of the murderer. The murderer's identity is unknown to both Jennifer and to readers, but readers are aware that he presents an ever-growing danger to Jennifer.

5. *Let the main character become aware of some information but keep it from the reader for a while.* While you must play fair with readers by eventually giving them every clue, there is no reason you can't heighten suspense by showing your reader that your main character knows something but is not yet ready to divulge it. In Chapter One of *The Stalker,* Jennifer, still in shock with news of the murder, questions her grandmother.

"Where is Bobbie? Did they say?"
"Good question. Police don't know where she is. Looks like she up and run away. Nobody on God's earth knows where that girl's gone off to."
Jennifer clutched the (freshly ironed) shirts to her chest, ducking into the smell of starch and scorch so that Grannie couldn't see her face. "I'll start supper," she mumbled, and hurried from the room.
Where was Bobbie? Suddenly, surely, Jennifer knew.

The chapter ends as the police question Jennifer, who is so angry that she keeps her knowledge from them, too.

There was a pause. The detective with the pad and pen leaned toward her just a fraction. The other one did, too. It was coming—the question Jennifer had expected, had been afraid of.
"Jennifer," he said, "do you know where Bobbie Trax is now?"
Jennifer looked at him without blinking, as steadily as she could manage. She gripped the arms of her chair so tightly that her fingers ached as she answered, "No, I don't."

418

It is not until Chapter Three, when Jennifer is on her way to join Bobbie, that readers are made aware of what Jennifer has known all along.

6. *Tantalize readers by hinting at other kinds of secrets that are up to them to uncover.* In *A Deadly Game of Magic,* Lisa and three companions seek refuge from a storm in a nearby house. From the beginning, Lisa, who is intuitive, feels uncomfortable in this house, sensing that though they thought they were alone, there is some other presence in the house with them; her fear zeros in on a room at the end of the bedroom wing—the only room in which the door stands open. Throughout the story an unseen person again and again attempts to lure them toward that room, but each time they manage to avoid entering it. While readers begin to suspect what might be in that room, the final clue isn't given until the last paragraph in the book, and readers must figure out the answer themselves.

7. *Let readers see your main character make a mistake, or choose a totally wrong course of action, as a result of a personality flaw.* In *The Stalker,* Jennifer has been characterized as loyal and loving, but impulsive and stubborn, too. Readers are well aware that she should stay away from the scene of the crime, but her impatient single-mindedness causes her to make the wrong choice. Without telling her detective-partner, Jennifer goes alone to the scene, placing herself in immediate danger.

8. *Description of the setting can help to create and maintain suspense.* Highly visual writing through active picturesque verbs is the essential tool here. In *The Ghosts of Now,* an empty house holds such an important place in the story that it deserves the detailed description which begins:

The Andrews place squats alone at the end of an empty, quiet street. Maybe it's because of the overlarge lot that surrounds it; maybe it's because the house looks like an unkempt, yellowed old man who badly needs a barber, but I feel that the other houses on the block have cringed away from this place, tucking in their tidy porches and neat walkways and dropping filmy curtains over blank eyes. . . .
Someone once lived in this house and loved it, and for a few moments I feel sad that it should be so neglected, left alone to die.
But the house is not dead.

419

There are small rustlings, creakings, and sounds barely loud enough to be heard as the house moves and breathes with the midday heat. I feel that it's watching me, waiting to see what I'll do. Or could someone be watching, listening, just as I listen?

9. *Sub-mysteries can aid suspense.* A sudden shadow on the porch, which is accounted for in the next chapter; a character whose actions are so peculiar that they frighten your main character; an aunt who is frantic to keep something hidden—such sub-mysteries tie in with the central mystery to be solved and heighten suspense. Sometimes they can do double duty by serving as red herrings. In *The Kidnapping of Christina Lattimore,* Christina, upstairs in bed and doing her homework, thinks she is alone in the house, until:

Maybe there was the click of a doorknob downstairs. If there was, I didn't notice it. I hold my breath and listen as I become aware that softly, very softly, through the thick plush carpeting on the stairway, footsteps are padding, patting, like little slaps with a power puff. And they are coming up the stairs!

Christina, preparing to defend herself, discovers it's only her father's secretary, Rosella, and relaxes. But as they talk, Rosella's inconsistent, nervous behavior arouses Christina's suspicions.

10. *A peculiar character can add suspense whenever he or she appears.* In *The Seance,* the daily life of Ila Hughes, grandmother of one of Lauren's friends, is built around superstitions, some of them creepy, such as the cat she has buried inside the walls of her house to keep the devil away. And her hobby?

My glance fell on something that made me automatically step back. On the mantel, on a level with my eyes, was a row of little gray skulls!
There was a chuckle close to my ear, and Mrs. Hughes touched my shoulders, moving me forward again. "Those are my little birds," she said, laughing. "Aren't they precious? Little bird skulls. I began finding them in the Thicket years ago."

11. *Old tricks can still be used.* We're all familiar with the *time is running out* technique, but it can still be effective. And so can the technique of *making the readers—but not the main characters—aware that someone is sneaking toward the house or slowly turning the knob on the bedroom door.* Pull out all the stops. Readers of young adult mysteries love it.

12. *Each chapter ending should be so intriguing that readers can't close the book.* These last sentences can whet curiosity or be downright terrifying, but their job is to lead readers from one chapter into the next, nonstop:

From *The Other Side of Dark:*

If I shot Jarrod, wouldn't it be self-defense? And wouldn't it end the trials and the questions and the badgering and the harassment and the nightmares and the worries and the years and years of fear?
Carefully I aim the gun.

From *A Deadly Game of Magic:*

I would have liked to comfort her. I would have loved it if someone had tried to comfort me. All I could do was lean against the door, hoping it would hold me. My legs were wobbly. My mind seemed to tremble as much as my body, but one thought came through clearly. "Whatever Sam saw," I said, "is still in this house. And like it or not, we're trapped in here with it."

To keep readers from becoming exhausted, you must have the suspense in your mystery build and peak, drop and build again. The valleys are a good place for humor, for development of the relationships between the main character and her family and friends, for her moments of introspection and attempts to handle the non-mystery problems that are part of her life.

But it's those peaks of suspense that will cause your readers to write, "I just couldn't put your book down. When is your next mystery coming out?"

‖ 84

Fantasy for Young Readers

By Shirley Rousseau Murphy

CREATIVE FANTASY," wrote Tolkien, "because it is mainly trying to do something else (make something new), may open your hoard and let all the locked things fly away like caged birds. The gems all turn into flowers or flames, and you will be warned that all you had (or knew) was dangerous and potent, not really effectively chained, free and wild; no more yours than they were you."

To touch such wonder as this is the dream of the fantasist. But dream and realization are far apart, and the journey not an easy one; few reach Tolkien's high and ragged peaks, and there are many paths. How to begin? How to map and give shape to your own inner worlds?

My own approach is rather haphazard. I sort through bits and pieces I've collected, through images that have stayed in my mind, through quickly written sketches, snatches of conversation, and notes from scattered reading:

Dragons too often evil. Otters use tools. Spiders lay eggs inside dead insects.

Though unrelated, some of the items in my collection have a mysterious affinity for one another that I do not at first see. The Dragonbard trilogy began with three unconnected images fomenting almost at an unconscious level. To foment is to cherish with heat; to encourage growth of; to stir up; instigate; incite. All this had been happening before they had any visible relationship or direction.

The dragon was there; I tried a dozen stories around her, all came to nothing. I had a recurring picture of otters idling in the sea, their paws busy cracking shellfish. I could fashion no story that suited them.

I had been reading some history, wanting to see the panorama of man's past completely connected and cohesive. I never did accomplish that goal, but I began to wonder what our world would be like if we

422

knew none of its past, if all history vanished from memory and record and we, like amnesiacs, became a civilization without a past.

Among the insistent images were green islands scattered on a blue sea. Now suddenly I saw them from the back of a winging dragon, and saw the progress of history in vision created by her. It was the dragon who would keep alive history in this island world. And the otters seemed a natural part of that world. Now the images had joined, and I was ready to shape the story. The heart of the Dragonbard trilogy had emerged. I had changed roles from collector to craftsman.

I wanted to write about the vulnerability of a world for which all knowledge of the past had been obscured. The world of Tirror would have no written history, its past would be brought alive only in telepathic visions made by the dragons; if they were driven out or destroyed, all history would die. I knew the enemy now; in her diary, the self-exiled Queen Meriden writes:

The dark captains move into the villages two and three at a time to take control, warping minds . . . in the cities their manipulations are more intricate as they win the allegiance of kings. [They] seek to destroy the mystery of our pasts within us and so destroy our sense of who we are . . . That is how they will enslave us, by creating a race without self knowledge.

It would be handy to lay everything out neatly at this point—plot, place, characters—and get to work. But still the story comes to me in pieces as jumbled as the scattered shards of a broken pot. Though now that I am directly concerned with otters and dragons, and with foxes, I am extending my reading about them.

I had now made a map of the island nations, which were the tips of larger continents long ago flooded. In the beginning of a fantasy novel I need not only to know the land intimately, but to know how it was formed. Place is vitally important, and must have its own geological past.

I named the lands, and named the first dragons and the otters. My notebook of words is ongoing, words lifted from a Welsh dictionary or from the phone book, from any source, but twisted to make new words. Certain sounds, certain groups of letters marked each race of animals. The naming of individual beasts evokes an age-old magic: they begin to come to life.

The act of construction is, for me, a quicksilver time of restlessness.

At first, after the map and the naming, I write unrelated scenes and conversations not knowing, often, where they came from or where they are going. I let each character speak as he will. From these sketches, outlines grow. I write more scenes and make new outlines as the random sketches take direction.

When the story has come sufficiently alive, and an outline has the substance and movement I want, I begin to write seriously, working usually ten hours a day. My habit is to write quickly, but turning back every morning to edit what I did the day before, discovering with each revision new facets of story and character; these help shape the coming day's work. So as I work I construct plot more carefully, discover more fully the story's direction and secondary conflicts. Story begets story. If I plotted fully at the beginning, I wouldn't write.

As I grew to know the otter nation of Nightpool, I saw the simple tools the otters used, and knew they did not have fire. I thought that soon a young boy would bring them fire, stirring sharp controversy within the otter nation. So Tebriel was born, a boy different from other boys, and alone. In the beginning he does not know that he was meant to travel with the singing dragons. As prisoner in his dead father's palace, when he hears his captors report the sighting of a singing dragon, he is powerfully and mysteriously stirred.

But it is a long time before he will understand that he belongs with the dragons and has talents like theirs. Long before he sets out to search for dragons, the speaking animals hide him and help him. The animal characters, the foxes and otters, owls and great cats, interacting with humans, solved many plot problems, sometimes surprising, always quite naturally. And they created a blending of cultures into one concerted effort against the common danger. I was comforted by their quick humor and by their solemn resistance to tyranny. I try to be true to the character of each animal, to see the world as he would. After Tebriel is wounded in battle, two otters hunting shellfish discover the boy lying unconscious.

"It's no bigger than we are," Mikk said, sniffing Teb's face. "It's just a child—a boy child."

"Is it alive?"

They put their noses to Teb's nose and could feel his breath.

It took the otters some time to decide what to do. Because the boy was small, he appealed to them more than an adult; they would likely have left an adult human to die. This boy was no older than they, and he was in need.

The journey that followed nearly killed Teb, for he almost drowned in the cold seas that lapped over him, choking him again and again. The otters had to stop pulling and pushing the raft each time and hold his head up until he could breathe. The salt water started his wounds bleeding harder, and stung fiercely.

Our senses are important. Story becomes real to us first when we smell smoke, feel the chill wind. It is after that, that our emotions take over, that we know anger, fear, the sharp feelings stirred by conflict, and then only if we truly care about the characters. That is the writer's first job, to make the reader care.

And perhaps the fantasy writer particularly must think about strong ties to the familiar. If the reader doesn't know the fantasy world through his senses, he won't believe in it. Sometimes, if an event in the fantasy world relates to something in our own world, there is recognition and thus willing belief. After the singing dragon breeds:

(The dragon) began to uproot trees from the countryside below and, on the highest peak of the Lair, to weave her nest from the trunks, curving the smaller branches and twigs inward to make a soft bed. She sensed the five young within her with a terrible joy of love and possession.

She killed two angora goats and three sheep, and laid them around the nest in a circle, then ripped their bellies open. These would receive her five eggs, to warm and nurture them. When all was ready, she crouched, bellowed again to shake the sky, and began to lay.

After the first draft is complete, I let the manuscript cool, go on to something else. I want to come back to the final polishing as if it were the work of a stranger, when new discovery is heightened. But from the first draft on, it is the warp of the story that is most vital, the heart of the story you have to tell; and the more patiently the writer hones his skills, the more clearly that heart will come alive.

Words, like threads, are frail. But the work can be strong, lasting centuries. Its strength comes from the durable warp hidden beneath. In a tapestry, if you pull the warp thread out, the bright woof will unravel, and the picture distort and fall away.

With simple words, Tolkien created Middle Earth. The warp of truth with which his words are woven makes Tolkien's work last: the truth of our deepest feelings, of good and evil, of courage and fear. You know them, they are your own warp, the stuff of which we all are made. To construct a world from the truth of his inner vision, that is the writer's journey.

85

DOUBLE VISION: A SPECIAL TOOL FOR YOUNG ADULT WRITERS

BY CHERYL ZACH

WRITING A YOUNG ADULT NOVEL with an authentic teen voice requires the author to see the world with double vision—both as the child he was and the adult he is now. We have all lived through adolescence, endured its pains, joys, and frustrations. Delving into your own teenage memories will enable you to relive those strong, sometimes overwhelming emotions and recreate them in your fiction, producing the immediacy and validity that the genre demands.

Do you remember your first date? (Could you ever forget it?) The first time someone asked you out? The first time that special person kissed you? The sweating palms, the rumbling stomach, the anguished attempts at achieving a poise that often failed you at the most crucial moments—these feelings are universal and timeless. Attributing such emotions to your characters will give them depth and reality, propel them off the page and into full dimension.

Adolescence involves a series of stages, changing year by year. Think back to the summer you were thirteen—what were your most pressing concerns? Girls with developing figures who snubbed you unmercifully? The low velocity in your fast ball that might keep you off the team?

Now jump to your sixteenth birthday! How have you changed? Have you achieved a reputation for being "cool" that makes you the envy of all the other guys, but might be lost if you reveal your attraction for the girl who smiles at you in chemistry class—a girl that not everyone admires? Or, from the feminine perspective, have you had your first date, your first kiss, and then—horrors—lost your first love to an older, more sophisticated girl? How will you ever recover, and who wants to? Has an essay you've written or a unique science project you've prepared drawn praise from your favorite teacher, causing you to dream for the first time of attending college—even though you know your parents can't afford to send you? Remember—and put it all into the characters you create.

Then, returning to your adult perspective, examine these characters. Reliving your own emotions will give your characters validity and elicit the essential reader sympathy. As the writer, you must add the exterior polish. Emotions do not change, nor do many of the "first" experiences—first date, first kiss, first car, etc. But the outer trappings—clothes, fads, slang—do.

To make your teen characters ring true to your young adult readers, now you must substitute observation for nostalgia. Watch today's teenagers in their natural settings—schools, restaurants, movies, malls, beaches, among others. Notice that they wear Reeboks or Nikes, not saddle shoes; acid-washed denim, not poodle skirts. Note the music coming from a teenager's Walkman, the activities that attract them as participants or observers. And if you don't enjoy spending time with teens, beware: writing YA novels may not be for you. Immersing yourself in the lives of your teenage characters as you write your novel will be difficult unless you have a genuine liking for this age group.

After creating strong, believable characters, you must grapple with the related question of conflict and plot. What is your character's problem, and how will he or she solve it? Looking at this from your perspective as a teenager will help you avoid a common pitfall among would-be YA authors: an adult-centered plot rather than one that is teen-centered. Again, think back to your own teen years. What was your biggest problem and how did you handle it? Did your older sister steal your boyfriends? What did you do about it? Were you and your best friend in love with the same person? How did you work it out? Allowing your character to cope with his or her problem in a manner consistent with the character's age shapes your plot outline.

Reverting to your adult viewpoint allows you to check your plot for possible flaws. Most of all, remember that the conflict must be solvable by your teen protagonist. Having an adult, friendly or not, step in to deal with your young hero's problem is a fatal mistake. When my shy, teenaged protagonist in *The Frog Princess* is elected class president because of a cruel joke, no adult can be allowed to solve her dilemma for her. Kelly has to solve her problem by herself, gaining self-confidence as well as the respect of her classmates in the process.

Having looked at your conflict through your young protagonist's eyes

427

should also protect you from another common pitfall—the condescension that creeps in when the writer's "adult" side has not been effectively exorcised. The problems you faced at thirteen or fifteen or seventeen were real and vital and soul-shaking: they mattered. The fact that getting a date for the big dance or outshining your older brother seems a minor worry now does not lessen its original importance. Remembering this should deter you from talking down to your teen readers, or, even worse, preaching to them. Problem-solving and moments of revelation can come only through your teen protagonist, and cannot be superimposed by an intrusive author. At the end of *The Frog Princess,* Kelly receives a compliment from Tony, the good-looking classmate she has secretly admired, despite the dirty trick he played on her earlier. But by now she has realized that "Tony would smile only for party-pretty girls in new dresses," and decides this guy is not worth any heartache.

Having believable characters, a strong but age-appropriate conflict and logical plotting, what next? Dialogue is just as crucial in teen fiction as in adult novels, with an added twist—challenge of "current" teen slang. Your child's eye will remind you of basic interests—friends, school, family problems—but dialogue is one element of your novel that may benefit most from your adult/detached writer's perspective.

Sit on a park bench, on a bus, at the beach or amusement park, and listen to teenagers talk. Write down what you hear. Will this give you good dialogue? Only if you cut the inconsequential chatting that forms a large part of real conversation. Good dialogue is not the same as real speech; it only sounds that way. Listen to how teenagers really speak— using lots of monosyllables and elliptical phrases, as in the following:

> "Butt out," Pete told me, his voice thick with anger. "What's it to you?"
> "She's my sister," I said.
> "So?"
> "So she's coming home, right now."

What about current slang—often a double-edged sword? Watch out for outdated expressions. An anachronistic slang word will alert readers—and editors—that the author isn't paying attention. Teen catchwords change quickly. The expression you hear today may be "out" by the time your book gets into print. So use even the most up-to-date slang judiciously, to add flavor but not overpower the other essentials.

What about setting? Unless your book takes place during a holiday period, school will probably be part of your background. In some ways, schools are unchanging, but in others, they may have altered greatly since your own school days. Take a look at the schools in your neighborhood. What are the kids studying, what are they doing for extra-curricular activities? Read student newspapers; they will inform you about student opinions, issues that concern them, their opinions, and interests.

Remember the first rule, however: Look at the school scene through the eyes of a teenager, not those of a curious adult. To a fourteen-year-old, the essential part of the school day will most likely take place before, between and after classes.

And when you return to your adult viewpoint, consider other, more novel settings. Editors sometimes complain about overused lunchroom scenes. This doesn't necessitate moving your story to exotic locales. My YA novel, *Too Many Cooks,* in which the action centers around a small catering business, won critical praise for its "vivid and unusual setting."

Last, point of view. Most YA novels are written either from first person—the "I" viewpoint—or third person limited—looking inside one or two main characters. Both have advantages and pitfalls. First person can lend an impression of immediacy and help the writer focus strongly on the protagonist. It can also be limiting, presenting only what your main character witnesses. Also, some Young Adult editors have grown tired of first-person viewpoint and are less likely to be impressed with a novel using it.

Using third person lets you present more than one viewpoint, widening the scope of your novel. But switching viewpoints must be done skillfully and not too often, or your book will sound choppy and confuse your reader. Accidental switches in points of view are one of the most obvious signs of a beginning writer and throw up a red flag to editors. While viewing the situation through your eyes as an adolescent will enable you to make the point of view authentic, you must go over your manuscript carefully from your perspective as an adult.

When you have brought your YA novel to a satisfying and believable conclusion and have rewritten, polished, and proofread it, how do you market it? With the same care that you would use for an adult novel, studying the marketplace and individual publishers' requirements.

The YA market changes just as the adult market does. Currently, series using continuing characters are "hot." While this may make it harder to sell your individual title, a strong novel may be adapted to a series concept. Why not sell four or six book ideas instead of one? And series do offer opportunities for beginning writers to break into the field, gaining valuable experience.

YA romance novels, which once occupied much of the bookstore shelf space, have lost ground to books in which romance is only one of many concerns facing teenage protagonists. Recent popular series titles reveal this diversity: *Sweet Valley High, Sisters, Sorority Girls, Roommates* all cover the full spectrum of teen life. Problem novels, dealing with darker conflicts of drugs, suicide, abortion, etc., are not presently being sought; humor, on the other hand, is very popular with readers and editors. YA hardcover sales have dropped, but the market for original YA paperbacks continues to grow.

The most essential requirement doesn't vary: a good manuscript with strong, believable characters and an authentic teen voice. Your double vision will aid you in crafting a satisfying and special YA novel.

86

WRITING FOR YOUNG ADULTS

BY NORMA FOX MAZER

WRITING for young adults today is particularly satisfying. These young people are going through the most intensely felt time of their lives. They are a devoted audience and, once caught by one of your books, they will read all of them and wait impatiently for the next one to appear. To write for this audience, it's not necessary to know their slang or the latest fad. It is important to understand their fears, dreams and hopes, but it is vital to know your *own* point of view: what you, the writer, think, feel, fear, understand and believe. You cannot write a deeply felt, satisfying book without a point of view on your material.

The storyteller brings order to events that in life might be random, purposeless, even meaningless. It's this sense of orderliness and meaning that makes the novel so satisfying. But to create that order, the writer should be aware of certain rhythms and patterns. To begin with, a story needs those simple classic elements: a beginning, a middle, and an ending. Most books have a beginning and an ending of sorts, but a great many fall down in the middle. If the writer flounders, the reader gets the sense of the writer's despair: I've come this far—what do I do now?

There are two things I think will help the new writer. One is to work with a unity of opposites as the foundation for your story—two characters locked together but intent on opposite goals. In my novel *Taking Terri Mueller,* Phil and Terri are father and daughter; that is their essential unity. They are further united by the deep love between them, and this, in turn, is reinforced by their life style, which isolates them from other people. This is the background of the struggle that ensues between them. Terri is determined to know the truth about her past. Phil is equally determined that she should not. There they are, united, unable and unwilling to get away from each other, and wanting completely different things.

431

When you first come up with an idea for a novel, test it by asking yourself a few questions: What is the basic unity? (It does not have to be two people. The unity of a character and an animal, or a character and nature, such as a landslide or a hurricane, is just as valid.) What is the opposition? Can I put the idea of the story into a paragraph that will suggest the unity of opposites? *Taking Terri Mueller* began with a single sentence. "A girl has been kidnapped by her own father."

When a writer works with a powerful unity of opposites, there are scenes that almost demand to be written. Long before I knew how I would develop the story to the point at which a confrontation about Phil's lying takes place between Terri and Phil, I knew that scene had to be written. All I had to do was work my way through the story toward that point. This key scene comes about midway through the novel, when the reader has been fully engaged with Terri's struggles and her father's painful desire to keep her ignorant of the truth.

The second thing I find helpful in writing a novel is to think in threes. Three is a magic number. Human beings respond to threes. A story must rise and fall three times to satisfy the reader. When I'm planning, I often divide the book into three sections. Then each section can also be divided twice into three parts. And in most chapters, there is a threefold rise and fall. Let me give one illustration from the key chapter in *Taking Terri Mueller*:

Terri and her father Phil have a close, affectionate and trusting relationship. Her only other relative is her Aunt Vivian. Now it's time for Aunt Vivian's once-a-year visit, a wonderful event to which Terri looks forward all year.

She wants to make the most of the visit, yet it's marred almost from the beginning. Three things happen. First, Vivian dislikes Nancy, Phil's new girlfriend, creating a strained atmosphere. Secondly, Terri sees a wallet snapshot of her aunt, who is said to have no other family, with two young boys. And finally, Terri overhears a conversation between her father and her aunt that strongly suggests there are secrets between them.

There are other ways to use the rhythm of three. For instance, a working rule of thumb for fixing a character in the reader's mind is to repeat something about that character three times. Although it needn't be a physical characteristic, the obvious and old example is the mole on the nose. Use a bit of subtlety in repeating the detail—certainly don't say it the same way each time—but within the first five or six chapters, working in the "mole" helps the reader visualize the character, especially if the detail can be used to shed light on the character's personality or state of mind.

In a description of Terri, I work on her appearance, but also on her state of mind.

She was a tall girl with long hair that she sometimes wore in a single braid down her back. . . . She was quiet and watchful and didn't talk a lot, although she liked to talk, especially to her father, with whom she felt she could talk about anything.

The end of that description reveals something much more important than that Terri has long hair: her trust in her father. That he betrayed this trust is one of the central themes of the book. In the next chapter, Nancy thinks Terri is older than she is. Terri says, "You only thought so . . . because I'm tall." Thus, through dialogue, I repeat one of the points of Terri's description. And through narration we also learn that Terri is almost always the tallest girl in her class. But what's important here is not Terri's height, but her emotional maturity. And this is reinforced when Nancy says that it isn't Terri's being tall—but her poise—that made her think Terri was older.

In creating characters, remember that key word—create. You are not making a real human being, but an illusion of a human being. It would be impossible, confusing, and boring to put down on paper all the elements that go into any one actual person. Your job as a writer is to make your readers believe. Therefore, on the one hand your character needs a certain consistency, and on the other hand those very contradictions that are part of being human.

It's good to give your readers a sense of how your characters look, but what's basic are words and actions. What the characters say. What the characters do. I, the author, tell you, the reader, that Terri is a warmhearted girl, but if what you see her do is trip up a little old lady, then you know I'm lying to you. When I'm struggling with a character, I remind myself of the basic dictum: show, don't tell. I wanted to show Terri's longing for a family. Rather than say it, I showed Terri looking at a friend's family snapshots. Terri's interest and eagerness bring home to the reader her underlying sense of isolation and loneliness.

I've been speaking here of the young adult novel, and yet most of the

433

things I'm saying should apply to any novel. Still, the young adult novel stands in a class by itself. Briefly, I'd like to mention what, in general, distinguishes the young adult novel from any other novel.

The first and most obvious point is the age of the protagonist. Nearly always, the main character is going to be a person the same age or slightly older than the people in your audience. In the young adult novel, there tends to be a very close identification between the reader and the protagonist. A reader wrote me recently, "I hope you know your book describes my life." Literally, it couldn't have, since story, setting, and characters were all products of my imagination. Yet this reader believed in the reality of the world I created. To achieve this sense of verisimilitude, when you write you cannot stand above or to one side of the character, you cannot comment as an older, "wiser" adult, but you must see and report the world through your protagonist's eyes. This limitation, more than anything else, makes the difference between a novel written for this audience and one written for an adult audience.

Although it's important to recognize who your audience is, it's simply death to allow a patronizing attitude to creep into your writing. Your readers deserve your best. The one time I focus on the fact that I'm writing for teenagers is in the early stages when I'm searching for the right idea. Clearly, some book ideas are better than others.

I consider this early stage of writing the novel, which is really an almost non-writing stage, the most important. Concept is all. A silly or unimportant concept can mean months of wasted work.

Questions: Is the idea about young people? Is there an opportunity for the characters to work out their own problems and destinies? Is there a chance for consideration of some serious subjects? Is there also a place for the playful scene or character? I like to achieve a balance. Even in *Taking Terri Mueller,* which is about the terribly serious problem of childnapping, there are a few funny scenes with her father, a scattering of amusing dialogues with her girlfriend.

There are rewards in writing for young adults. There is hardly a subject or an idea that can't be tackled. I have written short stories, serious realistic novels, a time fantasy and, in *Taking Terri Mueller,* a mystery.

Perhaps the first real lesson I learned about writing was that not only did I have something to say, but, whether I recognized it or not, it was there, inside me, waiting to be said. I'm convinced this is true for everyone. Each of us has a unique point of view on the world; the struggle is to get in touch with that uniqueness and bring it into our writing.

My method is to write a first draft in which I spill out everything. The inner censor is banished. I do not allow myself to ponder over the "right" word, to search for the felicitous phrase or struggle for the beautifully constructed sentence. For me, a first draft means putting the truth of a story before all else. It means digging down for all those unique, but what-if-no-one-else-agrees-with-me thoughts, bringing them into the light and onto paper.

Then there is your audience. Is there another group of readers who are quite so enthusiastic, who are ready to laugh and cry over your book, who will cheer you on and write to you in droves? What can compare with the thrill of receiving a letter like the one that came in my mail from a girl in Pennsylvania: "Once I began to read about Terri, I could not get my eyes away from the book."

Each time I approach the writing of a new young adult novel I wonder, "Can I do it again? Will I do this story justice? Will I write a book readers will enjoy? What does this story mean? And aren't there enough books in the world already?"

No, not as long as there are readers and writers. Not as long as there are people like me, like you, like all of us who, like the writer Katha Pollitt, believe that we "go to fiction for the revelation of character, the rich presentation of lived life and the daily clutter of things."

87

STORYTELLING: THE OLDEST AND NEWEST ART

BY JANE YOLEN

SOME time ago I received one of those wonderful letters from a young reader, the kind that are always signed mysteriously "Your fiend." This one had an opening that was an eye-opener. It read:

Dear Miss Yolen:
I was going to write to Enid Blyton or Mark Twain, but I hear they are dead so I am writing to you...

Of course I answered immediately—just in case. After all, I did not want that poor child to think that all the storytellers were dead. Because that was what the three of us—Enid Blyton, Mark Twain, and Miss Yolen—had in common. Not style. Not sense. Not subject. Not "message or moral." The link was clear in the child's mind just as it was in mine. Blyton, Twain, and Yolen. We were all storytellers.

Nowadays most of the storytellers *are* dead. Instead, we are overloaded with moralists and preachers disguised as tale tellers. Our medium has become a message.

So I want to talk to you today about the art of and the heart of storytelling; about tales that begin, go somewhere, and then end in a satisfying manner. Those are the tales that contain their own inner truth that no amount of moralizing can copy. The Chinese, the *New York Times* reported in 1968, were recruiting "an army of proletarian storytellers" who were ordered to fan out into the countryside and "disseminate the thoughts of Chairman Mao." They told the kind of stories that end: "As a result, the evil wind of planting-more-watermelons-for-profit was checked." These tales waste no time in getting their message across. But they are sorry excuses for stories. As Isaac Bashevis Singer has said: "In art, truth that is boring is not true."

Storytelling may be the oldest art. The mother to her child, the hunter to his peers, the survivor to his rescuers, the priestess to her followers, the seer to his petitioners. They did not just report, *they told a tale.* And the better the tale was told, the more it was believed. And the more it was believed, the truer it became. It spoke to the listener because it spoke not just to the ears but to the heart as well.

These same stories speak to us still. And without the story, would the tale's wisdom survive?

The invention of print changed the storyteller's art, gave it visual form. Since we humans are slow learners, it took a while to learn that the eye and ear are different listeners. It took a while to learn the limits and the limitlessness of two kinds of tellers—the author and the illustrator—in tandem. And it has taken us five centuries, dating from Gutenberg, to throw away the tale at last.

Children, the last audience for the storytellers who once entertained all ages, are finding it hard to read the new stories. Their literature today is full of realism without reality, diatribes without delight, information without incantation, and warning without wisdom or wit. And so the children—and the adults they grow into—are no longer reading at all. The disturbing figure I heard only last month is that 48% of the American people read no book at all in the past five years.

And so I dare. I dare to tell tales in the manner of the old story-tellers. I do not simply retell the old tales. I make up my own. I converse with mermaids and monsters and men who can fly, and I teach children to do the same. It is the only kind of teaching I allow in my tales.

What of these stories? There is a form. First, a story has a beginning, an opening, an incipit. Sometimes I will use the old magical words "Once upon a time." Sometimes I vary it to please my own ear:

Once many years ago in a country far to the East....

There was once a plain but goodhearted girl....

In ancient Greece, where the spirits of beautiful women were said to dwell in trees....

Once on the far side of yesterday....

In the time before time, the Rainbow Rider lives....

Once upon a maritime, when the world was filled with wishes the way the sea is filled with fishes....

But always a story begins at the beginning. That is surely a simple thing to remember. Yet my husband begins reading any book he picks up in the middle and, if he likes it, he will continue on. He says it does not matter where he begins, with modern books—and he is right. If stories and books no longer start at the beginning, why should the reader? And if, as Joyce Cary says, "... reading is a creative art subject to the same rules, the same limitations, as the imaginative process...," then a story that begins in the middle and meanders around and ends still in the middle encourages that kind of reading.

Now I am not saying that a story has to move sequentially in time to have a beginning. One does not have to start with the birth of the hero or heroine to start the story at the beginning. Still, there must be a reason, a discernible reason, for starting a tale somewhere and not just the teller's whim. The person who invented the words "poetic license" should have his revoked.

What of the story's middle? First it should not be filled with middle-age spread. But also, it should not be so tight as to disappear. Do you remember the nursery rhyme:

> I'll tell you a story
> About Jack O'Nory,
> And now my tale's begun.
> I'll tell you another
> Of Jack and his brother,
> And now my tale is done.

Where is the middle of that story? It should be the place in the tale that elicits one question from the reader—*what then*? The middle is the place that leads the reader inevitably on to the end.

Is that not a simple task? I run a number of writers' groups and conferences, and all persuasions of writers have passed through. There are the naive novices who think that children's books must be easier to write because they are shorter and the audience less discriminating. There are the passable writers, almost-pros who have had a story or two published in religious magazines and are ready to tackle a talking animal tale or—worse—a talking prune story where inanimate objects converse on a variety of uninteresting subjects. And there are the truly professional writers whose combined publications make a reasonable backlist for any publishing company. And they all have trouble with the middles of stories.

The problem is one of caring. Too few writers today care enough about storytelling. If they should happen in the throes of "inspiration" to come upon a beginning and an ending, then they simply link the two together, a tenuous lifeline holding two climbers onto a mountain.

Of course the middle *is* the mountain. It is the most important part of the book, the tale, the story. It is where everything important occurs. Perhaps that is why so few people do it well.

What of the end? Ecclesiastes says: "Better is the end of a thing than the beginning thereof." An overstatement perhaps. But if the end is not *just* right, and is not filled with both inevitability and surprise, then it is a bad ending.

Adults are quite willing to forgive bad endings. I saw only recently a review of an adult book that said, in essence, the ending is silly, unconvincing, and weak, but the book is definitely worth reading. Children will not forgive a weak ending. They demand a rounding off, and they are very vocal in this demand. I remember reading a story of mine in manuscript to my daughter, then age seven. It was a tale about three animals—a sow, a mare, and a cow—who, tired of men and their fences, decided to live together. When I finished reading, with great feeling and taking the dialogue in special voices, I looked up at my audience of one. She looked back with her big brown eyes.

"Is that all?" she asked.

"Well, that's all in this story," I said, quickly adding "Would you like another?"

She tried again. "Is that all that happens?"

"Well, they just...I mean they...yes, that's all."

She drew in a deep breath. "That *can't* be all," she said.

"Why?" I asked, defeated.

"Because if that's all, it's not a story."

And she was right. I have not yet worked out a good ending for that story, though I am still trying. G.K. Chesterton noted this about fairy tale endings, which are sometimes bloodier than an *adult* can handle. He wrote: "Children know themselves innocent and demand justice. We fear ourselves guilty and ask for mercy."

But lots of stories can still have a beginning, a middle, and an end and not be right. If they are missing that "inner truth," they are nothing. A tale, even a small children's tale filled with delight, is still

439

saying something. The best stories are, in Isak Dinesen's words, "a statement of our existence." Without meaning, without metaphor, without reaching out to touch the human emotion, a story is a pitiable thing; a few rags upon a stick masquerading as life.

I believe this last with all my heart. For storytelling is not only our oldest art, it is our oldest form of religion as well; our oldest way of casting out demons and summoning angels. Storytelling is our oldest form of remembering; remembering the promises we have made to one another and to our various gods, and the promises given in return; of recording our human-felt emotions and desires and taboos.

The story is, quite simply, an essential part of our humanness.

88

A SENSE OF AUDIENCE

BY JILL PATON WALSH

I FEEL DISTINCTLY uneasy about giving practical, down-to-earth advice about writing for children. There are many things in the world, like riding a bicycle, which one may be well able to do, about which one cannot offer a coherent explanation; in one sense one does not know how to do it, even while bowling along the road! Writing for children may be very like riding a bike.

Certainly in the case of the bike, if you become too self-conscious about it you fall off at once; and a similar Catch-22 really does apply to writing for children; if you think that because your audience is young, something special needs doing, or not doing, then you probably can't do it at all. I would like to pursue the heavy metaphor about bike riding a little further, because much of the advice about writing for children that one reads is like exhortations to remember your balance when riding. It is so often telling people to think deliberately about their audience, the vocabulary, the market, whereas, I believe, the sense of audience really is like a sense of balance: If you need to think about it, you haven't got it, and you can't get it by wrinkling your brows and thinking about it harder, because to do it properly you need to be thinking about something else, rather as the cyclist, unaware of how to ride, thinks about which way to take into town.

Let me elaborate on this a little further, though enough about the bike, I promise. I once read an article advising people to *"write for children as though they were your equals."* Does that startle you as much as it did me? Children *are* my equals. Many of them, in time, will turn out to be my superiors—in brain power, in sensitivity, in warmth of heart. By and large, I believe, one generation is pretty much like another, and belonging to an older one gives no ground for claiming superior status.

But, perhaps you won't feel easy with this statement. Perhaps you think that claiming to think of children as equals is a sign of lack of sophistication, or a form of swank, in the way that Damon Runyon was swanking when he said he had never met a boring person. If that is how you are reacting as you read these words, then my down-to-earth advice is that you should ask yourself whom you *do* think of as your equals, and write for them; they are your natural audience. For them you will be able to write without, metaphorically speaking, putting on a funny hat, adopting a curious vocal tone, or limiting your vocabulary.

I have often wondered in the course of what is now a twenty-year career as a children's writer, why some people instinctively take children seriously, and others—including some published writers for children—simply fool about, and I have arrived at a contentious theory, which is that it depends what sort of childhood you had. If you have half forgotten your own; if it was happy and uneventful, and nothing painful or dangerous happened, or if it tested you much until you reached your teens, then, when you write, your characters will be teen-agers or older. I was a child in the war; I think of childhood as the most important formative time of life. I don't think about children when I write; I just assume without thinking that some of the readers will be children and that things had best be told as simply as possible, because everyone, including me, prefers it that way.

You must by now be wondering what I do think about when working, and the answer is, the subject. Day and night, at the typewriter, off the typewriter, waiting at the bus stop, lying in the bath, while washing up, dusting, eating, I recommend thinking consciously about the *book.* Or, more accurately perhaps, having book-shaped thoughts about the subject. Not just any subject, either; not something concocted from worldly-wise assessments of publishers' stated needs, or deductions about what sells based on reading what has sold. Not something that someone thinks there ought to be a book about. But something that moves your mind to enthusiasm. That gives you that glow of real interest. I realize that this sounds wildly impractical—the other kind of advice sounds so *sensible;* and of course I am thinking, in what I say, only about fiction—nonfiction may be different, or may not, I don't know enough about writing it to say—but however airy-fairy it sounds, it has always worked for me. I write about things that move me deeply, I never try to write commercially salable work, I try to write the best book I possibly can about this wonderful subject; and I honestly think that the best book you can write is your best prospect of publication and commercial success. It is also your best prospect of noncommercial success—of that letter from a child who has never managed to finish a book until he reads yours, or who has read what you say about the war and found a sudden sympathy for a dreadful grandpa, or who just wants you to look at the picture he has drawn for you, of a scene in your book.

When I ask myself if my method is successful, I think of the flaws and shortcomings in my books—none of us can write as well as we wish we could—and then I remember the hundreds of loving letters I have received from children all over the world, and I feel like the most lucky and successful person I can possibly imagine.

Of course, it's all very well for me to tell you to burn with enthusiasm for your subject. Most people do that readily for their first book. But most first books don't get published. Keeping oneself supplied indefinitely with burning enthusiasms to make books out of is a problem for published and unpublished writers alike. And here comes my most practical piece of advice, my only really useful suggestion—do as I do, keep a notebook.

A notebook is not a diary, and doesn't have to be written in every day, or contain a note of anything dull. And everyone's notebook would contain a different balance of items. A notebook is a record of the activity of that part of your mind that produces ideas. Writing is a split personality activity: a "producer," which creates a huge output of thought and story and description, and a "controller," which carves and squashes and selects, and constructs a book from the raw material thrown up by the "producer." In my experience, the "controller" is easy to advise and improve and teach, and is sitting in your conscious mind, where you can talk to it. The notebook is an attempt to talk to the producer down in the unconscious depths, where it all comes from.

So what's in the notebook? Mine contains a good deal of description. I like places and often get ideas for books just from some interesting place. But I might come back from a week at the seaside with nothing in the notebook except a few sentences about the exact color of a breaking wave, and a list of the types of seaweed on a lee shore. I often try to write very exact descriptions of unusual weather, sky formations, effects of the light, and so on. The notebook entries are fragmentary and short, but in the year of the drought, for example, I made a lot of such notes. Three years ago I wrote a novel set in the summer of the Plague, when it didn't rain for three and a half months, and I reaped the benefit.

The next most frequent entry is fragments of overheard conversation, especially in any regional or highly demotic voice. I eavesdrop ruthlessly, wherever I am. Catching the tune of real voices—the English don't speak standard English—is terribly difficult. Months and months before I began work on *Gaffer Samson's Luck,* I had noted two children talking about a mouse their cat had caught: "What did you do with that?" "She put that in the bin, haven't she . . . ." The local children in my book never say "it." But if you don't eavesdrop, how will you know?

I also clip newspapers for stories that catch my attention, as in the item about a forest fire started deliberately to provide a rare bird with the hot pine cones it needed to nest; the fire went out of control and destroyed a small North American town. Hundreds of such fascinating possible starting points are printed free in the papers—local papers especially—every week. I clip or note the ones I like.

Finally I list reactions to the books I am reading, and sometimes make notes of states of mind—especially of frames of mind about the book I am writing; there is some comfort in looking back and seeing how gloomy I was about the last one, which is now in print and doing nicely, when I am feeling suicidal about the current one.

The point about a writer's notebook is writing it, of course—not reading it. I never read mine. I don't even, very often, consult it. If you went back and copied one of those exact descriptions, or conversations, directly into a book the words would be sure to stick out like a sore thumb. The tone of voice would be all wrong. But I find I can remember things I noted down, as I remembered the dusty surface of rivers and ponds in the year of the drought, all the way through till I needed that little detail. Perhaps your memory is marvelous anyway. But writing in a notebook regularly has an astonishing effect on your attention; things you would have no reason to notice, aspects of the world for which you have no present use, and which would normally float past you on the tide of weeks and days, will collect in your notebook. You will be like a child gathering handfuls of unremarkable special pebbles from a beach, and it will gradually enhance your powers of attention, and the vividness and realism with which you can write.

For really, writers have no special expertise. The only claim we have on the reader's time is that we have learned more, thought more, looked more carefully at some aspect of the human context, the human predicament, than most people have time for. There is a teaching method for very young children called "Look and Say." Look comes before Say. Otherwise what shall we have to tell each other stories *about*?

PLAYWRITING

89

ROLES IN COLLISION: A PLAY BEGINS

BY JEFFREY SWEET

MY SON CAME BACK from his visit to a department store Santa Claus with a handout from an elf—one of those infernal little plastic doodads containing three tiny BB's. On the floor of the container is a picture pocked by three shallow indentations. The object is to tip the container to and fro so as to propel the three BB's into the three indentations and thus complete the picture (in this case—a juggler with three balls overhead).

I had better things to do. So of course I picked up the game. More than half an hour evaporated as I jiggled and jostled and cussed. Finally, after countless near-misses, I had two of the three BB's snugly placed. Only one to go. I held my breath and tapped gingerly. And, with lazy grace, the third BB rolled across the face of the picture and settled into the third indentation with a plop.

There was something very familiar about that plop. It is with a similar sound that I find that the premises of my plays usually come together. After analogous jiggling, jostling, and tapping in my imagination, some small element drops into place, and I suddenly know how I'm going to be spending the next several months. Mind you, this is not primarily a matter of luck (though luck is never entirely absent in writing). Just as there is skill (however trivial) involved in the BB game, there is skill involved in taking images, hunches, and impulses that have lodged in one's mind and manipulating them into an arrangement that is sufficient grounds for typing "Act One" onto a piece of paper.

Different dramatists arrive at their starting points in different ways. Many rely on instinct and intuition, but I've always held to the belief that when performing surgery you're more likely to have a successful outcome if the lights are on in the operating room so you can see your

447

tools. I'd like to share a tool that I've found of particular use in building plays.

I had long ago been fascinated by the blacklisting of entertainers that occurred during the McCarthy era and wanted to find a way to deal with the subject dramatically. A friend of mine named Kate Draper had told me that her father Paul had been among those blacklisted in the fifties, so I asked her if we could arrange to get together so that I could fire a few questions at her. She was agreeable, and soon after, in a local coffee shop, she told me how her father, a famous dancer, had seen his career all but destroyed when someone accused him of being a Communist. After she had shared details of her family's ordeal and answered all of my prepared questions, the conversation shifted to chat about what was going on in our lives at the moment. She had good news. She had just been cast in a Broadway musical. Idly, I asked how she thought her father would react if it turned out that the director of the musical had been one of those who had cooperated with the House Committee on Un-American Activities, one of the forces responsible for the blacklist.

"The director didn't," said Kate.

"I know," I said. "I'm asking 'if.' "

She paused for a second, then replied, "He probably wouldn't say much of anything. He tends not to talk too much about those days."

My reaction was, "That's not dramatic."

This led me to wonder what would make it dramatic. The answer, of course, was if the father had quite a strong reaction indeed. Plop. There was the premise of my play. A year or so later, my play *The Value of Names* opened at the Actors Theatre of Louisville and has since been staged by a number of other companies and been published.

Thinking about the matter later, I realized that what I did when I asked Kate that question was construct the dilemma that would result if two important roles in her life—those of actress and daughter—were to come into conflict. This dilemma—the conflict between two or more of a central character's roles—is the dynamic element in most of the plays I write as well as those I admire.

Everybody plays several roles. Among the ones I count in my personal repertoire: my son's father, my wife's husband, my father's son, my mother's son, my agent's client, my students' teacher, and so on. Frequently, these roles come into conflict. For instance, as any dedi-

448

cated writer who is married knows, there inevitably come times when your spouse asks, "Are you married to me or your work?" How one responds to this question may determine whether one retains the role of husband and wife or takes on the challenge of the new role of a divorced person.

Characters in plays, too, must choose between roles. Their choices and the resulting fates are the stuff of drama.

Let's dive into the deep and look at *Hamlet*. Shakespeare loads him with several conflicting roles. Hamlet is simultaneously the ghost's appointed avenger, Gertrude's son, Claudius's nephew, Ophelia's boyfriend, Rosencrantz and Guildenstern's schoolmate, and so on. The impossibility of being all of these things at the same time and the choice he has to make between these roles are what make the action of the play possible. One of the many things Hamlet and the audience discover is that his role as avenger ultimately supersedes all of the other roles. Because he embraces this role and the attendant responsibility, Gertrude is poisoned, Claudius is stabbed, Ophelia drowns, Rosencrantz and Guildenstern are executed, and Hamlet himself dies.

In Sophocles' *Antigone*, the title character must choose between two mutually exclusive roles. Creon, the king of Thebes, has refused to allow the slain rebel Polyneices the dignity of funeral rites and has decreed that anybody contravening his order is to be executed. Antigone's dilemma is that she is both a citizen of Thebes (and thereby bound to obey Theban law) and Polyneices' sister (and thereby bound by family obligation to give her brother a proper funeral). The play centers on her determination that her role as sister takes precedence over her role as citizen. In burying her brother she condemns herself to death.

Much has been written about why one experiences a catharsis watching tragedy. How is it that witnessing the destruction of heroes produces in the audience not a profound depression but a kind of elation? My theory is that this feeling is a result of our knowledge that Hamlet, Antigone, Iphigenia, Romeo and Juliet, Macbeth, and Medea (to name but a few) meet and embrace their true natures. "To thine ownself be true" is an injunction few in real life have the courage to fulfill, and there is something liberating about seeing characters who, in full knowledge of the frequently cataclysmic consequences, choose to be their truest selves.

449

But this business of characters choosing their true selves is not limited to classical tragedy. Neil Simon's *The Odd Couple* is a comedy in which characters, again, have to determine their real roles. Felix and Oscar must battle their way to the understanding that their relationship is more truly that of good friends than bad roommates. The title character in Molière's *Tartuffe* meets his deserved comeuppance when he gives free rein to his usually-hidden lecherous nature. At the end of Ibsen's *A Doll House,* Nora walks out on her marriage having resolved to put aside the degrading part of Torvald's "doll-wife" in favor of the role of a mature and self-respecting adult.

I have found this construct useful not only for the analysis of others' plays, but for the synthesis of my own. Before I begin to write a script, I ask myself a number of questions about my central character's options. A play depicts the actions taken by the central character or characters. It is not enough, however, to know what my protagonist does. I have to know what my protagonist chooses *not* to do. After all, the choice of one road necessarily implies the rejection of at least one other. If a character's choice is to have any tension or resonance, the case for the road not taken must be very strong. In the case of *The Value of Names,* Norma, the daughter, knows that if she chooses to stay in the cast of the play being directed by her father's enemy, she puts her relationship with her father at risk. If she resigns from the play, she jeopardizes her career. It is the difficulty of the choice that attracted me to the story.

Because Norma ultimately decides to stay with the play, Benny, her father, then is faced with a choice: either to accept and forgive what he sees as a betrayal or to hold fast to his bitterness and, in essence, blacklist his daughter from his affections. During the writing of the play I found that this choice became the central question of the piece.

To summarize the process, what started as my speculation about which choice Paul Draper would make in a hypothetical situation led me to wonder which choice my character Norma would make if confronted over this issue by her father Benny, which, in turn, led me to wonder which choice Benny would make in reaction to Norma's choice.

I am not suggesting that one should blithely appropriate the private lives of friends. (As I hope I've established, my play, though derived from a speculation about how Kate and her father would handle a certain situation, is in no meaningful way a reflection of Kate's relationship with her father.) But everybody lives with contradictions in his or her life. Most of us are fairly nimble about keeping these contradictions from coming to too much of a head. But drama is found in the exploration of these contradictions, in asking what would happen if push were indeed to come to shove.

Get into the habit of this kind of speculation, and you may also find the third BB dropping into place in your imagination.

90

TEN GOLDEN RULES FOR PLAYWRIGHTS

BY MARSHA NORMAN

Budding playwrights often write to ask me advice on getting started—and succeeding—in writing plays. The following are a few basics that I hope aspiring playwrights will find helpful.—M.N.

1. Read at least four hours every day, and don't let anybody ask you what you're doing just sitting there reading.

2. Don't write about your present life. You don't have a clue what it's about yet. Write about your past. Write about something that terrified you, something you *still* think is unfair, something that you have not been able to forget in all the time that's passed since it happened.

3. Don't write in order to tell the audience how smart you are. The audience is not the least bit interested in the playwright. The audience only wants to know about the characters. If the audience begins to suspect that the thing onstage was actually written by some other person, they're going to quit listening. So keep yourself out of it!

4. If you have characters you cannot write fairly, cut them out. Grudges have no place in the theatre. Nobody cares about your grudges but you, and you are not enough to fill a house.

5. There must be one central character. One. Everybody write that down. Just one. And he or she must want something. And by the end of the play, he or she must either get it or not. Period. No exceptions.

6. You must tell the audience right away what is at stake in the evening, i.e. how they know when they can go home. They are, in a sense, the jury. You present the evidence, and then they say whether it seems true to them. If it does, it will run, because they will tell all their friends to come see this true thing, God bless them. If it does not seem true to them, try to find out why and don't do it any more.

7. If, while you are writing, thoughts of critics, audience members or family members occur to you, stop writing and go read until you have successfully forgotten them.

8. Don't talk about your play while you are writing it. Good plays are always the product of a single vision, a single point of view. Your friends will be helpful later, after the play's direction is established. A play is one thing you can get too much help with. If you must break this rule, try not to say what you have learned by talking. Or just let other people talk and you listen. Don't talk the play away.

9. Keep pads of paper near all your chairs. You will be in your chairs a good bit (see Rule 1), and you will have thoughts for your play. Write them down. But don't get up from reading to do it. Go right back to the reading once the thoughts are on the paper.

10. Never go to your typewriter until you know what the first sentence is that day. It is definitely unhealthy to sit in front of a silent typewriter for any length of time. If, after you have typed the first sentence, you can't think of a second one, go read. There is only one good reason to write a play, and that is that there is no other way to take care of it, whatever it is. There are too many made-up plays being written these days. So if it doesn't spill out faster than you can write it, don't write it at all. Or write about something that does spill out. Spilling out is what the theatre is about. Writing is for novels.

91

GUIDELINES FOR THE BEGINNING PLAYWRIGHT

By Louis E. Catron

YEARS OF teaching playwriting probably have been more educational for me than for my students. Several hundred young playwrights have taken one or more of my classes since I first started teaching at the College of William and Mary in 1966, and they have taught me that writing a play can be simplified—maybe not made "easy," but certainly "easier"—if certain boundaries are imposed.

We began experimenting with guidelines because so many playwrights were expending too much creative energy chasing nonproductive fireflies. We found that these limitations help playwrights over difficult hurdles. More, they are highly important for the overall learning process.

To be sure, for some writers the very idea of imposed limits appears to be a contradiction in significant terms. How, they ask, can I do creative writing if you fence me in?

Their objections have merit. Limitations often inhibit the creative mind, and many creative people expend a great deal of effort seeking clever ways of circumventing the rules. Certainly I've had students react to the guidelines with the fervor of a bull to a red flag and we've had to arm wrestle about the rules.

Nonetheless, imposition of limitations is a way of life in all creative arts. Theatre is no exception. As a play director, for example, I have found that one key portion of my job is establishing parameters of character for actors, holding these walls tightly in place during rehearsals, and encouraging the performers to create depth within those limitations.

We're talking about the contrast between the casual and sloppy meandering of a Mississippi River versus a tightly confined Colorado. The former changes directions so often that it confuses even experienced riverboat captains, but the latter is held so tightly in direction that it cuts the Grand Canyon. Discipline is essential for the creation of beauty.

454

The beginning playwright is encouraged to accept the following guidelines to write his or her first play. Later plays can be more free. Indeed, deliberately breaking selected guidelines later will help you better understand the nature of dramatic writing. For now, however, let these guidelines help you in your initial steps toward learning the art and craft of playwriting.

1. *Start with a one-act play.* A full-length play isn't merely three times longer and therefore only three times more difficult. And that a one-act is simpler doesn't mean it is insignificant. The one-act play can be exciting and vibrantly alive, as has been shown by plays such as *No Exit* (Sartre), *Zoo Story* (Albee), *The Maids* (Genet), *the Dumb Waiter* (Pinter) and *The Madness of Lady Bright* (Wilson).

Starting with the one-act lets the writer begin with a canvas that is easily seen at a glance, instead of a mural that covers such a huge space perception doesn't grasp it all.

The one-act typically has only a few characters, is an examination of a single dramatic incident, and runs about half an hour in length. It usually stays within one time frame and one place. Because there are fewer complexities, you'll be able to focus more upon the actual writing, and you'll have less concern about a number of stage problems which come with full-length plays.

2. *Write about something you care about.* Writing manuals usually tell the beginner to write "about what you know best." I think that can lead a beginner to think in terms of daily, mundane events. Better, I believe, is for the beginner to *care;* if the playwright is involved with the subject, that interest will pull an audience along.

3. *Conflict is essential to drama.* Quibble me no quibbles about plays which may not have conflict. For *your* first play, there should be conflict. Drama is the art of the showdown. Force must be opposed by force, person (or group) by person (or group), desire by desire.

If there's no conflict, the dramatic qualities are lost. The result may still hold the stage, but the odds against it are increased. More important, even if the one-act has no conflict and yet holds the stage, the playwright hasn't learned that all-significant lesson about showing conflict. You'll want to know that when you write more.

4. *Let there be emotion.* People *care,* in your first play, I hope; people feel strongly, whether it is love or hate, happiness or despair. If you are able to get them emotional, your characters more than likely are going to be active and going somewhere. The audience will care more about emotional people than those dull-eyed, unfeeling dramatic deadbeats.

5. *Stay within the "realistic" mode.* Realism deals with contemporary people, the sort who might live next door, in their contemporary activities, and with selective use of ordinary speech. It avoids the aside and the soliloquy. It is quite comfortable inside the traditional box set. Realism is selective, and sometimes critical, in its presentation of objective facts.

Realism is the familiar mode you've seen most often: it dominates television, and only a handful of movies break away from realism. No doubt you've also seen it on stage more than any other mode. Because you know it best, your first play will be easier to write if you stay in realism. Expressionism, absurdism, symbolism, epic: avoid these for your first experience with playwriting.

(Examples of realism would be full-length plays like *Ghosts* or *A Doll's House,* both by Ibsen, or one-acts like *Ile* and other sea plays by O'Neill. More recent plays tend to be eclectic—primarily but not totally realistic, like the full-length *Death of a Salesman,* by Arthur Miller, or the one-act *Gnadiges Fraulein* by Tennessee Williams.)

6. *Limit the number of characters.* Too many characters and you may lose some: they'll be on stage but saying and doing nothing, so you'll send them off to make dinner or fix the car while you focus on the remaining characters you like better. Consider eliminating those who are dead.

Strenuously avoid "utilitarian" characters—those people who make minor announcements (in older drawing-room plays they say little more than, "Dinner is served"), or deliver packages or messages (Western Union's delivery boy, remember, is as much a relic as the butler). Such characters tend to be flat and no fun for playwright, performer or audience.

Some utilitarians are confidants, on stage to serve as ears so the protagonist will be able to speak inner thoughts without resorting to the soliloquy. The confidant in this sort of case turns out to be about as vital as a wooden listening post.

456

Confidants, by the way, are easily recognized: their faces are covered with a huge question mark. They seem to be asking questions eternally, without any apparent interest in question or answer. The playwright uses the confidant to get to the answer. If such a person is necessary, let the character be more than a pair of ears.

Just how many characters should be in the play?

Three is a good number for the first play. The triangle is always helpful; three characters allow development of good action and conflict and variety. More, and there's the risk of excess baggage; less, and the characters may quickly become thin and tired.

7. *Keep them all on stage as long as you can.* All too often I've seen plays developing potentially exciting situations, only to be deflated by the exit of a prime character. The audience will feel let down—promised excitement evaporated through the swinging door.

A flurry of activity with entrances and exits is deceptive. There may be a feeling of action but in truth there's only movement of people at the door. The more such business, often the less the drama: in class we begin to comment jokingly about wanting a percentage of the turnstile concession.

The beginning writer needs to learn to keep all characters alive and actively contributing to the play's action. So, then, you need to try to keep them all on stage as long as you possibly can. If you have a character who keeps running out, perhaps he ought to be eliminated.

You needn't invent a supernatural force to keep them in the same room, by the way, although I've seen my student writers come up with fascinating hostage or kidnap situations and locked doors in order to justify keeping everyone present. All of that is clever, but all you need is action that involves all the characters.

8. *No breaks: no scene shifts, no time lapses.* Just as some playwrights have people leaving when stage action is growing, so also are there authors who cut from the forthcoming explosion with a pause to shift scenery or to indicate a passage of time. There is a break in the action and that always is disappointing. Such lapses are all too often barriers to the play's communication with the audience.

If you have in mind a play that takes place first in an apartment, then in a grocery store, then in a subway, you have let the motion pictures overly influence your theatrical concept. It just won't wash, not in a one-act stage play; with so many sets and breaks producers will shy away from your script. (Yes, yes, you can cite this or that exception, but we're talking about a beginner's first play, not a script by someone with an established reputation.)

Reduce the locales to the *one* place where the essential action occurs, and forget the travelogue. So also with the jumps in time: find the *single* prime moment for these events to take place.

Later you can jump freely in time and space, as Miller does so magnificently in *After the Fall*. Your first play, however, needs your concentrated attention on action, not on inventive devices for jumping around through time and space.

9. *Aim for a thirty-minute play.* One-act plays are delightfully free of the restrictions placed upon full lengths, and can run from only a few minutes to well over an hour. The freedom is heady stuff for a beginning writer.

Aim for around half an hour. Less than that and you probably only sketched the characters and action; much longer, and you might exhaust your initial energies (and your audience!). Your goal, of course, is to be sure you achieve adequate amplification; too many beginners start with a play only eight or ten minutes long, and it seems full of holes. Your *concept* should be one that demands around half an hour to be shown.

10. *Start the plot as soon as you can.* Let the exposition, foreshadowing, mood and character follow the beginning of the plot (the point of attack). Get into the action quickly, and let the other elements follow.

11. *Remember the advantage of the protagonist-antagonist structure.* Our era of the anti-hero apparently has removed the protagonist from the stage. Too bad. The protagonist is a very handy character indeed, and the protagonist-antagonist structure automatically brings conflict which, you recall, is essential for drama.

The protagonist is the "good guy," the one with whom we sympathize and/or empathize, the central character of the play. A better definition: *The one whose conscious will is driving to get a goal.* The antagonist stands firmly in the way. Both should be equal forces at the beginning of

458

the play: if one is obviously stronger, the conflict is over quickly and so should the play be.

(If you do not fully understand the personality of a true protagonist, look at Cyrano in Hooker's translation of Edmond Rostand's *Cyrano de Bergerac*. Cyrano is so strongly a conscious will moving actively that it takes several antagonists to balance him.)

12. *Keep speeches short.* Long speeches often grow boring. Sometimes they are didactic; the playwright delivering The Play's Message. Always they drag the tempo. But the worst sin of a long speech is that it means the playwright is thinking just of that one character and all the others are lying about dead.

Short speeches—quick exchanges between characters—on the other hand keep all of them alive and make the play appear to be more crisp and more vital. The play will increase in pace and you'll automatically feel a need to increase the complications.

How long is "short"? Let the dialogue carry but one idea per speech. Or, to give you another answer, let your ear "listen" to the other characters while one is talking, and see who wants to interrupt. A third answer: try to keep the speeches under, say, some twenty words.

One grants the effectiveness of the "Jerry and the Dog" speech in Albee's *Zoo Story*. It makes a nice exception to this guideline. But there are very few such examples, and there are many more examples of plays where the dialogue is rich and effective because the playwright disciplined the talky characters.

13. *Complications are the plot's heartbeat.* John wants Mary. Mary says fine. Her family likes the idea. Her dog likes John. His parrot likes Mary and the dog. So John and Mary get married. They have their 2.8 kids, two cars, a dishwasher, and they remember anniversaries. Happiness.

Interesting? Not very. Dramatic? Hardly.

John wants Mary. Mary is reluctant, wondering if John simply is in love with love. John is angry at the charge. Mary apologizes. John shows full romanticism. Mary worries again. Mary's grandmother advises Mary to take John to see what love really is by visiting Mary's older sis who everyone knows is happy in marriage. Mary and John visit. Sis and her husband Mike are having a violent fight; mental cruelty; damning ac-

459

cusations. Sis gets John to help her and he unwillingly does; Mike pulls John to his side; Mary yells at John for causing trouble.

That's the first ten minutes.

I think you'll grant it has more potential than the first sketch. *Complications* keep it vital, moving, alive. *A play depends upon conflict for its dramatic effect, and complications are the active subdivision of the basic conflict.*

So, then: the traditional baker's dozen—thirteen guidelines which will help you with your first play. They will help you avoid pitfalls which have lamed so many playwrights, and they will give you a basic learning experience which will help you with future plays.

92

THE S-N-A-P-P-E-R TEST FOR PLAYWRIGHTS

BY LAVONNE MUELLER

WHENEVER I finish a play, I check to see that I have applied to it every point from what I call the "S-N-A-P-P-E-R Formula." Here is my "Snapper" checklist.

Secret

Everyone loves to hear a secret. Have the main characters in your play tell something about themselves that is revealing and intimate.

In my play *The Only Woman General,* Olive Wiggins tells us that when she was in combat, she couldn't tell the winning from the losing; all battles seemed the same.

The secret Anne reveals (but only to her diary) in *The Diary of Anne Frank* is the physical change in her body that turns her into a woman. Willy Loman, in Arthur Miller's *Death of a Salesman,* tells Ben about his life insurance policy and also what his funeral will be like:

They'll come from Maine, Massachusetts, Vermont, New Hampshire! All the old timers with strange license plates.

In Tennessee Williams' *The Glass Menagerie,* Laura tells the Gentleman Caller her secret humiliation when she was going to school with a brace on her leg:

My seat was in the back row. I had to go clumping all the way up the aisle with everyone watching.

How would *Death of a Salesman* change, for example, if Willy's secret was that he wanted to be an artist? How would *The Glass Menagerie* change if the secret Laura confides to the Gentleman Caller was that she had successfully hid from the world the brace on her leg?

Names

Give your characters interesting names. Names can define a character. They can also function ironically and humorously. A cowboy in my play *Little Victories* is called Double Ugly because he's been in a fight that cut his face in two places. In *The Only Woman General*, the woman general is ironically named Olive—olive for peace.

Big Daddy in Tennessee Williams's *Cat on a Hot Tin Roof* is the head of a wealthy household, and not only does he command obedience and servitude, but the humorous overtones of his name add an ironic dimension. Big Daddy's sons are Gooper and Brick—the first is simpering, the second headstrong.

How would *Cat on a Hot Tin Roof* change if Tennessee Williams had named Big Daddy Herbert or Leslie or reversed the names of his sons?

If you wrote a one-act play about a dermatologist, would you want to call him Sam Lumpkin?

Action

Every play must have action. Drama is like a boxing match. Two characters go at each other until one is shoved up against the wall. Or knocked out. The image of a boxing match is actually used by author Shirley Lauro in her excellent play, *Open Admissions*. Ms. Lauro states: "The audience's experience from the start should be as if they had suddenly tuned in on the critical round of a boxing match."

In *Little Victories*, Joan wishes to be a successful general. She has to convince her adjutants that she is competent. She is constantly being pressured by them. In desperation, she uses many tricks of common sense that she learned as a farm girl. Her main goal is always a source of action: Joan pulls soldiers out of mudholes with the same skill she used on her cows. Because she can't read, she uses the lines in the palm of her hand as a map. She struggles to win over her troops. Action.

Make sure your main character wants something, and make sure somebody is keeping him/her from getting it. In *Cat on a Hot Tin Roof*, Big Daddy wants a son from Brick. Brick is obstinate. They struggle. Action!

Props

Props can be very effective. They are visual messages to the audience, and they are an extension of the character's personality. Try to think of props that are genuinely important to the development of your play. You don't want to use a prop that is gratuitous.

In my play *Breaking the Prairie Wolf Code,* Helen, a pioneer woman, takes a tea set with her on the westward journey. At every wagon stop, she has tea to remind herself of a former gentility. As the trip progresses, parts of the tea set are broken and lost. I use this prop to show graphically the hardships of the journey.

Hamlet speaks to the skull of Yorick. The Moor in *Othello* uses a handkerchief as proof of his suspicions of Desdemona's infidelity. In *The Diary of Anne Frank,* Anne tapes pictures of movie stars on the wall of her small hiding space. In Eugene O'Neill's *Long Day's Journey into Night,* Mary's faded wedding dress is her one tangible connection to the past.

It's hard to imagine these plays without their classic props. What if Hamlet delivered his monologue to a rock instead of Yorick's skull? What if Anne Frank had pictures of food instead of movie stars on her wall?

Plot

Plot is as important to a dramatist as it is to a novelist. The attention of the audience is held by a clear, strong story line. Shakespeare is a master of storytelling. We want to know, for example, what will happen to Romeo and Juliet. What will happen to Lear after he's turned over his power to his children?

The plot is closely related to what we call "the dramatic question." This question is something an audience wants answered. In *Hamlet,* the dramatic question is: Will Hamlet avenge his father? The answer to that dramatic question keeps each person interested enough to come back after the intermissions.

The plot/dramatic question does not have to be complex. In *Little Victories,* the question is simply: How will Joan win the battle? In the musical *A Chorus Line,* the plot/dramatic question is simply: Who will get chosen for the chorus line?

If you think of a question to ask on stage, it becomes easier to structure a plot around it. In *Breaking the Prairie Wolf Code,* my question is simply: Will the wagon train get to California? After I came up with the question, I began to imagine all the things that could

463

prevent this journey and make it more difficult. I invented obstacles and characters to "hang" on the story line of my dramatic question.

Ending

Give your characters a well-planned exit. They've come to the end of their tale, and it's very effective if they can leave the stage with some relevant words or actions.

Again, in *Little Victories,* the drama ends when Joan tells Susan that she must reach into the future and find somebody who can help her. Joan takes Susan's hand and points it to the audience, saying: "Take the dark."

In *Cat on a Hot Tin Roof,* Maggie says to Brick at the end of the play: "Oh, you weak, beautiful people who give up so easily. You need somebody to hand your life back to you like something gold."

Anne's father in *The Diary of Anne Frank* reads a last line from her diary entry: "In spite of everything I still believe that people are really good at heart."

How would *Cat on a Hot Tin Roof* change if the ending line were Brick's—perhaps saying that he didn't know if he had the strength to go on?

How would *The Diary of Anne Frank* change if her last diary entry were that people are basically corrupt?

Relatives

Let the characters tell us something about their relatives or background. It helps us to understand how they came to be the people they are.

Esther Bibbs, an ex-slave on the wagon train in *Breaking the Prairie Wolf Code,* tells us:

I used to make this pea soup for the Fenchler family. They were my marsters in Georgia. My folks was took to the South from Africa and sold into the Fenchler family, ya know. Course the North whupped the South and they made the Constitution signed. That's why I'm free—here in the west.

In *Death of a Salesman,* Willy tells us that his father lived for many years in Alaska and was an adventurous man. Willy adds: "We've got quite a little streak of self-reliance in our family."

Mary, in *Long Day's Journey into Night*, tells us that she was in a convent school for girls when she was young:

At the Convent I had so many friends. Girls whose families lived in lovely homes.

How would *Death of a Salesman* change if Willy's father had been a college professor? How would *Long Day's Journey into Night* change if Mary had gone to a public school?

Now you know the formula. It works for me, and it can work for you. Don't mail out your script until you give it the S-N-A-P-P-E-R test. And after you do so and send it off, begin immediately to think of your next play. Don't wait for the mail. Let your mind work on new ideas. The following test may help get your imagination rolling again. It is not meant to be an indicator of your creativity, but only a vector to point the way to your creative potential.

How's Your I. Q. (Imagination Quotient)?

(Give yourself 5 points for each YES answer. Give yourself 2 points for each SOMETIMES answer.)

1. When I see a person for the first time, I always observe the color of his eyes and hair.
YES   SOMETIMES   NO

2. I like to think about a person's name and how it is appropriate or not appropriate for that person.
YES   SOMETIMES   NO

3. I would definitely laugh (to myself) if I became acquainted with a Japanese man named John Smith.
YES   SOMETIMES   NO

4. When I look at a cloud in the sky, I often see more than just a cloud.
YES   SOMETIMES   NO

5. When I'm observing the behavior of animals, I am often reminded of certain human characteristics.
YES   SOMETIMES   NO

6. If I came across an empty food tray in a cafeteria, I would find it fun to *guess* by the leftovers what kind of person belonged to that tray.
YES   SOMETIMES   NO

7. If a person sits across from me on a bus or train or airplane for any length of time, I like to guess the occupation of that person by his appearance.
YES   SOMETIMES   NO

8. I find it fun to sit in an outdoor restaurant or park bench for long periods of time just to peoplewatch.
YES   SOMETIMES   NO

9. When I go into a person's house, I like to observe how that person added his own personality to the house by means of furniture, art objects, and color scheme.
YES   SOMETIMES   NO

10. If I see a person reading a particular book, I imagine what kind of person he is by the book he is reading.
YES   SOMETIMES   NO

11. If I observe a person carrying a large, wrapped box, I often imagine quite a few things that could be inside that box.
YES   SOMETIMES   NO

12. When someone I don't know is on the phone, I try to imagine what that person is like from the tone of his voice.
YES   SOMETIMES   NO

13. When I am at a large function such as a ball game, concert, or picnic, I often like to strike up a conversation with someone next to me because I find it interesting to know what they are thinking or what they might say to me.
YES   SOMETIMES   NO

14. If I see a movie I really like, I like to imagine what happens to the main character after the movie ends.
YES   SOMETIMES   NO

15. I always see variety in a rainy day. Rainy days are not all alike.
YES   SOMETIMES   NO

16. If I am outside and hear a jet going over, I like to imagine what the inside of the jet looks like and the people on it and what they might be doing at that instant.
YES   SOMETIMES   NO

17. I like to look at other people's picture albums and piece together their lives from the various photos.
YES   SOMETIMES   NO

18. I like to try strange and exotic foods just for the experience.
YES   SOMETIMES   NO

19. Whenever I go through a department store or grocery store, I have a strong desire to "touch" things so that I can feel as well as see objects.
YES   SOMETIMES   NO

20. An interesting smell such as that of perfume or food or flowers can suddenly bring back a memory to me.
YES   SOMETIMES   NO

WHAT IS YOUR IMAGINATION SCORE?

100–80 = Excellent
79–60 = Very Good
59–40 = Average
Below 40 = You need to be more observant about ways to improve your imagination.

93

CONFLICT: THE HEARTBEAT OF A PLAY

BY D. R. ANDERSEN

EVERY PLAYWRIGHT is a Dr. Frankenstein trying to breathe life into a page for the stage. In a good play, the heartbeat must be thundering. And the heartbeat of a play is conflict.

Simply put, conflict exists when a character wants something and can't get it. Conflict may sometimes be internal—as when a character struggles to choose between or among opposing desires. For example, Alma in Tennessee Williams's *Summer and Smoke* longs to yield to her sexual yearnings but is prevented by the repressed and conventional side of her nature.

Conflict in drama may also be external—as when a character struggles against another *character* (Oscar and Felix in Neil Simon's *The Odd Couple*); against *society* (Nora in Ibsen's *A Doll's House*); against *nature* (the mountain climbers in Patrick Meyers' *K2*); or against *fate* (Sophocles' *Oedipus*).

In most plays, the conflict is a combination of internal and external struggles. In fact, internal conflict is often externalized for dramatic impact. In Philip Barry's *Holiday,* for instance, the hero's inner dilemma is outwardly expressed in his attraction to two sisters—one who represents the safe but boring world of convention, and the other who is a symbol of the uncertain but exciting life of adventure.

Granted that a conflict may be internal or external; that a character may be in conflict with another character, society, nature or fate; and that most plays are a combination of internal and external conflict, many plays that have these basic elements of conflict do not have a thundering heartbeat. Why? These plays lack one, some, or all of the five magic ingredients of rousing, attention-grabbing-and-holding conflict.

The five magic ingredients

I. *Never let your audience forget what your protagonist wants.*

You can achieve this in a number of ways. Often the protagonist or another character states and periodically restates in dialogue what is at stake. Or in some plays, he explains what he wants directly to the audience in the form of a monologue. As you read or watch plays you admire, take note of the obvious and ingenious techniques playwrights use to tell the reader or audience what the characters' goals are.

Sometimes the method used to keep your audience alerted to your protagonist's goal/concern/need is a direct reflection of the protagonist's personality. In the following three short passages from my play *Graduation Day,*[1] a mother and father with very traditional values have a conversation while waiting to meet their rebellious daughter, who has told them she has a big surprise. Notice how the protagonist—Mrs. Whittaker—nervously and comically manipulates the conversation, reminding her husband and the audience of her concern for her daughter Jane:

MRS. WHITTAKER
(Knocking on the door)
Jane. Jane. It's Mom and Dad.
(Pause)
No answer. What should we do, Tom?
MR. WHITTAKER
Let's go in.
MRS. WHITTAKER
Suppose we find Jane in a compromising situation?
MR. WHITTAKER
Nobody at Smith College has ever been found in a compromising situation.

* * *

MRS. WHITTAKER
Tom, you know, this was my freshman room.
MR. WHITTAKER
Of course, I know.
MRS. WHITTAKER
And Jane's. It was Jane's freshman room too, Tom. Remember?

* * *

MR. WHITTAKER
Mary, you get in the craziest moods at these reunions. I may never bring you back again.

---

1. First produced by Playwrights Horizons in New York, starring Polly Holliday.

469

MRS. WHITTAKER

Do you know why you fell in love with me, Tom?

MR. WHITTAKER

I fell in love with you the minute I saw you eat pancakes.

MRS. WHITTAKER

That's a sound basis for a relationship. Tom, where do you suppose Jane is? And more frightening, what do you suppose she wants to tell us? She said just enough on the phone to suggest that she's going to be bringing a boy here for us to meet.

MR. WHITTAKER

A man, Mary, a man.

MRS. WHITTAKER

Oh, God. I never even considered that possibility. Suppose Jane brings a fiancé—our age—like Pia Zadora did.

MR. WHITTAKER

Don't you want Jane to live her own life?

MRS. WHITTAKER

No. Especially not her own life. Practically anyone else's. But not her own.

MR. WHITTAKER

What *do* you want for Jane?

MRS. WHITTAKER

I don't see why Jane can't fall in love with a plain Harvard Business School student, let's say. Someone who'll be steady and dependable.

And so it goes. The protagonist discusses a number of topics, but she inevitably leads the conversation back to her overriding concern. Mrs. Whittaker's desire to see her daughter do the right thing and marry wisely is always uppermost in the mind and conversation of the character.

In this one act, a comic effect is achieved by having Mrs. Whittaker insistently remind the audience what she wants. Once you have clearly established what a character wants, you can then write powerful and often hilarious scenes in which the audience, already knowing the character's point of view, is able to anticipate his reaction.

II. *Show your protagonist struggling to achieve what he wants.*

This principle is, of course, the basic writing advice to *show*, not tell, and it was a major concern for me when I was writing *The House Where I Was Born.*[2]

The plot: A young man, Leo, has returned from the Vietnam War, a psychosomatic mute because of the atrocities he witnessed. He comes back to a crumbling old house in a decaying suburb, a home populated

---

2. First produced by Playwrights Horizons in New York.

470

by a callous stepfather; a mother who survives on aphorisms and by bending reality to diminish her despair; a half-crazy aunt; and a grandfather who refuses to buckle under to the pressures from his family to sell the home.

I set out to dramatize Leo's painful battle to free himself of memories of the war and to begin a new life. However, each time I worked on the scene in the play when Leo first comes home, his dialogue seemed to trivialize his emotions.

Then it occurred to me that Leo should not speak at all during the first act; that his inability to speak would *show* an audience his suffering and pain far better than his words could.

At the end of the third act, when Leo regains some hope, some strength to go on, every speech I wrote for him also rang false. The problem, I eventually realized, was that as playwright, I was *telling* the audience that a change had taken place, instead of *showing* the change as it took place.

In the final draft, I solved this dramatic problem by having Leo, who had loved music all his life, sit down at the piano and begin playing and singing Christmas carols while his surprised and relieved family joined in.

First silence, then singing, served my play better than mere telling.

III. *Create honest, understandable, and striking obstacles against which your protagonist must struggle.*

Many plays fail because their characters' problems seem too easily solved. I wrestled with this issue when I was writing *Oh Promise Me!*[3] a play that takes place in a private boarding house for the elderly. The play's original title was *Mr. Farner Wants a Double Bed.* The plot involved the attempt of an elderly man and woman—an unmarried couple—to share a double bed in a rooming house run by a repressed and oppressive owner. I wanted to explore contemporary attitudes toward the elderly, particularly as they concerned sexuality.

The more I played with the idea, the more I repeatedly heard an inner voice saying, "Chances are the couple could find some place to live where nobody cared if they were married or not." This voice—like the

---

3. Winner of the Jane Chambers Memorial Playwriting Award.

audience watching a play without an honest, understandable, convincing obstacle for the protagonist—kept saying, "So what?"

The writer's response: "Suppose, instead of a man and a woman, the couple is two men." Here was a real obstacle: Two elderly, gay men, growing feeble, want to sleep together in a double bed under the roof of an unsympathetic and unyielding landlord.

Suddenly, the play was off and running.

IV. *In the final scene or scenes, make sure your protagonist achieves what he wants; comes to understand that there is something* else *he wants; or accepts (defiantly, humbly, etc.) that he cannot have what he wants.*

If we spend time in the theater watching a character battle for something, we want to know the outcome—whatever it may be.

In my psychological thriller *Trick or Treat*,[4] Kate, a writer in her forties, has been badly burned in a love affair and is unable to decide whether to accept or reject a new relationship. She is involved at present with Toby, a younger man, but—as the following dialogue reveals—she insists on keeping him at a cool distance.

KATE
That does it, Toby. We're getting out of this place.
TOBY
Okay. Tomorrow we'll check into the local Howard Johnson's.
KATE
I want to go home—to New York—to my own apartment.
TOBY
Okay. Okay. If you insist. Besides, Howard Johnson's is not to be entered into lightly.
KATE
Huh?
TOBY
It's an old college rule. You'd never shell out for a room at Howard Johnson's—unless you were *very* serious about the girl.
KATE
I'll remember that. The day I agree to check into a Howard Johnson's—you'll know I've made a serious commitment to our relationship.

In the course of the play, Kate faces a number of trials—including a threat to her life—as she tries to expose the fraudulent leader of a

---

4. First produced by the Main Street Theater, New York, New York.

religious cult. Through these trials—with Toby by her side—Kate comes to realize that she's ready to forget the past and give herself over to a new relationship. This critical decision is humorously expressed in the last seconds of the play:

KATE

Do you love me, Toby?

TOBY

Yes, I do. I found that out tonight . . . when I thought I might be losing you forever. Do you love me?

KATE

Yes. And I can prove it.

TOBY

How?

KATE

Take me to Howard Johnson's—please! Take me to Howard Johnson's!

The curtain falls and the audience knows that the heroine has made an unequivocal decision.

V. *Make sure that the audience ultimately sympathizes with the protagonist's yearning to achieve his goal, however outlandish his behavior.*

This may be the most important of the five magic ingredients of conflict. It may also be the most elusive. To oversimplify, in a good play, the protagonist must be very likable and/or have a goal that is universal.

In the plays I've had produced, one character seems to win the sympathy of the audience hands down. In my romantic comedy *Funny Valentines*,[5] Andy Robbins, a writer of children's books, is that character. Andy is sloppy, disorganized, and easily distracted, and—this is his likable trait—he's painfully aware of his shortcomings and admits them openly. Here's Andy speaking for himself:

ANDY

Judging by my appearance, you might take me to be a complete physical and emotional wreck. Well, I can't deny it. And it's gotten worse—much worse—since Ellen left. You know that's true.

---

5. Published by Samuel French; winner of the Cummings/Taylor Playwriting Award; produced in Canada under the title *Drôles de Valentins*.

473

Andy is willing to admit his failings to old friends and strangers alike. Here he's talking to an attractive young woman he's just met.

ANDY

You don't have to be consoling just because I haven't finished a book lately. I won't burst into tears or create a scene. No. I lied. I might burst into tears—I'm warning you.

ZAN

I didn't mean to imply . . . (*She laughs.*)

ANDY

Why are you laughing?

ZAN

You stapled your shirt.

ANDY

What's so odd about that? Millions of derelicts do it every day.

ZAN

And your glasses are wired together with a pipe cleaner.

ANDY

I didn't think twine would be as attractive.

In addition to liking Andy, audiences seem to sympathize with his goal of wanting to grow up and get back together with his collaborator and ex-wife, Ellen.

Whether you're wondering where to find an idea for a one-act play or beginning to refine the rough draft of a new full-length work or starting rehearsals of one of your plays, take your cue from the five magic ingredients of conflict. Whatever your experience as a playwright and whatever your current project, understanding the nature of dramatic conflict and how to achieve it will prove invaluable at every point in the writing and staging process.

* * *

Five exercises for creating dramatic conflict

Try these exercises to develop your skill in handling conflict.

1. Choose five plays you like. Summarize each in one sentence, stating what the protagonist wants. For example, Hamlet wants to avenge his father's murder.
2. Write one page of dialogue in which character A asks character B to do something that character B doesn't want to do. Have character A

474

make a request in three different ways, each showing a different emotion—guilt, enthusiasm, humility, anger.

3. Write a speech in which a character talks to another character and conveys what he wants without explicitly stating his goal.

4. Choose a famous play you enjoy. Rewrite the last page or two so that the outcome of the conflict for the protagonist is entirely different from the original.

5. Flip through today's newspaper until you find a story about a person—famous or unknown—who interests you. Then summarize the story in one sentence, stating what the person wants. For example: X wants to save an endangered species of bird. Next list the obstacles the person is facing in trying to get what he wants:

• A developer wants to build a shopping mall where the remaining members of the endangered species live.

• Pollution from a nearby factory is threatening the birds' food supply.

Finally, write several short scenes in which X (the protagonist) confronts the people (the antagonists) who represent the cause of each obstacle. (In this example, the antagonist would be the developer or the owner of the factory.) Decide which of the scenes you've written is the most dramatically satisfying. Identify the reasons you think it is the best scene.

EDITORS, AGENTS, AND BUSINESS

94

THE ABC'S OF COPYRIGHT

BY ELIZABETH PRESTON

THOUGH THE AREA OF COPYRIGHT PROTECTION and infringement tends to concern and often confuse many writers, the copyright law is actually quite straightforward, easy to comprehend, and generous in terms of copyright protection of literary property. The law was revised in 1978—the first complete revision since 1909—and the changes dramatically increased the rights of creators of copyrightable work. In this chapter we'll discuss some copyright basics, including what may be copyrighted, who may apply for copyright, duration of protection, and the rights of copyright owners. For answers to more complicated copyright questions, writers should get in touch directly with the Copyright Office.

What is copyright? What works can be copyrighted?

The copyright laws of the United States protect "original works of authorship"—both published and unpublished—including literary, dramatic, musical, artistic, and certain other "intellectual" works. Under the law, a work is protected as soon as it is set down on paper, or recorded, for the first time, and it becomes the sole property of the author who created it. What this means to you as the writer or "creator" of a work is that you own and control the rights to its publication and use, whether it's a four-line limerick, a story, an article, a play, or a novel.

There are several categories of material that may not be copyrighted, however: speeches or performances that have not been written or recorded; titles, names, and slogans; ideas, concepts, principles or devices, as distinguished from a description, explanation, or illustration; and works that consist entirely of information that is in the public domain and contains no original authorship, such as standard calendars, material from public documents or other common sources.

What's the procedure for copyright registration?

As noted earlier, your work is automatically protected by copyright from the time that it's put onto paper or in another physical form, and actual registration with the Copyright Office is not a requirement for protection. Nonetheless, there are several advantages to registration, and failure to register your work could be detrimental, particularly if the work becomes commercially valuable and there is increased possibility of infringement (unauthorized reprinting, filming, recording, or other uses). Among these advantages are the following:

• Registration establishes a public record of the copyright claim

• Registration is ordinarily necessary before any infringement suits may be filed in court

• If made before or within five years of publication, registration will establish evidence in court of the validity of the copyright

• If registration is made within three months after publication of the work or prior to an infringement of it, the court may award statutory damages and attorney's fees to the copyright owner. Otherwise, only an award of actual damages and profits is legally available to the copyright owners.

To register a work, send the following (in the same envelope or package) to the U.S. Copyright Office, Register of Copyrights, Library of Congress, Washington, DC 20559:

1. A properly completed application form (supplied free of charge by the Copyright Office)

2 A fee of $20 for each application (recently increased from $10)

3. A deposit (copy) of the work being registered (one if the work is unpublished, two if already published)

Be sure the application form is completed legibly, preferably type-written; since it becomes a part of the official permanent records of the Copyright Office, it must meet archival standards.

In general, you should register book manuscripts, play scripts, and other long works when they're completed. It's well worth the $20 registration fee to make sure that there's a public record of your copyright ownership. It's not necessary to register articles, short stories, poems, or other short work individually; you may use one application—and pay a single fee—to register several individual published works of the same nature. For instance, 20 short stories published in a single year may be registered on one $20 application. Write to the Copyright Office for further details on group registration.

Most writers will use application form TX—for published and unpublished non-dramatic literary works—or PA—for published and unpublished works of the performing arts. Other forms available include RE (for claims to renew copyright in works copyrighted under the old law); CA (for supplementary registration to correct or amplify information given in the Copyright Office record of an earlier registration); and GR/CP (an adjunct application for registration of a group of contributions to periodicals). When requesting forms from the Copyright Office, indicate exactly what type of work you wish to copyright so that you'll receive the proper information. The effective date of copyright registration is the day on which a completed application, deposit, and fee have been *received* in the Copyright Office. Once your application has been processed, you will receive an official certificate of copyright registration.

Who may file an application form?

The following individuals may submit an application form for a particular work:

• The author

• A person or organization that has obtained ownership of all the rights under the copyright initially belonging to the author

• The owner of exclusive right(s). Under the new law, any of the exclusive rights that make up a copyright—and any subdivision of them—can be transferred and owned separately, even though the transfer may be limited in time or place. For example, a magazine or book publisher that has purchased first rights in a work may apply for registration of a claim in the work for this use only.

• The duly authorized agent of an author, other copyright claimant, or the owner of exclusive right(s). For instance, book publishers usually apply for copyrights on behalf of their authors; of course, the author should always be sure that the work is copyrighted in his or her name.

How long does copyright last?

One of the major innovations in the U.S. copyright law is that it adopts the basic "life-plus-fifty" years system already in effect in most countries; that is, *a work created and "fixed in tangible form" after January 1, 1978, is protected for a term of the author's life, plus 50 years after the author's death.* Works created before January 1, 1978, but neither published nor registered for copyright before that date, are also automatically protected by statute for the life of the author plus 50 years.

The protection available for works copyrighted before 1978 depends on whether the copyright had already been renewed and was therefore in its second term when the new law came into effect, or was still in its first term on December 31, 1977. The copyright law before 1978 allowed for a work to be copyrighted for a first term of 28 years from the date it was secured, followed by a renewal for a second term of 28 years. This system of computing the duration of protection for works copyrighted before 1978 has been carried over into the present law, with one major change: the length of the second term is increased to 47 years. Thus, the maximum total term of protection for works already copyrighted (i.e., prior to 1978) is increased from 56 years (28-year first term plus 28-year renewal term) to 75 years (28-year first term plus 47-year renewal term).

Any copyright in its second term as of January 1, 1978 was automatically extended up to a maximum of 75 years from the end of the year in which it was originally secured, without the need for further renewal. Copyrights still in their first term as of January 1, 1978, must be renewed by the end of their 28th calendar year, or else they will expire, and the work will go into public domain. (For instance, the first term of a copyright registered for a work in 1970 will come up for renewal in 1998; if renewal is made by the end of that year, the work will then be protected for an additional 47 years.)

Should you put a copyright notice on your work?

Writers often wonder whether they should affix a copyright notice to unpublished works before submitting them to publishers. Technically, such a notice is not required on unpublished works, but most would agree that it's a good idea to include a copyright notice on the first page of a short manuscript, or the title page of a book manuscript. The notice should include the following three elements:

- The symbol © and/or the word "copyright"
- The year of first publication of the work
- The name of the owner of copyright in the work

Example: © 1990 by John Doe or Copyright © 1990 John Doe

Most magazines are copyrighted, so if your work is published in such a publication, it will automatically be protected. Even so, *you* remain the copyright owner of the work, since in most cases, periodicals buy "first rights" only.

What are the rights of copyright owners?

Copyright owners have the right to reproduce their work; to prepare derivative works based upon their work; to distribute copies of the work to the public by sale, rental, lease or lending; and to perform or display the work publicly, as in the case of literary, musical, and dramatic works and pantomimes, motion pictures, and other audiovisual works.

As the author of a copyrighted work, you may sell or transfer rights to it in any way that you choose. For example, you would usually sell "first rights" only to a magazine in which your poem, story, article, or filler is to be published. Later, you may choose to sell reprint or "second" rights in that work to another publication, or for some other use (movie or TV filming, for instance). The permission of the original publisher is not required, although it may be necessary for certain works copyrighted under the old law. A publisher may not buy "all rights" to your material unless you agree to such a sale and signify it in a signed written statement or "instrument of conveyance." In the absence of this signed statement, the publisher owns only first rights, or one-time use of your work.

A work written or prepared by an employee within the scope of his or her employment—called "work for hire"—is the property of the employer, who may register the work in his name or that of the company. However, as the result of a recent Supreme Court decision, the "work for hire" stipulation applies only to those writers who are actually in an employer-employee relationship with a publisher; it cannot be applied to the work of those who write on a free-lance basis unless they specifically agree to it.

If you're selling a book manuscript, be sure the contract your publisher offers specifically states the terms of the sale and which rights are included. Book contracts are somewhat standardized, though the language and terms will vary. For instance, as author you would declare that your work is original; that you are granting the publisher the right to publish your book; that you will deliver your manuscript in final form

481

on a specified date; that you will be responsible for obtaining permissions if the manuscript includes copyrighted work. The publisher promises to make timely payment of royalties; to give you as author a specified number of free copies of your published book; to share in the proceeds from sales to book clubs, and so forth. It's important to remember that the time to discuss any terms that are not satisfactory to you, or are at all unclear, is *before* the contract is signed. In most cases, the terms of book contracts are somewhat negotiable, and you shouldn't shy away from discussing possible changes with your editor.

A final note: Infringement of copyright is a relatively rare occurrence, and although writers should take precautions to protect their work, they should find reassurance not only in the fact that the revised copyright law represents their best interests, but also that reputable publishers will deal fairly and honestly with authors in all matters relating to the publication of their work.

95

A GOOD AGENT IS NOT
HARD TO FIND—
If You Know How, When, and Where to Look

BY TIMOTHY SCHAFFNER

THE INCREASED VOLUME OF SUBMISSIONS versus the limited time in which an editor has to consider manuscripts has caused many publishers to close their doors to unagented material. In the eyes of these publishers, the work has passed muster only when submitted by a reputable agent. Therefore, today, more than ever, writers need the services of a good literary agent. So, before even attempting to make a sale, the writer must find a good agent to represent his work.

Finding a good agent can, in many respects, be more difficult than getting the book published. Agents these days are a lot more choosy than they might have been in the past because of stricter publication standards, the narrowing list of viable publishers, and the decrease in the number of books published by each house within a given year. An agent's select list must be honed down to include only those writers of the highest quality in any given area of literature; for not only must the agent be able to place work successfully, he must also maintain a reputation among the publishers with whom he works in order to continue to do business with them in the future.

When submitting a manuscript to an agent, the writer must observe a high level of professionalism. Make sure all spelling, typing, and punctuation are correct; type on one side of each page, leave wide margins (2–2¼″), and be sure to paginate throughout. If using a word processor, use only a letter quality or "near-letter quality" printer—dot matrix is discouraged by most agents as it is extremely hard on the eyes. A full manuscript should be submitted unbound in a sturdy typing paper box; be sure to enclose a self-addressed, stamped envelope with sufficient postage for the manuscript's return.

Always query first. A six-hundred-page manuscript, even if it is the greatest work of literature since *War and Peace*, will not be looked upon favorably if it arrives unbidden at an agent's door; chances are, if it does not have the requisite postage for its return, it may very well end up in the trash. In the query letter, briefly describe the nature of the work in one paragraph, and include a short biography and any information that might be helpful to the agent: previous writing credentials and awards received in the last five years, a brief description of your background not only as a writer, but in general terms as well, i.e., where you live, your age, your profession other than writer, interests, etc.

There are several publications on the market to aid the writer in finding an agent. I suggest the *Literary Market Place* (a guide to publishing brought out annually by R. R. Bowker and available in every library reference department), *The Literary Agents of North America* (published by Author Aid Associates, 340 E. 52nd St., New York, NY 10022, this is especially helpful, as it gives a detailed list of each agent's interest as well as a brief rundown of recent titles sold through that agency), and the various books and pamphlets made available through such sources as the Society of Authors' Representatives (10 Astor Pl., 3rd Fl., New York, NY 10003), The Authors Guild (for members), Poets & Writers (72 Spring St., New York, NY 10012), and others. Some of these will provide a detailed description of a particular agent's field of activity. It will be fairly easy to glean from these which you should or should not try. Many of the bigger agencies will not take on any new clients unless they have been referred by someone they know, or better yet, someone who is already a client at that agency. Some agents will work only in a specific area, while others are more generalized. The guides will also point out who accepts unsolicited material, who charges reading fees, and what commission each agent takes. Though many of the big agencies still charge ten percent, most of the independent agents are now charging fifteen.

Trade magazines—such as *Publishers Weekly,* which often gives brief rundowns on the deals of the week (on the "Rights" page) and the agents involved—are also helpful, and you can always look for mention of an agent's name in the acknowledgments of a book you've recently enjoyed. If working in a particular genre, such as romance, science fiction, or mystery, you'll often find agents who are active in that field mentioned in the pages of the various fanzines. Word of mouth is always helpful if you know an agented author who can recommend some agents. Try not to call the agent to ask what kind of work he handles, as this can be determined easily in your research, and such calls can often interrupt the agent in his day-to-day tasks. An agent might be more receptive to your work if you inform him of the source through which you got his name and if you show that you know a little about his special interests.

Once you've selected a group of agents or a particular agent to query, write to them in the manner previously described. If you enclose a self-addressed stamped envelope, you'll be assured of a quick response. Some writers include a postcard with spaces for the agent to check off whether he or she wants to see the work, and if so, in what form, i.e., partial manuscript or complete manuscript. In the case of fiction, I generally ask to see the full manuscript, as it is essential to read the beginning, middle, and end to judge the work. But many agents ask only for partial manuscripts. With a partial, a full synopsis is required, or if it is a nonfiction work, sample chapters plus an outline and table of contents. When an agent asks to see your work, expect a good amount of time to elapse before you hear from him. I usually take between four to six weeks to respond, sometimes less if the author indicates the work is being submitted to more than one agent. When submitting your work to several agents simultaneously, be sure to inform each agent of this fact, and to keep each abreast of any early interest that may develop. Though simultaneous submission is an increasingly common practice, many agents refuse to consider an author's work unless offered to them exclusively.

Once an agent has offered to represent a writer, it is very important to determine the extent to which such representation is offered and under what terms. Many agents work in conjunction with co-agents in the areas of foreign dramatic rights, so it is a good idea to find out a little about this arrangement. Some agents might insist on handling all the author's work or on having a "first look" option, while others might not wish to peddle the writer's short fiction or articles to those magazines and literary journals that tend to offer little or no money and are slow to respond. Some agents have long binding contracts, while others work purely on the basis of a handshake or verbal agreement.

It is always a good idea to get to know the agent either by phone, correspondence, or ideally, in person. Arrange a brief appointment at the agent's office to judge the size of his operation and the sorts of books he has handled recently. The way the agent conducts business is by far the most important factor in your decision, but it is essential for you and the agent to see eye to eye. Though you may be primarily interested in getting your work-at-hand sold, bear in mind that you'll be working with each other for a long period of time beyond the first book. The agent you select should be interested in working with you as a *writer,* and not just in representing you for this one particular book.

Equally important to knowing *how* to find an agent is knowing *when* to get one. Virtually every writer, with the exception perhaps of beginning free-lance magazine writers, juvenile writers, and poets, needs an agent. Once you've reached the point in your career at which a book is evolving, for instance, you will need someone to protect your rights in negotiations and promote your work to insure its greatest possible success. Many well-known writers prefer to handle their books themselves, and some use the services of a lawyer. But, no matter how skilled you or your lawyer might be, it would be extremely difficult to exploit successfully all the additional rights in your work, and to market your book through all the necessary channels. An agent provides services beyond the preliminary negotiations and sale of a work that are vital to an author's career and success. Much of the agent's activity on your behalf is conducted in the day-to-day course of events and does not require the author's participation. The agent is there to handle all your literary business affairs so you can attend to the business of writing without worries and distractions.

Bringing an author out of obscurity into the literary limelight does not happen overnight, and the agent must therefore be thinking long term, beyond the first book, toward building an author's career. Sometimes that much-anticipated first novel might receive glowing reviews but sell only two thousand copies. It then becomes the agent's job to assure both editor and author that there is more to look forward to after the initial frustration and disappointment inherent in the publication of any first book. Similarly, an agent must be able to determine that point in an author's career at which it is necessary to make the great leap forward, to auction the new "break-out" novel for huge sums, and to take the daring gambles that he or she knows from experience will pay off for the writer. Over time, an author can develop a special relationship with his or her agent, a state of symbiosis based on trust, friendship, and an intuitive understanding by the agent of the writer's potential for the present and the future.

96

WRITING SUCCESSFUL PROPOSALS FOR THE ROMANCE MARKET

By Tahti Carter, Editor, *Harlequin Books*

I'D LIKE TO DESCRIBE for you a dream scenario of a successful proposal from a writer's rather than an editor's point of view. The ideal scenario goes something like this: The writer has a terrific idea for a romance novel, one that she thinks would be perfect for a specific category romance series. She has done her homework, read all the recent books for the line that she could get her hands on, and loved them all, or most of them anyway. She has decided that the Harlequin American Romance, Temptation, or Silhouette Desire line, or that of some other publisher, is the perfect one for her story. So she sits down at her typewriter or word processor, and writes a wonderful plot outline or synopsis. Then she goes to work with great enthusiasm, verve, and talent to write the first three chapters of the work. It's fantastically good, and she knows it.

Then, after querying her chosen publisher with a compelling and convincing letter, she gets a positive response and is asked to send in her proposal. She mails off her partial. It arrives safely on the editor's desk. By a combination of good luck and unusual circumstances, the editor reads it immediately and is bowled over by the author's likable characters, believable story line, creative plot, fresh new ideas, and the honest emotion that make it all shimmer with magic. The editor picks up the telephone and calls the author to offer her a contract. The author has made her sale and she happily sits down to write her book.

Now then, let me give you the editor's scenario, or the reality of the situation. Every day the mail is dropped on the editor's desk, and in it are numerous query letters from published and unpublished authors, outlining story ideas that they say are perfect for the line for which she buys manuscripts. The pile grows higher each day, and maybe once a week, or even only once a month, does the editor go through that pile,

488

looking for manuscripts that suit her line's specifications. First of all, any query outlining a plot that does not violate some obvious requirement for her specific line gets a positive response, and the writer gets a letter requesting to see the partial manuscript. But the editor knows, as should the writer, that only published authors are offered a contract on the basis of a partial submission. At Harlequin unpublished authors must submit a complete manuscript before they can make a sale. But since the editor is in the business of finding new authors, she is willing to give feedback to beginning writers, to guide them as to what will and will not work for her line. Communicating with a writer as the book develops will save time and energy for both author and editor. Hopefully this collaboration will prevent the book from going off the track and needing many revisions.

Let's see what happens to this partial category proposal when it does land on the editor's desk. More often than not it is put on the bottom of a pile of similar submissions that must wait for a quiet afternoon, when amazingly there is no pressing deadline to meet on the current books for the line, which are already in various stages of production—whether they are being revised, line edited, or being worked on for art sheets, front matter, or back cover copy. A time when there is no contract that demands to be negotiated, or a speech that needs to be written for an upcoming writers' conference.

What do you need to do as a writer to make the best use of that moment when your proposal is read by an already tired and jaded editor? What do you need to do to ensure that your category proposal will be a success, that it will get a positive reading, and will make the editor want to add your book to her publishing schedule? First of all, what are the things that an editor will *not* want to see? Although hopefully the positive elements of your proposal will outweigh any negative ones, the negatives, no matter how insignificant, seem to stand out the most. Of first importance is its physical appearance. Is the proposal professional looking, well typed on good quality paper, and error free? Second, does the synopsis begin with Chapter 1, rather than Chapter 4 as some writers have the terrible habit of doing? I always feel that a writer who does this shows great insecurity. It is as if to say, "I want to force you to read all three of my chapters, and if I give you a complete synopsis, I'm afraid that you won't bother." This psychological blackmail is one of my pet peeves. Another one is a single-spaced synopsis. I've never understood why writers, who know that manuscripts must be double spaced, still single space their synopses. Don't do it, for it makes difficult reading.

Let's look at the elements of the proposal itself that must be evident if it's to sell your manuscript. The two most important elements are characterization and plotting. The characters in a romance have to be likable, because who wants to read for pleasure and relaxation if the characters are not people you would like to meet? The heroine must be someone the reader can relate to and wants to see win in romance and succeed in her career. Regardless of the category romance line that the author chooses to write for, all heroines today must be independent in some way, and in charge of their own lives.

The hero must be a man you could easily fall in love with. The reader wants to know what life would be like if she could only meet and fall in love with the perfect man. Of course he will have some imperfections or flaws that will lead to conflict, but overall he must be likable in order to be lovable. And this rules out the instant antagonism cliché. The novel with a hero and heroine who hate each other from the start but later suddenly decide they are in love never works, as far as I'm concerned. Yes, I want to see tension, drama, and conflict, but certainly not constant sparring and chauvinistic bullying.

In the proposal it will be important to show how you bring your characters to life, and you may want to do this by including a character description of the hero and heroine. To become a master at characterization, you need to give your characters direction. And to make characters believable, they must appear to act of their own free will and not be manipulated. The simplest way to do this is to give each character a goal, one that will give him a rationale to behave the way that you want him to.

The second equally important element that an editor will examine in considering your category proposal will be the story line. Today's sophisticated readers want realistic situations, plots that mirror real life and deal with issues that concern them. This is particularly true for us at Harlequin American Romance. We know that our readers want a slice of life along with their romance, as a story about real people facing real problems—or life as it relates to their own.

What the editor will be looking for in your proposal is a story line that suits her publishing program. And here you need to do your homework and read many of the current books in that line to see if you are targeting your work for the right market. At American Romance we are looking for complex plots that deal with present-day issues and concerns of American women and embody realistic conflicts that arise from their everyday lives. Because of the longer length of our books (70,000 to 75,000 words), we also require a subplot. Something else has to be going on besides the romance. In your proposal indicate what your subplot is and how it relates to your primary characters. A solid roster of secondary characters is important in successfully implementing a subplot. When creating your characters, you must strive for contrast; individual characters must strike sparks off each other, they must interact and conflict because of differing sets of ideas and goals. Yet in order to be believable, a character needs to be consistent in his behavior, and consistent with his self image.

In order to write a successful romance, the writer must meet the emotional needs of the reader and provide the wish fulfillment of a love story with a happy ending. This emotional payoff, this feeling of uplift and satisfaction, is the necessary rationale behind romance novels. The fantasy element enters into the love relationship in that love in romance novels is always better and more wonderful than it may be in real life. Because readers seek out books that will satisfy their individual emotional needs, the writer must design characters that meet these needs. Category romance novels have a very specific audience and this audience has come to demand certain qualities. Although certain lines within the category romance field stress some elements over others— some are more sensuous, others more realistic, and some more fantasy-oriented—they all provide a reading experience in which a man and a woman meet and fall in love, face conflicts and resolve them, and then make a commitment to love each other forever. While in soap operas problems never end, conflicts continue to expand and multiply, and happiness is never lasting, category romance novels give the reader the reassurance that yes, life can be beautiful if the heroine meets the right man, a man who will fulfill all of her dreams. It is this reassurance that your readers are seeking and that you must learn to provide if you are to write the successful category proposal, the one that will sell.

Submission Procedure

For unagented and unsolicited submissions, we prefer to see a query letter first, in which you should ask if we are interested in seeing your complete or partial manuscript. Your letter should clearly state how many words are in your manuscript, and include a brief story synopsis as well as pertinent information about yourself, such as whether you have ever been published (and if so, what, where and when), how long you've been writing, how familiar you are with romance novels, whether you belong to any writer's groups, and why you feel your novel is right for us.

Ten elements to include when writing a Harlequin Intrigue

1. You need a dynamite opening that grabs the reader and puts her right into the middle of the intrigue. Start your intrigue with a story that is already in progress.

2. Be sure to involve your heroine in the intrigue itself. She needs to be actively taking part in solving the intrigue puzzle, and a take-charge, active participant in the action. A heroine in peril has great drama.

3. The heroine does not need to be suspicious of the hero. An adversarial relationship will hinder the romance. However, suspicion of a secondary character may be an element.

4. The romance and intrigue need to blend and develop at the same time. We want to see a romance that is convincing and believable.

5. Put down a layer of the mystery in each chapter and end all chapters with a mini cliff hanger. We want a page turner that will keep the reader motivated to find out what will happen next.

6. Lay down clues throughout the book. The plot should be full of unexpected turns, surprises, and red herrings.

7. Because a fast pace is necessary, use a lot of dialogue to move the story forward quickly. Don't get bogged down in too much introspection or narration. Avoid flowery imagery since it doesn't belong in an Intrigue format.

8. Solve the mystery through showing rather than telling. Don't solve the intrigue in great long speeches or stretches of narrative at the end. Use elements of discovery throughout the story instead.

9. Tie up all loose ends. Each clue that has been put down throughout the book needs to work and be explained. There must be a skillful blending of everexpanding clues that build to a bang-up climactic ending, where the mystery or intrigue is resolved.

10. The romance has to grow and build along with the intrigue and climax in a satisfactory, uplifting ending, as it does in a regular romance. The love scenes have to be woven in carefully so that they do not slow down the pace of the story. Build to an action-filled resolution that brings the intrigue to a satisfactory climax and the romance to a happy ending.

97

A LITERARY AGENT'S PERSPECTIVE

BY ANITA DIAMANT

IN THIS AGE of proliferating conglomerates, the publishing industry has followed suit: The former cottage industry has indeed become big business. The business department, the sales and marketing departments are apt to influence the acceptance of a manuscript by the publishing house. And so literary agents, following the trends, often become interested primarily in projects bearing the promise of a six-figure advance. Where does this leave the great majority of writers and would-be writers? Is it impossible for them to secure representation?

It is true that conservatively 75% of all manuscripts are sold through agents today, but it is also a fact that there remain many bona fide agents who are more interested in representing a writer than only in securing huge advances. I can think of no greater pleasure than to place a first novel that indubitably will bring a relatively small advance. And it is important and rewarding for an agent to be an integral part of building a successful career for a new writer. Does this mean that every agent will take on any project that is sent in to him or her? Of course, we have to be discriminating, and obviously we will all take on manuscripts and ideas that appeal to us and would seem to bear the promise of a sale. I would like to start by assuring writers that it is possible even for a neophyte to obtain representation by a professional agent; but a good deal depends upon the way in which the work is presented and of course on the feasibility of selling the material.

The author-agent relationship is a very personal one. There must be complete trust and respect between the writer and the agent. This is true financially as well as editorially. The agent receives all monies due the writer, deducts a percentage, and then sends the balance to the writer. This should be done as soon as the publisher's check has cleared, but I must admit that I have heard numerous stories about an undue length of time that elapses before the writer is paid by the agent.

All of this can be avoided if a writer secures a reference before deciding to have a particular agent represent him or her.

I also feel that an agent must have enough background in the publishing world to be able to offer some editorial assistance to a writer. I do not mean that it is an agent's job to edit or rewrite, but an agent should know whether a proposal is sufficiently effective; whether plot, style, and characterization are successful; whether a theme is handled with clarity. If there are problems, the agent should be willing and able to indicate where the problems lie and perhaps offer suggestions that would help correct them. Your agent should also be your friend. This does not mean that an agent should take the place of your psychiatrist, your attorney, or your financial adviser, although we generally listen carefully to problems in all these areas.

The value of agents obviously is their knowledge of the markets, of the changing editorial staffs, and, of course, the close contact with all of the people who are in the field at any one time. And this is certainly a changing scene: This past year has seen enormous changes in ownership of the large publishing companies and in the hiring and firing of editorial personnel. It is very often important to think not solely of the suitable publishing house for a project, but also of the editor who will be most empathic and whose interests are somewhat analogous to the material presented.

The question inevitably rises, "Is it necessary for a writer to have an agent?" Of course, there are always manuscripts submitted directly to publishers, which sell, but the fact remains that many houses simply will not read unsolicited manuscripts, and in the case of a book project, I would certainly advise a writer to get an agent, if it is at all possible. All successful agents work on a commission basis—from 10% to 15% on domestic sales, 15% to 20% on foreign sales—and this is how the agent makes a livelihood.

An agent will also know how best to handle a property. If it is a book project, the question arises whether it should be a hardcover book, a paperback, or perhaps it would be best to sell to a hard/soft firm. Since in the case of most book contracts, the writer must give up 50% of the monies secured on a softcover deal by a hardcover publisher, it is often advisable to sell both hard- and softcover rights to a publisher who offers this arrangement, in which case there will not be a 50% split on the softcover sale.

494

There is always the question of multiple submissions or auctions. Not every work should be auctioned; if we feel there is a particularly appropriate publisher or editor for a certain idea, we would rather give first crack at the work to that editor. We're told by many top editors today that they are really annoyed by auctions of books that are not top properties, and it seems totally unfair and a waste of time for them to read a manuscript that is also being read by a great many other editors simultaneously. Hence, the agent's decision on how the work should be presented becomes of the utmost importance.

An agent also often assumes the role of an arbiter—between the publisher and the writer and also, more importantly, between two writers on a project. We were asked recently to handle a manuscript that had been contracted for by a major publishing house, but later rejected because of the arguments between the writers. We resold the material for a larger advance and made a very good deal with the former publisher to pay back only a portion of the money advanced. However, we spent endless hours again trying to get the parties to agree to accepting responsibility for the share each had in the manuscript. At this moment, everything is signed and we hope the new publisher will receive a satisfactory revision and the work can get underway.

Now, how does a writer go about finding an agent? First, through recommendation from other writers, perhaps from a publisher. However, three good sources are the lists offered by The Society of Authors' Representatives (10 Astor Place, 3rd Floor, New York, NY 10003); The Independent Literary Agents Association (55 Fifth Avenue, New York, NY 10003); and *Literary Market Place,* published by R. R. Bowker Co., available in the reference department of most good public libraries. Also, there are always agents who speak at writers' conferences and even to writers' groups.

Once you decide on having an agent, you must write a good, selling query letter, indicating just what the idea may be, outlining the idea, as well as including something about your own background and authority for writing the book; your general vita; any previous publications you have had, and why you feel there is a market for this idea. DO NOT send manuscripts, and by all means make certain that you are approaching the agent who handles the kind of material you are writing. *Literary Market Place* indicates in the agents' section the type of manuscripts the agent will accept.

When we read a query letter that is intelligently written, we will ask to see either a proposal and sample chapters, or we may even ask to see the entire manuscript. We have been fortunate in finding even best-selling writers this way, the most notable of whom was V. C. Andrews, whose novels have sold over 30 million copies in this country alone. Consequently, even though realistically an agent will prefer to handle a writer who already has a track record, it is unrealistic for us not to take a chance at reading something that evokes our interest.

Each time I speak at a writers' conference, I am bombarded with requests for my address, and I realize that this will bring in numerous proposals and a good deal of mail. But I have found several very good writers through these conferences, and I would advise writers who are not living near the major markets to attend writers' conferences, for this gives them an opportunity to meet and talk to agents and editors and in this way make a professional contact.

Often writers ask me whether it is necessary to sign a contract with an agent. Many agents do require contracts, but I personally do not feel this is necessary, for like a marriage, the relationship between writer and agent is good only if they can work amicably together. If not, then a divorce is inevitable. Also, all book contracts have an agency clause stipulating that the agent has the right to negotiate for the author, and all monies due will be sent directly to the agent.

However, if problems develop between you and your agent, first discuss the situation with him or her. If this does not resolve the problem, send a registered letter detailing your complaints and stating that you are hereby ending your agreement. Even though there may not be a termination clause in your agreement with your agent, most agents will release a client if there is a bona fide reason for disagreement.

We find that writers today are shopping for agents as they might publishers. This is certainly legitimate, but we do resent having to take the time to read manuscripts if we have not been given them exclusively. And frankly, many agents have told me that they simply will not read anything if they know it has been given to many other agents. It is far better to select an agent, give that person a specified time to respond to the project and to your letter, and if you are not satisfied at that point, go on to seek another agent. After all, personalities do not always mesh, and you may be happier with one agent representing you than another.

It's important for the writer to be able to keep in touch with his agent, who, upon the writer's request, must make available a record of where a manuscript has been sent and what the rejections have been. Many writers ask whether it is advisable to seek an attorney as well as an agent, or perhaps in lieu of an agent. If an attorney has been dealing with literary properties, he can of course be very helpful, but the average attorney does not know the practices of the trade, and we find (as do publishers) that the average lawyer simply does not know what is negotiable in a contract and what must remain intact. Since agents spend so many hours attempting to sort out these problems, they are more knowledgeable about them. Recently, a deal was almost killed because of the inappropriate interference of an attorney who did not understand that his client must assume responsibility for what he presents in his manuscript.

The publishing business has become exceedingly complex, and it is because of the nature of the changes that I feel it is so important for a writer to find representation with a well-established agent. A good agent knows what rights must be protected for a writer in a contract and which houses offer better contracts than others. It is an interesting fact that in selling a manuscript, we find it easier to obtain a higher advance for a writer when the idea is so exciting that many publishers want it, than for a writer who has published many books but whose sales record is not very good. The first question editors ask when we submit an idea by a published writer is how many copies his or her last book sold. The fact is that editors are looking almost exclusively for book ideas that will sell in big numbers.

Since agents receive publishers' lists of their forthcoming books, we are also in a position to advise our writers whether they are zeroing in on an idea that has been presented before, and perhaps we can save the writer time in trying to work out that particular idea. The agent must be constantly in touch with the market, and this is where a writer receives the greatest benefit from that representation.

In spite of the fact that publishers prefer best sellers and blockbusters to anything of a literary nature, the market is still open for well-written, fresh works, and any legitimate agent will welcome the submission of a work that has a *good sales potential* or reveals a writer with a future.

Certainly, any writer who has the urge, the ability, and the time to pursue such a career should not be discouraged at this time. It was George Sand who once said, "The trade of authorship is a violent and indestructible obsession."

98

ERASING THE BLUE-PENCIL BLUES

BY DAVID PETERSEN

IF YOU'VE ever felt that too many of the magazine articles you've strived so diligently to create have wound up getting edited too harshly, then I don't need to tell you about the Blue-Pencil Blues. You know the ailment well, even if you've not heard the term before. While I'd never say that you should consider this potentially debilitating malady a blessing, I *will* suggest that your writing can benefit from it.

During more than a decade of straddling the publishing fence as both a free lancer and a magazine editor, I've identified five nonfiction problem areas that I feel comprise the most common reasons editors bring out their blue pencils. The good news is that by learning to recognize and weed out these troublemakers, you can significantly reduce the need for editing and—a delightful spin-off—increase sales.

Here, then, are what I perceive to be the five primary reasons editors edit—along with a few tips to help you eliminate them from your writing.

1. *Editors edit for grammar, punctuation, spelling, and all the other nuts and bolts that hold a manuscript together, but that too many free lancers too often fail to tighten.*

Many aspiring wordsmiths feel so blessed with talent that they think they needn't bother with the more mundane details of the writer's craft—things such as submitting clearly typed manuscripts free of punctuation errors, pronouns that disagree in number, misspellings, and the like. Some of these writers do show budding talent, but anyone who believes that just a good yarn is enough to win consistently at the free-lancing game is setting himself up for a fall.

The reality is that few magazine editors have the time or inclination to take on serious cosmetic surgery, no matter how beautiful the hidden message may be. Sloppily prepared pieces, peppered with mechanical glitches that could easily have been caught and corrected by the writer, are rarely going to sell—and the few that do are bound to be heavily edited.

The self-evident remedy, therefore, is to make sure that your copy is road-ready; that nary a screw that you can detect is left jangling loose for an editor to spot and tighten. If *you* don't take care of the mechanical essentials and your editors have to, consider their tinkering a blessing rather than a curse.

2. *Editors edit for style.*

No two publications speak with exactly the same voice. A serious free lancer knows this and—while making no attempt to parrot every stylistic inflection of a magazine—will avoid submitting seriously off-key articles. You wouldn't, for example, use a stiff, academic style in an article bound for a magazine whose voice is as informal and conversational as *The Mother Earth News,* but many free lancers have— only to be rejected or heavily edited for their trouble.

A submission written in a voice that's gratingly off-key tells an editor that the writer a) hasn't bothered to familiarize himself with the publication (a cardinal and surprisingly common free lancer's sin); or b) is unable to recognize a magazine's style when he sees it. An off-key article is far less likely to sell and, if it does, is certain to be returned to bring it into editorial harmony. So, familiarize yourself with your target publication's voice, and pitch your style accordingly.

3. *Editors edit for length.*

When I queried one of my favorite magazines about an article idea not long ago, the editors gave me a green light to submit the piece on speculation, but stipulated that I hold the length to around 1,500 words. Had I sent them the 2,500 tome I generated on the first draft (rather than the 1,500 words I eventually trimmed it to), I could hardly have taken umbrage had they cut the piece to the requested length—or even rejected it. The moral: When an editor is helpful enough to indicate a preferred length for an article, don't exceed it.

But many times you don't have a specified length to shoot for. What then? Here's a procedure that has worked well for me as a free lancer— and *with* me as an editor.

Begin by studying a few recent issues of the target magazine to determine the average word count of several articles similar in style and scope to the one you plan to submit. Next, send an SASE for writer's guidelines (which will probably suggest minimum and maximum lengths for different kinds of articles). Finally, a query. And in that query, suggest a length for your article based on what you've learned by studying the guidelines and the magazine itself. This procedure will significantly improve your chances of getting a go-ahead from the editor. If the editor is interested in your proposal but wants more or fewer words than you've suggested, he can say so in his response.

4. Editors edit for accuracy and completeness.

Consider this scenario: You've written and submitted an article in which you quote a fellow named Stewart. The piece sells, is published, and all is well . . . until the day the publication's editor sends you a copy of a letter received from Mr. Stewartt (two t's). No matter that the extra "t" is a somewhat unusual spelling; Mr. Stewartt is upset that you got his name wrong—and the editors are also upset because they feel compelled to print Stewartt's letter along with an apology. How eager do you think they'll be to purchase more of your work?

The most common inaccuracies are dates, figures, quotations, professional titles, and the names of persons and places. The free-lancing war is won or lost through many small battles. Verify, verify, verify!

Hand-in-hand with accuracy goes completeness. Never assume that readers will have sufficient foreknowledge of your topic to fill in informational blanks for themselves. When in doubt, err on the side of providing too much detail rather than too little.

5. Editors edit for clarity.

Clarity is the cornerstone of effective communication—and effective communication is the foundation of good writing. To achieve clarity, polish each of your manuscripts until you think it shines, then ask a reliable friend who's willing to play the part of candid literary critic to read it and point out any hazy spots. If your critic is confused by a passage, fails to chuckle at a joke you thought was an absolute knee-slapper, or otherwise misses a point you've tried to make, it's a fair bet that other readers—including editors—will have the same trouble. (If you don't have someone to read your work for you, the next best critic is *time*. The longer you can afford to let a piece rest after you've "completed" it, the more objective you'll be when you return to it for further editing.)

500

Sure, a good editor can shine up your slightly hazy prose for you—that's part of what he's trained and paid to do. But a serious writer won't expect him to, won't want him to, won't give him the need to. To increase sales and minimize editing, polish your product until even the filmiest patches of fog disappear. Then polish some more.

And there you have it—the five kinds of problems that most frequently prompt editors to reject or heavily edit manuscripts . . . along with a few suggestions for eliminating them from your writing.

Of course, all this talk of how to minimize having your work altered assumes that you'll be dealing with competent editors. A fair assumption, I believe. Slovenly and unqualified editors are as scarce as fur on a fish and as ephemeral as Halley's comet. In general, you can trust career blue-pencilers to be skilled professionals dedicated to making their publications the best they can be by making their free-lance contributors perform at their best. Both are essential.

When an editor improves my words without making them sound more like his than mine, I'm unabashedly grateful. But as much as I appreciate the help, I nonetheless set my sights on leaving no loose nuts and bolts to tighten, no fat to trim away, no murky prose to clarify, no inaccuracies to correct or blanks to fill in, and no off-key voice to bring my article into line with the magazine's style. I don't always succeed, but I always try. That's my duty as a writer.

And when I'm sitting on the other side of the editorial desk, I try to make every article I work with as good as it can be without destroying the writer's voice or betraying the style of my magazine. That's my duty as an editor.

I've never known a sadistic editor, and the unqualified are few and far between. In the majority of cases, therefore, the most effective way to avoid the feeling that your work is being edited too severely by others is to bear down a little harder with your own blue pencil.

99

WHAT EVERY WRITER NEEDS TO KNOW ABOUT LITERARY AGENTS

BY ELLEN LEVINE

Q. *At what stage in their careers should writers look for an agent— or will a good agent find them?*

A. Most agents prefer to begin a working relationship with a writer when there is a book-length work to market, rather than articles or short stories. Some agents prefer writers who already have publication credits, perhaps magazine publication of shorter work. However, a writer who has never published before, but who is offering a book which deals with a unique or popular topic may also have an excellent chance of securing an agent. Quite a number of agents are actively looking for new writers, and they comb the little magazines for talented writers of fiction. They also read general interest and specialty magazines for articles on interesting subjects, since they might contain the seeds for books. Some agents visit writers conferences and workshops with the express purpose of discovering talented authors who might be interested in representation.

Q. *How does a writer go about looking for a legitimate agent?*

A. Writers can obtain lists of agent members from two professional organizations—The Society of Authors' Representatives (SAR) or The Independent Literary Agents Association (ILAA)— by writing to these organizations at (for SAR) 10 Astor Place, 3rd Floor, New York, New York 10003 and (for ILAA) 55 Fifth Ave., New York, NY 10003. Writers can also obtain a more complete list of agents by checking the "Agents" section of *Literary Market Place* (LMP), available from R. R. Bowker, 205 E. 42nd St., New York, NY 10017, or as a reference work at the local library. Finally, the Authors Guild at 234 W. 44th St., New York, NY 10036 will supply a list of agents.

Q. *How important is it for an agent to be a member of SAR or ILAA?*

A. It is not essential for a good agent to belong to either organization, but membership is very helpful and adds credibility and professionalism to the agency. These organizations schedule meetings to discuss issues and problems common to the industry and their members work together to solve them. Expertise is often shared; panels and seminars are regularly scheduled, often including key publishing personnel. There are also certain codes of professional ethics, which members of each group subscribe to. This, of course, is to the writer's advantage.

Q. *Do literary agents specialize in particular types of material— novels, plays, nonfiction books, short stories, television scripts? Are there some categories that agents could not profitably handle that could better be marketed by the authors?*

A. Most of the agents' listings in LMP specify which kind of material the agency handles. A few agencies do have certain areas of specialization such as screenplays, or children's books, as well as more general fiction and nonfiction.

Q. *Should a writer query an agent (or several agents) before sending him or her his manuscript(s)?*

A. It is acceptable for a writer to query more than one agent before sending material, but it should be made clear to the agent that the writer is contacting several agents at one time. It is even more important for the writer to clarify whether he plans to make multiple submissions of a manuscript. Most agents prefer to consider material on an exclusive basis for a reasonable period of time, approximately four to eight weeks.

Q. *What do agents look for before accepting a writer as a client?*

A. An agent usually takes on a new client based on his or her enthusiasm for that writer's work and a belief that it will ultimately be marketable.

Q. *Once an agent has agreed to take a writer on as a client, what further involvement can the agent expect and legitimately ask of the writer?*

A. It may take longer to place the work of a new author, and the client should be patient in the process. If the writer has made contact with a specific editor or knows that there is interest in the work from a specific publisher, he or she should inform the agent. The writer should feel free to continue contacts with book editors with whom he or she has worked, and to discuss ideas with magazine editors.

Q. *Do most agents today ask for proposals, outlines, synopses, etc., of a book-length work before taking on the job of reading and trying to market the whole book? Do agents ever prepare this type of material, or is that solely the author's function?*

A. This varies among agents. A popular procedure for consideration of material from a prospective client is the request of an outline or proposal and the first 50 or 100 pages. If the book is complete, some agents might request the completed manuscript. It is common practice to submit a nonfiction work on the basis of one or more chapters and a synopsis or outline. The extent of the sample material needed is often based on the writer's previous credentials. It is generally the author's job to prepare the outline and the agent's to prepare the submission letter or the "pitch."

Q. *When, if ever, are multiple queries or submissions allowable, acceptable, desirable? By agent or by author?*

A. If an author is working without an agent, multiple submissions to publishers are acceptable only if the author informs the publisher that the book is being submitted on that basis. However, this can sometimes backfire since those publishers who will read unsolicited manuscripts may not care to waste the staff's reading time on a manuscript that is on simultaneous submission to five other publishers. Multiple queries with one-at-a-time submissions upon receipt of a favorable reply are probably more effective for a relatively new author. However, if a writer has a nonfiction project that is obviously very desirable or timely (an inside story, a current political issue), it is of course expedient to proceed with a multiple submission. This should be done carefully, informing all the participants of the deadline, ground rules, and so on. Agents must judge each project individually and decide on the appropriate procedure. If more than one publisher has expressed an interest in a specific writer or project, a multiple submission is not only appropriate, it is fair and in the author's best interest if there are competitive offers. If a book is very commercial, an auction may well be the result of a multiple submission. If other factors, such as a guaranteed print order or publicity plans are important, a multiple submission without the necessity of taking the highest bid may bring the best results. If an agent routinely makes multiple submissions of all properties, credibility may be lost. If this practice is reserved for the projects which warrant it, the procedure is more effective. It is usually not appropriate to send out multiple copies of a promising first novel. It may be for the inside story of last week's Congressional investigation.

Q. *What business arrangements should a writer make with an agent? Are contracts common to cover the relationship between author and agent? How binding should this be and for what period of time?*

A. Author-agent business arrangements vary among agencies. Some agents will discuss commission, expenses, and methods of operation with their authors, and this informal verbal agreement is acceptable to both parties. Others will write letters confirming these arrangements. Several agencies require contracts defining every detail of the business arrangements, and others require formal, but less extensive contracts. Written agreements often contain a notification of termination clause by either party with a period varying from 30 days to a full year. A few of the agency agreements require that the agency continue to control the subsidiary rights to a book even after the author and agent have parted. Most agents include what is known as an "agency clause" in each book contract the author signs, which provides for the agency to receive payments for the author due on that book for the complete life of the contract, whether or not the author or agent has severed the general agency agreement. In a few cases this clause will contain the provision mentioned above (compulsory representation of the author's retained subsidiary rights). It is important for a writer to discuss these and all aspects of the agency's representation at the beginning of the relationship. In addition to understanding clearly commission rates and expenses he or she will be required to pay, a writer might want to discuss such matters as expectations for consultation on marketing, choice of publishers, the number of submissions to be made, frequency of contact with agent, and so on. *Poets and Writers, Inc.* at 72 Spring

505

Street, New York, NY 10012 has published a helpful handbook entitled *Literary Agents: A Writers Guide* ($6.95), which addresses these issues. Commissions vary among agents. The range is often between 10% and 20%. Some agencies may vary the commission for different rights, charging 10% or 15% for domestic sales and 15% or 20% for foreign sales. Certain agencies have different rates for different authors, depending upon the length of time the author has been with the agency, the size of the publishing advance, or the amount of editorial and preparatory work the agent must do before marketing the book. Some agents work more extensively in an editorial capacity than others and may make detailed suggestions and ask for revisions before marketing a work.

Q. *Can a writer express a preference to the agent concerning the particular publishing house or kind of house he would prefer for his book?*

A. Writers should share with their agents any preferences or ideas they may have about their work, including which publishers would be most appealing, and in which format they envision their books. However, writers should not be dismayed if their agents feel in some cases that a particular preference may be unrealistic or inappropriate.

Q. *How much of the business side of publishing does the writer need to deal with, once he is in the hands of a competent agent?*

A. An agent acts as a writer's business representative for his publishing affairs. Most agents do not act as a writer's overall financial manager, and if an author begins to earn a substantial income, he or she may be well-advised to consult with a C.P.A. and/or tax attorney. The prudent writer, while entrusting his business affairs to his or her agent, will want to stay informed about these matters.

Q. *How much "reporting" can a writer legitimately expect from the agent who has agreed to handle his work?*

A. This would depend on the agent's individual style and the writer's need and preference. Many agents keep clients informed about the progress of submissions by sending copies of rejection letters; others do not, and will give the writer a summary periodically. A writer should be kept informed of all important events and conversations with editors and co-agents about his or her work; for instance, a favorable *Publishers Weekly* review that has come in, a substantial delay in publication, a paperback auction date that has been set. On the other hand, writers should not expect daily contact with an agent as an established routine.

Q. *What involvement, if any, should a writer have in the contract that the agent makes with a publisher? Does he have the right, responsibility to question the terms, change them, insist on higher royalty rates, advertising, etc., or is this left entirely to the agent, along with the sale of substantial rights?*

A. It is the agent's responsibility to consult with the author before accepting any of the basic terms of an offer such as the advance, royalties, subsidiary rights, and territories granted. If the author has any particular reasonable requests which he or she would like to include in the contract, such as approval or consultation on the jacket design, it is the author's responsibility to let the agent know before the start of negotiations. The choice of an agent should imply the author's trust and confidence in the agent's expertise in negotiating the contract and securing the best possible financial and legal terms for the author. Authors should read contracts carefully and ask questions about any provisions, if necessary. However, it is not reasonable for an author to ask for changes in every clause or expect provisions that are extremely difficult to obtain, particularly for authors who have not had best sellers. For instance, advertising guarantees in contracts are not common for new authors. If the author has chosen a skillful agent, he or she should have confidence in the agent's explanation of what is or is not feasible in a contract with a particular publisher.

Q. *If an agent feels that he cannot place a manuscript and the author feels that it is marketable, or, at least, worthy of publication, can the author try to sell it on his own?*

A. If this happens on occasion and the agent has no objection, the author should feel free to try after discussing what he or she plans to do. The agent will want to be informed so that no prior obligation, such as an option requirement, is breached. If the author's agent repeatedly

507

feels that the author's manuscripts cannot be placed, perhaps it is time for the author and agent to re-examine their relationship and discuss a change.

Q. *What services, other than the marketing of the manuscripts, negotiating the terms of their publishing contracts and related business arrangements may authors reasonably expect from their agents?*

A. In addition to marketing manuscripts, agents often help authors in formulating book ideas, passing along book ideas from editors when appropriate, and making introductions to appropriate editors if the author is between projects and free of contract obligations. Agents also follow up on various details of the publication process, such as production schedules, publicity, promotion, suggestions of other writers who might offer a quote for the jacket. The agent should also disseminate reviews, quotes, and information on subsidiary rights sales such as reprint and book club sales. Agents also examine royalty statements and, when necessary, obtain corrected statements.

Authors should not expect an agent to act as a secretary, travel agent, or bank. On the other hand, it is inevitable that a more personal bond may often form in the author/agent relationship, and in certain cases, agents do become involved to varying extents in friendships with their clients. In fact, hand-holding, "mothering" and counseling are not unfamiliar to many agents in dealing with certain authors. This is really a function of the agent's personality and often a conscious decision about how personally involved with his or her clients that particular agent wishes to be. A client should not expect that agent to solve his or her personal problems routinely.

Q. *How would you sum up the major role the agent plays in selling an author's work?*

A. If a manuscript is marketable, a good agent can short-circuit the random process of submissions by knowledge of the market, publishers, and the tastes and personalities of specific editors. However, an agent cannot place unsalable work. An agent can also be effective in the choice of marketing strategy for a particular work—should the book be sold as a trade paperback? Is a "hard-soft" deal best for the project? Would the author best be served by an auction, or would select individual submissions with editorial meetings be best?

508

❙ 100

Becoming Your Own Editor

By Moira Anderson Allen

WRITERS SPECULATE a lot about what editors really do. Some firmly believe that we are the final barricade between writers' excellent manuscripts and publication. Others seem to believe that the job of an editor is to clean up after writers and tell them what to do next.

To a certain extent, the latter is true. When a manuscript comes along that is so magnificent that no amount of typos can detract from its impact, we clean it up, gladly. Usually, though, we must weigh whether or not this "clean-up" time will be justified by the final product. Often the answer is no.

You can avoid this, however. If you follow these four easy steps, your editor will be able to judge your work using criteria that really count. Better yet, you'll never again have to speculate about what an editor does, because you'll be doing it yourself!

Step 1: **Get to the point.** The first thing an editor wants to learn from your manuscript is its purpose. What is the story you are going to tell, and why? Why is it important? Don't shroud your purpose in three or four cleverly written but pointless opening paragraphs.

If you're writing a story about Old Sam, a three-legged border collie who was the most unforgettable dog you've ever met, don't start your article with this kind of opener:

When I got out of college with a few courses of animal science under my belt, I had little idea how bleak the job outlook would be. I wandered from clinic to clinic, but no work was to be had. Then my old buddy Joe, who owned a sheep ranch out on the South Fork Road, offered me a job as a stablehand. . . .

This sort of opener may ramble on just like buddy Joe's ranch before the author finally gets to the point: "And that's where I met Old Sam."

All this information may be important, but it isn't the point of your piece: Old Sam is. If, on the other hand, your first sentence is "Old Sam was the most unforgettable dog I've ever met," your editor might not think you have the world's best knack for opening lines, but he will know what you plan to talk about up front, and be more inclined to read on. Find another way to work in all that background information, if it's really necessary.

Part of getting to the point is explaining to the editor, and the reader, why he should spend time reading what you have to say. Why are you writing this particular article? Why are you writing it now? The answer may lie in your credentials, your personal experience, or simply in your ability to express important ideas to the editor's readers.

Let's say you want to write an article about a new virus in cats. Why should the reader hear about this from you? The answer could be that you're a veterinarian who has handled several cases of the virus and can enlighten cat owners about it; or you might be a cat owner who chanced to learn about this new disease, and you want to share the information you've gathered about it. Or, as a writer with a "nose" for a good story, you might choose to interview both veterinarians and cat owners about the disease and its effects, providing an article with both human appeal and expert information.

The approach you choose will depend on your market and your audience, but you should make two things clear: why this topic is important, and why the editor should accept you as the best person to write about it. Then let your story tell itself.

Step 2: **Get organized.** One of my associates told me of a trick she had learned to help her organize her thoughts while writing: "Think in subheads." Just about every magazine or newspaper story of any length is broken up into smaller chunks, each set off with a subhead. These subheads make the page look better artistically and lead the reader through an organized series of ideas.

If you look at your article carefully, you'll probably find that it breaks down into three or four major component ideas. Thinking of subheads for these ideas gives you a chance to organize your thoughts into the appropriate categories, almost like creating an outline for the article after it has been written. You may find during this process that you need to flesh out one of your ideas in greater detail, cut back on another, or add yet a third. Your subheads don't have to be cute or catchy, and you may decide not to include them in the final draft; their primary purpose is to help you organize your material.

Step 3: **Get rid of the clutter.** When you break your article into subheads, you may find that you have some ideas that don't belong under any of the categories you've roughed out. This could mean one of two things: You need another subhead, or you don't need that information in the article. It might be the basis for another piece, but serves only as clutter in this particular manuscript.

It can be painful to look at a stack of notes and realize that, even though it took you hours to get the information, it just doesn't belong in your article. But part of your job is deciding precisely what is important about the material you've amassed, and presenting that—and only that—to your readers. If you leave it to an editor to pluck the gems from the clutter, he may simply pluck a rejection slip from the drawer instead.

So read through your work again. Once you've organized it, it's easier to spot ideas that are only tangential to the main subject, or identify background material that is interesting but doesn't contribute that much to the basic piece. Try pulling some of the material out of the main text and presenting it in sidebars. Suppose you are writing about cancer treatments at a particular clinic, for example, and you've found some interesting information about another clinic or some other methods that seem promising. If that information doesn't belong in the main body of your piece, write it up as a complementary sidebar. If the editor likes your sidebar and has room for it, you may even get paid extra for it. But if he doesn't, you won't have jeopardized the success of your main article by cluttering it with extra information.

Step 4: **Keep it "clean."** Whenever I receive an all-but-illegible manuscript, filled with typos, my first reaction is that the writer doesn't care enough about me or my audience to clean up his work, to present the best article he can. I'm prejudiced against that writer from the start, and he'll have to work twice as hard to prove that the content of his work outweighs his presentation.

Unfair? Maybe. But if a writer doesn't check for typos and grammatical errors—the easy stuff—I'm bound to wonder if he was any more careful where it counts. When a manuscript is littered with misspellings, what assurance do I have that the writer has checked his facts, verified every phone number and double-checked figures and spellings of names?

Editors also get irritated by the idiosyncrasies of computers. If your computer leaves peculiar codes on the page when you try to underline or capitalize, changes your quotation marks to brackets, or leaves huge spaces between your words because it's trying to justify your right-hand margins, do something about it. Be extra careful of inadvertent changes that result from corrections: Your text may rearrange itself in ways you never anticipated. And please, please don't leave your manuscript just the way it was printed on continuous-feed paper. No editor enjoys having to tear your pages apart before being able to read them.

Finally, editors like to know that *you* know they exist, and that you know what's going on with their publications. When I receive a manuscript addressed to my predecessor's predecessor at an address that we haven't used in two years, I can't help but wonder how recently that author has examined a copy of the magazine.

The penultimate sin, of course, is to leave out your self-addressed, stamped envelope. Make sure that you put enough postage on the SASE; I have seen writers put a 25-cent stamp on a large manila envelope that would require extra postage just to be delivered empty. The ultimate sin? Letting your manuscript arrive with postage due.

So take another look at that manuscript you're about to put in the mail. Did you read it through with an editor's eyes—the eyes of someone who has never seen it before and doesn't know yet what you're trying to say? Is your ribbon clean and dark? Is there enough postage on both envelopes? If you've answered "yes," congratulations! You've just removed another major barrier between you and success.

WHERE TO SELL

Where to stay

PART IV

Where to Sell

This year's edition of *The Writer's Handbook* includes a completely revised and updated list of free-lance markets, and writers at all levels of experience should be encouraged by the number and wide variety of opportunities available to them. Editors, publishers, and producers rely on free lancers for a wide range of material, from articles and fiction to play scripts, op-ed pieces, how-tos, and children's books, and they are very receptive to the work of newcomers.

The field of specialized publications, including travel, city and regional magazines, and those covering such areas as health, science, consumer issues, sports, and hobbies and crafts, remains one of the best markets for beginning free lancers. Editors of these magazines are in constant need of authoritative articles (for which the payment is usually quite high), and writers with experience in and enthusiasm for a particular field, whether it's gardening, woodworking, bicycling, stamp collecting, bridge, or car repair, will find their knowledge particularly helpful, as there is usually at least one publication devoted to every one of these areas. Such interests and activities can generate more than one article if a different angle is used for each magazine and the writer keeps the audience and editorial content firmly in mind.

The market for technical, computer, health, and personal finance writing is also very strong, with articles on these topics appearing in almost every publication on the newsstands today. For these subjects, editors are looking for writers who can translate technical material into lively, readable prose, often the most important factor in determining a sale.

While some of the more established markets may seem difficult to break into, especially for the beginner, there are thousands of lesser-known publications where editors will consider submissions from first-time free lancers. City and regional publications offer some of the best opportunities, since these editors generally like to work with local writers and often use a wide variety of material, from features to fillers. Many newspapers accept op-ed pieces, and are most receptive to pieces on topics not covered by syndicated columnists (politics, economics, and foreign affairs); pieces with a regional slant are particularly welcome here.

It is important for writers to keep in mind the number of opportunities that exist for nonfiction, because the paying markets for fiction are somewhat limited. Many general-interest and women's magazines do publish short stories; however, beginners will find these markets extremely competitive, with their work being judged against that of experienced professionals. We highly recommend that new writers look into the small, literary, and college publications, which always welcome the work of talented beginners. Payment usually is made only in copies, but publication in literary journals can lead to recognition by editors of larger circulation magazines, who often look to the smaller publications for new talent. A growing number of regional, specialized, and Sunday magazines use short stories and are particularly interested in local writers.

The market for poetry in general-interest magazines continues to be tight, and the advice for poets, as for fiction writers, is to try to get established and build up a list of publishing credits by submitting material to literary journals. Poets should look also to local newspapers, which often use verse, especially if it is related to holidays or other special occasions.

Community, regional, and civic theaters and college dramatic groups offer new playwrights the best opportunities for staged production in this competitive market. Indeed, many of today's well-known playwrights received their first recognition in regional theaters, and aspiring writers who can get their work produced by one of these have taken a significant step toward breaking into this field. In addition to producing plays and giving dramatic readings, many theaters also sponsor competitions or new play festivals.

Although the free-lance television market is also addressed in this section of the *Handbook,* writers should be aware of the fact that this market is inaccessible without an agent, and most writers break into it only after a careful study of the medium and a long apprenticeship.

While the book publishing field remains competitive, beginners should be especially encouraged by the many first novels published over the past few years, with more editors than ever before seeking out new works of fiction. An increasing number of publishers are broadening their nonfiction lines as well, and editors at many hardcover and paperback houses are on the lookout for new authors, especially those with a knowledge of or training in a particular field. Writers of juvenile and young adult books will be pleased to hear that in response to a growing audience of young readers and increased sales, many publishers are greatly expanding their lists of children's books.

Small presses across the country continue to flourish—in fact, they are currently publishing more books by name authors and more books on mainstream subjects, than at any time in recent years—offering writers an attractive alternative for their manuscripts.

All information in these lists concerning the needs and requirements of magazines, book publishing companies, and theaters comes directly from the editors, publishers, and directors, but editors move and addresses change, as do requirements. No published listing can give as clear a picture of editorial needs and tastes as a careful study of several issues of a magazine, and writers should never submit material without first thoroughly researching the prospective market. If a magazine is not available in the local library, write directly to the editor for a sample copy (often sent free or at a small cost). Contact the publicity department of a book publisher for an up-to-date catalogue or a theater for a current schedule. Many companies also offer a formal set of writers guidelines, available for an SASE upon request.

ARTICLE MARKETS

The magazines in the following list are in the market for free-lance articles of many types. Unless otherwise stated in these listings, a writer should submit a query first, including a brief description of the proposed article and any relevant qualifications or credits. A few editors want to see samples of published work, if available. Manuscripts must be typed double-space on good white bond paper (8½ x 11), with name, address, and telephone number at the top left- or right-hand corner of the paper. Do not use erasable or onion skin paper, since it is difficult to work with, and always keep a copy of the manuscript, in case it is lost in the mail. Submit photos or slides *only* if the editor has specifically requested them. A self-addressed envelope with sufficient postage to cover the return of the manuscript or the answer to a query should accompany all submissions. Response time may vary from two to eight weeks, depending on the size of the magazine and the volume of mail it receives. If an editor doesn't respond within what seems to be a reasonable amount of time, it's perfectly acceptable to send a polite inquiry. Many publications have writers guidelines, outlining their editorial requirements and submission procedures; these can be obtained by sending a self-addressed, stamped envelope (SASE) to the editor. Also, be sure to ask for a sample copy: Editors indicate the most consistent mistake free lancers make is failing to study several issues of the magazine to which they are submitting material.

GENERAL-INTEREST PUBLICATIONS

ACCENT—P.O. Box 10010, Ogden, UT 84409. Caroll Shreeve, Pub. Articles, 1,200 words, about destinations in the U.S. and Canada. Must include transparencies. Query. Pays 15¢ a word and $35 to $50 for photos, on acceptance.

ALCOHOLISM & ADDICTION MAGAZINE—P.O. Box 31329, Seattle, WA 98103. Neil Scott, Ed. Articles on all aspects of alcoholism: treatment, legislation, education, prevention, and recovery. Send SASE for guidelines.

ALLIED PUBLICATIONS—1776 Lake Worth Rd., Lake Worth, FL 33460. Articles, to 1,000 words: business, management, fashion, careers, travel (foreign and domestic), beauty, hairstyling, general interest, home, family, art and artists. Photos, cartoons, humor. Write for terms of payment. Guidelines. Publishes *Trip & Tour, Management Digest, Modern Secretary, Woman Beautiful, Home, Exhibit.*

THE AMERICAN LEGION MAGAZINE—Box 1055, Indianapolis, IN 46206. Michael D. LaBonne, Ed. Articles, 750 to 1,800 words, on current world affairs, public policy, and subjects of contemporary interest. Pays $100 to $1,000, on acceptance. Query.

AMERICAN VISIONS, THE MAGAZINE OF AFRO AMERICAN CULTURE—The Visions Foundation, Smithsonian Institution, The Carter G. Woodson House, Capitol Hill, Washington, DC 20560. Madelyn Bonsignore, Ed. Articles, 1,500 to 4,000 words, and columns, 750 to 2,000 words, on people and events that contribute significantly to black culture and heritage. Pays from $100 to $1,000, on publication. Query first.

AMERICAS—OAS, General Secretariat Bldg., 1889 F. St. N.W., Washington, DC 20006. Catherine Healy, Man. Ed. Features, to 2,500 words, on life in Latin America and the Caribbean. Wide focus: anthropology, the arts, travel, science, and development, etc. No political material. Query. Pays from $200, on publication.

AMTRAK EXPRESS—140 E. Main St., Suite 11, Huntington, NY 11743. Christopher Podgus, Ed. General-interest articles on business, health, books, sports, personal finance, lifestyle, entertainment, travel (within Amtrak territory), science for Amtrak travelers. Submit seasonal material three to six months in advance. Pays on publication, $300 to $700 for 1,500- to 2,000-word manuscript; $250 to $600 for department pieces of 1,500 to 2,500 words. Query with published clips.

THE ATLANTIC—745 Boylston St., Boston, MA 02116. William Whitworth, Ed. In-depth articles on public issues, politics, social sciences, education, business, literature, and the arts, with emphasis on information rather than opinion. Ideal length: 3,000 to 6,000 words, though short pieces (1,000 to 2,000 words) are also welcome. Pays excellent rates, on acceptance.

BETTER HOMES AND GARDENS—1716 Locust St., Des Moines, IA 50336. David Jordan, Ed. Articles, to 2,000 words, on home and family entertainment, building, decorating, food, money management, health, travel, pets, and cars. Pays top rates, on acceptance. Query.

BON APPETIT—5900 Wilshire Blvd., Los Angeles, CA 90036. Barbara Fairchild, Exec. Ed. Articles on fine cooking (menu format or single focus), cooking classes, and gastronomically-focused travel. Query with samples of published work. Pays varying rates, on acceptance.

CAPPER'S—616 Jefferson St., Topeka, KS 66607. Nancy Peavler, Ed. Articles, 300 to 500 words: human-interest, personal experience, for women's section, historical. Pays varying rates, on publication.

CHATELAINE—MacLean Hunter Bldg., 777 Bay St., Toronto, Ont., Canada M5W 1A7. Elizabeth Parr, Sr. Ed. Articles, 1,500 to 3,500 words, for Canadian women, on current issues, personalities, medicine, psychology, etc., covering all aspects of Canadian life. "Upfront" columns, 500 words, on relationships, health, nutrition, fitness, parenting. Pays from $350 for columns, from $1,200 for features, on acceptance.

THE CHRISTIAN SCIENCE MONITOR—One Norway St., Boston, MA 02115. David Holstrom, Feature Ed. Articles, 800 words, on arts, education, food, sports, science, and lifestyle; interviews, literaty essays for "Home Forum" page; guest columns for "Opinion Page." Pay varies, on acceptance. Original material only.

CLASS—27 Union Sq. W., New York, NY 10003. Rene John-Sandy, Ed. Articles, to 2,500 words, of interest to the Third World population living in the U.S., and inhabitants of the Caribbean Islands. Pays 5¢ to 20¢ a word, after acceptance. Guidelines.

COLUMBIA—1 Columbus Plaza, New Haven, CT 06507–0901. Richard McMunn, Ed. Journal of the Knights of Columbus. Articles, 500 to 1,500 words, on a wide variety of topics of interest to K. of C. members, their families, and the Catholic layman: current events, religion, education, art, etc. Must include substantial quotes from a variety of sources, and must be illustrated with color transparencies. Pays $250 to $500, inclusive of art, on acceptance.

CONNOISSEUR—Hearst Corp., 1790 Broadway, 18th Fl., New York, NY 10019. Sarah Scrymser, Man. Ed. Articles for readers "interested in learning about excellence in all areas of art." Topics include fine, decorative, and performing arts, architecture and design, food, fashion, and travel; include pertinent service data. Length varies; query required.

CONSUMERS DIGEST—5705 N. Lincoln Ave., Chicago, IL 60659. John Manos, Ed. Articles, 500 to 3,000 words, on subjects of interest to consumers:

products and services, automobiles, health, fitness, consumer legal affairs, and personal money management. Photos. Pays from 30¢ a word, extra for photos, on publication. Buys all rights. Query with resumé and published clips.

COSMOPOLITAN—224 W. 57th St., New York, NY 10019. Helen Gurley Brown, Ed. Guy Flatley, Man. Ed. Articles, to 3,500 words, and features, 500 to 2,500 words, on issues affecting young career women. Query.

COUNTRY—5400 S. 60th, Greendale, WI 53129. Bob James, Assoc. Ed. People-centered articles, 500 to 1,000 words, for a rural audience. (No articles on production techniques.) Fillers, 50 to 200 words. Taboos: tobacco, liquor, and sex. Pays $125 to $200, on acceptance. Query.

COUNTRY JOURNAL—P.O. Box 8200, 2245 Kohn Rd., Harrisburg, PA 17105. Peter V. Fossel, Ed. Tracey S. Lynn, Man. Ed. Articles, 2,500 to 3,000 words, for country and small town residents; practical, informative pieces, essays, humor, and reports on contemporary rural life. Pays $500 to $1,500, on acceptance. Query.

DALLAS LIFE MAGAZINE—*The Dallas Morning News,* Communications Center, Dallas, TX 75265. Melissa Houtte, Ed. Well-researched articles and profiles, 1,000 to 3,000 words, on contemporary issues, personalities, on subjects of strictly Dallas-related interest. Pays 20¢ and up a word, on acceptance. Query.

DIVERSION MAGAZINE—60 E. 42nd St., Suite 2424, New York, NY 10169. Stephen Birnbaum, Ed. Dir. Articles, 1,200 to 2,500 words, on travel, sports, hobbies, entertainment, food, etc., of interest to physicians at leisure. Photos. Pays from $400, on acceptance. Query. No recent report.

EBONY—820 S. Michigan, Chicago, IL 60603. Lerone Bennett, Jr., Exec. Ed. Articles, with photos, on blacks: achievements, civil rights, etc. Pays from $150, on publication. Query.

THE ELKS MAGAZINE—425 W. Diversey Parkway, Chicago, IL 60614. Fred D. Oakes, Ed. Articles, 3,000 words, on business, sports, and topics of current interest, for non-urban audience with above-average income. Informative or humorous pieces, to 2,500 words. Pays $150 to $500 for articles, on acceptance. Query.

ESQUIRE—1790 Broadway, New York, NY 10019. David Hirshey, Articles Ed. Lisa Grunwald, Features Ed. Articles, 2,500 to 4,000 words, for intelligent adult audience. Pay varies, on acceptance. Query with published clips; complete manuscripts from unpublished writers.

ESSENCE—1500 Broadway, New York, NY 10036. Susan L. Taylor, Ed.-in-Chief. Provocative articles, 1,500 to 2,500 words, about black women in America today: self-help, how-to pieces, business and finance, health, celebrity profiles, and political issues. Short items, 300 to 750 words, on work, parenting, and health. Pays varying rates, on acceptance.

EXHIBIT—See Allied Publications.

FAMILY CIRCLE—110 Fifth Ave., New York, NY 10010. Susan Ungaro, Articles Ed. Ellen Stoianoff, Sr. Ed., Leah Breier, Health Ed. Articles, to 2,500 words, on "women who have made a difference," marriage, family and child-rearing issues; consumer affairs, travel, humor, health and fitness, personal opinion essays. Query required. Pays top rates, on acceptance.

FORD TIMES—One Illinois Center, 111 E. Wacker Dr., Suite 1700, Chicago, IL 60601. John Fink, Ed. Articles for a family audience, particularly geared to ages 18 to 35: topical pieces (trends, lifestyles); profiles; first-person accounts of unusual vacation trips or real-life adventures; unusual sporting events or outdoor activities;

food and cooking; humor. Bright lively photos desired. "Road Show": travel and dining anecdotes; pays $50, on publication. Payment for articles, 1,200 to 1,700 words, is $550 to $800; $400 for 800 to 1,200 words; and $250 for short pieces (500 to 800 words), on acceptance. Query with SASE required for all but humor and anecdotes.

GENTLEMEN'S QUARTERLY—350 Madison Ave., New York, NY 10017. Eliot Kaplan, Man. Ed. Articles, 1,500 to 4,000 words, for a male audience, on politics, personalities, lifestyles, trends, grooming, sports, travel, business. Columns, 1,000 to 2,500 words: "Private Lives" (essays by men on life); "All about Adam" (nonfiction by women about men); "Games" (sports); "Health"; and "Humor"; also columns on fitness, nutrition, investments, music, wine and food. Pays $750 to $4,000, on acceptance. Query with clips.

GLAMOUR—350 Madison Ave., New York, NY 10017. Ruth Whitney, Ed.-in-Chief; Lisa Bain, Art. Ed. Articles on careers, health, psychology, interpersonal relationships, etc.; editorial approach is "how-to" for women ages 18 to 35. Fashion and beauty material staff-written. Pays from $1,000 for 1,500- to 2,000-word articles, from $1,500 for longer pieces, on acceptance.

GLOBE—5401 N.W. Broken Sound Blvd., Boca Raton, FL 33487. Robert Taylor, Exec. Ed. Factual articles, 500 to 1,000 words, with photos: exposés, celebrity interviews, consumer and human-interest pieces. Pays $50 to $1,500.

GOLDEN YEARS—233 E. New Haven Ave., Melbourne, FL 32902-0537. Carol Brenner Hittner, Ed. Bimonthly for people over the age of 50. Pieces on unique hobbies, beauty and fashion, sports, and travel, 500 words. Pays 10¢ a word, on publication.

GOOD HOUSEKEEPING—959 Eighth Ave., New York, NY 10019. Joan Thursh, Articles, Ed. Personal-experience articles, 2,500 words, on a unique or trend-setting event; family relationships; personal medical pieces dealing with an unusual illness, treatment, and result; personal problems and how they were solved. Short essays, 750 to 1,000 words, on family life or relationships. Pays top rates, on acceptance. Queries preferred. Guidelines.

GOOD READING MAGAZINE—Litchfield, IL 62056. Peggy Kuethe, Assoc. Ed. Articles, 500 to 1,000 words, with B&W photos, on current subjects of general interest; travel, business, personal experiences, relationships. Pays $10 to $100.

GRIT—208 W. Third St., Williamsport, PA 17701. Alvin Elmer, Assoc. Ed. Articles, to 800 words, with photos, on interesting people, communities, jobs, recreation, families, and coping. Pays 15¢ a word, extra for photos, on acceptance.

HARPER'S BAZAAR—1700 Broadway, New York, NY 10019. Anthony Mazzola, Ed.-in-Chief. Articles, 1,500 to 2,000 words, for active, sophisticated women. Topics include the arts, world affairs, food, wine, travel, families, education, personal finance, careers, health, and sexuality. No unsolicited manuscripts; query first with SASE. Payment varies, on acceptance.

HARPER'S MAGAZINE—666 Broadway, New York, NY 10012. Address managing editor. Articles, 2,000 to 5,000 words. Query first.

HG: HOUSE & GARDEN—350 Madison Ave., New York, NY 10017. Priscilla Flood, Man. Ed. Michael Boodro, Articles Ed. Articles on decorating, architecture, gardens, the arts. Rarely buys unsolicited manuscripts. Query.

HOME—See Allied Publications.

HORTICULTURE—Statler Bldg., 20 Park Plaza, Suite 1220, Boston, MA 02116. Debbie Starr, Articles Ed. Authoritative, well-written articles, 1,200 to 3,000 words, on all aspects of gardening and horticulture. Pays competitive rates. Query.

HOUSE BEAUTIFUL—1700 Broadway, New York, NY 10019. Joanna L. Krotz, Dir. Copy/Features. Service articles related to the home. Pieces on architecture, design, travel, and gardening; mostly staff-written. Pays varying rates, on acceptance. Query with detailed outline. Guidelines.

INQUIRER MAGAZINE—*Philadelphia Inquirer,* P.O. Box 8263, 400 N. Broad St., Philadelphia, PA 19101. Fred Mann, Ed. Local-interest features, 500 to 7,000 words. Profiles of national figures in politics, entertainment, etc. Pays varying rates, on publication. Query.

INSIDE MAGAZINE—226 S. 16th St., Philadelphia, PA 19102. Jane Biberman, Ed. Articles, 1,000 to 3,000 words, on Jewish issues and the arts. Queries required; send clips if available. Pays $75 to $600, within 4 weeks of acceptance.

KIWANIS—3636 Woodview Trace, Indianapolis, IN 46268. Chuck Jonak, Exec. Ed. Articles, 2,500 to 3,000 words, on home, family, international issues, the social and emotional needs of youth, career and community concerns of business and professional men. No travel pieces, interviews, profiles. Pays $400 to $1,000, on acceptance. Query.

LADIES' HOME JOURNAL—100 Park Ave., New York, NY 10017. Lynn Langway, Exec. Ed. Linda Peterson, Articles Ed. Jane Farrell, Sr. Ed. Articles on contemporary subjects of interest to women. Personal-experience and regional pieces. Query required. Not responsible for unsolicited manuscripts.

LISTEN MAGAZINE—6830 Laurel St. N.W., Washington, DC 20012. Gary B. Swanson, Ed. Articles, 1,000 to 1,500 words, on problems of alcohol and drug abuse, for teenagers; personality profiles. Photos. Pays 5¢ to 7¢ a word, extra for photos, on acceptance. Query. Guidelines.

MCCALL'S—230 Park Ave., New York, NY 10169. Anne Mollegen Smith, Ed.-in-Chief. Andrea Thompson, Articles Ed. Interesting, unusual, and topical narratives, reports on social trends relating to women of all ages, 1,000 to 3,000 words. Humor. Human interest stories. Pays top rates, on acceptance.

MADEMOISELLE—350 Madison Ave., New York, NY 10017. Michelle Stacey, Man. Ed. Articles, 1,500 to 2,000 words, on subjects of interest to single, working women in ther 20s. Pays from $1,750 for full-length articles, on acceptance. Query.

MAGAZINE OF THE MIDLANDS—*The Omaha World-Herald,* World Herald Sq., Omaha, NE 68102. David Hendee, Ed. Regional-interest articles and profiles, 400 to 2,000 words, with tie-in to Omaha and the Midwest. Pays $40 to $150, on publication. Query.

MANAGEMENT DIGEST—See Allied Publications.

MARRIAGE & FAMILY—Abbey Press Publishing Div., St. Meinrad, IN 47577. Kass Dotterweich, Man. Ed. Articles, 1,500 to 1,700 words, on husband-wife and parent-child relationships; faith dimension essential. Pays 7¢ a word, on acceptance. Query.

MD MAGAZINE—3 E. 54th St., New York, NY 10022. Sharon AvRutick, Ed. Articles, 750 to 2,500 words, for doctors, on the arts, history, other aspects of culture; fresh angle required. Pays from $200 to $700, on acceptance. Query by mail only.

METROPOLITAN HOME—750 Third Ave., New York, NY 10017. Service and informational articles for residents of houses, co-ops, lofts, and condominiums, on real estate, equity, wine and spirits, collecting, trends, travel, etc. Interior design and home furnishing articles with emphasis on lifestyle. Pay varies. Query.

MODERN MATURITY—3200 East Carson St., Lakewood, CA 90712. Ian Ledgerwood, Ed. Articles on careers, workplace, human interest, living, finance, relationships, and consumerism, for persons over 50 years, to 2,000 words. Photos. Pays $500 to $2,500, extra for photos, on acceptance. Query first.

MODERN SECRETARY—See Allied Publications.

THE MOTHER EARTH NEWS—105 Stoney Mt. Rd., Hendersonville, NC 28793. Articles, with photos, for rural and urban readers: home improvements, how-tos, indoor and outdoor gardening, family pastimes, etc. Also, self-help, health, food-related, ecology, energy, and consumerism pieces. Pays varying rates, on acceptance. Guidelines.

MOTHER JONES—1663 Mission St., San Francisco, CA 94103. Doug Foster, Ed. Investigative articles, political essays, cultural analyses. "OutFront" pieces, 50 to 200 words, about "change, whether good, bad, or strange"; "Out of Pocket" pieces on economy and personal finance. Pays $750 to $2,000, after acceptance. Query in writing only.

MS.—One Times Square, New York, NY 10036. Address Manuscript Ed. Articles relating to women's roles and changing lifestyles; general interest, how-to, self-help, profiles. Pays market rates. Query with SASE required.

NATIONAL ENQUIRER—Lantana, FL 33464. Articles, of any length, for mass audience: topical news, the occult, how-to, scientific discoveries, human drama, adventure, personalities. Photos. Pays from $325. Query; no unsolicited manuscripts accepted.

NATIONAL EXAMINER—5401 N.W. Broken Sound Blvd., Boca Raton, FL 33431. Cliff Linedecker, Exec. Ed. Celebrity interviews and human-interest pieces, 500 to 1,000 words. Must be well documented. Pays varying rates, on acceptance. Query required.

NEW WOMAN—215 Lexington Ave., New York, NY 10016. Gay Bryant, Ed. "Read the magazine in order to become familiar with our needs before querying." Articles on new lifestyles. Features on financial and legal advice, building a business, marriage, relationships, surviving divorce, innovative diets. Pays varying rates, on acceptance. Query with SASE.

NEW YORK—755 Second Ave., New York, NY 10017. Edward Kosner, Ed. Laurie Jones, Man. Ed. Feature articles of interest to New Yorkers. Pays from $850 to $3,500, on acceptance. Query required; not responsible for unsolicited material.

THE NEW YORK ANTIQUE ALMANAC—Box 335, Lawrence, NY 11559. Carol Nadel, Ed. Articles on antiques, shows, shops, art, investments, collectibles, collecting suggestions, nostalgia, related humor. Photos. Pays $5 to $75, extra for photos, on publication.

THE NEW YORK TIMES MAGAZINE—229 W. 43rd St., New York, NY 10036. Address Articles Ed. Timely articles approximately 4,000 words, on news items, forthcoming events, trends, culture, entertainment, etc. Pays $350 to $500 for short pieces, $1,000 to $2,500 for major articles, on acceptance. Query with clips.

THE NEW YORKER—25 W. 43rd St., New York, NY 10036. Address the Editors. Factual and biographical articles, for "Profiles," "Reporter at Large,"

"Annals of Crime," "Onward and Upward with the Arts," etc. Pays good rates, on acceptance. Query.

NEWSWEEK—444 Madison Ave., New York, NY 10022. Original opinion essays, 1,000 to 1,100 words, for "My Turn" column: must contain verifiable facts. Submit manuscript with SASE. Pays $1,000, on publication.

OMNI—1965 Broadway, New York, NY 10023–5965. Patrice Adcroft, Ed. Articles, 2,500 to 3,000 words, on scientific aspects of the future: space, machine intelligence, ESP, origin of life, future arts, lifestyles, etc. Pays $750 to $4,000, less for short features, on acceptance. Query.

ORBIT VIDEO—8330 Boone Blvd., Vienna, VA 22180. Phil Swann, Sr. Ed. Video and movie personality and hardware articles, 750 to 2,500 words. Query with clips. Pay varies, on acceptance.

PARADE—750 Third Ave., New York, NY 10017. Fran Carpentier, Sr. Articles Ed. National Sunday newspaper supplement. Factual and authoritative articles, 1,000 to 1,500 words, on subjects of national interest: health, education, consumer and environmental issues, science, the family, sports, etc. Profiles of well-known personalities and service pieces. No fiction, poetry, games, or puzzles. Photos with captions. Pays from $1,000. Query.

PENTHOUSE—1965 Broadway, New York, NY 10023–5965. Peter Bloch, Exec. Ed. Robert Sabat, Man. Ed. General-interest or controversial articles, to 5,000 words. Pays from 20¢ a word, on acceptance.

PEOPLE IN ACTION—Box 10010, Ogden, UT 84409. Caroll Shreve, Pub. Features, 1,200 words, on nationally noted individuals in the fine arts, literature, entertainment, communications, business, sports, education, etc. Must exemplify positive values. Manuscripts should be accompanied by high-quality color transparencies. Query. Pays 15¢ a word and $35 to $50 for photos, on acceptance.

PEOPLE WEEKLY—Time-Life Bldg., Rockefeller Ctr., New York, NY 10020. Hal Wingo, Asst. Man. Ed. Considers article proposals only, 3 to 4 paragraphs, on timely, entertaining, and topical personalities. Pays good rates, on acceptance. Most material staff written.

PLAYBOY—680 N.Lakeshore Dr., Chicago, IL 60611. John Rezek, Articles Ed. Sophisticated articles, 4,000 to 6,000 words, of interest to urban men. Humor: satire. Pays to $3,000, on acceptance. Query.

PLAYGIRL—801 Second Ave., New York, NY 10017. Nancie S. Martin, Ed.-in-Chief. Articles, 2,000 to 2,500 words, for women ages 18 to 34. Celebrity interviews, 1,500 to 2,000 words. Pays negotiable rates. Query with clips to nonfiction editor.

PRIME TIMES—2802 International Ln., Suite 120, Madison, WI 53704. Joan Donovan, Exec. Ed. Articles, 500 to 1,800 words, for dynamic, creative midlifers. Departments, 850 to 1,000 words. Pays $125 to $750, on publication. Query. Guidelines with SASE.

PSYCHOLOGY TODAY—80 Fifth Ave., New York, NY 10011. T. George Harris, Ed.-in-Chief. Lively, useful articles, 2,500 to 3,000 words, and short news items about timely subjects, based on the research findings of social scientists and the clinical insights of practicing psychotherapists; jargon free. Department pieces, 1,200 to 1,500 words, on health, work, relationships, the brain, etc. Pays good rates, on acceptance.

READER'S DIGEST—Pleasantville, NY 10570. Kenneth O. Gilmore, Ed.-

in-Chief. Unsolicited manuscripts will not be read or returned. General-interest articles already in print and well-developed story proposals will be considered. Send reprint or query to any editor on the masthead.

REDBOOK—224 W. 57th St., New York, NY 10019. Annette Capone, Ed.-in-Chief. Diane Salvatore, Articles Ed. Articles, 1,000 to 3,500 words, on subjects related to relationships, sex, current issues, marriage, the family, and parenting. Pays from $750, on acceptance. Query.

ROLLING STONE—745 Fifth Ave., New York, NY 10151. Magazine of modern American culture, politics, and art. No fiction. Query; "rarely accepts free-lance material." No recent report.

THE ROTARIAN—1560 Sherman Ave., Evanston, IL 60201. Willmon L. White, Ed. Articles, 1,200 to 2,000 words, on international social and economic issues, business and management, human relationships, travel, sports, environment, science and technology; humor. Pays good rates, on acceptance. Query.

SATELLITE ORBIT—8330 Boone Blvd., Vienna, VA 22180. Mike Doan, Ed. Television-related articles, 750 to 2,500 words; personality profiles; and articles of interest to the satellite and cable TV viewer. Query with clips. Pay varies, on acceptance.

THE SATURDAY EVENING POST—1100 Waterway Blvd., Indianapolis, IN 46202. Ted Kreiter, Exec. Ed. Family-oriented articles, 1,500 to 3,000 words: humor, preventive medicine, destination-oriented travel pieces (not personal experience), celebrity profile, the arts, and sciences. Pieces on sports and home repair (with photos). Photo essays. Pays varying rates, on publication. Queries preferred.

SELF—350 Madison Ave., New York, NY 10017. Alexandra Penney, Ed. Articles for young women with a particular interest in health, nutrition, fitness, and related lifestyle subjects. Pays from $1 a word. Query.

SOAP OPERA DIGEST—45 W. 25th St., New York, NY 10010. Lynn Davey, Man. Ed. Investigative reports, profiles, and humor, to 1,500 words, for people interested in daytime and nighttime New York- or Los Angeles-based soaps. Pays from $225, on acceptance. Query.

SOAP OPERA UPDATE—158 Linwood Plaza, Ft. Lee, NJ 07024. Allison J. Waldman, Man. Ed. Soap-opera oriented articles, 750 to 1,250 words; fillers to 500 words. Pays $100 to $175, on publication. Queries preferred.

SPORTS ILLUSTRATED—1271 Ave. of the Americas, New York, NY 10020. No unsolicited material.

STAR—660 White Plains Rd., Tarrytown, NY 10591. Topical articles, 50 to 800 words, on human-interest subjects, show business, lifestyles, the sciences, etc., for family audience. Pays varying rates.

SUCCESS—342 Madison Ave., New York, NY 10175. Scott Degarmo, Ed.-in-Chief. Profiles of successful executives, entrepreneurs; management science, psychology, behavior, and motivation articles, 500 to 3,500 words. Query.

SUNDAY JOURNAL MAGAZINE—*Providence Sunday Journal,* 75 Fountain St., Providence, RI 02902. Doug Cumming, Ed. Features and essays, 300 to 2,000 words, with emphasis on prose style; articles on some aspect of life in New England, especially Rhode Island and S.E. Massachusetts. Short fiction, with regional flavor. Pays $75 to $750, on acceptance. Query preferred; send published clips.

TOWN & COUNTRY—1700 Broadway, New York, NY 10019. Address

Features Dept. Considers one page proposals for articles. Rarely buys unsolicited manuscripts.

TRAVEL & LEISURE—1120 Ave. of the Americas, New York, NY 10036. Pamela Fiori, Ed.-in-Chief. Articles, 800 to 3,000 words, on destinations and leisure-time activities. Regional pieces for regional editions. Pays $600 to $3,000, on acceptance. Query.

TRIP & TOUR—See Allied Publications.

TROPIC—*The Miami Herald,* One Herald Plaza, Miami, FL 33132. Tom Shroder, Ed. Essays and articles on current trends and issues, light or heavy, 1,000 to 4,000 words, for sophisticated audience. No fiction or poetry. Limited humor. Pays $200 to $1,000, on publication. Query with SASE; 4 to 6 weeks for reponse.

TV GUIDE—Radnor, PA 19088. Andrew Mills, Asst. Man. Ed. Short, light, brightly-written pieces about humorous or offbeat angles of television. Pays on acceptance. Query.

US MAGAZINE—One Dag Hammarskjold Plaza, New York, NY 10017. Steven Redicliffe, Man. Ed. Cyndi Stivers, Sr. Ed. Articles, 750 to 3,500 words, on celebrities and entertainment-related topics. Pays from $500, on publication. Query with published clips required.

VILLAGE VOICE—842 Broadway, New York, NY 10003. Sarah Jewler, Man. Ed. Articles, 500 to 2,000 words, on current or controversial topics. Pays $75 to $450, on acceptance. Query or send manuscript with SASE.

VISTA—999 Ponce, Suite 600, Coral Gables, FL 33134. Renato Perez, Sr. Ed. Articles, 2,000 words, for English-speaking Hispanic Americans, on job advancement, bilingualism, immigration, the media, fashion, education, medicine, sports, and food. Profiles, 100 words, of Hispanic Americans in unusual jobs; photos welcome. Pays 20¢ a word, on acceptance. Query required.

VOGUE—350 Madison Ave., New York, NY 10017. Address Features Ed. Articles, to 1,500 words, on women, entertainment and the arts, travel, medicine, and health. General features. Query.

VOLKSWAGEN'S WORLD—Volkswagen of America, Troy, MI 48099. Marlene Goldsmith, Ed. Articles, 600 to 1,000 words, for Volkswagen owners: profiles of well-known personalities; inspirational or human-interest pieces; travel; humor; high-tech German product pieces; German travel. Photos. Pays $150 per printed page, on acceptance. Query. Guidelines.

WASHINGTON JOURNALISM REVIEW—2233 Wisconsin Ave. N.W., Washington, DC 20007. Bill Monroe, Ed. Articles, 500 to 3,000 words, on print or electronic journalism. Pays 20¢ a word, on publication. Query.

WASHINGTON POST MAGAZINE—*The Washington Post,* 1150 15th St. N.W., Washington, DC 20071. Stephen L. Petranek, Man. Ed. Essays, profiles and general-interest pieces, to 5,000 words, on business, arts and culture, politics, science, sports, education, children, relationships, behavior, etc. Pays from $1,000, after acceptance.

WEEKLY WORLD NEWS—600 S. East Coast Ave., Lantana, FL 33462. Joe West, Ed. Human-interest news pieces, about 500 to 1,000 words: human adventure, unusual situations. Pays $125 to $500, on publication.

WISCONSIN—*The Milwaukee Journal Magazine,* P.O. Box 661, Milwaukee, WI 53201. Alan Borsuk, Ed. Trend stories, essays, humor, personal-experience pieces, profiles, 500 to 2,000 words, with strong Wisconsin emphasis. Pays $75 to $500, after publication.

WOMAN BEAUTIFUL—See Allied Publications.

WOMAN'S DAY—1515 Broadway, New York, NY 10036. Rebecca Greer, Articles Ed. Articles, 500 to 3,000 words, on subjects of interest to women: marriage, education, family health, child rearing, money management, interpersonal relationships, changing lifestyles, etc. Dramatic first-person narratives about women who have experienced medical miracles or other triumphs, or have overcome common problems, such as alcoholism. "Reflections": short, provocative personal essays, 1,000 to 1,500 words, humorous or serious, dealing with concerns of interest and relevance to women. Pays $2,000 for essays, top rates for articles, on acceptance.

WOMAN'S WORLD—270 Sylvan Ave., Englewood Cliffs, NJ 07632. Articles, 600 to 1,800 words, on interest to middle-income women between the ages of 18 and 60, on love, romance, careers, medicine, health, psychology, family life, travel, dramatic stories of adventure or crisis, investigative reports. Pays $300 to $750, on acceptance. Query.

WORKING WOMAN—342 Madison Ave., New York, NY 10173. Anne Mollegen Smith, Ed. Articles, 1,000 to 2,500 words, on business and personal aspects of working women's lives. Pays from $400, on acceptance.

YANKEE—Dublin, NH 03444. Judson D. Hale, Ed. Articles, to 3,000 words, with New England angle. Photos. Pays $150 to $1,000 (average $750), on acceptance.

YOUR HOME/INDOORS & OUT—Box 10010, Ogden, UT 84409. Caroll Shreeve, Pub. Articles, 1,200 words, with fresh ideas for home decor, construction, management, ownership, and working with a realtor. No do-it-yourself articles. Prefer color transparencies. Pays 15¢ a word, $35 to $50 for pictures, on acceptance. Query.

CURRENT EVENTS, POLITICS

AFRICA REPORT—833 U.N. Pl., New York, NY 10017. Margaret A. Novicki, Ed. Well-researched articles by specialists, 1,000 to 4,000 words, with photos, on current African affairs. Pays $150 to $250, on publication.

THE AMERICAN LEGION MAGAZINE—Box 1055, Indianapolis, IN 46206. Michael D. LaBonne, Ed. Articles, 750 to 1,800 words, on current world affairs, public policy, and subjects of contemporary interest. Pays $100 to $1,000, on acceptance. Query.

THE AMERICAN SCHOLAR—1811—St. N.W., Washington, DC 20009. Joseph Epstein, Ed. Non-technical articles and essays, 3,500 to 4,000 words, on current affairs, the American cultural scene, politics, arts, religion, and science. Pays $450, on acceptance.

THE AMICUS JOURNAL—Natural Resources Defense Council, 40 W. 20th St., New York, NY 10168. Peter Borrelli, Ed. Investigative articles, book reviews, and poetry related to national and international environmental policy. Pays varying rates, on acceptance. Queries required.

THE ATLANTIC—745 Boylston St., Boston, MA 02116. William Whitworth, Ed. In-depth articles on public issues, politics, social sciences, education, business, literature, and the arts, with emphasis on information rather than opinion.

Ideal length: 3,000 to 6,000 words, though short pieces (1,000 to 2,000 words) are also welcome. Pays excellent rates, on acceptance.

COMMENTARY—165 E. 56th St., New York, NY 10022. Norman Podhoretz, Ed. Articles, 5,000 to 7,000 words, on contemporary issues, Jewish affairs, social sciences, community life, religious thought, cultural. Serious fiction; book reviews. Pays on publication.

COMMONWEAL—15 Dutch St., New York, NY 10038. Margaret O'Brien Steinfels, Ed. Catholic. Articles, to 3,000 words, on political, social, religious, and literary subjects. Pays 3¢ a word, on acceptance.

THE CRISIS—260 Fifth Ave., 6th Fl., New York, NY 10001. Fred Beauford, Ed. Articles to 1,500 words on the arts, civil rights, and problems and achievements of blacks and other minorites. Pays $75 to $500, on acceptance.

ENVIRONMENT—4000 Albemarle St. N.W., Washington, DC 20016. Barbara T. Richman, Man. Ed. Articles, 2,500 to 5,000 words, on environmental, scientific, and technological policy and decision-making issues. Pays $100 to $300, on publication. Query.

FOREIGN POLICY JOURNAL—11 Dupont Circle N.W., Washington, DC 20036. Charles William Maynes, Ed. Articles, 3,000 to 5,000 words, on international affairs. Honorarium, on publication. Query.

FOREIGN SERVICE JOURNAL—2101 E. St. N.W., Washington, D.C. 20037. Articles on American diplomacy, foreign affairs, and subjects of interest to Americans representing U.S. abroad. Query.

THE FREEMAN—Foundation for Economic Education, Irvington-on-Hudson, NY 10533. Brian Summers, Sr. Ed. Articles, to 3,500 words, on economic, political, and moral implications of private property, voluntary exchange, and individual choice. Pays 10¢ a word, on publication.

INQUIRER MAGAZINE—*Philadelphia Inquirer,* P.O. Box 8263, 400 N. Broad St., Philadelphia, PA 19101. Fred Mann, Ed. Local-interest features, 500 to 7,000 words. Profiles of national figures in politics, entertainment, etc. Pays varying rates, on publication. Query.

IRISH AMERICA—432 Park Ave. S., Suite 1000, New York, NY 10016. Sean O'Murchu, Ed. Articles, 1,500 to 2,000 words, of interest to Irish-American audience; preferred topics include history, sports, the arts, and politics. Pays 10¢ a word, after publication. Query.

MIDSTREAM—515 Park Ave., New York, NY 10022. Murray Zuckoff, Ed. Articles on politics and their relationship to the Jewish experience. Pays 5¢ a word, after publication.

MOMENT—3000 Connecticut Ave., Suite 300, Washington, DC 20008. Charlotte Anker, Man. Ed. Sophisticated articles, 2,500 to 5,000 words, on politics and Jewish topics. Pays $150 to $400, on publication.

MOTHER JONES—1663 Mission St., San Francisco, CA 94103. Doug Foster, Ed. Investigative articles, political essays, cultural analyses. "OutFront" pieces, 50 to 200 words, about change, either good, bad, or strange." Pays $750 to $2,000, after acceptance. Query in writing only.

THE NATION—72 Fifth Ave., New York, NY 10011. Victor Navasky, Ed. Articles, 1,500 to 2,500 words, on politics and culture from a liberal/left perspective. Pays $75 per published page, to $300, on publication. Query.

THE NEW YORK TIMES MAGAZINE—229 W. 43rd St., New York, NY 10036. Address Articles Ed. Timely articles, approximately 4,000 words, on news items, trends, culture, etc. Pays $350 to $500 for short pieces, $1,000 to $2,500 for major articles, on acceptance. Query with clips.

THE NEW YORKER—25 W. 43rd St., New York, NY 10036. Address the Editors. Factual and biographical articles, for "Profiles," "Reporter at Large," "Annals of Crime," "Onward and Upward with the Arts," etc. Pays good rates, on acceptance. Query.

NEWSWEEK—444 Madison Ave., New York, NY 10022. Original opinion essays, 1,000 to 1,100 words, for "My Turn" column: must contain verifiable facts. Submit manuscript with SASE. Pays $1,000, on publication.

PRESENT TENSE—165 E. 56th St., New York, NY 10022. Murray Polner, Ed. Serious articles, 2,000 to 3,000 words, with photos, concerning Jews throughout the world; first person encounters and personal experience pieces. Literary-political reportage. Contemporary themes only. Pays $200 to $300, on publication. Query.

THE PROGRESSIVE—409 E. Main St., Madison, WI 53703. Erwin Knoll, Ed. Articles, 1,000 to 3,500 words, on political, social problems. Light features. Pays $75 to $300, on publication.

PUBLIC CITIZEN MAGAZINE—2000 P St. N.W., Suite 610, Washington, DC 20036. Ana Radelat, Ed. Investigative reports and articles of timely political interest, for members of Public Citizen: consumer rights, health and safety, environmental protection, safe energy, tax reform, and government and corporate accountability. Photos, illustrations. Pays to $500.

REGARDIE'S—1010 Wisconsin Ave. N.W., Suite 600, Washington, DC 20007. Brian Kelly, Ed. Profiles and investigations of the "high and mighty" in the DC area: "We require aggressive reporting and imaginative, entertaining writing." Pays 50¢ a word, on publication. Queries required.

ROLL CALL: THE NEWSPAPER OF CAPITOL HILL—900 2nd St. N.E., Washington, DC 20002. James K. Glassman, Ed.-in-Chief. Factual, breezy articles with political or Congressional angle: Congressional historical and human-interest subjects, political lore, etc. Political satire and humor. Pays on publication.

THE ROTARIAN—1560 Sherman Ave., Evanston, IL 60201. Willmon L. White, Ed. Articles, 1,200 to 2,000 words, on international social and economic issues, business and management, environment, science and technology. "No direct political or religious slants." Pays good rates, on acceptance. Query.

SATURDAY NIGHT—36 Toronto St., Suite 1160, Toronto, Ont., Canada M5C 2C5. John Fraser, Ed. Canada's oldest magazine of politics, social issues, culture, and business. Features, 1,000 to 3,000 words, and columns, 800 to 1,000 words; fiction, to 3,000 words. Must have Canadian tie-in. Payment varies, on acceptance.

TROPIC—*The Miami Herald,* One Herald Plaza, Miami, FL 33132. Tom Shroder, Assoc. Ed. Essays and articles on current trends and issues, light or heavy, 1,000 to 4,000 words, for sophisticated audience. Pays $200 to $1,000, on publication. Query with SASE; 4 to 6 weeks for response.

VFW MAGAZINE—406 West 34th St., Kansas City, MO 64111. Richard K. Kolb, Ed. Magazine for Veterans of Foreign Wars and their families. Articles, 1,000 words, on current issues and history, with veteran angle. Photos. Pays from $400, extra for photos, on acceptance. Guidelines.

VILLAGE VOICE—842 Broadway, New York, NY 10003. David Herndon, Man. Ed. Articles, 500 to 2,000 words, on current or controversial topics. Pays $75 to $450, on acceptance. Query or send manuscript with SASE.

THE WASHINGTON MONTHLY—1611 Connecticut Ave. N.W., Washington, DC 20009. Charles Peters, Ed. Investigative articles, 1,500 to 5,000 words, on politics, government and the political culture. Pays 10¢ a word, on publication. Query.

WASHINGTON POST MAGAZINE—*The Washington Post,* 1150 15 St. N.W., Washington, DC 20071. Stephen L. Petranek, Man. Ed. Essays, profiles and general-interest pieces, to 5,000 words, on politics and related issues. Pays from $1,000, after acceptance.

REGIONAL AND CITY PUBLICATIONS

ADIRONDACK LIFE—P.O. Box 97, Jay, NY 12941. Christopher Shaw, Ed. Features, to 3,000 words, on outdoor and environmental activities and issues, arts, wilderness, profiles, and history; focus is on the Adirondack region and North Country of New York State. Pays to 25¢ a word, on acceptance. Query.

ALASKA—808 E St., Suite 200, Anchorage, AK 99501. Ron Dalby, Ed. Articles, 1,500 words, on life in Alaska and Northwestern Canada. Pays varying rates, on acceptance. Guidelines.

ALOHA, THE MAGAZINE OF HAWAII—P.O. Box 3260, Honolulu, HI 96801. Cheryl Chee Tsutsumi, Ed. Articles, 1,500 to 4,000 words, on the life, customs, and people of Hawaii and the Pacific. Poetry. Fiction. Pays $150 to $400, on publication. Query first.

AMERICAN WEST—7000 E. Tanque Verde Rd., Tucson, AZ 85715. Mae Reid-Bills, Man. Ed. Articles, 2,500 to 3,000 words, and department pieces, 900 to 1,000 words, that celebrate the West, past and present; emphasis on travel. Pays $200 to $800, on acceptance. Query required.

ANGELES—11601 Wilshire Blvd., Los Angeles, CA 90025. Joanne Jaffe, Ed. Features on design, art, architecture, food, and fashion aimed at Los Angeles' Westside population. Pays good rates, on acceptance.

ARIZONA HIGHWAYS—2039 W. Lewis Ave., Phoenix, AZ 85009. Merrill Windsor, Ed. Articles, 2,000 words, on travel in Arizona; pieces on adventure, humor, lifestyles, nostalgia, history, archaeology, nature, etc. Pays 30¢ to 45¢ a word, on acceptance. Query first.

ARKANSAS TIMES—Box 34010, Little Rock, AR 72203. Mel White, Ed. Articles, to 6,000 words, on Arkansas history, people, travel, politics. All articles must have strong AR orientation. Pays to $500, on acceptance.

ATLANTA—1360 Peachtree St., Suite 1800, Atlanta, GA 30309. Lee Walburn, Ed. Articles, 1,500 to 5,000 words, on Atlanta subjects or personalities. Pays $600 to $1,200, on publication. Query.

ATLANTIC CITY MAGAZINE—1637 Atlantic Ave., Atlantic City, NJ 08401. Tom McGrath, Ed. Lively articles, 500 to 5,000 words, on Atlantic City and Southern New Jersey for locals and tourists: entertainment, casinos, business, personalities, environment, local color, crime. Pays $100 to $600, on acceptance. Query.

AUSTIN MAGAZINE—P.O. Box 4368, Austin, TX 78765. Annette Wysocki, Ed. Profiles, civic affairs, and general-interest articles, 750 to 3,000 words, with local business focus. Query preferred. Pays $75 to $400, on publication.

BAKERSFIELD LIFESTYLE—123 Truxtun Ave., Bakersfield, CA 93301. Steve Walsh, Ed. Articles and fiction with local slant, 1,500 to 2,000 words. Pays $15, on publication.

BALTIMORE MAGAZINE—26 S. Calvert St., Baltimore, MD 21202. Stan Heuisler, Ed. Articles, 500 to 3,000 words, on people, places, and things in the Baltimore metropolitan area. Consumer advice, investigative pieces, profiles, humor, and personal experience pieces. Payment varies, on publication. Query required.

BIRMINGHAM—2027 First Ave. N., Birmingham, AL 35203. Joe O'Donnell, Ed. Personality profiles, features, business, and nostalgia pieces (to 8 pages) with Birmingham tie-in. Pays $50 to $175, on publication.

BOCA RATON—JES Publishing, Amtec Center, Suite 100, 6413 Congress Ave., Boca Raton, FL 33487. Christina Houlihan, Ed. Articles, 800 to 3,000 words, on Florida topics, personalities, and travel. Pays $75 to $500, on publication. Query with clips required.

THE BOSTON GLOBE MAGAZINE—*The Boston Globe*, Boston, MA 02107. Ande Zellman, Ed. General-interest articles, interviews, and profiles, 2,500 to 5,000 words. Query and SASE required.

BOSTON MAGAZINE—300 Massachusetts Ave., Boston, MA 02115. David Rosenbaum, Ed. Informative, entertaining features, 1,000 to 4,000 words, on Boston area personalities, institutions, and phenomena. Pays $250 to $2,000, on publication. Query Betsy Buffington, Man. Ed., or Janice Brand, Service Features Ed.

BOUNDARY WATERS JOURNAL—Route 1, Box 1740, Ely, MN 55731. Stuart Osthoff, Ed. Articles, 2,000 to 3,000 words, on recreation and natural resources in Minnesota's Boundary Waters region, including canoe routes, lifestyles of residents, hiking, and events. Pays $200 to $400, on publication.

BUFFALO SPREE MAGAZINE—Box 38, Buffalo, NY 14226. Johanna Shotell, Ed. Articles, to 1,800 words. Pays $75 to $100, $25 for poetry, on publication.

BUSINESS IN BROWARD—1040 Bayview Dr., Suite 210, Ft. Lauderdale, FL 33304. T. Constance Coyne, Ed. Small business regional bi-monthly; 2,500-word articles for eastern Florida county. Pay varies, on acceptance.

CALIFORNIA—11601 Wilshire Blvd., Los Angeles, CA 90025. Rebecca Levy, Man. Ed. Features with a California focus, on politics, business, environmental issues, ethnic diversity, travel, style, fashions, restaurants, the arts, and sports. Service pieces, profiles, and well-researched investigative articles. Pays $500 to $2,500 for features, $250 to $500 for shorter articles, on acceptance. Query first.

CALIFORNIA BASKETBALL MAGAZINE—See *California Football Magazine.*

CALIFORNIA FOOTBALL MAGAZINE—1330 E. 223rd St., Suite 501, Carson, CA 90745. David Raatz, Ed. Articles, 250 to 2,000 words, related to California high school, junior college, college, and professional football programs and standout Californians playing in other states. Pays $25 to $300, on acceptance. Query with writing samples. Same requirements for *California Basketball Magazine.*

CAPE COD LIFE—P.O. Box 222, Osterville, MA 02655. Brian F. Shortsleeve, Pub. Articles on Cape Cod current events, business, art, history, and gardening, 2,000 words. Pays 10¢ a word, 30 days after publication. Queries preferred.

CAPITAL MAGAZINE—(formerly *California Region Magazine*) 4 Central Ave., Albany, NY 12210. Dardis McNamee, Ed.-in-Chief. News, features, and profiles angled to the Albany, New York, region (1,000 to 5,000 words); anecdotes, vignets, short profiles, and humor (250 to 500 words). Pays 10¢ a word, on acceptance. Query required.

CARIBBEAN TRAVEL AND LIFE—8403 Colesville Rd., Silver Spring, MD 20910. Veronica Gould Stoddart, Ed. Articles, 500 to 3,000 words, on all aspects of travel, recreation, leisure, and culture in the Caribbean, Bahamas, and Bermuda. Pays $75 to $550, on publication. Query with published clips.

CENTURY CITY MAGAZINE—23919 Ventura Blvd., Calabasas, CA 91302. A. Henry Shaw, Exec. Ed. Articles, 500 to 2,000 words, and 60- to 100-word anecdotes on business for executives in the Century City business area of Los Angeles. Payment varies, on publication. Query.

CHESAPEAKE BAY MAGAZINE—1819 Bay Ridge Ave., Annapolis, MD 21403. Betty D. Rigoli, Ed. Articles, 8 to 10 typed pages, related to the Chesapeake Bay area. Profiles. Photos. Pays $75 to $125, on publication. Query first.

CHESTER COUNTY LIVING MAGAZINE—See *Mainline Style Magazine.*

CHICAGO—414 N. Orleans, Chicago, IL 60610. Joanne Trestrail, Man. Ed. Articles, 1,000 to 5,000 words, related to Chicago. Pays varying rates, on acceptance. Query.

CHICAGO HISTORY—Clark St. at North Ave., Chicago, IL 60614. Russell Lewis, Ed. Articles, to 4,500 words, on urban, political, social, and cultural history. Pays to $250, on publication. Query.

CITY MAGAZINE—5563 W. 73rd St., Indianapolis, IN 46268. Jane Graham, Man. Ed. Articles on health, business, sports, people, etc., with regional tie-in. Lengths vary, to 12 pages. Pays $40 to $300, on publication. Query required.

CITY SPORTS—P.O. Box 3693, San Francisco, CA 94119. Jane McConnell, Ed. Articles, 500 to 2,000 words, on participant sports, family recreation, travel, and the active lifestyle. Pays $100 to $650, on publication. Query.

CLINTON STREET QUARTERLY—Box 3588, Portland, OR 97208. David Milholland, Ed. Articles (to 15 pages) and creative fiction (2 to 20 pages). "Eclectic blend of politics, culture, humor, and art." Compelling first-person accounts welcome. Pays $50 to $200, on publication.

COLORADO BUSINESS—5951 S. Middlefield Rd., Littleton, CO 80123. Paulette Whitcomb, Man. Ed. Articles,varying length, on business and economic trends in Colorado. Pays on publication. Query.

COLORADO HOMES & LIFESTYLES—2250 31st St., Suite 154, Denver, CO 80216. Darla J. Worden, Exec. Ed. Articles on topics related to Colorado: travel, fashion, design and decorating, gardening, luxury real estate, art, celebrity lifestyles, people, food, and entertaining. Pays to 20¢ a word, on acceptance.

CONNECTICUT—789 Reservoir Ave., Bridgeport, CT 06606. Sara J. Cuneo, Ed. Articles, 1,500 to 2,500 words, on Connecticut topics, issues, people, and lifestyles. Pays $500 to $800, on publication.

COOSA VALLEY VIEW—102 W. Second Ave., Rome, GA 30161. John Willis, Man. Ed. Articles, 500 to 750 words, on business and economic developments in Northwest Georgia; profiles, 500 to 750 words. Pays 5¢ to 10¢ a word, on publication.

THE COVENTRY JOURNAL—P.O. Box 124, Andover, CT 06232. Bill Cisowski, Ed. Articles, to 2,000 words, about the New England (especially Eastern

Connecticut) region: historical, unusual persons, businesses, and events. Pays $250, on acceptance.

CRAIN'S DETROIT BUSINESS—1400 Woodbridge, Detroit, MI 48207. Mary Kramer, Ed. Business articles, 500 to 1,000 words, about Detroit, for Detroit business readers. Pays $100 to $200, on publication. Query required.

CREATING EXCELLENCE—New World Publishing, P.O. Box 2084, S. Burlington, VT 05403. David Robinson, Ed. Self-help and inspirational articles, profiles, and essays related to Northern Vermont. Pays $50 to $250, on publication.

D—3988 N. Central Expressway, Suite 1200, Dallas, TX 75204. Ruth Fitzgibbons, Ed. In-depth investigative pieces on current trends and problems, personality profiles, and general-interest articles on the arts, travel, and business, for upper-class residents of Dallas. Pays $350 to $500 for departments, $800 to $1,200 for features. Written queries only.

DALLAS MAGAZINE—1201 Elm, Suite 2000, Dallas, TX 75270. Jeff Hampton, Ed. Features, 2,500 words, on business and businesses in Dallas. Department pieces, 1,500 words. Pays $100 to $600, on acceptance. Query required.

DELAWARE TODAY—P.O. Box 4440, Wilmington, DE 19807. Lise Monty, Ed. Service articles, profiles, news, etc., on topics of local interest. Pays $75 to $125 for department pieces, $125 to $300 for features, on publication. Queries with clips required.

DETROIT FREE PRESS MAGAZINE—*Detroit Free Press,* 321 W. Lafayette Blvd., Detroit, MI 48231. Articles, to 4,000 words, with a Detroit-area or Michigan focus, on issues, lifestyles. Personality profiles; essays; humor. Pays from $100. Query required.

DETROIT MONTHLY—1400 Woodbridge, Detroit, MI 48207. Diane Brozek, Ed. Articles on Detroit-area people, issues, lifestyles, and business. Payment varies. Query required.

DOMAIN—P.O. Box 1569, Austin, TX 78767. Catherine Chadwick, Ed. Bimonthly lifestyle supplement to *Texas Monthly.* Articles of Texas architecture, art, home design, gardens, travel, and cuisine. Features (750 to 2,500 words) and department pieces (2,500 words or less). Payment varies, on acceptance. Query.

DOWN EAST—Camden, ME 04843. Davis Thomas, Ed. Articles, 1,500 to 2,500 words, on all aspects of life in Maine. Photos. Pays to 20¢ a word, extra for photos, on acceptance. Query.

ERIE & CHAUTAUQUA MAGAZINE—Charles H. Strong Bldg., 1250 Tower La., Erie, PA 16505. Kim Kalvelage, Man. Ed. Feature articles, to 2,500 words, on issues of interest to upscale readers in the Erie, Warren, and Crawford counties (PA), and Chautauqua (NY) county. Pieces with regional relevance. Pays after publication. Query preferred, with writing samples. Buys all rights. Guidelines available.

FLORIDA GULF COAST HOMEBUYER'S GUIDE—1311 N. Westshore Blvd., Suite 109, Tampa, FL 33607. Paula L. Maguire, Relocation/Production Dir. Articles, 750 to 1,200 words, for the active home buyer on the Gulf Coast: home-related articles, moving tips, financing, etc. Pays 7¢ to 10¢ a word, on acceptance. Query preferred.

FLORIDA HOME & GARDEN—600 Brickell Ave., Suite 207, Miami, FL 33131. Kathryn Howard, Ed. Features,1,000 to 2,000 words, and department pieces, 1,000 words, about Florida interior design, architecture, landscape architecture, gardening, cuisine, fashion, trendy new products, art, travel (Florida and Caribbean), and home entertaining. Pays $300 to $400, photos extra.

FLORIDA KEYS MAGAZINE—505 Duval St., Upper Suite, Key West, FL 33040. David Ethridge, Ed. Articles, 1,000 to 4,000 words, on the Florida Keys: history, environment, natural history, profiles, etc. Fillers, humor. Photos. Pays varying rates, on publication. Query preferred.

FLORIDA TREND—Box 611, St. Petersburg, FL 33731. Tom Billitteri, Man. Ed. Articles on Florida business and businesspersons. Query letter required.

'GBH MAGAZINE—352 Congress St., Boston, MA 02210. Jack Curtis, Man. Ed. Member magazine for WGBH of Boston's public TV and radio channels. Articles, 700 to 1,000 words, based on WGBH programming, written in first- or third-person. Pays from $500 to $1,000, on acceptance.

GEORGIA JOURNAL—Grimes Publications, P.O. Box 27, Athens, GA 30603–0027. Articles, 1,200 words, on people, events, travel, etc. in and around GA. Poetry, to 20 lines. Pays $50 to $150, on acceptance.

GO: THE AUTHENTIC GUIDE TO NEW ORLEANS—541 Julia St., New Orleans, LA 70130. Suzy G. Lauderdale, Ed. Articles, 1,200 words, of interest to New Orleans visitors. Pays $150, on publication. Query required.

GREAT LAKES SAILOR—572 W. Market St., Suite 6, P.O. Box 2234, Akron, OH 44309. Drew Shippy, Ed. Department pieces: "Destinations" (2,500 to 3,000 words, on cruises); "Trailor Sailor" (trips for day sailors, to 1,500 words); and "First Person" (profiles, 2,500 to 3,000 words). How-to pieces on sailing and navigational techniques, human-interest stories. Photos. Pays to 25¢ a word, on publication. Queries required. Guidelines.

GULF COAST GOLFER—See *North Texas Golfer.*

GULFSHORE LIFE—2975 S. Horseshoe Dr., Naples, FL 33942. Janis Lyn Johnson, Ed. Articles, 800 to 3,000 words, on personalities, travel, sports, business, architecture and design, the arts, investment, nature, in southwestern Florida. Pays $150 to $300. Query.

HAWAII—Box 6050, Mission Viejo, CA 92690. Dennis Shattuck, Ed. Articles related to Hawaii. Pays 7¢ a word, on publication. Query.

HIGH COUNTRY NEWS—Box 1090, Paonia, CO 81428. Betsy Marston, Ed. Articles on environmental land management, energy, and natural resource issues; profiles of western innovators; pieces on western politics. Poetry. B&W photos. Pays $2 to $4 per column inch, on publication, for 750-word roundups and 2,000-word features. Query first.

HONOLULU—36 Merchant St., Honolulu, HI 96813. Brian Nicol, Ed. Features highlighting life in the Hawaiian islands—politics, sports, history, people, events are all subjects of interest. Pays $400, on acceptance. Columns and department pieces are mostly staff-written. Queries are required.

HOUSTON METROPOLITAN MAGAZINE—P.O. Box 25386, Houston, TX 77265. Barbara Burgower, Man. Ed. Gabrielle Cosgriff, Ed. Dir. Articles with strong Houston-area angles. Gardening and design pieces; department columns (City Insight, Art Beat, Metropolitan Marketplace); issue-oriented features, profiles, lifestyle pieces. Pays $50 to $500 for columns; $600 to $1,000 for features.

ILLINOIS ENTERTAINER—2200 E. Devon, Suite 192, Des Plaines, IL 60018. Bill Dalton, Ed. Articles, 500 to 1,500 words, on local and national entertainment (emphasis on popular music) in the greater Chicago area. Personality profiles; interviews; reviews. Photos. Pays varying rates on publication. Query preferred.

ILLINOIS TIMES—Box 3524, Springfield, IL 62708. Fletcher Farrar, Jr., Ed. Articles, 1,000 to 2,500 words, on people, places, and activities of Illinois, outside the Chicago metropolitan area. Pays 4¢ a word, on publication. Query required.

IMAGE—*San Francisco Examiner,* 110 Fifth St., San Francisco, CA 94103. Articles, 1,200 to 3,000 words, on lifestyles, issues, business, history, events, and people in Northern California. Query first. Pays varying rates.

INDIANA HORIZONS—5563 W. 73rd St., Indianapolis, IN 46268. Jane Graham, Man. Ed. Quarterly. Articles, 750 to 2,000 words, of interest to active Indiana residents, 50 years and older. Profiles, 250 words, for "Indiana Achievers." Pays $100 to $350, $30 for profiles, on publication.

INDIANAPOLIS MONTHLY—8425 Keystone Crossing, Indianapolis, IN 46240. Deborah Paul, Ed./Pub. Sam Stall, Man. Ed. Articles, 1,000 words, on health, sports, politics, business, interior design, travel, and Indiana personalities. All material must have a regional focus. Pays varying rates, on publication.

INDUSTRY MAGAZINE—441 Stuart St., Boston, MA 02116. Alan R. Earls, Ed./Pub. Articles, 1,200 to 1,500 words, related to industry in Massachusetts. Pays negotiable rates, on acceptance. Queries required.

INLAND—Inland Steel Co., 18 South Home Ave., Park Ridge, IL 60068. Sheldon A. Mix, Man. Ed. Articles, varying lengths, of interest to Midwestern readers. History, folklore, commentaries, nature, humor. Send completed manuscripts. Pays on acceptance.

INQUIRER MAGAZINE—*Philadelphia Inquirer,* 400 N. Broad St., Philadelphia, PA 19101. Fred Mann, Ed. Articles, 1,500 to 2,000 words, and 3,000 to 7,000 words, on politics, science, arts and culture, business, lifestyles, and entertainment, sports, health, beauty, psychology, education, religion, and humor. Short pieces, 850 words, for "Up Front" department. Pays varying rates. Query.

INSIDE CHICAGO—2501 W. Peterson Ave., Chicago, IL 60659. Barbara Young, Man. Ed. Features, to 3,000 words, on Chicago-related trends, profiles of Chicagoans, entrepreneuring, architecture (to 1,500 words). Short reports, 200 to 700 words. Department pieces, 1,000 to 1,500 words. Pays varying rates. Query.

THE IOWAN MAGAZINE—108 Third St., Suite 350, Des Moines, IA 50309. Charles W. Roberts, Ed. Articles, 1,000 to 3,000 words, on business, arts, people, and history of Iowa. Photos a plus. Pays $200 to $600, on publication. Query required.

ISLAND LIFE—P.O. Box X, Sanibel Island, FL 33957. Joan Hooper, Ed. Articles, 500 to 1,200 words, with photos, on unique or historical places in Florida, wildlife, architecture, fashions, home decor, cuisine, on barrier islands off Florida's S.W. Gulf Coast. Pays on publication. SASE.

JACKSONVILLE MAGAZINE—P.O. Box 329, Jacksonville, FL 32201. Carolyn Carroll, Ed. Articles of interest to the Northeast Florida community: strong regional slant a must. Pays $100 to $300, on acceptance. Query required.

KANSAS!—Kansas Dept. of Commerce, 400 W. Eighth Ave., 5th Fl., Topeka, KS 66603–3957. Andrea Glenn, Ed. Quarterly. Articles of 5 to 7 typed pages on the people, places, history, and events of Kansas. Color slides. Pays to $150, on acceptance. Query.

L/A TODAY—One Auburn Center, Suite 203, Auburn, ME 04210. John C. Turner, Pub. Articles, 500 to 2,000 words, on Maine-related topics, for readers in

Lewiston/Auburn area: personalities, profiles, places, and activities (contemporary or historical). Short poetry and fillers. Pays 10¢ a word, on publication.

LAKE SUPERIOR MAGAZINE—325 Lake Ave. S., #100, Duluth, MN 55802. Paul Hayden, Ed. Articles with unusual twists on regional subjects; historical pieces that highlight the people, places, and events that have affected the Lake Superior region. Pictorial essays; humor and occasional poetry. Pays to $400, after publication. Query first.

LONG ISLAND MONTHLY—CMP Publications, 600 Community Dr., Manhasset, NY 11030. John Atwood, Ed. "We seek to cover all aspects of Long Island, from politics and environment to food and fashion." Payment varies, on acceptance. Query with clips.

LOS ANGELES MAGAZINE—1888 Century Park E., Los Angeles, CA 90067. Lew Harris, Exec. Ed. Articles, to 3,000 words, of interest to sophisticated, affluent southern Californians, preferably with local focus on a lifestyle topic. Pays from 10¢ a word, on acceptance. Query.

LOS ANGELES READER—12224 Victory Blvd., N. Hollywood, CA 91606. James Vowell, Ed. Articles, 750 to 2,500 words, on subjects relating to the Los Angeles area; special emphasis on entertainment, feature journalism, and the arts. Pays $25 to $300, on publication. Query preferred.

LOS ANGELES TIMES MAGAZINE—Times Mirror Sq., Los Angeles, CA 90053. Linda Mathews, Ed. General-interest news features, photo spreads, profiles, and interviews focusing on people and events of interest in Southern California, to 3,500 words. Pays to $2,500, on acceptance. Query required.

L.A. WEST MAGAZINE—L.A. West Media Magazine, Inc., 919 Santa Monica Blvd., #245, Santa Monica, CA 90401. Jan Loomis, Ed. Essays, travel, and lifestyle articles, 800 to 1,000 words, for upscale, well-educated audience. Pays $75 to $500, on acceptance. Queries required.

LOUISVILLE—One Riverfront Plaza, Louisville, KY 40202. Betty Lou Amster, Ed. Articles, 1,000 to 2,000 words, on community issues, personalities, and entertainment in the Louisville area. Photos. Pays from $50, on acceptance. Query; articles on assignment only. Limited free-lance market.

MAGAZINE OF THE MIDLANDS—*Omaha World-Herald,* World Herald Sq., Omaha, NE 68102. David Hendee, Ed. General-interest articles, 400 to 2,000 words, and profiles tied to the Midwest. Photos. Pays $40 to $150, on publication. Query.

MAGNETIC NORTH—Thorn Books, Inc., Franconia, NH 03580. Jim McIntosh, Ed. Well-researched, offbeat articles, 500 to 1,500 words, for residents and visitors to New Hampshire's White Mountains. Pays $50 to $150, on publication. Query with SASE.

MAINLINE STYLE MAGAZINE—P.O. Box 350, Wayne, PA 19087. Articles, 100 to 1,400 words, on leisure, business, history, travel, dining, food, sports, education, real estate, lifestyles, health, etc., with southern Pennsylvania regional tie-in. Pays 15¢ a word, 30 days after publication. Same requirements for *Chester County Living Magazine.*

MARYLAND—c/o Dept. of Economic and Employment Development, 217 E. Redwood St., 9th Fl. , Baltimore, MD 21202. Bonnie Joe Ayers, Ed. Articles, 800 to 2,200 words, on Maryland subjects. Pay varies, on acceptance. Query preferred. Guidelines.

MEMPHIS—MM Corp., Box 256, Memphis, TN 38101. Larry Conley, Ed. Articles, 1,500 to 4,000 words, on a wide variety of topics related to Memphis and the Mid-South region: politics, education, sports, business, etc. Profiles; investigative pieces. Pays $75 to $1,000, on publication. Query. Guidelines available.

MICHIGAN BUSINESS—26111 Evergreen, Suite 303, Southfield, MI 48076. Ron Garbinski, Ed. Business news features on Michigan businesses. Query. Pay varies, on publication.

MICHIGAN LIVING—17000 Executive Plaza Dr., Dearborn, MI 48126. Len Barnes, Ed. Travel articles, 500 to 1,500 words, on tourist attractions and recreational opportunities in the U.S. and Canada, with emphasis on Michigan: places to go, things to do, costs, etc. Color photos. Pays $100 to $350, extra for photos, on acceptance.

MICHIGAN, THE MAGAZINE OF THE DETROIT NEWS—615 W. Lafayette Blvd., Detroit, MI 48231. Beaufort Cranford, Ed. Articles, from 750 words, on business, politics, arts and culture, science, people, sports, education, etc., with a Michigan slant. Cover articles, to 3,000 words. Some fiction. Pays $200 to $600, on publication.

MICHIGAN WOMAN—30400 Telegraph Rd., Suite 374, Birmingham, MI 48010. Monica Smiley, Ed. Articles, 750 words, highlighting the achievements and contributions of Michigan women in helping others enjoy more fulfilling careers and personal lives. Pays 10¢ a word, on publication. Michigan writers only. Query first.

MID-WEST OUTDOORS—111 Shore Dr., Hinsdale, IL 60521. Gene Laulunen, Ed. Articles, 1,500 words, with photos, on where, when, and how to fish, within 500 miles of Chicago. Pays $25, on publication.

MILWAUKEE—312 E. Buffalo, Milwaukee, WI 53202. Judith Woodburn, Ed. Profiles, investigative articles, and historical pieces, 3,000 to 4,000 words; local tie-in a must. Some regional fiction. Pays $400 to $600, on publication. Query required.

MPLS. ST. PAUL—12 S. 6th St., Suite 400, Minneapolis, MN 55402. Claude Peck, Man. Ed. In-depth articles, features, profiles, and service pieces, 400 to 3,000 words, with Minneapolis-St. Paul focus. Pays to $600.

MONROE—477 N. Dixie Hwy., Monroe, MI 48161. David M. Meagher, Man. Ed. The Monroe County, Michigan, area monthly. Aritcles on local history, community projects, area homes, and nearby fairs and festivals. Stories, 750 to 1,500 words, and poetry. Pays $50, on publication.

MONTANA MAGAZINE—P.O. Box 5630, Helena, MT 59604. Carolyn Cunningham, Ed. Where-to-go items, regional profiles, photo essays. Montana-oriented only. B&W prints, color slides. Pays $75 to $350, on publication.

NEVADA—101 South Fall, Carson City, NV 89710. Kirk Whisler, Ed. Articles, 500 to 700 or 1,500 to 1,800 words, on topics related to Nevada: travel, history, profiles, humor, and places—with or without photos. Pay varies, on publication.

THE NEVADAN—*The Las Vegas Review-Journal,* Box 70, Las Vegas, NV 89125–0070. A.D. Hopkins, Ed. Feature articles, 2,000 to 2,500 words, on social trends and people in Nevada. Pieces, 1,000 to 2,000 words, on history in Nevada, Southwest Utah, Northeast Arizona, and Death Valley area of California, accompanied by B&W photos. Pays $175 for cover piece, $125-$150 for articles, $20 per photos, on publication. Queries required.

NEW ALASKAN—Rt. 1, Box 677, Ketchikan, AK 99901. R.W. Pickrell, Ed.

Articles, 1,000 to 5,000 words, and fiction must be related to S.E. Alaska. Pays 1 ½¢ a word, on publication.

NEW HAMPSHIRE PROFILES—90 Fleet St., Portsmouth, NH 03801. Jack Savage, Ed. Articles, 500 to 2,500 words, on New Hampshire people, events, arts, and life styles. Pays $100 to $300, on publication. Query.

NEW JERSEY MONTHLY—P.O. Box 920, Morristown, NJ 07963–0920. Patrick Sarver, Exec. Ed. Articles, profiles, and service pieces, 2,000 to 3,000 words; department pieces on health, business, education, travel, sports, local politics, and arts, 1,200 to 1,800 words, with New Jersey tie-in. Pays $35 to $100 for shorts, $450 to $1,500 for features, on acceptance. Query with SASE and clips. Guidelines.

NEW JERSEY REPORTER—The Center for Analysis of Public Issues, 16 Vandeventer Ave., Princeton, NJ 08542. Rick Sinding, Ed. Alice Chasan, Man. Ed. In-depth articles, 2,000 to 6,000 words, on New Jersey politics and public affairs. Pays $100 to $250, on publication. Query required.

NEW MEXICO MAGAZINE—Joseph M. Montoya Bldg., 1100 St. Francis Dr., Santa Fe, NM 87503. Address Ed. Articles, 250 to 2,000 words, on New Mexico subjects. Pays about 20¢ a word, on acceptance.

NEW ORLEANS MAGAZINE—111 Veterans Blvd., New Orleans, LA 70124. Sherry Spear, Ed. Articles, 3 to 15 triple-spaced pages, on New Orleans area people and issues. Photos. Pays $50 to $500, extra for photos, on publication. Query.

NEW YORK—755 Second Ave., New York, NY 10017. Edward Kosner, Ed. Laurie Jones, Man. Ed. Feature articles on New York City subjects. Payment negotiated and on acceptance. Query required.

NEW YORK ALIVE—152 Washington Ave., Albany, NY 12210. Mary Grates Stoll, Ed. Articles aimed at developing knowledge of and appreciation for New York State. Features, 3,000 words maximum, on lifestyle, sports, travel and leisure, history, and the arts. Department pieces for regular columns, including "Great Escapes" (travel ideas) and "Expressly New York" (unusual places, products or events in New York). Pays $200 to $350 for features, $50 to $150 for departments. Query preferred.

NORTH DAKOTA HORIZONS—P.O. Box 2467, Fargo, ND 58108. Sheldon Green, Ed. Quarterly. Articles, about 3,000 words, on the people, places, and events that affect life in North Dakota. Photos. Pays $75 to $300, on publication.

NORTH GEORGIA JOURNAL—110 Hunters Mill, Woodstock, GA 30188. Olin Jackson, Pub./Ed. Historic features, 2,000 to 3,000 words, on north Georgia, with human-interest approach. Travel pieces, 1,000 words, on regional historic sites. Folkloric fiction, 1,500 to 3,000 words. Fillers and humor, 100 to 500 words. Pays $50 to $300, extra for photos and drawings, on acceptance. Query required.

NORTH TEXAS GOLFER—P.O. Box 162079, Irving, TX 75016. Bob Gray, Ed. Articles, 800 to 1,500 words, involving local golfers or related directly to North Texas. Pays from $50 to $250, on publication. Query. Same requirements for *Gulf Coast Golfer* (related to South Texas).

NORTHCOAST VIEW—Blarney Publishing, Box 1374, Eureka, CA 95502. Scott K. Ryan, Damon Maguire, Eds. Fiction, 2 to 20 pages; local news articles, 4 to 10 pages; poetry. Pays $5 per typed page, on publication.

NORTHEAST MAGAZINE—*The Hartford Courant,* 285 Broad St., Hartford, CT 06115. Lary Bloom, Ed. Articles and short essays that reflect the concerns of Connecticut residents, 750 to 3,000 words. Pays $250 to $1,000, on acceptance.

NORTHERN LIGHTS—Box 8084, Missoula, MT 59807–9962. Address Editor. Thoughtful articles, 500 to 3,000 words, about the West. Occasional fiction. "We're open to virtually any subject as long as it deals with our region (the Rocky Mountains) in some way." Pays to 10¢ a word, on publication.

NORTHWEST—1320 S.W. Broadway, Portland, OR 97201. Jack R. Hart, Ed. Sunday magazine of *The Sunday Oregonian.* Articles, to 3,000 words, on Pacific Northwest issues and personalities: regional travel, science and business, outdoor recreation, and lifestyle trends. Personal essays. Local angle essential. Pays $75 to $1,000. Query first.

NORTHWEST LIVING!—130 Second Ave. S., Edmonds, WA 98020. Terry W. Sheely, Ed. Lively, informative articles, 400 to 1,000 words, on the natural resources of the Northwest: homes, gardens, people, travel, history, etc. Color photos essential. Shorts, 100 to 400 words. Pays $50 to $400, on acceptance. Query, SASE required.

OH! IDAHO—Peak Media, Box 925, Hailey, ID 83333. Colleen Daly, Ed. "Articulate, image-oriented" features, 2,000 to 2,500 words, on Idaho's residents and recreation. Department pieces, 1,200 to 1,500 words, on food and travel in Idaho. Humor, 1,500 words. Pays from 10¢ a word, on publication. Query with clips. Guidelines.

OHIO MAGAZINE—40 S. Third St., Columbus, OH 43215. Ellen Stein Burbach, Man. Ed. Profiles of people, cities, and towns of Ohio; pieces on historic sites, tourist attractions, little-known spots. Lengths and payment vary. Query.

OKLAHOMA TODAY—Box 53384, Oklahoma City, OK 73152. Sue Carter, Ed. Travel articles; profiles, history, nature and outdoor recreation, and arts articles. All material must have regional tie-in. Queries for 1,000- to 2,000-word articles preferred. Pays $100 to $300, on acceptance. SASE for guidelines.

ORANGE COAST—245-D Fisher, Suite 8, Costa Mesa, CA 92626. Janet Eastman, Ed. Articles of interest to educated, affluent Southern Californians. Pieces, 1,000 to 1,500 words, for regular departments: "Profile," "Coasting" (op-ed), "Media," "Business" (hard news about the regional business community), and "Nightlife." Feature articles run 1,500 to 2,500 words. Query. Pays $150 for features, $100 for columns, on acceptance. Guidelines.

ORLANDO MAGAZINE—P.O. Box 2207, Orlando, FL 32802. Michael Candelaria, Ed. Articles and profiles, 1,000 to 1,500 words, related to growth, development, and business Central Florida. Photos a plus. Pays $100 to $200, on publication. Query required.

PALM SPRINGS LIFE—Desert Publications, 303 N. Indian Ave., Palm Springs, CA 92262. Becky Kurtz, Ed. Articles, 1,000 to 2,000 words, of interest to "wealthy, upscale people who live and/or play in the desert": food, interior design, luxury cars, shopping, sports, homes, personalities, arts, and culture. Pays $150 to $200 for features, $30 for short profiles, on publication. Query required.

PENNSYLVANIA MAGAZINE—Box 576, Camp Hill, PA 17011. Albert E. Holliday, Ed. General-interest features with a Pennsylvania flavor. All articles must be illustrated. Send photocopies of possible illustrations. Guidelines.

PHILADELPHIA—1500 Walnut St., Philadelphia, PA 19102. Bill Tonelli, Exec. Ed. Articles, 1,000 to 5,000 words, for sophisticated audience, relating to Philadelphia area. No fiction. Pays on acceptance. Query.

PHOENIX METRO MAGAZINE—4707 N. 12th St., Phoenix, AZ 85014. Robert J. Early, Ed. Articles, 1,000 to 3,000 words, on topics of interest to Phoenix-area residents. Pays $75 to $300, on publication. Written queries preferred.

PORTLAND MONTHLY—578 Congress St., Portland, ME 04101. Colin Sargent, Sr. Ed. Articles on local people, fashion, culture, trends, commercial and residential real estate. Fiction, to 2,500 words. Pays on publication. Query preferred.

PRIME TIMES—Senior World, Inc., 2819 First Ave., Seattle, WA 98121. Anthony E. Thein, Pub./Ed. Articles to address active, affluent residents of King County, WA, ages 55 to 70. Pays $50 to $75, on publication.

REGARDIE'S—1010 Wisconsin Ave. N.W., Suite 600, Washington, DC 20007. Brian Kelly, Ed. Profiles and investigations of the "high and mighty" in the DC area: "We require aggressive reporting and imaginative, entertaining writing." Pays 50¢ a word, on publication. Queries required.

ROCKFORD MAGAZINE—211 W. State St., Box 197, Rockford, IL 61105. John Harris, Ed. Lively regional magazine covering northern Illinois and southern Wisconsin. Feature articles 3,000 words, and columns, 1,000 to 2,000 words, on area personalities, events, arts, business, nostalgia, family and more. Pays from 10¢ a word, on publication. Query with samples.

RURAL LIVING—4201 Dominion Blvd., Suite 101, Glen Allen, VA 23060. Richard G. Johnstone, Jr., Ed. Features, 1,000 to 1,500 words, on people, places, historic sites in Virginia and Maryland's Eastern Shore. Queries preferred. Pays $100 to $150 for articles, on publication.

RURALITE—P.O. Box 558, Forest Grove, OR 97116. Address Ed. or Feature Ed. Articles, 800–1,000 words, of interest to a primarily rural and small-town audience in Oregon, Washington, Idaho, Nevada, Northern California, and Alaska. Upbeat articles: biographies, local history and celebrations, self-help, etc. Humorous articles and animal pieces. No fiction or poetry. No sentimental nostalgia. Pays $30 to $130, on acceptance. Queries preferred.

SACRAMENTO MAGAZINE—P.O. Box 2424, Sacramento, CA 95811. Ann McSisemore, Man. Ed. Features, 2,500 words, on a broad range of topics related to the region. Department pieces, 1,200 to 1,500 words, and short pieces, 400 words, for "City Lights" column. Pays $150 to $300, on acceptance. Query first.

SAN DIEGO MAGAZINE—4206 W. Point Loma Blvd., P.O. Box 85409, San Diego, CA 92138. Martin Hill, Sr. Ed. Articles, 1,500 to 3,000 words, on local personalities, politics, lifestyles, business, history, etc., relating to San Diego area. Photos. Pays $250 to $600, on publication. Query with clips.

SAN DIEGO READER—P.O. Box 80803, San Diego, CA 92138. Jim Holman, Ed. Articles, 2,500 to 10,000 words, on the San Diego region. Pays $500 to $2,000, on publication.

SAN FRANCISCO BUSINESS TIMES—325 Fifth St., San Francisco, CA 94107. Tim Clark, Assoc. Ed. Business-oriented articles, about 20 column inches. Limited free-lance market. Pays $75 to $100, on publication. Query.

SAN FRANCISCO FOCUS—680 Eighth St., San Francisco, CA 94103. Mark Powelson, Ed. Service features, profiles of local newsmakers, and investigative pieces of local issues, 2,500 to 3,000 words. Short stories, 1,500 to 5,000 words. Pays $250 to $750, on acceptance. Query required.

SAN FRANCISCO: THE MAGAZINE—45 Belden Pl., San Francisco, CA 91404. Warren Sharpe, Ed. "We are the city magazine for San Francisco. We are looking for stories on the people, places, power, and issues that effect the Bay Area." Pays varying rates, on publication.

SEATTLE'S CHILD—P.O. Box 22578, Seattle, WA 98122. Ann Bergman,

538

Ed. Articles (400 to 2,500 words) of interest to parents, educators, and childcare providers of children under 12, plus investigative reports and consumer tips on issues affecting families in the Puget Sound region. Pays $75 to $400, on publication. Query required.

SENIOR MAGAZINE—3565 S. Higuera St., San Louis Obispo, CA 93401. Personality profiles and health articles, 600 to 900 words, humorous fillers, and book reviews (of new books or outstanding older titles) of interest to senior citizens of Santa Barbara and San Luis Counties. Pays $1.50 per inch, on publication.

7 DAYS—36 Cooper Sq., New York, NY 10003. Adam Moss, Ed. Short articles reflecting the New York City scene. Weekly. Payment varies, on acceptance. Query preferred.

SOUTH CAROLINA WILDLIFE—P.O. Box 167, Columbia, SC 29202. Address Man. Ed. Articles, 1,000 to 3,000 words, with regional outdoors focus: conservation, natural history and wildlife, recreation. Profiles, natural history. Pays from 10¢ a word. Query.

SOUTHERN MAGAZINE—See *Southpoint.*

SOUTHERN OUTDOORS—N. 1, Bell Rd., Montgomery, AL 36141. Larry Teague, Ed. How-to articles, 200 to 600 words or 1,500 to 2,000 words, on hunting and fishing, for fishermen and hunters in the 16 southern states. Pays 15¢ a word, on acceptance. Query.

SOUTHPOINT—(formerly *Southern Magazine*) 1760 Peachtree Rd. N.W., Atlanta, GA 30309. Susan Taylor, Ed. The Metropolitan Monthly. Features exploring all facets of the contemporary South; no fiction or poetry. Pays varying rates, on acceptance.

SOUTHWEST ART—Franklin Tower, 5444 Westheimer, Suite 1440, Houston, TX 77056. Susan McGarry, Ed. Articles, 1,800 to 2,200 words, on the artists, museums, galleries, history, and art trends west of the Mississippi River. Particularly interested in representational or figurative arts. Pays from $300, on acceptance. Query.

THE STATE: DOWN HOME IN NORTH CAROLINA—P.O. Box 2169, Raleigh, NC 27602. Jim Duff, Ed. Articles, 600 to 2,000 words, on people, history, and places in North Carolina. Photos. Pays on acceptance.

SUNDAY—*Chicago Tribune,* 435 N. Michigan Ave., Rm. 532, Chicago, IL 60611. Ruby Scott, Man. Ed. Profiles and articles, to 6,000 words, on public and social issues on the personal, local, or national. Prefer regional slant. Query. Pays varying rates, on publication.

SUNDAY MAGAZINE—*Providence Sunday Journal,* 75 Fountain St., Providence, RI 02902. Doug Cumming, Ed. Profiles, personal-experience pieces, fiction, New England features, 1,000 to 3,000 words. Pays $75 to $750, on publication. Query.

SUNSET MAGAZINE—80 Willow Rd., Menlo Park, CA 94025. William Marken, Ed. Western regional. Queries not encouraged.

SUNSHINE: THE MAGAZINE OF SOUTH FLORIDA—*The Sun-Sentinel,* 101 N. New River Dr., Ft. Lauderdale, FL 33301–2293. John Parkyn, Ed. Articles, 1,000 to 4,000 words, on topics of interest to South Floridians. Pays $250 to $1,000, on acceptance. Query first. Guidelines.

SUSQUEHANNA MONTHLY MAGAZINE—Box 75A, RD1, Marietta, PA 17547. Richard S. Bromer, Ed. Well-documented articles, 1,000 to 4,000 words, on regional (PA, DE, MD, DC) biographical history. Pays to $75, on publication. Query required. No fiction or poetry.

TALLAHASSEE MAGAZINE—P.O. Box 12848, Tallahassee, FL 32317. Marion McDanield, Ed. Articles, 800 to 1,100 words, with a positive outlook on the life, people, and history of the North Florida area. Pays 10¢ a word, on publication. Query.

TAMPA BAY LIFE—900 Bayport Plaza, 6200 Courtney Campbell Causeway, Tampa, FL 33607. Bonnie Dyson, Ed. Articles, 1,200 to 2,000 words, on the people, events, and issues shaping the region's future. Pays $250 to $400 for department pieces; $450 to $1,000 for features, on acceptance.

TEXAS HIGHWAYS MAGAZINE—State Dept. of Highways and Public Transportation, 11th and Brazos, Austin, TX 78701–2483. Frank Lively, Ed. Texas travel, history, and scenic features, 200 to 1,800 words. Pays 40¢ to 60¢ a word, on acceptance, extra for photos. Guidelines.

TIMELINE—1985 Velma Ave., Columbus, OH 43211–2497. Christopher S. Duckworth, Ed. Articles, 1,000 to 6,000 words, on Ohio history (politics, economics, social, and natural history) for lay readers in the Midwest. Pays $100 to $900, on acceptance. Queries preferred.

TOLEDO MAGAZINE—*The Blade,* Toldeo, OH 43660. Sue Stankey, Ed. Articles, to 5,000 words, on Toledo area personalities, events, etc. Pays $50 to $500, on publication. Query with SASE.

TORONTO LIFE—59 Front St. E., Toronto, Ont., Canada M5E 1B3. Marq De Villiers, Ed. Articles, 1,500 to 4,500 words, on Toronto. Pays $1,500 to $3,500, on acceptance. Query.

TROPIC—*The Miami Herald,* One Herald Plaza, Miami, FL 33132. Gene Weingarten, Exec. Ed. Tom Shroder, Ed. General-interest articles, 750 to 3,000 words, for South Florida readers. Pays $200 to $1,000, on acceptance. Send SASE.

TUCSON LIFESTYLE—Old Pueblo Press, 7000 E. Tanque Verde, Tucson, AZ 85715. Sue Giles, Ed. Features on local businesses, lifestyles, the arts, homes, and fashion. Payment varies, on acceptance. Query preferred.

TWIN CITIES READER—5500 Wayzata Blvd., Minneapolis, MN 55416. D.J. Tice, Ed.-in-Chief. Articles, 2 to 4 printed pages, on cultural phenomena, city politics, and general-interest subjects, for local readers aged 25 to 44. Pays to $3 to $5 per inch, on publication.

VALLEY MAGAZINE—16800 Devonshire, Suite 275, Granada Hills, CA 91344. Manley Witten, Ed. Articles, 1,000 to 1,500 words, on celebrities, issues, education, health, business, dining, and entertaining, etc., in the San Fernando Valley. Pays $100 to $350, within 8 weeks of acceptance.

VENTURA COUNTY & COAST REPORTER—1583 Spinnaker Dr., Suite 213, Ventura, CA 93001. Nancy Cloutier, Ed. Articles, 3 to 5 pages, on any locally slanted topic. Pays $10, on publication.

VERMONT LIFE—61 Elm St., Montpelier, VT 05602. Tom Slayton, Ed.-in-Chief. Articles, 500 to 3,000 words, about Vermont subjects only. Pays 20¢ a word, extra for photos. Query perferred.

VIRGINIA BUSINESS—411 E. Franklin St., Suite 105, Richmond, VA 23219. James Bacon, Ed. Articles, 1,000 to 2,500 words, related to the business scene in Virginia. Pays varying rates, on acceptance. Query required.

THE VIRGINIAN—P.O. Box 8, New Hope, VA 24469. Hunter S. Pierce, IV, Man. Ed. Articles, 1,000 words, relating to VA, WV, MD, NC, and DC, with emphasis on first person or personality profiles of Virginians.

WASHINGTON—200 W. Thomas, Seattle, WA 98119. J. Kingston Pierce, Senior Ed. Articles (500 to 4,000 words) on the people, places, and issues of Washington State. Pays from 15¢ to 25¢ a word, on acceptance. Query required.

WASHINGTON DOSSIER—1015 31st St N.W., Fifth Fl., Washington, DC 20007. Laura Goldstein, Assoc. Ed. Feature articles (4,000 words), profiles and department pieces (1,500 words), including "quick profiles, restaurant news, and extraordinary itineraries" (200 to 500 words). Pays good rates, on acceptance. Query required.

WASHINGTON POST MAGAZINE—*The Washington Post,* 1150 15th St. N.W., Washington, DC 20071. Stephen L. Petranek, Man. Ed. Personal-experience essays, profiles, and general-interest pieces, to 6,000 words, on business, arts and culture, politics, science, sports, education, children, relationships, behavior, etc. Articles should be of interest to people living in Washington, D.C. Pays from $300, on acceptance.

THE WASHINGTONIAN—1828 L St. N.W., Suite 200, Washington, DC 20036. John Limpert, Ed. Helpful, informative articles, 1,000 to 4,000 words, on Washington-related topics. Pays 30¢ a word. Query.

WE ALASKANS MAGAZINE—*Anchorage Daily News,* Box 149001, Anchorage, AK 99514. George Benson, Ed. Articles, 2,000 words, and features, 3,000 to 4,000 words, on Alaska topics only. Profiles, narratives, fiction, and humor. Pays $75—$125 for articles, $300 for features, on publication.

THE WEEKLY, SEATTLE'S NEWS MAGAZINE—1931 Second Ave., Seattle, WA 98101. David Brewster, Ed. Articles, 700 to 4,000 words, with a Northwest perspective. Pays $75 to $800, on publication. Query. Guidelines.

WEST—*San Jose Mercury News,* 750 Ridder Park Dr., San Jose, CA 05190. Charles Matthews, Man. Ed. Sunday magazine. Pieces related to San Francisco Bay, Monterey Bay, and Northern California, including personalities, places, and events. Pays $150, on acceptance.

WESTERN SPORTSMAN—P.O. Box 737, Regina, Sask., Canada S4P 3A8. Rick Bates, Ed. Informative articles, to 2,500 words, on outdoor experiences in Alberta and Saskatchewan. How-tos, humor, cartoons. Photos. Pays $20 to $325, on publication.

WESTWAYS—Box 2890, Terminal Annex, Los Angeles, CA 90051. Mary Ann Fisher, Ed. Articles, 1,000 to 1,500 words, and photo essays, on western U.S., Canada, and Mexico: history, contemporary living, travel, personalities, etc. Photos. Pays from 20¢ a word, extra for photos, 30 days before publication. Query.

WISCONSIN—*The Milwaukee Journal Magazine,* Newspapers, Inc., Box 661, Milwaukee, WI 53201. Alan Borsuk, Ed. Articles, 500 to 2,000 words, on business, politics, arts, science with strong Wisconsin emphasis. Personal-experience essays and investigative articles. Pays $75 to $500, on publication. Query.

WISCONSIN TRAILS—P.O. Box 5650, Madison, WI 53705. Geri Nixon, Man. Ed. Articles, 1,500 to 3,000 words, on regional topics: outdoors, lifestyle, events, adventure, travel; profiles of artists and craftspeople, and regional personalities. Fiction, with regional slant. Fillers. Pays $100 to $450, on acceptance and on publication. Query.

WISCONSIN WEST MAGAZINE—P.O. Box 381, Eau Claire, WI 54702–0381. Jane Hieb, Features Ed. Articles on contemporary issues for residents of western Wisconsin; profiles of towns, neighborhoods, families in the region; and historical pieces. Short humor. Payment varies, on publication.

WORCESTER MONTHLY—One Exchange Pl., Worcester, MA 01608. Michael Warshaw, Ed. Articles, to 3,000 words, on the arts, entertainment, fashion, events, and issues specific to Central Massachusetts. Pays $200, on publication. Query required.

YANKEE—Yankee Publishing Co., Dublin, NH 03444. Judson D. Hale, Ed. Articles and fiction, about 2,500 words, on New England and residents. Pays about $600 for features, $1,000 for fiction, on acceptance.

YANKEE MAGAZINE'S TRAVEL GUIDE TO NEW ENGLAND AND ITS NEIGHBORS—Main St., Dublin, NH 03444. Elizabeth Doyle, Ed. Articles, 500 to 2,000 words, on activities, attractions, places to visit in New England, New York State, and Atlantic Canada. Photos. Pays $50 to $300, on acceptance. Query with outline and writing samples.

TRAVEL ARTICLES

AAA WORLD—1000 AAA Dr., Heathrow, VA 32746–5064. Douglas Damerst, Ed.-in-Chief. Articles, 600 to 1,500 words, on consumer automotive and travel concerns. Pays $200 to $800, on acceptance. Query with writing samples only.

ACCENT—Box 10010, Ogden, UT 84409. Melody Haakenson and Libby Hyland, Eds. Articles, 1,200 words, on travel destinations, ways to travel, and travel tips. Pays 15¢ a word, $35 for photos, on acceptance. Query first.

ADVENTURE ROAD—The Condé Nast Publications, 360 Madison Ave., New York, NY 10017. Marilyn Holstein, Ed. Official publication of the Amoco Motor Club. Articles, 1,500 words, on destinations in North America, Mexico, and the Caribbean. Photos. Pays $300 to $800, on acceptance. Query required.

AIRFARE INTERLINE MAGAZINE—4 Park Ave., New York, NY 10016. Ratu Kamlani, Ed. Travel articles, 1,000 to 2,500 words, with photos, on shopping, sightseeing, dining, and night life for airline employees. Prices, discount information, and addresses must be included. Pays $75, after publication.

ARIZONA HIGHWAYS—2039 W. Lewis Ave., Phoenix, AZ 85009. Richard G. Stahl, Man. Ed. Informal, well-researched travel articles, 2,000 to 2,500 words, focusing on a specific city or region in Arizona and environs. Also articles dealing with nature, environment, flora and fauna, history, anthropology, archaeology, hiking, boating, industry. Pays 30¢ to 45¢ a word, on acceptance. Query with published clips. Guidelines.

BRITISH HERITAGE—P.O. Box 8200, Harrisburg, PA 17105. Gail Huganir, Ed. Travel articles on places to visit in the British Isles, 800 to 1,000 words. Include detailed historical information with a "For the Visitor" sidebar. Pays $100 to $200, on acceptance.

CALIFORNIA HIGHWAY PATROLMAN—2030 V St., Sacramento, CA 95818. Carol Perri, Ed. Travel articles, to 2,000 words, focusing on places in California and the West Coast. Pays 2 ½¢ a word, extra for black and white photos, on publication.

THE CAMPER TIMES—Royal Productions, Inc., Box 6294, Richmond, VA 23230. Alice P. Supple, Ed. Articles and fiction, 500 to 2,000 words, related to outdoor or leisure activities, travel attractions in the MD, VA, NC, NJ, NY, DE, and TN area. Pays $25 to $50, on publication. Queries preferred.

CARIBBEAN TRAVEL AND LIFE—8403 Colesville Rd., Suite 830, Silver Spring, MD 20910. Veronica Gould Stoddart, Ed. Lively, informative articles, 500 to 2,500 words, on all aspects of travel, leisure, recreation, and culture in the Caribbean, Bahamas, and Bermuda, for up-scale, sophisticated readers. Photos. Pays $75 to $550, on publication. Query.

DISCOVERY—One Illinois Center, 111 E. Wacker Dr., Suite 1700, Chicago, IL 60601. John Fink, Ed. Articles, 1,000 to 2,500 words, on travel topics that explore continental North America and its people; pieces should be geared to the automotive traveler. Photos on assignment only. Pays from $800, on acceptance. Query with published clips required.

EARLY AMERICAN LIFE—Box 8200, Harrisburg, PA 17105. Frances Carnahan, Ed. Travel features about historic sites and country inns, 1,000 to 3,000 words. Pays $50 to $500, on acceptance. Query.

ENDLESS VACATION—Box 80260, Indianapolis, IN 46280. Helen A. Wernle, Ed. Travel features, to 2,000 words; international scope. Pays on acceptance. Query preferred. Guidelines.

FAMILY CIRCLE—110 Fifth Ave., New York, NY 10011. Susan Ungaro, Articles Ed. Travel articles, to 2,000 words. Destination pieces should appeal to a national audience and focus on affordable activities; prefer area roundups, theme-oriented travel pieces or first-person family vacation stories. Pay rates vary, on acceptance. Query first.

FORD TIMES—One Illinois Center, 111 E. Wacker Dr., Suite 1700, Chicago, IL 60601. John Fink, Ed. Articles, 500 to 1,500 words, on current trends, lifestyles, profiles, places of interest, travel, outdoor activities, food, and humor, appealing to drivers age 18 to 35. Pays from $550 for 1,200 to 1,500 words, on acceptance. Query with SASE required.

FRIENDLY EXCHANGE—Locust at 17th, Des Moines, IA 50336. Adele Malott, Ed. Articles, 1,000 to 1,800 words, of interest to the active Western family, on travel and leisure. Photos. Pays $300 to $800, extra for photos. Query preferred. Guidelines.

GO: THE AUTHENTIC GUIDE TO NEW ORLEANS—541 Julia St., New Orleans, LA 70130. Suzy G. Lauderdale, Ed. Articles, to 1,200 words, of interest to New Orleans visitors. Pays to $150, on publication. Query required.

GREAT EXPEDITIONS—Box 8000–411, Sumas, WA 98295–8000. Craig Henderson, Ed. Articles, 700 to 2,500 words on independent, adventurous, budget-conscious travel and unusual destinations. Pays $20 to $40, on publication. Guidelines.

GUIDE TO LIVING OVERSEAS—See *Transitions Abroad.*

GULFSHORE LIFE—Collier Park of Commerce, 2975 S. Horseshoe Dr., Naples, FL 33942. Janis Lyn Johnson, Ed. Destination-oriented travel articles focusing on the unusual and unique, 1,800 to 2,400 words. Don't want "typical" destinations. Pay negotiable, on publication. Queries required.

INTERNATIONAL LIVING—824 E. Baltimore St., Baltimore, MD 21202. Bruce Totaro, Ed. Newsletter. Short pieces and features, 200 to 2,000 words, with useful information on investing, shopping, travel, employment, real estate, and lifestyles overseas. Pays $50 to $200 after publication.

ISLANDS—3886 State St., Santa Barbara, CA 93105. Articles on island-related topics written from a historical, exploratory, or cultural point of view, 3,000 words, 2,500 words, or 1,000 words. Pays 50¢ a word, half on acceptance, half on publication. Query required. Guidelines.

MICHIGAN LIVING—Automobile Club of Michigan, 17000 Executive Plaza Dr., Dearborn, MI 48126. Len Barnes, Ed. Informative travel articles, 500 to 1,500 words, on U.S. Canadian tourist attractions and recreational opportunities; special interest in Michigan.

THE MIDWEST MOTORIST—12901 N. Forty Dr., St. Louis, MO 63141. Jean Kennedy, Man. Ed. Articles 1,000 to 1,500 words, with color slides, on domestic and foreign travel. Pays from $150, on acceptance.

MODERN BRIDE—475 Park Ave. S., New York, NY 10016. Geri Bain, Travel Ed. Articles, 1,800 to 2,000 words, on honeymoon travel, covering the U.S., Caribbean, Bahamas, Bermuda, Canada, Mexico, South Pacific, and Europe. Queries preferred. Pays $600 to $1,200, on acceptance.

NATIONAL GEOGRAPHIC—17th and M Sts. N.W., Washington, DC 20036. Wilbur E. Garrett., Ed. First-person articles on geography, exploration, natural history, archeology, and science. Half staff written; half written by recognized authorities and published authors. Does not review manuscripts.

NATIONAL GEOGRAPHIC TRAVELER—National Geographic Society, 17th and M Sts., N.W., Washington, DC 20036. Richard Busch, Ed. Dir. Articles 1,500 to 4,000 words, that highlight specific places. Query with 1–2 page proposal, resumé, and published clippings required. Pays $1 a word, on acceptance.

NATIONAL MOTORIST—Bayside Plaza, 188 The Embarcadero, San Francisco, CA 94105. Jane Offers, Ed. Illustrated articles, 500 to 1,100 words, for California motorists, on motoring in the West, car care, roads, personalities, places, etc. Photos. Pays from 10¢ a word, extra for photos, on acceptance. SASE required.

NEW ENGLAND GETAWAYS—215 Newbury St., Peabody, MA 01960. Features, 1,000 to 2,500 words, designed to lure travelers to New England; include specific information such as addresses, phone numbers, hours of business, etc. Pays $100 to $250, after publication.

NEW WOMAN—215 Lexington Ave., New York, NY 10016. Gay Bryant, Ed. Armchair travel pieces; personal experience and "what I learned from this experience" pieces, 2,000. Pays $500 to $2,000, on acceptance. Query required.

NEW YORK DAILY NEWS—220 E. 42nd St., New York, NY 10017. Harry Ryan, Travel Ed. First-person impressions, anecdotes, 600 to 1,200 words on all manner of travel. Price information must be included. Black and white photos preferred. Pays $100 to $200, on publication, extra for photos.

NORTHWEST—*The Sunday Oregonian,* 1320 S.W. Broadway, Portland, OR 97201. Travel articles, 1,000 to 1,500 words, third-person perspective. All material must pertain to the Northwest (OR, WA, ID, and MT). Include details about where to go, what to see, plans to make, with specific information about reservations, ticket reservations, purchases, etc. Pays $150 to $250, on acceptance. Query with clips. Experienced writers only.

NORTHWEST LIVING!—130 Second Ave., South Edmonds, WA 98020–3588. Terry W. Sheely, Ed. Articles, 400 to 1,500 words, on regional travel and natural resources. Color slides or B&W prints. Query with SASE required.

OFF DUTY MAGAZINE—3303 Harbor Blvd., Suite C-2, Costa Mesa, CA

92626. Gary Burch, U.S. Ed. Travel articles, 1,800 to 2,000 words, for active duty military Americans (ages 20 to 40) and their families, on U.S. regions or cities. Must have wide scope; no out-of-the-way places. Military angle essential. Photos. Pays from 13¢ a word, extra for photos, on acceptance. Query required. Send for guidelines. European and Pacific editions. Foreign travel articles for military Americans and their families stationed abroad. Send SASE for guidelines. Limited market.

THE ORIGINAL NEW ENGLAND GUIDE—The Jolicoeur Companies, Inc., 177 East Industrial Dr., Manchester, NH 03103. Annual. Articles on special events, sightseeing, travel destinations, and activites, focusing on a particular attraction or theme. Pay varies, on acceptance. Query with clips required.

SACRAMENTO MAGAZINE—P.O. Box 2424, Sacramento, CA 95812–2424. Nancy Curley, Ed. Destination-oriented articles in the Sacramento area (or within a 6 hour drive) 1,000 to 1,500 words. Pay varies, on acceptance. Query first, to Jan Haag.

TEXAS HIGHWAYS MAGAZINE—State Dept. of Highways and Public Transportation, 11th and Brazos, Austin, TX 78701–2483. Frank Lively, Ed. Travel, historical, cultural, scenic features on Texas, 1,000 to 1,800 words. Pays 40¢ to 75¢, on acceptance; photos $80-$400.

TOURS & RESORTS—World Publishing Co., 990 Grove St., Evanston, IL 60201–4370. Ray Gudas, Man. Ed. Features on international vacation destinations and resorts, 1,500 words; also essays, nostalgia, humor, tour company profiles, travel tips, and service articles, 800 to 1,500 words. Pays up to $350, on acceptance. Top-quality color slides a must. Query.

TRANSITIONS ABROAD—18 Hulst Rd., Box 344, Amherst, MA 01004. Dr. Clayton A. Hubbs, Ed. Articles for travelers overseas who seek an in-depth experience of the culture: work, study, travel, budget tips. Include practical, first-hand information. Emphasis on establishing meaningful contact with people (home stays and exchanges, schools, specialty holiday courses, volunteer work, etc.). B&W photos a plus. Pays $2 per column inch, after publication. Same requirements for *Guide to Living Overseas,* for nontourist (educational, cultural, vocational) travel aboard.

TRAVEL AGE WEST—100 Grant Ave., San Francisco, CA 94108. Donald Langley, Man. Ed. Articles, 800 to 1,000 words, with photos, on any aspect of travel useful to travel agents, including names, addresses, prices, etc.; news or trend angle preferred. Pays $2 per column inch, after publication.

TRAVEL & LEISURE—1120 Ave. of the Americas, New York, NY 10036. Pamela Fiori, Ed-in Chief. Articles, 800 to 3,000 words on destinations and travel related activities. Regional pieces for regional editions. Pays $600 to $3,000, on acceptance. Query; articles on assignment.

TRAVEL HOLIDAY—Travel Publication, Inc., 28 W. 23rd St., 10th Floor, NewYork, NY 10010. Diane Marshall, Man. Ed. Informative, lively features, 1,400 to 1,600 words, on foreign and domestic travel to well-known or little-known places; featurettes, 1,000 to 1,200 words, on special-interest subjects: museums, shopping, smaller cities or islands, special aspects of destination. Pays to $400 for featurettes, to $750 for features, on acceptance. Query with published clips.

TRAVEL SMART—Dobbs Ferry, NY 10522. Short pieces, 250 to 1,000 words, about interesting, unusual and/or economical places: give specific details on hotels, restaurants, transportation, and costs. Pays on publication.

TRAVEL SMART FOR BUSINESS—Dobbs Ferry , NY 10522. H.J. Teison,

Ed. Articles, 200 to 1,000 words, for company executives and business travel managers, on lowering travel costs and increasing travel convenience. Pays on publication.

VISTA/USA—Box 161, Convent Station, NJ 07961. Kathleen M. Caccavale, Ed. Travel articles, 1,200 to 2,000 words, on U.S., Canada, Mexico, and the Caribbean. Plus, general interest, hobby/collecting, culture, and Americana. "Flavor of the area, not service, oriented." Shorts, 500 to 1,000 words, on "Minitrips," "CloseFocus," "American Vignettes." Pays from $500, for features, from $150 for shorts, on acceptance. Query with writing sample and outline. Limited market.

VOLKSWAGEN'S WORLD—Volkswagen of America, Inc., P.O. Box 3951, 888 W. Big Beaver, Troy, MI 48007–3951. Marlene Goldsmith, Ed. Travel articles on unique places or with a unique angle, to 750 words. Pays $150 per printed page, on acceptance. Query.

WESTWAYS—P.O. Box 2890, Terminal Annex, Los Angeles, CA 90051. Mary Ann Fisher, Exec. Ed. Travel articles on where to go, what to see, and how to get there, 1,500 words. Domestic travel articles are limited to Western U.S., Canada, and Hawaii; foreign travel articles are also of interest. Quality color transparencies should be available. Pays 20¢ a word, 30 days before publication.

YACHT VACATIONS MAGAZINE—P.O. Box 1657, Palm Harbor, FL 34682–1657. Sandra Tracey, Ed. Articles and photography on chartered yacht vacations worldwide, 1,000 to 1,800 words. Pays varying rates, on publication. Query first.

YANKEE MAGAZINE'S TRAVEL GUIDE TO NEW ENGLAND AND ITS NEIGHBORS—Main St., Dublin, NH 03444. Elizabeth Doyle, Ed. Articles 500 to 2,000 words, on unusual activities, restaurants, places to visit in New England, New York, and Atlantic Canada. Photos. Pays $50 to $300, on acceptance. Query with outline and writing samples.

INFLIGHT MAGAZINES

ABOARD—North-South Net, Inc., 777 41st St., P.O. Box 40–2763, Miami Beach, FL 33140. Cristina Arencibia, Ed. Inflight magazine of nine Latin American international airlines. Articles, with photos, on Chile, Panama, Paraguay, Dominican Republic, Ecuador, Guatemala, El Salvador, Bolivia, Venezuela, and Honduras. Pieces on science, sports, home, fashion, and gastronomy, 1,200 to 1,500 words. Pays $150, with photos, on acceptance and on publication. Query required.

AMERICAN WAY—P.O. Box 619616, MD 2G23, DWF Airport, TX 75261–9616. Rod Davis, Ed. American Airline's inflight magazine. Features of interest to the business traveler, emphasizing travel, adventure, business, and the arts/culture. Pays from $450, on acceptance. Query.

AMERICANA WEST AIRLINES MAGAZINE—Skyward Marketing, Inc., 7500 N. Dreamy Draw Dr., Suite 236, Phoenix, AZ 85020. Michael Derr, Ed. Articles celebrating creativity, 750 to 2,000 words; regional angle helpful. Pays from $250 to $750, on publication. Query required. Guidelines.

HORIZON—See *Midway.*

MIDWAY—Skies Publishing Co., Plaza West, 9600 S.W. Oak St., Suite 310, Portland, OR 97223. Terri Wallo, Ed. Articles, 1,000 to 1,300 words; and columns, 500 to 700 words, of interest to business travelers. Pays $200 to $400 for features, $50 to $100 for columns, on publication. Query letters preferred. Same requirements for *United Express* and *Horizon.*

SKY—12955 Biscayne Blvd., North Miami, FL 33181. Lidia de Leon, Ed. Delta Air Lines' inflight magazine. Articles on business, life style, high tech, sports, the arts, etc. Color slides. Pays varying rates, on acceptance. Query.

SPIRIT—East/West Network, 34 E. 51st St., New York, NY 10022. John Cade, Ed. Southwest Airlines. Articles, 1,000 to 2,000 words, on business, arts, profiles, and lifestyles in Southwest U.S. Pays $900, on acceptance. Query.

UNITED EXPRESS—See *Midway.*

USAIR—1301 Carolina St., Greensboro, NC 27401. Maggie Oman, Ed. Articles, 1,500 to 3,000 words, on travel, business, sports, entertainment, food, health, and other general-interest topics. No downbeat or extremely controversial subjects. Pays $350 to $800, on acceptance. Query first.

VIS A VIS—East/West Network, 34 E. 51st St., New York, NY 10022. Susan C. Shipman, Ed. First-person articles, 600 to 700 words, on profiles, resorts, and luxury vacations. Pays varying rates, on acceptance. No photos. Queries required. Guidelines.

WOMEN'S PUBLICATIONS

BBW: BIG BEAUTIFUL WOMAN—9171 Wilshire Blvd., Suite 300, Beverly Hills, CA 90210. Carole Shaw, Ed.-in-Chief. Articles, 2,500 words, of interest to large-size women, including interviews with successful large-size women and self-pieces on how to cope with difficult situations. Tips on restaurants, airlines, stores, etc., that treat large women with respect. Payment varies, on publication. Query.

BEAUTY DIGEST—95 Madison Ave., New York, NY 10016. Tricia McMahon Drain, Ed. Innovative angles for pieces on beauty, health, fitness, emotional self-help for women. Submit queries with published clips. Pay varies.

BLACK ELEGANCE—475 Park Ave. S., New York, NY 10016. Sharyn J. Skeeter, Ed. Articles, 1,000 to 2,000 words, on fashion, beauty, relationships, home design, careers, personal finance, and personalities for black women age 25 to 45. Short interviews. Include photos if available. Pays $150 to $225, on publication. Query. Guidelines.

BRIDAL GUIDE—Globe Communications Corp., 441 Lexington Ave., New York, NY 10017. Deborah Harding, Ed. Bimonthly covering wedding planning, fashion, beauty, contemporary relationships, honeymoon travel, and plans for the first home. Regular departments include: finance, sex, remarriage, and advice for the groom. Prefers queries for articles 800 to 1,600 words. Pays $200 to $600, on acceptance.

BRIDE'S—350 Madison Ave., New York, NY 10017. Andrea Feld, Man. Ed. Articles, 800 to 2,500 words, for engaged couples or newlyweds, on communication, sex, housing, finances, careers, remarriage, step-parenting, health, birth control, pregnancy, babies, religion, in-laws, relationships, and wedding planning. Pays $300 to $800, on acceptance.

CAPPER'S—616 Jefferson St., Topeka, KS 66607. Nancy Peavler, Ed. Human interest, personal experience, historical articles, 300 to 700 words. Poetry, to 15 lines, on nature, home, family. Novel-length fiction for serialization. Letters on women's interests, recipes, hints, for "Heart of the Home." Jokes. Children's writing and art section. Pays varying rates, on publication.

CHATELAINE—Maclean Hunter Bldg., 777 Bay St., Toronto, Ont., Canada M5W 1A7. Elizabeth Parr, Sr. Ed. Articles, 2,500 words, on current issues and

547

personalities of interest to Canadian women. Pays from $1,200 for 1,500 to 3,000 words; from $350 for 500-word "Up-front" columns (relationships, health, parents/kids), on acceptance. Send query with outline, or manuscript with international reply coupon.

COMPLETE WOMAN—1165 N. Clark, Chicago, IL 60610. Susan Handy, Sr. Ed. Articles, 1,500 to 2,000 words, with how-to sidebars, giving practical advice to women on careers, health, personal relationships, etc. Inspirational profiles of successful women. Pays varying rates, on publication. Send manuscript or query with SASE.

COSMOPOLITAN—224 W. 57th St., New York, NY 10019. Helen Gurley Brown, Ed. Betty Nichols Kelly, Fiction and Books Ed. Articles, to 3,500 words, and features, 500 to 2,500 words, on issues affecting young career women. Fiction on male-female relationships: short shorts, 1,500 to 3,000 words; short stories, 3,000 to 4,000 words; condensed published novels, 25,000 words. Pays from $750 to $3,500 for full-length articles, $1,500-$2,500 for short stories, on acceptance.

COUNTRY WOMAN—P.O. Box 643, Milwaukee, WI 53201. Kathy Pohl, Man. Ed. Profiles of country women (photo/feature packages), inspirational, reflective pieces. Personal-experience, humor, service-oriented articles, and how-to features, to 1,000 words, of interest to country women. Pays $40 to $150, on acceptance.

ENTREPRENEURIAL WOMAN—2392 Morse Ave., Irvine, CA 92714. Rieva Lesonsky, Ed. Profiles, 2,000 words, of women entrepreneurs; how-tos on running a business, and pieces on coping as a woman business owner. Payment varies, on acceptance.

ESSENCE—1500 Broadway, New York, NY 10036. Harriette Cole, Contemporary Living Ed. Provocative articles, 800 to 2,500 words, about black women in American today: self-help, how-to pieces, business and finance, health, celebrity profiles, and political issues. Short items, 500 to 750 words, on work, parenting, and health. Features and fiction, 800 to 2,500 words. Pays varying rates, on acceptance. Query for articles.

EXECUTIVE FEMALE—127 W. 24th St., New York, NY 10011. Mary Elizabeth Terzella, Ed. Features, 6 to 12 pages, on managing people, time, and careers, for women in business. Articles, 6 to 8 pages, for "More Money," "Horizons," "Profiles," and "Entrepreneur's Corner." Pays varying rates, on publication. Limited market.

FAMILY CIRCLE—110 Fifth Ave., New York, NY 10011. Susan Ungaro, Articles Ed. Susan Sherry, Sr. Ed. Leah Breier, Health Ed. Articles, to 2,500 words, on "women who have made a difference," marriage, family, and child-rearing issues; consumer affairs, travel, humor, health and fitness, personal opinion essays. Query required. Fiction: limited market. Seeks quality short stories that reflect real-life situations. Pays top rates, on acceptance.

FIRST FOR WOMEN—P.O. Box 1649, Englewood Cliffs, NJ 07632. Dennis Neeld, Ed. Articles, 1,200 words, and fiction, 5,000 to 6,000 words: "Real-life stories illustrating dire or uplifting situations any woman might find herself in." Address queries to Johnene Granger. Pay varies, on acceptance.

FLARE—777 Bay St., Toronto, Ontario, Canada M5W 1A7. Service articles, 1,500 to 2,000 words, on health, careers, relationships, and contemporary problems; articles on home decor, food, and entertaining for Canadian women age 18 to 34. Profiles, 200 to 800 words, of up-and-coming Canadians. Pays on acceptance. Query.

GLAMOUR—350 Madison Ave., New York, NY 10017. Ruth Whitney, Ed.-in-Chief. Barbara Coffey, Man. Ed. How-to articles, from 1,500 words, on careers, health, psychology, interpersonal relationships, etc., for women aged 18 to 35. Fashion and beauty pieces staff-written. Submit queries to Lisa Bain, Articles Ed. Pays from $500.

GOOD HOUSEKEEPING—959 Eighth Ave., New York, NY 10019. Joan Thursh, Articles Ed. Naome Lewis, Fiction Ed. In-depth articles and features on controversial problems, topical social issues; dramatic personal narratives with unusual experiences of average families; new or unusual medical information, personal medical stories. No submissions on food, beauty, needlework, and crafts. Short stories, 2,000 to 5,000 words, with strong identification for women, by published writers and "beginners with demonstrable talent." Pays top rates, on acceptance.

IDEALS—Nelson Place at Elm Hill Pike, P.O. Box 140300, Nashville, TN 37214-0300. Cynthia Wyatt, Ed. Articles, 600 to 800 words; poetry, 12 to 50 lines, no free verse. Light, reminiscent pieces of interest to women. Pays $10 for poems. Guidelines.

LADIES' HOME JOURNAL—100 Park Ave., New York, NY 10017. Myrna Blyth, Pub. Dir./Ed.-in-Chief. Articles of interest to women. Send queries with outlines to Lynn Langway, Exec. Ed. (news/celebrities); Linda Peterson, Articles Ed. (psychology/ human interest); Nelly Edmondson Gupta (health/medical); Lois Johnson (beauty/fashion/fitness); Marilyn Glass (decorating); Jan Hazard (food). Fiction and poetry accepted through literary agents only.

LEAR'S—655 Madison Ave., New York, NY 10021. Audreen Ballard, Exec. Ed. "Literate, lively, and compelling" articles, 800 to 1,200 words, for women over 40, on health, finance, personalities, and leisure. Query with clips and SASE. Pays $1 a word, on acceptance.

MCCALL'S—230 Park Ave., New York, NY 10169. Andrea Thompson, Ed. Articles, 1,000 to 3,000 words, on current issues, human interest, family relationships. Pays top rates, on acceptance.

MADEMOISELLE—350 Madison Ave., New York, NY 10017. Michelle Stacey, Man. Ed., Articles; Eileen Schnurr, Fiction Ed. Fiction and books. Pays $800 to $1,000 for short articles, from $1,750 for full-length features; $1,000 for short-short stories; from $2,000 for short stories, on acceptance.

MODERN BRIDE—475 Park Ave. South, New York, NY 10016. Mary Ann Cavlin, Man. Ed. Articles, 1,800 to 2,000 words, for bride and groom, on wedding planning, financial planning, juggling career and home, etc. Query Travel Editor Geri Bain with articles on honeymoon travel. Pays $600 to $1,200, on acceptance.

MS.—One Times Sq., New York, NY 10036. Address Manuscript Editor with SASE. Articles relating to women's roles and changing lifestyles; profiles, self-help, and general interest. Poetry and fiction neither accepted, acknowledged, nor returned. Pays competitive rates.

NA'AMAT WOMAN—200 Madison Ave., Suite 2120, New York, NY 10016. Judith Sokoloff, Ed. Articles on Jewish culture, women's issues, social and political topics, and Israel, 1,500 to 2,500 words. Short stories, with a Jewish theme. Pays 8¢ a word, on publication. Query or send manuscript.

NEW WOMAN—215 Lexington Ave., New York, NY 10016. Gay Bryant, Ed. Self-help/inspirational articles, on psychology, relationships, money, careers. Travel features, with personal discovery angle. Lifestyle, health, and fitness features. Profiles of celebrities, business women. Pays to $1 a word, on acceptance. Query with SASE.

NEW YORK WOMAN—2 Park Ave., New York, NY 10016. Betsy Carter, Ed. Articles, 500 to 3,000 words, for women age 25 to 45, living in the metropolitan New York area. Pays $1 a word, on publication. Queries with SASE required.

PLAYGIRL—801 Second Ave., New York, NY 10017. Nancie S. Martin, Ed.-in-Chief. In-depth articles for contemporary women. Fiction, 2,500 words. Humor, celebrity interviews. Pays varying rates. Query first with clips. Guidelines.

QUARANTE—P.O. Box 2875, Arlington, VA 22202. Michele Linden, Articles Ed. *The Magazine of Style and Substance for the Woman Who Has Arrived.* Features and fiction (to 3,000 words), poetry (3 to 18 lines), and short profiles for "Women of Substance" column. Topics include fashion, politics, health, cuisine, and finance geared to women over 30. Pays to $150, on publication. SASE required. Guidelines.

REDBOOK—224 W. 57th St., New York, NY 10019. Deborah Purcell, Fiction Ed. Diane Salvatore, Articles Ed. Fiction and articles for women ages 25 to 40. Pays from $1,000 for short stories to 25 typed pages; to $850 for short shorts, to 9 typed pages; $750 for personal-experience pieces, 1,000 to 2,000 words, on solving problems in marriage, family life, or community, for "Young Mother's Story." Query for articles only. SASE required.

SELF—350 Madison Ave., New York, NY 10017. Alexandra Penney, Ed. Query for articles on current women's issues. No poetry. Payment varies. Include SASE.

VIRTUE—P. O. Box 850, Sisters, OR 97759. Becky Durost-Fish, Ed. Articles, 1,000 to 1,500 words, on the family, marriage, self-esteem, working mothers, opinions, food, decorating. Fiction. Pays 10¢ a word, on publication. Query required.

WOMAN'S DAY—1515 Broadway, New York, NY 10036. Rebecca Greer, Articles, Ed. Eileen Herbert Jordan, Fiction Ed. Human-interest or helpful articles, to 3,500 words, on marriage, child-rearing, health, careers, relationships, money management. Dramatic narratives of medical miracles, rescues, etc. Pays top rates, on acceptance. Query.

WOMAN'S WORLD—270 Sylvan Ave., Englewood Cliffs, NJ 07632. Marilyn Webb, Feature Ed. Articles, 600 to 1,800 words, of interest to middle-income women between the ages of 18 and 60, on love, romance, careers, psychology, family life, investigative stories, dramatic adventures or crises. Pays $300 to $750, on acceptance. Query.

WOMEN IN BUSINESS—American Business Women's Assn., 900 Ward Pkwy., Box 8728, Kansas City, MO 64114. Laura M. Luckert, Ed. Features, 1,000 to 1,500 words, for working women between 35 and 55 years. No profiles. Pays on acceptance. Written query required.

WOMEN'S CIRCLE—P.O. Box 299, Lynnfield, MA 01940. Marjorie Pearl, Ed. Success stories on home-based female entrepreneurs. How-to articles on contemporary craft and needlework projects. Unique money-saving ideas and recipes. Pays varying rates, on acceptance.

WOMEN'S SPORTS & FITNESS—P.O. Box 2456, Winter Park, FL 32789. Lewis Rothlein, Ed. How-tos, profiles, and sports reports, 500 to 3,000 words, for active women. Fitness, nutrition, and health pieces also considered. Pays on publication. Query first

WORKING MOTHER—Working Woman/McCall's Group, 230 Park Ave., New York, NY 10169. Address Editorial Dept. Articles, to 1,000 words, that help women in their task of juggling job, home, and family. "We like humorous pieces that solve or illuminate a problem unique to our readers." Payment varies, on acceptance.

WORKING WOMAN—342 Madison Ave., New York, NY 10173. Lisa Higgins, Man. Ed. Articles, 1,000 to 2,500 words, on business and personal aspects of working women's lives. Pays from $400, on acceptance.

HOME AND LIFESTYLE PUBLICATIONS

THE AMERICAN ROSE MAGAZINE—P.O. Box 30,000, Shreveport, LA 71130. Harold S. Goldstein, Ed. Articles on home rose gardens: varieties, products, etc. Pays in copies.

BETTER HOMES AND GARDENS—1716 Locust St. , Des Moines, IA 50336. David Jordan, Ed. Articles, to 2,000 words, on home and family entertainment, money management, health, travel, pets, and cars. Pays top rates, on acceptance. Query.

CHILD—110 Fifth Ave., New York, NY 10011. Kate White, Ed. Bi-monthly magazine. Articles on the lifestyles of children and families. Departments: Fashion, Home Environment, Baby Best, and Travel. Pays from $750. Query.

CHOCOLATIER—Haymarket, Ltd. 45 W. 34th St., New York, NY 10001. Barbara Albright, Ed. Articles related to chocolate and desserts; cooking and baking techniques. Pays varying rates, on acceptance. Query required. Guidelines.

THE CHRISTIAN SCIENCE MONITOR—One Norway St., Boston, MA 02115. David Holmstrom, Features Ed. Articles on lifestyle trends, women's rights, family, parenting, consumerism, fashion, and food. Pays varying rates, on acceptance.

CONNOISSEUR—Hearst Corp., 1790 Broadway, 18th Fl., New York, NY 10019. Sarah Scrymser, Man. Ed. Articles for readers "interested in learning about excellence in all areas of art." Topics include fine, decorative, and performing arts, architecture and design, food, fashion, and travel; include pertinent service data. Length varies; query required. Pays about $1 a word, on acceptance.

CONSUMERS DIGEST—5705 N. Lincoln Ave., Chicago, IL 60659. John Manos, Ed. Articles, 500 to 3,000 words, on subjects of interest to consumers: products and services, automobiles, health, fitness, consumer legal affairs, and personal money management. Photos. Pays from 30¢ a word, extra for photos, on publication. Buys all rights. Query with resumé and published clips.

THE COOK'S MAGAZINE—2710 North Ave., Bridgeport, CT 06604. Deborah Hartz, Exec. Ed. Articles on trends in home and restaurant food and cooking. Query with brief outline, published clips, and sample recipe (for writing and recipe style). Pays $200 to $500, on acceptance. SASE required.

COUNTRY—5400 S. 60th St., Greendale, WI 53129. Address Jean Van Dyke. Pieces on interesting rural and country people who have unusual hobbies or businesses, 500 to 1,500 words; liberal use of direct quotes. Good, candid, color photos required. Pays on acceptance. Queries preferred.

DECORATING REMODELING—110 Fifth Ave., New York, NY 10011. Carol Sama Sheehan, Ed. Columns on finance and for "Man About the House" and "Where to Live." Articles on home decorating, remodeling, and gardening. Query first. Payment varies, on acceptance.

FARM AND RANCH LIVING—5400 S. 60th St., Greendale, WI 53129. Bob

Ottum, Ed. Articles, 2,000 words, on rural people and situations; nostalgia pieces, profiles of interesting farms and farmers, ranches and ranchers. Poetry. Pays $15 to $400, on acceptance and on publication.

FLORIDA HOME & GARDEN—600 Brickell Ave., Suite 207, Miami, FL 33131. Kathryn Howard, Ed. Features, 800 to 1,000 words, and department pieces, 500 to 900 words, about Florida interior design, architecture, landscape architecture, gardening, cuisine, fashion, trendy new products, and home entertaining. Pays $200 to $400, extra for photos.

FLOWER & GARDEN MAGAZINE—4251 Pennsylvania, Kansas City, MO 64111. Mr. A. Cort Sinnes, Ed. How-to articles, to 1,200 words, with photos, on indoor and outdoor home gardening. Pays varying rates, on acceptance. Query preferred.

FOOD & WINE—1120 Ave. of the Americas, New York, NY 10036. Ila Stanger, Ed.-in-Chief. Warren Picower, Man. Ed. Current culinary or beverage ideas for dining and entertaining at home and out. Submit detailed proposal.

GARDEN—The Garden Society, Botanical Garden, Bronx, NY 10458. Ann Botshon, Ed. Articles, 1,000 to 2,500 words, on botany, horticulture, ecology, agriculture. Photos. Pays to $300, on publication. Query.

GARDEN DESIGN—4401 Connecticut Ave. N.W., Fifth Floor, Washington, DC 20008. Karen D. Fishler, Ed. Articles, 1,500 to 2,000 words, on classic and contemporary examples of residential landscape design, garden art, and garden history. Pays $350 for features, $250 for departments, on publication. Query.

HARROWSMITH/USA—Ferry Rd., Charlotte, VT 05445. Tom Rawls, Ed. Investigative pieces, 4,000 to 5,000 words, on ecology, energy, health, gardening, do-it-yourself projects, and the food chain. Short pieces for "Screed" (opinions); and "Gazette" (news briefs). Pays $500 to $1,500 for features, from $50 to $600 for department pieces, on acceptance. Query required. Send SASE for guidelines.

THE HERB QUARTERLY—P. O. Box 548, Boiling Springs, PA 17007. Linda Sparrow, Ed. Articles, 2,000 to 10,000 words, on herbs: practical uses, cultivation, gourmet cooking, landscaping, herb tradition, unique garden designs, profiles of herb garden experts, practical how-tos for the herb businessperson. Include garden design when possible. Pays on publication. Guidelines.

HG: HOUSE & GARDEN—350 Madison Ave., New York, NY 10017. Nancy Novogrod, Ed.-in-Chief. Ellen Cannon Peck, Man. Ed. Articles on decorating, style, design, architecture, and the arts. No unsolicited articles.

HOME MAGAZINE—5900 Wilshire Blvd., 15th Fl., Los Angeles, CA 90036. Joseph Ruggiero, Ed. Articles of interest to homeowners: architecture, remodeling, decorating, how-tos, project ideas, landscaping, taxes, insurance, conservation, and solar energy. Pays varying rates, on acceptance. Query, with 50- to 200-word summary.

HOMEOWNER—3 Park Ave., New York, NY 10016. Joe Carter, Ed. Articles, 500 to 1,500 words, with photos, on home improvement, remodeling, landscaping, and do-it-yourself projects. Pays $400 to $1,000 for feature stories, on acceptance. Query.

HOMEOWNERS—8520 Sweetwater, Suite F57, Houston, TX 77037. Theresa Seegers, Man. Ed. Articles, 200 to 500 words, on buying and selling real estate, mortgages, investments, home improvement, interior design, consumer and business trends: "material should emphasize the importance of consulting a real estate professional on any real estate matter." Pays 10¢ to 20¢ a word, on acceptance. Query.

HORTICULTURE—Statler Bldg., 20 Park Plaza, Suite 1220, Boston, MA 02116. Debbie Starr, Articles Ed. Authoritative, well-written articles, 1,000 to 2,500 words, on all aspects of gardening. Pays competitive rates. Query first.

HOUSE BEAUTIFUL—1700 Broadway, New York, NY 10019. Joanna L. Krotz, Features Dir. Service articles related to the home. Pieces on design, travel and gardening mostly staff-written. Send for writer's guidelines. Query with detailed outline. SASE required.

HOUSTON METROPOLITAN MAGAZINE—(formerly *Houston Home & Garden*) 5615 Kirby, Suite 600, P.O. Box 25386, Houston, TX 77265. Gabrielle Cosgriff, Ed. Dir. Barbara Burgower, Man. Ed. Articles on home design and gardening, real estate, arts, lifestyles, health, travel; profiles. All material must have a strong Houston-area angle. Pays $50 to $500 for columns; $600 to $1,000 for feature articles. Query.

INDEPENDENT LIVING—44 Broadway, Greenlawn, NY 11740. Anne Kelly, Ed. Articles, 1,000 to 2,000 words, addressing lifestyles of persons who have disabilities. Possible topics: home health care, travel, sports, cooking, hobbies, family life, and sexuality. Pays 10¢ a word, on publication. Query.

LIFE IN THE TIMES—The Times Journal Co. , Springfield, VA 22159–0200. Barry Robinson, Ed. Travel articles, 900 words; features on food, 500 to 1,000 words; and short, personal-experience pieces, 750 words, of interest to military people and their families around the world. Pays from $25 to $150 for short pieces, to $350 for general-interest features up to 2,000 words, on acceptance.

LOG HOME GUIDE FOR BUILDERS & BUYERS—Rt. 2, Box 581, Cosby, TN 37722. Articles, 500 to 1,500 words, on building new, or restoring old, log homes, especially with solar or alternative heating systems, as well as pieces on decorating or profiles of interesting builders of log homes. Pays 20¢ a word, extra for photos, on publication. Limited market. Query first.

LOG HOME LIVING—610 Herndon Pkwy., Suite 500, Herndon, VA 22070. Roland Sweet, Man. Ed. Articles, 1,000 to 1,500 words, on modern manufactured and handcrafted kit log homes: home owner profiles; design and decor features; home producer profiles; historical features; technical articles. Pays $200 to $1,000, on acceptance.

MATURE HEALTH—45 W. 34th St., Suite 500, New York, NY 10001. David Allikas, Ed. Articles, 1,200 to 1,500 words, on exercise, the heart, sex, hypertension, fatigue, diabetes, arthritis, low back pain, nutrition, cholesterol reduction, mental wellnes, and health care costs; for people in their forties through their sixties. Fillers, 200 to 600 words. Query with clips. Pays 40¢ a word, on publication.

MATURE OUTLOOK—Meredith Corp., 1716 Locust, Des Moines, IA 50336. Marjorie P. Groves, Ed. Articles, 500 to 2,000 words, for "energetic" readers over the age of 50: covers travel and leisure topics, health, food, gardening, and personalities. Pays $200 to $1,500, on acceptance.

METROPOLITAN HOME—750 Third Ave., New York, NY 10017. Barbara Graustark, Articles Ed. Service and informational articles for metropolitan dwellers in apartments, houses, co-ops, lofts, and condos. Pays varying rates. Query.

MILITARY LIFESTYLE MAGAZINE—1732 Wisconsin Ave. N.W., Washington, DC 20007. Hope Daniels, Ed. Articles, 1,000 to 2,000 words, for military families in the U.S. and overseas; pieces on child raising, marriage, health, fitness, food, and issues concerning young military families; home decor and "portable" or "instant" gardening articles; fiction. Pays $200 to $600, on publication. Query first.

THE MOTHER EARTH NEWS—105 Stoney Mt. Rd., Hendersonville, NC

28791. Bruce Woods, Ed. Articles on country living: home improvement and construction, how-tos, indoor and outdoor gardening, crafts and projects, etc. Also self-help, health, food-related, ecology, energy, and consumerism pieces; profiles. Pays from $100 per published page, on acceptance. Address Submissions Ed.

NATIONAL GARDENING MAGAZINE—180 Flynn Ave., Burlington, VT 05401. Ms. Kit Anderson, Ed. Articles, 300 to 3,000 words: seed-to-table profiles of major crops; firsthand reports from experienced gardeners in this country's many growing regions; easy-to-follow gardening techniques; garden food recipes; coverage of fruits, vegetables, and ornamentals. Pays $75 to $450, extra for photos, on acceptance. Query preferred.

NEW AGE JOURNAL—342 Western Ave., Brighton, MA 02135. Florence Graves, Ed./Assoc. Pub. Features, 2,000 to 4,000 words; columns, 750 to 1,500 words; short news items, 500 words; and first-person narratives, 750 to 1,500 words, for readers who take an active interest in holistic health, personal and spiritual growth, social responsibility, and contemporary social issues. Pays varying rates. Query or send completed manuscript.

NEW CHOICES FOR THE BEST YEARS—28 W. 23rd St., New York, NY 10010. Carol Mauro, Exec. Ed. Lifestyle/service magazine for people aged 50 and over. Articles, 1,500 to 2,500 words: careers, health/fitness, travel, gardening, relationships, entertaining, and finance. Columns, 1,000 to 1,500 words: "Decisions," "Comfort Zone," "Generations," "Collecting," and "Back Talk" (humor). Send complete manuscript with SASE. Payment varies, on acceptance.

NEW HOME—P.O. Box 2008, Laconia, NH 03247. Steven Maviglio, Man. Ed. Articles, 250 to 2,500 words, "that give upscale new homeowners whatever they need to make their home more comfortable, practical, and personal." Department pieces on lawn care, roofing, and interviews with professionals in their homes. Pays $200 to $1,000, on acceptance. Query required.

1001 HOME IDEAS—3 Park Ave., New York, NY 10016. Ellen Frankel, Ed. General-interest articles, 500 to 2,000 words, on home decorating, furnishings, food, household tips, crafts, remodeling, gardening. How-to and problem-solving decorating pieces. Pays varying rates, on acceptance. Query.

PALM SPRINGS LIFE—Desert Publications, 303 N. Indian Ave., Palm Springs, CA 92262. Rebecca Kurtz, Ed. Articles (1,000 to 1,500 words) of interest to "wealthy, upscale people who live and/or play in the desert." Pays $150 to $200 for features, $30 for short profiles, on publication. Query required.

PEOPLE IN ACTION—P.O. Box 10010, Ogden, UT 84409. Address Editor. Cover stories, 1,200 words, on living, renowned individuals in fine arts, entertainment, communications, business, sports, education, health, science, and technology. "People featured must exemplify positive values, overcome obstacles, help others, advance culture, and create solutions." Send high-quality, color transparencies illustrating manuscript. Query first with SASE.

SELECT HOMES—3835 W. 30th Ave., Vancouver, B.C., Canada V6S 1W9. Pam Withers, Western Ed. How-to articles, profiles of Canadian homes, 750 to 1,200 words. Pays from $250 to $700 (Canadian), on acceptance. Query regional editors: Pam Withers, Western Ed. (address above), or Diane McDougall, Ed., 2300 Yonge St., #410, Toronto, Canada M4P 1E4. Include International Reply Coupons. Send SASE for guidelines.

WEIGHT WATCHERS MAGAZINE—360 Lexington Ave., New York, NY 10017. Ruth Papazian, Articles Ed. Articles on nutrition and health. Pays from $250, on acceptance. Query with clips required. Guidelines.

WORKBENCH—4251 Pennsylvania, Kansas City, MO 64111. Robert N. Hoffman, Ed. Illustrated how-to articles on home improvement and woodworking, with detailed instructions. Pays from $150 per printed page, on acceptance. Send SASE for writers' guidelines.

YOUR HOME/INDOORS & OUT—P.O. Box 10010, Ogden, UT 84409. Articles, 1,200 words, with fresh ideas in all areas of home decor: the latest in home construction (exteriors, interiors, building materials, design); the outdoors at home (landscaping, pools, patios, gardening); home management, buying and selling. "We are especially interested in articles on choosing a realtor or home builder." No do-it-yourself pieces. Manuscripts, 1,200 words, with quality color transparencies. Query first with SASE to editor.

SPORTS, OUTDOORS, RECREATION

AAA WORLD—AAA Headquarters, 1000 AAA Dr., Heathrow, FL 32746–5064. Douglas Damerst, Ed. Automobile and travel concerns, including automotive travel, maintenance and upkeep, 750 to 1,500 words. Pays $300 to $600, on acceptance. Query with clips preferred.

THE AMERICAN FIELD—542 S. Dearborn, Chicago, IL 60605. William F. Brown, Ed. Yarns about hunting trips, bird-shooting; articles to 1,500 words, on dogs and field trials, emphasizing conservation of game resources. Pays varying rates, on acceptance.

AMERICAN GOLF MAGAZINE—4500 S. Lakeshore Dr., Suite 336, Tempe, AZ 85282. Michael A. Cox, Ed. Articles, 800 to 2,000 words, aimed at public golfers; "we never write about courses that the general golfer cannot play." Travel pieces (1,500 to 2,500 words), course reviews, profiles (600 to 800 words), and shorts (150 words). Pays $50 to $300, on publication. Query preferred. Guidelines.

AMERICAN HANDGUNNER—591 Camino de la Reina, Suite 200, San Diego, CA 92108. Cameron Hopkins, Ed. Semi-technical articles on shooting sports, gun repair and alteration, handgun matches and tournaments, for lay readers. Pays $100 to $500, on publication. Query.

AMERICAN HUNTER—470 Spring Park Place, Suite 1000, Herndon, VA 22070. Tom Fulgham, Ed. Articles, 1,400 to 2,500 words, on hunting. Photos. Pays on acceptance. Guidelines.

AMERICAN MOTORCYCLIST—American Motorcyclist Assn., Box 6114, Westerville, OH 43081–6114. Greg Harrison, Ed. Articles and fiction, to 3,000 words, on motorcycling: news coverage, personalities, tours. Photos. Pays varying rates, on publication. Query with SASE.

THE AMERICAN RIFLEMAN—470 Spring Park Place, Suite 1000, Herndon, VA 22070. Bill Parkerson, Ed. Factual articles on use and enjoyment of sporting firearms. Pays on acceptance.

AMERICAN SQUAREDANCE MAGAZINE—216 Williams St., P.O. Box 488, Huron, OH 44839. Cathie Burdick, Ed. Articles and fiction, 1,000 to 1,500 words, related to square dancing. Poetry. Fillers to 100 words. Pays $2 per column inch.

ARCHERY WORLD—See *Bowhunting World*.

THE ATLANTIC SALMON JOURNAL—1435 St. Alexandre, Suite 1030, Montreal, Quebec, Canada H3A 2G4. Terry Davis, Ed. Material related to Atlantic salmon: conservation, ecology, travel, politics, biology, how-tos, anecdotes, cuisine. Articles, 1,500 to 3,000 words. Pays $100 to $350, on publication.

BACKPACKER MAGAZINE—Rodale Press, 33 Minor St., Emmaus, PA 18098. John Viehman, Exec. Ed. Articles, 250 to 3,000 words, on backpacking, technique, kayaking/canoeing, mountaineering, alpine/nordic skiing, health, natural science. Photos. Pays varying rates. Query.

THE BACKSTRETCH—19363 James Couzens Hwy., Detroit, MI 48235. Ruth LeGrove, Man. Ed. Ann Moss, Ed. United Thoroughbred Trainers of America. Feature articles, with photos, on subjects involved with thoroughbred horse racing. Pays after publication.

BASEBALL ILLUSTRATED—See *Hockey Illustrated.*

BASSIN'—15115 S. 76th E. Ave., Bixby, OK 74008. Gordon Sprouse, Man. Ed. Articles, 1,500 to 1,800 words, on how-to and where-to bass fish, for the average fisherman. Pays $275 to $400, on acceptance.

BASSMASTER MAGAZINE—B.A.S.S. Publications, P.O. Box 17900, Montgomery, AL 36141. Dave Precht, Ed. Articles, 1,500 to 2,000 words, with photos, on freshwater black bass and striped bass. "Short Casts" pieces, 400 to 800 words, on news, views, and items of interest. Pays $200 to $400, on acceptance. Query.

BAY & DELTA YACHTSMAN—2019 Clement Ave., Alameda, CA 94501. Bill Parks, Ed. Cruising stories and features. Must have Northern California tie-in. Photos and illustrations. Pays varying rates.

BC OUTDOORS—1132 Hamilton St., #202, Vancouver, B.C., Canada V6B 2S2. George Will, Ed. Articles, to 2,000 words, on fishing, hunting, conservation, and all forms of non-competitive outdoor recreation in British Columbia and Yukon. Photos. Pays from 15¢ to 25¢ a word, on acceptance.

BICYCLE GUIDE—711 Boylston St., Boston, MA 02116. Theodore Costantino, Ed. "Our magazine covers, from an enthusiast's perspective, all aspects of cycling: racing, touring, sport riding, product reviews, and technical information. We depend on free lancers for touring articles, personality profiles, and race coverage." Queries are preferred. Pays varying rates, on publication.

BICYCLING—33 E. Minor St., Emmaus, PA 18098. James C. McCullagh, Ed. Articles, 500 to 2,500 words, on recreational riding, fitness training, nutrition, bike maintenance, equipment, racing and touring, for serious cyclists. Photos, illustrations. Pays $25 to $1000, on acceptance. Guidelines.

BIKEREPORT—Bikecentennial, P.O. Box 8308, Missoula, MT 59807. Daniel D'Ambrosio, Ed. Accounts of bicycle tours in the U.S. and overseas, interviews, personal-experience pieces, humor, and news shorts, 1,200 to 2,500 words. Pays $25 to $65 per published page.

BIRD WATCHER'S DIGEST—P.O Box 110, Marietta, OH 45750. Mary B. Bowers, Ed. Articles, 600 to 2,500 words, for bird watchers: first-person accounts; how-tos; pieces on endangered species; profiles. Cartoons. Pays to $50, on publication.

BLACK BELT—P.O. Box 7728, 1813 Victory Pl., Burbank, CA 91510-7728. Articles related to self-defense: how-tos on fitness and technique; historical, travel, philosophical subjects. Pays $100 to $200, on publication. Query required. Guidelines.

BOAT PENNSYLVANIA—Pennsylvania Fish Commission, P.O. Box 1673,

Harrisburg, PA 17105–1673. Articles, 200 to 2,500 words, with photos, on boating in Pennsylvania: motorboating, sailing, waterskiing, canoeing, kayaking, and rafting. No pieces on fishing. Pays $50 to $300, on acceptance. Query. Guidelines.

BOUNDARY WATERS JOURNAL—Route 1, Box 1740, Ely, MN 55731. Stuart Osthoff, Ed. Articles, 2,000 to 3,000 words, on recreation and natural resources in Minnesota's Boundary Waters Canoe area wilderness and Ontario's Quetico Provincial Park. Regular features include canoe route journals, fishing, camping, hiking, cross-country skiing, wildlife and nature, regional lifestyles, history, and events. Pays $200-$400, on publication; $50-$150 for photos.

BOW & ARROW HUNTING—Box HH, 34249 Camino Capistrano, Capistrano Beach, CA 92624. Roger Combs, Ed. Dir. Articles, 1,200 to 2,500 words, with photos, on bowhunting; profiles and technical pieces. Pays $50 to $300, on acceptance. Same address and mechanical requirements for *Gun World.*

BOWHUNTER MAGAZINE—2245 Kohn Rd., Box 8200, Harrisburg, PA 17105–8200. M.R. James, Ed. Informative, entertaining features, 500 to 5,000 words, on bow and arrow hunting. Fillers. Photos. Pays $25 to $300, on acceptance. Study magazine first.

BOWHUNTING WORLD—(formerly *Archery World*) 319 Barry Ave. S., Suite 101, Wayzata, MN 55391. Tim Dehn, Ed. Articles, 1,000 to 2,500 words, on all aspects of bowhunting, with photos. Pays from $200, extra for photos, on publication.

BOWLERS JOURNAL—101 E. Erie St., Chicago, IL 60611. Mort Luby, Ed. Trade and consumer articles, 1,200 to 2,200 words, with photos, on bowling. Pays $75 to $200, on acceptance.

BOWLING—5301 S. 76th St., Greendale, WI 53129. Dan Matel, Ed. Articles, to 1,500 words, on amateur league and tournament bowling. Profiles. Pays varying rates, on publication.

CALIFORNIA ANGLER—1921 E. Carnegie St., Suite N, Santa Ana, CA 92705. Jim Matthews, Ed. How-to and where-to articles, 2,000 words, for freshwater and saltwater anglers in California: travel, new products, fishing techniques, profiles. Photos. Pays $75 to $350, on acceptance. Query first.

CALIFORNIA BASKETBALL MAGAZINE—See *California Football Magazine.*

CALIFORNIA FOOTBALL MAGAZINE—1330 E. 223rd St., Suite 501, Carson, CA 90745. David Raatz, Ed. Articles, 250 to 2,000 words, related to California high school, junior college, college, and professional football programs and standout Californians playing in other states. Pays $25 to $300, on acceptance. Query with writing samples. Same requirements for *California Basketball Magazine.*

CALIFORNIA HORSE REVIEW—P.O. Box 2437, Fair Oaks, CA 95628. Articles, 750 to 2,500 words, on horse training, for professional horsemen; profiles of prominent West Coast horses and riders. Pays $35 to $125, on publication.

CANOE—P.O. Box 3146, Kirkland, WA 98083. David F. Harrison, Ed.-in-Chief. Features, 2,000 to 4,000 words; department pieces, 500 to 2,000 words, on competition, political and environmental affairs, equipment, health, how-tos, etc. Pays $5 per column inch, on publication. Query preferred.

CAR AND DRIVER—2002 Hogback Rd., Ann Arbor, MI 48105. William Jeanes, Ed. Articles, to 2,500 words, for enthusiasts, on car manufacturers, new developments in cars, etc. Pays to $2,000, on acceptance. Query with clips.

CAR CRAFT—8490 Sunset Blvd., Los Angeles, CA 90069. Cameron Benty, Ed. Articles and photofeatures on unusual street machines, drag cars, racing events; technical pieces; action photos. Pays from $150 per page, on publication.

CASCADES EAST—716 N.E. Fourth St., P.O. Box 5784, Bend, OR 97708. Geoff Hill, Ed./Pub. Articles, 1,000 to 2,000 words, on outdoor activities, (fishing, hunting, golfing, backpacking, rafting, skiing, snowmobiling, etc.), history, special events, and scenic tours in Cascades region. Photos. Pays 3¢ to 10¢ a word, extra for photos, on publication.

CHESAPEAKE BAY MAGAZINE—1819 Bay Ridge Ave., Annapolis, MD 21403. Betty Rigoli, Ed. Technical and how-to articles, to 1,500 words, on boating, fishing, conservation, in Chesapeake Bay. Photos. Pays $85 to $125, on publication.

CITY SPORTS—P.O Box 3693, San Francisco, CA 94119. Jane McConnell, Ed. Articles, 200 to 2,000 words, on the active lifestyle, including service pieces, trend pieces, profiles, and business. Pays $50 to $650, on publication. Query appropriate editor.

CROSS COUNTRY SKIER—33 E. Minor St., Emmaus, PA 18049. Tom Shealey, Man. Ed. Articles, to 3,000 words, on all aspects of cross-country skiing. Departments, 1,000 to 1,500 words, on ski maintenance, skiing techniques, health and fitness. Published October through February. Pays $300 to $700 for features, $100 to $350 for departments, on publication. Query.

CRUISING WORLD—524 Thames St., Newport, RI 02840. George Day, Ed. Articles on sailing, 1,000 to 2,500 words: technical and personal narratives. No fiction, poetry, or logbook transcripts. 35mm slides. Pays $100 to $600, on acceptance. Query preferred.

CYCLING U.S.A.—U.S. Cycling Federation, 1750 E. Boulder St., Colorado Springs, CO 80909. Diane Fritschner, Ed. Articles, 500 to 1,500 words, on bicycle racing. Pays 10¢ a word, on publication. Query first.

CYCLIST—20816 Higgins Ct., Torrance, CA 90501. John Francis, Ed. Articles on all aspects on bicycling: touring, travel, and equipment. Query required.

THE DIVER—P.O. Box 249, Cobalt, CT 06414. Bob Taylor, Ed. Articles on divers, coaches, officials, springboard and platform techniques, training tips, etc. Pays $15 to $40, extra for photos ($5 to $25 for cartoons), on publication.

EQUUS—Fleet Street Corp., 656 Quince Orchard Rd., Gaithersburg, MD 20878. Emily Kilby, Ed. 1,000- to 3,000-word articles on all breeds of horses, covering their health, care, the latest advances in equine medicine and research, and horse-world events. "Attempt to speak as one horse-person to another." Pays $100 to $400, on acceptance.

FIELD & STREAM—2 Park Ave., New York, NY 10016. Duncan Barnes, Ed. Articles, 1,500 to 2,500 words, with photos, on hunting, fishing. Fillers, 250 to 1000 words. Cartoons. Pays from $800 for feature articles with photos, $250 to $450 for fillers, $100 for cartoons, on acceptance. Query for articles.

FINS AND FEATHERS—318 W. Franklin Ave., Minneapolis, MN 55404. James F. Billig, Ed. Articles, 2,000 to 2,500 words, on a wide variety of recreational activities, including hunting, fishing, camping, and environmental issues. Pays $100 to $500, on publication. Query.

FISHING WORLD—51 Atlantic Ave., Floral Park, NY 11001. Keith Gardner, Ed. Features, to 2,500 words, with color transparencies, on fishing sites, technique, equipment. Pays to $500 for major features, $200 for shorter destination articles. Query preferred.

THE FLORIDA HORSE—P.O. Box 2106, Ocala, FL 32678. Bernie Dickman, Ed. Articles, 1,500 words, on Florida Thoroughbred breeding and racing. Pays $100 to $200, on publication.

FLY FISHERMAN—Box 8200, Harrisburg, PA 17105. John Randolph, Ed. Articles, to 3,000 words, on how to and where to fly fish. Fillers, to 100 words. Pays from $50 to $500, on acceptance. Query.

THE FLYFISHER—1387 Cambridge, Idaho Falls, ID 83401. Dennis G. Bitton, Ed. Articles, 500 to 3,000 words, on techniques, lore, history, and flyfishing personalities; how-pieces. Serious or humorous short stories related to flyfishing. Pays from $50 to $200, after publication. Queries are preferred. Guidelines.

FLYFISHING NEWS, VIEWS AND REVIEWS—1387 Cambridge, Idaho Falls, ID 83401. Dennis G. Bitton, Ed. Articles 500–3,500 words on flyfishing, fiction, humor, nonfiction reports, or where tos/ how tos. Guest opinion articles and letters to the editor. Pays $50 to $150 for articles, $25 to $50 for prints or drawings. Queries preferred.

FLYING MAGAZINE—1515 Broadway, New York, NY 10036. William Garvey, Ed.-in-Chief. Articles, 1,500 words, on personal flying experiences. Pays varying rates, on acceptance.

FOOTBALL DIGEST—Century Publishing Co., 990 Grove St., Evanston, IL 60201. Michael K. Herbert, Ed.-in-Chief. Profiles of pro stars, "think" pieces, 1,500 words, aimed at the pro football fan. Pays on publication.

FOOTBALL FORECAST—See *Hockey Illustrated.*

FUR-FISH-GAME—2878 E. Main St., Columbus, OH 43209. Mitch Cox, Ed. Illustrated articles, 800 to 2,500 words, preferably with how-to angle, on hunting, fishing, trapping, dogs, camping, or other outdoor topics. Some humorous or where-to articles. Pays $40 to $150, on acceptance.

GAME AND FISH PUBLICATIONS—P.O. Box 741, Marietta, GA 30061. Publishes 34 monthly outdoors magazines for 48 states. Articles, 1,500 to 2,500 words, on hunting and fishing. How-tos, where-tos, and adventure pieces. Profiles of successful hunters and fishermen. No hiking, canoeing, camping, or backpacking pieces. Pays $125 to $175 for state-specific articles, $200 to $300 for multi-state articles, before publication. Pays, $25 to $75 for photos.

GOAL—650 Fifth Ave., 33rd Fl., New York, NY 10019. Michael A. Berger, Ed. Official magazine of the National Hockey League. Player profiles and trend stories, 1,000 to 1,800 words, for hockey fans with knowledge of the game and players, by writers with understanding of the sport. Pays $150 to $300, on acceptance. Query.

GOLF DIGEST—5520 Park Ave., Trumbull, CT 06611. Jerry Tarde, Ed. Instructional articles, tournament reports, and features on players, to 2,500 words. Fiction, 1,000 to 3,000 words. Poetry, fillers, humor, photos. Pays varying rates, on acceptance. Query preferred.

GOLF FOR WOMEN—426 S. Lamar Blvd., Oxford, MS 38655. Geoge Kehoe, Ed.-in-Chief. Golf-related articles of interest to women; fillers and humor. Instructional pieces staff written. Pays from 25¢ a word, on publication. Query first.

GOLF ILLUSTRATED—3 Park Ave., New York, NY 10016. Al Barkow, Ed. Hal Goodman, Man. Ed. Golf-related features, 1,000 to 2,000 words: instruction, profiles, photo essays, travel, technique, nostalgia, opinion. Pays $750 to $1,500, on acceptance. Query preferred.

GOLF JOURNAL—Golf House, Far Hills, NJ 07931. Robert Sommers, Ed.

U.S. Golf Assn. Articles on golf personalities, history, travel. Humor. Photos. Pays varying rates, on publication.

GOLF MAGAZINE—2 Park Ave., New York, NY 10016. James Frank, Exec. Ed. Articles, 1,500 words with photos, on golf. Shorts, to 500 words. Pays $500 to $1,000 for articles, $75 to $150 for shorts, on publication.

GREAT LAKES SAILOR—572 W. Market St., Suite 6, P.O. Box 951, Akron, OH 44309. Drew Shippy, Ed. How-to pieces on sailing and navigational techniques; human-interest stories; and department pieces. "Destinations" (2,500 to 3,000 words, on cruises), "Trailor Sailor" (trips for day sailors, 1,500 words), and "First Person" (profiles, 2,500 to 3,000 words). Photos. Pays to 20¢ a word, on publication. Queries required. Guidelines.

THE GREYHOUND REVIEW—National Greyhound Association, Box 543, Abilene, KS 67410. Tim Horan, Man. Ed. Articles, 1,000 to 10,000 words, pertaining to the greyhound racing industry: how-to, historical nostalgia, interviews. Pays $85 to $150, on publication.

GULF COAST GOLFER—See *North Texas Golfer.*

GUN DIGEST AND HANDLOADER'S DIGEST—4092 Commercial Ave., Northbrook, IL 60062. Ken Warner, Ed. Well-researched articles, to 5,000 words, on guns and shooting, equipment, etc. Photos. Pays from 10¢ a word, on acceptance. Query.

GUN DOG—P.O. Box 35098, Des Moines, IA 50315. Bob Wilbanks, Man. Ed. Features, 1,000 to 2,500 words, with photos, on bird hunting: how-tos, where-tos, dog training, canine medicine, breeding strategy. Fiction Humor. Pays $50 to $150 for fillers and short articles, $150 to $350 for features, on acceptance.

GUN WORLD—See *Bow & Arrow Hunting.*

GUNS & AMMO—8490 Sunset Blvd., Los Angeles, CA 90069. E. G. Bell, Jr., Ed. Technical and general articles, 1,500 to 3,000 words, on guns, ammunition, and target shooting. Photos, fillers. Pays from $150, on acceptance.

HANG GLIDING—U.S. Hang Gliding Assn., P.O. Box 500, Pearblossom, CA 93553. Gilbert Dodgen, Ed. Articles and fiction, 2 to 3 pages, on hang gliding. Pays to $50, on publication. Query.

HOCKEY ILLUSTRATED—Lexington Library, Inc., 355 Lexington Ave., New York, NY 10017. Stephen Ciacciarelli, Ed. Articles, 2,500 words, on hockey players, teams. Pays $125, on publication. Query. Same address and requirements for *Baseball Illustrated, Wrestling World, Pro Basketball Illustrated, Pro Football Illustrated, Basketball Annual* (college), *Baseball Preview, Baseball Forecast, Pro Football Preview, Football Forecast,* and *Basketball Forecast.*

HORSE & RIDER—941 Calle Negocio, San Clemente, CA 92672. Ray Rich, Ed. Articles, 500 to 3,000 words, with photos, on Western riding and general horse care geared to the performance horse: training, feeding, grooming, etc. Pays varying rates, on publication. Buys all rights. Guidelines.

HORSE WORLD USA—P.O. Box 249, Huntington Station, NY 11746. Diana DeRosa, Ed. Horse-related articles of varying lengths of interest to horse enthusiasts. Pays on publication. Query.

HORSEMAN—25025 I 45N, Suite 390, Spring, TX 77380. David T. Gaines, Ed./Pub. Instructional articles, to 2,500 words, with photos, for Western trainers and riders. Pays from $50.

HORSEMEN'S YANKEE PEDLAR—785 Southbridge St., Auburn, MA 01501. Nancy L. Khoury, Pub. News and feature-length articles, about horses and horsemen in the Northeast. Photos. Pays $2 per published inch, on publication. Query.

HORSEPLAY—P.O. Box 130, Gaithersburg, MD 20877. Cordelia Doucet, Ed. Articles, 1,800 to 3,000 words, on eventing, show jumping, horse shows, dressage, driving, and fox hunting, for horse enthusiasts. Pays 10¢ a word for all rights, 9¢ a word for first American rights, after publication. Query. SASE required.

HOT BIKE—2145 W. La Palma, Anaheim, CA 92801. Buck Lovell, Ed. Articles, 250 to 2,500 words, with photos, on motorcycles (contemporary and antique). Event coverage on high performance street and track and sport touring motorcycles, with emphasis on Harley Davidsons. Pays $50 to $100 per printed page, on publication.

HOT BOAT—Sport Publications 500 Harrington St., Suite I, Corona, CA 91720. Kevin Spaise, Exec. Ed. Family-oriented articles on motorized water sport events and personalities: general-interest, how-to, and technical features, 600 to 1,000 words. Pays $85 to $300, on publication. Query.

HOT ROD—8490 Sunset Blvd., Los Angeles, CA 90069. Jeff Smith, Ed. How-to pieces and articles, 500 to 5,000 words, on auto mechanics, hot rods, track and drag racing. Photo-features on custom or performance-modified cars. Pays to $250 per page, on publication.

HUNTING—8490 Sunset Blvd., Los Angeles, CA 90069. Craig Boddington, Ed. How-to articles on practical aspects of hunting. At least 15 photos required with articles. Pays $250 to $400 for articles with B&W photos, extra for color photos, on publication.

INSIDE CYCLING—See *Velonews.*

INSIDE RUNNING & FITNESS—See *Inside Texas Running.*

INSIDE TEXAS RUNNING—(formerly *Inside Running & Fitness*) 9514 Bristlebrook Dr., Houston, TX 77083. Joanne Schmidt, Ed. Articles and fillers on running, cycling, and triathlons in Texas. Pays $35 to $100, $10 for photos, on acceptance.

KEEPIN' TRACK OF VETTES—P.O. Box 48, Spring Valley, NY 10977. Shelli Finkel, Ed. Articles of any length, with photos, relating to Corvettes. Pays $25 to $200, on publication.

KITPLANES—P.O. Box 6050, Mission Viejo, CA 92690. Dave Martin, Ed. Articles geared to the growing market of aircraft built from kits and plans by home craftsmen, on all aspects of design, construction, and performance, 1,000 to 4,000 words. Pays $100 to $300, on publication.

LAKELAND BOATING—1600 Orrington Ave., Suite 500, Evanston, IL 60201. Douglas Seibold, Ed. Articles for boat owners on the Great Lakes and other area waterways, on long distance cruising, short trips, maintenance, equipment, history, regional personalities and events, and environment. Photos. Pays on acceptance. Query first. Guidelines.

MEN'S FITNESS—21100 Erwin St., Woodland Hills, CA 91367. Jim Rosenthal, Features Ed. Features, 1,500 to 2,500 words, and department pieces, 1,000 to 1,500 words: "authoritative and practical articles dealing with fitness, health, and men's lifestyles." Pays $200 to $400, on acceptance.

MEN'S HEALTH—Rodale Press, 33 E. Minor Dr., Emmaus, PA 18098.

Michael Lafavore, Exec. Ed. Articles, 1,000 to 2,500 words, on fitness, diet, health, relationships, sports, and travel, for men ages 25 to 55. Pays 50¢ a word, on acceptance. Query first.

MICHIGAN OUT-OF-DOORS—P.O. Box 30235, Lansing, MI 48909. Kenneth S. Lowe, Ed. Features, 1,500 to 2,500 words, on hunting, fishing, camping, and conservation in Michigan. Pays $75 to $150, on acceptance.

MID-WEST OUTDOORS—111 Shore Dr., Hinsdale, IL 60521. Gene Laulunen, Ed. Articles, 1,500 words, with photos, on where, when, and how to fish and hunt in the Midwest. Fillers, 500 words. Pays $15 to $35, on publication.

MOTOR TREND—8490 Sunset Blvd., Los Angeles, CA 90069. Mike Anson, Ed. Articles, 250 to 2,000 words, on autos, racing, events, and profiles. Photos. Pay varies, on acceptance. Query.

MOTORCYCLIST—8490 Sunset Blvd., Los Angeles, CA 90069. Art Friedman, Ed. Articles, 1,000 to 3,000 words. Action photos. Pays varying rates, on publication.

MOTORHOME MAGAZINE—29901 Agoura Rd., Agoura, CA 91301. Bob Livingston, Ed. Articles, to 2,000 words, with color slides, on motorhomes; travel and how-to pieces. Pays to $600, on acceptance.

MOUNTAIN BIKE—Rodale Press, 33 E. Minor St., Emmaus, PA 18098. Ed Pavelka, Ed. Dir. Articles, 1,200 to 2,000 words, on mountain bike touring; major off-road events; political, sport, or land-access issues; riding techniques; fitness and training tips. Pays $200 to $400, on publication. Query first.

MUSCULAR DEVELOPMENT—351 W. 45th St., New York, NY 10019. Alan Paul, Ed. Articles, 1,000 to 2,500 words, on competitive body building and weight training, personality profiles, training features, and diet and nutrition pieces. Photos. Pays $100 to $300 for articles; $25 for photos and $300 to $400 for cover photos.

MUSHING—P.O. Box 149, Ester, AK 99725. Todd Hoener, Ed. How-tos, profiles, and features (1,500 to 2,000 words) and department pieces (500 to 1,000 words) for competitive and recreational mushers and skijorers. Humor and photos. Pays $25 to $250, after acceptance. Queries preferred. Guidelines.

NATIONAL RACQUETBALL—400 Douglas Ave., Suite B, Dunedin, FL 34698. Helen Quinn, Pub./Man. Ed. Articles, 800 to 1,200 words, on health and conditioning. How-tos. Profiles. Fiction. Material must be related to racquetball, health/fitness, diet, etc. Pays $25 to $150, on publication. Photos.

NAUTICAL QUARTERLY—Pratt St., Essex, CT 06426. Joseph Gribbins, Ed. In-depth articles, 3,000 to 7,000 words, about boats and boating, U.S. and foreign. Pays $500 to $1,000, on acceptance.

THE NEW ENGLAND SKIERS GUIDE—Box 1125, Waitsfield, VT 05673. Karla Hostetter, Assoc. Ed. Annual (September closing). Articles on alpine and nordic skiing, equipment, and winter vacations at New England resorts. Color slides helpful. Rates vary.

NORTH TEXAS GOLFER—9182 Old Katy Rd., Suite 212, Houston, TX 77055. Bob Gray, Ed. Articles, 800 to 1,500 words, of interest to golfers in North Texas. Pays $50 to $250, on publication. Queries required. Same requirements for *Golf Coast Golfer.*

NORTHEAST OUTDOORS—P.O. Box 2180, Waterbury, CT 06722–2180. Jean Wertz, Ed. Articles, 500 to 1,800 words, preferably with B&W photos, on camping in Northeast U.S.: recommended private campgrounds, camp cookery, recreational vehicle hints. Stress how-to, where-to. Cartoons. Pays $20 to $80, on publication. Guidelines.

OFFSHORE—220 Reservoir St., Needham Heights, MA 02194. Martha Lostrom, Ed. Articles, 1,200 to 2,500 words, on boats, people, and places along the New England, New York, and New Jersey coasts. Photos a plus. Pays $100 to $300.

ON TRACK—17165 Newhope St., "M," Fountain Valley, CA 92708. Andrew Crask and Craig Fisher, Eds. Features and race reports, 500 to 2,500 words. Pays $4 per column inch, on publication.

OPEN WHEEL—P.O. Box 715, Ipswich, MA 01938. Dick Berggren, Ed. Articles, to 6,000 words, on open wheel drivers, races, and vehicles. Photos. Pays to $400 on publication.

OUTDOOR AMERICA—1401 Wilson Blvd., Level B, Arlington, VA 22209. Quarterly publication of the Izaak Walton League of America. Articles, 1,500 to 2,000 words, on natural resource conservation issues and outdoor recreation; especially fishing, hunting, and camping. Pays 20¢ a word for features. Query Articles Ed. with published clippings.

OUTDOOR LIFE—2 Park Ave., New York, NY 10016. Clare Conley, Ed. Articles on hunting, fishing, and related subjects. Pays top rates, on acceptance.

OUTSIDE—1165 N. Clark, Chicago, IL 60610. High-quality articles, with photos, on sports, nature, wilderness travel, adventure, etc. Pays varying rates. Query.

PENNSYLVANIA ANGLER—Pennsylvania Fish Commission, P.O. Box 1673, Harrisburg, PA 17105–1673. Address Ed. Articles, 250 to 2,500 words, with photos, on freshwater fishing in Pennsylvania. Pays $50 to $300, on acceptance. Must send SASE with all material. Query. Guidelines.

PENNSYLVANIA GAME NEWS—Game Commission, Harrisburg, PA 17110–9797. Bob Bell, Ed. Articles, to 2,500 words, with photos, on outdoor subjects, except fishing and boating. Photos. Pays from 5¢ a word, extra for photos, on acceptance.

PERFORMANCE HORSEMAN—Gum Tree Corner, Unionville, PA 19375. Miranda Lorraine, Articles, Ed. Factual how-to pieces for the serious western rider, on training, improving riding skills, all aspects of care and management, etc. Pays from $300, on acceptance.

PETERSEN'S FISHING—8490 Sunset Blvd., Los Angeles, CA 90069. Robert Robb, Ed. "We're interested primarily in how-to articles (2,000 to 2,500 words), though pieces on where to fish, unusual techniques and equipment, and profiles of successful fisherman will also be considered. Photos must accompany all manuscripts, and we prefer to be queried first." Pays $300 to $400, on acceptance.

PGA MAGAZINE—The Quartron Group, 2701 Troy Center Dr., #430, Troy, MI 48084. Articles, 1,500 to 2,500 words, on golf-related subjects. Pays $300 to $500, on acceptance. Query.

PLEASURE BOATING—1995 N.E. 150th St., North Miami, FL 33181. Gord Lomer, Man. Ed. Articles, 1,000 to 2,500 words, on fishing cuising, recreational boating, travel, offshore racing, covering the coastline from Texas to New York and the islands. Special sections on Florida Keys, Bahamas, Jamaica and Cayman Islands. Pays varying rates, on publication. Query first. Study sample copies. Guidelines.

563

POPULAR LURES—15115 S. 76th E. Ave., Bixby, OK 74008. T. Smith, Ed. Articles, 1,500 to 1,800 words, on lure and techniques for catching all freshwater and saltwater fish. Pays $200 to $300, on acceptance.

POWERBOAT—15917 Strathern St., Van Nuys, CA 91406. Randy Scott, Ed. Articles, to 1,500 words, with photos, for powerboat owners, on outstanding achievements, water-skiing, competitions; technical articles on hull developments; how-to pieces. Pays $300 to $500, on acceptance. Query.

PRACTICAL HORSEMAN—Gum Tree Corner, Unionville, PA 19375. Miranda D. Lorraine, Articles Ed. How-to articles on English riding, training, and horse care. Pays on acceptance. Query.

PRIVATE PILOT—P.O. Box 6050, Mission Viejo, CA 92690. Mary R. Silitch, Ed. Technically based aviation articles for pilots and aircraft owners, 1,000 to 4,000 words, for aviation enthusiasts. Photos. Pays $75 to $250, on publication. Query.

PRO BASKETBALL ILLUSTRATED—See *Hockey Illustrated.*

PRO FOOTBALL ILLUSTRATED—See *Hockey Illustrated.*

PURE BRED DOGS/AMERICAN KENNEL GAZETTE—51 Madison Ave., New York, NY 10010. Marion Lane, Exec. Ed.; Judy Hartop, Sen. Ed. Articles, 1,000 to 2,500 words, relating to pure-bred dogs. Pays from $100 to $300, on publication. Queries preferred.

RESTORATION—3153 E. Lincoln, Tucson, AZ 85714-2017. W.R. Haessner, Ed. Articles, 1,200 to 1,800 words, on restoration of autos, trucks, planes, trains, etc. Photos. Pays varying rates (from $50 per page) on publication. Queries required.

RIDER—29901 Agoura Rd., Agoura, CA 91301. Mark Tuttle, Jr., Ed. Articles, with slides, to 3,000 words, with emphasis on travel, touring, commuting, and camping motorcyclists. Pays $100 to $500, on publication. Query.

RIVER RUNNER—P.O. Box 2073, Durango, CO 81302. Ken Hulick, Ed. Illustrated articles, 1,500 to 3,000 words, on canoeing, rafting, kayaking, and topics related to U.S. rivers. Pieces for departments on current legislation, short subjects, opinion, "River Towns," and "History." Pays from 5¢ a word, on publication. Query. Guidelines.

ROW MAGAZINE—401 Washington St., Suite D, Petaluma, CA 94952. Greg Sabourin, Ed. Bi-monthly. Articles (1,000–3,000 words) and fillers offering the latest information on equipment, training, and technique; fiction (1,000–2,000 words); photos. Pays 15¢ to 35¢ a word, on publication.

RUNNER'S WORLD—Rodale Press, 33 E. Minor St., Emmaus, PA 18098. Bob Wischnia, Sr. Ed. Articles for "Human Race" (submit to Eileen Shoulin), "Finish Line" (to Cristina Negron), and "Health Watch" (to Kate Delhagen) columns. Send feature articles or queries to Bob Wischnia. Payment varies, on acceptance. Query.

SAIL—Charlestown Navy Yard, 100 First Ave., Charlestown, MA 02129. Patience Wales, Ed. Articles, 1,500 to 3,500 words, features, 1,000 to 1,500 words, with photos, on sailboats, equipment, racing, and cruising. How-tos on navigation, sail trim, etc. Pays $75 to $1,000 on publication. Guidelines sent on request.

SAILING—125 E. Main St., Port Washington, WI 53074. William F. Schanen, III, Ed. Features, 700 to 1,500 words, with photos, on cruising and racing; first-person accounts; profiles of boats and regattas. Query for technical or how-to pieces. Pays varying rates, 30 days after publication. Guidelines.

SALT WATER SPORTSMAN—280 Summer St., Boston, MA 02210. Barry Gibson, Ed. Articles, 1,200 to 1,500 words, on how anglers can improve their skills, and on new places to fish off the coast of U.S. and Canada, Central America, the Caribbean, and Bermuda. Photos a plus. Pays $350 to $700, on acceptance. Query.

SCORE, CANADA'S GOLF MAGAZINE—287 MacPherson Ave., Toronto, Ont., Canada M4V 1A7. John Gordon, Man. Ed. Articles, 800 to 2,000 words, on travel, golf equipment, golf history, personality profiles, or prominent professionals. (Canadian content only.) Pays $125 to $600 for features, on assignment and publication. Query with published clips.

SEA KAYAKER—1670 Duranleau St., Vancouver, B.C., Canada V6H 3S4. John Dowd, Ed. Articles, 400 to 4,500 words, on ocean kayaking. Fiction. Pays 5¢ to 10¢ a word, on publication. Query with clips and international reply coupons.

SEA, THE MAGAZINE OF WESTERN BOATING—P. O. Box 1579, Newport Beach, CA 92663. Linda Yuskaitis, Exec. Ed. Features, 800 to 2,500 words, and news articles, 200 to 400 words, of interest to West Coast boating enthusiasts: profiles of boating personalities, cruise destinations, analyses of marine environmental issues, technical pieces on navigation and seamanship, news from Western harbors. No fiction, first-person, poetry, or cartoons. Pays varying rates, on publication.

SHOTGUN SPORTS—P.O. Box 6810, Auburn, CA 95604. Frank Kodl, Ed. Official publication of The United States Sporting Clays Assoc. Articles with photos, on trap and skeet shooting, sporting clays, hunting with shotguns, reloading, gun tests, and instructional shooting. Pays $25 to $200, on publication.

SKI MAGAZINE—2 Park Ave., New York, NY 10016. Dick Needham, Ed. Articles, 1,300 to 2,000 words, for experienced skiers: profiles, humor, "it-happened-to me" stories, and destination articles. Short, 100- to 300-word, news items for "Ski Life" column. Equipment and racing articles are staff written. Query first (with clips) for articles. Pays from $200, on acceptance.

SKI RACING—Box 1125, Rt. 100, Waitsfield, VT 05673. Articles on alpine and nordic racing, training, personalities. Photos. Rates vary.

SKIING MAGAZINE—2 Park Ave., New York, NY 10016. Bill Grote, Ed. Personal adventures on skis, from 2,500 words (no first time on skis stories); profiles and interviews, 50 to 300 words. Pays $150 to $300 per printed page, on acceptance.

SKIN DIVER MAGAZINE—8490 Sunset Blvd., Los Angeles, CA 90069. Bill Gleason, Ed. Illustrated articles, 500 to 2,000 words, on scuba diving activities, equipment, and dive sites. Pays $50 per published page, on publication.

SKYDIVING MAGAZINE—P. O. Box 1520, DeLand, FL 32721. Michael Truffer, Ed. Timely news articles, 300 to 800 words, relating to sport and military parachuting. Fillers. Photos. Pays $25 to $200, extra for photos, on publication.

SNOWBOARDER—P.O. Box 1028, Dana Point, CA 92629. Casey Sheahan, Man. Ed. Published four times yearly from Sept. to Jan. Articles, 1,000 to 1,500 words, on snowboarding personalities, techniques, and events; four-color transparencies or B&W prints. Occasional fiction, 1,000 to 1,500 words. Pays $150 to $800, on acceptance and on publication.

SNOWMOBILE—319 Barry Ave., S., Suite. 101, Wayzata, MN 55391. Dick Hendricks, Ed. Articles, 700 to 2,000 words, with B&W color photos, related to snowmobiling: races and rallies, trail rides, personalities, travel. How-tos, humor; cartoons. Pays to $450, on publication. Query.

SNOWEST—(formerly *Snowmobile West*) 520 Park Ave., Idaho Falls, ID

565

83402. Steve Janes, Ed. Articles, 1,200 words, on snowmobiling in the western states. Pays to $100, on publication.

SOCCER AMERICA MAGAZINE—P. O. Box 23704, Oakland, CA 94623. Lynn Berling-Manuel, Ed. Articles, to 500 words, on soccer: news, profiles, coaching tips. Pays $25 to $50, for features, within 60 days on publication.

SOUTH CAROLINA WILDLIFE—P. O. Box 167, Columbia , SC 29202. John E. Davis, Ed. Articles, 1,000 to 3,000 words, with regional outdoor focus: conservation, natural history, wildlife, and recreation. Profiles, how-tos. Pays on acceptance.

SPORT MAGAZINE—8490 Sunset Blvd., Los Angeles, CA 90069. Kelly Garrett, Exec. Ed. Query with clips. No fiction, poetry, or first person.

SPORTS AFIELD SPECIALS—250 W. 55th St., New York, NY 10019. Well-written, informative fishing and hunting articles, 2,000 to 2,500 words, with photos, with primary focus on how-to techniques: includes lively anecdotes, and good sidebars, charts. Pays to $450 for features, on acceptance.

SPORTS ILLUSTRATED—1271 Avenue of the Americas, New York, NY 10020. Chris Hunt, Articles Ed. No unsolicited material.

SPUR MAGAZINE—P. O. Box 85, Middleburg, VA 22117. Address Editorial Dept. Articles, 300 to 5,000 words, on Thoroughbred racing, breeding, polo, show jumping, eventing, and steeplechasing. Profiles of people and farms. Historical and nostalgia pieces. Pays $50 to $400, on publication. Query.

STOCK CAR RACING—P. O. Box 715, Ipswich, MA 01938. Dick Berggren, Feature Ed. Articles, to 6,000 words, on stock car drivers, races, and vehicles. Photos. Pays to $400, on publiction.

SURFER MAGAZINE—P. O. Box 1028, Dana Point, CA 92629. Steve Pezman, Pub. Paul Holmes, Ed. Articles, 500 to 5,000 words, on surfing, surfers, etc. Photos. Pays 10¢ to 15¢ a word, $10 to $600 for photos, on publication.

SURFING—P. O. Box 3010, San Clemente, CA 92672. Bill Sharp, Ed. Eric Fairbanks, Assoc. Ed. First-person travel articles, 1,500 to 2,000 words, on surfing locations; knowledge of sport essential. Pays varying rates, on acceptance.

SWIMSUIT INTERNATIONAL—Swimsuit Publishers, 801 Second Ave., New York, NY 10017. Barbara Haigh, Man. Ed. Articles, 1,000–2,000 words, on swimwear-related topics. Pays $350, on acceptance. Query.

TENNIS—5520 Park Ave., P. O. Box 0395, Trumbull , CT 06611–0395. Alex McNab, Ed. Instructional articles, features, profiles of tennis stars, 500 to 2,000 words. Photos. Pays From $100 to $750, on publication. Query.

TENNIS U.S.A.—3 Park Ave., New York, NY 10016. Steven C. Prince, Man. Ed. Articles, 750 to 1,000 words, on local, sectional, and national tennis personalities and news events. Pays $50 to $100, on publication. Query; uses very little free-lance material.

TENNIS WEEK—124 E. 40th St., Suite 1101, New York, NY 10016. Eugene L. Scott, Pub. Heather Thiermann, Ed. In-depth, researched articles, from 1,000 words, on current issues and personalities in the game. Pays $125, on publication.

TRAILER BOATS—20700 Belshaw Ave., P. O. Box 5427, Carson, CA 90249–5427. Chuck Coyne, Ed. Technical and how-to articles, 500 to 2,000 words, on boat, trailer, or tow vehicle maintenance and operation; skiing, fishing, and cruising. Fillers, humor. Pays 10¢ to 15¢ a word, on publication.

TRAILER LIFE—29901 Agoura Rd., Agoura, CA 91301. Bill Estes, Ed. Articles, to 2,500 words, with photos, on trailering, truck campers, motorhomes, hobbies, and RV lifestyles. How-to pieces. Pays to $600, on acceptance. Send for guidelines.

TRAILS-A-WAY—120 S. Lafayette St., Greenville, MI 48838. Martha Higbie, Ed. RV-related travel articles, 1,000 to 1,200 words, for "the newspaper dedicated to Midwest camping families." Pays $75 to $125, on publication.

VELONEWS—5595 Arapahoe, Suite G, Boulder, CO 80303. John Wilcockson, Ed. Articles, 500 to 1,500 words, on competitive cycling, profiles, training, nutrition, interviews. No how-to or touring articles. "We focus on the elite of the sport." Pays 10¢ a word, on publication.

VOLKSWAGEN'S WORLD—Volkswagen of America, Troy, MI 28007. Marlene Goldsmith, Ed. Articles, 750 to 1,000 words, accompanied by color slides. Pays $150 to $325 per printed page, on acceptance. Query required. Guidelines.

THE WALKING MAGAZINE—711 Boylston St., Boston, MA 02116. Bradford Ketchum, Ed. Articles, 1,500 to 2,000 words, on fitness, health, equipment, nutrition, travel, and adventure, famous walkers, and other walking-related topics. Shorter pieces, 500 to 1,500 words, and essays for "Ramblings" page. Photos welcome. Pays $750 to $2,500 for features, $100 to $600 for department pieces. Guidelines.

WASHINGTON FISHING HOLES—P.O. Box 32, Sedro Wolley, WA 98284. Detailed articles, with specific maps, 800 to 1,500 words, on fishing in Washington. Local Washington fishing how-tos. Photos. Pays on publication. Query. Send SASE for guidelines.

THE WATER SKIER—749 Overlook Dr., Winter Haven, FL 33884. Duke Cullimore, Ed. Offbeat articles on waterskiing. Pays varying rates, on acceptance.

THE WESTERN BOATMAN—20700 Belshaw Ave., P.O. Box 5427, Carson, CA 90249–5427. Ralph Poole, Ed. Articles, to 1,500 words, for boating enthusiasts from Alaska to Mexico, on subjects from waterskiing and salmon fishing to race boats and schooners. Photos required. Pays $5 per column inch, $20 to $300 (cover) for color photos, on publication. Queries preferred.

THE WESTERN HORSEMAN—P.O. Box 7980, Colorado Springs, CO 80933. Randy Witte, Ed. Articles, around 1,500 words, with photos, on care and training of horses. Pays to $250, on acceptance.

WESTERN OUTDOORS—3197-E Airport Loop, Costa Mesa, CA 92626. Timely, factual articles on fishing and hunting, 1,500 to 1,800 words, of interest to western sportsmen. Pays $400 to $500, on acceptance. Query. Guidelines.

WESTERN SPORTSMAN—P.O. Box 737, Regina, Sask., Canada S4P 3A8. Roger Francis, Ed. Articles, to 2,500 words, on outdoor experiences in Alberta and Saskatchewan; how-to pieces. Photos. Pays $75 to $325, on publication.

WILDBIRD—Box 6050, Mission Viejo, CA 92690. Tim Gallagher, Man. Ed. Features, 1,500 to 2,000 words, and columns, 700 to 1,000 words, for field birders and garden birders. "No pieces on taming wild birds." Pays $25 for reader columns, from $100 for articles, extra for photos. Guidelines.

WIND SURF—P.O. Box 561, Dana Point, CA 92629. Drew Kampion, Ed. Articles on all aspects of windsurfing. Pays 10¢ to 20¢ a word, on publication.

WINDRIDER—P.O. Box 2456, Winter Park, FL 32790. Debbie Snow, Ed. Features, instructional pieces, and tips, by experienced boardsailors. Fast action photos. Pays $50 to $75 for tips, $250 to $300 for features, extra for photos. Send guidelines first.

WOMAN BOWLER—5301 S. 76th St., Greendale, WI 53129. Karen Sytsma, Ed. Profiles, interviews, and news articles, to 1,000 words, for women bowlers. Pays varying rates, on acceptance. Query with outline.

WOMEN'S SPORTS & FITNESS—P.O. Box 2456, Winter Park, FL 32790. Lewis Rothlein, Ed. How-tos, profiles, and sports reports, 500 to 3,000 words, for active women. Fitness, nutrition, and health pieces also considered. Pays on publication.

WORLD TENNIS—Family Media, Inc., 3 Park Ave., New York, NY 10016. Peter Coan, Man. Ed. Articles, 750 to 1,500 words, on tournaments, technique, celebrities, equipment, player profiles, tennis resorts, and related subjects. Payment varies, on acceptance. Query.

WRESTLING WORLD—See *Hockey Illustrated.*

YACHTING—2 Park Ave., New York, NY 10016. Roy Attaway, Ed. Articles, 2,000 words, on recreational power and sail boating. How-to and personal-experience pieces. Photos. Pays $350 to $1,000, on acceptance. Queries preferred.

AUTOMOTIVE MAGAZINES

AAA WORLD—AAA Headquarters, 1000 AAA Dr., Heathrow, FL 32746–5064. Douglas Damerst, Ed. Automobile and travel concerns, including automotive travel, maintenance and upkeep, 750 to 1,500 words. Pays $300 to $600, on acceptance. Query with clips preferred.

AMERICAN MOTORCYCLIST—American Motorcyclist Assn., Box 6114, Westerville, OH 43081–6114. Greg Harrison, Ed. Articles and fiction, to 3,000 words, on motorcycling: news coverage, personalities, tours. Photos. Pays varying rates, on publication. Query with SASE.

CAR AND DRIVER—2002 Hogback Rd., Ann Arbor, MI 48105. William Jeanes, Ed. Articles, to 2,500 words, for enthusiasts, on car manufacturers, new developments in cars, etc. Pays to $2,000, on acceptance. Query with clips.

CAR AUDIO AND ELECTRONICS—21700 Oxnard St., Woodland Hills, CA 91367. Bill Neill, Ed. "We want articles that cover complicated topics simply." Features (1,000 to 2,000 words) on electronic products for the car: audio, cellular telephones, security systems, CBs, radar detectives, etc.; how to buy them; how they work; how to use them. Pays $300 to $1,000, on acceptance. Send manuscript or query.

CAR CRAFT—8490 Sunset Blvd., Los Angeles, CA 90069. Cameron Benty, Ed. Articles and photofeatures on unusual street machines, drag cars, racing events; technical pieces; action photos. Pays from $150 per page, on publication.

CYCLE MAGAZINE—5706 Corsa Ave., Westlake Village, CA 91362. Phil Schilling, Ed. Articles, 6 to 20 manuscript pages, on motorcycle races, history, touring, technical pieces; profiles. Photos. Pays on publication. Query.

CYCLE WORLD—853 W. 17th St., Costa Mesa, CA 92627. Paul Dean, Ed. Technical and feature articles, 1,500 to 2,500 words, for motorcycle enthusiasts. Photos. Pays $100 to $200 per page, on publication. Query.

HOT BIKE—2145 W. La Palma, Anaheim, CA 92801. Buck Lovell, Ed. Articles, 250 to 2,500 words, with photos, on motorcycles (contemporary and antique). Event coverage on high performance street and track and sport touring motorcycles, with emphasis on Harley Davidsons. Pays $50 to $100 per printed page, on publication.

HOT ROD—8490 Sunset Blvd., Los Angeles, CA 90069. Jeff Smith, Ed. How-to pieces and articles, 500 to 5,000 words, on auto mechanics, hot rods, track and drag racing. Photo features on custom or performance-modified cars. Pays $250 per page, on publication.

KEEPIN' TRACK OF VETTES—P.O. Box 48, Spring Valley, NY 10977. Shelli Finkel, Ed. Articles of any length, with photos, relating to Corvettes. Pays $25 to $200, on publication.

MOTOR TREND—8490 Sunset Blvd., Los Angeles, CA 90069. Mike Anson, Ed. Articles, 250 to 2,000 words, on autos, racing, events, and profiles. Photos. Pay varies, on acceptance. Query.

MOTORCYCLIST—8490 Sunset Blvd., Los Angeles, CA 90069. Art Friedman, Ed. Articles, 1,000 to 3,000 words. Action photos. Pays varying rates, on publication.

OPEN WHEEL—See *Stock Car Racing.*

RESTORATION—3153 E. Lincoln, Tucson, AZ 85714–2017. W.R. Haessner, Ed. Articles, 1,200 to 1,800 words, on restoration of autos, trucks, planes, trains, etc. Photos. Pays from $50 per page, on publication. Queries required.

RIDER—29901 Agoura Rd., Agoura, CA 91301. Mark Tuttle, Jr., Ed. Articles, with slides, to 3,000 words, with emphasis on travel, touring, commuting, and camping motorcyclists. Pays $100 to $500, on publication. Query.

STOCK CAR RACING—P.O. Box 715, Ipswich, MA 01938. Dick Berggren, Ed. Features, technical automotive pieces, up to ten typed pages, for oval track racing enthusiasts. Fillers. Pays $75 to $350, on publication. Same requirements for *Open Wheel.*

VOLKSWAGEN'S WORLD—Volkswagen of America, Troy, MI 28007. Marlene Goldsmith, Ed. Articles, 750 to 1,000 words, accompanied by color slides. Pays $150 per printed page, on acceptance. Query required. Guidelines.

FITNESS MAGAZINES

AMERICAN FITNESS—15250 Ventura Blvd., Suite 310, Sherman Oaks, CA 91403. Peg Jordan, Ed. Rhonda Wilson, Man. Ed. Articles, 500 to 1,500 words, on exercise, health, sports, nutrition, etc. Illustrations, photos, cartoons.

AMERICAN HEALTH—80 Fifth Ave., New York, NY 10011. Address Editorial Dept. Lively, authoritative articles, 1,000 to 3,000 words, on scientific and lifestyle aspects of health and fitness; 100- to 500-word news reports. Query with clips. Pays $250 ($50 kill fee) for news stories; 75¢ per word for features (kill fee is 25% of assigned fee); on acceptance.

EAST WEST: THE JOURNAL OF NATURAL HEALTH & LIVING—17 Station St., Box 1200, Brookline, MA 02147. Features, 1,500 to 2,500 words, on holistic health, natural foods, gardening, etc. Material for "Body," "Healing," "In the Kitchen," and "Beauty and Fitness." Interviews. Photos. Pays 10¢ a word, extra for photos, on publication.

HEALTH—3 Park Ave., New York, NY 10016. Articles, 800 to 2,500 words, on fitness and nutrition. Pays up to $2,000 on acceptance. Query.

INSIDE TEXAS RUNNING—9514 Bristlebrook Dr., Houston, TX 77083. Joanne Schmidt, Ed. Articles and fillers on running, cycling, and triathlons in Texas. Pays $35 to $100, $10 for photos, on acceptance.

MEN'S FITNESS—21100 Erwin St., Woodland Hills, CA 91367. Jim Rosenthal, Features Ed. Features, 1,500 to 2,500 words, and department pieces, 1,000 to 1,500 words: "authoritative and practical articles dealing with fitness, health, and men's lifestyles." Pays $200 to $400, on acceptance.

MEN'S HEALTH—Rodale Press, 33 E. Minor Dr., Emmaus, PA 18098. Michael Lafavore, Exec. Ed. Articles, 1,000 to 2,500 words, on fitness, diet, health, relationships, sports, and travel, for men ages 25 to 55. Pays 50¢ a word, on acceptance. Query first.

MUSCULAR DEVELOPMENT—351 W. 45th St., New York, NY 10019. Alan Paul, Ed. Articles, 1,000 to 2,500 words, on competitive bodybuilding and power lifting for serious weight training athletes: personality profiles, training features, and diet and nutrition pieces. Photos. Pays $100 to $300 for articles; $25 for photos and $300 to $400 for cover photos.

NEW BODY—888 Seventh Ave., New York, NY 10106. Kate Staples, Ed. Lively, readable service-oriented articles, 800 to 1,500 words, on exercise, nutrition, lifestyle, diet, and health for women aged 18 to 25. Writers should have some background in or knowledge of the health field. Pays $100 to $300, on publication. Query.

THE PHYSICIAN AND SPORTSMEDICINE—4530 W. 77th St., Minneapolis, MN 55435. Debra Giel Adams, Features Ed. News and feature articles, 500–3,000 words, on fitness, sports, and exercise. Medical angle necessary. Pays $150 to $900, on acceptance. Guidelines.

SHAPE—21100 Erwin St., Woodland Hills, CA 91367. Jennifer Koch, Asst. Ed. Articles, 1,200 to 1,500 words, with new and interesting ideas on the physical and mental side of getting and staying in shape; reports, 300 to 400 words, on journal research. Expert bylines only. Payment varies, on publication. Guidelines.

VEGETARIAN TIMES—P.O. Box 570, Oak Park, IL 60603. Paul Obis, Pub. Articles, 750 to 2,500 words, on health, nutrition, exercise and fitness, meatless meals, etc. Personal-experience and historical pieces, profiles. Pays $25 to $500, on publication.

VIM & VIGOR—8805 N. 23rd Ave., Suite 11, Phoenix, AZ 85021. Leo Calderella, Ed. Positive articles, with accurate medical facts, on health and fitness, 1,200 words, by assignment only. Pays $250 to $350, on publication. Query.

THE WALKING MAGAZINE—711 Boylston St., Boston, MA 02116. Bradford Ketchum, Ed. Articles, 1,500 to 2,500 words, on fitness, health, equipment, nutrition, travel and adventure, famous walkers, and other walking-related topics. Shorter pieces, 150 to 800 words, and essays for "Ramblings" page. Photos welcome. Pays $750 to $1,200 for features, $100 to $500 for department pieces. Guidelines.

WEIGHT WATCHERS MAGAZINE—360 Lexington Ave., New York, NY 10017. Ruth Papazian, Articles Ed. Articles on nutrition and health. Pays from $250, on acceptance. Query with clips required. Guidelines.

WOMEN'S SPORTS & FITNESS—P.O. Box 2456, Winter Park, FL 32790. Lewis Rothlein, Ed. How-tos, profiles, and sports reports, 500 to 3,000 words, for active women. Fitness, nutrition, and health pieces also considered. Pays on publication.

YOGA JOURNAL—2054 University Ave., Berkeley, CA 94704. Stephan Bodian, Ed. Articles, 1,200 to 3,000 words, on holistic health, meditation, consciousness, spirituality, and yoga. Pays $50 to $350, on publication.

CONSUMER/PERSONAL FINANCE

BETTER HOMES AND GARDENS—1716 Locust St., Des Moines, IA 50336. Articles, 750 to 1,000 words, on "any and all topics that would be of interest to family-oriented, middle-income people." Address Margaret V. Daly, Money Management, Automotive and Features Ed., *Better Homes and Garden*, 750 Third Ave., New York, NY 10017.

BLACK ENTERPRISE—130 Fifth Ave., New York, NY 10011. Earl G. Graves, Ed. Articles on money management, careers, political issues, entrepreneurship, high technology, and lifestyles for black professionals. Profiles. Pays on acceptance. Query.

CHANGING TIMES—1729 H St. N.W., Washington, DC 20006. Articles on personal finance (i.e., buying a stereo, mutual funds). Length and payment vary. Query required. Pays on acceptance.

CONSUMERS DIGEST—5705 N. Lincoln Ave., Chicago, IL 60659. John Manos, Ed. Articles, 500 to 3,000 words, on subjects of interest to consumers: products and services, automobiles, travel, health, fitness, consumer legal affairs, and personal money management. Photos. Pays from 30¢ a word, extra for photos, on acceptance. Query with resumé and clips.

CZESCHIN'S MUTUAL FUND OUTLOOK & RECOMMENDATIONS —P.O. Box 1423, Baltimore, MD 21203–1423. Robert W. Czeschin, Ed. Short features, to 1,000 words, on all aspects of mutual funds and mutual fund investing: IRA's, switching strategies, non-U. S. funds, taxes, etc. Pays $100, on acceptance.

FAMILY CIRCLE—110 Fifth Ave., New York, NY 10011. Susan Ungaro, Articles Ed. Susan Sherry, Sr. Ed. Enterprising, creative, and practical articles (1,000 to 1,500 words) on investing, starting your own business, secrets of successful entrepreneurs, and consumer news that helps one be a smarter shopper. Query first with clips. Pays $1 a word, on acceptance.

GOLDEN YEARS—233 E. New Haven Ave., Melbourne, FL 32902–0537. Carol Brenner Hittner, Ed. "We consider articles (to 500 words) on preretirement, retirement planning, real estate, travel, celebrity profiles, humor, and contemporary issues of particular interest to affluent people over 50." Pays on publication.

KIWANIS—3636 Woodview Trace, Indianapolis, IN 46468. Chuck Jonak, Exec. Ed. Articles (2,500 to 3,000 words) on financial planning for younger families in a variety of areas; pieces on financial planning for retirees and small business owners. Pays $400 to $1,000, on acceptance. Query required.

MODERN MATURITY—3200 E. Carson St., Lakewood, CA 90712. Ian Ledgerwood, Ed. Articles, 1,000 to 2,000 words, on a wide range of financial topics of interest to people over 50. Pays to $2,500. Queries required.

MONEY MAKER—5705 N. Lincoln Ave., Chicago, IL 60659. Dennis Fertig, Ed. Informative, jargon-free articles, to 2,500 words, for beginning-to-sophisticated investors, on investment opportunities, personal finance, and low-priced investments. Pays 25¢ a word, on acceptance. Query with clips for assignment.

THE MONEYPAPER—930 Mamaroneck Ave., Mamaroneck, NY 10543. Vita Nelson, Ed. Financial news and money-saving ideas. Brief, well-researched articles on personal finance, money management: saving, earning, investing, taxes, insurance, and related subjects. Pays $75 for articles, on publication. Query with resumé and writing sample.

MOTHER JONES—1663 Mission St., San Francisco, CA 94103. Doug Foster, Ed. Articles for "Out of Pocket" section, on economy and personal finance. Pays 60 cents a word, after acceptance. Query in writing only.

SELF—350 Madison Ave., New York, NY 10017. Susan Ochshorn, Money/Careers Ed. Articles, 1,200 to 1,500 words, on money matters for career women in their 20s and 30s. Pays from $1,000, on acceptance. Query first.

WOMAN'S DAY—1515 Broadway, New York, NY 10036. Rebecca Greer, Articles Ed. Articles, to 3,000 words, on financial matters of interest to a broad range of women. Pays top rates, on acceptance. Query first.

WOMAN'S ENTERPRISE—28210 Dorothy Dr., Agoura Hills, CA 91301. Caryne Brown, Ed. Articles, 1,500 to 2,000 words, on women who own small businesses; features on business management. "The more specific income, expenditure, and profit figures are, the better." No personal profiles. Pays 20¢ a word, on acceptance. Query preferred.

PROFESSIONAL/TRADE PUBLICATIONS

ACCESS CONTROL—6255 Barfield Rd., Atlanta, GA 30328. Steven Lasky, Ed./Assoc. Pub. Comprehensive case studies on large-scale access control installations in an industrial, commercial, governmental, utilities, retail, and transportational environment. Each issue includes special monthly features on door and card entry, gates and operators, turnstiles and portals, perimeter security fencing and its accessories, perimeter and interior sensors, and CCTU tecchnology. Photos. Pays from 10¢ a word, extra for photos, on publication. Query.

ACCESSORIES MAGAZINE—50 Day St., Norwalk, CT 06854. Reenie Brown, Ed. Dir. Articles, with photos, for women's fashion accessories buyers and manufacturers. Profiles of retailers, designers, manufacturers; articles on merchandising and marketing. Pays $75 to $100 for short articles, from $100 to $300 for features, on publication. Query.

ACROSS THE BOARD—845 Third Ave., New York, NY 10022. Sarasue French, Asst. Ed. Articles, to 5,000 words, on a variety of topics of interest to business executives; straight business angle not required. Pays $100 to $750 on publication.

ALTERNATIVE ENERGY RETAILER—P.O. Box 2180, Waterbury, CT 06722. Ed Easley, Ed. Feature articles, 2,000 words, for retailers of alternative and energy products: wood, coal, and fireplace products and services. Interviews with successful retailers, stressing the how-to. B&W photos. Pays $200, extra for photos, on publication. Query first.

AMERICAN BANKER—One State Street Plaza, New York, NY 10004. William Zimmerman, Ed., Patricia Stunza, Features Ed. Articles, 1,000 to 3,000 words, on banking and financial services, technology in banking, consumer financial services, human resources, management techniques. Pays varying rates, on publication. Query preferred.

AMERICAN BAR ASSOCIATION JOURNAL—750 N. Lake Shore Dr., Chicago, IL 60611. Robert Yates, Man. Ed. Practical articles, to 3,000 words, on law-related topics: current events in the law and ideas that will that will help lawyers in small firms better their practices. Writing should be in an informal, journalistic style. Pays $750 to $950, on acceptance; buys all rights.

AMERICAN COIN-OP—500 N. Dearborn St., Chicago, IL 60610. Ben Russell, Ed. Articles, to 2,500 words, with photos, on successful coin-operated laundries: management, promotion, decor, maintenance, etc. Pays from 6¢ a word, $6 per B&W photo, two weeks prior to publication. Query. Send SASE for guidelines.

AMERICAN DEMOGRAPHICS—P.O. Box 68, Ithaca, NY 14851. Caroline Arthur, Man. Ed. Articles, 3,000 to 5,000 words, on demographic trends and business demographics for strategists in industry, government, and education. Pays $300, on publication. Query.

AMERICAN FARRIERS JOURNAL—63 Great Rd., Maynard, MA 01754. Susan G. Philbrick, Ed. Articles, 800 to 5,000 words, on general farriery issues, hoof care, tool selection, equine lameness, and horse handling. Pays 30¢ per published line, $10 per published illustration or photo, on publication. Query.

AMERICAN MEDICAL NEWS—535 N. Dearborn St., Chicago, IL 60610. Flora Johnson Skelly, Assistant Exec. Ed. Features, 1,000 to 3,000 words, of interest to physicians across the country. No pieces on health, clinical treatments, or research. Query required. Pays $50 to $1,000, on acceptance. Guidelines.

THE AMERICAN SALESMAN—424 N. Third St., Burlington, IA 52601–5224. Barbara Boeding, Ed. Articles, 900 to 1,200 words, on techniques for increasing sales. Pays 3¢ a word, on publication. Guidelines.

AMERICAN SALON—7500 Old Oak Blvd., Cleveland, OH 44130. Jody Byrne, Ed. Official publication of the National Cosmetology Assoc. Articles of varying lengths for salon professionals. Payment varies, on publication. Query.

AREA DEVELOPMENT MAGAZINE—525 Northern Blvd., Great Neck, NY 11021. Tom Bergeron, Ed. Articles for top executives of manufacturing companies, on industrial and office facility planning. Pays $40 per manuscript page. Query.

ART BUSINESS NEWS—60 Ridgeway Plaza, P.O. Box 3837, Stamford, CT 06905. Jo Yanow-Schwartz, Ed. Articles, 1,000 words, for art dealers and framers, on trends and events of national importance to the art industry, and relevant business subjects. Pays $75 plus, on publication. Query preferred.

ART MATERIAL TRADE NEWS—6255 Barfield Rd., Atlanta, GA 30328. Anthony Giometti, Ed. Articles, from 800 words, for dealers, wholesalers, and manufacturers of artist materials; must be specific to trade. Pays to 15¢ a word, on publication. Query.

AUTOMATED BUILDER—(formerly *Automation in Housing and Manufactured Home Dealer*) P.O. Box 120, Carpinteria, CA 93013. Don Carlson, Ed. Articles, 500 to 750 words, on various types of home manufacturers and dealers. Query required. Pays $350, on acceptance, for articles with slides.

AUTOMOTIVE EXECUTIVE—8400 Westpark Dr., McLean, VA 22102. Joe Phillips, Man. Ed. National Automobile Dealers Assn. Articles, 1,500 to 2,500 words, on management of automobile and heavy-duty truck dealerships and general business management and automotive issues. Color photos. Pays on publication. Query.

BANKING WEEK—1 State Street Plaza, New York, NY 10004. William Zimmerman, Ed. Articles, 3 to 5 typed pages, on important news and trends in the banking industry; profiles of interesting bankers. Pays varying rates, on acceptance. Query.

BARRISTER—American Bar Assn., 750 N. Lake Shore Dr., Chicago, IL 60611. Anthony Monahan, Ed. Articles, to 3,500 words, on legal and social affairs, for young lawyers. Pays to $700, on acceptance.

BARRON'S—200 Liberty St., New York, NY 10281. Alan Abelson, Ed. National-interest articles, 1,200 to 2,500 words, on business and finance. Query.

BETTER BUSINESS—235 East 42nd St., New York, NY 10017. John F. Robinson, Pub. Articles, 10 to 12 double-spaced pages, for the small business/ minority business markets. Query.

BOATING INDUSTRY—390 Fifth Ave., New York, NY 10018. Paul C. Larsen, Ed. Articles, 1,000 to 1,500 words, on marine management, merchandising, and selling, for boat dealers. Photos. Pays varying rates, on publication. Query.

BUILDER—Hanley-Wood, Inc., 655 15th St. NW, Suite 475, Washington, DC 20005. Mitchell B. Rouda, Ed. Articles, to 1,500 words, on trends and news in home building: design, marketing, new products, etc. Pays negotiable rates, on acceptance. Query.

BUSINESS AGE—135 W. Wells St., 7th Floor, Milwaukee, WI 53203. Claire A. Bremer, Ed. The Magazine for Small Business. Articles, 1,500 to 2,000 words, providing information the small-business person can use to improve day-to-day operations; department pieces, 200 to 1,000 words. Pays $50 to $250, on publication. Departments: accounting, finance, personnel management, taxes, management, business law, marketing, technology, and planning. Queries are required. Guidelines and editorial calendar available.

BUSINESS DIGEST OF GREATER NEW HAVEN—20 Grand Ave., New Haven, CT 06513. Jean McAndrews, Ed. Feature articles, 1,500 to 2,000 words, on successful New Haven-area businesses and owners. Pays $2.75 per published inch, on publication. Query required.

BUSINESS MARKETING—220 E. 42nd St., New York, NY 10017. Bob Donath, Ed. Articles on selling, advertising, and promoting products and services to business buyers. Pays competitive rates, on acceptance. Queries are required.

BUSINESS MONTH—488 Madison Ave, New York, NY 10022. John Van Doorn, Ed.-in-Chief. Articles, to 5,000 words: profiles of CEOs, large corporations; articles on trends and key issues in management. Pays to $1 a word, on acceptance.

BUSINESS TODAY—P.O. Box 10010, 1720 Washington Blvd., Ogden, UT 84409. Melody Haakenson, Libby Hyland, Eds. Articles, 1,200 words; profiles of businessmen and women, informative articles on business concerns of the businessperson/entrepeneur. Pays 15¢ a word, $35 for color photos, on acceptance. Query. Guidelines.

BUSINESS VIEW—P.O. Box 9859, Naples, FL 33941. Eleanor K. Somer, Pub. Innovative articles and columns, 750 to 1,500 words, on business, economics, finance; profiles of business leaders; new trends in technology and advances in management techniques. Real estate and banking trends. Southwest Florida regional angle preferred. Pays $100 to $300, on publication. Query.

CALIFORNIA LAWYER—1390 Market St., Suite 1016, San Francisco, CA 94102. Thomas Brom, Man. Ed. Articles, 2,500 to 3,000 words, for attorneys in California, on legal subjects (or the legal aspects of a given political or social issue);

how-tos on improving legal skills and law office technology. Pays $300 to $1,200, on acceptance. Query.

CAMPGROUND MANAGEMENT—100 Corporate North, Suite 100, Bannockburn, IL 60015–1253. Mike Byrnes, Ed. Detailed articles, 500 to 2,000 words, on managing recreational vehicle campgrounds. Photos. Pays $50 to $200, after publication.

CASHFLOW—6255 Barfield Rd., Atlanta, GA 30328. Richard Gamble, Ed. Articles, 1,250 to 2,500 words, for treasury managers in public and private institutions: cash management; investments; domestic and international financing; credit and collection management; developments in law, economics, and tax. Pays $125 per published page, on publication. Query.

CENTURY CITY MAGAZINE—23919 Ventura Blvd., Calabasas, CA 91302. A. Henry Shaw, Exec. Ed. Articles, 500 to 2,000 words, and 60- to 100-word anecdotes on business for executives in the Century City business area of Los Angeles. Payment varies, on publication. Query.

CERAMIC SCOPE—3632 Ashworth N., Seattle, WA 98103. Michael Scott, Ed. Articles, 800 to 1,500 words, on retail or wholesale business operations of hobby ceramic studios. Photos. Pays 10¢ a word, extra for photos, on publication. Query.

CHIEF EXECUTIVE—205 Lexington Ave., New York, NY 10016. J.P. Donlon, Ed. CEO bylines. Articles, 2,500 to 3,000 words, on management, financial, or business strategy. Departments on investments, amentites, and travel, 1,200 to 1,500 words. Features on CEOs at leisure, Q&A's with CEOs, other topics. Pays varying rates, on acceptance. Query required.

CHINA, GLASS & TABLEWARE—P.O. Box 2147, Clifton, NJ 07015. Amy Stavis, Ed. Case histories and interviews, 1,500 to 2,500 words, with photos, on merchandising of china and glassware. Pays $50 per page, on publication. Query.

CLEANING MANAGEMENT—15550-D Rockfield, Irvine, CA 92718. R. Daniel Harris, Jr., Pub. Articles, 1,000 to 1,500 words, on managing efficient cleaning and maintenance operations. Photos. Pays 10¢ a word, extra for photos, on publication.

COMMERCIAL CARRIER JOURNAL—Chilton Way, Radnor, PA 19089. Jerry Standley, Ed. Factual articles on private fleets and for-hire trucking operations. Pays from $50, on acceptance. Queries required.

COMPUTER DECISIONS MAGAZINE—(formerly *Computer & Communication Decisions Magazine*) Glenpointe Center E., DeGraw Ave., Teaneck, NJ 07666. Robin Nelson, Ed. Articles, 800 to 4,000 words, on corporate applications of computer systems. Pays $500 to $1,500 per article, on acceptance. Queries are required.

COMPUTER GRAPHICS WORLD—One Technology Park Dr., Westford, MA 01886. Stephen Porter, Man. Ed. Articles, 1,000 to 3,000 words, on computer graphics technology and its use in science, engineering, architecture, and graphic areas. Photos. Pays $600 to $1,000 per article, on acceptance. Query.

CONCRETE INTERNATIONAL: DESIGN AND CONSTRUCTION—Box 19150, 22400 W. Seven Mile Rd., Detroit, MI 48219. William J. Semioli, Ed. Articles, 6 to 12 double-spaced pages, on concrete construction and design, with drawings and photos. Pays $100 per printed page, on publication. Query.

CONTRACTORS MARKET CENTER—Box 2029, Tuscaloosa , AL 35403.

Robert Ruth, Ed. Features, 500 to 1,500 words, for contractors who buy and sell used heavy equipment; stories offering tips to used equipment buyers and sellers. Pays $10 to $50, on acceptance.

CONVENIENCE STORE NEWS—254 W. 31st St., New York, NY 10001. Monica Battagliola, Ed. Features and news items, 500 to 750 words, for convenience store owners, operators, and suppliers. Photos, with captions. Pays $3 per column inch, extra for photos, on publication. Query.

COOKING FOR PROFIT—P.O. Box 267, Fond du Lac, WI 54936–0267. Colleen Phalen, Ed. Practical how-to articles, 1,000 words, on commercial food preparation, energy management; case studies, etc. Pays $75 to $250, on publication.

CRAIN'S CHICAGO BUSINESS—740 Rush St., Chicago, IL 60611. Dan Miller, Ed. Business articles about the Midwest exclusively. Pays $11.50 per column inch, on acceptance.

CREATING EXCELLENCE—New World Publishing, P.O. Box 2084, S. Burlington, VT 05403. David Robinson, Ed. Self-help and inspirational articles: profiles and essays related to personal development. "Purpose is to inform and inspire people to be their best, personally and professionally." Pays $75 to $250, on acceptance. Queries preferred.

CREDIT AND COLLECTION MANAGEMENT BULLETIN—Bureau of Business Practice, 24 Rope Ferry Rd., Waterford, CT 06386. Russell Case, Ed. Interviews, 500 to 1,250 words, for commercial and consumer credit managers, on innovations, successes and problem solving. Query.

D & B REPORTS—299 Park Ave., New York, NY 10171. Patricia W. Hamilton, Ed. Articles, 1,500 to 2,000 words, for top management of smaller businesses: government regulations, export opportunities, employee relations; how-tos on cash management, sales, productivity; profiles, etc. Pays on acceptance.

DAIRY FOODS MAGAZINE—Gorman Publishing Co., 8750 W. Bryn Mawr, Chicago, IL 60631. Jerry Dryer, Ed. Articles, to 2,500 words, on innovative dairies, dairy processing operations, marketing successes, new products, for milk handlers, and makers of dairy products. Fillers, 25 to 150 words. Pays $25 to $300, $5 to $25 for fillers, on publication. Same requirements for *Cheese Market News.*

DELUXE—Maxwell Custom Publishing, 1999 Shepard St., St. Paul, MN 55116. George Ashfield, Ed. Distributed to employees of financial institutions. Articles, 1,000 to 1,400 words, on personal improvement, professional development/business interest; lifestyle; foods, recipes, and activities. Pays $300 to $600, on acceptance. Query with SASE.

DENTAL ECONOMICS—P.O. Box 3408, Tulsa, OK 74101. Dick Hale, Ed. Articles, 1,200 to 3,500 words, on business side of dental practice, patient and staff communication, personal investments, etc. Pays $100 to $400, on acceptance.

DOMESTIC ENGINEERING—385 N. York Rd., Elmhurst, IL 60126. Stephen J. Shafer, Ed. Articles, to 3,000 words, on plumbing, heating, air conditioning, and process piping. Photos. Pays $20 to $35 per printed page, on publication.

DRAPERIES & WINDOW COVERINGS—450 Skokie Blvd., Suite 507, Northbrook, IL 60062. Katie Renckens, Ed. Articles, 1,000 to 2,000 words, for retailers, wholesalers, designers, and manufacturers of draperies and window coverings. Profiles, with photos, of successful businesses in the industry. Pays $150 to $250, after acceptance. Query.

EARNSHAW'S INFANTS & CHILDREN'S REVIEW—393 Seventh Ave.,

New York, NY 10001. Christina Gruber, Ed. Articles on retailers, retail promotions, and statistics for children's wear industry. Pays $50 to $200, on publication. Query. Limited market.

ELECTRICAL CONTRACTOR—7315 Wisconsin Ave., Bethesda, MD 20814. Larry C. Osius, Ed. Articles, 1,000 to 1,500 words, with photos, on construction or management techniques for electrical contractors. Pays $100 per printed page, before publication. Query.

ELECTRONIC MANUFACTURING NEWS—1350 E. Touhy Ave., Box 5080, Des Plaines, IL 60018. Diane Pirocanac, Man. Ed. Articles, 500 to 750 words, of interest to engineers and managers in the electronic manufacturing industry. Payment varies, on acceptance. Query required.

EMERGENCY—P.O. Box 159, Carlsbad, CA 92008–0032. Laura Gilbert, Ed. Features (to 3,000 words) and department pieces (to 1,000 words) of interest to paramedics, emergency medical technicians, and EMS personnel: disaster management, advanced first-aid, and medical assessment. Pays $100 to $400 for features, $50 to $250 for department pieces. Photos are a plus. Guidelines available.

EMPLOYEE SERVICES MANAGEMENT—NESRA, 2400 S. Downing, Westchester, IL 60154. Pamela A. Tober, Ed. Articles, 800 to 2,500 words, for human resource, fitness, and employee service professionals.

ENGINEERED SYSTEMS—7314 Hart St., Mentor, OH 44060. Robert L. Schwed, Ed. Articles, case histories, product information related to engineered hvac systems in commercial, industrial, or institutional buildings. Pays $4.75 per column inch, $12 per illustration, on publication. Query.

THE ENGRAVERS JOURNAL—26 Summit St., Box 318, Brighton, MI 48116. Michael J. Davis, Man. Ed. Articles, of varying lengths, on topics related to the engraving industry or small business. Pays $60 to $175, on acceptance. Query.

ENTREE—825 7th Ave., New York, NY 10019. Jeanne Muchnick, Ed. Articles, 100 to 800 words, on trends and people in better housewares industry, both retailers and manufacturers. Pays from $300, on acceptance.

ENTREPRENEUR—2392 Morse Ave., Irvine, CA 92714. Rieva Lesonsky, Ed. Articles for established and aspiring independent business owners, on all aspects of running a business. Pays $100 to $500, on acceptance. Queries required.

ENTREPRENEURIAL WOMAN—2392 Morse Ave., Irvine, CA 92714. Rieva Lesonsky, Ed. Profiles, 2,000 words, of women entrepreneurs; how-tos on running a business, and pieces on coping as a woman business owner. Payment varies, on acceptance.

EXPORT MAGAZINE—386 Park Ave. South, New York, NY 10016. Jack Dobson, Ed. Articles, 1,000 to 1,200 words. From U.S.-based free lancers: articles on developments in hardware and appliances, air conditioning and refrigeration, sporting goods and leisure products. From overseas-based free lancers: articles on merchandising techniques of foreign retailers who import above-described items from U.S. Pays $300 to $400 with photos, on acceptance. Query required.

FARM JOURNAL—230 W. Washington Sq., Philadelphia, PA 19105. Practical business articles on growing crops and producing livestock. Pays $50 to $500, on acceptance. Query required.

THE FINANCIAL MANAGER—Warren, Gorham & Lamont, 1 Penn Plaza, New York, NY 10119. Joseph P. Burns, Ed.-in-Chief. Articles, 1,500 to 3,000 words, on corporate taxation, corporate accounting, corporate finance, career development, and information systems and computers for financial and accounting professionals. Payment varies, on acceptance.

FINANCIAL WORLD—1450 Broadway, New York, NY 10018. Douglas A. McIntyre, Pub. Features and profiles of large companies and financial institutions and the people who run them. Pays varying rates, on publication. Queries are required.

FITNESS MANAGEMENT—P.O. Box 1198, Solana Beach, CA 92075. Edward H. Pitts, Ed. Authoritative features, 750 to 2,500 words, and news shorts, 100 to 750 words, for owners, managers, and program directors of fitness centers. Content must be in keeping with current medical practice; no fads. Pays 8¢ a word, on publication. Query.

FLORIST—29200 Northwestern Hwy., P.O. Box 2227, Southfield, MI 48037. Susan Nicholas, Man. Ed. Articles, to 2,000 words, with photos, on retail florist business improvement. Photos. Pays 8¢ a word.

FLOWERS &—Teleflora Plaza, Suite 260, 12233 W. Olympic Blvd., Los Angeles, CA 90064. Marie Moneysmith, Ed.-in-Chief. Articles, 1,000 to 3,500 words, with how-to information for retail florists. Pays from $500, on acceptance. Query with clips.

FOOD MANAGEMENT—747 Third Ave., New York, NY 10017. Donna Boss, Ed. Articles on foodservice in healthcare, schools, colleges, prisons, business and industry. Trends and how-to pieces, with management tie-in. Query.

FOOD PEOPLE—P.O. Box 3763, Seattle, WA 98124. Robb Zerr, Ed. Business news and trends pieces (10 to 500 words) for retail and wholesale grocers; features on employees, food, entertaining, supermarkets, and shopping. Fillers, to 200 words. Pays varying rates, on publication. Query.

FOREIGN TRADE—8208 W. Franklin, Minneapolis, MN 55426. John Freivalds, Ed. Articles and interviews, 1,700 to 2,100 words, on topics related to international trade that examine problems managers have faced, and deal with how they solved them. Pays $400, on publication. Guidelines.

THE FOREMAN'S LETTER—24 Rope Ferry Rd., Waterford, CT 06386. Carl Thunberg, Ed. Interviews, with photos, with top-notch supervisors and foremen. Pays 10¢ to 14¢ a word, extra for photos, on acceptance.

FREQUENT FLYER—888 Seventh Ave., New York, NY 10106. Jane L. Levere, Man. Ed. Articles, 1,000 to 3,000 words, on all aspects of frequent business travel, international trade, aviation, etc. Few pleasure travel; no personal experience pieces. Pays up to $500, on acceptance. Query required.

GARDEN DESIGN—4401 Connecticut Ave. N.W., Fifth Fl., Washington, DC 20008. Karen Fishler, Ed. Society of American Landscape Architects. Articles, 1,500 to 2,000 words, on classic and contemporary examples of residential landscape, garden, art, history, and design. Interviews. Pays $350, on publication. Query.

GLASS DIGEST—310 Madison Ave., New York, NY 10017. Charles Cumpston, Ed. Articles, 1,200 to 1,500 words, on building projects and glass/metal dealers, distributors, storefront and glazing contractors. Pays varying rates, on publication.

GLASS NEWS—P.O. Box 7138, Pittsburgh, PA 15213. Liz Scott, Man. Ed. Articles, to 1,500 words, on developments in glass manufacturing, glass factories, types of glass. Personality profiles. Pays 5¢ to 10¢ a word, on publication. Query with SASE.

GOLF COURSE NEWS—7901 Fourth St. North, St. Petersburg, FL 33702. Mark Leslie, Man. Ed. Features, 1,000 to 1,500 words, and news stories of any length, on all aspects of golf course design, building, and management. Pays $300 to $400, on acceptance.

GOLF SHOP OPERATIONS—5520 Park Ave., Box 395, Trumbull, CT 06611–0395. Dave Gould, Ed. Articles, 200 to 800 words, with photos, on successful golf shop operations; new ideas for merchandising, display, bookkeeping. Short pieces on golf professionals and retailers. Pays $250 to $350, on publication. Query with outline.

GOVERNMENT EXECUTIVE—1730 M St. N.W., 6th Fl., Washington, DC 20036. Timothy Clark, Ed. Articles, 1,500 to 3,000 words, for civilian and military government workers at the management level.

GREENHOUSE MANAGER—P.O. Box 1868, Fort Worth, TX 76101. Kevin Neal, Man. Ed. How-to articles, success stories, 500 to 1,800 words, accompanied by color slides, of interest to professional greenhouse growers. Profiles. Pays $50 to $300, on acceptance. Query required.

HARVARD BUSINESS REVIEW—Harvard Graduate School of Business Administration, Boston, MA 02163. Query editors on new ideas about management of interest to senior executives. Pays on publication.

HEALTH FOODS BUSINESS—567 Morris Ave., Elizabeth, NJ 07208. Mary Jane Dittmar, Ed. Articles, 1,500 words, with photos, on managing health food stores. Shorter pieces on trends, research findings, preventive medicine, alternative therapies. Interviews with doctors and nutritionists. Brief items for "Quote/Unquote" (include source). Pays on publication. Query. Send for guidelines.

HEATING/PIPING/AIR CONDITIONING—2 Illinois Center, Chicago, IL 60601. Robert T. Korte, Ed. Articles, to 5,000 words, on heating, piping, and air conditioning systems in industrial plants and large buildings; engineering information. Pays $60 per printed page, on publication. Query.

HOMEOWNERS—8520 Sweetwater, Suite F57, Houston, TX 77037. Theresa Seegers, Man. Ed. Articles, 200 to 500 words, on buying and selling real estate, mortgages, investments, home improvement, interior design, consumer and business trends: "material should emphasize the importance of consulting a real estate professional on any real estate matter." Pays 10¢ to 20¢ a word, on acceptance. Query.

HOSPITAL GIFT SHOP MANAGEMENT—7628 Densmore, Van Nuys, CA 91406. Barbara Feiner, Ed. Articles, 750 to 2,500 words, with managerial tips and sales pointers; hospital and merchandise profiles. Pays $10 to $100, on acceptance. Query required.

HOSPITAL SUPERVISOR'S BULLETIN—24 Rope Ferry Rd., Waterford, CT 06386. Michele Dunaj, Ed. Interviews, articles with non-medical hospital supervisors on departmental problem solving. Pays 12¢ a word. Query.

HOSPITALS—211 E. Chicago Ave., Suite 700, Chicago, IL 60611. Frank Sabatino, Ed. Articles, 500 to 800 words, for hospital administrators. Pays varying rates, on acceptance. Query.

HUMAN RESOURCE EXECUTIVE—Axon Group, 1035 Camphill Rd., Fort Washington, PA 19034. David Shadovitz, Ed. Profiles, case stories, and opinion pieces (1,800 to 2,200 words) of interest to people in the personnel profession. Pays varying rates, on acceptance. Queries required.

INC.—38 Commercial Wharf, Boston, MA 02110. George Gendron, Ed. Feature articles about how owners and managers of growing companies solve common problems. Pays to $1,500, on acceptance. Query.

INCENTIVE MAGAZINE—633 Third Ave., New York, NY 10017. Mary Riordan, Man. Ed. Articles on marketing, incentive travel, and product categories; motivation and incentive sales and merchandising strategies. Pays $125 to $800, on acceptance.

INCOME OPPORTUNITIES—380 Lexington Ave., New York, NY 10017. Stephen Wagner, Ed. Helpful articles, 1,000 to 2,500 words, on how to make money full or part-time; how to run a successful small business, improve sales, etc. Pays varying rates, on acceptance.

INDUSTRIAL DESIGN—330 W. 42nd St., New York, NY 10036. Annetta Hanna, Ed. Articles to 2,000 words, on product development, design management, graphic design, design history, fashion, art, and environments for designers and marketing executives. Profiles of designers and corporations that use design effectively. Pays $250 to $600, on publication.

INSTANT & SMALL COMMERCIAL PRINTER—P.O. Box 368, Northbrook, IL 60065. Patricia Cronin, Ed. Articles, 3 to 5 typed pages, for operators and employees of printing businesses specializing in retail printing and/or small commercial printing: case histories, how-tos, technical pieces. Opinion pieces, 1 to 2 typed pages. Photos. Pays $150 to $250 ($25 to $50 for opinion pieces), extra for photos, on publication. Query.

INSTITUTIONAL RESEARCH—See *Research Magazine.*

INTV JOURNAL—80 Fifth Ave., New York, NY 10011. William Dunlap, Ed. Features and short pieces on trends in independent television. Pays to $650, after publication. Query.

JEMS, JOURNAL OF EMERGENCY MEDICAL SERVICES—P.O. Box 1026, Solana Beach, CA 92075. Rick Minerd, Man. Ed. Articles (1,500 to 3,000 words) should address a wide audience (nurses, paramedics, EMTs, and physicians) exploring topics so that each group better understands the role and responsibilities of the others. Pays 10¢ a word. Guidelines available. Queries are required.

LOTUS—P.O. Box 9123, Cambridge, MA 02139. John Campbell, Ed. Dir. Articles, 1,500 to 3,000 words, for business and professional people using Lotus software. Query with outline required. Pay varies, on final approval.

LP-GAS MAGAZINE—131 W. First St., Duluth, MN 55802. Zane Chastain, Ed. Articles, 1,500 to 2,500 words, with photos, on LP-gas dealer operations: marketing, management, etc. Photos. Pays to 15¢ a word, extra for photos, on acceptance. Query.

MACHINE DESIGN—Penton Publications, 1100 Superior Blvd., Cleveland, OH 44114. Richard Beercheck, Exec. Ed. Articles, to 10 typed pages, on design-related topics for engineers. Pays varying rates, on publication. Submit outline or brief description.

MAGAZINE DESIGN & PRODUCTION—8340 Mission Rd., Suite 106, Prairie Village, KS 66206. Maureen Waters, Man. Ed. Articles, 6 to 10 typed pages, on magazine design and production: printing, typesetting, design, computers, layout, etc. Pays $100 to $200, on acceptance. Query required.

MAINTENANCE TECHNOLOGY—1300 S. Grove Ave., Barrington, IL 60010. Robert C. Baldwin, Ed. Articles with how-to information on maintenance of electrical and electronic systems, mechanical systems and equipment, and plant facilities. Readers are maintenance professionals in industrial plants and hospitals. Payment varies, on acceptance. Query required.

MANAGE—2210 Arbor Blvd., Dayton, OH 45439. Doug Shaw, Ed. Articles, 1,500 to 2,200 words, on management and supervision for first-line and middle managers. Pays 5¢ a word.

MANUFACTURING SYSTEMS—191 S. Gary, Carol Stream, IL 60188. Tom Inglesby, Ed. Articles, 500 to 2,000 words, on computer and information systems for industry executives seeking to increase productivity in manufacturing firms. Pays 10¢ to 20¢ a word, on acceptance. Query required.

MEMPHIS BUSINESS JOURNAL—88 Union, Suite 102, Memphis, TN 38103. Barney DuBois, Ed. Articles, to 2,000 words, on business, industry trade, agri-business and finance in the Mid-South trade area. Pays $80 to $200, on acceptance.

MINIATURES DEALER—633 W. Wisconsin Ave., Suite 304, Milwaukee, WI 53203. Geraldine Willems, Ed. Articles, 1,000 to 1,500 words, on advertising, promotion, merchandising of miniatures and other small business concerns. Interviews with miniatures dealers. Pays to $200, on publication.

MIX MAGAZINE—6400 Hollis St., Suite 12, Emeryville, CA 94608. David Schwartz, Ed. Articles, varying lengths, for professionals, on audio, video, and music entertainment technology. Pays 12 ½¢ a word, on publication. Query required.

MODERN HEALTHCARE—740 N. Rush St., Chicago, IL 60611. Clark Bell, Ed. Features on management, finance, building design and construction, and new technology for hospitals, health maintenance organizations, nursing homes, and other health care institutions. Pays $7 per column inch, on publication. Query.

MODERN OFFICE TECHNOLOGY—1100 Superior Ave., Cleveland, OH 44114. Lura Romei, Ed. Articles (3 to 4 double-spaced, typed pages) on new concepts, management techniques, technologies, and applications for management executives. Payment varies, on acceptance. Query preferred.

MODERN TIRE DEALER—P.O. Box 5417, 110 N. Miller Rd., Akron, OH 44313. Lloyd Stoyor, Ed. Tire retailing and automotive service articles, 1,000 to 1,500 words, with photos, on independent tire dealers and retreaders. Pays $300 to $350, on publication.

NANNY TIMES—P.O. Box 31, Rutherford, NJ 07070. Gillian Gordon, Ed. & Pub. How-to articles, 1,000 to 1,500 words, on childcare or anything related to the business of being or employing a nanny: safety, first aid, entertainment, nutrition, psychology, etc. Pays 5¢ to 10¢ a word, on publication.

NATIONAL FISHERMAN—120 Tillson Ave., Rockland, ME 04841. James W. Fullilove, Ed. Articles, 200 to 2,000 words, aimed at commercial fishermen and boat builders. Pays $3 per inch, extra for photos, on publication. Query preferred.

NATION'S BUSINESS—1615 H St. N.W., Washington, DC 20062. Articles on business-related topics, including management advice and success stories aimed at small- to medium-sized businesses. Pays negotiable rates, after acceptance. Guidelines available.

NEPHROLOGY NEWS & ISSUES—18582 Beach Blvd., Suite 201, Huntington Beach, CA 92648. David G. Anast, Ed. "We publish strictly news articles and opinion essays on dialysis, kidney transplantations, and kidney disease. We are not interested in patient testimonials, poems, humor, or any other 'soft' journalism." Pays varying rates, on publication. Photos a plus. Queries required.

NEVADA BUSINESS JOURNAL—3800 Howard Hughes Pkwy, Suite 120, Las Vegas, NV 89109. Lyle Brennan, Ed. Business articles, 1,000 to 3,000 words, of interest to Nevada readers; profiles, how-to articles. Pays $150 to $250 on acceptance. Query. Guidelines.

NEW CAREER WAYS NEWSLETTER—67 Melrose Ave., Haverhill, MA 01830. William J. Bond, Ed. How-to articles, 1,500 to 2,000 words, on new ways to succeed in business careers. Pays varying rates, on publication. Query with outline.

NORTHEAST INTERNATIONAL BUSINESS—401 Theodore Fremd Ave., Rye, NY 10580. David E. Moore, Exec. Ed. Articles, 1,000 to 1,500 words, on global marketing strategies, and short (500 words) pieces with tips on operating abroad. Profiles, 750 to 3,000 words, on individuals or companies. Pays $12 a column inch, on acceptance and on publication. Query required.

NSGA RETAIL FOCUS—National Sporting Goods Assoc., 1699 Wall St., Suite 700, Mt. Prospect, IL 60056. Larry Weindruch, Ed. Members magazine. Articles, 700 to 1,000 words, on sporting goods industry news and trends, the latest in new product information, and management and store operations. Payment varies, on publication. Query.

NURSINGWORLD JOURNAL—470 Boston Post Rd., Weston, MA 02193. Shirley Copithorne, Ed. Articles, 800 to 1,500 words, for nurses, nurse educators, and students of nursing, etc., on all aspects of nursing. B&W photos. Pays from 25¢ per column inch, on publication.

OPPORTUNITY MAGAZINE—6 N. Michigan Ave., Suite 1405, Chicago, IL 60602. Jack Weissman, Ed. Articles, 900 words, on sales psychology, sales techniques, self-improvement. Pays $20 to $40, on publication.

PAPER SALES—One East First St., Duluth, MN 55802. Jane Seybolt, Ed. Articles, 2,000 words, covering markets for all grades of paper, sanitary maintenance products, and plastics; read by paper distributors and sales representatives. Pays $250 to $300, on publication.

PC WEEK—800 Boylston St., Boston, MA 02119. Jennifer DeJong, Exec. Ed. No free-lance submissions.

PET BUSINESS—5728 Major Blvd., Suite 200, Orlando, FL 32819. Amy Jordan Smith, Ed. Brief documented articles on animals and products found in pet stores; research findings; legislative/regulatory actions. Pays $4 per column inch, on publication. Photos, $10 to $20.

PETS/SUPPLIES/MARKETING—One E. First St., Duluth, MN 55802. David D. Kowalski, Ed. Articles, 1,000 to 1,200 words, with photos, on pet shops, and pet and product merchandising. Pays 10¢ a word, extra for photos. No fiction or news clippings. Query.

PHOTO MARKETING—3000 Picture Pl., Jackson, MI 49201. Margaret Hooks, Man. Ed. Business articles, 1,000 to 3,500 words, for owners and managers of camera/video stores or photo processing labs. Pays $150 to $500, extra for photos, on publication.

PHYSICAL THERAPY/OCCUPATIONAL THERAPY JOB NEWS— 470 Boston Post Rd., Weston, MA 02193. John C. Hinds, Jr. Articles, case studies, and profiles (1,500 to 2,500 words) of interest to professional and student physical therapists. Guidelines available. Pays on publication.

PHYSICIANS FINANCIAL NEWS—McGraw-Hill Health Care Group, 800 Second Ave., New York, NY 10017. Joseph Lisanti, Sr. Ed. Articles (1,000 words) on investment and personal finance and non-clinical medical economic subjects. Pays $400, after acceptance. Queries required.

PHYSICIAN'S MANAGEMENT—7500 Old Oak Blvd., Cleveland, OH 44130. Bob Feigenbaum, Ed. Articles, about 2,500 to 3,000 words, on finance, investments, malpractice, and office management for primary care physicians. No clinical pieces. Pays $125 per printed page, on acceptance. Query with SASE.

PIZZA TODAY—P.O. Box 114, Santa Claus, IN 47579. Amy Lorton, Assoc. Ed. Business management articles, to 2,500 words, of use to pizza entrepreneurs. Pays $50 to $125 per published page, on publication.

PNG REPORT—P.O. Box 337, 121 North Main, Iola, WI 54945. Deb Lengkeek, Ed. Professional Numismatists Guild publication, for coin and bullion dealers. Management advice and business articles (2,000 to 3,000 words) aimed at improving work-related issues. Payment varies, on publication. Query.

P.O.B.—5820 Lilley Rd., Suite 5, Canton, MI 48187. Victoria L. Dickinson, Assoc. Ed. Technical and business articles, 1,000 to 4,000 words, for professionals and technicians in the surveying and mapping fields. Technical tips on field and office procedures and equipment maintenance. Pays $150 to $400, on acceptance.

POLICE MAGAZINE—P.O. Box 847, Carlsbad, CA 92008-9970. Glenn Hare, Ed. Articles and profiles (1,000 to 3,000 words) on specialized groups, equipment, issues and trends of interest to people in the law enforcement profession. Pays $100 to $400, on acceptance.

POOL & SPA NEWS—3923 W. Sixth St., Los Angeles, CA 90020. News articles for the swimming pool, spa, and hot tub industry. Pays from 8¢ to 12¢ a word, extra for photos, on publication. Query first.

PRIVATE PRACTICE—Box 12489, Oklahoma City, OK 73157. Cindy Wickersham, Asst. Ed. Articles, 1,500 to 2,000 words, on state or local legislation affecting medical field. Pays $250 to $350, on publication.

PRO—1233 Janesville Ave., Fort Atkinson, WI 53538. Rod Dickens, Ed. Articles, 1,000 to 1,500 words on business management for owners of lawn maintenance firms. Pays $150 to $300, on publication. Query.

PROFESSIONAL OFFICE DESIGN—111 Eighth Ave., New York, NY 10011. Muriel Chess, Ed. Articles, to 1,500 words, on space planning and design for offices in the fields of law, medicine, finance, accounting, advertising, and architecture/design. Pays competitive rates, on publication. Query required.

PROGRESSIVE GROCER—Four Stamford Forum, Stamford, CT 06901. Michael J. Sansolo, Man. Ed. Articles related to retail food operations; ideas for successful merchandising, promotions, and displays. Short pieces preferred. Cartoons and photos. Pay varies, on acceptance.

THE QUALITY REVIEW—253 W. 73rd St., New York, NY 10023. Brenda Niemand, Man. Ed. Articles, 2,000 to 4,000 words, on "relationship of quality to public policy, global business, and growing concerns about competitiveness." Pieces should be nontechnical; include case studies for illustration. Pay varies, on acceptance.

QUICK PRINTING—1680 S. W. Bayshore Blvd., Port St. Lucie, FL 34984. Bob Hall, Ed. Articles, 1,500 to 3,000 words, of interest to owners and operators of quick print shops, copy shops, and small commercial printers, on how to make their businesses more profitable; include figures. Pays $100, on acceptance.

REAL ESTATE TODAY—National Association of Realtors, 430 N. Michigan Ave., Chicago, IL 60611. Educational, how-to articles on all aspects of residential, finance, commercial-investment, and brokerage-management real estate, to 2,000 words. Query required. Pays in copies.

REMODELING—Hanley-Wood, Inc., 655 15th St., Suite 475, Washington, DC 20005. Wendy A. Jordan, Ed. Articles, 250 to 1,700 words, on remodeling and industry news for residential and light commercial remodelers. Pays 20¢ a word, on acceptance. Query.

RESEARCH MAGAZINE—2201 Third St., P.O. Box 77905, San Francisco, CA 94107. Anne Evers, Ed. Articles of interest to stock brokers, 1,000 to 3,000 words, on financial products, selling, how-tos, and financial trends. Pays from $300 to $900, on publication. Same requirements for *Institutional Research,* for institutional investors. Query.

RESTAURANTS USA—1200 17th St. N.W., Washington, DC 20036–3097. Sylvia Rivchun-Somerville, Ed. Articles, 2,500 to 3,500 words, on the food service and restaurant business. Pays $350 to $750, on acceptance. Query.

ROOFER MAGAZINE—P.O. Box 06253, Ft. Myers, FL 33906. Mr. Shawn Holiday, Ed. Technical and non-technical articles, human-interest pieces, 500 to 1,500 words, on roofing-related topics: new roofing concepts, energy savings, pertinent issues, industry concern. No general business or computer articles. Pays negotiable rates, on publication. Guidelines.

RV BUSINESS—29901 Agoura Rd., Agoura, CA 91301. Katherine Sharma, Exec. Ed. Articles, 1,500 to 2,500 words, on manufacturing, financing, selling, and servicing recreational vehicles. Articles on legislative matters affecting the industry. Pays varying rates.

THE SAFETY COMPLIANCE LETTER—24 Rope Ferry Rd., Waterford, CT 06386. Margot Levin, Ed. Interview-based articles, 800 to 1,250 words, for safety professionals, on solving OSHA-related safety and health problems. Pays to 15¢ a word, on acceptance. Query.

SALES & MARKETING MANAGEMENT—Bill Communications, Inc., 633 Third Ave., New York, NY 10017. A.J. Vogl, Ed. Short and feature articles of interest to sales and marketing executives. Looking for practical "news you can use." Pays varying rates, on acceptance. Queries preferred.

SALTWATER DEALER—One Bell Rd., Montgomery, AL 36117. Dave Ellison, Ed. Articles (300 to 1,250 words) for merchants who carry saltwater tackle and marine equipment: business focus is required, and writers should provide practical information for improving management and merchandising. Pays varying rates, on acceptance.

SIGN BUSINESS—P.O. Box 1416, Broomfield, CO 80020. Emerson Schwartzkopf, Ed. Articles specifically targeted to the sign business. Pays $50 to $200, on publication.

SNACK FOOD MAGAZINE—131 W. First St., Duluth, MN 55802. Jerry Hess, Ed. Articles, 600 to 1,500 words, on trade news, personalities, promotions, production in snack food manufacturing industry. Short pieces; photos. Pays 12¢ to 15¢ a word, $15 for photos, on acceptance. Query.

SOUTHERN LUMBERMAN—P.O. Box 1627, Franklin, TN 37064. Nanci P. Gregg, Ed. Articles on hardwood sawmill operations, interviews with industry leaders, how-to technical pieces with an emphasis on increasing sawmill production and efficiency. Pays $100 to $250 for articles with B&W photos. Queries preferred.

SOUVENIRS AND NOVELTIES—7000 Terminal Square, Suite 210, Upper Darby, PA 19082. Articles, 1,500 words, quoting souvenir shop managers on items that sell, display ideas, problems in selling, industry trends. Photos. Pays from $1 per column inch, extra for photos, on publication.

SPECIALTY STORE SERVICE BULLETIN—6604 W. Saginaw Hwy., Lansing, MI 48917. Jill Powell, Man. Ed. Articles on how to run a business, fashion trends, sales training, etc., for women's clothing store owners and managers. Payment varies, on acceptance. Query.

SUCCESSFUL FARMING—1716 Locust St., Des Moines, IA 50336. Loren Kruse, Ed. Articles, to 2,000 words, for farming families, on all areas of business farming: money management, marketing, machinery, soils and crops, livestock, and buildings; profiles. Pays from $300, on acceptance. Query required.

TAVERN SPORTS INTERNATIONAL—101 E. Erie St., Suite 850, Chicago, IL 60611. Jocelyn Hathaway, Man. Ed. Personality profiles and news features, 1,000 to 2,000 words, with color photos if possible, on organized amateur sports (darts, pool, shuffleboard, etc.) and issues concerning the coin-operated game industry. Payment varies, on publication.

TEA & COFFEE TRADE JOURNAL—130 W. 42nd St., New York, NY 10036. Jane P. McCabe, Ed. Articles, 3 to 5 pages, on trade issues reflecting the tea and coffee industry. Query first. Pays $5 per published inch, on publication.

TEXTILE WORLD—4170 Ashford-Dunwoody Rd. N.E., Suite 420, Atlanta, GA 30319. L.A. Christiansen, Ed. Articles, 500 to 2,000 words, with photos, on manufacturing and finishing textiles. Pays varying rates, on acceptance.

TILE WORLD/STONE WORLD—485 Kinderkamack Rd., Oradell, NJ 07649–1502. John Sailer, Man. Ed. Articles, 750 to 1,500 words, on new trends in installing and designing with tile and stone. For architects, interior designers, and design professionals. Pays $80 per printed page, on publication. Query.

TOP SHELF—199 Ethan Allen Hwy., Ridgefield, CT 06877. Jane Tougas, Ed. Dir. Trade news and advice (1,000 to 2,500 words) for bar owners and managers. "The emphasis is on personalities; taboos include irresponsible marketing of alcohol and promotion of overconsumption." Pays $300 to $600, on acceptance. Query.

TOURIST ATTRACTIONS AND PARKS—7000 Terminal Square, Suite 210, Upper Darby, PA 19082. Articles, 1,500 words, on successful management of parks and leisure attractions. News items, 250 and 500 words. Pays 7¢ a word, on publication. Query.

TRAILER/BODY BUILDERS—1602 Harold St., Houston, TX 77006. Paul Schenck, Ed. Articles on engineering, sales, and management ideas for truck body and truck trailer manufacturers. Pays from $100 per printed page, on acceptance.

TRAINING, THE MAGAZINE OF HUMAN RESOURCES DEVELOPMENT—50 S. Ninth St., Minneapolis, MN 55402. Jack Gordon, Ed. Articles, 1,000 to 2,500 words, for managers of training and development activities in corporations, government, etc. Pays to 15¢ a word, on acceptance. Query.

TRAVEL PEOPLE—CMP Publications, 600 Community Dr., Manhassett, NY 11030. Linda Ball, Ed. Personality profiles, 1,000 to 1,500 words, of successful travel industry workers. Pay varies, on acceptance.

TRUCKER/USA—P.O. Box 2029, Tuscaloosa, AL 35403. Phil Willis, Ed.

Features, 250 to 1,000 words, for heavy-duty truck drivers. Pays $10 to $50, on acceptance.

VENDING TIMES—545 Eighth Ave., New York, NY 10018. Arthur E. Yohalem, Ed. Feature and news articles, with photos, on vending machines. Pays varying rates, on acceptance. Query.

VIEW—80 Fifth Ave., Suite 501, New York, NY 10011. Peter Caranicas, Ed. Dir. Features and short pieces on trends in the business of television programming (network, syndication, cable, and pay). Profiles. Pays to $600, after publication.

VIRGINIA BUSINESS—411 E. Franklin St., Richmond, VA 23219. James Bacon, Ed. Articles, 1,000 to 2,500 words, related to the business scene in Virginia. Pays varying rates, on acceptance. Query required.

WESTERN INVESTOR—400 S.W. Sixth Ave., Suite 1115, Portland, OR 97204. Business and investment articles, 800 to 1,200 words, about companies and their leaders listed in the "Western Investor" data section. Pays from $50, on publication. Query first.

WINES & VINES—1800 Lincoln Ave., San Rafael, CA 94901. Philip E. Hiaring, Ed. Articles, 1,000 words, on grape and wine industry, emphasizing marketing and production. Pays 5¢ a word, on acceptance.

WOMAN'S ENTERPRISE—28210 Dorothy Dr., Agoura Hills, CA 91301. Caryne Brown, Ed.-in-Chief. Articles, 1,500 to 2,000 words, on the management of businesses owned by women; features on specific businesses and all aspects of their operation, including success factors, pitfalls, income expenditure, and profit figures. Pays 20¢ a word, on acceptance.

WOMEN IN BUSINESS—9100 Ward Parkway, Box 8728, Kansas City, MO 64114. Margaret E. Horan, Ed. Publication of the American Business Women's Association. Features, 1,000 to 2,000 words, for career women from 25 to 55 years old; no profiles. Pays 15¢ a word, on acceptance. Query.

WOOD "N ENERGY—P.O. Box 2008, Laconia, NH 03247. Jason Perry, Ed. Profiles and interviews, 1,000 to 2,500 words, with retailers and manufacturers of fireplace and wood stove equipment. Pays $150 to $250, on acceptance.

WOODSHOP NEWS—Pratt St., Essex, CT 06426–1122. Ian C. Bowen, Ed. Features (1 to 3 typed pages) for and about people who work with wood: business stories, profiles, news. Pays from $2 per column inch, on publication. Queries preferred.

THE WORK BOAT—P.O. Box 1348, Mandeville, LA 70470. Marilyn Barrett, Assoc. Ed. Features (to 2,000 words) and shorts (500 to 1,000 words) providing current, lively information for work boat employees, suppliers, and regulators: topics include construction and conversion; politics and industry; new products; and profiles. Payment varies, on acceptance and on publication. Queries preferred.

WORLD OIL—Gulf Publishing Co., P.O. Box 2608, Houston, TX 77252. T.R. Wright, Jr., Ed. Engineering and operations articles, 3,000 to 4,000 words, on petroleum industry exploration, drilling or producing. Photos. Pays from $50 per printed page, on acceptance. Query.

WORLD SCREEN NEWS—80 Fifth Ave., Suite 401, New York, NY 10011. Peter Caranicas, Ed. Features and short pieces on trends in the business of international television programming (network, syndication, cable, and pay). Pays to $500, after publication.

WORLD WASTES—6255 Barfield Rd., Atlanta, GA 30328. Bill Wolpin,

Ed./Pub. Lourdes Zamota, Assoc. Ed. Case studies, 1,000 to 2,000 words, with photos, of refuse haulers, landfill operators, resource recovery operations, and transfer stations, with solutions to problems in field. Pays from $125 per printed page, on publication. Query preferred.

YOUNG FASHIONS—119 Fifth Ave., New York, NY 10003. Articles, 2,000 to 4,000 words, that help store owners and department store buyers of children's clothes with merchandising or operations; how-to pieces. Payment varies, on acceptance. Query required.

IN-HOUSE MAGAZINES

Publications circulated to company employees (sometimes called house magazines or house organs) and to members of associations and organizations are excellent, well-paying markets for writers at all levels of experience. Large corporations publish these magazines to promote good will, familiarize readers with the company's services and products, and interest customers in these products. And, many organizations publish house magazines designed to keep their members abreast of the issues and events concerning a particular cause or industry. Always read an in-house magazine before submitting an article; write to the editor for a sample copy (offering to pay for it) and the editorial guidelines. Stamped, self-addressed envelopes should be enclosed with any query or manuscript. The following list includes only a sampling of publications in this large market.

AMERICAN BAR ASSOCIATION JOURNAL—750 N. Lake Shore Dr., Chicago, IL 60611. Robert Yates, Man. Ed. Practical articles, to 3,000 words, on law-related topics: current events in the law and ideas that will that will help lawyers in small firms better their practices. Writing should be in an informal, journalistic style. Pays $750 to $950, on acceptance; buys all rights.

AMTRAK EXPRESS—140 E. Main St., Suite 11, Huntington, NY 11743. Christopher Podgus, Ed. General-interest articles on business, health, books, sports, personal finance, lifestyle, entertainment, travel (within Amtrak territory), science for Amtrak travelers. Submit seasonal material three to six months in advance. Pays on publication, $300 to $700 for 1,500- to 2,000-word manuscript; $250 to $600 for department pieces of 1,500 to 2,500 words. Query with published clips.

CALIFORNIA HIGHWAY PATROLMAN—2030 V St., Sacramento, CA 95818. Carol Perri, Ed. Articles on transportation safety, California history, travel, consumerism, humor, general items, etc. Photos a plus. Pays 2 ½¢ a word, extra for B&W photos, on publication. Guidelines with SASE.

CATHOLIC FORESTER—425 W. Shuman Blvd., Naperville, IL 60566. Barbara Cunningham, Ed. Official publication of the Catholic Order of Foresters, a fraternal life insurance company for Catholics. Articles, to 2,000 words, of interest to Middle America. Fiction, to 3,000 words, that deals with contemporary issues; no sex or violence. Pays from 5¢ a word, on acceptance.

COLUMBIA—1 Columbus Plaza, New Haven, CT 06507–0901. Richard McMunn, Ed. Journal of the Knights of Columbus. Articles, 1,500 words, for Catholic families. Must be accompanied by color photos or transparencies. No fiction. Pays to $500 for articles and photos, on acceptance.

THE COMPASS—Mobil International Aviation and Marine Sales, Inc., 150 E. 42nd St., New York, NY 10017. T.F. Gerrety, Ed. Articles, to 3,500 words, on the sea and deep sea trade; also articles on aviation. Photos. Pays to $250, on acceptance. Query.

THE ELKS MAGAZINE—425 W. Diversey Pkwy., Chicago, IL 60614. Fred D. Oakes, Ed. Articles, to 2,500 words, on business, sports, and topics of current interest; for non-urban audience with above-average income. Informative or humorous pieces, to 2,500 words. Pays $150 to $500 for articles, on acceptance. Query.

FIREHOUSE—PTN Publishing Company, 210 Crossways Park Dr., Woodbury, NY 11797. Janet Kimmerly, Exec. Ed. Articles, 500 to 2,000 words: on-the-scene accounts of fires, trends in firefighting equipment, controversial fire service issues, and lifestyles of firefighters. Pays $100 per typeset page. Also pays for photos. Query.

FOCUS—Turnkey Publications, 4807 Spicewood Springs Rd., Suite 3150, Austin, TX 78759. Greg Farman, Ed. Magazine of the North American Data General Users Group. Articles, 700 to 4,000 words, on Data General computers. Photos a plus. Pays to $100, on publication. Query required.

FORD NEW HOLLAND NEWS—Ford New Holland, Inc., New Holland, PA 17557. Gary Martin, Ed. Articles, to 1,500 words, with strong color photo support, on production, agriculture, research, and rural living. Pays on acceptance. Query.

THE FURROW—Deere & Company, John Deere Rd., Moline, IL 61265. George R. Sollenberger, Exec. Ed. Specialized, illustrated articles on farming. Pays to $1,000, on acceptance.

GEOBYTE—P.O. Box 979, Tulsa, OK 74101. Ken Milam, Man. Ed. Publication of the American Association of Petroleum Geologists. Articles, 20 typed pages, on computer applications in exploration and production of oil, gas, and energy minerals for geophysicists, geologists, and petroleum engineers. Pay varies, on acceptance. Queries preferred.

INLAND—Inland Steel Co., 18 South Home Ave., Park Ridge, IL 60068. Sheldon A. Mix, Man. Ed. Articles, varying lengths, of interest to Midwestern readers. History, folklore, commentaries, nature, humor. Send completed manuscripts. Pays on acceptance.

KIWANIS—3636 Woodview Trace, Indianapolis, IN 46268. Chuck Jonak, Exec. Ed. Articles, 2,500 words (sidebars, 250 to 350 words) on lifestyle, relationships, world view, education, trends, small business, religion, health, etc. No travel pieces, interviews, profiles. Pays $400 to $1,000, on acceptance. Query.

THE LION—300 22nd St., Oak Brook, IL 60570. Robert Kleinfelder, Sr. Ed. Official publication of Lions Clubs International. Articles, 800 to 2,000 words, and photo essays, on Club activities. Pays from $50 to $400, including photos, on acceptance. Query.

THE MODERN WOODMEN—Modern Woodmen of America, Mississippi River at 17th St., Rock Island, IL 61201. Gloria Bergh, Manager, Public Relations. Family- and community-oriented, general-interest articles; some quality fiction. Color photos. Pays from $50, on acceptance. Publication not copyrighted.

OPTIMIST MAGAZINE—4494 Lindell Blvd., St. Louis, MO 63108. Gary S. Bradley, Ed. Articles, to 1,500 words, on activities of local Optimist club, and techniques for personal and club success; also articles of general interest to the membership. Pays from $100, on acceptance. Query.

RESTAURANTS USA—1200 17th St. N.W., Washington, DC 20036–3097. Sylvia Rivchun-Somerville, Ed. Publication of the National Restaurant Association. Articles, 2,500 to 3,500 words, on the food service and restaurant business. Pays $350 to $750, on acceptance. Query.

THE ROTARIAN—1560 Sherman Ave., Evanston, IL 60201. Willmon L. White, Ed. Publication of Rotary International, world fellowship of business and professional men. Articles, 1,200 to 2,000 words, on international social and economic issues, business and management, human relationships, travel, sports, environment, science and technology; humor. Pays good rates, on acceptance. Query.

WOODMEN OF THE WORLD MAGAZINE—1700 Farnam St., Omaha, NE 68102. Leland A. Larson, Ed. Articles on history, travel, sports, do-it-yourself projects, health, science, etc. Photos. Pays 5¢ a word, extra for photos, on acceptance.

RELIGIOUS AND DENOMINATIONAL

ADVANCE—1445 Boonville Ave., Springfield, MO 65802. Gwen Jones, Ed. Articles, 1,200 words, slanted to ministers, on preaching, doctrine, practice; how-to features. Pays to 5¢ a word, on acceptance.

AGLOW MAGAZINE—P.O. Box 1548, Lynnwood, WA 98046–1557. Gwen Weising, Ed. Articles and testimonials, 1,000 to 2,000 words, that encourage, instruct, inform, or entertain Christian women of all ages, and relate to the work of the Holy Spirit. Should deal with contemporary issues. Pays 8¢ to 10¢ a word, on acceptance. Queries required.

AMERICA—106 W. 56th St., New York, NY 10019. George W. Hunt, S.J., Ed. Articles, 1,000 to 2,500 words, on current affairs, family life, literary trends. Pays $75 to $150, on acceptance.

AMERICAN BIBLE SOCIETY RECORD—1865 Broadway, New York, NY 10023. Clifford P. Macdonald, Man. Ed. Material related to work of American Bible Society: translating, publishing, distributing. Pays on acceptance. Query.

ANNALS OF ST. ANNE DE BEAUPRÉ—P.O. Box 1000, St. Anne de Beaupré, Quebec, Canada G0A 3C0. Roch Achard, C.Ss.R., Ed. Articles, 1,100 to 1,200 words, on Catholic subjects and on St. Anne. Pays 2¢ to 4¢ a word, on acceptance.

BAPTIST LEADER—American Baptist Churches, P.O. Box 851, Valley Forge, PA 19482–0851. L. Isham, Ed. Practical how-to or thought-provoking articles, 1,200 to 1,600 words, for local church education lay leaders and teachers.

THE B'NAI B'RITH INTERNATIONAL JEWISH MONTHLY—1640 Rhode Island Ave. N.W., Washington, DC 20036. Jeff Rubin, Ed. Original, lively articles, 500 to 3,000 words, on trends, politics, personalities, and culture of the Jewish community. Fiction, 1,000 to 4,000 words. Pays 10¢ to 25¢ a word, on publication. Query.

BREAD—6401 The Paseo, Kansas City, MO 64131. Karen De Sollar, Ed. Church of the Nazarene. Devotional, Bible study, and Christian guidance articles, to 1,200 words, for teenagers. Religious short stories, to 1,500 words. Pays from 3 ½¢ a word for first rights, 3¢ a word for reprints, on acceptance. Guidelines.

BRIGADE LEADER—Box 150, Wheaton, IL 60189. Steve Neideck, Ed. Inspirational articles, 1,000 to 1,800 words, for Christian men who lead boys. Pays $60 to $150. Query only.

CATECHIST—2451 E. River Rd., Dayton, OH 45439. Patricia Fischer, Ed. Informational and inspirational articles, 1,200 to 1,500 words, for Catholic teachers, coordinators, and administrators in religious education programs. Pays $25 to $75, on publication.

589

CATHOLIC LIFE—35750 Moravian Dr., Fraser, MI 48026. Robert C. Bayer, Ed. Articles, 600 to 1,200 words, on Catholic missionary work in Hong Kong, India, Latin America, Africa, etc. Photos. No fiction or poetry. Pays 4¢ a word, extra for photos, on publication.

CATHOLIC TWIN CIRCLE—12700 Ventura Blvd., Suite 200, Studio City, CA 91604. Mary Louise Frawley, Ed. Articles and interviews of interest to Catholics, 1,000 to 2,000 words, with photos. Strict attention to Catholic doctrine required. Enclose SASE. Pays 10¢ a word, on publication.

CHARISMA & CHRISTIAN LIFE—600 Rinehart Rd., Lake Mary, FL 32746. Paul Thigpen, Ed. Dir. Charistmatic/Evangelical Christian articles, 1,000 to 2,000 words, for developing the spiritual life. Photos. Pays varying rates, on publication.

THE CHRISTIAN CENTURY—407 S. Dearborn St., Chicago, IL 60605. James M. Wall, Ed. Ecumenical. Articles, 1,500 to 2,500 words, with a religious angle, on political and social issues, international affairs, culture, the arts. Poetry, to 20 lines. Photos. Pays about $25 per printed page, extra for photos, on publication.

CHRISTIAN HERALD—40 Overlook Dr., Chappaqua, NY 10514. Bob Chuvala, Ed. Interdenominational. Articles, personal-experience pieces, to 1,500 words, on biblically oriented topics. Pays from 10¢ a word for full-length features, from $25 for short pieces, after acceptance. Query or send complete manuscript. No poetry.

CHRISTIAN SINGLE—127 Ninth Ave. N., Nashville, TN 37234. Cliff Allbritton, Ed. Articles, 600 to 1,200 words, on leisure activities, inspiring personal experiences, for Christian singles. Humor. Pays 5¢ a word, on acceptance. Query. Send 9 x12 SASE with 85¢ postage for guidelines and sample issue.

CHRISTIAN SOCIAL ACTION—100 Maryland Ave. NE, Washington, DC 20002. Lee Ranck, Ed. Articles, 1,500 to 2,000 words, on social issues for concerned persons of faith. Pays $75 to $100, on publication.

CHRISTIANITY TODAY—465 Gundersen Dr., Carol Stream, IL 60188. Lyn Cryderan, Ed. David Neff, Sr. Assoc. Ed. Doctrinal social issues and interpretive essays, 1,500 to 3,000 words, from evangelical Protestant perspective. Pays $300 to $500, on acceptance. Query required.

CHURCH & STATE—8120 Fenton St., Silver Spring, MD 20910. Joseph L. Conn, Man. Ed. Articles, 600 to 2,600 words, on religious liberty and church-state relations issues. Pays varying rates, on acceptance. Query.

CHURCH ADMINISTRATION—127 Ninth Ave. N., Nashville, TN 37234. Gary Hardin, Ed. Southern Baptist. How-to articles, 1,500 to 1,800 words, on administrative planning, staffing, pastoral ministry, organization, and financing. Pays 5¢ a word, on acceptance. Query.

CHURCH EDUCATOR—Educational Ministries, Inc., 2861-C Saturn St., Brea, CA 92621. Robert G. Davidson, Ed. Articles, 200 to 3,000 words, with a personal approach to Christian education; articles on youth programs; Advent or Lenten material. How-tos for adult and juvenile Christian education. Pays 3¢ a word, on publication.

THE CHURCH HERALD—6157 28th St. S.E., Grand Rapids, MI 49506. John Stapert, Ed. Reformed Church in America. Articles, 500 to 1,500 words, on Christianity and culture, politics, marriage, and home. Pays $40 to $125, on acceptance. Query required.

THE CHURCH MUSICIAN—127 Ninth Ave. N., Nashville, TN 37234. W. M. Anderson, Ed. Articles for spiritual enrichment, testimonials, human-interest pieces, and other subjects of interest to music directors, pastors, organists, pianists, choir coordinators, and members of the music council in local churches. No clippings. Pays to 5¢ a word, on acceptance. Same address and requirements for *Glory Songs* (for adults), and *Opus One* and *Opus Two* (for teenagers).

THE CIRCUIT RIDER—P.O. Box 801, Nashville, TN 37202. Keith Pohl, Ed. Articles for United Methodist Pastors, 800 to 1,600 words. Pays $25 to $100, on acceptance. Query, with SASE, preferred.

COLUMBIA—1 Columbus Plaza, New Haven, CT 06507–0901. Richard McMunn, Ed. Knights of Columbus. Articles, 1,500 words, for Catholic families. Must be accompanied by color photos or transparencies. No fiction. Pays to $500 for articles with photos, on acceptance.

COMMENTARY—165 E. 56th St., New York, NY 10022. Norman Podhoretz, Ed. Articles, 5,000 to 7,000 words, on contemporary issues, Jewish affairs, social sciences, religious thought, culture. Serious fiction; book reviews. Pays on publication.

COMMONWEAL—15 Dutch St., New York, NY 10038. Margaret O'Brien Steinfels, Ed. Catholic. Articles, to 3,000 words, on political, religious, social, and literary subjects. Pays 3¢ a word, on acceptance.

CONFIDENT LIVING—Box 82808, Lincoln, NE 68501. Jan Reeser, Man. Ed. Articles, to 1,500 words, on relating biblical truths to daily living. Photos. Pays 4¢ to 10¢ a word, extra for photos, on acceptance. No simultaneous submissions or reprints. SASE required.

DAILY MEDITATION—Box 2710, San Antonio, TX 78299. Ruth S. Paterson, Ed. Inspirational nonsectarian articles, 650 to 2,000 words. Fillers, to 350 words; verse, to 20 lines. Pays ½¢ to 2¢ a word for prose; 14¢ a line for verse, on acceptance.

DECISION—Billy Graham Evangelistic Association, 1300 Harmon Pl., Minneapolis, MN 55403. Roger C. Palms, Ed. Articles, Christian testimonials, 1,800 to 2,000 words. Poems, 4 to 20 lines, preferably free verse; narratives, 500 to 1,000 words. Pays varying rates, on publication.

THE DISCIPLE—Box 179, St. Louis, MO 63166. James L. Merrell, Ed. Articles on Christian living; devotionals, 150 words. Poetry; short humor. Pays $10 to $35 for articles, $2 to $10 for poetry, on publication.

DISCOVERIES—6401 The Paseo, Kansas City, MO 64131. Fiction for children, grades 3 to 6, 400 to 500 words, defining Christian experiences and demonstrating Christian values and beliefs. Pays 3½¢ a word for first rights, on acceptance.

THE EVANGEL—999 College Ave., Winona Lake, IN 46590. Vera Bethel, Ed. Free Methodist. Personal-experience articles, 1,000 words. Short, devotional items, 300 to 500 words. Fiction, 1,200 words, on Christian solutions to problems. Serious poetry, 8 to 12 lines. Pays $25 for articles, $45 for fiction, $5 for poetry, on publication. Return postage required.

EVANGELICAL BEACON—1515 E. 66th St., Minneapolis, MN 55423. George Keck, Ed. Evangelical Free Church. Articles, 250 to 1,750 words, on religious topics: testimonials, pieces on current issues from an evangelical perspective, short inspirational and evangelistic devotionals. Pays 3¢ to 4¢ a word, on publication. Send SASE for writers' guidelines.

FAITH TODAY—Box 8800, Sta. B, Willowdale, Ontario, Canada M2K 2R6. Brian C. Stiller, Ed. Audrey Dorsch, Man. Ed. Articles, 1,500 words, on current issues relating to the church in Canada. Pays negotiable rates, on publication. Queries are preferred.

THE FUNDAMENTALIST JOURNAL—2220 Langhorne Rd., Lynchburg, VA 24514. Deborah Huff, Ed. Articles, 500 to 2,000 words, that examine matters of contemporary interest to all Fundamentalist Christians: news articles, profiles, human-interest pieces; moral and religious issues; Bible studies; short articles for "Family Living" and "Preaching & Pastoring" sections. Payment varies and is made on publication. Query.

THE GEM—Box 926, Findlay, OH 45839. Marilyn Rayle Kern, Ed. Articles, 300 to 1,600 words, and fiction, 1,000 to 1,600 words: true-to-life experiences of God's help, of healed relationships, and of growing maturity in faith. For adolescents through senior citizens. Pays $15 for articles and fiction, $5 to $10 for fillers, after publication.

GLORY SONGS—See *The Church Musician.*

GROUP, THE YOUTH MINISTRY MAGAZINE—Box 481, Loveland, CO 80539. Joani Schultz, Ed. Dir. Interdenominational magazine for leaders of junior and senior high school Christian youth groups. Articles, 500 to 1,700 words, about successful youth groups or youth group projects. Short how-to pieces, to 300 words, for "Try This One"; news items, to 500 words, for "News, Trends, and Tips." Pays to $150 for articles, $15 to $25 for department pieces, on acceptance. Guidelines available.

GUIDE MAGAZINE—Review and Herald Publishing Co., 55 W. Oak Ridge Dr., Hagerstown, MD 21740. Stories and articles, to 1,800 words, for Christian youth, ages 10 to 14. Pays 3¢ to 4¢ a word, on acceptance.

GUIDEPOSTS—747 Third Ave., New York, NY 10017. True first-person stories, 250 to 1,500 words, stressing how faith in God helps people cope with life. Anecdotal fillers, to 250 words. Pays $100 to $400, $50 for fillers, on acceptance.

HOME LIFE—127 Ninth Ave. N., Nashville, TN 37234. Charlie Warren, Ed. Mary P. Darby Asst. Ed. Southern Baptist. Articles, preferably personal-experience, and fiction, to 1,500 words, on Christian marriage, parenthood, and family relationships. Human-interest pieces, 200 to 500 words; cartoons and short verse. Pays to 5¢ a word, on acceptance.

INSIDE MAGAZINE—226 S. 16th St., Philadelphia, PA 19102. Jane Biberman, Ed. Articles, 1,500 to 3,000 words, and fiction, 2,000 to 3,000 words, of interest to Jewish men and women. Pays $100 to $500, on acceptance. Query.

INSIGHT—55 West Oak Ridge Dr., Hagerstown, MD 21740. Christopher Blake, Ed. Seventh-day Adventist. Personal-experience narratives, articles, and humor, to 1,500 words, for high school students. Parables; shorts; poetry. Pays 10¢ to 15¢ a word, extra for photos, on acceptance. Same requirements for *Insight/Out,* for Christian non-denominational readers.

JOURNEY—Christian Board of Publication, Box 179, St. Louis, MO 63166. Michael E. Dixon, Ed. Fiction, 100 to 1,200 words; articles, 600 to 1,000 words; and poetry, to 20 lines. Accepts material for 12- to 16-year-olds. Pays 3¢ a word for prose, from $3 for poetry, on acceptance. Guidelines available.

KEY TO CHRISTIAN EDUCATION—8121 Hamilton Ave., Cincinnati, OH 45231. Marjorie Miller, Ed. Articles, on teaching methods, and success stories for workers in Christian education. Pays varying rates, on acceptance.

LIBERTY MAGAZINE—12501 Old Columbia Pike, Silver Spring, MD 20904–1608. Roland R. Hegstad, Ed. Timely articles, to 2,500 words, and photo essays, on religious freedom and church-state relations. Pays 6¢ to 8¢ a word, on acceptance. Query.

LIGHT AND LIFE—901 College Ave., Winona Lake, IN 46590. Robert Haslam, Ed. Fresh, lively articles about practical Christian living, and sound treatments of vital issues facing the Evangelical in contemporary society. Pays 4¢ a word, on publication. Query.

LIGUORIAN—Liguori, MO 63057. Rev. Allan Weinert, Ed. Francine O'Connor, Man. Ed. Catholic. Articles and short stories, 1,500 to 2,000 words, on Christian values in modern life. Pays 10¢ to 12¢ a word, on acceptance.

LIVE—1445 Boonville Ave., Springfield, MO 65802. John T. Maempa, Adult Ed. Sunday school paper for adults. Fiction, 1,500 to 2,000 words, and articles, 1,000 to 1,500 words, on applying Bible principles to everyday living. Pays 2¢ to 3¢ a word, on acceptance. Send SASE for guidelines.

THE LIVING LIGHT—United States Catholic Conference, Dept. of Education, 3211 4th St. N.W., Washington, DC 20017–1194. Berard L. Marthaler, Exec. Ed. Theoretical and practical articles, 1,500 to 4,000 words, on religious education, catechesis, and pastoral ministry.

LIVING WITH CHILDREN—127 Ninth Ave. N., Nashville, TN 37234. Articles, 800, 1,450, or 2,000 words, on parent-child relationships, told from a Christian perspective. Pays 5¢ a word, after acceptance.

LIVING WITH PRESCHOOLERS—127 Ninth Ave. N., Nashville, TN 37234. Articles, 800, 1,450, or 2,000 words, and fillers, to 300 words, for Christian families. Pays 5¢ a word, on acceptance.

LIVING WITH TEENAGERS—127 Ninth Ave. N., Nashville, TN 37234. Articles told from a Christian perspective for parents of teenagers; first-person approach preferred. Poetry, 4 to 16 lines. Pays 5¢ a word, on acceptance.

THE LOOKOUT—8121 Hamilton Ave., Cincinnati, OH 45231. Mark A. Taylor, Ed. Articles, 1,000 to 1,500 words, on families and people overcoming problems by applying Christian principles. Inspirational or humorous shorts, 500 to 800 words; fiction. Pays 4¢ to 6¢ a word, on acceptance.

THE LUTHERAN—8765 W. Higgins Rd., Chicago, IL 60631. Edgar R. Trexler, Ed. Articles, to 2,000 words, on Christian ideology, personal religious experiences, social and ethical issues, family life, church, and community. Pays $100 to $600, on acceptance. Query.

MARRIAGE & FAMILY—Division of Abbey Press, St. Meinrad, IN 47577. Kass Dotterweich, Man. Ed. Expert advice, personal-experience articles with moral, religious, or spiritual slant, to 2,500 words, on marriage and family relationships. Pays 7¢ a word, on acceptance.

MATURE LIVING—127 Ninth Ave. N., Nashville, TN 37234. General-interest and travel articles, nostalgia and fiction, 900 words, for Christians, 60 years and older. Profiles, 25 lines; must include a B&W action photo. Brief, humorous items for "Cracker Barrel." Pays 5¢ a word, $25 for profile and photo, $5 for humor on acceptance. Buys all rights.

MATURE YEARS—201 Eighth Ave. S., P.O. Box 801, Nashville, TN 37202. United Methodist. Articles on retirement or related subjects, 1,500 to 2,000 words. Humorous and serious fiction, 1,500 to 1,800 words, for adults. Poetry, to 14 lines. Include Social Security number. with manuscript. Buys all rights.

MESSENGER OF THE SACRED HEART—661 Greenwood Ave., Toronto, Ont., Canada M4J 4B3. Articles and short stories, about 1,500 words, for American and Canadian Catholics. Pays from 4¢ a word, on acceptance.

MIDSTREAM—515 Park Ave., New York, NY 10022. Murray Zuckoff, Ed. Jewish-interest articles and book reviews. Fiction, to 3,000 words, and poetry. Pays 5¢ a word, after publication.

THE MIRACULOUS MEDAL—475 E. Chelten Ave., Philadelphia, PA 19144. Robert P. Cawley, C.M. Ed. Dir. Catholic. Fiction, to 2,400 words. Religious verse, to 20 lines. Pays from 2¢ a word for fiction, from 50¢ a line for poetry, on acceptance.

MODERN LITURGY—160 E. Virginia St., #290, San Jose, CA 95112. Ken Guentert, Ed. Creative material for worship services; religious parables, to 1,000 words; how-tos, essays on Roman Catholic worship, 750 to 1,600 words. Plays. Pays in copies and subscription.

MOMENT—3000 Connecticut Ave., Suite 300, Washington, DC 20008. Charlotte Anker, Man. Ed. Sophisticated articles and some fiction, 2,500 to 5,000 words, on Jewish topics. Pays $150 to $400, on publication.

MOMENTUM—National Catholic Educational Assn., 1077 30th St. N.W., Suite 100, Washington, DC 20007–3852. Patricia Feistritzer, Ed. Articles, 500 to 1,500 words, on outstanding programs, issues, and research in education. Book reviews. Pays 2¢ a word, on publication. Query.

MOODY MONTHLY—820 N. La Salle Dr., Chicago, IL 60610. Andrew Scheer, Sr. Ed. Anecdotal articles, 1,200 to 1,800 words, on the Evangelical Christian experience in school, the home, and the workplace. Pays 10¢ to 15¢ a word, on acceptance. Query.

THE NATIONAL CHRISTIAN REPORTER—See *The United Methodist Reporter.*

NEW ERA—50 E. North Temple, Salt Lake City, UT 84150. Richard M. Romney, Man. Ed. Articles, 150 to 3,000 words, and fiction, to 3,000 words, for young Mormons. Poetry; photos. Pays 5¢ to 10¢ a word, 25¢ a line for poetry, on acceptance. Query.

NEW WORLD OUTLOOK—475 Riverside Dr., Rm. 1351, New York, NY 10115. Sherrie Boyens, Man. Ed. Articles, 1,500 to 2,500 words, on Christian missions, religious issues, and public affairs. Pays on publication.

OBLATES—15 S. 59th St., Belleville, IL 62222–9978. Address Jacqueline Lowery Corn, Man. Ed. Articles, 500 to 600 words, for mature Catholics, that inspire, uplift, and motivate through positive Christian values in everyday life. Inspirational poetry, to 16 lines. Pays $75 for articles, $25 for poems, on acceptance. Send complete manuscript only. Guidelines.

OPUS ONE AND OPUS TWO—See *The Church Musician.*

OUR FAMILY—Box 249, Battleford, Sask., Canada S0M 0E0. Nestor Gregoire, Ed. Articles, 1,000 to 3,000 words, for Catholic families, on modern society, family, marriage, current affairs, and spiritual topics. Humor; verse. Pays 7¢ to 10¢ a word for articles, 75¢ to $1 a line for poetry, on acceptance. SASE with international reply coupons required with all submissions. Guidelines.

OUR SUNDAY VISITOR—Huntington, IN 46750. Robert Lockwood, Ed. In-depth features, 1,000 to 1,200 words, on the Catholic church in America today. Pays $150 to $250, on acceptance

PARISH FAMILY DIGEST—Noll Plaza, Huntington, IN 46750. George P. Foster, Ed. Articles, 750 to 900 words, fillers and humor, for Catholic families and parishes. Pays 5¢ a word, on acceptance.

PENTECOSTAL EVANGEL—1445 Boonville Ave., Springfield, MO 65802. Richard Champion, Ed. Assemblies of God. Religious personal experience and devotional articles, 500 to 1,500 words. Verse, 12 to 30 lines. Pays 4¢ a word, on publication.

PRESBYTERIAN SURVEY—100 Witherspoon, Louisville, KY 40202. Vic Jameson, Ed. Articles, 1,200 words, of interest to members of the Presbyterian Church or ecumenical individuals. Pays to $150, on acceptance.

PRESENT TENSE—165 E. 56th St., New York, NY 10022. Murray Polner, Ed. Serious articles, 2,000 to 3,000 words, with photos, on news concerning Jews throughout the world; first person encounters and personal experience pieces. Literary-political reportage. Contemporary themes only. Pays $200 to $300, on publication. Query.

THE PRIEST—200 Noll Plaza, Huntington, IN 46750. Articles, to 2,500 words, on life and ministry of priests, current theological developments, etc., for priests, permanent deacons, and seminarians. Pays $35 to $100, on acceptance.

PURPOSE—616 Walnut Ave., Scottdale, PA 15683–1999. James E. Horsch, Ed. Articles, 350 to 1,200 words, on Christian discipleship themes, with good photos; pieces of history, biography, science, hobbies, from a Christian perspective. Fiction, to 1,200 words, on Christian problem solving. Poetry, 3 to 12 lines. Pays to 5¢ a word, to $1 a line for poetry, on acceptance.

QUEEN—26 S. Saxon Ave., Bay Shore, NY 11706. James McMillan, M.M.M., Ed. Publication of Montfort Missionaries. Articles and fiction, 1,000 to 2,000 words, related to the Virgin Mary. Poetry. Pay varies, on acceptance.

THE QUIET HOUR—850 N. Grover Ave., Elgin, IL 60120. Janette L. Pearson, Ed. Short devotionals. Pays $15, on acceptance. By assignment only; query required.

THE RECONSTRUCTIONIST—Church Road & Greenwood Ave., Wyncote, PA 19095. Rabbi Joy Levitt, Ed. Articles and fiction, 2,000 to 3,000 words, relating to Judaism. Poetry. Pays $18 to $36, on publication.

ST. ANTHONY MESSENGER—1615 Republic St., Cincinnati, OH 45210. Norman Perry, O.F.M., Ed. Articles, 2,000 to 3,000 words, on personalities, major movements, education, family, and social issues. Human interest pieces. Humor; fiction (2,000 to 3,000 words). Pays 14¢ a word, on acceptance. Query for nonfiction.

ST. JOSEPH'S MESSENGER—P.O. Box 288, Jersey City, NJ 07303. Sister Ursula Maphet, Ed. Inspirational articles, 500 to 1,000 words, and fiction, 1,000 to 1,500 words. Verse, 4 to 40 lines.

SEEK—8121 Hamilton Ave., Cincinnati, OH 45231. Eileen H. Wilmoth, Ed. Articles and fiction, to 1,200 words, on inspirational and controversial topics and timely religious issues. Christian Testimonials. Pays to 3¢ a word, on acceptance. Guidelines.

SHARING THE VICTORY—8701 Leeds Rd., Kansas City, MO 64129. Skip Stogsdill, Ed. Articles, interviews, and profiles, to 1,000 words, for coed Christian athletes and coaches in high school and college. Pays from $75, on publication. Query required.

SIGNS OF THE TIMES—P. O. Box 7000, Boise, ID 83707. Kenneth J.

Holland, Ed. Feature articles on Christians who have performed community services; current issues from a biblical perspective; health, home, marriage, human-interest pieces; inspirational articles, 500 to 2,000 words. Pays 12¢ to15¢ a word, on acceptance. Seventh-Day Adventists.

SISTERS TODAY—The Liturgical Press, St. John's Abbey, Collegeville, MN 56321. Sister Mary Anthony Wagner, O.S.B., Ed. Articles, 500 to 3,500 words, on Roman Catholic theology, religious issues for women and the Church. Poetry, to 34 lines. Pays $5 per printed page, $10 per poem, on publication. Send articles to Editor at St. Benedict's Convent, St. Joseph's MN 56374. Send poetry to Sister Audrey Synnott, R.S.M., 1437 Blossom Rd., Rochester, NY 14610.

SOCIAL JUSTICE REVIEW—3835 Westminster Pl., St. Louis, MO 63108. Rev. John H. Miller, C.S.C., Ed. Articles 2,000 to 3.000 words, on social problems in light of Catholic teaching and current scientific studies. Pays 2¢ a word, on publication.

SPIRITUAL LIFE—2131 Lincoln Rd. N.E., Washington, DC 20002-1199. Steven Payne, O.C.D., Ed. Professional religious journal. Religious essays, 3,000 to 5,000 words, on spirituality in contemporary life. Pays from $50, on acceptance. Guidelines.

SPIRITUALITY TODAY—7200 W. Division St., River Forest, IL 60305. Richard Woods, O.P., Ed. Quarterly. Biblical, liturgical, theological, ecumenical, historical, and biographical articles, 4,000 words, about the challenges of contemporary Christian life. Pays from 1 ½¢ a word, on publication. Query required, with SASE. Guidelines.

STANDARD—6401 The Paseo, Kansas City, MO 64131. Articles, 300 to 1,700 words; True experiences; poetry, to 20 lines; fiction with Christian emphasis but not overtly preachy; fillers; short articles with devotional emphasis; cartoons in good taste. Pays 3 ½¢ a word, on acceptance.

SUNDAY DIGEST—850 N. Grove Ave., Elgin, IL 60120. Articles, 1,000 to 1,800 words, on Christian faith in contemporary life; inspirational and how-to articles; free-verse poetry. Anecdotes, 500 words. Pays $40 to $190 (less for reprints), on acceptance.

SUNDAY SCHOOL COUNSELOR—1445 Boonville Ave., Springfield, MO 65802-1894. Sylvia Lee, Ed. Articles, 1,000 to 1,500 words, on teaching and Sunday school people, for local Sunday school teachers. Pays 3¢ to 5¢ a word, on acceptance.

SUNSHINE MAGAZINE—Sunshine Press, Litchfield, IL 62056. Peggy Kuethe, Ed. Inspirational articles, to 600 words. Short stories, 1,000 words, and juveniles, 400 words. No heavily religious material or "born again" pieces. Pays varying rates, on acceptance.

TEACHERS INTERACTION—1333 S. Kirkwood Rd., St. Louis, MO 63122. Martha S. Jander, Ed. Articles, 800 to 1,200 words; how-to pieces, to 100 words, for Lutheran volunteer church school teachers. Pays $10 to $35, on publication. Limited free-lance market.

TEENS TODAY—Church of the Nazarene, 6401 The Paseo, Kansas City, MO 64131. Karen DeSollar, Ed. Short stories that deal with teens demonstrating Christian principles, 1,200 to 1,500 words. Pays 3 ½¢ a word for first rights, 3¢ a word for reprints, on acceptance. Guidelines.

THEOLOGY TODAY—Box 29, Princeton, NJ 08542. Hugh T. Kerr, Ed. Articles, 1,500 to 3,500 words, on theology, religion, and related social issues. Literary criticism. Pays $50 to $100, on publication.

THE UNITED CHURCH OBSERVER—85 St. Clair Ave. E., Toronto, Ont., Canada M4T 1M8. Factual articles, 1,500 to 2,500 words, on religious trends, human problems, social issues. No poetry. Pays after publication. Query.

UNITED EVANGELICAL ACTION—P. O. Box 28, Wheaton, IL 60189. Don Brown, Ed. National Assn. of Evangelicals. News-oriented expositions and editorials, 750 to 1,000 words, on current events of concern and consequence to the evangelical church. Pays about 7¢ to 10¢ a word, on publication. Query with writing samples required.

THE UNITED METHODIST REPORTER—P.O. Box 660275, Dallas, TX 75266–0275. Spurgeon M. Dunnam, III, Ed. John Lovelace, Man. Ed. United Methodist. Religious features, to 500 words. Religious verse, 4 to 12 lines. Photos. Pays 4¢ a word, on publication. Send for guidelines. Same address and requirements for *The National Christian Reporter* (interdenominational).

UNITED SYNAGOGUE REVIEW—155 Fifth Ave., New York, NY 10010. Lois Goldrich, Ed. Articles, 1,000 to 1,200 words, on issues of interest to Conservative Jewish community. Query.

UNITY MAGAZINE—Unity School of Christianity, Unity Village, MO 64065. Philip White, Ed. Articles and poems: inspirational, religious, metaphysical, 500 to 1,500 words. Pays 5¢ to 9¢ a word, on acceptance.

VIRTUE—P. O. Box 850, Sisters, OR 97759. Articles and fiction for Christian women. Query only, except for "One Woman's Journal," "In My Opinion."

VISTA MAGAZINE—P. O. Box 50434, Indianapolis, IN 46250–0434. Articles and adult fiction, on current Christian concerns and issues. First-person pieces, 750 to 1,200 words. Opinion pieces from an Evangelical perspective, 500 to 750 words. Pays from 2¢ to 4¢ a word.

YOUNG SALVATIONIST—The Salvation Army, 799 Bloomfield Ave., Verona, NJ 07044. Robert R. Hostetler, Ed. Articles, 600 to 1,200 words, teach the Christian view to everyday living, for teenagers. Short shorts, first-person testimonies, 600 to 800 words. Pays 4¢ to 5¢ a word, on acceptance. SASE required. Guidelines.

THE YOUNG SOLDIER—The Salvation Army, 799 Bloomfield Ave., Verona, NJ 07044. Robert R. Hostetler, Ed. For children 8 to 12. Must carry a definite Christian message or teach a biblical truth. Fiction, 800 to 1,000 words. Some poetry. Fillers, puzzles, etc. Pays 4¢ a word, $3 to $5 for fillers, puzzles, on acceptance.

HEALTH

ACCENT ON LIVING—P. O. Box 700, Bloomington, IL 61702. Raymond C. Cheever, Pub. Betty Garee, Ed. Articles, 250 to 1,000 words, about physically disabled people, including their careers, recreation, sports, self-help devices, and ideas that can make daily routines easier. Good photos a plus. Pays 10¢ a word, on publication. Query.

AMERICAN BABY—475 Park Ave. S., New York, NY 10016. Judith Nolte, Ed. Articles, 1,000 to 2,000 words, for new or expectant parents on prenatal or infant care. Pays varying rates, on acceptance.

AMERICAN FITNESS—15250 Ventura Blvd., Suite 310, Sherman Oaks, CA 91403. Peg Jordan, Ed. Rhonda Wilson, Man. Ed. Articles, 500 to 1,500 words, on exercise, health, sports, nutrition, etc. Illustrations, photos, cartoons.

AMERICAN HEALTH—80 Fifth Ave., New York, NY 10011. Address Editorial Dept. Lively, authoritative articles, 1,000 to 3,000 words, on scientific and lifestyle aspects of health and fitness; 100- to 500-word news reports. Query with clips. Pays $250 ($50 kill fee) for news stories; 75¢ per word for features (kill fee is 25% of assigned fee); on acceptance.

AMERICAN JOURNAL OF NURSING—555 W. 57th St., New York, NY 10019. Mary B. Mallison, R.N., Ed. Articles, 1,500 to 2,000 words, with photos, on nursing. Query.

ARTHRITIS TODAY—The Arthritis Foundation, 1314 Spring St. N.W., Atlanta, GA 30309. Cindy McDaniel, Ed. Self-help, how-to, general interest, and inspirational articles (1,000 to 2,500 words), "slice-of-life" fiction (750 to 2,500 words), and short fillers (100 to 250 words) to help people with arthritis live more productive, independent, and pain-free lives. Pays from $350, on acceptance.

BESTWAYS—P.O. Box 570, Oak Park, IL 60303. Sally Cullen, Ed. Articles, 1,000 to 1,500 words, on healthy cooking, natural food, general health, lifestyles, exercise, nutrition. Pays from $150, on publication. Query.

CHILDBIRTH EDUCATOR—475 Park Ave. S., New York, NY 10016. Marsha Rehns, Ed. Articles, 2,000 words, on maternal and fetal health, child care, child development, and teaching techniques for teachers of childbirth and baby care classes. Pays $500, on acceptance. Query with detailed outline.

EAST WEST: THE JOURNAL OF NATURAL HEALTH & LIVING—17 Station St., Box 1200, Brookline, MA 02147. Features, 1,500 to 2,500 words, on holistic health, natural foods, gardening, etc. Material for "Body," "Healing," "In the Kitchen," and "Beauty and Fitness." Interviews. Photos. Pays 10¢ to 15¢ a word, extra for photos, on publication.

HEALTH—3 Park Ave., New York, NY 10016. Articles, 800 to 2,500 words, on medicine, nutrition, fitness, emotional and psychological well-being. Pays up to $2,000, on acceptance. Query.

HEALTH PROGRESS—4455 Woodson Rd., St. Louis, MO 63134. Judy Cassidy, Ed. Journal of the Catholic Health Association. Features, 1,500 to 2,000 words, on hospital management and administration, medical-moral questions, health care, public policy, technological developments in health care and their impacts, nursing, financial and human resource management for health care administrators, and innovative programs in hospitals and long-term care facilities. Payment negotiable. Query.

HEART CORPS—American Health Publications, 2899 Agoura Rd., Suite 142, West Lake Village, CA 91361. Bill Bush, Ed. "A Self-Care Journal for Heart Patients and Those Who Love Them." Articles, 1,000 to 1,500 words, and short fillers on heart health. Pay varies, on publication.

HIPPOCRATES—See *In Health*.

IDEA TODAY—6190 Cornerstone Ct. East, Suite 204, San Diego, CA 92121-3773. Patricia Ryan, Ed. Practical articles, 1,000 to 3,000 words, on new exercise programs, business management, nutrition, sports medicine, and dance-exercise and one-to-one training techniques. Payment negotiable, on acceptance. Query preferred.

IN HEALTH—(formerly *Hippocrates*) 475 Gate Five Rd., Suite 225, Sausalito, CA 94965. Sylvia Quesada, Ed. Articles, 850 to 5,000 words, on health and medicine; pieces for "Food," "Sports," "Drugs," "Mind," "Family," and "Housecalls" departments. Pays 50¢ to 80¢ a word, on acceptance. Query required.

LET'S LIVE—P.O. Box 74908, Los Angeles, CA 90004. Debra A. Jenkins, Ed. Articles, 1,000 to 1,500 words, on preventive medicine and nutrition, alternative medicine, diet, exercise, recipes, and natural beauty. Pays $150, on publication. Query.

MATURE HEALTH—45 W. 34th St., Suite 500, New York, NY 10001. David Allikas, Ed. Articles, 1,200 to 1,500 words, on exercise, the heart, sex, hypertension, fatigue, diabetes, arthritis, low back pain, nutrition, cholesterol reduction, mental wellness, and health care costs; for people in their forties through their sixties. Fillers, 200 to 600 words. Query with clips. Pays 40¢ a word, on publication.

NEW BODY—888 Seventh Ave., New York, NY 10106. Kate Staples, Ed. Well-researched, service-oriented articles, 800 to 1,500 words, on exercise, nutrition, lifestyle, diet, and health for women aged 18 to 35. Writers should have some background in or knowledge of the health field. Pays $100 to $300, on publication. Query.

NURSING 90—1111 Bethlehem Pike, Springhouse, PA 19477. Maryanne Wagner, Ed. Most articles are clinically oriented, and are written by nurses for nurses. Covers legal, ethical, management, and career aspects of nursing. No poetry. Pays $25 to $250, on publication. Query.

NURSINGWORLD JOURNAL—470 Boston Post Rd., Weston, MA 02193. Eileen Devito, Man. Ed. Articles, 500 to 1,500 words, for and by nurses and nurse-educators, on aspects of current nursing issues. Pays from 25¢ per column inch, on publication.

PATIENT CARE—690 Kinderkamack Rd., Oradell, NJ 07649. Robert L. Edsall, Ed. Articles on medical care, for physicians; mostly staff written. Pays varying rates, on publication. Query; all articles assigned.

THE PHYSICIAN AND SPORTSMEDICINE—4530 W. 77th St., Minneapolis, MN 55435. Debra Giel Adams, Features Ed. News and feature articles, 500 to 3,000 words, on fitness, sport, and exercise. Medical angle necessary. Pays $150 to $900, on acceptance. Guidelines.

A POSITIVE APPROACH—1600 Malone, Municipal Airport, Millville, NJ 08332. Ann Miller, Ed. Articles, 500 words, on all aspects of the positive-thinking disabled/handicapped person's private and business life. Well-researched articles of interest to the visually and hearing impaired, veterans, the arthritic, and all categories of the disabled and handicapped, on interior design, barrier-free architecture, gardening, wardrobe, computers, and careers. No fiction or poetry. Pays in copies.

PSYCHOLOGY TODAY—80 Fifth Ave., New York, NY 10011. T. George Harris, Ed.-in-Chief. Lively, useful articles, 2,500 to 3,000 words, and short news items about timely subjects, based on the research findings of social scientists and the clinical insights of practicing psychotherapists; jargon free. Department pieces, 1,200 to 1,500 words, on health, work, relationships, the brain, etc. Pays good rates, on acceptance.

RECOVERY LIFE—P.O. Box 31329, Seattle, WA 98103. Neil Scott, Ed. Articles, to 1,500 words, for recovering alcoholics, on how to meet the challenge of sobriety. First-person recovery stories, with helpful how-tos for others, 500 to 1,000 words. SASE for guidelines.

RN—Oradell, NJ 07649. Articles, to 2,000 words, preferably by R.N.s, on nursing, clinical care, etc. Pays 10¢ to 15¢ a word, on acceptance. Query.

VEGETARIAN TIMES—P.O. Box 570, Oak Park, IL 60603. Paul Obis, Pub. Articles, 750 to 2,500 words, on health, nutrition, exercise and fitness, meatless meals, etc. Personal-experience and historical pieces, profiles. Pays $25 to $500, on publication.

VIBRANT LIFE—55 W. Oak Ridge Dr., Hagerstown, MD 21740. Features, 1,000 to 2,000 words, on total health: physical, mental, and spiritual. No disease-related articles or manuscripts geared to people over 50. Seeks upbeat articles on how to live happier and healthier lives; Christian slant. Pays $150 to $300, on acceptance.

VIM & VIGOR—8805 N. 23rd Ave., Suite 11, Phoenix, AZ 85021. Leo Calderella, Ed. Positive articles, with accurate medical facts, on health and fitness, 1,200 words, by assignment only. Pays $250 to $350, on publication. Query.

THE WALKING MAGAZINE—711 Boylston St., Boston, MA 02116. Bradford Ketchum, Ed. Articles, 1,500 to 2,500 words, on fitness, health, equipment, nutrition, travel, and adventure, famous walkers, and other walking-related topics. Shorter pieces, 150 to 800 words, and essays for "Ramblings" page. Photos welcome. Pays $750 to $1,200 for features, $100 to $500 for department pieces. Guidelines.

YOGA JOURNAL—2054 University Ave., Berkeley, CA 94704. Stephan Bodian, Ed. Articles, 1,200 to 4,000 words, on holistic health, meditation, consciousness, spirituality, and yoga. Pays $50 to $350, on publication.

YOUR HEALTH—1720 Washington Blvd., Box 10010, Ogden, UT 84409. Carroll Shreeve, Pub. Articles, 1,200 words, on individual health care needs: prevention, treatment, fitness, nutrition, etc. Photos required. Pays 15¢ a word, on acceptance. Guidelines.

EDUCATION

AMERICAN SCHOOL & UNIVERSITY—401 N. Broad St., Philadelphia, PA 19108. Joe Agron, Ed. Articles and case studies, 1,200 to 1,500 words, on design, construction, operation, and management of school and college facilities. Payment varies.

THE BIG APPLE PARENTS' PAPER—928 Broadway, Suite 707, New York, NY 10010. Helen Rosengren Freedman, Ed. Articles (600 to 750 words) for NYC parents. Pays $50 to $75, withing 60 days of acceptance (plus $25 cover bonus). Buys first NY area rights.

CAPSTONE JOURNAL OF EDUCATION—P.O. Box 870231, Tuscaloosa, AL 35487–0231. Alexia M. Kartis, Asst. Ed. Articles, to 5,000 words, on contemporary ideas in educational research. Guidelines.

CHANGE—4000 Albemarle St. N.W., Suite 500, Washington, DC 20016. Columns, 700 to 2,000 words, and in-depth features, 2,500 to 3,500 words, on programs, people, and institutions of higher education. Payment varies.

CLASSROOM COMPUTER LEARNING—Peter Li, Inc., 2169 Francisco Blvd. E., Suite A-4, San Rafael, CA 94901. Holly Brady, Ed. Articles, to 3,000 words, for teachers of grades K through12, related to uses of computers in the classroom: human-interest and philosophical articles, how-to pieces, software reviews, and hands-on ideas. Pay varies, on acceptance.

FOUNDATION NEWS—1828 L St. N.W., Washington, DC 20036. Arlie W. Schardt, Ed. Articles, to 2,000 words, on national or regional activities supported by, or of interest to, grant makers. Pays to $1,500, on acceptance. Query.

GIFTED EDUCATION PRESS—P.O. Box 1586, 10201 Yuma Ct., Manassas, VA 22110. Maurice Fisher, Pub. Articles, to 1,200 words, written by educators, laypersons, and parents of gifted children, on the problems of identifying and teaching gifted children and adolescents. "Interested in incisive analyses of current programs for the gifted, and recommendations for improving the education of gifted students. Particularly interested in the problems of teaching Humanities to the gifted." Pays with subscription.

HOME EDUCATION MAGAZINE—P.O. Box 1083, Tonasket, WA 98855. Mark J. Hegener, Ed. Positive, informative articles, 1,000 to 3,500 words, on home schooling or alternative education. (Most articles 1,000 to 2,500 words.) Poetry with a home-schooling slant. Pays $10 per printed page for article, $5 to $10 for poems, within 15 days of publication. Send complete manuscript.

THE HORN BOOK MAGAZINE—14 Beacon St., Boston, MA 02108. Anita Silvey, Ed. Articles, 600 to 2,800 words, on books for young readers, and related subjects, for librarians, teachers, parents, etc. Pays $25 per printed page, on publication. Query.

INSTRUCTOR MAGAZINE—Scholastic, Inc., 730 Broadway, New York, NY 10003. Attn: Manuscripts Ed. How-to articles on elementary classroom teaching, and computers in the classroom, with practical suggestions and project reports. Pays varying rates, on acceptance. SASE required.

ITC COMMUNICATOR—International Training in Communication, 4249 Elzevir Rd., Woodland Hills, CA 91364. JoAnn Levy, Ed. Educational articles, 200 to 800 words, on leadership, language, speech presentation, meetings procedures, personal and professional development, written and spoken communication techniques. SASE required. Pays in copies.

JOURNAL OF CAREER PLANNING & EMPLOYMENT—62 Highland Ave., Bethlehem, PA 18017. Patricia A. Sinnott, Ed. Quarterly. Articles, 3,000 to 4,000 words, on topics related to college career planning, placement, and recruitment. Pays $200 to $400, on acceptance. Query first with clips. Guidelines available.

KEY TO CHRISTIAN EDUCATION—8121 Hamilton Ave., Cincinnati, OH 45231. Marjorie Miller, Ed. Fillers, articles, to 1,500 words, on Christian education; tips for teachers in the local church. Pays varying rates, on acceptance.

LEARNING 89/90—1111 Bethlehem Pike, Springhouse, PA 19477. Charlene Gaynor, Ed. How-to, why-to, and personal-experience articles, to 3,000 words, for teachers of grades K through 8. Tested classroom ideas for curriculum roundups, to 600 words. Pays to $300 for features, on acceptance.

MEDIA & METHODS—1429 Walnut St., Philadelphia, PA 19102. Michele Sokoloff, Ed. Articles, 800 to 1,500 words, on media, technologies, and methods used to enhance instruction and learning in high school and university classrooms. Pays $50 to $100, on publication. Query.

THE MINORITY ENGINEER—44 Broadway, Greenlawn, NY 11740. James Schneider, Ed. Articles, 1,000 to 1,500 words, for college students, on career opportunities in engineering, scientific, and technological fields; techniques of job hunting; developments in and applications of new technologies. Interviews. Profiles. Pays 10¢ a word, on publication. Query. Same address and requirements for *The Woman Engineer,* a career-guidance quarterly; query Editor Anne Kelly.

PHI DELTA KAPPAN—8th and Union St., Box 789, Bloomington, IN 47402. Pauline Gough, Ed. Articles, 1,000 to 4,000 words, on educational research, service, and leadership; issues, trends, and policy. Pays from $250, on publication.

SCHOOL ARTS MAGAZINE—50 Portland St., Worcester, MA 01608. Kent Anderson, Ed. Articles, 800 to 1,000 words, on art education with special application to the classroom. Photos. Pays varying rates, on publication.

SCHOOL SAFETY—National School Safety Center, 16830 Ventura Blvd., Encino, CA 91436. Stuart Greenbaum, Ed. Published three times during the school year. Articles, 2,000 to 3,000 words, of use to educatiors, law enforcers, judges, and legislators on the prevention of drugs, gangs, weapons, bullying, discipline problems, and vandalism; also on site security and character development as they relate to students and schools. Pays to $500, on publication.

SCHOOL SHOP—Box 8623, Ann Arbor, MI 48107. Alan H. Jones, Pub./ Exec. Ed. Articles, 1 to 10 double-spaced typed pages, for teachers and administrators in industrial, technical, and vocational educational fields, with particular interest in classroom projects and computer uses. Pays $25 to $150, on publication. Guidelines.

TEACHING AND COMPUTERS—Scholastic, Inc., 730 Broadway, New York, NY 10003. Ms. Mickey Revenaugh, Ed. Articles, 300 to 500 words, for computer-using teachers in grades K through 8. Payment varies, on acceptance.

TODAY'S CATHOLIC TEACHER—2451 E. River Rd., Dayton, OH 45489. Stephen Brittan, Ed. Articles, 600 to 800 words and 1,200 to 1,500 words, on Catholic education, parent-teacher relationships, innovative teaching, teaching techniques, etc. Pays $15 to $75, on publication. SASE required. Query first. Guidelines.

WILSON LIBRARY BULLETIN—950 University Ave., Bronx, NY 10452. Mary Jo Godwin, Ed. Articles, 2,500 to 3,000 words, on libraries, communications, and information systems. News, reports, features. Pays from $250, extra for photos, on publication.

THE WOMAN ENGINEER—See *The Minority Engineer.*

FARMING AND AGRICULTURE

ACRES USA—10008 E. 60 Terrace, Kansas City, MO 64133. Articles on biological agriculture. Pays 6¢ a word, on accepted. Query.

AMERICAN BEE JOURNAL—51 N. Second St., Hamilton, IL 62341. Joe M. Graham, Ed. Articles on beekeeping, for professionals. Photos. Pays 75¢ a column inch, extra for photos, on publication.

BEEF—1999 Shepard Rd., St. Paul, MN 55116. Paul D. Andre, Ed. Articles on beef cattle feeding, cowherds, stocker operations, and related phases of the cattle industry. Pays to $300, on acceptance.

BUCKEYE FARM NEWS—Ohio Farm Bureau Federation, Two Nationwide Plaza, Box 479, Columbus, OH 43216. George D. Robey, Man. Ed. Occasional articles and humor, to 600 words, related to agriculture. Pays on publication. Query.

FARM AND RANCH LIVING—5400 S. 60th St., Greendale, WI 53129. Bob Ottum, Ed. Articles, 2,000 words, on rural people and situations; nostalgia pieces; profiles of interesting farms and farmers, ranches and ranchers. Poetry. Pays $15 to $400, on acceptance and on publication.

FARM INDUSTRY NEWS—1999 Shepard Rd., St. Paul, MN 55116. Joe Degnan, Ed. Articles for farmers, on new products, buying, machinery, equipment, chemicals, and seeds. Pays $175 to $400, on acceptance. Query required.

FARM JOURNAL—230 W. Washington Sq., Philadelphia, PA 19105. Earl

Ainsworth, Ed. Articles, 500 to 1,500 words, with photos, on the business of farming, for farmers. Pays 20¢ to 50¢ a word, on acceptance. Query.

FLORIDA GROWER & RANCHER—1331 N. Mills Ave., Orlando, FL 32803. Frank H. Abrahamson, Ed. Articles and case histories on farmers, growers, and ranchers. Pays on publication. Query; buys little freelance material.

THE FURROW—Deere & Company, John Deere Rd., Moline, IL 61265. George Sollenberger, Exec. Ed. Specialized, illustrated articles on farming. Pays to $1,000, on acceptance.

HARROWSMITH—Telemedia Publishing, Inc., Camden East, Ont., Canada K0K 1J0. Wayne Grady, Ed. Articles, 700 to 4,000 words, on country life, homesteading, husbandry, organic gardening, and alternative energy with a Canadian slant. Pays $150 to $1,500, on acceptance. Query with SASE/international reply coupon.

HARROWSMITH/USA—The Creamery, Ferry Rd., Charlotte, VT 05445. Tom Rawls, Ed. Investigative pieces, 4,000 to 5,000 words, on ecology, energy, health, gardening, do-it-yourself projects, and the food chain. Short pieces for "Screed" (opinions), and "Gazette" (news briefs). Pays $500 to $1,500 for features, $50 to $600 for department pieces, on acceptance. Query required. Send SASE for guidelines.

NORDEN NEWS—601 W. Cornhusker Hwy., Lincoln, NE 68521. Kathleen Etchison, Ed. Technical articles, 1,200 to 1,500 words, and clinical features, 500 words, on veterinary medicine. Photos. Pays $200 to $250, $100 for shorter pieces, extra for photos, on publication.

THE OHIO FARMER—1350 W. Fifth Ave., Columbus, OH 43212. Andrew L. Stevens, Ed. Articles on farming, rural living, etc., in Ohio. Pays $20 per column, on publication.

PEANUT FARMER—P.O. Box 95075, Raleigh, NC 27625. Dayton Matlick, Ed./Pub. Articles, 500 to 1,500 words, on production and management practices in peanut farming. Pays $50 to $350, on publication.

PENNSYLVANIA FARMER—704 Lisburn Rd., Camp Hill, PA 17011. John R. Vogel, Ed. Articles on farmers in PA, NJ, DE, MD, and WV; timely business-of-farming concepts and successful farm management operations.

RURAL HERITAGE—P.O. Box 516, Albia, IA 52531. Allan Young, Ed./Pub. How-to and feature articles, 300 to 2,500 words, related to draft horses and rural living. Pays 3¢ to 10¢ a word, $5 to $25 for photos, on publication.

SHEEP! MAGAZINE—W. 2997 Market Rd., Helenville, WI 53137. Dave Thompson, Ed. Articles, to 1,500 words, on successful shepherds, woolcrafts, sheep raising, and sheep dogs. Photos. Pays $80 to $250, extra for photos, on publication.

SMALL FARMER'S JOURNAL—P.O. Box 2805, Eugene, OR 97402. Address the Editors. How-tos, humor, practical work horse information, livestock and produce marketing, and articles appropriate to the independent family farm. Pays negotiable rates, on publication. Query first.

SUCCESSFUL FARMING—1716 Locust St., Des Moines, IA 50336. Gene Johnston, Man. Ed. Articles on farm production, business, and families; also farm personalities, health, leisure, and outdoor topics. Pays varying rates, on acceptance.

WALLACES FARMER—1501 42nd St., #501, W. Des Moines, IA 50265. Monte Sesker, Ed. Features, 600 to 700 words, on farming in IA, MN, NE, KS, ND, and SD; methods and equipment; interviews with farmers. Query.

ENVIRONMENT, CONSERVATION, WILDLIFE, NATURAL HISTORY

THE AMERICAN FIELD—542 S. Dearborn, Chicago, IL 60605. William F. Brown, Ed. Yarns about hunting trips, bird-shooting; articles to 1,500 words, on dogs and field trials, emphasizing conservation of game resources. Pays varying rates, on acceptance.

AMERICAN FORESTS—1516 P St. N.W., Washington, DC 20005. Bill Rooney, Ed. Well-documented articles, to 2,000 words, with photos, on recreational and commercial uses and management of forests. Photos. Pays on acceptance.

THE AMICUS JOURNAL—Natural Resources Defense Council, 40 W. 20th St., New York, NY 10168. Peter Borrelli, Ed. Investigative articles, book reviews, and poetry related to national and international environmental policy. Pays varying rates, on acceptance. Queries required.

ANIMAL KINGDOM—New York Zoological Society, Bronx, NY 10460. Nancy Christie, Sr. Ed. First-person articles, 1,500 to 2,000 words, on "popular" natural history, "based on author's research and experience as opposed to textbook approach." Payment varies, on acceptance. Guidelines.

ANIMALS—Massachusetts Society for the Prevention of Cruelty to Animals, 350 S. Huntington Ave., Boston, MA 02130. Diana Levey, Ed. Asst. Informative, well-researched articles, to 3,000 words, on animal welfare and pet care, conservation, international wildlife, and environmental issues affecting animals; no personal accounts or favorite pet stories. Pays to $300, on publication. Query.

ATLANTIC SALMON JOURNAL—1435 St. Alexandre, Suite 1030, Montreal, Quebec, Canada H3A 2G4. Terry Davis, Ed. Articles, 1,500 to 3,000 words. Material related to Atlantic salmon: conservation, ecology, travel, politics, biology, how-tos, anecdotes, cuisine. Pays $100 to $350, on publication.

BIRD WATCHER'S DIGEST—P.O. Box 110, Marietta, OH 45750. Mary B. Bowers, Ed. Articles, 600 to 2,500 words, for bird watchers: first-person accounts; how-tos; pieces on endangered species; profiles. Cartoons. Pays to $50, on publication.

ENVIRONMENTAL ACTION—1525 New Hampshire Ave. N.W., Washington, DC 20036. News and features, varying lengths, on a broad range of political and/or environmental topics: energy, toxics, self-sufficiency, etc. Book reviews; environmentally-related consumer goods. Pays $120 to $300 for features, $25 book reviews, $40 to $70 for short news articles, $25 for photos, on publication. Query required.

EQUINOX—7 Queen Victoria Rd., Camden East, Ont., Canada K0K 1J0. Jody Morgan, Asst. Ed. Articles, 3,000 to 6,000 words, on popular geography, wildlife, astronomy, science, the arts, travel, and adventure. Department pieces, 300 to 500 words, for "Nexus" (science and medicine), and "Habitat" (man-made and natural environment). Pays $1,250 to $2,000, for features, $100 to $300 for short pieces, on acceptance.

HARROWSMITH/USA—The Creamery, Ferry Rd., Charlotte, VT 05445. Tom Rawls, Ed. Investigative articles, 4,000 to 5,000 words, on ecology, energy, health, gardening, and the food chain. Short pieces for "Screed" (opinions) and "Gazette" (news briefs). Do-it-yourself projects. Pays $500 to $1,500 for features, from $50 to $600 for department pieces, on acceptance. Query required; SASE. Guidelines.

THE LOOKOUT—Seamen's Church Institute, 50 Broadway, New York, NY

10004. Carlyle Windley, Ed. Factual articles on the sea and merchant seafarers. Features, 200 to 1,500 words, on the merchant marines, sea oddities, etc. Photos. Pays $25 to $100, on publication.

NATIONAL GEOGRAPHIC—17th and M Sts. N.W., Washington, DC 20036. Wilbur E. Garrett, Ed. First-person, general-interest, heavily-illustrated articles on science, natural history, exploration, and geographical regions. Query required.

NATIONAL PARKS MAGAZINE—1015 31st St. N.W., Washington, DC 20007. Michele Strutin, Ed. Articles, 1,000 to 2,000 words, on natural history, wildlife, outdoors activities, travel, and conservation as they relate to national parks: illustrated features on the natural, historic, and cultural resources of the National Park System. Pieces about legislation and other issues and events related to the parks. Pays $100 to $500, on acceptance. Query. Send for guidelines.

NATIONAL WILDLIFE & INTERNATIONAL WILDLIFE—8925 Leesburg Pike, Vienna, VA 22184. Mark Wexler, Man. Ed., Nat. Wildlife. Jon Fisher, Man. Ed., Inter. Wildlife. Articles, 1,000 to 2,500 words, on wildlife, conservation, environment; outdoor how-to pieces. Photos. Pays on acceptance. Query.

NATURAL HISTORY—American Museum of Natural History, Central Park West at 79th St., New York, NY 10024. Alan Ternes, Ed.-in-Chief. Informative articles, to 3,000 words, by experts, on anthropology and natural sciences. Pays $1,000 for features, on acceptance. Query.

OUTDOOR AMERICA—1401 Wilson Blvd., Level B, Arlington, VA 22209. Quarterly publication of the Izaak Walton League of America. Articles, 1,500 to 2,000 words, on natural resource conservation issues and outdoor recreation; especially fishing, hunting, and camping. Pays 20¢ a word for features. Query Articles Ed. with published clips.

SEA FRONTIERS—4600 Rickenbacker Causeway, Virginia Key, Miami 33149. Jean Bradfisch, Exec. Ed. Illustrated articles, 500 to 3,000 words, on scientific advances related to the sea, biological, physical, chemical, or geological phenomena, ecology, conservation, etc., written in a popular style for lay readers. Send SASE for guidelines. Pays $75 to $500, on acceptance. Query.

SIERRA—730 Polk St., San Francisco, CA 94109. Jonathan F. King, Ed.-in-Chief. Articles, 250 to 2,500 words, on environmental and conservation topics, politics, hiking, backpacking, skiing, rafting, cycling. Book reviews and children's departments. Photos. Pays from $75 to $1,500, extra for photos, on acceptance. Query with SASE.

SMITHSONIAN MAGAZINE—900 Jefferson Dr., Washington, DC 20560. Marlane A. Liddell, Articles Ed. Articles on history, art, natural history, physical science, profiles, etc. Query.

SPORTS AFIELD—250 W. 55th St., New York, NY 10019. Tom Paugh, Ed. Articles, 2,000 words, with quality photos, on hunting, fishing, natural history, conservation, personal experiences, new hunting/fishing spots. How-to pieces; humor, fiction. Pays top rates, on acceptance.

MEDIA AND THE ARTS

AHA! HISPANIC ARTS NEWS—Assoc. of Hispanic Arts, 173 E. 116th St., New York, NY 10029. Dolores Prida, Ed. Interviews and book reviews with Hispanic authors, to 500 words. Pays on publication. Query required.

AIRBRUSH ACTION—400 Madison Ave., Lakewood, NJ 08701. Address the editors. Articles, 500 to 3,000 words, on airbrush, graphics, and art-related topics. Pays $75 to $300, on publication. Query.

THE AMERICAN ART JOURNAL—40 W. 57th St., 5th Fl., New York, NY 10019. Jane Van N. Turano, Ed. Quarterly. Scholarly articles, 2,000 to 10,000 words, on American art of the 17th through 20th centuries. Photos. Pays $200 to $400, on acceptance.

AMERICAN INDIAN ART MAGAZINE—7314 E. Osborn Dr., Scottsdale, AZ 85251. Roanne P. Goldfein, Man. Ed. Detailed articles, 10 typed pages, on American Indian arts—painting, carving, beadwork, basketry, textiles, ceramics, jewelry, etc. Pays varying rates for articles, on publication. Query.

AMERICAN THEATRE—355 Lexington Ave., New York, NY 10017. Jim O'Quinn, Ed. Features, 500 to 4,000 words, on the theater and theater-related subjects. Payment negotiable, on publication. Query.

ART & ANTIQUES—89 Fifth Ave., New York, NY 10003. Jeffrey Schaire, Ed. Investigative pieces or personal narratives, 1,500 words, and news items, 300 to 500 words, on art or antiques. Pays 50¢ a word, on publication. Query first.

ART GALLERY INTERNATIONAL: THE CONTEMPORARY COLLECTORS MAGAZINE—P.O. Box 52940, Tulsa, OK 74152. Debra Carter Nelson, Ed. Articles, 1,500 to 2,500 words, on contemporary artists and their recent works; no restrictions on artists' style, medium, or subject matter; a "gallery in print" for readers. Query with clips, visual samples, and SASE. Pays 10¢ a word or $50 per printed page, after publication.

ARTS ATLANTIC—P.O. Box 848, Charlottetown, P.E.I., Canada C1A 7L9. Joseph Sherman, Ed. Articles and reviews, 800 to 2,500 words, on visual, performing, and literary arts, crafts in Atlantic Canada. Also, "idea and concept" articles of universal appeal. Pays from 15¢ a word, on publication. Query.

BLUEGRASS UNLIMITED—Box 111, Broad Run, VA 22014. Peter V. Kuykendall, Ed. Articles, to 3,500 words, on bluegrass and traditional country music. Photos. Pays 6¢ to 8¢ a word, extra for photos.

BROADCASTER—7 Labatt Ave., Toronto, Ont., Canada M5A 3P2. Lynda Ashley, Ed. Articles, 500 to 2,000 words, on broadcasting, satellites, and the cable industry. Rates negotiable. Payment on publication.

CLAVIER MAGAZINE—200 Northfield Rd., Northfield, IL 60093. Kingsley Day, Man. Ed. Practical articles, interviews, master classes, and humor pieces, 2,000 words, for keyboard performers and teachers. Pays $35 to $45 per page of magazine text, on publication.

DANCE MAGAZINE—33 W. 60th St., New York, NY 10023. Richard Philp, Ed.-in-Chief. Features on dance, personalities, techniques, health issues, and trends. Photos. Query; limited free-lance market.

DANCE TEACHER NOW—3020 Beacon Blvd., West Sacramento, CA 95691–3436. K.C. Patrick, Ed. Articles, 1,000 to 3,000 words, for professional dance educators, dancers, and other dance professionals on practical information for the teacher and/or business owner, economic and historical issues related to the profession. Profiles of schools, methods, and people who are leaving their mark on dance. Must be thoroughly researched. Pays $200 to $300, on publication. Query preferred.

DARKROOM PHOTOGRAPHY—9171 Wilshire Blvd., Suite 300, Beverly Hills, CA 90210. Thom Harrop, Ed. Articles on post-camera photographic techniques, 1,000 to 2,500 words, with photos, for all levels of photographers. Pays $100 to $500. Query.

DESIGN MANAGEMENT—(formerly *Design Graphics World*), Communications Channels, 6255 Barfield Rd., Atlanta, GA 30328. Eric Torrey, Ed. Articles, 1,500 to 2,000 words, on news, trends concerning CAD, engineering and architecture, computer graphics, reprographics, and related design fields. Pays on publication. Query required.

THE DRAMA REVIEW—See *TDR: A Journal of Performance Studies.*

DRAMATICS—International Thespian Society, 3368 Central Pkwy., Cincinnati, OH 45225-2392. Don Corathers, Ed. Articles, interviews, how-tos, 750 to 4,000 words, for high school students on the performing arts with an emphasis on theater practice: acting, directing, playwriting, tech. subjects. Prefer articles that "could be used by a better than average high school teacher to teach students something about the performing arts." Pays $15 to $200 honorariums. Manuscripts preferred; graphics and photos accepted.

THE ENGRAVERS JOURNAL—26 Summit St., Box 318, Brighton, MI 48116. Michael J. Davis, Man. Ed. Articles, varying lengths, on topics related to the engraving industry and small business operations. Pays $60 to $175, on acceptance. Query first.

FILM QUARTERLY—University of California Press, 2120 Berkeley Way, Berkeley, CA 94720. Ernest Callenbach, Ed. Film reviews, historical and critical articles, book reviews, to 6,000 words. Pays on publication. Query.

FLUTE TALK—Instrumentalist Publishing Co., 200 Northfield Rd., Northfield, IL 60093. Kathleen Goll-Wilson, Ed. Articles, 6 to 12 typed pages, on flute performance and pedagogy; flute-related poetry; fillers; photos and line drawings. Thorough knowledge of the instrument a must. Pays $45 per page, on publication. Queries preferred.

HANDMADE ACCENTS—488-A River Mountain Rd., Lebanon, VA 24266. Steve McCay, Ed./Pub. Profiles, 1,500 words, and essays, 750 to 1,000 words, on subjects of concern to arts consumers and patrons. Pays 5¢ a word, on publication.

INDUSTRIAL PHOTOGRAPHY—210 Crossways Park Dr., Woodbury, NY 11797. Steve Shaw, Ed. Articles on techniques and trends in current professional photography; audio visuals, etc., for industrial photographers and executives. Query.

INTERNATIONAL MUSICIAN—Paramount Bldg., 1501 Broadway, Suite 600, New York, NY 10036. Articles, 1,500 to 2,000 words, for professional musicians. Pays varying rates, on acceptance. Query.

JAZZIZ—P. O. Box 8309, Gainesville, FL 32605. Michael Fagien, Ed. Feature articles on all aspects of adult contemporary: interviews, profiles, concept pieces. Departments include "Reviews," "Video," and "Audio." Emphasis on new releases. Pays varying rates, on acceptance. Query.

KEYBOARD MAGAZINE—20085 Stevens Creek, Cupertino, CA 95014. Dominic Milano, Ed. Articles, 1,000 to 5,000 words, on keyboard instruments and players. Photos. Pays $175 to $500, on acceptance. Query.

MEDIA HISTORY DIGEST—c/o Editor & Publisher, 11 W. 19th St., New York, NY 10011. Hiley H. Ward, Ed. Articles, 1,500 to 2,000 words, on the history of print media, for wide consumer interest. Puzzles and humor related to media history. Pays varying rates, on publication. Query.

MODERN DRUMMER—870 Pompton Ave., Cedar Grove, NJ 07009. Ronald L. Spagnardi, Ed. Articles, 500 to 2,000 words, on drumming: how-tos, interviews. Pays $50 to $500, on publication.

MUSIC MAGAZINE—P. O. Box 96, Station R, Toronto, Ont., Canada M4G 3Z3. Articles, with photos, on musicians, conductors, and composers, for all classical music buffs. Pays $100 to $300, on publication. Query required. Guidelines.

MUSICAL AMERICA/OPUS—825 Seventh Ave., New York, NY 10019. Shirley Fleming, Ed. Authoritative articles, 1,000 to 1,500 words, on classical music subjects. Pays around 15¢ a word, on acceptance.

NEW ENGLAND ENTERTAINMENT DIGEST—c/o *Mariner Newspapers,* P.O. Box 682, Marshfield, MA 02050. Paul J. Reale, Ed. News features and reviews on arts and entertainment in New England. Light verse. Pays $10 to $25, $1 to $2 for verse, on publication.

OPERA NEWS—The Metropolitan Opera Guild, 1865 Broadway, New York, NY 10023. Patrick J. Smith, Ed. Articles, 600 to 2,500 words, on all aspects of opera. Pays 20¢ a word for articles, on publication. Query.

PETERSEN'S PHOTOGRAPHIC—8490 Sunset Blvd., Los Angeles, CA 90069. Bill Hurter, Ed. Articles and how-to pieces, with photos, on travel, video, and darkroom photography, for beginners, advanced amateurs, and professionals. Pays $60 per printed page, on publication.

PHOTOMETHODS—1090 Executive Way, Des Plaines, IL 60018. Alfred DeBat, Ed. Articles, 1,500 to 3,000 words, on innovative techniques in imaging (still, film, video), working situations, and management. Pays from $75, on publication. Query.

PLAYBILL—71 Vanderbilt Ave., New York, NY 10169. Joan Alleman, Ed.-in-Chief. Sophisticated articles, 700 to 2,000 words, with photos, on theater and subjects of interest to theater-goers. Pays $100 to $500, on acceptance.

POPULAR PHOTOGRAPHY—1633 Broadway, New York, NY 10019. Jason Schneider, Ed. Dir. How-to articles, 500 to 2,000 words, for amateur photographers. Query first with outline and photos.

PREVUE—P.O. Box 974, Reading, PA 19603. J. Steranko, Ed. Lively articles on films and film-makers; entertainment features and celebrity interviews. Length: 4 to 25 pages. Pays varying rates, on acceptance. Query with clips.

PROFESSIONAL STAINED GLASS—245 W. 29th St., 13th Fl., New York, NY 10001–5208. Chris Peterson, Man. Ed. Practical articles of interest to stained glass professionals. Abundant opportunity for energetic and enterprising free lancers. Pays $100 to $150, on publication. Query required.

RIGHTING WORDS—P.O. Box 6811, F.D.R. Sta., New York, NY 10150. Jonathan S. Kaufman, Ed. Journal of Language and Editing. Articles (3,000 words) on topics of interest to professional editors. Pays from $100, on acceptance.

ROLLING STONE—745 Fifth Ave., New York, NY 10151. Articles on American culture, art, and politics. Query required. Rarely accepts free-lance material.

SHEET MUSIC MAGAZINE—223 Katonah Ave., Katonah, NY 10536. Josephine Sblendorio, Man. Ed. Pieces, 1,000 to 2,000 words, for pianists and organists, on musicians and composers, how-tos, and book reviews (to 500 words); no hard rock or heavy metal subjects. Pays $75 to $200, on publication.

SPLASH—561 Broadway, 4B, New York, NY 10012. Jordan Crandall, Ed. Articles, 750 to 2,000 words, on art and contemporary culture. Reviews, 500 to 750 words; interviews; editorials, 450 to 1,250 words. Sophisticated and black humor, 250 to 500 words. Pays $50 to $1,000, on publication.

SUN TRACKS—Box 2510, Phoenix, AZ 85002. David Koen, Music Ed. Music section of *New Times*. Long and short features, record reviews, and interviews. Pays $25 to $500, on publication. Query.

TDR: A JOURNAL OF PERFORMANCE STUDIES—(formerly *The Drama Review*) 721 Broadway, 6th Fl., New York, NY 10003. Rebecca Schneider, Man. Ed. Eclectic articles on experimental performance and performance theory; cross-cultural, examining the social, political, historical, and theatrical contexts in which performance happens. Submit query or manuscript with SASE. Pays 3¢ a word, on publication.

THEATRE CRAFTS MAGAZINE—135 Fifth Ave., New York, NY 10010. Patricia MacKay, Ed. Articles, 500 to 2,500 words, for professionals in the business, design, and production of theater, film, video, and the performing arts. Pays on acceptance. Query.

VIDEO CHOICE—Connell Communications, Inc., Rt. 202S, 331 Jaffrey Rd., Peterborough, NH 03458. Deborah Navas, Ed. Articles, 200 to 500 words, on theatrical videos newly released at consumer prices; special-interest, high-profile video reviews. Pays varying rates, on acceptance. Query required.

VIDEO MAGAZINE—460 W. 34th St., New York, NY 10001. Art Levis, Ed.-in-Chief. How-to and service articles on home video equipment, technology, and programming. Interviews and human-interest features related to non-broadcast television, from 800 to 2,500 words. Pays varying rates, on acceptance. Query.

VIDEOMAKER—P.O. Box 4591, Chico, CA 95927. Bradley Kent, Ed. Authoritative, how-to articles geared at hobbyist and professional video camera/camcorder users: instructionals, innovative applications, tools and tips, industry developments, new products, etc. Pays varying rates, on publication. Queries preferred.

WASHINGTON JOURNALISM REVIEW—2233 Wisconsin Ave. N.W., Washington, DC 20007. Bill Monroe, Ed. Articles, 500 to 3,000 words, on print or electronic journalism. Pays 20¢ a word, on publication. Query.

HOBBIES, CRAFTS, COLLECTING

ANTIQUE MONTHLY—2100 Powers Ferry Road, Atlanta, GA 30339. Elizabeth McKenzie, Man. Ed. Articles, 750 to 1,200 words, on the exhibition and sales (auctions, antique shops, etc.) of decorative arts and antiques more than 100 years old, with B&W photos or color slides. Pays varying rates, on publication.

THE ANTIQUE TRADER WEEKLY—Box 1050, Dubuque, IA 52001. Kyle D. Husfloen, Ed. Articles, 1,000 to 2,000 words, on all types of antiques and collectors' items. Photos. Pays from $5 to $150, extra for photos, on publication. Query preferred. Buys all rights.

ANTIQUES & AUCTION NEWS—P.O. Box 500, Mount Joy, PA 17552. Weekly newspaper. Factual articles, 600 to 1,500 words, on antiques, collectors, and collections. Photos. Pays $5 to $20, after publication.

ANTIQUEWEEK—P.O. Box 90, Knightstown, IN 46148. Tom Hoepf, Ed. Weekly antique, auction, and collectors newspaper. Articles, 500 to 1,500 words, on antiques, collectibles, restorations, genealogy, auction and antique show reports. Photos. Pays from $1 per inch, $75 to $125 for in-depth articles, on publication. Query. Guidelines.

AQUARIUM FISH—P.O. Box 6050, Mission Viejo, CA 92690. Edward Bauman, Ed. Articles, 2,000 words, on freshwater, saltwater, and pond fish, with or without color transparencies. (No "pet fish" stories, please.) Payment varies, on publication.

THE AUTOGRAPH COLLECTOR'S MAGAZINE—P.O. Box 55328, Stockton, CA 95205. Joe Kraus, Ed. Articles, 100 to 1,500 words, on all areas of autograph collecting: preservation, framing, and storage, specialty collections, documents and letters, collectors and dealers. Queries preferred. Pays 5¢ a word, $3 for illustrations, $10 for photos, and $25 for cartoons, on publication.

BIRD TALK—Box 6050, Mission Viejo, CA 92690. Karyn New, Ed. Articles for pet bird owners: care and feeding, training, outstanding personal adventures. Pays 7¢ to 10¢ a word, after publication. Query or manuscript with good transparency illustrations preferred.

BIRD WATCHER'S DIGEST—P.O. Box 110, Marietta, OH 45740. Mary B. Bowers, Ed. Articles, 600 to 3,000 words, on bird-watching experiences and expeditions: information about rare sightings; updates on endangered species. Pays to $50, on publication.

THE BLADE MAGAZINE—P.O. Box 22007, Chattanooga, TN 37422. J. Bruce Voyles, Ed. Articles, 500 to 3,000 words: historical pieces on knives and old knife factories, etc.; interviews with knifemakers; how-to pieces. Pays from 5¢ a word, on publication. Study magazine first.

CHESS LIFE—186 Route 9W, New Windsor, NY 12550. Don Maddox, Ed. Articles, 500 to 3,000 words, for members of the U.S. Chess Federation, on news, profiles, technical aspects of chess. Features on all aspects of chess: history, humor, puzzles, etc. Fiction, 500 to 2,000 words, related to chess. Photos. Pays varying rates, on acceptance. Query; limited free-lance market. Also publishes *School Mates* for juvenile or novice members of U.S.C.F. Jennie L. Simon, Ed. Query.

COLLECTOR EDITIONS—170 Fifth Ave., New York, NY 10010. Joan Muyskens Pursley, Man. Ed. Articles, 750 to 1,500 words, on collectibles, mainly glass and porcelain. Pays $150 to $350, within 30 days of acceptance. Query with photos.

COUNTRY HANDCRAFTS—5400 S. 60th St., Greendale, WI 53129. Jill Nickerson, Ed. How-to articles on all types of crafts (needlepoint, quilting, woodworking, etc.) with complete instructions and patterns. Pays from $50 to $500, on acceptance.

CRAFTS 'N THINGS—14 Main St., Dept. W, Park Ridge, IL 60068. Nancy Tosh, Ed. How-to articles on all kinds of crafts projects, with instructions. Pays $35 to $200, on publication. Send manuscript with instructions and photograph of the finished item.

DOLLS, THE COLLECTOR'S MAGAZINE—170 Fifth Ave., New York, NY 10010. Krystyna Poray Goddu, Ed. Articles, 500 to 2,500 words, for knowledgeable doll collectors: sharply focused with a strong collecting angle, and concrete information: value, identification, restoration. etc. Pays $100 to $350, after acceptance. Query.

FINESCALE MODELER—P.O. Box 1612, Waukesha, WI 53187. Bob Hayden, Ed. How-to articles for people who make nonoperating scale models of aircraft, automobiles, boats, figures. Photos and drawings should accompany articles. One-page model-building hints and tips. Pays from $30 per published page, on acceptance. Query preferred.

GAMBLING TIMES—16760 Stagg St., #213, Van Nuys, CA 91406. Dwight Chuman, Ed. Gambling-related articles, 1,000 to 6,000 words. Pays $100 to $150, on publication.

GAMES—810 Seventh Ave., New York, NY 10019. R. Wayne Schmittberger, Ed. Articles on games and puzzles. Quizzes, tests, brainteasers, etc. Photos. Pays varying rates, on acceptance.

THE HOME SHOP MACHINIST—2779 Aero Park Dr., Box 1810, Traverse City, MI 49685. Joe D. Rice, Ed. How-to articles, on precision metalworking and foundry work. Accuracy and attention to detail a must. Pays $40 per published page, extra for photos and illustrations, on publication. Send SASE for writer's guidelines.

KITPLANES—P.O. Box 6050, Mission Viejo, CA 92690. Dave Martin, Ed. Articles geared to the growing market of aircraft built from kits and plans by home craftsmen, on all aspects of design, construction and performance, 1,000 to 4,000 words. Pays $100 to $300, on publication.

THE LEATHER CRAFTSMAN—Box 1386, Fort Worth, TX 76101. Nancy Sawyer, Ed. Articles on leather crafters, helpful hints, and projects of varying difficulty. Pays $50 to $200, on publication.

LOST TREASURE—P.O. Box 1589, Grove, OK 74344. Kathy Dyer, Man. Ed. Factual articles, 1,000 to 3,000 words, on treasure hunting, metal detecting, prospecting techniques, and legendary lost treasure. Profiles. Photos. Pays 4¢ a word; preference given stories with photos.

MINIATURE COLLECTOR—170 Fifth Ave., New York, NY 10010. Chris Revi, Ed. Articles, 800 to 1,200 words, with photos, on outstanding 1/12-scale (dollhouse) miniatures and the people who make and collect them. Original, illustrated how-to projects for making miniatures. Pays varying rates, within 30 days of acceptance. Query with photos.

MODEL RAILROADER—1027 N. Seventh St., Milwaukee, WI 53233. Russ Larson, Ed. Articles, with photos of layout and equipment, on model railroads. Pays $75 per printed page, on acceptance. Query.

NATIONAL DOLL WORLD—306 E. Parr Rd., Berne, IN 46711. Rebekah Montgomery, Ed. Informational articles about doll collecting.

NEW ENGLAND ANTIQUES JOURNAL—4 Church St., Ware, MA 01082. Rufus Foshee, Ed. Well-researched articles, to 2,500 words, on antiques of interest to collectors and/or dealers, auction and antiques show reviews, to 1,000 words, antiques market news, to 500 words; photos desired. Pays to $150, on publication. Query or send manuscript. Reports in 2 to 4 weeks.

THE NEW YORK ANTIQUE ALMANAC—Box 335, Lawrence, NY 11559. Carol Nadel, Ed. Articles on antiques, shows, shops, art, investments, collectibles, collecting suggestions; related humor. Photos. Pays $5 to $75, extra for photos, on publication.

NOSTALGIA WORLD—Box 231, North Haven, CT 06473. Bonnie Roth, Ed. Articles, 500 to 3,000 words, on all kinds of collectibles: records, TV memorabilia ("Munsters," "Star Trek," "Dark Shadows," Elvira, etc.), comics, gum cards, toys, sheet music, monsters, magazines, dolls, movie posters, etc. Pays $10 to $50, on publication.

NUTSHELL NEWS—21027 Crossroads Cir., P.O. Box 1612, Waukesha, WI 53187. Sybil Harp, Ed. Articles, 1,200 to 1,500 words, for architectural scale miniatures enthusiasts, collectors, craftspeople, and hobbyists. Pays 10¢ a word, on publication. Query first.

PETERSEN'S PHOTOGRAPHIC—8490 Sunset Blvd., Los Angeles, CA 90069. Bill Hurter, Ed. How-to articles on all phases of still photography of interest to the amateur and advanced photographer. Pays $60 per printed page for article accompanied by photos, on publication.

PLATE WORLD—9200 N. Maryland Ave., Niles, IL 60648. Alyson Sulaski Wyckoff, Ed. Articles on artists, collectors, manufacturers, retailers of limited-edition (only) collector's plates. No antiques. Internationally oriented. Pays varying rates, on acceptance. Query first with writing samples.

POPULAR MECHANICS—224 W. 57th St., New York, NY 10019. Bill Hartford, Man. Ed. Articles, 300 to 2,000 words, on latest developments in mechanics, industry, science; features on hobbies with a mechanical slant; how-tos on home, shop, and crafts projects. Photos and sketches a plus. Pays to $1,000, $25 to $100 for short pieces, on acceptance. Buys all rights.

POPULAR PHOTOGRAPHY—1633 Broadway, New York, NY 10019. Jason Schneider, Ed. Dir. Illustrated articles of interest to serious amateur photographers, especially how-to picture taking pieces, 500 to 2,000 words. Payment varies. Query with outline.

THE PROFESSIONAL QUILTER—Oliver Press, Box 75277, St. Paul, MN 55175. Jeannie M. Spears, Ed. Articles, 500 to 1,500 words, for small businesses related to the quilting field: business and marketing skills, personality profiles. Graphics, if applicable; no how-to quilt articles. Pays $25 to $75, on publication. Guidelines.

RAILROAD MODEL CRAFTSMAN—P.O. Box 700, Newton, NJ 07860. William C. Schaumburg, Ed. How-to articles on scale model railroading; cars, operation, scenery, etc. Pays on publication.

R/C MODELER MAGAZINE—P.O. Box 487, Sierra Madre, CA 91024. Patricia E. Crews, Ed. Technical and semi-technical how-to articles on radio-controlled model aircraft, boats, helicopters, and cars. Query.

RESTORATION—3153 E. Lincoln, Tucson, AZ 85714–2017. W.R. Haessner, Ed. Articles, 1,200 to 1,800 words, on restoring autos, trucks, planes, trains, etc. Pays $10 per page, on publication. Query.

THE ROBB REPORT—1 Acton Pl., Acton, MA 01720. Attn: Geoffrey Douglas. Feature articles on investment opportunities, classic and collectible autos, art and antiques, home interiors, boats, travel, etc. Pays on publication. Query with SASE and published clips.

SCHOOL MATES—See *Chess Life*.

73 AMATEUR RADIO—WGE Center, Hancock, NH 03449. Bryan Hastings, Ed. Articles, 1,500 to 3,000 words, for electronics hobbyists and amateur radio operators. Pays $100 per printed page for construction articles, $50 to $75 per printed page for others.

SEW NEWS—P.O. Box 1790, News Plaza, Peoria, IL 61656. Linda Turner

Griepentrog, Ed. Articles, to 3,000 words, "that teach a specific technique, inspire a reader to try new sewing projects, or inform a reader about an interesting person, company, or project related to sewing, textiles, or fashion." Emphasis is on fashion (not craft) sewing. Pays $25 to $400, on acceptance. Queries required.

SPORTS COLLECTORS DIGEST—Krause Publications, 700 E. State St., Iola, WI 54990. Tom Mortenson, Ed. Articles, 750 to 2,000, on old baseball card sets and other collectibles. Pays $50 to $100, on publication.

STORYBOARD MAGAZINE—2512 Artesia Blvd., Redondo Beach, CA 90278. Glenn Shaffer, Ed. Articles, to 2,500 words, on "Disneyana": Disney studio and theme park history, movie history, travel, Disney-related art, and collectors or collections. Fillers and humor. Payment varies, on publication. Query required.

TEDDY BEAR REVIEW—P.O. Box 1239, Hanover, PA 17331. Chris Revi, Ed. Articles on antique and contemporary teddy bears for makers, collectors, and enthusiasts. Pays $50 to $200, within 30 days of acceptance. Query with photos.

THREADS MAGAZINE—Taunton Press, 63 S. Main St., Box 355, Newtown, CT 06470. Address the Editors. A bimonthly devoted to design, materials, and techniques in the fiber and textile arts. Articles and department pieces about materials, tools, techniques, people, and design, especially in sewing, knitting, and stitchery. Pays $150 per published page, on publication.

TREASURE—6745 Adobe Rd., Twenty-Nine Palms, CA 92277. Jim Williams, Ed. Articles, to 2,500 words, and fillers, 300 words, of interest to treasure hunters: How-to (building projects and hunting techniques); Search (where to look for treasure); and Found (stories of discovered treasure). Photos and illustrations welcome. Pays from $30 for fillers, to $125 for features, on publication. Same address and requirements for *Treasure Search* and *Treasure Found.*

TROPICAL FISH HOBBYIST—211 W. Sylvania Ave., Neptune City, NJ 07753. Ray Hunziker, Ed. Articles, 500 to 3,000 words, for beginning and experienced tropical and marine fish enthusiasts. Photos. Pays $35 to $250, on acceptance. Query.

WEST ART—Box 6868, Auburn, CA 95604. Martha Garcia, Ed. Features, 350 to 700 words, on fine arts and crafts. No hobbies. Photos. Pays 50¢ per column inch, on publication. SASE required.

WESTERN & EASTERN TREASURES—P.O. Box 1095, Arcata, CA 95521. Rosemary Anderson, Man. Ed. Illustrated articles, to 1,500 words, on metal detecting, treasure hunting, rocks, and gems. Pays 2¢ a word, extra for photos, on publication.

THE WINE SPECTATOR—Opera Plaza, Suite 2014, 601 Van Ness Ave., San Francisco, CA 94102. Jim Gordon, Man. Ed. Features, 600 to 2,000 words, preferably with photos, on news and people in the wine world. Pays from $100, extra for photos, on publication. Query required.

WOMEN'S CIRCLE COUNTED CROSS-STITCH—306 E. Parr Rd., Berne, IN 46711. Denise Lohr, Ed. How-to and instructional counted cross-stitch. Short stories, interviews, and photos of top designers, book reviews, tips, humor. Pays varying rates, on publication.

WOMEN'S CIRCLE COUNTRY NEEDLECRAFT—306 E. Parr Rd., Berne, IN 46711. Jenine Howard Nuwer, Ed. How-to and instructional needlecrafts, humor, book reviews, and tips. Photos. Pays varying rates, on publication.

WOODEN BOAT—P.O. Box 78, Brooklin, ME 04616. Jonathan Wilson, Ed.

How-to and technical articles, 4,000 words, on construction, repair, and maintenance of wooden boats; design, history, and use of wooden boats; and profiles of outstanding wooden boat builders and designers. Pays $6 per column inch. Query preferred.

THE WORKBASKET—4251 Pennsylvania, Kansas City, MO 64111. Roma Jean Rice, Ed. Instructions and models for original knit, crochet, and tat items. (Designs must fit theme of issue.) How-tos on crafts and gardening, 400 to 1,200 words, with photos. Pays 7¢ a word for articles, extra for photos, on acceptance; negotiable rates for instructional items.

WORKBENCH—4251 Pennsylvania Ave., Kansas City, MO 64111. Robert N. Hoffman, Ed. Articles on do-it-yourself home improvement and maintenance projects and general woodworking articles for beginning and expert craftsmen. Complete working drawings with accurate dimensions, step-by-step instructions, lists of materials, and photos of the finished product must accompany submission. Queries welcome. Pays from $150 per published page, on acceptance.

YELLOWBACK LIBRARY—P.O. Box 36172, Des Moines, IA 50315. Gil O'Gara, Ed. Articles, 300 to 2,000 words, on boys/girls series literature (Hardy Boys, Nancy Drew, Tom Swift, etc.) for collectors, researchers, and dealers. "Especially welcome are interviews with, or articles by past and present writers of juvenile series fiction." Pays in copies and ads.

YESTERYEAR—P.O. Box 2, Princeton, WI 54968. Michael Jacobi, Ed. Articles on antiques and collectibles, for readers in WI, IL, IA, MN, and surrounding states. Photos. Will consider regular columns on collecting or antiques. Pays from $10, on publication.

ZYMURGY—Box 287, Boulder, CO 80306. Charles N. Papazian, Ed. Articles appealing to beer lovers and homebrewers. Pays $25 to $75, for pieces 750 to 2,000 words, on publication. Query.

POPULAR & TECHNICAL SCIENCE; COMPUTERS

AD ASTRA—(formerly *Space World*) National Space Society, 922 Pennsylvania Ave. S.E., Washington, DC 20003. Leonard David, Ed.-in-Chief. Lively, non-technical features (to 3,000 words) on all aspects of international space program. Particularly interested in "Living in Space" articles; space settlements; lunar and Mars bases. Pays $150 to $300, on publication. Query; guidelines available.

AIR & SPACE—370 L'Enfant Promenade, 10th Fl., Washington, DC 20024–2518. George Larson, Ed. General-interest articles, 1,000 to 3,500 words, on aerospace experience, past, present, and future; travel, space, history, biographies, essays, commentary. Pays varying rates, on acceptance. Query first.

AMIGA WORLD—IDG Communications, 80 Elm St., Peterborough, NH 03458. Linda Barrett, Acquisitions Ed. Articles, 1,500 to 3,000 words, on programming and product reviews (including games) on the Amiga systems. Pays $350 to $800, on publication. Query first.

ANTIC, THE ATARI RESOURCE—544 Second St., San Francisco, CA 94107. Nat Friedland, Ed. Programs and information for the Atari computer user/owner. Reviews, 500 words, of hardware and software, original programs, etc. Game reviews, 400 words. Pays $50 per review, $60 per published page, on publication. Query.

ARCHAEOLOGY—15 Park Row, New York, NY 10038. Peter A. Young, Ed.-in-Chief. Articles on archaeology by professionals or lay people with a solid knowledge of the field. Pays $500 to $1,000, on acceptance. Query required.

ASTRONOMY—P.O. Box 1612, Waukesha, WI 53187. Richard Berry, Ed.-in-Chief. Articles on astronomy, astrophysics, space programs, research. Hobby pieces on equipment; short news items. Pays varying rates, on acceptance.

BIOSCIENCE—American Institute of Biological Science, 730 11th St. N.W., Washington, DC 20001. Laura Tangley, Features Ed. Articles, 2 to 4 journal pages, on new developments in biology or on science policy, for professional biologists. Pays $200 per journal page, on publication. Query required.

BYTE MAGAZINE—One Phoenix Mill Ln., Peterborough, NH 03458. Frederic Langa, Ed. Features on new technology, how-to articles, and reviews of computers and software, varying lengths, for sophisticated users of personal computers. Payment is competitive. Query. Guidelines.

CBT DIRECTIONS—Weingarten Publications, 38 Chauncy St., Boston, MA 02111. Mark Fritz, Ed. Articles (2,500 words) and news items (from 500 words) on computer-based training and interactive video for industry and government professionals in program development. Pays $100 to $600, on acceptance. Query.

COMPUTE!—324 W. Wendover Ave., Suite 200, Greensboro, NC 27408. Peter Scisco, Ed. In-depth feature articles on using the personal computer at home, work, and school. Industry news, interviews with leaders in the pc field, product information, hardware and software reviews. For users of Amiga, Apple, Commodore 64/128, IBM, Tandy, and compatibles. Also: *Compute's PC Magazine*, Lance Elko, Ed.

COMPUTE!'S GAZETTE—324 W. Wendover Ave., Suite 200, Greensboro, NC 27408. Kathleen Martinek, Man. Ed. Patrick Parrish, Assoc. Ed. Articles, to 2,000 words, on Commodore 64/128, including home, education, and business applications, games, and programming. Original programs also accepted.

DATA COMMUNICATIONS INTERNATIONAL—1221 Ave. of the Americas, New York, NY 10020. Joseph Braue, Ed.-in-Chief. Technical articles, 2,000 words, on communications networks. Readers are managers of multinational computer networks. Payment varies; made on acceptance and on publication.

DATACENTER MANAGER—International Computer Programs, Inc., 9100 Keystone Crossing, Suite 200, Indianapolis, IN 46240. Mark Taber, Ed. Articles, 2,000 to 3,000 words, on the software and utilities that drive computer systems, communications, and data center operations. Pays $600 to $800, on acceptance.

DIGITAL NEWS—33 West St., Boston, MA 02111. Charles Babcock, Ed. Newspaper articles of varying lengths, covering products, applications, and events related to Digital's VAX line of computers. Pay varies, on acceptance. Query required.

DISCOVER MAGAZINE—Family Media, Inc., 3 Park Ave., New York, NY 10016. Query.

ENVIRONMENT—4000 Albemarle St. N.W., Washington, DC 20016. Barbara T. Richman, Man. Ed. Factual articles, 2,500 to 5,000 words, on scientific, technological, and environmental policy and decision-making issues. Pays $100 to $300. Query.

FINAL FRONTIER—P.O. Box 11519, Washington, DC 20008. Tony Reich-

615

hardt, Ed. Articles (1,500 to 3,000 words), columns (800 words), and shorts (250 words) about people, events, and "exciting possibilities" of the world's space programs. Pays about 25¢ a word, on acceptance. Query.

FOCUS—Turnkey Publications, 4807 Spicewood Springs Rd., Suite 3150, Austin, TX 78759. Greg Farman, Ed. Articles, 700 to 4,000 words, on Data General computers. Photos a plus. Pays to $100, on publication. Query required.

THE FUTURIST—World Future Society, 4916 Elmo Ave., Bethesda, MD 20814. Timothy Willard, Man. Ed. Features, 1,000 to 5,000 words, on subjects pertaining to the future: environment, education, science, technology, etc. Pays in copies.

GENETIC ENGINEERING NEWS—1651 Third Ave., New York, NY 10128. John Sterling, Man. Ed. Articles on all aspects of biotechnology; feature articles and news articles. Pays varying rates, on acceptance. Query.

GEOBYTE—American Association of Petroleum Geologists, P.O. Box 979, Tulsa, OK 74101. Ken Milam, Man. Ed. Articles, 20 typed pages, on computer applications in exploration and production of oil, gas, and energy minerals for geophysicists, geologists, and petroleum engineers. Pay varies, on acceptance. Queries preferred.

HAM RADIO—Main St., Greenville, NH 03048. Terry Northup, Man. Ed. Articles, to 2,500 words, on amateur radio theory and construction. Pays $40 per printed page, on publication. Query. Guidelines.

INCIDER—IDG Communications/Peterborough, 80 Elm St., Peterborough, NH 03458. Paul Statt, Sr. Ed. Features, 2,000 to 2,500 words, and product reviews, 1,000 to 1,500 words, of interest to Apple II computer users. Short hints and news, to 100 words. Pays from $25 to $500, on acceptance. Query.

LINK-UP—143 Old Marlton Pike, Medford, NJ 08055. Joseph A. Webb, Ed. Dir. How-to pieces, hardware and software reviews, and current trends, 600 to 2,500 words, for business and education professionals who use computers and modems at work and at home. Pays $90 to $220, on publication. Photos a plus.

LOTUS—P. O. Box 9123, Cambridge, MA 02139. John Campbell, Ed. Dir. Articles, 1,500 to 3,000 words, on business and professional applications of Lotus software. Query with outline required. Pays $700 to $1500, on acceptance.

MACINTOSH HANDS ON—(formerly Nibble Mac) 52 Domino Dr., Concord, MA 01742. Steve Sarsfield, Man. Ed. Articles using Macintosh programs; product reviews, tutorials, and general-interest articles for Macintosh users. Articles on use of Hyper Card stackware and publishable Hyper Card stacks. Pays $40 to $500, after acceptance. Programs must be submitted on disk. Send SASE for guidelines.

MACWORLD—Editorial Proposals, 501 Second St., Suite 600, San Francisco, CA 94107. Reviews, news, consumer, and how-to articles relating to Macintosh personal computers; varying lengths. Query or send outline with screenshots, if applicable. Pays from $300 to $3,000, on acceptance. Send SASE for writers guidelines.

MODERN ELECTRONICS—76 N. Broadway, Hicksville, NY 10081. Art Salsberg, Ed.-in-Chief. How-to features, technical tutorials, and construction projects related to latest consumer and industrial electronics circuits, products, and personal computer equipment. Lengths vary. Query with outline required. Pays $80 to $150 per published page, on acceptance.

NETWORK WORLD—Box 9171, Framingham, MA 01701. John Gallant, Ed. Articles, to 2,500 words, about applications of communications technology for management level users of data, voice, and video communications systems. Pays varying rates, on acceptance.

NIBBLE—52 Domino Dr., Concord, MA 01742. Rich Williams, Man. Ed. Programs and programming methods, as well as short articles, reviews, and general-interest pieces for Apple II Computer users. Include program and article on disk. Send short cover letter and sample program runs with manuscript. Pays $75 to $500 for articles, $50 to $250 for shorter pieces. Send SASE for writers' guidelines.

NIBBLE MAC—See *Macintosh Hands On.*

OMNI—1965 Broadway, New York, NY 10023. Patrice Adcroft, Ed. Articles, 1,000 to 3,500 words, on scientific aspects of the future: space colonies, cloning, machine intelligence, ESP, origin of life, future arts, lifestyles, etc. Pays $800 to $4,000, $150 for short items, on acceptance. Query.

PCM MAGAZINE—Falsoft, Inc., 9509 US Highway 42, P.O. Box 385, Prospect, KY 40059. Judi Hutchinson, Ed. Articles and computer programs for Tandy portables and MS-DOS computers. Pays varying rates, on publication.

PERSONAL COMPUTING—VNLL Business Publications, Inc., 10 Holland Dr., Hasbrouck Heights, NJ 07604. Fred Abatemarco, Ed.-in-Chief. Articles for managerial-level business audience and savvy personal compute users. Pays on acceptance.

PERSONAL PUBLISHING—191 S. Gary Ave., Carol Stream, IL 60188. Dan Brogan, Ed. Articles, 1,500 to 2,000 words, on desktop publishing technology. Queries required. Pay varies, on publication.

POPULAR ELECTRONICS—500-B Bi County Blvd., Farmingdale, NY 11735. Julian S. Martin, Ed. Features, 1,500 to 2,500 words, for electronics hobbyists and experimenters. "Our readers are science oriented, understand computer theory and operation, and like to build projects." Fillers and cartoons. Pays $25 to $350, on acceptance.

PUBLISH!—PCW Communications, 501 Second St., San Francisco, CA 94107. Susan Gubernat, Ed.-in-Chief. Features (700 words; 1,200 to 2,000 words) and reviews (800 to 2,500 words) with how-to information on the practical aspects of desktop publishing. Pays $300 for short articles and reviews, $600 and up for full-length features and reviews, on acceptance. Query Leslie Steere, Man. Ed.

RADIO-ELECTRONICS—500-B Bi-County Blvd., Farmingdale, NY 11735. Brian C. Fenton, Ed. Technical articles, 1,500 to 3,000 words, on all areas related to electronics. Pays $50 to $500, on acceptance.

THE RAINBOW—Falsoft, Inc., 9509 U. S Highway 42, P. O. Box 385, Prospect, KY 40059. Tony Olive, Submissions Ed. Articles and computer programs for Tandy color computers. Pays varying rates, on publication.

RUN—CW Communications, 80 Elm St., Peterborough, NH 03458. Dennis Brisson, Ed.-in-Chief. Articles, 6 to 10 typed pages, geared to Commodore home computer users: applications, program listings, hints, and tips to "help readers get the most out of their Commodore." Query first for technical subjects. Pays $100 per printed page.

THE SCIENCES—2 E. 63rd St., New York, NY 10021. Paul T. Libassi, Ed. Essays and features, 300 to 4,000 words, and book reviews, on all scientific disciplines. Pays honorarium, on publication. Query.

SEA FRONTIERS—4600 Rickenbacker Causeway, Virginia Key, Miami, FL 33149. Jean Bradfisch, Exec. Ed. Illustrated articles, 500 to 3,000 words, on scientific advances related to the sea, biological, physical, chemical, or geological phenomena, ecology, conservation, etc., written in a popular style for lay readers. Send SASE for guidelines. Pays $50 to $450, on acceptance. Query.

SHAREWARE MAGAZINE—1030D E. Duane Ave., Sunnyvale, CA 94086. Michelle Rainage, Ed. Reviews of shareware programs and articles on related topics, 1,000 to 4,000 words. Payment varies, on publication. Query.

SPACE WORLD—See *Ad Astra.*

START MAGAZINE—Antic Publishing, 544 Second St., San Francisco, CA 94107. Andrew Reese, Ed. Articles, to 4,000 words, and programming features, 1,500 to 2,500 words, for beginning and experienced users of Atari ST computers. Submit hard copy and disk. Pay varies, on publication. Guidelines.

TECHNOLOGY REVIEW—M.I.T., W59–200, Cambridge, MA 02139. Jonathan Schlefer, Ed. General-interest articles and more technical features, 1,500 to 5,000 words, on technology, the environment, and society. Pay varies, on publication. Query.

VOICE PROCESSING MAGAZINE—P.O. Box 42382, Houston, TX 77242. Tim Cornitius, Ed. Quarterly. Technical articles, 2,000 to 2,400 words, and applications of voice mail and messaging, voice response, call processing, and voice/data networking. Pays 15¢ per word, on publication. Query.

ANIMALS

AMERICAN FARRIERS JOURNAL—63 Great Rd., Maynard, MA 01754. Susan G. Philbrick, Ed. Articles, 800 to 5,000 words, on general farriery issues, hoof care, tool selection, equine lameness, and horse handling. Pays 30¢ per published line, $10 per published illustration or photo, on publication. Query.

ANIMAL KINGDOM—New York Zoological Society, Bronx, NY 10460. Nancy Christie, Sr. Ed. First-person articles, 1,500 to 2,000 words, on "popular" natural history, "based on author's research and experience as opposed to textbook approach." Payment varies, on acceptance. Guidelines.

AQUARIUM FISH—P.O. Box 6050, Mission Viejo, CA 92690. Edward Bauman, Ed. Articles, 2,000 words, on freshwater, saltwater, and pond fish, preferably with color transparencies (no "pet fish" stories, please). Payment varies, on publication.

BIRD TALK—Box 6050, Mission Viejo, CA 92690. Karyn New, Ed. Articles for pet bird owners: care and feeding, training, outstanding personal adventures. Pays 7¢ to 12¢ a word, after publication. Query or send manuscript with good transparency illustrations.

BIRD WATCHER'S DIGEST—P.O. Box 110, Marietta, OH 45740. Mary B. Bowers, Ed. Articles, 600 to 3,000 words, on bird-watching experiences and expeditions: information about rare sightings; updates on endangered species. Pays to $50, on publication.

CAT FANCY—P.O. Box 6050, Mission Viejo, CA 92690. Linda Lewis, Ed. Articles, from 1,500 to 3,000 words, on cat care, health, grooming, etc. Pays 5¢ a word, or $150 to $300 for photo story with quality color slides or B&W prints, on publication.

DOG FANCY—P. O. Box 6050, Mission Viejo, CA 92690. Kim Thornton, Ed. Articles, 1,500 to 3,000 words, on dog care, health, grooming, breeds, activities, events, etc. Photos. Pays from 5¢ a word, on publication.

EQUUS—Fleet Street Corp., 656 Quince Orchard Rd., Gaithersburg, MD 20878. Emily Kilby, Ed. 1,000- to 3,000-word articles on all breeds of horses, covering their health, care, the latest advances in equine medicine and research. "Attempt to speak as one horse-person to another." Pays $100 to $400, on acceptance.

HORSE & RIDER—941 Calle Negocio, San Clemente, CA 92672. Ray Rich, Ed. Articles, 500 to 3,000 words, with photos, on Western riding and general horse care: training, feeding, grooming, etc. Pays varying rates, on publication. Buys all rights. Guidelines.

HORSEMAN—25025 I 45N, Suite 390, Spring, TX 77380. David T. Gaines, Ed./Pub. Instructional articles, to 2,500 words, with photos, for Western trainers and riders. Pays from $50.

HORSEMEN'S YANKEE PEDLAR—785 Southbridge St., Auburn, MA 01501. Nancy L. Khoury, Pub. News and feature-length articles, about horses and horsemen in the Northeast. Photos. Pays $2 per published inch, on publication. Query.

HORSEPLAY—P.O. Box 130, Gaithersburg, MD 20877. Cordelia Doucet, Ed. Articles, 1,000 to 3,000 words, on eventing, show jumping, horse shows, dressage, driving, and fox hunting, for horse enthusiasts. Pays 10¢ a word, buys all rights, after publication.

HORSEWORLD USA—P.O. Box 249, Huntington, NY 11746. Diana DeRosa, Ed. Horse-related articles of varying lengths of interest to horse enthusiasts. Pays on publication. Query.

MUSHING—P.O. Box 149, Ester, AK 99725. Todd Hoener, Ed. How-tos, profiles, and features (1,500 to 2,000 words) and department pieces (500 to 1,000 words) for competitive and recreational mushers and skijorers. Humor and photos. Pays $25 to $250, after acceptance. Queries preferred. Guidelines.

PERFORMANCE HORSEMAN—Gum Tree Corner, Unionville, PA 19375. Miranda Lorraine, Articles Ed. Factual how-to pieces for the serious western rider, on training improving riding skills, all aspects of care and management, etc. Pays from $300, on acceptance.

PRACTICAL HORSEMAN—Gum Tree Corner, Unionville, PA 19375. Miranda D. Lorraine, Articles Ed. How-to articles on horse care, English riding, and training. Pays on acceptance. Query.

PURE BRED DOGS/AMERICAN KENNEL GAZETTE—51 Madison Ave., New York, NY 10010. Marion Lane, Exec. Ed. Judy Hartop, Sr. Ed. Articles, 1,000 to 2,500 words, relating to pure-bred dogs. Pays from $100 to $300, on publication. Query preferred.

SHEEP! MAGAZINE—W. 2997 Market Rd., Helenville, WI 53137. Dave Thompson, Ed. Articles, to 1,500 words, on successful shepherds, woolcrafts, sheep raising, and sheep dogs. Photos. Pays $80 to $250, extra for photos, on publication.

TROPICAL FISH HOBBYIST—211 W. Sylvania Ave., Neptune City, NJ 07753. Ray Hunziker, Ed. Articles, 500 to 3,000 words, for beginning and experienced tropical and marine fish enthusiasts. Photos. Pays $35 to $250, on acceptance. Query.

WILDBIRD—Box 6050, Mission Viejo, CA 92690. Tim Gallagher, Man. Ed. Features, 1,500 to 2,000 words, and columns, 700 to 1,000 words, for field birders and garden birders. "No pieces on taming wild birds." Pays from $100 for features, $25 for columns, extra for photos. Guidelines.

PARENTING, CHILD CARE, AND DEVELOPMENT

AMERICAN BABY—475 Park Ave. S., New York, NY 10016. Judith Nolte, Ed. Articles, 1,000 to 2,000 words, for new or expectant parents on prenatal and infant care. Pays varying rates, on acceptance.

BABY TALK—636 Ave. of the Americas, New York, NY 10011. Susan Strecker, Ed. Articles, 1,500 to 3,000 words, by parents or professionals, on babies, baby care, etc. Pays varying rates, on acceptance. SASE required.

CHILD—110 Fifth Ave., New York, NY 10011. Kate White, Ed. Bi-monthly magazine. Articles on lifestyles of children and family. Departments: Fashion, Home Environment, Baby Best, and Travel. Pays from $750. Query.

GROWING CHILD/GROWING PARENT—22 N. Second St., Lafayette, IN 47902. Nancy Kleckner, Ed. Articles to 1,500 words on subjects of interest to parents of children under 6, with emphasis on the issues, problems, and choices of being a parent. No personal-experience pieces or poetry. Pays 8¢ to 15¢ a word, on acceptance. Query.

LIVING WITH CHILDREN—127 Ninth Ave. N., Nashville, TN 37234. Articles, 800, 1,450, or 2,000 words, on parent-child relationships, told from a Christian perspective. Pays 5¢ a word, after acceptance.

LIVING WITH PRESCHOOLERS—127 Ninth Ave. N., Nashville, TN 37234. Articles, 800, 1,450, or 2,000 words, and fillers, to 300 words, for Christian families. Pays 5¢ a word, on acceptance.

LIVING WITH TEENAGERS—127 Ninth Ave. N., Nashville, TN 37234. Articles told from a Christian perspective for parents of teenagers; first-person approach preferred. Poetry, 4 to 16 lines. Pays 5¢ a word, on acceptance.

MARRIAGE & FAMILY—Abbey Press Publishing Div., St. Meinrad, IN 47577. Kass Dotterweich, Man. Ed. Expert advice, personal-experience articles with moral, religious, or spiritual slant, to 2,500 words, on husband-wife and parent-child relationships. Pays 7¢ a word, on acceptance.

NEW YORK FAMILY—420 E. 79th St., New York, NY 10021. Felice Shapiro, Susan Ross, Eds. Articles related to family life in New York City. Pays $50 to $100, on publication. Same requirements for *Westchester Family,* for parents in Westchester County, NY.

PARENTING—501 Second St., San Francisco, CA 94107. David Markus, Ed. Articles, 500 to 2,500 words, for parents of children up to 10-years-old, especially under 6-years-old. Topics include education, health, fitness, nutrition, child development, psychology, and social issues. Pays to $2,000. Query.

PARENTS—685 Third Ave., New York, NY 10017. Ann Pleshette Murphy, Ed.-in-Chief. Articles, 1,500 to 3,000 words, on growth and development of infants, children, teens; family; women's issues; community; current research. Informal style with quotes from experts. Pays from $1,000, on acceptance. Query.

THINKING FAMILIES—605 Worcester Rd., Towson, MD 21204. Marjory Spraycar, Ed. Articles (500 to 1,500 words) about elementary school children: their social, intellectual, and physical development and their lives in school. Pays $50 to $1,000, on publication. Query required.

WESTCHESTER FAMILY—See *New York Family.*

WORKING MOTHER—230 Park Ave., New York, NY 10169. Address Editorial Dept. Articles, to 1,000 words, that help women in their task of juggling job, home, and family. Payment varies, on acceptance.

MILITARY

THE AMERICAN LEGION MAGAZINE—Box 1055, Indianapolis, IN 46206. Michael D. LaBonne, Ed. Articles, 750 to 1,800 words, on current world affairs, public policy, and subjects of contemporary interest. Pays $100 to $1,000, on acceptance. Query.

ARMY MAGAZINE—2425 Wilson Blvd., Arlington, VA 22201-3385. L. James Binder, Ed.-in-Chief, Features, to 5,000 words, on military subjects. Essays, humor, history, news reports, first-person anecdotes. Pays 12¢ to 18¢ a word, $10 to $25 for anecdotes, on publication.

LIFE IN THE TIMES—The Times Journal Co., Springfield, VA 22159–0200. Barry Robinson, Ed. Articles, to 2,000 words, on current military family life. Pays $100 to $350, on acceptance.

MILITARY LIFESTYLE MAGAZINE—1732 Wisconsin Ave. N.W., Washington, DC 20007. Hope Daniels, Ed. Articles, 1,000 to 2,000 words, for military families in the U.S. and overseas, on lifestyles, travel, fashion, nutrition, and health; fiction. Pays $200 to $800, on publication. Query first.

OFF DUTY MAGAZINE—3303 Harbor Blvd., Suite C-2, Costa Mesa, CA 92626. Bruce Thorstad, U.S. Ed. Informative, entertaining and useful articles, 900 to 1,800 words, for military service personnel and their dependents, on making the most of off-duty time and getting the most out of service life: military living, travel, personal finance, sports, military people, American trends, etc. Military angle essential. Pays 13¢ to 16¢ a word, on publication. European and Pacific editions also. Query required. Guidelines.

THE RETIRED OFFICER MAGAZINE—201 N. Washington St., Alexandria, VA 22314. Articles, 750 to 2,000 words, of interest to military retirees and their families. Current military/political affairs: recent military history (especially Vietnam and Korea), humor, travel, hobbies, military family lifestyles, wellness, and second-career job opportunities. Photos a plus. Pays to $500, extra for photos, on acceptance. Queries required, no unsolicited manuscripts; address Manuscript Ed. Guidelines.

VFW MAGAZINE—406 West 34th St., Kansas City, MO 64111. Richard K. Kolb, Ed. Magazine for Veterans of Foreign Wars and their families. Articles, 1,000 words, on current issues and history, with veteran angle. Photos. Pays up to $400, extra for photos, on acceptance. Guidelines.

WESTERN

AMERICAN WEST—7000 E. Tanque Verde Rd., Suite 30, Tucson, AZ 85715. Mae Reid-Bills, Man. Ed. Well-researched, illustrated articles, 1,000 to 2,500 words, linking the contemporary West with its historic past and emphasizing places to see and things to do for the Western traveler. Pays from $200, on acceptance. Query required.

OLD WEST—See *True West.*

PERSIMMON HILL—1700 N.E. 63rd St., Oklahoma City, OK 73111. Marcia Preston, Ed. Published by the National Cowboy Hall of Fame. Articles, 1,500 to 3,000 words, on Western history and art, cowboys, ranching, and nature. Top quality illustrations a must. Pays from $100 to $250, on acceptance.

TRUE WEST—P.O. Box 2107, Stillwater, OK 74076. John Joerschke, Ed. True stories, 500 to 4,500 words, with photos, about the Old West to 1930. Some contemporary stories with historical slant. Source list required. Pays 3¢ to 5¢ a word, extra for B&W photos, on acceptance. Same address and requirements for *Old West.*

HISTORICAL

AMERICAN HERITAGE—60 Fifth Ave., New York, NY 10011. Byron Dobell, Ed. Articles, 750 to 5,000 words, on U.S. history and background of American life and culture from the beginning to recent times. No fiction. Pays from $300 to $1,500, on acceptance. Query. SASE.

AMERICAN HERITAGE OF INVENTION & TECHNOLOGY—60 Fifth Ave., New York, NY 10011. Frederick Allen, Ed. Articles, 2,000 to 5,000 words, on history of technology in America, for the sophisticated general reader. Query. Pays on acceptance.

AMERICAN HISTORY ILLUSTRATED—2245 Kohn Road, P.O. Box 8200, Harrisburg, PA 17105. Articles, 3,000 to 5,000 words, soundly researched. Style should be popular, not scholarly. No travelogues, fiction, or puzzles. Pays $300 to $650, on acceptance. Query with SASE required.

CHICAGO HISTORY—Clark St. at North Ave., Chicago, IL 60614. Russell Lewis, Ed. Articles, to 4,500 words, on political, social, and cultural history. Pays to $250, on publication. Query.

EARLY AMERICAN LIFE—Box 8200, Harrisburg, PA 17105. Frances Carnahan, Ed. Illustrated articles, 1,000 to 3,000 words, on early American life: arts, crafts, furnishings, architecture; travel features about historic sites and country inns. Pays $50 to $500, on acceptance. Query.

HEARTLAND JOURNAL—Box 55115, Madison, WI 53705. Jeri McCormick and Lenore Coberly, Eds. Articles, 100 to 4,000 words, on "times and places that are gone." Writers must be over 60 years old. Pays in copies.

HISTORIC PRESERVATION—1785 Massachusetts Ave. N.W., Washington, DC 20036. Thomas J. Colin, Ed. Lively feature articles from published writers, 1,500 to 4,000 words, on residential restoration, preservation issues, and people involved in saving America's built environment. High-quality photos. Pays $300 to $1,000, extra for photos, on acceptance. Query required.

COLLEGE, CAREERS

AMPERSAND—303 N. Glenoaks Blvd., Suite 600, Burbank, CA 91502. Stewart Weiner, Exec. Ed. Articles, 1,000 to 2,000 words, of interest to college students. Focus on films and popular entertainment. Query.

THE BLACK COLLEGIAN—1240 S. Broad St., New Orleans, LA 70125. K. Kazi-Ferrouillet, Man. Ed. Articles, to 2,000 words, on experiences of black students, careers, and how-to subjects. Pays on publication. Query.

CAMPUS LIFE—465 Gundersen Dr., Carol Stream, IL 60188. Jim Long, Man. Ed. Articles reflecting Christian values and world view, for high school and college students. Humor and general fiction. Photo essays, cartoons. Pays from $150, on acceptance. Limited free-lance market. Query.

CAMPUS USA—1801 Rockville Pike, Suite 216, Rockville, MD 20852. Gerald S. Snyder, Ed. Articles (500 to 1,500 words) on the tastes, feelings, and moods of today's college students: careers, college financing, travel, movies, fashion, autos, and sports. Pays $150 to $500, on publication. Query required.

CIRCLE K—3636 Woodview Trace, Indianapolis, IN 46268. Nicholas K. Drake, Exec. Ed. Serious and light articles, 2,000 to 2,500 words, on community service and involvement, self-help, leadership development, youth issues, and careers. Pays $200 to $300, on acceptance. Queries required.

COLLEGE WOMAN—303 N. Glenoaks Blvd., Suite 600, Burbank, CA 91502. Stewart Weiner, Exec. Ed. Articles, 2,500 words, of interest to college women, on topics from controversial on-campus issues to fashion and sports. Fillers, to 500 words. Query required.

THE MINORITY ENGINEER—44 Broadway, Greenlawn, NY 11740. James Schneider, Ed. Articles, 1,000 to 1,500 words, for college students, on career opportunities in engineering, scientific and technological fields; techniques of job hunting; developments in and applications of new technologies. Interviews. Profiles. Pays 10¢ a word, on publication. Query. Same address and requirements for *The Woman Engineer.*

MOVING UP—303 N. Glenoaks Blvd., Suite 600, Burbank, CA 91502. Stewart Weiner, Exec. Ed. Articles, 500 to 2,500 words, of interest to college men, concerning careers, relationships, fitness, personal style, and self-awareness; profiles; opinion pieces; humor. Pays on acceptance. Query required.

UCLA MAGAZINE—405 Hilgard Ave., Los Angeles, CA 90024. Mark Wheeler, Ed. Quarterly. Articles (2,000 words) related to UCLA through research, alumni, students, etc. Queries required. Pays to $750, on acceptance.

WHAT'S NEW MAGAZINE—Multicom, Inc., 11 Allen Rd., Boston, MA 02135. Bob Leja, Ed. General-interest articles, 150 to 300 words, on music, movies, books, cars, travel, sports, food, wine, consumer electronics, computers, arts, and entertainment. Pays $25 to $250, on publication. Query required.

THE WOMAN ENGINEER—See *The Minority Engineer.*

ALTERNATIVE MAGAZINES

EAST WEST: THE JOURNAL OF NATURAL HEALTH & LIVING—17 Station St., Box 1200, Brookline, MA 02147. Features, 1,500 to 2,500 words, on holistic health, natural foods, gardening, etc. Material for "Body," "Healing," "In the Kitchen," and "Beauty and Fitness." Interviews. Photos. Pays 10¢ to 15¢ a word, extra for photos, on publication.

FATE—P.O. Box 64383, St. Paul, MN 55164–0383. Donald Michael Kaag, Ed. Factual fillers and true stories, to 300 words, on strange or psychic happenings and mystic personal experiences. Pays $2 to $15.

NEW AGE—342 Western Ave., Brighton, MA 02135. Address Manuscript Ed. Articles for readers who take an active interest in social change, contemporary issues, health, and personal growth. Features, 2,000 to 4,000 words; columns, 750 to 1,500 words; short news items, 50 words; and first-person narratives, 750 to 1,500 words. Pays varying rates. Query.

NEW REALITIES—4000 Albemarle St. N.W., Washington, DC 20016. Neal Vahle, Ed. Articles on holistic health, personal growth, parapsychology, alternative lifestyles, new spirituality. Query or send complete manuscript.

WILDFIRE—Bear Tribe Publishing, P.O. Box 9167, Spokane, WA 99209. Matthew Ryan, Ed. Articles (1,000 to 2,500 words) with a strong nature-based focus on spirituality, personal development, alternative lifestyles, natural healings, and ecology. Fiction (900 to 4,500 words) and poetry (20 lines). Pays to $250, on publication.

YOGA JOURNAL—2054 University Ave., Berkeley, CA 94704. Stephan Bodian, Ed. Articles, 1,200 to 3,000 words, on holistic health, spirituality, yoga, and transpersonal psychology; "new age" profiles; interviews. Pays $75 to $200, on publication.

OP-ED MARKETS

Op-ed pages in newspapers (those that run opposite the editorials) offer writers an excellent opportunity to air their opinions, views, ideas, and insights on a wide spectrum of subjects and in styles, from the highly personal and informal essay to the more serious commentary on politics, foreign affairs, and news events. Humor and nostalgia often find a place here.

THE ATLANTA CONSTITUTION—P.O. Box 4689, Atlanta, GA 30302. Patricia Carr, Op-Ed Ed. Articles related to the Southeast, Georgia or the Atlanta metropolitan area, 200 to 800 words, on a variety of topics: law, economics, politics, science, environment, performing and manipulative arts, humor, education; religious and seasonal topics. Pays $50 to $150, on publication. Submit complete manuscript.

THE BALTIMORE SUN—501 N. Calvert St., Baltimore, MD 21278. Harold Piper, Op-Ed Ed. Articles, 750 to 1,000 words, for Opinion Commentary page, on a wide range of topics: politics, education, foreign affairs, lifestyles, etc. Humor. Pays $75 to $125, on publication.

BOSTON HERALD—One Herald Sq., Boston, MA 02106. Shelly Cohen, Editorial Page Ed. Pieces, 600 to 800 words, on human-interest, political, regional, lifestyle, and seasonal topics. Pays $50 to $75, on publication. Prefer submissions from regional writers.

THE CHICAGO TRIBUNE—435 N. Michigan Ave., Chicago, IL 60611. Richard Liefer, Op-Ed Ed. Pieces, 500 to 800 words, on politics, government, economics, education, environment, foreign and domestic affairs. Writers must have experience in their fields. Pays $100 to $250, on publication.

THE CHRISTIAN SCIENCE MONITOR—One Norway St., Boston, MA 02115. Cynthia Hanson, Op. Page Coord. Pieces, 600 to 700 words, for "Opinion and Commentary" page, on politics, domestic and foreign affairs. Humor. Payment varies. Query preferred.

THE CHRONICLE—901 Mission St., San Francisco, CA 94103. Ms. Lyle York, "This World" Ed. Articles, 1,500 to 2,500 words, on a wide range of subjects. Pays $75 to $150, on publication. SASE required.

DALLAS MORNING NEWS—Communications Center, P.O. Box 655237, Dallas, TX 75265. Carolyn Barta, "Viewpoints" Ed. Pieces, 750 words, on politics, education, foreign and domestic affairs, seasonal and regional issues. Pay averages $75, on publication. SASE required.

DES MOINES REGISTER—Box 957, Des Moines, IA 50304. "Opinion" Page Ed. Articles, 600 to 800 words, on all topics. Humor. Pays $25 to $250, on publication.

THE DETROIT FREE PRESS—321 W. Lafayette St., Detroit, MI 48231. Address Op-Ed Editor. Opinion pieces, 750 to 800 words, on topics of local interest. Pays varying rates, on publication.

THE DETROIT NEWS—615 Lafayette Blvd., Detroit, MI 48231. Richard Burr, Ed. Pieces, 500 to 900 words, on science, economics, foreign and domestic affairs, education, environment, regional topics, religion, and politics. Humor. Priority to local writers and local issues. Pays varying rates, on publication.

THE LOS ANGELES HERALD EXAMINER—Box 2416, Terminal Annex, Los Angeles, CA 90051–0416. Editorial Page Ed. Articles, to 800 words, on local topics not covered by syndicated columnists. Humor. Pays $100 to $150, on publication.

LOS ANGELES TIMES—Times Mirror Sq., Los Angeles, CA 90053. J.D. Jones, Op. Ed. Commentary pieces, to 800 words, on many subjects. Pays $150 to $250, on publication. SASE required.

MILWAUKEE JOURNAL—Box 661, Milwaukee, WI 53201. James P. Cattey, Op-Ed Ed. Infrequent pieces, 600 to 700 words, on various subjects. Pays $30 to $35, on publication.

THE NEW YORK TIMES—229 W. 43rd St., New York, NY 10036. Leslie H. Gelb, Op-Ed Ed. Pieces, 750 words, on topics including public policy, science, lifestyles, and ideas. Pays $150, on publication.

NEWSDAY—Long Island, NY 11747. James Lynn, "Viewpoints" Ed. Pieces, 600 to 1,500 words, on foreign and domestic affairs, politics, economics, lifestyles, law, education, and the environment. Seasonal pieces. Prefer policy experts and local writers. Pays $150 to $400, on publication.

THE OAKLAND TRIBUNE—Box 24424, Oakland, CA 94623. Jonathan Marshall, Editorial Page Ed. Articles, 800 words, on a wide range of political and social topics; no humor or lifestyle materials. Pays $20 to $50, on publication.

PITTSBURGH POST GAZETTE—50 Blvd. of the Allies, Pittsburgh, PA 15222. Michael McGough, Editorial Page Ed. Articles, to 800 words, on politics, law, economics, lifestyle, religion, foreign and domestic affairs. Pays varying rates, on publication. SASE required.

THE REGISTER GUARD—P.O. Box 10188, Eugene, OR 97440. Don Robinson, Editorial Page Ed. All subjects; regional angle preferred. Pays $10 to $25, on publication. Very limited use of non-local writers.

THE SACRAMENTO BEE—21st and Q, P.O. Box 15779, Sacramento, CA 95852. Rhea Wilson, Opinion Ed. Op-ed pieces, to 1,000 words; topics of state and regional interest only. Pays $150, on publication. Query.

ST. LOUIS POST-DISPATCH—900 N. Tucker Blvd., St. Louis, MO 63101. Articles on economics, education, science, politics, foreign and domestic affairs, and the environment. Pays $70, on publication.

ST. PAUL PIONEER PRESS DISPATCH—345 Cedar St., St. Paul, MN 55101. Robert J.R. Johnson, Ed. Uses occasional pieces, to 750 words, on topics related to Minnesota and western Wisconsin. Pays $50, on publication. Query first.

ST. PETERSBURG TIMES—Box 1121, 490 First Ave. S., St. Petersburg, FL

33731. Jack Reed, "Perspective" Section Ed. Authoritative articles, to 2,000 words, on current political, economic, and social issues. Payment varies, on publication. Query first.

SEATTLE POST-INTELLIGENCER—101 Elliott Ave. W., Seattle, WA 98119. Charles J. Dunsire, Editorial Page Ed. Current events articles, 800 to 1,000 words, with Pacific Northwest themes. Pays $75 to $100, on publication.

THE WALL STREET JOURNAL—World Financial Center, 200 Liberty St., New York, NY 10281. Tim Ferguson, Editorial Features Ed. Articles, 850 to 1,100 words, on politics, economics, lifestyles, law, education, environment, humor, nostalgia, science, foreign and domestic affairs, religion, human-interest, and seasonal topics. Submit manuscript with SASE. Single bylines only.

ADULT MAGAZINES

CAVALIER—2355 Salzedo St., Coral Gables, FL 33134. Nye Willden, Man. Ed. Articles with photos, and fiction, 1,500 to 3,000 words, for sophisticated young men. Pays to $400 for articles, to $250 for fiction, on publication. Query for articles.

CHIC—9171 Wilshire Blvd., Suite 300, Beverly Hills, CA 90210. Doug Oliver, Exec. Ed. Articles, interviews, erotic fiction, 2,500 to 4,000 words. Pays $750 for articles, $500 for fiction, on acceptance.

GALLERY—401 Park Ave. S., New York, NY 10016. Marc Lichter, Ed.-in-Chief. Barry Janoff, Man. Ed. Articles, investigative pieces, interviews, profiles, to 3,500 words, for sophisticated men. Short humor, satire, service pieces. Photos. Pays varying rates, half on acceptance, half on publication. Query.

GEM—G&S Publications, 1472 Broadway, New York, NY 10036. Will Martin, Ed. Sex-related (not pornographic) articles and fiction, 500 to 2,500 words. Straight treatment as well as humor, satire, and spoofs of sexual subjects. Pays $50 to $100, after acceptance. All submissions must be accompanied by SASE.

GENESIS—22 West 27th St., 8th Fl., New York, NY 10001. J.J. Kelleher, Ed.-in-Chief. Articles, 2,500 words; celebrity interviews, 2,500 words. Sexually-explicit nonfiction features, 3,000 words. Photo essays. Pays 60 days after acceptance. Query.

HARVEY FOR LOVING PEOPLE—Suite 2305, 450 Seventh Ave., New York, NY 10001. Harvey Shapiro, Ed./Pub. Sexually-oriented articles and fiction, to 2,500 words. Pays on publication. Query for articles.

PENTHOUSE—1965 Broadway, New York, NY 10023. Peter Bloch, Exec. Ed. General-interest or investigative articles, to 5,000 words. Interviews, 5,000 words, with introductions. Pays to 50¢ a word, on acceptance.

PLAYBOY—680 N. Lakeshore Dr., Chicago, IL 60611. John Rezek, Articles Ed. Alice K. Turner, Fiction Ed. Articles, 3,500 to 6,000 words, and sophisticated fiction, 1,000 to 10,000 words (6,000 preferred), for urban men. Humor; satire. Science fiction. Pays to $5,000 for articles, to $5,000 for fiction ($1,000 for short-shorts), on acceptance.

PLAYERS—8060 Melrose Ave., Los Angeles, CA 90046. H.L. Sorrell, Ed. Articles, 1,000 to 3,000 words, for black men: politics, economics, travel, fashion, grooming, entertainment, sports, interviews, fiction, humor, satire, health, and sex. Photos a plus. Pays on publication.

PLAYGIRL—801 Second Ave., New York, NY 10017. Nancie S. Martin, Ed. Articles, 2,000 to 2,500 words, for women age 18 to 34. Celebrity interviews, 1,500 to 2,000 words. Humor. Cartoons. Pays varying rates, on acceptance.

FICTION MARKETS

This list gives the fiction requirements of general- and special-interest magazines, including those that publish detective and mystery, science fiction and fantasy, romance and confession stories. Other good markets for short fiction are the *College, Literary and Little Magazines* where, though payment is modest (usually in copies only), publication can help a beginning writer achieve recognition by editors at the larger magazines. Juvenile fiction markets are listed under *Juvenile, Teenage, and Young Adult Magazines.* Publishers of book-length fiction manuscripts are listed under *Book Publishers.*

All manuscripts must be typed double-space and submitted with self-addressed envelopes bearing postage sufficient for the return of the material. Use good white paper; onion skin and erasable bond are not acceptable. *Always* keep a copy of the manuscript, since occasionally a manuscript is lost in the mail. Magazines may take several weeks—often longer—to read and report on submissions. If an editor has not reported on a manuscript after a reasonable amount of time, write a brief, courteous letter of inquiry.

ABORIGINAL SF—P.O. Box 2449, Woburn, MA 01888–0849. Charles C. Ryan, Ed. Stories, 2,500 to 4,500 words, with a unique scientific idea, human or alien character, plot, and theme of lasting value; "must be science fiction, no fantasy, horror, or sword and sorcery." Pays $250. Send SASE for guidelines.

AIM MAGAZINE—P.O. Box 20554, Chicago, IL 60620. Ruth Apilado, Ed. Short stories, 800 to 3,000 words, geared to promoting racial harmony and peace. Pays from $15 to $25, on publication. Annual contest.

ALFRED HITCHCOCK'S MYSTERY MAGAZINE—380 Lexington Ave., New York, NY 10017. Cathleen Jordan, Ed. Well-plotted, plausible mystery, suspense, detection and crime stories, to 14,000 words; "ghost stories, humor, private eye, atmospheric tales are all possible, as long as they include a crime or the suggestion of one." Pays 5¢ a word, on acceptance. Guidelines.

ALOHA, THE MAGAZINE OF HAWAII AND THE PACIFIC—49 S. Hotel St., Suite 309, Honolulu, HI 96813. Cheryl Tsutsumi, Ed. Fiction to 4,000 words, with a Hawaii focus. Pays $150 to $300, on publication. Query.

AMAZING STORIES—Box 111, Lake Geneva, WI 53147. Patrick L. Price, Ed. Science fiction and fantasy, to 25,000 words. No unagented or unsolicited manuscripts. Pays 6¢ to 8¢ a word, on acceptance.

ANALOG: SCIENCE FICTION/SCIENCE FACT—380 Lexington Ave., New York, NY 10017. Stanley Schmidt, Ed. Science fiction, with strong characters in believable future or alien setting: short stories, 2,000 to 7,500 words; novelettes, 10,000 to 20,000 words; serials, to 70,000 words. Pays 5¢ to 8¢ a word, on acceptance. Query for novels.

THE ATLANTIC—745 Boylston St., Boston, MA 02116. William Whitworth, Ed. Short stories, 2,000 to 6,000 words, of highest literary quality, with "fully developed narratives, distinctive characterization, freshness in language, and a resolution of some kind." Pays excellent rates, on acceptance.

THE ATLANTIC ADVOCATE—P.O. Box 3370, Fredericton, N.B., Canada E3B 5A2. H.P. Wood, Ed. Fiction, 1,000 to 1,500 words, with regional angle. Pays to 10¢ a word, on publication.

ATLANTIC SALMON JOURNAL—1435 St. Alexandre, Suite 1030, Montreal, Quebec, Canada H3A 2G4. Terry Davis, Ed. Fiction, 1,500 to 2,500 words, related to angling or conservation of Atlantic salmon. Pays $100 to $325, on publication.

THE BOSTON GLOBE MAGAZINE—*The Boston Globe,* Boston, MA 02107. Ande Zellman, Ed. Short stories, to 3,000 words. Include SASE. Pays on publication.

BOYS' LIFE—1325 Walnut Hill Ln., P.O. Box 152079, Irving, TX 75015–2079. W.E. Butterworth IV, Fiction Ed. Publication of the Boy Scouts of America. Humor, mystery, SF, adventure, 750 to 1,500 words, for 8- to 18-year-old boys; study back issues. Pays from $750, on acceptance. Send SASE for guidelines.

BUFFALO SPREE MAGAZINE—Box 38, Buffalo, NY 14226. Johanna V. Shotell, Ed. Fiction and humor, to 1,800 words, for readers in the western New York region. Pays $75 to $100, on publication.

CAMPUS LIFE—465 Gundersen Dr., Carol Stream, IL 60188. James Long, Man. Ed. Fiction and humor, reflecting Christian values (no overtly religious material), 1,000 to 4,000 words, for high school and college students. Pays from $150 to $400, on acceptance. Limited free-lance market. Queries only; SASE.

CAPPER'S—616 Jefferson Ave., Topeka, KS 66607. Nancy Peavler, Ed. Short novel-length family-oriented or romance stories. Also limited market for short stories, 5,000 to 7,500 words, that can be divided into two or three installments. Pays $75 to $200. Submit complete manuscript.

CAT FANCY—P.O. Box 6050, Mission Viejo, CA 92690. K.E. Segnar, Ed. Fiction, to 3,000 words, about cats. Pays 5¢ a word, on publication.

CATHOLIC FORESTER—425 W. Shuman Blvd., Naperville, IL 60566. Barbara A. Cunningham, Ed. Official publication of the Catholic Order of Foresters. Fiction, to 3,000 words (prefer shorter); "looking for more contemporary, meaningful stories dealing with life today." No sex or violence or "preachy" stories; religious angle not essential. Pays from 5¢ a word, on acceptance.

CAVALIER—2355 Salzedo St., Coral Gables, FL 33134. Maurice DeWalt, Fiction Ed. Sexually-oriented fiction, to 3,000 words, for sophisticated young men. Pays to $250, on publication.

CHESAPEAKE BAY MAGAZINE—1819 Bay Ridge Ave., Annapolis, MD 21403. Betty Rigoli, Ed. Short stories, to 15 pages; must be related to Chesapeake Bay area. Pays $95 to $150, on publication.

CLINTON STREET QUARTERLY—P.O. Box 3588, Portland, OR 97208. David Milholland, Ed. Short stories, 2 to 20 pages: "First-person accounts, thought-provoking, non-rhetorical essays, and idea pieces." Pays varying rates, on publication.

COBBLESTONE—20 Grove St., Peterborough, NH 03458. Carolyn P.

Yoder, Ed. Fiction, related to monthly theme, 500 to 1,200 words, for children aged 8 to 14 years. Pays 10¢ to 15¢ a word, on publication. Send SASE for editorial guidelines.

COMMENTARY—165 E. 56th St., New York, NY 10022. Marion Magid, Ed. Fiction, of high literary quality, on contemporary social or Jewish issues. Pays on publication.

THE COMPASS—Mobil International Aviation and Marine Sales, Inc. 150 E. 42nd St., New York, NY 10017. J.A. Randall, Ed. True stories, to 2,500 words, on the sea, sea trades, and aviation. Pays to $600, on acceptance. Query.

COSMOPOLITAN—224 W. 57th St., New York, NY 10019. Betty Kelly, Fiction and Books Ed. Short shorts, 1,500 to 3,000 words, and short stories, 4,000 to 6,000 words, focusing on contemporary man-woman relationships. Solid, upbeat plots, sharp characterization; female protagonists preferred. Pays $800 for short shorts; $1,500 to $2,500 for short stories.

COUNTRY WOMAN—P.O. Box 643, Milwaukee, WI 53201. Kathy Pohl, Man. Ed. Fiction, 750 to 1,000 words, of interest to rural women; protagonist must be a country woman. "Stories should focus on life in the country, its problems and joys, as experienced by country women; must be upbeat and positive." Pays $90 to $125, on acceptance.

CRICKET—Box 300, Peru, IL 61354. Marianne Carus, Ed.-in-Chief. Fiction, 200 to 1,500 words, for 6- to 12-year-olds. Pays to 25¢ a word, on publication. Return postage required.

DISCOVERIES—6401 The Paseo, Kansas City, MO 64131. Address Middler Ed. Fiction, 600 to 1,000 words, for children grades 3 to 6, defining Christian experiences and values. Pays 3 ½¢ a word, on acceptance.

DIVER MAGAZINE—295–10991 Shellbridge Way, Richmond, B.C., Canada V6X 3C6. Peter Vassilopoulos, Pub./Ed. Fiction, related to diving. Humor. Pays $2.50 per column inch, on publication. Query.

EASYRIDERS MAGAZINE—P. O. Box 3000, Agoura Hills, CA 91301–0800. Lou Kimzey, Ed. Fiction, 3,000 to 5,000 words. Pays from 10¢ a word, on acceptance.

ELLERY QUEEN'S MYSTERY MAGAZINE—380 Lexington Ave., New York, NY 10017. Eleanor Sullivan, Ed. High-quality detective, crime, and mystery stories, 4,000 to 6,000 words; "we like a mix of classic detection and suspenseful crime." "First Stories" by unpublished writers. Pays 3¢ to 8¢ a word, on acceptance.

ENTERTAINER MAGAZINE—9420 Towne Sq. Ave., Suite 15, Cincinnati, OH 45242. Monica Hawley, Pub. General comedy, 750 words. Pays $15 and copies, on publication.

ESQUIRE—1790 Broadway, New York, NY 10019. Lee Eisenberg, Ed.-in-Chief. We accept unsolicited manuscripts.

FAMILY CIRCLE—110 Fifth Ave., New York, NY 10011. Kathy Sagan, Fiction Ed. Limited market: seeks quality short stories and short shorts that reflect real life situations. No unsolicited manuscripts.

FAMILY MAGAZINE—P.O. Box 4993, Walnut Creek, CA 94596. Address Editors. Short stories, to 2,000 words, of interest to high school-educated military wives between 20 and 35. Pays from $100 to $300, on publication.

FICTION INTERNATIONAL—English Dept., San Diego State Univ., San Diego, CA 92182. Harold Jaffe and Larry McCaffery, Eds. Post-modernist and politically-committed fiction and theory. Submit between Sept. 1st and Jan. 15th.

FIRST FOR WOMEN—P.O. Box 1649, Englewood Cliffs, NJ 07632. Dennis Neeld, Ed. Realistic and believable fiction, 5,000 to 6,000 words, reflecting the concerns of contemporary women; no formula or experimental fiction. Pay varies, on acceptance.

GALLERY—401 Park Ave. S., New York, NY 10016. Marc Lichter, Ed. Dir. John Bowers, Fiction Ed. Fiction, to 4,000 words, for sophisticated men. Pays varying rates, half on acceptance, half on publication.

GENTLEMEN'S QUARTERLY—350 Madison Ave., New York, NY 10017. Tom Jenks, Literary Ed. Fiction, to 3,000 words. Pays on acceptance. No unsolicited manuscripts.

GOLF DIGEST—5520 Park Ave., Trumbull, CT 06611. Jerry Tarde, Ed. Unusual or humorous stories, to 2,000 words, about golf; golf "fables," to 1,000 words. Pays 50¢ a word, on acceptance.

GOOD HOUSEKEEPING—959 Eighth Ave., New York, NY 10019. Naome Lewis, Fiction Ed. Short stories, 1,000 to 3,000 words, with strong identification figures for women, by published writers and "beginners with demonstrable talent." Novel condensations or excerpts. Pays top rates, on acceptance.

GUN DOG—1901 Bell Ave., Des Moines, IA 50315. Bob Wilbanks, Man. Ed. Occasional fiction, humor related to gun dogs and bird hunting. Pays $100 to $350, on acceptance.

HICALL—1445 Boonville Ave., Springfield, MO 65802. Sinda Zinn, Ed. Fiction, to 1,500 words, for 15- to 19-year-olds. Strong evangelical emphasis a must: believable characters working out their problems according to biblical principles. Pays 3¢ a word for first rights, on acceptance.

HIGHLIGHTS FOR CHILDREN—803 Church St., Honesdale, PA 18431. Kent L. Brown Jr., Ed. Fiction on sports, humor, adventure, mystery, etc., 900 words, for 9- to 12-year-olds. Easy rebus form, 100 to 150 words, and easy-to-read stories, to 600 words, for beginning readers. "We are partial to stories in which the protagonist solves a dilemma through his own resources, rather than through luck or magic." Pays from 14¢ a word, on acceptance. Buys all rights.

HOMETOWN PRESS—2007 Gallatin St., Huntsville, AL 35801. Jeffrey C. Hindman, MD, Ed.-in-Chief. Fiction, 800 to 2,500 words, well-crafted and tightly written, suitable for family reading. New and unpublished writers welcome. SASE for guidelines.

ISAAC ASIMOV'S SCIENCE FICTION MAGAZINE—380 Lexington Ave., New York, NY 10017. Gardner Dozios, Ed. Short science fiction and fantasies, to 15,000 words. Pays 6¢ to 8¢ a word, on acceptance.

LADIES' HOME JOURNAL—100 Park Ave., New York, NY 10017. Fiction with strong identification for women. Short stories and full-length manuscripts accepted through agents only.

LIVE—1445 Boonville Ave., Springfield, MO 65802. John T. Maempa, Adult Ed. Fiction, 1,100 to 2,000 words, on applying Bible principles to everyday living; include Soc. Sec. no. Send SASE for guidelines. Pays 2¢ to 3¢ a word, on acceptance.

LOLLIPOPS—Good Apple, Inc., P. O. Box 299, Carthage, IL 62321–0299.

Jerry Aten, Ed. Teaching ideas and activites covering all areas of the curriculum for preschool to second grade children. Rates vary.

THE LOOKOUT—8121 Hamilton Ave., Cincinnati, OH 45231. Mark Taylor, Fiction Ed. Inspirational short-shorts, 1,000 to 1,800 words. Pays to 6¢ a word, on acceptance.

MCCALL'S—230 Park Ave., New York, NY 10169. Helen Delmonte, Fiction Ed. Short stories, to 2,500 words; short-shorts, 1,000 words: contemporary themes with strong identification for intelligent women. Family stories, love stories, holiday stories, humor, suspense; must have strong plots. Pays from $2,000 for stories, $1,500 for short-shorts, on acceptance. Occasionally buys stories for Silver Edition, a special supplement aimed at older readers. Stories must be short (1,000 to 1,500 words), upbeat, and geared to concerns of mature readers, aged 50 to 65. Pays from $500 to $1,200 on acceptence. No unsolicited manuscripts. Query.

MADEMOISELLE—350 Madison Ave., New York, NY 10017. Eileen Schnurr, Fiction Ed. Short stories, 1,500 to 5,000 words, of interest to young single women. Looking for strong voices, fresh insights, generally classic form—no genre fiction. Male point-of-view about personal relationships welcome. Pays $1,000 for short shorts, to $2,000 for stories, on acceptance.

MATURE LIVING—127 Ninth Ave. N., Nashville, TN 37234. Judy Pregel, Asst. Ed. Fiction, 900 to 1,200 words, for senior adults. Must be consistent with Christian principles. Pays 5¢ a word, on acceptance.

MIDSTREAM—515 Park Ave., New York, NY 10022. Murray Zuckoff, Ed. Fiction on Jewish themes, to 3,000 words. Pays 5¢ a word, after publication.

MILITARY LIFESTYLE MAGAZINE—1732 Wisconsin Ave. N.W., Washington, DC 20007. Hope Daniels, Ed. Fiction, to 2,000 words, for military families in the U.S. and overseas. Pays from $300 to $500, on publication.

MODERN SHORT STORIES—500-B Bi-County Blvd., Farmingdale, NY 11735. Glenn Steckler, Ed. Serious fiction, humor, romance, and science fiction (1,000 to 5,000 words) and shorter stories (1,000 to 2,500 words). "We are interested in publishing the widest variety of material possible and exposing our readership to the newest trends in fiction." Pays $25 to $75 for stories, $5 to $15 for fillers and short humor, on acceptance.

MS.—One Times Square, New York, NY 10036. No unsolicited fiction.

NA'AMAT WOMAN—200 Madison Ave., 21st Fl., New York, NY 10016. Judith A. Sokoloff, Ed. Short stories, approx. 2,500 words, with Jewish theme. Pays 8¢ a word, on publication.

NATIONAL RACQUETBALL—400 Douglas Ave., Suite B, Dunedin, FL 34698. Helen Quinn, Pub. Judi Schmidt, Man. Ed. Fiction, related to racquetball. Pays $1.65 per column inch, $50 per printed page, on publication.

NEVADAN—P.O. BOX 70, Las Vegas, NV 89125–0070. A.D. Hopkins, Ed. Sunday magazine of the *Las Vegas Review Journal.* Fiction with regional angle: Nevada, Southwestern Utah, Northwestern Arizona and the California desert region adjacent to Southern Nevada. Pays $200 to $650, on publication.

THE NEW YORKER—25 W. 43rd St., New York, NY 10036. Fiction Dept. Short stories, humor, and satire. Pays according to length, on acceptance. Include SASE.

NORTH GEORGIA JOURNAL—110 Hunters Mill, Woodstock, GA 30188.

Olin Jackson, Pub./Ed. Folkloric fiction, 1,500 to 3,000 words, on north Georgia region. Pays to $300, on publication.

NORTHEAST MAGAZINE—*The Hartford Courant,* 285 Broad St., Hartford, CT 06115. Lary Bloom, Ed. Short stories, to 4,000 words; must have Connecticut tie-in, or be universal in theme and have non-specific setting. Pays $300 to $600, on acceptance.

OMNI—1965 Broadway, New York, NY 10023–5965. Ellen Datlow, Fiction Ed. Strong, realistic science fiction, to 12,000 words. Some contemporary hard-edged fantasy. Pays to $2,000, on acceptance.

PENTHOUSE—1965 Broadway, New York, NY 10023. No unsolicited manuscripts.

PLAYBOY—680 N.Lakeshore Dr., Chicago, IL 60611. Alice K. Turner, Fiction Ed. Quality fiction, 1,000 to 8,000 words (average 6,000): suspense, mystery, adventure, and sports short stories; stories about contemporary relationships; science fiction. Active plots, masterful pacing, and strong characterization. Pays from $2,000 to $5,000, on acceptance.

PLAYGIRL—801 Second Ave., New York, NY 10017. Mary Ellen Strote, Fiction Ed. Contemporary, romantic fiction, 1,000 to 4,000 words. Pays from $500, after acceptance.

PLOUGHSHARES—Box 529, Cambridge, MA 02139. Address Editors. Serious fiction, to 7,000 words. Poetry. Pays $10 to $50, on publication. Reading periods and themes vary. Query.

PRIME TIMES—2802 International Ln., Suite 210, Madison, WI 53704. Joan Donovan, Exec. Ed. Circulates to approx. 300,000 mid-life readers. Excellent fiction, to 4,000 words, shorter lengths preferred; general themes. Pays varying rates, on publication. Query first.

PURPOSE—616 Walnut Ave., Scottdale, PA 15683–1999. James E. Horsch, Ed. Fiction, 1,200 words, on problem solving from a Christian point of view. Poetry, 3 to 12 lines. Pays up to 5¢ a word, to $1 per line for poetry, on acceptance.

RANGER RICK—8925 Leesburg Pike, Vienna, VA 22184–0001. Betty Blair and Deborah Churchman, Fiction Eds. Nature- and conservation-related fiction, for 7- to 12-year-olds. Maximum: 900 words. Pays to $550, on acceptance. Buys all rights.

REDBOOK—224 W. 57th St., New York, NY 10019. Deborah Purcell, Fiction Ed. Fresh, distinctive short stories, of interest to women, about love and relationships, friendship, careers, parenting, family dilemmas, confronting basic problems of contemporary life issues. Pays $850 for short-shorts (up to 9 manuscript pages), from $1,000 for short stories (to 20 pages). Allow 8 to 12 weeks for reply. Manuscripts without SASE will not be returned. No unsolicited novellas or novels accepted.

ROAD KING—P.O. Box 250, Park Forest, IL 60466. George Friend, Ed. Short stories, 1,200 to 1,500 words, for and/or about truck drivers. Pays to $400, on acceptance.

ST. ANTHONY MESSENGER—1615 Republic St., Cincinnati, OH 45210. Norman Perry, O.F.M., Ed. Barbara Beckwith, Man. Ed. Fiction that makes readers think about issues, lifestyles, and values. Pays 14¢ a word, on acceptance. Queries or manuscripts accepted.

SASSY—One Times Square, New York, NY 10036. Catherine Gysin, Fiction Ed. Short stories written in the magazine's style, 1,000 to 3,000 words, for girls age 14 to 19. Pays $1,000, on acceptance.

SCHOLASTIC SCOPE—Scholastic, Inc., 730 Broadway, New York, NY 10003. Fiction for 15- to 18-year-olds, with 4th to 6th grade reading ability. Short stories, 400 to 1,200 words, on teenage interests and relationships; family, job, and school situations. Plays to 5,000 words. Pays good rates, on acceptance.

SEA KAYAKER—1670 Duranleau St., Vancouver, B.C., Canada V6H 3S4. John Dowd, Ed. Short stories exclusively related to ocean kayaking, 1,000 to 3,000 words. Pays on publication. Include international reply coupons and SAE.

SEVENTEEN—850 Third Ave., New York, NY 10022. Adrian LeBlanc, Fiction Ed. High-quality, literary short fiction focusing on the teenage experience. Pays on acceptance.

SNOWBOARDER—P.O. Box 1028, Dana Point, CA 92629. Casey Sheahan, Man. Ed. Published four times yearly from Sept. to Jan. Uses occasional fiction (1,000 to 1,500 words) related to snowboarding. Pays $150 to $800, on acceptance and on publication.

SPORTS AFIELD—250 W. 55th St., New York, NY 10019. Tom Paugh, Ed. Fiction, on hunting, fishing, and related topics. Outdoor adventure stories. Humor. Pays top rates, on acceptance.

STRAIGHT—8121 Hamilton Ave., Cincinnati, OH 45231. Carla Crane, Ed. Well-constructed fiction, 1,000 to 1,500 words, showing Christian teens using Bible principles in everyday life. Contemporary, realistic teen characters a must. Most interested in school, church, dating, and family life stories. Pays about 3¢ a word, on acceptance. Send SASE for guidelines.

SUNDAY DIGEST—850 N. Grove Ave., Elgin, IL 60120. Janette L. Pearson, Ed. Short stories, 1,000 to 1,500 words, with evangelical religious slant. Pays 10¢ a word, on acceptance. Query.

SUNSHINE MAGAZINE—Sunshine Press, Litchfield, IL 62056. Peggy Kuethe, Ed. Wholesome fiction, 900 to 1,200 words; short stories for youths, 400 words. Pays to $100, on acceptance. Guidelines. Include SASE.

SWANK—888 Seventh Ave., New York, NY 10106. Bob Rosen, Fiction Ed. Graphic erotic short stories, to 2,500 words. Study recent issue before submitting material. Pays on publication. Limited market.

TAMPA BAY LIFE—990 Bayport Plaza, 6200 Courtney Campbell Causeway, Tampa, FL 33607. Bonnie Dyson, Ed. Fiction, 1,200 to 2,000 words, with a regional flavor. Payment varies, on acceptance.

'TEEN—8490 Sunset Blvd., Los Angeles, CA 90069. Address Fiction Dept. Short stories, 2,500 to 4,000 words: mystery, teen situations, adventure, romance, humor for teens. Pays from $100, on acceptance.

TEENS TODAY—Nazarene Publishing House, 6401 The Paseo, Kansas City, MO 64131. Karen DeSollar, Ed. Short stories, 1,200 to 1,500 words, that deal with teens demonstrating Christian principles in real-life situations; adventure stories. Pays 3 ½¢ a word, on acceptance. (Pays 3¢ a word for reprints.)

TQ/TEEN QUEST—Box 82808, Lincoln, NE 68501. Barbara Comito, Man. Ed. Fiction, 1,000 to 2,000 words, for Christian teens. Pays 4¢ to 10¢ a word, on acceptance.

VANITY FAIR—350 Madison Ave., New York, NY 10017. Address Fiction Ed. Fiction of high literary quality. Very limited market.

VIRTUE—P.O. Box 850, Sisters, OR 97759. Becky Durost Fish, Ed. Fiction with a Christian slant. Pays 10¢ a word, on publication. Query required.

WASHINGTON—200 W. Thomas, Seattle, WA 98119. Kenneth A. Gould-thorpe, Ed. Bimonthly for Washington State residents. Fiction, 1,500 to 3,000 words. Pays 15¢ to 25¢ a word, on acceptance.

WESTERN PEOPLE—Box 2500, Saskatoon, Sask., Canada S7K 2C4. Short stories, 1,000 to 2,500 words, on subjects or themes of interest to rural readers in Western Canada. Pays $40 to $150, on acceptance. Enclose international reply coupons and SAE.

WILDFOWL—1901 Bell Ave., Suite #4, Des Moines, IA 50315. B. Wil-banks, Man. Ed. Occasional fiction, humor, related to duck hunters and wildfowl. Pays $200 to $350, on acceptance.

WOMAN'S WORLD—270 Sylvan Ave., Englewood Cliffs, NJ 07632. Jeanne Muchnick, Fiction Ed. Fast-moving short stories, about 4,500 words, with light romantic theme. Mini-mysteries, 1,600 to 1,700 words, with "whodunit" or "how-dunit" theme. No science fiction, fantasy, or historical romance. Pays $1,000 for short stories, $500 for mini-mysteries, on acceptance. Submit manuscript with SASE.

WOODMEN OF THE WORLD MAGAZINE—1700 Farnam St., Omaha, NE 68102. Leland A. Larson, Ed. Family-oriented fiction. Pays 5¢ a word, on acceptance.

YANKEE—Yankee Publishing Co., Dublin, NH 03444. Judson Hale, Ed. Edie Clark, Fiction Ed. High-quality, literary short fiction, to 4,000 words, with setting in or compatible with New England; no sap buckets or lobster pot stereo-types. Pays $1,000, on acceptance.

DETECTIVE AND MYSTERY

ALFRED HITCHCOCK'S MYSTERY MAGAZINE—380 Lexington Ave., New York, NY 10017. Cathleen Jordan, Ed. Well-plotted mystery, detective, sus-pense, and crime fiction, 1,000 to 14,000 words. Submissions by new writers strongly encouraged. Pays 5¢ a word, on acceptance.

ARMCHAIR DETECTIVE—129 W. 56th St., New York, NY 10019. Kathy Daniel, Ed. Articles on mystery and detective fiction; biographical sketches, reviews, etc. Pays $10 a printed page, except for reviews.

ELLERY QUEEN'S MYSTERY MAGAZINE—380 Lexington Ave., New York, NY 10017. Eleanor Sullivan, Ed. Detective, crime, and mystery fiction, approximately 4,000 to 6,000 words. No sex, sadism, or sensationalism. Particularly interested in new writers and "first stories." Pays 3¢ to 8¢ a word, on acceptance.

FRONT PAGE DETECTIVE—See *Inside Detective.*

INSIDE DETECTIVE—Reese Communications, Inc., 460 W. 34th St., New York, NY 10001. Rose Mandelsberg, Ed. Timely, true detective stories, 5,000 to 6,000 words, or 10,000 words. No fiction. Pays $250 to $500, extra for photos, on acceptance. Query. Same address and requirements for *Front Page Detective.*

MASTER DETECTIVE—460 W. 34th St., New York, NY 10001. Art Crock-ett, Ed. Detailed articles, 5,000 to 6,000 words, with photos, on current cases, emphasizing human motivation and detective work. Pays to $250, on acceptance. Query.

OFFICIAL DETECTIVE STORIES—460 W. 34th St., New York, NY 10001. Art Crockett, Ed. True detective stories, 5,000 to 6,000 words, on current investigations, strictly from the investigator's point of view. No fiction. Photos. Pays $250, extra for photos, on acceptance. Query.

P.I. MAGAZINE—755 Bronx Ave., Toledo, OH 43609. Bob Mackowiak, Ed. Fiction, 2,500 to 5,000 words, and profiles of professional investigators containing true accounts of their most difficult cases; puzzles. Pays $10 to $25, plus copies, on publication.

TRUE DETECTIVE—460 W. 34th St., New York, NY 10001. Art Crockett, Ed. Articles, from 5,000 words, with photos, on current police cases, emphasizing detective work and human motivation. No fiction. Pays $250, extra for photos, on acceptance. Query.

SCIENCE FICTION AND FANTASY

ABORIGINAL SF—P.O. Box 2449, Woburn, MA 01888–0849. Charles C. Ryan, Ed. Short stories, 2,500 to 5,500 words, and poetry, 1 to 2 typed pages, with strong science content, lively, unique characters, and well-designed plots. No sword and sorcery or fantasy. Pays $250 for fiction, $20 for poetry, $4 for SF jokes, and $20 for cartoons, on publication.

AMAZING STORIES—Box 111, Lake Geneva, WI 53147. Patrick L. Price, Ed. Science fiction and fantasy, to 15,000 words. Also general-interest science articles; query first on nonfiction. Pays 6¢ to 8¢ a word, on acceptance.

ANALOG: SCIENCE FICTION/SCIENCE FACT—380 Lexington Ave., New York, NY 10017. Stanley Schmidt, Ed. Science fiction, with strong characters in believable future or alien setting: short stories, 2,000 to 7,500 words; novelettes, 10,000 to 20,000 words; serials, to 80,000 words. Also uses future-related articles. Pays to 7¢ a word, on acceptance. Query on serials and articles.

THE ASYMPTOTICAL WORLD—P.O. Box 1372, Williamsport, PA 17703. Michael H. Gerardi, Ed. Psychodramas, fantasy, experimental fiction, 1,500 to 2,500 words. Illustrations, photographs. Pays 2¢ a word, on acceptance.

BEYOND: SCIENCE FICTION & FANTASY—P.O. Box 1124, Fair Lawn, NJ 07410. Roberta Rogow, Ed. Science fiction and fantasy: original, exciting, thought-provoking fiction (3,000 to 5,000 words), and poems (10 to 20 lines). Pays ¼¢ a word, on publication.

DRAGON MAGAZINE—P.O. Box 111, Lake Geneva, WI 53147. Roger E. Moore, Ed.-in-Chief; Barbara G. Young, Fiction Ed. Articles, 1,500 to 10,000 words, on fantasy and SF role-playing games. Fiction, 1,500 to 8,000 words. Pays 6¢ to 8¢ a word for fiction, slightly lower for articles, on publication. Guidelines (specify article or fiction).

FANTASY MACABRE—P.O. Box 20610, Seattle, WA 98102. Jessica Salmonson, Ed. Fiction, to 3,000 words, including translations. "We look for a tale that is strong in atmosphere, with menace that is suggested and threatening rather than the result of dripping blood and gore." Pays 1¢ a word, to $30 per story, on publication.

GRUE MAGAZINE—Box 370, Times Square Sta., New York, NY 10108. Peggy Nadramia, Ed. Fiction, 3,500 words, and macabre/surreal poetry of any length. "We seek very visceral, original horror stories with an emphasis on characterization and motivation." Pays ½¢ per word for fiction, $5 per poem, on publication.

HAUNTS—Nightshade Publications, Box 3342, Providence, RI 02906. Joseph K. Cherkes, Ed. Horror, science/fantasy, and supernatural short stories with strong characters, 1,500 to 8,000 words. No explicit sexual scenes or gratuitous violence. Pays ¼¢ to ⅓¢ a word, on publication. Submit June 1—Dec. 1.

THE HORROR SHOW—Phantasm Press, 14848 Misty Springs Lane, Oak Run, CA 96069. David B. Silva, Ed. Contemporary horror fiction, to 6,000 words, with a style that keeps the reader's hand trembling as he turns the pages. Pays 1¢ to 2¢ per word, on acceptance. Send SASE for guidelines.

ISAAC ASIMOV'S SCIENCE FICTION MAGAZINE—380 Lexington Ave., New York, NY 10017. Gardner Dozois, Ed. Short, character-oriented science fiction and fantasy, to 15,000 words. Pays 5¢ to 8¢ a word, on acceptance. Send SASE for requirements.

THE LEADING EDGE—3163 JKHB, Provo, UT 84602. Russell W. Asplund, Ed. Tri-annual science fiction and fantasy magazine. Short stories (3,000–12,000 words) and some experimental fiction; poems (to 200 lines); and articles (to 8,000 words) on science, scientific speculation, and literary criticism. Fillers and comics. "Do not send originals; manuscripts are marked and critiqued by staff." Pays ½¢ per word with a minimum of $5 for fiction; $4 per published page of poetry; $2 to $4 for fillers; on publication. Guidelines.

THE MAGAZINE OF FANTASY AND SCIENCE FICTION—Box 56, Cornwall, CT 06753. Edward Ferman, Ed. Fantasy and science fiction stories, to 10,000 words. Pays 5¢ to 7¢ a word, on acceptance.

MAGICAL BLEND—Box 11303, San Francisco, CA 94101. Silma Smith, Literary Ed. Positive, uplifting articles on spiritual exploration, lifestyles, occult, white magic, new age thought, and fantasy. Fiction and features to 5,000 words. Poetry, 4 to 40 lines. Pays in copies.

NEW BLOOD—540 W. Foothill Blvd., Suite 3730, Glendora, CA 91740. Chris Lacher, Ed. Fiction and poetry considered "too strong" for other periodicals. Interviews and reviews. Pays from 3¢ a word, on acceptance. Eager to work with beginning, less established writers.

OMNI—1965 Broadway, New York, NY 10023–1965. Ellen Datlow, Ed. Strong, realistic science fiction, 2,000 to 10,000 words, with good characterizations. Some fantasy. No horror, ghost, or sword and sorcery tales. Pays $1,250 to $2,000, on acceptance.

OWLFLIGHT—1025 55th St., Oakland, CA 94608. Millea Kenin, Ed. Science fiction and fantasy, 3,000 to 8,000 words. Science fiction/fantasy poetry, 8 to 100 lines. Photos, illustrations. Pays 1¢ a word, extra for illustrations, on publication. Send 45¢ SASE for guidelines.

PORTENTS—12 Fir Pl., Hazlet, NJ 07730. Deborah Rasmussen, Ed. Fiction —contemporary horror, dark fantasy, exceptional gothic, and supernatural horror —to 3,000 words. No werewolves, vampires, ghouls, religion, or sex. Pays ¼¢ a word, on publication.

SCIENCE FICTION CHRONICLE—P.O. Box 2730, Brooklyn, NY 11202. Andrew Porter, Ed. News items, 200 to 1,000 words, for SF and fantasy readers, professionals, and booksellers. Photos and short articles on author signings, events, conventions. Pays 3¢ to 5¢ a word, on publication.

SPACE AND TIME—138 W. 70th St., #4B, New York, NY 10023. Fantasy fiction, to 12,000 words; science fiction, supernatural, sword and sorcery. Pays ½¢ a word, on acceptance.

THRUST: SCIENCE FICTION & FANTASY REVIEW—8217 Langport Terrace, Gaithersburg, MD 20877. D. Douglas Fratz, Ed. Articles, interviews, 2,000 to 6,000 words, for readers familiar with SF and related literary and scientific topics. Book reviews, 100 to 800 words. Pays 1¢ to 2¢ a word, on publication. Query preferred. SASE for guidelines.

TWISTED—22071 Pinewood Dr., Antioch, IL 60002. Christine Hoard, Ed. Fiction and articles (to 5,000 words); poetry (to 1 page). "No sword and sorcery, or hard science fiction. We prefer horror and dark fantasy." Pays in copies.

2 AM—P.O. Box 6754, Rockford, IL 61125–1754. Gretta M. Anderson, Ed. Fiction, of varying lengths. "We prefer dark fantasy/horror; great science fiction and sword and sorcery stories are welcome." Profiles and intelligent commentaries. Poetry, to 50 lines. Pays from ½¢ a word, on acceptance. Guidelines.

WAYSTATION FOR THE SF WRITER—1025 55th St., Oakland, CA 94608. Millea Kenin, Ed. Articles, 2,000 words preferred, on the craft of writing science fiction and fantasy. Cartoons, illustrations, poetry. Pays negotiable rates, on publication. Query. Send envelope with 45¢ postage for guidelines.

CONFESSION AND ROMANCE

INTIMACY—355 Lexington Ave., New York, NY 10017. Nathasha Brooks, Ed. Fiction, 2,000 to 3,000 words, for women age 18 to 45; must have contemporary, glamorous plot and contain two romantic and intimate love scenes. Pays $75 to $100, on publication. Same address for *Jive,* geared toward younger women seeking adventure, glamour, and romance.

JIVE—See *Intimacy.*

MODERN ROMANCES—215 Lexington Ave., New York, NY 10016. Colleen Brennan, Ed. Confession stories with reader-identification and strong emotional tone, 1,500 to 7,500 words. Articles for blue-collar, family-oriented women, 300 to 1,500 words. Pays 5¢ a word, after publication. Buys all rights.

TRUE CONFESSIONS—215 Lexington Ave., New York, NY 10016. Helen Atkocius, Ed. Timely, emotional, first-person stories, 2,000 to 10,000 words, on romance, family life, and problems of today's young blue-collar women. Pays 5¢ a word, after publication.

TRUE EXPERIENCE—215 Lexington Ave., New York, NY 10016. Jean Press Silberg, Ed. Betsy Shanahan, Assoc. Ed. Realistic first-person stories, 4,000 to 8,000 words (short shorts, to 2,000 words), on family life, single life, love, romance, overcoming hardships, psychic/occult occurrences, mysteries. Pays 3¢ a word, after publication.

TRUE LOVE—215 Lexington Ave., New York, NY 10016. Marcia Pomerantz, Ed. Fresh, young, romance stories, on love and topics of current interest. Pays 3¢ a word, a month after publication.

TRUE ROMANCE—215 Lexington Ave., New York, NY 10016. Jean Sharbel, Ed. True, romantic first-person stories, 2,000 to 10,000 words. Love poems. Articles, 300 to 700 words, for young wives and singles. Pays 3¢ a word, a month after publication.

POETRY MARKETS

The following list includes markets for both serious and light verse. Although major magazines pay good rates for poetry, the competition to break into print is very stiff, since editors use only a limited number of poems in each issue. On the other hand, college, little, and literary magazines use a great deal of poetry, and though payment is modest—usually in copies—publication in these journals can establish a beginning poet's reputation, and can lead to publication in the major magazines. Poets will also find a number of competitions offering cash awards for unpublished poems in the *Literary Prize Offers* list.

Poets should also consider local newspapers as possible verse markets. Although they may not specifically seek poetry from free lancers, newspaper editors often print verse submitted to them, especially on holidays and for special occasions.

The market for book-length collections of poetry at commercial publishers is extremely limited. There are a number of university presses that publish poetry collections, however (see *University Presses*), and many of them sponsor annual competitions. Consult the *Literary Prize Offers* list for more information.

ALCOHOLISM & ADDICTION MAGAZINE—P.O. Box 31329, Seattle, WA 98103. Allison Crawford, Poetry Ed. Positive verse on recovery from chemical or other addictions. Wants upbeat, not negative, poetry.

ALOHA, THE MAGAZINE OF HAWAII—828 Fort St. Mall, Suite 640, Honolulu, HI 96813. Cheryl Chee Tsutsumi, Ed. Poetry relating to Hawaii. Pays $25 per poem, on publication.

AMAZING STORIES—Box 111, Lake Geneva, WI 53147. Patrick Lucien Price, Ed. Serious and light verse, with SF/fantasy tie-in. Pays $1 per line for short poems, somewhat less for longer ones, on acceptance.

AMERICA—106 W. 56th St., New York, NY 10019. Patrick Samway, S.J., Literary Ed. Serious poetry, preferably in contemporary prose idiom, 10 to 25 lines. Occasional light verse. Submit 2 or 3 poems at a time. Pays $1.40 per line, on publication. Guidelines.

THE AMERICAN SCHOLAR—1811—St. N.W., Washington, DC 20009. Joseph Epstein, Ed. Highly original poetry, 10 to 32 lines, for college-educated, intellectual readers. Pays $50, on acceptance.

THE ATLANTIC—745 Boylston St., Boston, MA 02116. Peter Davison, Poetry Ed. Previously unpublished poetry of highest quality. Limited market; only 3 to 4 poems an issue. Interest in new poets. Occasionally uses light verse. Pays excellent rates, on acceptance.

CAPPER'S—616 Jefferson St., Topeka, KS 66607. Nancy Peavler, Ed. Traditional poetry and free verse, 4 to 16 lines. Submit up to 6 poems at a time, with SASE. Pays $3 to $6, on acceptance.

CHILDREN'S PLAYMATE—P.O. Box 567, Indianapolis, IN 46206. Elizabeth A. Rinck, Ed. Poetry for children, 5 to 7 years old, on good health, nutrition, exercise, safety, seasonal and humorous subjects. Pays from $10, on publication. Buys all rights.

THE CHRISTIAN SCIENCE MONITOR—One Norway St., Boston, MA 02115. Fred Hunter, Ed., The Home Forum. Fresh, vigorous nonreligious poems of high quality, on various subjects. Short poems preferred. Pays varying rates, on acceptance. Submit no more than 3 poems at a time.

CLASS—27 Union Sq. West, New York, NY 10003. Jennifer Charles, Ed. Poetry, 8 to 20 lines, related to the Third World population in the U.S., general interest items, international affairs. Pays fixed rate, after publication.

COBBLESTONE—20 Grove St., Peterborough, NH 03458. Carolyn P. Yoder, Ed. Poetry, to 100 lines, must relate to monthly themes, for 8- to 14-year-olds. Pays varying rates, on publication. Send SASE for guidelines and themes.

COMMONWEAL—15 Dutch St., New York, NY 10038. Rosemary Deen, Poetry Ed. Catholic. Serious, witty poetry. Pays 50¢ a line, on publication. SASE required.

COMPLETE WOMAN—1165 N. Clark St., Chicago, IL 60610. Address Assoc. Ed. Poetry. Pays $10, on publication. SASE necessary for return of material.

COSMOPOLITAN—224 W. 57th St., New York, NY 10019. Teri Karush, Poetry Ed. Poetry about relationships and other topics of interest to young, active women. Pays from $25, on acceptance. SASE required.

DECISION—Billy Graham Evangelistic Assn., 1300 Harmon Pl., Minneapolis, MN 55403. Roger C. Palms, Ed. Poems, 5 to 20 lines, on Christian themes; preference for free verse. Pays on publication.

THE DISCIPLE—Box 179, St. Louis, MO 63166. Journal of the Christian Church (Disciples of Christ). Poetry on religious, seasonal, and historical subjects. Pays $7.50, on publication.

EVANGEL—999 College Ave., Winona Lake, IN 46590. Vera Bethel, Ed. Free Methodist. Devotional or nature poetry, 8 to 16 lines. Pays $5, on publication.

THE EVANGELICAL BEACON—1515 E. 66th St., Minneapolis, MN 55423. George Keck, Ed. Denominational publication of Evangelical Free Church of America. Some poetry related to Christian faith. Pays 4¢ a word, $2.50 minimum, on publication.

FARM AND RANCH LIVING—5400 S. 60th St., Greendale, WI 53129. Bob Ottum, Ed. Poetry, to 20 lines, on rural people and situations. Photos. Pays $35 to $75, extra for photos, on acceptance and on publication. Query.

GOLF DIGEST—5520 Park Ave., Trumbull, CT 06611–0395. Lois Hains, Asst. Ed. Humorous golf-related verse, 4 to 8 lines. Pays $50, on acceptance. Send SASE.

GOOD HOUSEKEEPING—959 8th Ave., New York, NY 10019. Rosemary Leonard, Ed. Light, humorous verses, quips, and poems. Pays $25 for four lines, $50 for six to eight lines, on acceptance.

JOURNEY—Christian Board of Publication, Box 179, St. Louis, MO 63166. Short poems for 12- to 15-year-olds. Pays 25¢ a line, on publication.

LADIES' HOME JOURNAL—100 Park Ave., New York, NY 10017. Short, humorous poetry for Last Laughs page only. Must be accessible to women in general. Pays $50 for accepted poetry.

LEATHERNECK—Box 1775, Quantico, VA 22134. W.V. H. White, Ed. Poetry overstocked at present.

MARRIAGE & FAMILY—Abbey Press Publishing Div., St. Meinrad, IN 47577. Kass Dotterweich, Man. Ed. Verse on marriage and family. Pays $15, on publication.

MATURE YEARS—201 Eighth Ave. S., P.O. Box 801, Nashville, TN 37202. Donn C. Downall, Ed. United Methodist. Poetry, to 14 lines, on pre-retirement, retirement, seasonal subjects, aging. No saccharine poetry. Pays 50¢ to $1 per line.

MCCALL'S—230 Park Ave., New York, NY 10169. Overstocked.

MIDSTREAM—515 Park Ave., New York, NY 10022. Murray Zuckoff, Ed. Poetry of Jewish interest. Pays $25, on publication.

THE MIRACULOUS MEDAL—475 E. Chelten Ave., Philadelphia, PA 19144. Robert P. Cawley, C.M., Ed. Catholic. Religious verse, to 20 lines. Pays 50¢ a line, on acceptance.

MODERN BRIDE—475 Park Ave. South, New York, NY 10016. Mary Ann Cavlin, Man. Ed. Short verse of interest to bride and groom. Pays $25 to $35, on acceptance.

THE NATION—72 Fifth Ave., New York, NY 10011. Grace Schulman, Poetry Ed. Poetry of high quality. Pays after publication.

NATIONAL ENQUIRER—Lantana, FL 33464. Jim Allan, Asst. Ed. Short poems, with traditional rhyming verse, of an amusing, philosophical or inspirational nature; longer poems of a serious or humorous nature. No experimental poetry. Submit seasonal/holiday material at least 2 months in advance. Pays from $20 after publication.

PENTECOSTAL EVANGEL—1445 Boonville, Springfield, MO 65802. Richard G. Champion, Ed. Journal of Assemblies of God. Religious and inspirational verse, 12 to 30 lines. Pays to 50¢ a line, on acceptance.

PURPOSE—616 Walnut Ave., Scottdale, PA 15683–1999. James E. Horsch, Poetry Ed. Poetry, to 8 lines, with challenging Christian discipleship angle. Pays 50¢ to $1 a line, on acceptance.

ST. JOSEPH'S MESSENGER—P.O. Box 288, Jersey City, NJ 07303. Sister Ursula Maphet, Ed. Light verse and traditional poetry, 4 to 40 lines. Pays $5 to $15, on publication.

THE SATURDAY EVENING POST—1100 Waterway Blvd., Indianapolis, IN 46202. Address Post Scripts Ed. Light verse and humor. Pays $15, on publication.

SEVENTEEN—850 Third Ave., New York, NY 10022. Karen Bokram, Teen Features Ed. Poetry, to 40 lines, by writers aged 21 and under. Submit up to 5 poems. Pays $15 to $30, after acceptance.

THE UNITED METHODIST REPORTER—P.O. Box 660275, Dallas, TX 75266–0275. Spurgeon M. Dunnam III, Ed. Religious verse, 4 to 16 lines. Pays $2, on acceptance.

YANKEE—Yankee Publishing Co., Dublin, NH 03444. Jean Burden, Poetry Ed. Serious poetry of high quality, to 30 lines. Pays $50 per poem for all rights, $35 for first rights, on publication.

POETRY SERIES

The following university presses publish book-length collections of poetry by writers who have never had a book of poems published. Each has specific rules for submission, so before submitting any material, be sure to write well ahead of the deadline dates for further information. Some organizations sponsor competitions for groups of poems; see *Literary Prize Offers*.

CLEVELAND STATE UNIVERSITY POETRY SERIES—Dept. of English, Rhodes Tower, Room 1815, Cleveland, OH 44115. Best volume of poetry submitted between December 15 to March 1 receives publication and $1,000. There is a $10 reading fee. Guidelines recommended before submission.

PITT POETRY SERIES—University of Pittsburgh Press, Pittsburgh, PA 15260. Poets who have never had a full-length book of poetry published may enter a 48- to 120-page collection of poems to the Agnes Lynch Starrett Poetry Prize between March and April. There is a $10 reading fee. $2,000 and publication of the winning manuscript is offered.

UNIVERSITY OF GEORGIA PRESS POETRY SERIES—Athens, GA 30602. Poets who have never had a book of poems published may submit book-length poetry manuscripts for possible publication. Open during the month of September each year. Manuscripts from poets who have published at least one volume of poetry (chapbooks excluded) are considered during the month of January. Send SASE for guidelines before submitting. There is a $10 reading fee.

WESLEYAN UNIVERSITY PRESS—110 Mt. Vernon St., Middletown, CT 06457. Considers unpublished book-length poetry manuscripts by poets who have never had a book published, for publication in the Wesleyan New Poets Series. There is no deadline. Submit manuscript, $15 reading fee, and SASE.

YALE UNIVERSITY PRESS—Box 92A, Yale Sta., New Haven, CT 06520. Address Editor, Yale Series of Younger Poets. Conducts Yale Series of Younger Poets Competition, in which the prize is publication of a book-length manuscript of poetry, written by a poet under 40 who has not previously published a volume of poems. Closes in February.

GREETING CARD MARKETS

Greeting card companies often have their own specific requirements for submitting ideas, verse, and artwork. The National Association of Greeting Card Publishers, however, gives the following general guidelines for submitting material: Each verse or message should be typed, double-space, on a 3x5 or 4x6 card. Use only one side of the card, and be sure to put your name and address in the upper left-hand corner. Keep a copy of every verse or idea you send. (It's also advisable to keep a record of what you've submitted to each publisher.) Always enclose an SASE, and do not send out more than ten verses or ideas in a group to any one publisher.

The Greeting Card Association brings out a booklet for free lancers, *Artists and Writers Market List,* with the names, addresses, and editorial guidelines of greeting card companies. Send a self-addressed stamped envelope and $5.00 to The Greeting Card Association, 1350 New York Ave. N.W., Suite 615, Washington, DC 20005.

AMBERLEY GREETING CARD COMPANY—11510 Goldcoast Dr., Cincinnati, OH 45249–1695. Ned Stern, Ed. Humorous ideas for birthday, illness, friendship, congratulations, "miss you," etc. Pays $40. Buys all rights.

BLUE MOUNTAIN ARTS, INC.—P.O. Box 1007, Boulder, CO 80306. Attn: Editorial Staff, Dept. TW. Poetry and prose about love, friendship, family, philosophies, etc. Also material for special occasions and holidays: birthdays, get well, Christmas, Valentine's Day, Easter, etc. No artwork or rhymed verse. Pays $200 per poem published on a notecard.

FREEDOM GREETING CARD COMPANY—P.O. Box 715, Bristol, PA 19007. Submit to Jay Levitt. Verse, traditional, humorous, and love messages. Inspirational poetry for all occasions. Pays negotiable rates, on acceptance. Query with SASE.

GALLANT GREETINGS CORPORATION—2654 West Medill, Chicago, IL 60647. Ideas for humorous and serious greeting cards. Pays $50 per idea, in 90 days.

HALLMARK CARDS, INC.—2501 McGee, Box 419580, Mail Drop 276, Kansas City, MO 64141. Query Carol King; no samples. Humor for everyday and seasonal greeting cards. Mostly staff-written; "free lancers must show high degree of skill and originality." Guidelines with SASE.

KALAN—97 S. Union Ave., Lansdowne, PA 19050. Address the Editors. Ideas for greeting cards, novelty copy (for buttons, key rings, bumper stickers, etc.) and new products. Copy should be humorous, of the everyday, risqué, and X-rated varieties; birthday and friendship cards are most wanted. Pays $50 per card idea, $25 per novelty item, made on acceptance; payment for new product ideas varies. Guidelines recommended.

THE MAINE LINE COMPANY—P.O. Box 418, Rockport, ME 04856. Attn: Perri Ardman. Untraditional humorous cards. Send SASE with three first-class stamps for guidelines. Pays $50 per card.

OATMEAL STUDIOS—Box 138 TW, Rochester, VT 05767. David Stewart, Ed. Humorous, clever, and new ideas needed for all occasions. Query with SASE.

OUTREACH PUBLICATIONS—P.O. Box 1010, Siloam Springs, AR 72761. Address Creative Ed. Christian greeting cards for most occasions. Pays varying rates, on acceptance.

RED FARM STUDIOS—P.O. Box 347, 334 Pleasant St., Pawtucket, RI 02862. Traditional cards for graduations, weddings, birthdays, get-wells, anniversaries, friendship, new baby, sympathy, Christmas, and Valentines. No studio humor. Pays varying rates. SASE required.

VAGABOND CREATIONS, INC.—2560 Lance Dr., Dayton, OH 45409. George F. Stanley, Jr., Ed. Greeting cards with graphics only on cover (no copy) and short tie-in copy punch line on inside page: birthday, everyday, Valentine, Christmas, and graduation. Mildly risqué humor with double entendre acceptable. Ideas for illustrated theme stationery. Pays $15, on acceptance.

WARNER PRESS PUBLISHERS—1200 E. Fifth St., Anderson, IN 46012. Cindy M. Grant, Product Ed. Sensitive prose and inspirational verse card ideas for boxed assortments; religious themes. Submit everyday ideas in Jan.-March; Christmas material May-July. Pays $15 to $30, on acceptance. Guidelines with SASE.

WEST GRAPHICS PUBLISHING—238 Capp St., San Francisco, CA 94110. Address Editorial Dept. Outrageous humor concepts, all occasions (especially birthday) and holidays, for photo and illustrated card lines. Submit on 3x5 cards: concept on one side; name, address, and phone number on other. Pays $60 per idea, 30 days after publication.

WILLIAMHOUSE-REGENCY, INC.—28 W. 23rd St., New York, NY 10010. Query Nancy Boecker. Captions for wedding invitations. Payment varies, on acceptance. SASE required.

COLLEGE, LITERARY AND LITTLE MAGAZINES

FICTION, NONFICTION, POETRY

The thousands of literary journals, little magazines, and college quarterlies published today welcome work from novices and pros alike; editors are always interested in seeing traditional and experimental fiction, poetry, essays, reviews, short articles, criticism, and satire, and as long as the material is well-written, the fact that a writer is a beginner doesn't adversely affect his or her chances for acceptance.

Most of these smaller publications have small budgets and staffs, so they may be slow in their reporting time—several months is not unusual. In addition, they usually pay only in copies of the issue in which published work appears and some— particularly college magazines—do not read manuscripts during the summer.

Publication in the literary journals can, however, lead to recognition by editors of large-circulation magazines, who read the little magazines in their search for new talent. There is also the possibility of having one's work chosen for reprinting in one of the prestigious annual collections of work from the little magazines.

Because the requirements of these journals differ widely, it is always important to study recent issues before submitting work to one of them. Copies of magazines may be in large libraries, or a writer may send a postcard to the editor and ask the price of a sample copy. When submitting a manuscript, always enclose a self-addressed envelope, with sufficient postage for its return.

For a complete list of literary and college publications and little magazines, writers may consult such reference works as *The International Directory of Little Magazines and Small Presses,* published annually by Dustbooks (P.O. Box 100, Paradise, CA 95967).

THE AGNI REVIEW—Boston University, Creative Writing Program, 236 Bay State Rd., Boston, MA 02215. Askold Melnyozuk, Ed. Short stories, poetry, essays, and artwork. Pays $8 per page.

ALASKA QUARTERLY REVIEW—Dept. of English, Univ. of Alaska, 3211 Providence Dr., Anchorage, AK 99508. Address Eds. Short stories, novel excerpts, poetry (traditional and unconventional forms). Submit manuscripts between August 15 and May 15. Pays in copies.

THE ALBANY REVIEW—4 Central Ave., Albany, NY 12210. Short fiction (1,750 to 5,000 words), essays, interviews with major writers, and articles (750 to 1,000 words); poetry and satire. Pays in copies.

ALBATROSS—4014 SW 21st Rd., Gainesville, FL 32607. Richard Smyth, Richard Brobst, Eds. High-quality poetry: especially interested in ecological and nature poetry written in narrative form. Interviews with well-known poets. Submit 3 to 5 poems at a time with brief bio. Pays in copies.

ALTERNATIVE FICTION & POETRY—7783 Kensington Ln., Hanover Park, IL 60103. Philip Athans, Ed./Pub. Wildly experimental/avant-garde/underground/marginal short fiction, poetry, prose, etc. Send Poetry to Andrew Gettler, Poetry Editor, 2663 Heath Ave., #6D, Bronx, NY 10463. Queries appreciated. Pays in copies.

AMELIA—329 E St., Bakersfield, CA 93304. Poetry, to 100 lines; critical essays, to 2,000 words; reviews, to 500 words; belles lettres, to 1,000 words; fiction, to 3,500 words; fine pen and ink sketches; photos. Pays $35 for fiction and criticism, $10 to $25 for other nonfiction and artwork, $2 to $25 for poetry. Annual contest.

THE AMERICAN BOOK REVIEW—Publications Center, Univ. of

Colorado, English Dept., Box 226, Boulder, CO 80309. Don Laing, Man. Ed. John Tytell, Rochelle Ratner, Ronald Sukenick, Eds. Book reviews, 700 to 1,200 words. Pays $50 honorarium and copies. Query first.

THE AMERICAN POETRY REVIEW—1704 Walnut St., Philadelphia, PA 19103. Address Eds. Highest quality contemporary poetry. Responds in 10 weeks. SASE a must.

AMERICAN QUARTERLY—National Museum of American History, Smithsonian Institution, Washington, DC 20560. Gary Kulik, Ed. Scholarly essays, 5,000 to 10,000 words, on any aspect of U.S. culture. Pays in copies.

THE AMERICAN SCHOLAR—1811 Q St. N.W., Washington, DC 20009. Joseph Epstein, Ed. Articles, 3,500 to 4,000 words, on science, politics, literature, the arts, etc. Book reviews. Pays $450 for articles, $100 for reviews, on publication.

THE AMERICAN VOICE—332 W. Broadway, Suite 1215, Louisville, KY 40202. Frederick Smock, Ed. Short stories and essays, to 10,000 words; free verse. Radical, feminist, and unpredictable material. Pays $400 for prose, $150 for poetry, on publication.

AMHERST REVIEW—P.O. Box 1811, Amherst College, Amherst, MA 01002. Josh Jacobs, Ed. Fiction, to 8,000 words, and poetry, to 160 lines. Photos, paintings, and drawings. Pays in copies. Submit material September through March only.

ANOTHER CHICAGO MAGAZINE—Box 11223, Chicago, IL 60611. Fiction, essays on literature, and poetry. Pays $5 to $25, on acceptance.

ANTIETAM REVIEW—82 W. Washington St., Hagerstown, MD 21740. Ann Knox, Ed.-in-Chief. Fiction, to 5,000 words; poetry and photography. Submissions from regional artists only (MD, PA, WV, VA, DC), from Oct. through Feb. Pays from $25 to $100. Annual Literary Award for fiction.

THE ANTIGONISH REVIEW—St. Francis Xavier Univ., Antigonish, N.S., Canada. George Sanderson, Ed. Poetry; short stories, essays, book reviews, 1,800 to 2,500 words. Pays in copies.

ANTIOCH REVIEW—P.O. Box 148, Yellow Springs, OH 45387. Robert S. Fogarty, Ed. Timely articles, 2,000 to 8,000 words, on social sciences, literature, and humanities. Quality fiction. Poetry. No inspirational poetry. Pays $10 per printed page, on publication.

APALACHEE QUARTERLY—Apalachee Press, P.O. Box 20106, Tallahassee, FL 32316. Barbara Hamby, Pamela Ball, Claudia Johnson, Bruce Boehrer, Paul McCall, Eds. Fiction, to 30 manuscript pages; poems (Submit 3 to 5). Pays in copies.

APOCALYPSO—673 Ninth Ave., New York, NY 10036. Articles and fiction, to 3,000 words. Poetry, any length. Archival material and graphics. Pays in copies.

THE ARCHER—Pro Poets, 2285 Rogers Ln. N.W., Salem, OR 97304. Winifred Layton, Ed. Contemporary poetry, to 30 lines. Pays in copies.

ARIZONA QUARTERLY—Univ. of Arizona, Main Library B-541, Tucson, AZ 85721. Edgar A. Dryden, Ed. Criticism of American literature and culture from a theoretical perspective. No poetry or fiction. Pays in copies.

THE ATAVIST—P.O. Box 5643, Berkeley, CA 94705. Robert Dorsett, Loretta Ko, Eds. Poetry and poetry criticism, any length. Translations of original poetry. Pays in copies.

AURA LITERARY/ARTS REVIEW—P.O. Box 76, Univ. Center, UAB, Birmingham, AL 35294. Wendy Freeman Miles, Ed. Fiction and essays on literature, to 7,000 words; book reviews to 4,000 words; poetry; photos and drawings. Pays in copies.

BALL STATE UNIVERSITY FORUM—Ball State Univ., Muncie, IN 47306. Bruce W. Hozeski, Ed.-in-Chief. High quality criticism, essays, short fiction, drama, and poetry. Pays in copies.

BELLES LETTRES—Box 987, Arlington, VA 22216. Janet Mullaney, Ed. Reviews and essays, 250 to 2,000 words, on literature by women. Literary puzzles, interviews, rediscoveries, retrospectives. Query required. Pays in copies.

BELLOWING ARK—P.O. Box 45637, Seattle, WA 98145. Robert R. Ward, Ed. Short fiction, and poetry and essays of varying lengths, that portray life as a positive, meaningful process. B&W photos; line drawings. Pays in copies.

THE BELOIT FICTION JOURNAL—Box 11, Beloit College, Beloit, WI 53511. Clint McCown, Ed. Short fiction, 1 to 35 pages, on all themes (no pornography, political propaganda, religious dogma). Manuscripts read year round. Pays in copies.

BELOIT POETRY JOURNAL—RFD 2, Box 154, Ellsworth, ME 04605. First-rate contemporary poetry, of any length or mode. Pays in copies. Send SASE for guidelines.

BITTERROOT—P.O. Box 489, Spring Glen, NY 12483. Menke Katz, Ed.-in-Chief. Poetry, to 50 lines; poetry book reviews; B&W camera-ready drawings. Pays in copies. Annual contests. Send SASE for information.

BLACK RIVER REVIEW—855 Mildred Ave., Lorain, OH 44052. Kaye Coller, Ed. Contemporary poetry, fiction, essays, short book reviews, B&W artwork. No greeting card verse or slick magazine prose. Submit between Jan. 1 and May 1. Pays in copies. Contests. Guidelines. SASE required.

THE BLACK WARRIOR REVIEW—P.O. Box 2936, Tuscaloosa, AL 35486–2936. Mark Dawson, Ed. Fiction; poetry; translations; reviews and essays. Pays per printed page. Annual awards.

THE BLOOMSBURY REVIEW—1028 Bannock St., Denver, CO 80204. Tom Auer, Ed. Ray Gonzalez, Poetry Ed. Book reviews, publishing features, interviews, essays, poetry, up to 800 words. Pays $5 to $25, on publication.

BLUELINE—English Dept., SUNY, Potsdam, NY 13676. Anthony Tyler, Ed. Reading period Sept. 1-Dec. 1. Essays, fiction, to 2,500 words, on Adirondack region or similar areas. Poetry, to 44 lines. No more than 5 poems per submission. Pays in copies.

BOSTON REVIEW—33 Harrison Ave., Boston, MA 02111. Margaret Ann Roth, Ed.-in-Chief. Reviews and essays, 800 to 3,000 words, on literature, art, music, film, photography. Original fiction, to 5,000 words. Poetry. Pays $40 to $150.

BUCKNELL REVIEW—Bucknell Univ., Lewisburg, PA 17837. Interdisciplinary journal in book form. Scholarly articles on arts, science, and letters. Pays in copies.

CAESURA—English Dept., Auburn Univ., Auburn, AL 36849. R. T. Smith, Man. Ed. Short stories, to 3,000 words; narrative and lyric poetry, to 150 lines. Pays in copies.

CALLALOO—Dept. of English, University of Virginia, Charlottesville, VA

22903. Charles H. Rowell, Ed. Fiction and poetry by, and critical studies on Afro-American, Caribbean, and African artists and writers. Payment varies, on publication.

CALLIOPE—Creative Writing Program, Roger Williams College, Bristol, RI 02809. Martha Christina, Ed. Short stories, to 2,500 words; poetry. Pays in copies. No submissions April through July.

CANADIAN FICTION MAGAZINE—Box 946, Sta. F, Toronto, Ontario, Canada M4Y 2N9. High-quality short stories, novel excerpts, and experimental fiction, to 5,000 words, by Canadians. Interviews with Canadian authors; translations. Pays $10 per page, on publication. Annual prize.

THE CAPILANO REVIEW—Capilano College, 2055 Purcell Way, North Vancouver, B.C., Canada V7J 3H5. Pierre Coupey, Ed. Fiction; poetry; drama; visual arts. Pays $12 to $50.

THE CARIBBEAN WRITER—Univ. of the Virgin Islands, RR 02, Box 10,000, Kingshill, St. Croix, Virgin Islands, U.S. 00850. Erika J. Smilowitz, Ed. Annual. Fiction (to 15 pages, submit up to 2 stories) and poems (no more than five); the Caribbean should be central to the work. Blind submissions policy: place title only on manuscript; name, address, and title of ms. on separate sheet. Reading period is through Oct. for Spring issue of the following year. Pays in copies.

CAROLINA QUARTERLY—Greenlaw Hall CB#3520, Univ. of North Carolina, Chapel Hill, NC 27599–3520. Allison Bulsterbaum, Ed. Fiction, to 7,000 words, by new or established writers. Poetry (no restrictions on length, though limited space makes inclusion of works of more than 300 lines impractical). Pays $3 per printed page for fiction, $5 per poem, on acceptance.

CATALYST—Atlanta-Fulton Public Library, 1 Margaret Mitchell Sq., Carnegie & Forsyth Sq., Atlanta, GA 30303–1089. Pearl Cleage, Ed. Fiction (to 3,000 words) and poetry by Southern writers, primarily black writers; biannual. Pays to $200, on publication. Send SASE for guidelines and themes.

THE CENTENNIAL REVIEW—110 Morrill Hall, Michigan State Univ., East Lansing, MI 48824–1036. R.K. Meiners, Ed. Articles, 3,000 to 5,000 words, on sciences, humanities, and interdisciplinary topics. Pays in copies.

THE CHARITON REVIEW—Creative Writing Program, University of California-Riverside, Riverside, CA 92521. Jim Barnes, Ed. Highest quality poetry and fiction, to 6,000 words. Modern and contemporary translations. Book reviews. Pays $5 per printed page for fiction and translations.

THE CHICAGO REVIEW—Univ. of Chicago, Faculty Exchange Box C, Chicago, IL 60637. Elizabeth Arnold, Emily McKnight, Jane Hoogestraat, Eds. Essays, interviews, reviews, fiction, translations, poetry. Pays in copies.

CHIMERA CONNECTIONS—See *Jabberwocky.*

CHIRON REVIEW—Rt. 2, Box 111, St. John, KS 67576. Michael Hathaway, Ed. Contemporary fiction (to 4,000 words) and articles (500 to 1,000 words), and poetry to 30 lines. Photos. Pays in copies.

CICADA—329 E St., Bakersfield, CA 93304. Single haiku, sequences or garlands, essays about the forms, haibun and fiction related to haiku or Japan. Pays in copies.

CIMARRON REVIEW—205 Morrill Hall, Oklahoma State Univ., Stillwater, OK 74078–0135. Deborah Bransford, Man. Ed. Poetry, fiction, essays, graphics/artwork. Seeks an individual, innovative style that focuses on contemporary themes. Pays in copies.

COLORADO REVIEW—English Dept., 359 Eddy, Colorado State Univ., Fort Collins, CO 80523. Poetry, short fiction, translations, interviews, articles on contemporary themes. Submit from September through May 1.

COLUMBIA, A MAGAZINE OF POETRY & PROSE—404 Dodge, Columbia Univ., New York, NY 10027. Address the Editors. Fiction and nonfiction to 5,000 words; poetry; essays; interviews; visual art. Pays in copies. SASE required. Guidelines and annual awards. Reading period: September 1 to April 1.

CONFRONTATION—Dept. of English, C.W. Post of L. I. U., Greenvale, NY 11548. Martin Tucker, Ed. Serious fiction, 750 to 6,000 words. Crafted poetry, 10 to 200 lines. Pays $10 to $100, on publication.

THE CONNECTICUT POETRY REVIEW—P.O. Box 3783, New Haven, CT 06525. J. Claire White and James Wm. Chichetto, Eds. Poetry, 5 to 20 lines, and reviews, 700 words. Pays $5 per poem, $10 for a review, on acceptance.

CONNECTICUT RIVER REVIEW—P.O. Box 112, Stratford, CT 06497. Rebecca Thompson, Ed. Poetry journal published twice yearly. Submit 3 to 5 poems, 40 lines or less. Pays in two copies. Guidelines.

COTTON BOLL/ATLANTA REVIEW—Sandy Springs P.O. Box 76757, Atlanta, GA 30358. Mary Hollingsworth, Ed. Short stories to 3,500 words; poetry, to 2 pages. Interviews with known writers. SASE for guidelines

CRAZY QUILT—3341 Adams Ave., San Diego, CA 92116. Address the Editors. Fiction, to 4,000 words, poetry, one-act plays, and literary criticism. Also B&W art, photographs. Pays in copies.

THE CREAM CITY REVIEW—Box 413, Univ. of Wisconsin, Milwaukee, WI 53201. Ron Tanner, Ed. "We serve a national and regional audience that seeks the best in fiction, poetry, and nonfiction; and we publish work by established and emerging writers." Submit up to three poems. Payment varies.

CRITICAL INQUIRY—Univ. of Chicago Press, Wieboldt Hall, 1050 E. 59th St., Chicago, IL 60637. W. J. T. Mitchell, Ed. Critical essays that offer a theoretical perspective on literature, music, visual arts, and popular culture. No fiction, poetry, or autobiography. Pays in copies.

CUBE LITERARY MAGAZINE—P.O. Box 5165, Richmond, VA 23220. Eric Mathews, Ed. Victoria Aracri, Assoc. Ed. Michele Maroney, Fiction Ed. Mike Malone, Poetry Ed. Fiction, to 5,000 words, poetry, to 50 lines, and creative or humorous essays. No romance fiction or poetry. Pays in copies.

CUMBERLAND POETRY REVIEW—P.O. Box 120128, Acklen Sta., Nashville, TN 37212. Address Eds. High-quality poetry and criticism; translations. No restrictions on form, style, or subject matter. Pays in copies.

DENVER QUARTERLY—Univ of Denver, Denver, CO 80208. Donald Revell, Ed. Literary, cultural essays and articles; poetry; book reviews; fiction. Pays $5 per printed page, after publication.

DESCANT—Texas Christian Univ., T.C.U. Sta., Fort Worth, TX 76129. Betsy Colquitt, Stanley Trachtenberg, Eds. Fiction, to 6,000 words. Poetry to 40 lines. No restriction on form or subject. Pays in copies. Submit Sept. through May only.

THE DEVIL'S MILLHOPPER—The Devil's Millhopper Press, Coll. of Humanities, U. of South Carolina/Aiken, 171 University Pkwy., Aiken, SC 29801. Stephen Gardner, Ed. Poetry. Send SASE for guidelines. Pays in copies.

EMBERS—Box 404, Guilford, CT 06437. Katrina Van Tassel, Mark Johnston, Charlotte Garrett, Eds. A poetry journal published twice yearly. Interested in original new voices as well as published poets.

EVENT—Douglas College, Box 2503, New Westminister, BC, Canada V3L 5B2. Dale Zieroth, Ed. Short fiction, short plays, poetry. Pays modest rates, on publication.

FARMER'S MARKET—P.O. Box 1272, Galesburg, IL 61402. Short stories, essays, and novel excerpts, to 40 pages, and poetry, related to the Midwest. Pays in copies.

FICTION INTERNATIONAL—English Dept., San Diego State Univ., San Diego, CA 92182. Harold Jaffe, Larry McCaffery, Eds. Post-modernist and politically committed fiction and theory. Manuscripts read from September to January 15. Payment varies.

THE FIDDLEHEAD—Old Arts Bldg., Univ. of New Brunswick, Fredericton, N.B., Canada E3B 5A3. Serious fiction, 2,500 words, preferably by Canadians. Pays about $10 per printed page, on publication.

FIELD—Rice Hall, Oberlin College, Oberlin, OH 44074. Stuart Friebert, David Young, Eds. Serious poetry, any length, by established and unknown poets; essays on poetics by poets. Translations by qualified translators. Pays $20 to $30 per page, on publication.

FINE MADNESS—P.O. Box 15176, Seattle, WA 98115. Poetry, any length; short fiction; occasional reviews. Pays varying rates.

FOOTWORK—Cultural Affairs Office, Passaic County Comm. College, College Blvd., Paterson, NJ 07509. Maria Gillan, Ed. High quality fiction, to 8 pages, and poetry, to 3 pages, any style. Pays in copies.

FREE INQUIRY—P.O. Box 5, Buffalo, NY 14215–0005. Paul Kurtz, Ed. Tim Madigan, Man. Ed. Articles, 500 to 5,000 words, for "literate and lively readership. Focus is on criticisms of religious belief systems, and how to lead an ethical life without a supernatural basis." Pays in copies.

THE GAMUT—1216 Rhodes Tower, Cleveland State Univ., Cleveland, OH 44115. Lively articles on general-interest topics preferably concerned with the region, 2,000 to 6,000 words. Quality fiction and poetry. Photos. Pays $25 to $250, on publication. Send SASE for guidelines.

GARGOYLE—P.O. Box 30906, Bethesda, MD 20814. Richard Peabody, Ed. Fiction, 3 to 30 typed pages; poetry, 5 to 25 lines. Photos. Pays in copies.

THE GEORGIA REVIEW—Univ. of Georgia, Athens, GA 30602. Stanley W. Lindberg, Ed., Stephen Corey, Assoc. Ed. Short fiction; interdisciplinary essays on arts, sciences, and the humanities; book reviews; poetry. No submissions in June, July, or August.

GREAT RIVER REVIEW—211 W. 7th St., Winona, MN 55987. Fiction and creative prose, 2,000 to 10,000 words. Quality contemporary poetry; send 4 to 8 poems. Special interest in Midwestern writers and themes.

GREEN'S MAGAZINE—P.O. Box 3236, Regina, Sask., Canada S4P 3H1. David Green, Ed. Fiction for family reading, 1,500 to 4,000 words. Poetry, to 40 lines. Pays in copies.

THE GREENSBORO REVIEW—Univ. of North Carolina, Greensboro, NC 27412. Jim Clark, Ed. Semi-annual. Poetry and fiction. Submission deadlines: Sept. 15 and Feb. 15. Pays in copies.

HALF TONES TO JUBILEE—Pensacola Junior College, English Dept., 1000 College Blvd., Pensacola, FL 32504. Walter F. Spara, Ed. Fiction, to 10,000 words, and poetry, to 60 lines. Pays in copies.

THE HAVEN, NEW POETRY—5969 Avenida la Barranca NW, Albuquerque, NM 87114. Miquel Montano, Ed. Poetry, to 20 lines. Contests. Pays $5 to $15, on acceptance.

HAWAII REVIEW—Dept. of English, Univ. of Hawaii, 1733 Donagho Rd., Honolulu, HI 96882. Dellzell Chenoweth, Ed.-in-Chief. Quality fiction, poetry, interviews, nonfiction essays, and literary criticism reflecting both regional and universal concerns.

HEARTLAND JOURNAL—Box 55115, Madison, WI 53705. Lenore Coberly, Ed. Fiction, poetry, children's page, articles, essays, B&W drawings, color slides of artwork. Open-minded about subject matter and length. Writers must be over 60 years old. Pays in copies. Contest.

HERESIES—Box 1306, Canal Street Sta., New York, NY 10013. Feminist art/political slant; thematic issues. Fiction, to 12 typed pages; nonfiction; poetry; art; photography.

HOME LIFE—127 Ninth Ave. N., Nashville, TN 37234. Charlie Warren, Ed. Southern Baptist. Short lyrical verse, humorous, marriage and family, seasonal, and inspirational. Pays to $24 for poetry, 5¢ a word for articles, on acceptance.

HURRICANE ALICE: A FEMINIST QUARTERLY—207 Lind Hall, 207 Church St. SE, Minneapolis, MN 55455. Articles, fiction, essays, interviews, and reviews, 500 to 3,000 words, with feminist perspective. Pays in copies.

INDIANA REVIEW—316 N. Jordan Ave., Bloomington, IN 47405. Russell Roby, Fiction Ed. Jon Tribble, Poetry Ed. Fiction with an emphasis on an honest voice as well as style. Poems that are well executed and ambitious. Pays $5 a page for poetry; $25 per story.

INLET—Dept. of English, Virginia Wesleyan Coll., Norfolk, VA 23502. Joseph Harkey, Ed. Short fiction, 1,000 to 3,000 words (short lengths preferred). Poems of 4 to 40 lines; all forms and themes. Submit between September and March 1st, each year. Pays in copies.

THE IOWA REVIEW—EPB 308, Univ. of Iowa, Iowa City, IA 52242. David Hamilton, Ed. Essays, poems, stories, reviews. Pays $10 a page for fiction and nonfiction, $1 a line for poetry, on publication.

JABBERWOCKY—(formerly *Chimera Connections*) 7701 S.W. 7th Pl., Gainesville, FL 32607. Jeff VanderMeer, Duane Bray, Eds. Fiction (to 8,000 words), poetry and humor. Fantasy, science fiction, and horror only. Query first with SASE. Pays $20 for fiction and poetry. Guidelines.

JAM TO-DAY—372 Dunstable Rd., Tyngsboro, MA 01879. Don Stanford and Judith Stanford, Eds. High-quality poetry and fiction, particularly from unknown and little-known writers. Interested in poems written in traditional forms, concrete/shaped poetry and found poetry. No traditional light verse. Short fiction, to 7,000 words. Pays $5 per page for fiction, $5 per poem, plus copies, on publication.

KANSAS QUARTERLY—Dept. of English, Denison Hall 122, Kansas State Univ., Manhattan, KS 66506. Literary criticism, art, and history. Fiction and poetry. Pays in copies. Two series of annual awards. Query for articles and special topics.

KARAMU—Dept. of English, Eastern Illinois Univ., Charleston, IL 61920. Peggy Brayfield, Ed. Contemporary or experimental fiction. Poetry. Pays in copies.

LAKE EFFECT—P.O. Box 315, Oswego, NY 13126. Jean O'Connor Fuller, Man. Ed. Short stories, essays, poetry, and humor for a general audience. Pays $25 for fiction and nonfiction, $5 for poems, on acceptance. Query for nonfiction only.

THE LEADING EDGE—3163 JKHB, Provo, UT 84602. Russell W. Asplund, Ed. Tri-annual science fiction and fantasy magazine. Short stories (3,000 to 12,000 words); poetry (to 200 lines); and articles (to 8,000 words) on science, scientific speculation, and literary criticism. Fillers and comics. "Do not send originals; manuscripts are marked and critiqued by staff." Pays ½¢ per word with $5 minimum for fiction; $4 per published page of poetry; $2 to $4 for fillers; on publication. SASE for guidelines.

LIFE BEAT—Blanchardville, WI 53516. Kathy Vaillancourt, Ed. Articles, art, and poetry. Guidelines. Pays varying rates, on acceptance.

LILITH—250 W. 57th St., New York, NY 10107. Susan Weidman Schneider, Ed. Fiction, 1,500 to 2,000 words, on issues of interest to Jewish women.

THE LION AND THE UNICORN—English Dept., Brooklyn College, Brooklyn, NY 11210. Geraldine DeLuca, Roni Natov, Eds. Articles, from 2,000 words, offering criticism of children's and young adult books, for teachers, scholars, artists, and parents. Query preferred. Pays in copies.

LITERARY MAGAZINE REVIEW—English Dept., Kansas State Univ., Manhattan, KS 66506. Reviews and articles concerning literary magazines, 1,000 to 1,500 words, for writers and readers of contemporary literature. Pays modest fees and copies. Query.

THE LITERARY REVIEW—Fairleigh Dickinson Univ., 285 Madison Ave., Madison, NJ 07940. Walter Cummins, Martin Green, Harry Keyishian, William Zander, Eds. Serious fiction; poetry; translations; reviews; essays on contemporary literature. Pays in copies.

THE LONG STORY—11 Kingston St., N. Andover, MA 01845. Stories, 8,000 to 20,000 words; prefer committed fiction. Pays $1 a page, on publication.

THE MALAHAT REVIEW—Univ. of Victoria, P.O. Box 1700, Victoria, B.C., Canada V8W 2Y2. Constance Rooke, Ed. Fiction and poetry, including translations. Pays from $20 per page, on acceptance.

THE MANHATTAN REVIEW—440 Riverside Dr., #45, New York, NY 10027. Highest quality poetry. Pays in copies.

MASSACHUSETTS REVIEW—Memorial Hall, Univ. of Massachusetts, Amherst, MA 01003. Literary criticism; articles on public affairs, scholarly disciplines. Short fiction. Poetry. No submissions between June and October. Pays modest rates, on publication. SASE required.

MEMPHIS STATE REVIEW—See *River City.*

MICHIGAN HISTORICAL REVIEW—Clark Historical Library, Central Michigan Univ., Mt. Pleasant, MI 48859. Address Ed. Articles related to Michigan's political, social, economic, and cultural history; articles on American, Canadian, and Midwestern history that directly or indirectly explore themes related to Michigan's past. SASE.

THE MICKLE STREET REVIEW—328 Mickle St., Camden, NJ 08102. Articles, poems, and artwork related to Walt Whitman. Pays in copies.

MID-AMERICAN REVIEW—Dept. of English, Bowling Green State Univ., Bowling Green, OH 43403. Ken Letko, Ed. High-quality fiction, poetry, articles, translations, and reviews of contemporary writing. Fiction to 20,000 words. Reviews, articles, 500 to 2,500 words. Pays to $50, on publication.

MIDWEST QUARTERLY—Pittsburg State Univ., Pittsburg, KS 66762. James B. M. Schick, Ed. Scholarly articles, 2,500 to 5,000 words, on contemporary issues. Pays in copies.

THE MINNESOTA REVIEW—English Dept., SUNY-Stony Brook, Stony Brook, NY 11794. Address the Editors. "Politically committed fiction (3,000 to 6,000 words), nonfiction (5,000 to 7,500 words), and poetry (3 pages maximum), for socialist, marxist, or feminist audience." Pays in copies.

MISSISSIPPI REVIEW—Center for Writers, Univ. of Southern Mississippi, Southern Sta., Box 5144, Hattiesburg, MS 39406–5144. Frederick Barthelme, Ed. Serious fiction, poetry, criticism, interviews. Pays in copies.

THE MISSISSIPPI VALLEY REVIEW—Dept. of English, Western Illinois Univ., Macomb, IL 61455. Forrest Robinson, Ed. Short fiction, to 20 typed pages. Poetry; send 3 to 5 poems. Pays in copies.

THE MISSOURI REVIEW—Dept. of English, 107 Tate Hall, Univ. of Missouri-Columbia, Columbia, MO 65211. Greg Michalson, Man. Ed. Poems, of any length. Fiction and essays. Pays $10 per printed page, on publication.

MODERN HAIKU—P.O. Box 1752, Madison, WI 53701. Robert Spiess, Ed. Haiku and articles about haiku. Pays $1 per haiku, $5 a page for articles.

MONTHLY REVIEW—122 W. 27th St., New York, NY 10001. Paul M. Sweezy, Harry Magdoff, Eds. Analytical articles, 5,000 words, on politics and economics, from independent socialist viewpoint. Pays $50, on publication.

THE MOUNTAIN—P.O. Box 1010, Galax, VA 24333. Address the Editors. Fiction (3,000 to 8,000 words) and general-interest nonfiction (500 to 6,000 words) reflecting mountain region life and of a national political interest. Humor, 10 to 150 words. Pays $10 to $750, on publication.

MOVING OUT—P.O. Box 21249, Detroit, MI 48221. Poetry, fiction, articles, and art by women. Submit 4 to 6 poems at a time. Pays in copies.

MUSE—(formerly *The Muse Letter*) P.O. Box 45, Burlington, NC 27216–0045. J. William Griffin, Ed. Poems (up to 36 lines preferred) of any subject, form, or style. Send up to five poems, typed single spaced. Pays $5 per poem, on publication.

THE NATIONAL STORYTELLING JOURNAL—P.O. Box 309, Jonesborough, TN 37659. Articles, 800 to 3,000 words, related to storytelling: "Articles can have folkloric, historical, personal, educational, travel bias, as long as it is related to storytelling." Poetry. Pays in copies.

NEBO—Dept. of English, Arkansas Tech. Univ., Russellville, AR 72801. Poetry; mainstream fiction to 20 pages; critical essays to 10 pages. Pays in two copies.

NEGATIVE CAPABILITY—62 Ridgelawn Dr. E., Mobile, AL 36608. Sue Walker, Ed. Poetry, any length; fiction, essays, art. Pays in copies. Annual Eve of St. Agnes poetry competition and annual fiction and essay contest.

NEW LETTERS—5216 Rockhill Rd., Kansas City, MO 64110. James

McKinley, Ed. Fiction, 10 to 25 pages; nonfiction, 10 to 25 pages. Poetry; submit 3 to 6 at a time.

NEW MEXICO HUMANITIES REVIEW—Box A, New Mexico Tech, Socorro, NM 87801. Poetry, any length, any theme; essays dealing with southwestern and native American themes. Pays with subscription.

NEW ORLEANS REVIEW—Loyola Univ., New Orleans, LA 70118. John Mosier, Ed. Literary or film criticism, to 6,000 words. Serious fiction and poetry.

THE NEW RENAISSANCE—9 Heath Rd., Arlington, MA 02174. Louise T. Reynolds, Ed. An international magazine of ideas and opinions, emphasizing literature and the arts. Query for articles; overstocked in fiction and poetry. Payment varies, after publication.

NEXUS—Wright State Univ., 006 Univ. Center, Dayton, OH 45435. Bob Moore, Ed. Poetry, hard-hitting fiction, surreal graphics and photography, "meaty" science essays. Guidelines. Pays in copies.

NIMROD—2210 S. Main St., Tulsa, OK 74114. Quality poetry and fiction, experimental and traditional. Publishes two issues annually, one awards and one thematic. Pays in copies. Annual awards for poetry and fiction. Send SASE for guidelines.

THE NORTH AMERICAN REVIEW—University of Northern Iowa, Cedar Falls, IA 50614. Peter Cooley, Poetry Ed. Poetry of high quality. Pays 50¢ a line, on acceptance.

THE NORTH DAKOTA QUARTERLY—Univ. of North Dakota, Box 8237, Grand Forks, ND 58202. Nonfiction essays in the humanities; fiction, reviews, graphics, and poetry. Limited market. Pays in copies.

THE NORTHERN REVIEW—Dept. of English, Univ. of Wisconsin/Stevens Point, Stevens Point, WI 54481. Address Man. Ed. Essays, articles (1,200 to 4,000 words), interviews, reviews, fiction, and poetry on or exploring northern themes. Pays in copies.

THE NORTHLAND QUARTERLY—(formerly *The Northland Review*) 51 E. Fourth St., Suite 412, Winona, MN 55987. Jody Wallace, Ed. Articles and fiction (1,500 to 3,500 words) on progressive issues, contemporary relationships, experimental fiction. Also includes reviews, art, essays. Poetry, any length. Query for articles. Pays in copies.

NORTHWEST REVIEW—369 PLC, Univ. of Oregon, Eugene, OR 97403. Cecelia Hagen, Fiction Ed. Serious fiction, commentary, and poetry. Reviews. Pays in copies. Send SASE for guidelines.

NYCTICORAX—1616 Wood St., Jonesboro, AR 72401. John A. Youril, Ed. Poetry (submit 4 to 8 poems at a time). Query about essays on literary criticism. Pays in copies.

OAK SQUARE—Box 1238, Allston, MA 02134. Anne E. Pluto, Fiction Ed. Scott Getchell, Poetry Ed. Experimental and traditional stories, 2,500 to 4,000 words; some poetry; nonpolitical essays and interviews. Manuscripts read Jan. 1 to June 1. Pays in copies.

THE OHIO REVIEW—Ellis Hall, Ohio Univ., Athens, OH 45701–2979. Wayne Dodd, Ed. Short stories, poetry, essays, reviews. Pays $5 per page for prose, $1 a line for poetry, plus copies, on publication. SASE required. Submissions not read in June, July or August.

ONIONHEAD—Arts on the Park, Inc., 115 N. Kentucky Ave., Lakeland, FL 33801. Short stories (to 4,000 words), essays (to 2,500 words), and poetry (to 60 lines), on provocative social, political, and cultural observations and hypotheses. Address manuscripts to the Editorial Council. Pays in copies.

OREGON EAST—Hoke College Center, EOSC, La Grande, OR 97850. Short fiction, nonfiction (to 3,000 words), and poetry (to 60 lines). Regional angle preferred. Pays in copies. Submissions by March 1, notification by June.

ORPHIC LUTE—526 Paul Pl., Los Alamos, NM 87544. Patricia Doherty Hinnebusch, Ed. Well-crafted lyric poetry, traditional and contemporary, third person perspective. Submit 4 to 5 poems at a time. Pays in copies.

OTHER VOICES—820 Ridge Rd., Highland Park, IL 60035. Dolores Weinberg, Lois Hauselman, Sharon Fiffer, Eds. Semi-annual. Fresh, accessible short stories and novel excerpts, to 5,000 words. Pays in copies and modest honorarium.

OUROBOROS—3912 24th St., Rock Island, IL 61201. Erskine Carter, Ed. Short stories (to 3,500 words) and poetry (submit 7 to 10 poems at a time). Guidelines. Pays in copies.

PAINTED BRIDE QUARTERLY—230 Vine St., Philadelphia, PA 19106. Louis Camp, and Joanne DiPaolo, Eds. Fiction, nonfiction, and poetry of varying lengths. Pays in copies and subscription.

PANDORA—2844 Grayson, Ferndale, MI 48220. Meg Mac Donald, Ed. Ruth Berman, Poetry Ed. Polly Vedder, Art Ed. Science fiction and speculative fantasy, to 4,000 words; poetry. Pays to 4¢ a word, on publication.

PARNASSUS—41 Union Sq. W., Rm. 804, New York, NY 10003. Herbert Leibowitz, Ed. Critical essays and reviews on contemporary poetry. International in scope. Pays in cash and copies.

PARTISAN REVIEW—Boston Univ., 236 Bay State Rd., Boston, MA 02215. William Phillips, Ed. Serious fiction, poetry and essays. Payment varies. No simultaneous submissions.

PASSAGES NORTH—William Bonifas Fine Arts Ctr., Escanaba, MI 49829. Elinor Benedict, Ed. Quality short fiction and contemporary poetry. Pays in copies, frequent prizes and honoraria.

THE PENNSYLVANIA REVIEW—Univ. of Pittsburgh, Dept. of English, 526 Cathedral of Learning, Pittsburgh, PA 15260. Fiction, to 5,000 words, book reviews, interviews with authors, and poetry (send as many as six at once). Pays $5 a page for prose, $5 for poetry.

PERMAFROST—English Dept., Univ. of Alaska, Fairbanks, AK 99775. Poetry, short fiction to 7,500 words, essays, and B&W photos and graphics. Reading period: Dec. 1-April 1. Pays in copies.

PIEDMONT LITERARY REVIEW—Bluebird Lane, Rt. #1, Box 512, Forest, VA 24551. Evelyn Miles, Man. Ed. Fiction, to 4,000 words. (Submit fiction to Dr. Olga Kronmeyer, 25 West Dale Dr., Lynchburg, VA 24501.) Poems, of any length and style. Special interest in young poets. (Submit up to 5 poems to Gail White, 100 Live Oak Dr., Lafayette, LA 70503.) Pays in copies.

PIG IRON—P.O. Box 237, Youngstown, OH 44501. Nate Leslie, Jim Villani, Eds. Fiction and nonfiction, to 8,000 words. Poetry, to 100 lines. Pays $5 per published page, on publication. Query for themes.

PINCHPENNY—4851 Q St., Sacramento, CA 95819. Tom Miner, Elisabeth

Goossens, Eds. Prose poems, tiny poems, short-short stories, B&W art. New writers welcome. Pays in copies.

PLAINS POETRY JOURNAL—Box 2337, Bismarck, ND 58502. Jane Greer, Ed. Poetry using traditional conventions in vigorous, compelling ways; no "greeting card"-type verse. No subject is taboo. Pays in copies.

PLOUGHSHARES—Box 529, Dept. M, Cambridge, MA 02139. Pays $10 to $50, on publication. Reading periods vary, check recent issue; guidelines.

POEM—c/o English Dept., U.A.H., Huntsville, AL 35899. Nancy Frey Dillard, Ed. Serious lyric poetry, any length. Pays in copies.

POET AND CRITIC—203 Ross Hall, Iowa State Univ., Ames, IA 50011. Neal Bowers, Ed. Poetry, reviews, essays on contemporary poetry. Pays in copies.

POET LORE—7815 Old Georgetown Rd., Bethesda, MD 20814. Sunil Freeman, Man. Ed. Original poetry, all kinds. Translations, reviews. Pays in copies. Annual narrative contest.

POETRY—60 West Walton St., Chicago, IL 60610. Joseph Parisi, Ed. Poetry of highest quality. Pays $2 a line, on publication.

PORTENTS—12 Fir Pl., Hazlet, NJ 07730. Deborah Rasmussen, Ed. Short stories (contemporary horror, dark fantasy, and supernatural horror) to 3,000 words. No werewolves, vampires, ghouls, religion, or sex. Pays ¼¢ a word. No poetry. Artists welcome.

PRAIRIE SCHOONER—201 Andrews Hall, Univ. of Nebraska, Lincoln, NE 68588. Hilda Raz, Ed. Short stories, poetry, essays, book reviews, and translations, to 6,000 words. Pays in copies. Annual contests. SASE required.

PRISM INTERNATIONAL—E459–1866 Main Mall, Dept. of Creative Writing, Univ. of British Columbia, Vancouver, B.C., Canada V6T 1W5. Janis McKenzie, Exec. Ed. High-quality fiction, poetry, drama, and literature in translation, varying lengths. Include international reply coupons. Pays $25 per published page. Annual short fiction contest.

PROOF ROCK—P.O. Box 607, Halifax, VA 24558. Don Conner, Fiction Ed., Serena Fusek, Poetry Ed. Fiction, to 2,500 words. Poetry, to 32 lines. Reviews. Pays in copies.

PUDDING—60 N. Main St., Johnstown, OH 43031. Jennifer Welch Bosveld, Ed. Poems on popular culture and social concerns, especially free verse and experimental, with fresh language, concrete images, and specific detail. Short articles about poetry in human services.

PUERTO DEL SOL—New Mexico State Univ., Box 3E, Las Cruces, NM 88003. Kevin McIlvoy, Ed. Short stories, to 30 pages; novel excerpts, to 65 pages; articles, to 45 pages, and reviews, to 15 pages. Poetry, photos. Pays in copies.

QUEEN'S QUARTERLY—Queens Univ., Kingston, Ont., Canada K7L 3N6. Articles, to 6,000 words, on a wide range of topics, and fiction, to 5,000 words. Poetry: send no more than 6 poems. B&W art. Pays to $150, on publication.

RACCOON—Ion Books, Inc., Box 111327, Memphis, TN 38111–1327. David Spicer, Ed. Poetry and poetic criticism, varying lengths. Pays in subscription for poetry, $50 for criticism, fiction.

RAMBUNCTIOUS REVIEW—1221 W. Pratt Blvd., Chicago, IL 60626. Mary Dellutri, Richard Goldman, Nancy Lennox, Beth Housler, Eds. Fiction to 15 pages, poetry (submit up to 5 at a time), short drama. Pays in copies. Submit material September through May.

RED CEDAR REVIEW—Dept. of English, Morrill Hall, Michigan State Univ., East Lansing, MI 48825. Fiction, 10 to 15 pages; poetry; interviews; book reviews; graphics. Pays in copies.

RELIGION AND PUBLIC EDUCATION—N155 Lagomarcino Hall, Iowa State Univ., Ames, IA 50011. Charles R. Kniker, Ed.-in-Chief. Paul Blakeley, Poetry Ed. Poems with mythological or religious values or themes. Pays in copies.

RHINO—1040 Judson Ave., Evanston, IL 60202. Enid Baron and Carole Hayes, Eds. "Authentic emotion in well-crafted poetry and prose poems." January to June reading period. Pays in copies.

RIVER CITY—(formerly *Memphis State Review*) Dept. of English, Memphis State Univ., Memphis, TN 38152. Short stories, novel excerpts, to 4,500 words; poetry, to one page. Pays in copies. Annual award.

RIVERSIDE QUARTERLY—P.O. Box 464, Waco, TX 76703. Science fiction and fantasy, to 3,500 words; criticism; poetry; reviews. Send fiction to Redd Boggs, Box 1111, Berkeley, CA 94701; poetry to Sheryl Smith, 515 Saratoga, Santa Clara, CA 95050. Pays in copies.

ROANOKE REVIEW—Roanoke College, Salem, VA 24153. Robert R. Walter, Ed. Quality short fiction, to 10,000 words, and poetry, to 100 lines. Pays in copies.

SAN FERNANDO POETRY JOURNAL—18301 Halstead St., Northridge, CA 91325. Richard Cloke, Ed. Quality poetry, 20 to 100 lines, with social content; scientific, philosophic, and historical themes. Pays in copies.

SAN JOSE STUDIES—San Jose State Univ., San Jose, CA 95192. Fauneil J. Rinn, Ed. Poetry, fiction, and essays on interdisciplinary topics. Pays in copies. Annual awards.

SANSKRIT LITERARY/ART PUBLICATION—Univ. of North Carolina/Charlotte, Charlotte, NC 28223. Tina McEntire, Ed.-in-Chief. Poetry, short fiction, photos, and fine art. Published annually. Pays in copies. Contest.

SCANDINAVIAN REVIEW—127 E. 73rd St., New York, NY 10021. Essays on contemporary Scandinavia. Fiction and poetry, translated from Nordic languages. Pays from $100, on publication.

SCRIVENER—McGill Univ., 853 Sherbrooke St. W., Montreal, Quebec, Canada H3A 2T6. Ernest Alston, Julie Crawford, Lisa Stankovic, Eds. Poetry, 5 to 15 lines; prose, to 20 pages; reviews, to 5 pages; essays, to 10 pages. Photography and graphics. Pays in copies.

THE SEATTLE REVIEW—Padelford Hall, GN-30, Univ. of Washington, Seattle, WA 98195. Donna Gerstenberger, Ed. Short stories (to 20 pages), poetry, essays on the craft of writing, and interviews with northwest writers. Payment varies.

SENECA REVIEW—Hobart & William Smith Colleges, Geneva, NY 14456. Poetry, translations, and essays on contemporary poetry. Pays in copies.

SHENANDOAH—Washington and Lee Univ., P.O. Box 722, Lexington, VA 24450. Dabney Stuart, Ed. Highest quality fiction, poetry, criticism, essays and interviews. Annual contests.

SHOOTING STAR REVIEW—7123 Race St., Pittsburgh, PA 15208. Sandra Gould Ford, Pub. Fiction and folktales, to 3,500 words, essays, to 2,500 words, and poetry, to 50 lines, on the African-American experience. Query for book reviews only. Pays $8 to $30, and in copies. Send SASE for topic deadlines.

SING HEAVENLY MUSE! WOMEN'S POETRY & PROSE—P.O. Box 13299, Minneapolis, MN 55414. Short stories and essays, to 5,000 words. Poetry. Query for themes and reading periods. Pays in copies.

SLIPSTREAM—Box 2071, New Market Sta., Niagara Falls, NY 14301. Fiction, 2 to 18 pages, and contemporary poetry, any length. Pays in copies. Query for themes. (Also accepting audio poetics cassette tape submissions for audio tape series: spoken word, collaborations, songs, audio experimentation.)

SMALL PRESS REVIEW—Box 100, Paradise, CA 95969. Len Fulton, Ed. News pieces and reviews, to 200 words, about small presses and little magazines. Pays in copies.

SNOWY EGRET—R.R. #1, Box 354, Poland, IN 47868. Karl Barnebey, Ed. Poetry, fiction, and nonfiction to 10,000 words. Natural history from artistic, literary, philosophical, and historical perspectives. Pays $2 per page for prose; $2 to $4 for poetry, on publication. Send poetry to Alan Seaburg, Poetry Ed., 67 Century St., West Medford, MA 02155.

SONORA REVIEW—Dept. of English, Univ. of Arizona, Tucson, AZ 85721. Martha Ostheimer, Laurie Schorr, Eds. Fiction, poetry, translations, interviews, literary nonfiction. Pays in copies. Annual prizes for fiction and poetry.

SOUTH DAKOTA REVIEW—Box 111, Univ. Exchange, Vermillion, SD 57069. John R. Milton, Ed. Exceptional fiction, 3,000 to 5,000 words, and poetry, 10 to 25 lines. Critical articles, especially on American literature, Western American literature, theory and esthetics, 3,000 to 5,000 words. Pays in copies.

SOUTHERN HUMANITIES REVIEW—9088 Haley Center, Auburn Univ., AL 36849. Thomas L. Wright, Dan R. Latimer, Eds. Short stories, essays, and criticism, 3,500 to 5,000 words; poetry, to 2 pages.

SOUTHERN POETRY REVIEW—Dept. of English, Univ. of North Carolina, Charlotte, NC 28223. Robert W. Grey, Ed. Poems. No restrictions on style, length, or content.

SOUTHERN REVIEW—43 Allen Hall, Louisiana State Univ., Baton Rouge, LA 70803. Fred Hobson, James Olney, Eds. Emphasis on contemporary literature in United States and abroad and with special interest in southern culture and history. Fiction and essays, 4,000 to 8,000 words. Serious poetry of highest quality. Pays $12 a page for prose, $20 a page for poery, on publication.

SOUTHWEST REVIEW—Southern Methodist Univ., Dallas, TX 72575. Willard Spiegelman, Ed. Fiction and essays, 3,000 to 7,500 words. Poetry. Pays varying rates.

SOU'WESTER—Dept. of English, Southern Illinois Univ. at Edwardsville, Edwardsville, IL 62026–1438. Dickie Spurgeon, Ed. Fiction, to 10,000 words. Poetry, especially poems over 100 lines. Pays in copies.

SPECTRUM—Anna Maria College, Box 72-A, Paxton, MA 01612. Robert H. Goepfert, Ed. Scholarly articles (3,000 to 15,000 words); short stories (to 10 pages) and poetry (to two pages); book reviews, photos and artwork. Pays $20 plus 2 copies.

THE SPIRIT THAT MOVES US—P.O. Box 1585 TW, Iowa City, IA 52244. Morty Sklar, Ed. Biannual. Fiction, poetry, that is expressive rather than formal or sensational. Send SASE for themes and guidelines.

SPSM&H—329 E St., Bakersfield, CA 93304. Frederick A. Raborg, Jr., Ed. Single sonnets, sequences, essays about the form, short fiction in which the sonnet plays a part, books and anthologies. Pays in copies.

STAND MAGAZINE—Box 1161, Florence, AL 35631. John and Pam Kingsbury, Eds. Fiction, 3,500 to 4,000 words, and poetry to 100 lines. No formulaic verse. Pays varying rates, on publication.

STONE COUNTRY—P.O. Box 132, Menemsha, MA 02552. Judith Neeld, Ed. High-quality contemporary poetry in all genres. Pays in copies. Semi-annual award. SASE required. Guidelines.

STORY QUARTERLY—P.O. Box 1416, Northbrook, IL 60065. Anne Brashler, Diane Williams, Eds. Short stories and interviews. Pays in copies.

STUDIES IN AMERICAN FICTION—English Dept., Northeastern Univ., Boston, MA 02115. James Nagel, Ed. Reviews, 750 words; scholarly essays, 2,500 to 6,500 words, on American fiction. Pays in copies.

SUNRUST—P.O. Box 58, New Wilmington, PA 16142. James Ashbrook Perkins, Nancy Esther James, Eds. Nonfiction, to 2,000 words, and poetry, to 75 lines, about rural life, nature, memories of the past, and small communities. Submissions accepted December 1 to January 31 and June 1 to July 31. Pays in copies.

SYCAMORE REVIEW—Purdue Univ. Dept. of English, West Lafayette, IN 47907. Address the Editors. Poetry, short fiction (no genre fiction), personal essays, and translations for biannual publication; manuscripts to 10,000 words. Pays in copies. Reading period: September to April.

TAR RIVER POETRY—Dept. of English, East Carolina Univ., Greenville, NC 27834. Peter Makuck, Ed. Poems, all styles. Interested in skillful use of figurative language. No flat statement poetry. Submit between September and May. Pays in copies.

TESTIMONY—P.O. Box 495, Montclair, NJ 07042. Sandra West, Ed. Poetry related to the Afro-American experience: "creative, soul-stirring poetry; sonnets, haiku, and political poetry." Pays in copies.

THE TEXAS REVIEW—English Dept., Sam Houston State Univ., Huntsville, TX 77341. Paul Ruffin, Ed. Fiction, poetry, articles, to 20 typed pages. Reviews. Pays in copies.

THE THREEPENNY REVIEW—P.O. Box 9131, Berkeley, CA 94709. Wendy Lesser, Ed. Fiction, to 5,000 words. Poetry, to 100 lines. Essays, on books, theater, film, dance, music, art, television, and politics, 1,500 to 3,000 words. Pays to $100, on acceptance. Limited market. Query first with SASE.

TOUCHSTONE—P.O. Box 8308, Spring, TX 77387. Bill Laufer, Pub. Quarterly. Fiction, 750 to 2,000 words: mainstream, experimental. Interviews, essays, reviews. Poetry, to 40 lines. Pays $2 to $5 for poems; $5 reviews; to $5 per page for prose.

TRANSLATION—The Translation Center, 412 Dodge Hall, Columbia Univ., New York, NY 10028. Frank MacShane, Dir. Diane G. H. Cook, Man. Ed. Semiannual. New translations of contemporary foreign fiction and poetry.

TRIQUARTERLY—Northwestern Univ., 2020 Ridge Ave., Evanston, IL 60208. Serious, aesthetically informed and inventive poetry and prose, for an international and literate audience. Pays $40 per page for prose, $2 per line for poetry. Reading period Oct. 1-April 30.

2 AM—P.O. Box 6754, Rockford, IL 61125–1754. Gretta Anderson, Ed. Poetry, articles, reviews, and personality profiles (500 to 2,000 words), as well as fantasy, horror, and some science fiction/sword and sorcery short stories (500 to 5,000 words). Pays ½¢ a word, on acceptance.

THE UNIVERSITY OF PORTLAND REVIEW—Univ. of Portland, Portland, OR 97203. Thompson H. Faller, Ed. Scholarly articles and contemporary fiction, 500 to 2,500 words. Poetry. Book reviews. Pays in copies.

UNIVERSITY OF WINDSOR REVIEW—Dept. of English, Univ. of Windsor, Windsor, Ont., Canada N9B 3P4. Joseph A. Quinn, Ed. Short stories, poetry, criticism, reviews. Pays $10 to $25, on publication.

THE VILLAGER—135 Midland Ave., Bronxville, NY 10708. Amy Murphy, Ed. Fiction, 900 to 1,500 words: mystery, adventure, humor, romance. Short, preferably seasonal poetry. Pays in copies.

VIRGINIA QUARTERLY REVIEW—One W. Range, Charlottesville, VA 22903. Quality fiction and poetry. Serious essays and articles, 3,000 to 6,000 words, on literature, science, politics, economics, etc. Pays $10 per page for prose, $1 per line for poetry, on publication.

WASCANA REVIEW—c/o Dept. of English, Univ. of Regina, Regina, Sask., Canada S4S OA2. Joan Givner, Ed. Short stories, 2,000 to 6,000 words; critical articles; poetry. Pays $3 per page for prose, $10 for poetry, after publication.

WASHINGTON REVIEW—P.O. Box 50132, Washington, DC 20004. Clarissa Wittenberg, Ed. Poetry; articles on literary, performing and fine arts in the Washington, D.C., area. Fiction, 1,000 to 2,500 words. Area writers preferred. Pays in copies.

WEBSTER REVIEW—Webster Univ., 470 E. Lockwood, Webster Groves, MO 63119. Nancy Schapiro, Ed. Fiction; poetry; interviews; essays; translations. Pays in copies.

WEST BRANCH—Bucknell Hall, Bucknell Univ., Lewisburg, PA 17837. Karl Patten, Robert Taylor, Eds. Poetry and fiction. Pays in copies and subscriptions.

THE WINDLESS ORCHARD—Dept. of English, Indiana-Purdue Univ., Ft. Wayne, IN 46805. Robert Novak, Ed. Contemporary poetry. Pays in copies. SASE required.

WITHOUT HALOS—Ocean County Poets Collective, P.O. Box 1342, Point Pleasant Beach, NJ 08742. Frank Finale, Ed. Submit poems (to 2 pages) between Jan. 1 and June 30. Pays in copies.

WOMAN OF POWER—Box 827, Cambridge, MA 02238–0827. Char McKee, Ed. A magazine of feminism, spirituality, and politics. Fiction and nonfiction, to 3,500 words. Poetry; submit up to 5 poems at a time. Send SASE for themes and guidelines. Pays in copies.

WRITERS FORUM—Univ. of Colorado, Colorado Springs, CO 80933–7150. Alex Blackburn, Ed. Annual. Mainstream and experimental fiction, 1,000 to 10,000 words. Poetry (1 to 5 poems per submission). Emphasis on Western themes and writers. Send material October through May. Pays in copies.

WYOMING, THE HUB OF THE WHEEL—The Willow Bee Publishing House, Box 9, Saratoga, WY 82331. Lenore A. Senior, Man. Ed. Fiction and nonfiction, to 2,500 words; poetry, to 80 lines. "An international literary/art magazine devoted to peace, the human race, positive relationships, and the human spirit and possibilities." Pays in copies.

YALE REVIEW—1902A Yale Sta., New Haven, CT 06520. Penelope Laurans, Ed. Serious poetry, to 200 lines, and fiction, 3,000 to 5,000 words. Pays nominal sum.

ZYZZYVA—41 Sutter, Suite 1400, San Francisco, CA 94104. Howard Junker, Ed. Publishes work of West Coast writers only: fiction, essays, and poetry. Pays $25 to $100, on acceptance.

HUMOR, FILLERS, SHORT ITEMS

Magazines noted for their excellent filler departments, plus a cross-section of publications using humor, short items, jokes, quizzes, and cartoons, follow. However, almost all magazines use some type of filler material, and writers can find dozens of markets by studying copies of magazines at a library or newsstand.

ALCOHOLISM & ADDICTION MAGAZINE—P. O. Box 31329, Seattle, WA 98103. News briefs, program updates, and personnel changes of interest to professionals in the addictions field.

THE AMERICAN FIELD—542 S. Dearborn, Chicago, IL 60605. W.F. Brown, Ed. Short farce items and anecdotes on hunting dogs, and field trials for bird dogs. Pays varying rates, on acceptance.

THE AMERICAN LEGION MAGAZINE—Box 1055, Indianapolis, IN 46206. Parting Shots Page: short, humorous anecdotes appealing to military veterans and their families. General humor: no sex, religion, ethnic humor, or political satire. Pays $15 for definitions, anecdotes, and gags, on acceptance. No poetry.

THE AMERICAN NEWSPAPER CARRIER—P.O. Box 15300, Winston-Salem, NC 27103. Short, humorous pieces, to 1,200 words, for preteen and teenage newspaper carriers. Pays $25, on publication.

ARMY MAGAZINE—2425 Wilson Blvd., Arlington, VA 22201–3385. L. James Binder, Ed.-in-Chief. True anecdotes on military subjects. Pays $10 to $35, on publication.

THE ATLANTIC—745 Boylston St., Boston, MA 02116. Sophisticated humorous or satirical pieces, 1,000 to 3,000 words. Some light poetry. Pays excellent rates, on acceptance.

ATLANTIC SALMON JOURNAL—1435 St. Alexandre, Suite 1030, Montreal, Quebec, Canada H3A 2G4. Terry Davis, Ed. Fillers, 50 to 100 words, on salmon politics, conservation, and nature. Cartoons. Pays $10 for fillers, $25 for cartoons, on publication.

BICYCLING—33 E. Minor St., Emmaus, PA 18098. Anecdotes, helpful cycling tips, and other items for "Paceline" section, 150 to 250 words. Pays $50, on publication.

BIKEREPORT—Bikecentennial, P.O. Box 8308, Missoula, MT 59807. Daniel D'Ambrosio, Ed. News shorts from the bicycling world for "In Bicycle Circles." Pays $5 to $10, on publication.

CAPPER'S—616 Jefferson St., Topeka, KS 66607. Nancy Peavler, Ed. Household hints, recipes, jokes. Pays varying rates, on publication.

CASCADES EAST—716 N. E. 4th St., P. O. Box 5784, Bend, OR 97708.

Geoff Hill, Ed. Fillers, related to travel, history, and recreation in Central Oregon. Pays 3¢ to 10¢ a word, extra for photos, on publication.

CASHFLOW—6255 Barfield Rd., Atlanta, GA 30328. Dick Gamble, Ed. Fillers, to 1,000 words, on varied aspects of treasury financial management and corporate finance, for treasury managers in public and private institutions. Pays on publication. Query.

CATHOLIC DIGEST—P.O. Box 64090, St. Paul, MN 55164. Features, to 300 words, on instances of kindness rewarded, for "Hearts Are Trumps." Stories about conversions, for "Open Door." Reports of tactful remarks or actions, for "The Perfect Assist." Accounts of good deeds, for "People Are Like That." Humorous pieces on parish life, for "In Our Parish." Amusing signs, for "Signs of the Times." Jokes; fillers. Pays $4 to $50, on publication. Manuscripts cannot be acknowledged or returned.

CHEESE MARKET NEWS—Gorman Publishing Co., 8750 W. Bryn Mawr, Chicago, IL 60631. Jerry Dryer, Ed. Fillers, 25 to 150 words, on innovative dairies, dairy processing operations, marketing successes, for milk handlers and makers of dairy products. Pays $25, on publication.

CHIC—9171 Wilshire Blvd., Suite 300, Beverly Hills, CA 90210. Visual fillers, short humor, with photos, 100 to 125 words, for "Odds and Ends." Pays on acceptance.

CHICKADEE—56 The Esplanade, Suite 306, Toronto, Ont., Canada M5E 1A7. Humorous poetry, 10 to 15 lines, about animals and nature, for children. Pays on publication. Enclose international reply coupons.

CHILDREN'S PLAYMATE—1100 Waterway Blvd., P. O. Box 567, Indianapolis, IN 46206. Elizabeth Rinck, Ed. Puzzles, games, mazes for 5- to 7-year-olds, emphasizing health, safety, and nutrition. Pays about 8¢ a word (varies on puzzles), on acceptance.

CHRISTIAN HERALD—40 Overlook Dr., Chappaqua, NY 10514. Bob Chuvala, Ed. For "The Two of Us": memorable, humorous, or touching moments in the life of a Christian marriage. For "Kids of the Kingdom": funny or revealing things that happened to you in the process of raising, teaching, or working with Christian kids. Both columns, pieces 75 to 200 words. Pay $25, on acceptance.

THE CHURCH MUSICIAN—127 Ninth Ave. N., Nashville, TN 37234. W. M. Anderson, Ed. For Southern Baptist music leaders. Humorous fillers with a music slant. No clippings. Pays around 5¢ a word, on acceptance. Same address and requirements for *Glory Songs* (for adults) and *Opus One* and *Opus Two* (for teenagers).

COLUMBIA JOURNALISM REVIEW—Columbia University, 700 Journalism Bldg., New York, NY 10027. Gloria Cooper, Man. Ed. Amusing mistakes in news stories, headlines, photos, etc. (original clippings required), for "Lower Case." Pays $10, on publication.

COUNTRY—5400 S. 60th St, Greendale, WI 53129. Fillers, 50 to 200 words, for rural audience. Pays on acceptance. Address Jean VanDyke.

COUNTRY WOMAN—P. O. Box 643, Milwaukee, WI 53201. Kathy Pohl, Man. Ed. Short verse, 4 to 20 lines, and fillers, to 250 words, on the rural experience. Pays $10 to $50, on acceptance.

CURRENT COMEDY FOR SPEAKERS—(formerly *Orben's Current Comedy*) 165 W. 47th St., New York, NY 10036. Gary Apple, Ed. Original, funny, performable one-liners and brief jokes on news, fads, topical subjects, etc. Jokes for roasts, retirement dinners, and for speaking engagements. Humorous material specifically geared for public speaking situations such as microphone feedback, hecklers, etc. Pays $12, after publication.

CYCLE WORLD—853 W. 17th St., Costa Mesa, CA 92627. David Edwards, Ed. News items on motorcycle industry, legislation, trends. Pays on acceptance.

CZESCHIN'S MUTUAL FUND OUTLOOK & RECOMMENDATIONS —P.O. Box 1423, Baltimore, MD 21203–1423. Robert W. Czeschin, Ed. Short features, to 1,000 words, on all aspects of mutual funds and mutual fund investing: IRA's, switching strategies, non-U. S. funds, taxes, etc. Pays $100, on acceptance.

DOWN EAST—Camden, ME 04843. Anecdotes about Maine, to 1,000 words, for "I Remember." Humorous anecdotes, to 300 words, for "It Happened Down East." Pays $25 to $75, on acceptance

THE ELKS MAGAZINE—425 W. Diversey Pkwy., Chicago, IL 60614. Fred D. Oakes, Exec. Ed. Informative or humorous pieces, to 2,500 words. Pays from $150, on acceptance. Query.

FACES—20 Grove St., Peterborough, NH 03458. Carolyn Yoder, Ed. Puzzles, mazes, crosswords, and picture puzzles, related to monthly themes, for children. Send SASE for list of themes before submitting.

FARM AND RANCH LIVING—5400 S. 60th St., Greendale, WI 53129. Bob Ottum, Ed. Fillers on rural people and living, 200 words. Pays from $15, on acceptance and publication.

FATE—P.O. Box 64383, St. Paul, MN 55164–0383. Donald Michael Kaag, Ed. Factual fillers, to 300 words, on strange or psychic happenings. True stories, to 300 words, on psychic or mystic personal experiences. Pays $2 to $15.

FIELD & STREAM—2 Park Ave., New York, NY 10016. Duncan Barnes, Ed. Fillers on hunting, fishing, camping, etc., to 1,000 words. Cartoons. Pays $250 to $750 for fillers, $100 for cartoons, on acceptance.

FLARE—777 Bay St., Toronto, Ont., Canada M5W 1A7. Career-related items, profiles, 100 to 150 words, for young Canadian working women ages 18 to 34. Pays on acceptance. Query.

FLY FISHERMAN—Harrisburg, PA 17105. Jack Russell, Assoc. Ed. Fillers, 100 words, on equipment tackle tips, knots, and fly-tying tips. Pays from $35, on acceptance.

FORD TIMES—One Illinois Center, 111 E. Wacker Dr., Suite 1700, Chicago, IL 60601. John Fink, Ed. Short, 150 words, vacation/travel/dining anecdotes for "Road Show." Pays $50, on publication.

GALLERY—401 Park Ave. S., New York, NY 10016–8802. Marc Lichter, Ed. Dir., Barry Janoff, Man. Ed. Short humor, satire, and short service features for men. Pays varying rates, on acceptance and publication. Query.

GAMES—810 Seventh Ave., New York, NY 10019. R. Wayne Schmittberger, Ed. Short articles on playful subjects and original games and puzzles. Pays varying rates, on acceptance. Query.

GLAMOUR—350 Madison Ave., New York, NY 10017. Articles, 1,000 words, for "Viewpoint" section: opinion pieces for women. Pays $500, on acceptance. Send SASE.

GLORY SONGS—See *The Church Musician.*

GOLF DIGEST—5520 Park Ave., Trumbull, CT 06611. Topsy Siderowf, Ed. Asst. Short fact items, anecdotes, quips, jokes, light verse related to golf. True humorous or odd incidents, to 200 words. Pays from $25, on acceptance.

GOLF ILLUSTRATED—3 Park Ave., New York, NY 10016. Golf-related fillers; one- to two-paragraph news or personal-experience snippets, preferably of humorous or offbeat nature. Pays $25 to $100, on acceptance.

GOLF MAGAZINE—2 Park Ave., New York, NY 10016. James Frank, Exec. Ed. Shorts, to 500 words, on golf. Pays $75 to $150, on publication.

GOOD HOUSEKEEPING—959 Eighth Ave., New York, NY 10019. Rosemary Leonard, Ed. Two to eight lines of witty poetry, light verse, and quips with broad appeal, easy to illustrate for "Light Housekeeping" page. Seasonal material welcome. Pays $25 to $50, on acceptance.

GUIDEPOSTS—747 Third Ave., New York, NY 10017. Rick Hamlin, Features Ed. Inspirational anecdotes, to 250 words. Pays $10 to $50, on acceptance.

HEARTH & HOME—(formerly *Wood 'n Energy*) P. O. Box 2008, Laconia, NH 03247. Jason Perry, Ed. Short pieces, 150 to 500 words, for columns: "Reports" (energy news); "Regulations" (Safety and standards news); and "Retailers Corner" (tips on running a retail shop). Pays to $50, on publication.

HOME LIFE—127 Ninth Ave. N., Nashville, TN 37234. Charlie Warren, Ed. Southern Baptist. Personal-experience pieces, 100 to 500 words, on Christian marriage and family relationships. Pays to 5¢ a word, on acceptance.

HOME MECHANIX—2 Park Ave., New York, NY 10016. Michael Morris, Ed. Time- or money-saving tips for the home, garage, or yard; seasonal reminders for homeowners. Pays $50, on acceptance.

INDEPENDENT LIVING—44 Broadway, New York, NY 11740. Anne Kelly, Ed. Short humor, to 500 words, for magazine addressing lifestyles and home health care of persons who have disabilities. Pays 10¢ a word, on publication. Query.

LADIES' HOME JOURNAL—"Last Laughs," 100 Park Ave., New York, NY 10017. Brief, true anecdotes about the amusing things children say for "Out of the Mouths of Babes" column and short poetry about the funny business of being a woman today. All material must be original. Pays $25 for children's anecdotes; $50 for poems and other humor. Submissions cannot be acknowledged; will return if accompanied by SASE.

MCCALL'S—Child Care Dept., 230 Park Ave., New York, NY 10169. Parenting tips and ideas, or words of wisdom on raising children. Pays $10. Include home phone and Social Security number with submission.

MAD MAGAZINE—485 Madison Ave., New York , NY 10022. Humorous pieces on a wide variety of topics. Two- to eight-panel cartoons; sketches not necessary. SASE for Guidelines. Pays top rates, on acceptance.

MATURE LIVING—127 Ninth Ave. N., MSN 140, Nashville, TN 37234. Brief, humorous, original items; 25 line profiles with action photos; "Grandparents Brag Board" items; inspirational pieces for senior adults, 125 words. Pays $5 to $15.

MATURE YEARS—201 Eighth Ave. S., P.O. Box 801, Nashville, TN 37202. Donn C. Downall, Ed. Poems, cartoons, puzzles, jokes, anecdotes, to 300 words, for older adults. Allow two months for manuscript evaluation. Include name, address, Social Security number with all submissions.

MID-WEST OUTDOORS—111 Shore Dr., Hinsdale, IL 60521. Gene Laulunen, Man. Ed. Where to and how to fish in the Midwest, 400 to 1,500 words, with two photos. Pays $15 to $35, on publication.

MODERN MATURITY—3200 E. Carson St., Lakewood, CA 90712. Ian Ledgerwood, Ed. Money-saving tips; jokes, cartoons; etc. Submit seasonal material 6 months in advance. Pays from $50, on acceptance. Query.

MODERN SHORT STORIES—500-B Bi-County Blvd., Farmingdale, NY 11735. Glenn Steckler, Ed. Fillers and short humor. Pays $5, on acceptance.

NATIONAL ENQUIRER—Lantana , FL 33464. Jim Allan, Asst. Ed. Short, humorous or philosophical fillers, witticisms, anecdotes, jokes, tart comments. Original items preferred. Short poetry with traditional rhyming verse, of amusing, philosophical, or inspirational nature. No obscure or arty poetry. Occasionally uses longer poems of a serious or humorous nature. Submit seasonal/holiday material at least two months in advance. SASE with all submissions. Pays from $20, after publication.

NEW CHOICES FOR THE BEST YEARS—28 W. 23rd St., New York, NY 10010. Carol Mauro, Exec. Ed. Lifestyle/service magazine for people ages 50 and up. Humor pieces, 1,000 to 1,500 words, for "Back Talk" column. Payment varies, on acceptance.

NEW JERSEY MONTHLY—P.O. Box 920, Morristown, NJ 07963–0920. Patrick Sarver, Exec. Ed. Short pieces related to life in New Jersey. Pays 30¢ a word, on acceptance.

NEW YORK—755 Second Ave. , New York, NY 10017. Daniel Shaw, Assoc. Ed. Short, lively pieces, to 400 words, highlighting events and trends in New York City for "Fast Track." Profiles to 300 words for "Brief Lives." Pays $25 to $300, on publication. Include SASE.

THE NEW YORKER—25 W. 43rd St., New York, NY 10036. Amusing mistakes in newspapers, books, magazines, etc. Pays from $10, extra for headings and tags, on acceptance. Address Newsbreaks Dept. Material returned only with SASE.

NORTH GEORGIA JOURNAL—110 Hunters Mill, Woodstock, GA 30188. Olin Jackson, Pub./Ed. Fillers and humor, 100 to 500 words, on north Georgia region. Pays $50, on acceptance.

NORTHWEST LIVING!—130 Second St. S., Edmonds, WA 98020. Terry S. Heely, Ed. Shorts, 100 to 400 words, related to the natural resources of the Northwest. Query first with SASE. Pays on publication.

OPUS ONE AND OPUS TWO—See *The Church Musician.*

ORBEN'S CURRENT COMEDY—See *Current Comedy For Speakers.*

OUTDOOR LIFE—2 Park Ave., New York, NY 10016. Clare Conley, Ed. Short instructive items and one-pagers on hunting, fishing, camping gear, boats, outdoor equipment. Photos. Pays on acceptance.

PARISH FAMILY DIGEST—200 Noll Plaza, Huntington, IN 46750. George P. Foster, Ed. Family- or Catholic parish-oriented humor. Anecdotes, to 250 words, of unusual parish experiences. Pays $5, on acceptance.

PENNYWHISTLE PRESS—Box 500-P, Washington, DC 20044. Anita Sama, Ed. Puzzlers, word games, stories, for 6- to 12-year-olds. Pays varying rates, on acceptance.

PEOPLE IN ACTION—P.O. Box 10010, Ogden, UT 84409. Profiles of gourmet chefs, first-class restaurant managers, food or nutrition experts, and celebrity cooks; 700 words, including recipe plus color photos of the finished dish, and the cook. Query with SASE to editor.

PGA MAGAZINE—The Quarton Group, 2701 Troy Center Dr., #430, Troy, MI 48084. Humorous pieces related to golf, to 1,500 words. Pays to $300, on acceptance.

PHILIP MORRIS MAGAZINE—153 Waverly Pl., 3rd Floor, New York, NY 10014. Frank Gannon, Ed. Tobacco trivia, products, anecdotes, history. Pays on publication.

PLAYBOY—680 N.Lakeshore Dr., Chicago, IL 60611. Address Party Jokes Ed. or After Hours Ed. Jokes; short original material on new trends, lifestyles, personalities; humorous new items. Pays $100 for jokes, on publication; $50 to $350 for "After Hours" items, on publication.

PLAYGIRL—801 Second Ave., New York, NY 10017. Humorous looks at daily life and relationships from male or female perspective, to 1,000 words, for "The Men's Room" and "The Women's Room." Query Nonfiction Ed. Cartoons dealing with women and women's issues. Susan Bax, Cartoon Ed. Pays varying rates.

POPULAR MECHANICS—224 W. 57th St., New York, NY 10019. Bill Hartford, Man. Ed. How-to pieces, from 300 words, with photos and sketches, on home improvement and shop and craft projects. Pays $25 to $300, on acceptance. Buys all rights.

REAL PEOPLE—950 Third Ave., New York, NY 10022–2705. Alex Polner, Ed. Briefs (to 100 words) on "people now living who have exhibited uncommon courage in the face of adversity to help others." Submit with clear color or B&W photo or slide. Pays $25, on publication.

RECOVERY LIFE—P. O. Box 31329, Seattle, WA 98103. Stories, poetry, and fillers of interest to those recovering from alcohol and other addictions. SASE required.

RIVER RUNNER—P.O. Box 2073, Durango, CO 81302. Ken Hulick, Ed. Tips for whitewater boaters of all levels. Pays from 10¢ a word, on publication.

ROAD KING—P. O. Box 250, Park Forest, IL 60466. Address Features Ed. Trucking-related cartoons for "Loads of Laughs"; anecdotes to 200 words, for "Trucker's Life." Pays $25 for cartoons, $25 for anecdotes, on publication. SASE required.

THE ROTARIAN—1560 Sherman Ave., Evanston, IL 60201. Willmon L. White, Ed. Occasional humor articles. Payment varies, on acceptance.

SACRAMENTO—1021 Second St., Sacramento, CA 95814. "City Lights," interesting and unusual people, places, and behind-the-scenes news items, 75 to 250 words. All material must have Sacramento tie-in. Pays on acceptance.

THE SATURDAY EVENING POST—1100 Waterway Blvd., Indianapolis, IN 46202. Jack Gramling, Post Scripts Ed. Humor and satire, to 300 words; light verse, cartoons, jokes, for "Post Scripts." Pays $15, on publication.

SCHOOL SHOP—Prakken Publishing, Box 8623, 416 Longshore Dr., Ann Arbor, MI 48107. Alan H. Jones, Pub. and Exec. Ed. Puzzles and cartoons of interest to technology and industrial education teachers and administrators. Pay varies, on publication.

SCORE, CANADA'S GOLF MAGAZINE—287 MacPherson Ave.,

Toronto, Ont., Canada M4V 1A4. John Gordon, Man. Ed. Fillers, 50 to 100 words, related to Canadian golf scene. Rarely uses humor or poems. Pays $10 to $25, on publication. Include international reply coupons.

SELECT HOMES—3835 W. 30th Ave., Vancouver, B.C., Canada V6S 1W9. Pam Withers, Ed. Humorous pieces, 650 words, on homeowning and home renovating, for "Back Porch." Pays from $200 (Canadian), on acceptance. Query regional editors: Pam Withers, Western Editor (address above); or Diane McDougall, Ed., 2300 Yonge St., Suite 401, Toronto, Ontario, Canada M4P 1E4.

SKI MAGAZINE—2 Park Ave., New York, NY 10016. Dick Needham, Ed. Short, 100- to 300-word items on events and people in skiing, for "Ski Life" department. Humor, 300 to 2,000 words, related to skiing. Pays on acceptance.

SNOWMOBILE—319 Barry Ave. S. Suite 101, Wayzata, MN 55391. Dick Hendricks, Ed. Short humor and cartoons on snowmobiling and winter "Personality Plates" sighted. Pays varying rates, on publication.

SOAP OPERA UPDATE—158 Linwood Plaza, Ft. Lee, NJ 97024. Allison J. Walsman, Man. Ed. Soap-opera oriented fillers, to 500 words. Payment varies, on publication.

SOUTHERN OUTDOORS—1 Bell Rd., Montgomery, AL 35117. Larry Teague, Ed. Humor, 800 to 1,200 words, related to the outdoors. Pays 15¢ to 20¢ a word, on acceptance.

SPORTS AFIELD—250 W. 55th St., New York, NY 10019. Unusual, useful tips, anecdotes, 100 to 300 words, for "Almanac" section: hunting, fishing, camping, boating, etc. Photos. Pays 10¢ per column inch, on publication.

STAR—660 White Plains Rd., Tarrytown, NY 10591. Topical articles, 50 to 800 words, on human-interest subjects, show business, lifestyles, the sciences, etc., for family audience. Pays varying rates.

TOUCH—Box 7259, Grand Rapids, MI 49510. Carol Smith, Man. Ed. Bible puzzles on themes from NIV version, for Christian girls aged 8 to 14. Pays $5 to $10 per puzzle, on acceptance. Send SASE for theme update.

TRAILER BOATS MAGAZINE—20700 Belshaw Ave., Carson, CA 90746. Chuck Coyne, Ed. Fillers and humor, preferably with illustrations, on boating and related activities. Pays $5 per column inch, extra for photos, on publication.

TRAVEL SMART—Dobbs Ferry, NY 10522. Interesting, unusual travel-related tips. Practical information for vacation or business travel. Query for over 250 words. Pays $5 to $50.

TRUE CONFESSIONS—215 Lexington Ave., New York, NY 10016. Helen Atkocius, Ed. Warm, inspirational first-person fillers, 300 to 700 words, about love, marriage, family life, for "The Feminine Side of Things." Pays after publication. Buys all rights.

THE VIRGINIAN—P.O. Box 8, New Hope, VA 24469. Hunter S. Pierce, IV, Ed. Fillers, related to Virginia and adjacent regions of the South. Anecdotes and nostalgia preferred. Pays on publication.

VOLKSWAGEN'S WORLD—P. O. Box 3951, 888 W. Big Beaver, Troy, MI 48007–3951. Marlene Goldsmith, Ed. Anecdotes, to 100 words, about Volkswagen owners' experiences; humorous photos of current model Volkswagens. Pays from $15 to $40, on acceptance.

WASHINGTON'S ALMANAC—200 W. Thomas, Seattle, WA 98119. J.

Kingston Pierce, Sr. Ed. Fillers and short humor pieces related to Washington state. Pays varying rates, on publication.

WISCONSIN TRAILS—P. O. Box 5650, Madison, WI 53705. Short fillers about Wisconsin: places to go, things to see, etc., 500 words. Pays $100, on publication.

WOMAN'S DAY—1515 Broadway, New York, NY 10036. Heart-warming anecdotes about a "good neighbor"; creative solutions to community or family problems. For "Tips to Share": short pieces of personal, instructive or family experiences, practical suggestions for homemakers. Pays $75, on publication.

WOODENBOAT MAGAZINE—Box 78, Brooklin, ME 04616. Jon Wilson, Ed. News of wooden boat-related activities and projects. Pays $5 to $50, on publication.

JUVENILE, TEENAGE, AND YOUNG ADULT MAGAZINES

JUVENILE MAGAZINES

CHICKADEE—The Young Naturalist Foundation, 56 The Esplanade, Suite 306, Toronto, Ont., Canada M5E 1A7. Janis Nostbakken, Ed. Animal and adventure stories, 200 to 800 words, for children aged 3 to 8. Also, puzzles, activities, and observation games, 50 to 100 words. Pays varying rates, on publication. Send complete manuscript and international postal coupons. No outlines.

CHILDREN'S ALBUM—P.O. Box 6086, Concord, CA 94524. Kathy Madsen, Ed. Fiction and poetry by children 8 to 14. Science and crafts projects, with step-by-step instructions. Pays $50 per page. Guidelines.

CHILDREN'S DIGEST—1100 Waterway Blvd., P.O. Box 567, Indianapolis, IN 46202. Elizabeth Rinck, Ed. Health publication for children aged 8 to 10. Informative articles, 500 to 1,200 words, and fiction (especially realistic, adventure, mystery, and humorous), 500 to 1,500 words, with health, safety, exercise, nutrition, or hygiene as theme. Historical and biographical articles. Poetry. Pays 8¢ a word, from $10 for poems, on publication.

CHILDREN'S PLAYMATE—Editorial Office, 1100 Waterway Blvd., P.O. Box 567, Indianapolis, IN 46206. Elizabeth Rinck, Ed. Humorous and health-related short stories, 500 to 700 words, for 5- to 7-year-olds. Simple science articles and how-to crafts pieces with brief instructions. "All About" features, about 500 words, on health, nutrition, safety, and exercise. Poems. Pays about 8¢ a word, $10 minimum for poetry, on publication.

CHILDREN'S SURPRISES—P.O. Box 236, Chanhassen, MN 55317. Peggy Simenson, Jeanne Palmer, Eds. "Activities for today's kids and parents." Educational activities, puzzles, games in reading, language, math, science, cooking, music, and art. Articles about history, animals, and geography. Pays $15 to $35, on publication.

666

CLUBHOUSE—Berrien Springs, MI 49103. Elaine Trumbo, Ed. Action-oriented Christian stories: features, 800 to 1,200 words. Children in stories should be wise, brave, funny, kind, etc. Pays to $30 to $35 for stories.

COBBLESTONE—20 Grove St., Peterborough, NH 03458. Carolyn Yoder, Ed. Theme-related biographies, fiction, poetry, and short accounts of historical events, to 1,200 words, for children aged 8 to 14 years. Pays 10¢ to 15¢ a word for prose, varying rates for poetry, on publication. Send SASE for editorial guidelines with monthly themes.

CRICKET—Box 300, Peru, IL 61354. Marianne Carus, Ed.-in-Chief. Articles and fiction, 200 to 1,500 words, for 6- to 12-year-olds. Poetry, to 30 lines. Pays to 25¢ a word, to $3 a line for poetry, on publication. SASE required. Guidelines.

DISCOVERIES—6401 The Paseo, Kansas City, MO 64131. Stories, 400 to 500 words, for 3rd to 6th graders, with Christian emphasis. Poetry, 4 to 20 lines. Cartoons. Pays 3 ½¢ a word (2¢ a word for reprints), 25¢ a line for poetry (minimum of $2), on acceptance. Send SASE with manuscript.

THE DOLPHIN LOG—The Cousteau Society, 8440 Santa Monica Blvd., Los Angeles, CA 90069. Pam Stacey, Ed. Articles, 500 to 1,200 words, on a variety of topics related to our global water system: marine biology, ecology, natural history, and water-related stories, for children aged 7 to 15. Pays $25 to $150, on publication. Query.

THE FRIEND—50 E. North Temple, 23rd Floor, Salt Lake City, UT 84150. Vivian Paulsen, Man. Ed. Stories and articles, 1,000 to 1,200 words. (Prefers completed manuscripts.) "Tiny tot" stories, to 250 words. Pays from 8¢ a word, from $15 per poem, on acceptance.

HIGHLIGHTS FOR CHILDREN—803 Church St., Honesdale, PA 18431. Kent L. Brown, Ed. Fiction and articles, to 900 words, for 2- to 12-year-olds. Fiction should have strong plot, believable characters, story that holds reader's interest from beginning to end. No crime or violence. For articles, cite references used and qualifications. Easy rebus-form stories. Easy-to-read stories, 400 to 600 words, with strong plots. Pays from 14¢ a word, on acceptance.

HOPSCOTCH—P.O. Box 1292, Saratoga Springs, NY 12866. Donald P. Evans, Ed. Bimonthly. Articles and fiction (600 to 1,200 words) and short poetry for girls ages 6 to 12. "We believe young girls deserve the right to enjoy a season of childhood before they become young adults; we are not interested in such topics as sex, romance, cosmetics, hair-styles, etc." Pays 5¢ per word; $150 for cover photos, made on publication.

HUMPTY DUMPTY'S MAGAZINE—1100 Waterway Blvd., P.O. Box 567, Indianapolis, IN 46206. Christine French Clark, Ed. Health publication for children ages 4 to 6. Easy-to-read fiction, to 600 words, some with health and nutrition, safety, exercise, or hygiene as theme; humor and light approach preferred. Creative nonfiction, including photo stories. Crafts with clear, brief instructions. No-cook recipes using healthful ingredients. Short verse, narrative poems. Pays about 8¢ a word, from $10 for poems, on publication. Buys all rights.

JUNIOR TRAILS—1445 Boonville Ave., Springfield, MO 65802. Cathy Ketcher, Ed. Fiction (1,000 to 1,800 words) with a Christian focus, believable characters, and moral emphasis. Articles (500 to 1,000 words) on science, nature, biography. Pays 2¢ or 3¢ a word, on acceptance.

KID CITY—See *3-2-1 Contact.*

LOLLIPOPS—Good Apple, Inc., P.O. Box 299, Carthage, IL 62321–0299.

Learning games and activities covering all areas of the curriculum; arts and crafts ideas; stories, for ages 4 to 7. Pays varying rates, on publication. Query first.

NATIONAL GEOGRAPHIC WORLD—1145 17th St. N.W., Washington, DC 20036. Pat Robbins, Ed. Picture magazine for young readers, ages 8 and older. Games and puzzles; proposals for picture stories. Pays $25 for games. Queries required for stories.

ODYSSEY—1027 N. 7th St., Milwaukee, WI 53233. Nancy Mack, Ed. Features, 600 to 1,500 words, on astronomy and space science for 8- to 14-year-olds. Short experiments, projects, and games. Pays $100 to $350, on publication.

ON THE LINE—616 Walnut, Scottdale, PA 15683–1999. Virginia A. Hostetler, Ed. Weekly paper for 10- to 14- year olds. Uses nature and how-to articles, 500 to 650 words; fiction, 900–1,200 words; poetry, puzzles, cartoons. Pays to 4¢ a word, on acceptance.

OWL—The Young Naturalist Foundation, 56 The Esplanade, Suite 306, Toronto, Ont., Canada M5E 1A7. Sylvia Funston, Ed. Articles, 500 to 1,000 words, for children ages 8 to 12 about animals, science, people, technology, new discoveries, activities. Pays varying rates, on publication. Send for guidelines.

PENNYWHISTLE PRESS—Box 500-P, Washington, DC 20044. Anita Sama, Ed. Short fiction, 850 words, for 8- to 12-year-old children, 400 words for 5- to 8-year-olds. Puzzles and word games. Payment varies, on publication.

PLAYS, THE DRAMA MAGAZINE FOR YOUNG PEOPLE—120 Boylston St., Boston, MA 02116. Elizabeth Preston, Man. Ed. Needs one-act plays, programs, skits, creative dramatic material, suitable for school productions at junior high, middle, and lower grade levels. Plays with one set preferred. Uses comedies, dramas, satires, farces, melodramas, dramatized classic, folktales and fairy tales, puppet plays. Pays good rates, on acceptance. Buys all rights. Guidelines. SASE.

POCKETS—1908 Grand Ave., Box 189, Nashville, TN 37202. Janet Bugg, Ed. Ecumenical magazine for children ages 6 to 12. Fiction and scripture stories, 600 to 1,500 words; short poems; and articles about the Bible, 400 to 600 words. Pays from 10¢ a word, $25 to $50 for poetry, on acceptance. Guidelines.

RADAR—8121 Hamilton Ave., Cincinnati, OH 45231. Margaret Williams, Ed. Articles, 400 to 650 words, on nature, hobbies, crafts. Short stories, 900 to 1,000 words: mystery, sports, school, family, with 12-year-old as main character; serials of 2,000 words. Christian emphasis. Poems to 12 lines. Pays to 3¢ a word, to 40¢ a line for poetry, on acceptance.

RANGER RICK—1400 16th St. N.W., Washington, DC 20036. Gerald Bishop, Ed. Articles, to 900 words, on wildlife, conservation, natural sciences, and kids in the outdoors, for 6- to 12-year-olds. Nature-related fiction and science fiction welcome. Games, crafts, poems, and puzzles. Pays to $550, on acceptance.

SESAME STREET MAGAZINE—See *3–2–1 Contact.*

SHOFAR—43 Northcote Dr., Melville, NY 11747. Gerald H. Grayson, Ed. Short stories, 500 to 750 words; articles, 250 to 750 words; poetry, to 50 lines; short fillers, games, puzzles, and cartoons, for Jewish children, 8 to 13. All material must have a Jewish theme. Pays 10¢ a word, on publication. Submit holiday pieces at least three months in advance.

THE SMALL STREET JOURNAL—405 E. Colorado Ave., Colorado Springs, CO 80903. Jan Mathis, Assoc. Ed. Animal-related fiction and nonfiction,

300 words, 4- to 8-line poetry, fillers, jokes, and puzzles. Pays $5 to $25, on publication. Send SASE for themes.

STONE SOUP, THE MAGAZINE BY CHILDREN—Box 83, Santa Cruz, CA 95063. Gerry Mandel, Ed. Stories, poems, plays, book reviews by children under 14. Pays in copies.

STORY FRIENDS—Mennonite Publishing House, Scottdale, PA 15683. Marjorie Waybill, Ed. Stories, 350 to 800 words, for 4- to 9-year-olds, on Christian faith and values in everyday experiences. Quizzes, riddles. Poetry. Pays to 5¢ a word, to $5 per poem, on acceptance.

3–2–1 CONTACT—Children's Television Workshop, 1 Lincoln Plaza, New York, NY 10023. Jonathan Rosenbloom, Ed. Entertaining and informative articles, 600 to 1,000 words, for 8- to 14-year-olds, on all aspects of science, computers, scientists, and children who are learning about or practicing science. Pays $75 to $400, on acceptance. No fiction. Also publishes *Kid City* and *Sesame Street Magazine.* Query.

TOUCH—Box 7259, Grand Rapids, MI 49510. Carol Smith, Man. Ed. Upbeat fiction and features, 1,000 to 1,500 words, for Christian girls ages 8 to 14; personal life, nature, crafts. Poetry, fillers, puzzles. Pays 2 ½¢ a word, extra for photos, on acceptance. Query with SASE.

TURTLE MAGAZINE FOR PRESCHOOL KIDS—1100 Waterway Blvd., Box 567, Indianapolis, IN 46206. Beth Wood Thomas, Ed. Stories about safety, exercise, health, and nutrition, for preschoolers. Humorous, entertaining fiction, 600 words. Simple poems. Stories-in-rhyme; easy-to-read stories, to 500 words, for beginning readers. Pays about 8¢ a word, on publication. Buys all rights. Send SASE for guidelines.

U.S. KIDS—245 Long Hill Rd., Middletown, CT 06457. Nancy Webb, Ed. Articles and fiction, 250 to 400 words, on issues related to kids age 5 to 10, true life adventures, science and nature topics, shorts. Pays $150 to $400, on acceptance. Query. Guidelines.

WEE WISDOM—Unity Village, MO 64065. Judy Gehrlein, Ed. Character-building stories, to 800 words, for children through age 12. Pays varying rates, on acceptance.

WONDER TIME—6401 The Paseo, Kansas City, MO 64131. Evelyn J. Beals, Ed. Stories, 200 to 600 words, for 6- to 8-year-olds, with Christian emphasis to correlate with Sunday School curriculum. Features, to 300 words, on nature, crafts, etc. Poetry, 4 to 12 lines. Pays 3 ½¢ a word, from 25¢ a line for verse, $2.50 minimum, on acceptance.

YOUNG AMERICAN, AMERICA'S NEWSPAPER FOR KIDS—P.O. Box 12409, Portland, OR 97212. Kristina T. Linden, Ed. Upbeat, positive, sophisticated material for children ages 4 to 15. Fiction, to 1,000 words; articles, to 350 words, on science, humor, history, and newsworthy young people; poetry. Pays 7¢ a word, $5 for photos, on publication.

TEENAGE AND YOUNG ADULT

ALIVE NOW!—P.O. Box 189, Nashville, TN 37202. Mary Ruth Coffman, Ed. Short essays, 250 to 400 words, with Christian emphasis for adults and young adults. Poetry, one page. Photos. Pays $5 to $20, on publication.

BOP—3500 W. Olive Ave., Suite 850, Burbank, CA 91505. Julie Laufer, Ed. Interviews and features, 500 to 1,000 words, for teenage girls, on stars popular with teenagers. Photos. Pays varying rates, on acceptance. Query preferred. Same requirements for *The Big Bopper.*

BOYS' LIFE—1325 Walnut Hill Ln., Irving, TX 75038–3096. William B. McMorris, Ed. Publication of Boy Scouts of America. Articles and fiction, 1,500 words, for 8- to 18-year-old boys. Photos. Pays from $500 for major articles and fiction, on acceptance. Query first.

CHRISTIAN LIVING FOR SENIOR HIGH—850 N. Grove, Elgin, IL 60120. Anne E. Dinnan, Ed. Articles and fiction, 1,000 to 1,500 words, of interest to Christian teens. Don't preach. Pays 10¢ a word, on acceptance.

EXPLORING—1325 Walnut Hill Ln., Box 152079, Irving, TX 75015–2079. Scott Daniels, Exec. Ed. Publication of Boy Scouts of America. Articles, 500 to 1,800 words, for 14- to 21-year-old boys and girls, on education, careers, Explorer post activities (hiking, canoeing, camping) and program ideas for meetings. No controversial subjects. Pays $150 to $500, on acceptance. Query. Send SASE for guidelines.

FREEWAY—Box 632, Glen Ellyn, IL 60138. Billie Sue Thompson, Ed. First-person true stories, personal experience, how-tos, fillers, and humor, to 1,000 words, with photos, for 13- to 22-year-olds. Must have Christian emphasis. Pays to 8¢ a word.

GRIT—208 W. Third St., Williamsport, PA 17701. Joanne Decker, Assignment Ed. Articles, 300 to 500 words, with photos, on young people involved in unusual hobbies, occupations, athletic pursuits, and personal adventures. Pays 15¢ a word, extra for photos, on acceptance.

HICALL—1445 Boonville Ave., Springfield, MO 65802. Sinda Zinn, Ed. Articles, 500 to 1,000 words, and fiction, to 1,500 words, for 12- to 19-year-olds; strong evangelical emphasis. Pays on acceptance.

IN TOUCH—Box 50434, Indianapolis, IN 46250–0434. Angelyn Rodriguez, Ed. Articles, 500 to 1,000 words, on contemporary issues, athletes, and singers from conservative Christian perspective, for 13- to 19-year-olds. Pays 2¢ to 4¢ a word. Send SASE for guidelines.

KEYNOTER—3636 Woodview Trace, Indianapolis, IN 46268. Jack Brockley, Exec. Ed. Articles, 1,500 to 2,500 words, for high school leaders: general-interest features; self-help; pieces on contemporary teenage problems. Photos. Pays $75 to $250, extra for photos, on acceptance. Query preferred.

LIGHTED PATHWAY—922 Montgomery Ave., Cleveland, TN 37311. Marcus V. Hand, Ed. Human-interest and inspirational articles, 800 to 1,000 words, for teenagers and young adults. Short pieces, 600 to 800 words. Fiction, 1,000 to 1,200 words. Pays 3¢ to 6¢ a word, on acceptance.

LISTEN MAGAZINE—6830 Laurel St. N.W., Washington, DC 20012. Gary B. Swanson, Ed. Articles (1,500 to 2,000 words) providing teens with "a vigorous, positive, educational approach to the problems arising out of the use of tobacco, alcohol, and other drugs." Pays 5¢ to 7¢ a word, on acceptance.

MERLYN'S PEN, THE NATIONAL MAGAZINE OF STUDENT WRITING—P.O. Box 1058, East Greenwich, RI 02818. R. James Stahl, Ed. Writing by students in grades 7 through 10 only. Short stories, to 3,500 words; reviews, travel pieces and poetry, to 100 lines. Pays in copies. Guidelines available.

NEW ERA—50 E. North Temple, Salt Lake City, UT 84150. Brian Kelly, Ed. Articles, 150 to 3,000 words, and fiction, to 3,000 words, for young Mormons. Poetry. Photos. Pays 5¢ to 20¢ a word, 25¢ a line for poetry, on acceptance. Query.

PIONEER—1548 Poplar Ave., Memphis, TN 38104. Tim Bearden, Ed. Southern Baptist. Articles, to 1,500 words, for 12- and 14-year-old boys, on teen problems, current events. Photo essays on Baptist sports personalities. Pays 4¢ a word, extra for photos, on acceptance.

QUE PASA—1086 Teaneck Rd., Teaneck, NJ 07666. Celeste Gomes, Ed. Articles (two to four pages) in Spanish or English on popular music stars, actors and actresses, and lifestyles of Latin celebrities for the Hispanic community. Fillers and humor. Pays from $50, on publication. For photographs, pays $75 for color and $25 for B&W.

SCHOLASTIC SCOPE—730 Broadway, New York, NY 10003. Fran Claro, Ed. For 15- to 18-year-olds with 4th to 6th grade reading ability. Realistic fiction, 400 to 1,200 words, and plays, to 5,000 words, on teen problems. Profiles, 400 to 800 words, of interesting teenagers, with B&W photos. (No sermons, coincidences, random happenings, or major changes in personality or values.) Pays $125 for 500- to 600-word articles, from $200 for plays and short stories, from $150 for longer pieces, on acceptance.

SEVENTEEN—850 Third Ave., New York, NY 10022. Roberta Myers, Articles Ed. Articles, to 2,500 words, on subjects of interest to teenagers. Sophisticated, well-written fiction, 1,500 to 3,500 words, for young adults. Poetry, to 40 lines, by teens. Short news and features, to 750 words, for "Talk." Articles, 1,000 words, by teenagers, for "View." Pays varying rates, on acceptance.

STRAIGHT—8121 Hamilton Ave., Cincinnati, OH 45231. Carla J. Crane, Ed. Articles on current situations and issues, humor, for Christian teens. Well-constructed fiction, 1,000 to 1,200 words, showing teens using Christian principles. Poetry by teenagers. Photos. Pays about 3¢ a word, on acceptance. Guidelines.

TEEN POWER—Box 632, Glen Ellyn, IL 60138. Mark Oestreicher, Ed. First person (as told to), true teen experience stories with Christian insights and conclusion, 700 to 1,000 words. Include photos. Pays 7¢ to 10¢ a word, extra for photos, on acceptance.

TEENS TODAY—Nazarene Headquarters, 6401 The Paseo, Kansas City, MO 64131. Karen DeSollar, Ed. Short stories, 1,200 to 1,500 words, dealing with teens demonstrating Christian principles in real-life situations. Adventure stories; stories about relationships and ethics. Pays 3 ½¢ a word, on acceptance.

TIGER BEAT—1086 Teaneck Rd., Teaneck, NJ 07666. Diane Umansky, Ed. Articles, to 4 pages, on young people in show business and music industry. Pays varying rates, on acceptance. Query. Unsolicited manuscripts sent without SASE will not be returned.

TIGER BEAT STAR—1086 Teaneck Rd., Teaneck, NJ 07666. Nancy O'Connell, Ed. Light celebrity fan pieces and interviews (pop/rock, movies and TV); occasional serious articles on topics of interest to teens. For articles, 300 words, payment is $50 per published page. Query.

TQ/TEEN QUEST—Box 82808, Lincoln, NE 68501. Barbara Comito, Ed. Articles, to 1,800 words, and well-crafted fiction, to 2,500 words, for conservative Christian teens. B&W photos and color slides. Pays 4¢ to 10¢ a word, extra for photos, on publication.

WRITING!—60 Revere Dr., Northbrook, IL 60062–1563. Alan Lenhoff, Ed.

671

Interviews, 1,200 words, for "Writers at Work" department, for high school students. Pays $200, on publication. Query.

YM—685 Third Ave., New York, NY 10017. David Keeps, Sr. Articles Ed. Entertainment, fashion, beauty, relationships, medical topics, and sports articles (to 1,500 words) for women ages 14 to 22; also uses humor. Send complete manuscript, or query with published clips; SASE required. Payment varies, on acceptance.

YOUNG AND ALIVE—4444 S. 52nd St., Lincoln, NE 68506. Richard Kaiser, Ed. Feature articles, 800 to 1,400 words, for blind and visually impaired young adults, on adventure, biography, camping, health, hobbies, and travel. Photos. Pays 3¢ to 5¢ a word, extra for photos, on acceptance. Write for guidelines.

YOUNG SALVATIONIST—The Salvation Army, 799 Bloomfield Ave., Verona, NJ 07044. Capt. Robert R. Hostetler, Ed. Articles for teens, 800 to 1,200 words, with Christian perspective; fiction, 800 to 1,200 words; short fillers. Young Soldier Section: fiction, 600 to 800 words; games and puzzles for children. Pays 3¢ to 5¢ a word, on acceptance.

THE DRAMA MARKET

REGIONAL AND UNIVERSITY THEATERS

Community, regional, and civic theaters and college dramatic groups offer the best opportunities today for playwrights to see their plays produced, whether for staged production or for dramatic readings. Indeed, aspiring playwrights who can get their work produced by any of these have taken an important step toward breaking into the competitive dramatic field—many well-known playwrights received their first recognition in the regional theaters. Payment is generally nominal, but regional and university theaters usually buy only the right to produce a play, and all further rights revert to the author. Since most directors like to work closely with the authors on any revisions necessary, theaters will often pay the playwright's expenses while in residence during rehearsals. The thrill of seeing your play come to life on the stage is one of the pleasures of being on hand for rehearsals and performances.

Aspiring playwrights should query college and community theaters in their region to find out which ones are interested in seeing original scripts. Dramatic associations of interest to playwrights include the Dramatists Guild (234 W. 44th St., New York, NY 10036), Theatre Communications Group, Inc. (355 Lexington Ave., New York, NY 10017), which publishes the annual *Dramatists Sourcebook,* and The International Society of Dramatists, publishers of *The Dramatist's Bible* (P.O. Box 1310, Miami, FL 33153). *The Playwright's Companion,* published by Feedback Theatrebooks, P.O. Box 5187, Bloomington, IN 47402–5187, is an annual directory of theatres and prize contests seeking scripts.

Some of the theaters on the following list require that playwrights submit all or some of the following with scripts—cast list, synopsis, resumé, recommendations, return postcard—and with scripts and queries, SASEs must always be enclosed. Playwrights may also wish to register their material with the U.S. Copyright Office.

For additional information about this, write Register of Copyrights, Library of Congress, Washington, DC 20559.

REGIONAL AND UNIVERSITY THEATERS

ACADEMY THEATRE—P.O. Box 77070, Atlanta, GA 30357. Linda C. Anderson, Lit. Mgr. "Plays that stretch the boundaries of imagination, with elements of surrealism, poetic language, and imagery in comedy and drama format." Prefers local playwrights for Genesis Series Productions. Considers regional and national playwrights for new play premiers in subscription series productions. Royalty is negotiable.

A. D. PLAYERS—2710 W. Alabama, Houston, TX 77098. Jeannette Clift George, Artistic Dir. Carol E. Anderson, Lit. Mgr. Full-length or one-act comedies, dramas, musicals, children's plays, and adaptations with Christian world view. Submit script with SAS postcard, resumé, cast list, and synopsis (Christmas plays should be submitted before Oct.). Reports in 2 months. Readings. Pays negotiable rates.

ALLEY THEATRE—615 Texas Ave., Houston, TX 77002. Robert Strane, Lit. Mgr. Full-length plays and musicals, including translations and adaptations, plays for young audiences. Query with synopsis, production requirements, and resumé before Feb. 1. Pay varies.

ALLIANCE THEATRE COMPANY—1280 Peachtree St. N.E., Atlanta, GA 30309. Sandra Deer, Lit. Mgr. Full-length comedies, dramas, musicals, and adaptations. Query with synopsis and cast list. Pay varies.

AMERICAN LIVING HISTORY THEATER—P.O. Box 2677, Hollywood, CA 90078. Dorene Ludwig, Artistic Dir. One-act, historically accurate (primary source materials only) dramas. Submit script with SASE. Reports in 1 to 6 months. Pays varying rates.

AMERICAN REPERTORY THEATRE—64 Brattle St., Cambridge, MA 02138. Arthur Holmberg, Lit. Mgr. No unsolicited manuscripts. Submit one-page description of play, 10 page sample; nothing returned without SASE; 3 to 4 months for response.

AMERICAN STAGE COMPANY—P.O. Box 1560, St. Petersburg, FL 33731. Victoria Holloway, Artistic Dir. Full-length comedies and dramas. Send synopsis with short description of cast and production requirements with SAS postcard. Pays negotiable rates. Submit Sept. to Jan.

AMERICAN STAGE COMPANY—FDU, Box 336, Teaneck, NJ 07666. Ted Rawlins, Prod. Dir. Full-length comedies, dramas, and musicals for cast of 5 or 6 and single set. Submit synopsis with resumé, cast list, and return postcard to Sheldon Epps, Art. Assoc. Read in Spring, reports in 2–3 months. No unsolicited scripts.

AMERICAN STANISLAVSKI THEATRE—485 Park Ave., #6A, New York, NY 10022. Sonia Moore, Artistic Dir. Full-length or one-act drama with important message. No offensive language. For cast aged 16 to 45. Submit script with SAS postcard in April and May; reports in Sept. No payment.

AMERICAN THEATRE OF ACTORS—314 W. 54th St., New York, NY 10019. James Jennings, Art. Dir. Full-length dramas for a cast of 2 to 6. Submit complete play and SASE. Reports in 1 to 2 months.

THE APPLE CORPS.—336 W. 20th St., New York, NY 10011. Bob Del

673

Pazzo, Coordinator. All types of one-act and full-length plays. Send bio, synopsis with SASE. Committed to non-traditional casting. Allow 4 to 6 months for response. Payment varies. No phone calls.

ARENA STAGE—Sixth and Maine Ave. S.W., Washington, DC 20024. Laurence Maslon, Lit. Mgr./Dramaturg. Submit one-page synopsis, first 10 pages of dialogue and resumé. No unsolicited manuscripts. Allow 1 month reply for queries, 3 months for manuscripts.

ARKANSAS ARTS CENTER CHILDREN'S THEATRE—Box 2137, Little Rock, AR 72203. Bradley Anderson, Artistic Dir. Seeks solid, professional (full-length or one-act) scripts, especially work adapted from contemporary and classic literature. Some original work. Pays flat rate.

ARKANSAS REPERTORY THEATRE COMPANY—601 S. Main, P.O. Box 110, Little Rock, AR 72203–0110. Cliff Fannin Baker, Artistic Dir. Full-length comedies, dramas, and musicals; prefer up to 10 characters. Send synopsis, cast list, resumé, and return postage. Reports in 5 to 6 months.

ARTREACH TOURING THEATRE—3074 Madison Rd., Cincinnati, OH 45209. Kathryn Schultz Miller, Artistic Dir. One-act dramas and adaptations for touring children's theater; cast to 3, simple sets. Submit script with synopsis, cast list, resumé, recommendations and SASE. Payment varies.

ASOLO STATE THEATRE—P.O. Drawer E, Sarasota, FL 34230. John Ulmer, Artistic Dir. Full-length dramas, comedies, musicals, and children's plays. Small stage. Pays royalty or varying rates. Readings and workshops offered. No unsolicited manuscripts. Query with synopsis.

AT THE FOOT OF THE MOUNTAIN—2000 S. Fifth St., Minneapolis, MN 55454. Nayo Watkins, Exec. Dir. Full-length, one-act, and musical plays by women. Query with synopsis, SAS postcard. Reports in 6 weeks. Pays royalty.

BAILIWICK REPERTORY—3212 N. Broadway, Chicago, IL 60657. Rosa Graham, Lit. Mgr. Full-length dramas, musicals, and children's plays. "Be creative and persistent. We look for innovative, challenging writing and topics." Submit script or synopsis with return postcard. Reports in 4 months. Payment varies.

BARTER THEATER—P.O. Box 867, Abingdon, VA 24210. Rex Partington, Producing Dir. Full-length dramas, comedies, adaptations, musicals, and children's plays. Full workshop and reading productions. Allow 6 to 8 months for report. Payment rates negotiable.

BERKELEY REPERTORY THEATRE—2025 Addison St., Berkeley, CA 94704. Sharon Ott, Artistic Dir. Mame Hunt, Lit. Mgr. No unsolicited manuscripts; agent submissions or professional recommendations only. Reporting time: 3 to 4 months.

BERKSHIRE THEATRE FESTIVAL—Box 797, Stockbridge, MA 02162. Richard Dunlap, Artistic Dir. Full-length comedies, musicals, and dramas; cast to 8. Submit through agent only.

BOARSHEAD THEATER—425 S. Grand Ave., Lansing, MI 48933. John Peakes, Artistic Dir. Full-length and one-act comedies and dramas with simple sets. Send precis, 5–10 pages of dialogue, cast list to 12 with descriptions, and resumé. SASE for reply.

CALIFORNIA UNIVERSITY THEATRE—California, PA 15419. Dr. Roger C. Emelson, Chairman. Unusual, avant-garde, or experiemental one-act and full-length comedies, dramas, children's plays, and adaptations. Cast sizes vary from

2 to 5. Submit synopsis in March or April with cast list, resumé, recommendations, and short sample scene. Payment varies.

CENTER STAGE—700 N. Calvert St., Baltimore, MD 21202. Rick Davis, Resident Dramaturg. Full-length and one-act comedies, dramas, translations, adaptations. No unsolicited manuscripts. Send synopsis, a few sample pages, resumé, cast list, recommendations and production history, with return postcard and SASE. Pays varying rates. Allow 4 to 8 weeks for reply.

CHILDSPLAY—Box 517, Tempe, AZ 85281. David Saar, Art. Dir. Plays running 45–90 minutes: dramas, musicals, children's plays, and adaptations. Sets must travel. Cast size, 4 to 8. Submissions accepted November through February. Reports in 2 to 6 months. Payment varies.

CIRCLE IN THE SQUARE/UPTOWN—1633 Broadway, New York, NY 10019. Theodore Mann, Artistic Dir. Full-length comedies, dramas, and adaptations. Send synopsis with resumé, cast list, and 10 page dialogue sample to Seth Goldman, Literary Advisor. No unsolicited scripts. SASE required.

CIRCLE REPERTORY COMPANY—161 Ave. of the Americas, New York, NY 10013. B. Rodney Marriott, Assoc. Artistic Dir. Send full-length dramas with cast list. Offers criticism "as often as possible." Pays $2,500. Reports in 5 months. Readings.

CITY THEATRE COMPANY—Bellefield Annex, 315 S. Bellefield Ave., Pittsburgh, PA 15260. Scott Cummings, Lit. Dir. Full-length comedies and dramas; query Sept. to May. Cast to 12; simple sets. Readings. Royalty.

CLASSIC STAGE COMPANY—136 E. 13th St., New York, NY 10003. Ellen Novack, Managing Dir. Carey Perloff, Artistic Dir. Full-length adaptations and translations of existing classic literature. Submit synopsis with cast list and SASE, Sept. to May. Offers workshops and readings. Pays on royalty basis.

COLUMBIA COLLEGE—Theatre-Music Center 72 E. 11th St., Chicago, IL 60605. Sheldon Patinkin, Art. Dir. Full-length musicals and plays by African American playwrights. Submit musicals to Chuck Smith, plays by African Americans to Sheldon Patinkin, with synopsis, resumé, and return postcard. Payment varies.

CREATIVE THEATRE—102 Witherspoon St., Princeton, NJ 08540. Laurie Huntsman, Artistic Director. One-act participatory plays for children, grades K through 6, and one-act plays for children grades 7 to 12; cast of 5 to 9; arena or proscenium staging. Submit manuscript with synopsis and cast list. Pays $300 for music and $300 for lyrics.

THE CRICKET THEATRE—9 W. 14th St., Minneapolis, MN 55403. William Partlan, Art. Dir. Send synopsis, resumé, and 10 page sample of work; "prefer contemporary plays." Cast to 11. Reports in 6 months.

CROSSROADS THEATRE CO.—320 Memorial Pkwy., New Brunswick, NJ 08901. Rick Khan, Producing Art. Dir. Sydné Mahone, Lit. Man. Full-length and one-act dramas, comedies, musicals, and adaptations; issue-oriented experimental pieces that offer honest, imaginative, and insighful examinations of the African-American experience. Also interested in African, Caribbean, and interracial plays. Queries only, with synopsis, cast list, resumé, and SASE.

DELAWARE THEATRE COMPANY—P.O. Box 516, Wilmington, DE 19899. Cleveland Morris, Artistic Dir. Full-length comedies, dramas, musicals, and adaptations, with cast to 10; prefer single set. Send cast list, synopsis, and SASE. Reports in 6 months. Pays royalty.

DENVER CENTER THEATRE COMPANY—1050 13th St., Denver, CO 80204. Barbara Sellers, Producing Dir. Send full-length comedies and dramas (cast to 12): June-Dec. Include cast list, resumé. Pay varies.

DETROIT REPERTORY THEATRE—13103 Woodrow Wilson Ave., Detroit, MI 48238. Barbara Busby, Lit. Mgr. Full-length comedies and dramas. Enclose SASE. Pays royalty.

DORSET THEATRE FESTIVAL—Box 519, Dorset, VT 05251. Jill Charles, Art. Dir. Full-length comedies, musicals, dramas, and adaptations; cast to 8; simple set preferred. Agent submissions and professional recomendations only. Pays varying rates. Residencies at Dorset Colony House for Writers available Sept. to May. Inquire. See *Writers Colonies* list for details.

DRIFTWOOD SHOWBOAT—Box 1032, Kingston, NY 12401. Fred Hall, Resident Company Art. Dir. Full-length family comedies for 2- to 6-person cast; single setting. No profanity. Sept. to June. Submit cast list, synopsis, and return postcard.

EAST WEST PLAYERS—4424 Santa Monica Blvd., Los Angeles, CA 90029. Full-length comedies, dramas, and musicals, dealings with Asian American issues and/or including important roles for Asian actors. Cast up to 10. Send manuscript with synopsis, cast list, resumé, and SASE. Pays varying rates. Offers workshops and readings. Allow 3 months for reply.

ECCENTRIC CIRCLES THEATRE—400 W. 43rd St., #4N, New York, NY 10036. Rosemary Hopkins, Art. Dir. Full-length comedies, dramas, and musicals with simple sets and a cast size to 10. Submit manuscript with resumé and SASE. Reports in 6 weeks.

EMPIRE STATE INSTITUTE FOR THE PERFORMING ARTS—Empire State Plaza, Albany, NY 12223. Patricia B. Snyder, Prod. Dir. Query for new musicals and plays for family audiences, with synopsis, cast list. Submit between June and August. Payment varies.

THE EMPTY SPACE THEATRE—P.O. Box 1748, Seattle , WA 98111–1748. Kurt Beattie, Lit. Mgr. Unsolicited scripts accepted only from WA, OR, WY, MT, and ID. Outside five-state N.W. region: scripts accepted through agents or established theater groups only.

ENSEMBLE STUDIO THEATRE—549 W. 52nd St., New York, NY 10019. Address Literary Mgr. Send full-length or one-act comedies and dramas, with cast list, resumé, and SASE, Sept. to April. Pay varies. Readings.

ENSEMBLE THEATRE COMPANY OF MARIN—c/o Tamalpais High School, Mill Valley, CA 94941. David Smith, Art. Dir. Comedies, dramas, children's plays, adaptations, and scripts addressing high school issues for largely female cast (approx. 3 women per man). Send synopsis and resumé.

THE FAMILY REPERTORY CO.—9 Second Ave., New York, NY 10003. J. J. Johnson, Art. Dir. Contemporary, social works on a variety of topics. Full-length dramas and musicals for young people and adults. Submit manuscript with synopsis, resumé, and return postcard. Pays small fee.

FLORIDA STUDIO THEATRE—1241 N. Palm Ave., Sarasota, FL 33577. Jack Fournier, New Play Development. Innovative smaller cast plays that are pertinent and contemporary. Query first with synopsis and SASE.

GE VA THEATRE—75 Woodbury Blvd., Rochester, NY 14607. Ann Patrice Carrigan, Lit. Dir. Query for comedies and dramas with synopsis and cast list. Readings.

GEER THEATRICUM BOTANICUM, WILL—Box 1222, Topanga, CA 90290. All types of scripts for outdoor theater, with large playing area. Submit synopsis with SASE. Pays varing rates.

GIFFORD CHILDREN'S THEATRE, EMMY—3504 Center St., Omaha, NE 68105. James Larson, Artistic Dir. Unsolicited scripts accepted with SASE.

THE GOODMAN THEATRE—200 S. Columbus Dr., Chicago, IL 60603. Tom Creamer, Dramaturg. Queries required for full-length comedies or dramas. Include synopsis, cast list, resumé, recommendations, and to 10 pages of dialogue. Reports in 3 months. Readings and workshops.

THE GROUP THEATRE—See Seattle Group Theatre.

THE GUTHRIE THEATER—725 Vineland Pl., Minneapolis, MN 55403. Mark Bly, Lit. Mgr. Full-length comedies, dramas, and adaptations. Manuscripts accepted only from recognized theatrical agents. Query with detailed synopsis, cast size, resumé, return postcard, and recommendations. Pays negotiable rates, and travel/residency expenses. Reports in 1 to 2 months.

HARRISBURG COMMUNITY THEATRE—513 Hurlock St., Harrisburg, PA 17110. Thomas G. Hostetter, Artistic Dir. Full-length comedies, dramas, musicals, and adaptations; cast to 20; prefers simple set. Submit script with cast list, resumé, synopsis, and SAS postcard. Best time to submit: June to August. Reporting time: 6 months. Pays negotiable rates.

HARTFORD STAGE COMPANY—50 Church St., Hartford, CT 06103. Nadia Zonis, Lit. Assoc. Full-length plays of all types, for cast up to 12. No unsolicited manuscripts; submit through agent or send synopsis. Pays varying rates.

HEDGEROW THEATRE—146 Rose Valley Rd., Moylan, PA 19086. David Zum Brunnen, Art. Dir. Full-length comedies, dramas, muscials, children's plays, and adaptations for 15-person cast. Small theater seats 150. Send script in the spring or summer with resumé, return postcard, cast list, and SASE. Reports in 2 months.

HIPPODROME STATE THEATRE—25 S.E. Second Pl., Gainesville, FL 32601. Mary Hausch, Producing Art. Dir. Full-length plays with unit sets and casts up to 15. Submit in summer and fall. Enclose return postcard and synopsis.

HOLLYWOOD THEATER COMPANY—12838 Kling St., Studio City, CA 91604. Rai Tasco, Art. Dir. Full-length comedies and dramas for integrated cast. Include cast list and stamped return postcard with submission.

HONOLULU THEATRE FOR YOUTH—Box 3257, Honolulu, HI 96801. John Kauffman, Art. Dir. Plays, 60 to 90 minutes playing time, for young people/ family audiences. Adult casts. Contemporary issues, Pacific themes, etc. Unit sets, small cast. Query or send manuscript with synopsis, cast list, and SASE. Royalties negotiable.

HORIZON THEATRE COMPANY—P. O. Box 5376, Station E, Atlanta, GA 30307. Jeffrey and Lisa Adler, Co-Artistic Directors. Full-length comedies, dramas, and satires that utilize "heightened" realism and other highly theatrical forms. Cast to 10. Submit synopsis with cast list, resumé, and recommendations. Pays percentage. Readings. Reports in 3 months.

HUDSON GUILD THEATRE—441 W. 26th St., New York, NY 10001. Geoffrey Sherman, Art. Dir. Full-length comedies, dramas, and musicals for 8-person cast. (No fly or wing space in theater.) Submit script to Steven Ramay with synopsis, return postcard, resumé, recommendations, and SASE. Reports in 2 to 3 months. Pays $1000.

HUNTINGTON THEATRE COMPANY—252 Huntington Ave., Boston,

MA 02115. Full-length comedies and dramas. Query with synopsis, cast list, resumé, recommendations, and return postcard.

ILLINOIS THEATRE CENTER—400 Lakewood Blvd., Park Forest, IL 60466. Steve S. Billig, Artistic Dir. Full-length comedies, dramas, musicals, and adaptations, for unit/fragmentary sets, and cast to 8. Send summary and return postcard. No unsolicited manuscripts. Pays negotiable rates. Workshops and readings offered.

ILLUSTRATED STAGE COMPANY—Box 640063, San Francisco, CA 94164–0063. Steve Dobbins, Art. Dir. Full-length comedies, dramas, and musicals for a cast to 18. Query with synopsis and SASE. No unsolicited manuscripts. Offers workshops and readings.

INVISIBLE THEATRE—1400 N. First Ave, Tucson, AZ 85719. Deborah Dickey, Literary Mgr. Reads queries for full-length comedies, dramas, musicals, adaptations, Jan. to May. Cast to 10; simple set. Pays royalty.

JEWISH REPERTORY THEATRE—344 E. 14th St., New York, NY 10003. Ran Avni, Artistic Dir. Full-length comedies, dramas, musicals, and adaptations, with cast to 10, relating to the Jewish experience. Pays varying rates. Enclose return postcard.

LAMB'S PLAYERS THEATRE—500 Plaza Blvd., P. O. Box 26, National City , CA 92050. Kerry Cederberg, Lit. Mgr. Full-length dramas, translations, adaptations, musicals. Special interest in works with Christian world view. Query with synopsis required.

LITTLE BROADWAY PRODUCTIONS—c/o Jill Shawn, P. O. Box 15068, N. Hollywood, CA 91615. Musicals and other plays for children performed by adult actors; 55 minutes, no intermission. Cast of 5 to 10. Submit manuscript with synopsis, return postcard, resumé, and SASE. Pays negotiable rates.

LONG ISLAND STAGE—P. O. Box 9001, Rockville Centre, New York 11571–9001. Clinton J. Atkinson, Art. Dir. Full-length dramas and adaptations. Query with SASE in late spring/early summer. Pays varying rates.

LOS ANGELES DESIGNERS' THEATRE—P. O. Box 1883, Studio City, CA 91614–0883. Richard Niederberg, Artistic Dir. Full-length comedies, dramas, muscials, fantasies, or adaptations. Religious, political, social, and controversial themes encouraged. Nudity, "adult" language, etc., O.K. Payment varies.

LOS ANGELES THEATRE UNIT—P. O. Box 429, Los Angeles, CA 90078. Steve Itkin, Man. Dir. Kate Ward, Lit. Dir. Full-length and one-act comedies and dramas. Submit script and SASE. Reports in 2 to 3 months. Pays varying rates.

MCCARTER THEATRE COMPANY—91 University Pl., Princeton, NJ 08540. Robert Lanchester, Assoc. Art. Dir. Full-length comedies, dramas, adaptations. Pays to $500 for readings; varying rates for production.

THE MAGIC THEATRE—Bldg. D, Fort Mason, San Francisco, CA 94123. Eugenie Chan, Literary Mgr. Comedies and dramas, ethnic-American, workshop productions. Query with synopsis, resumé, and 3 to 5 pages of sample dialogue. Pays varying rates.

MANHATTAN PUNCH LINE—410 W. 42nd St., New York, NY 10036. Steve Kaplan, Art. Dir. Comedies. Showcase contract. SASE required.

MANHATTAN THEATRE CLUB—453 W. 16th, New York, NY 10011. Address Tom Szentgyorgyi. Full-length and one-act comedies, dramas, and musicals. No unsolicited manuscripts. Send synopsis with 10 to 15 pages of dialogue, cast

list, resumé, recommendations and SASE. Pays negotiable rates. Allow 6 months for reply.

MAXWELL ANDERSON PLAYWRIGHTS SERIES, INC.—6 Sagmore Rd., Stamford, CT 06902. Dr. Philip Devine, Exec. Prod. Send script with SASE. Reports in 2 months. Pays travel expenses, to $100, for playwright to attend rehearsals.

MCCADDEN PLACE THEATRE—1157 N. McCadden Pl., Los Angeles, CA 90038. Joy Rerialdi, Art. Dir. Full-length comedies and dramas for a cast of 10 and a single set. "Nothing extravagant in sets, costumes, etc., will work!" Send script with cast list and SASE. Reports in 2 to 6 months. Pays small rates.

MIDWEST PLAYLABS—c/o The Playwrights' Center, 2301 Franklin Ave. E., Minneapolis, MN 55406. Full-length, previously unproduced scripts (no musicals). Query. Pays stipend, room and board, and travel for two-week August conference.

MILL MOUNTAIN THEATRE—Center in the Square, One Market Square, Roanoke, VA 24011. Jo Weinstein, Lit. Mgr. Full-length or one-act comedies, dramas, musicals; include publicity, resumé. One act plays limited to 25–40 minutes. Payment varies.

MISSOURI REPERTORY THEATRE—4949 Cherry St., Kansas City, MO 64110. Felicia Londré, Dramaturg. Full-length comedies and dramas. Query with synopsis, cast list, resumé, and return postcard. Pays standard royalty.

MUSIC THEATRE GROUP AT LENOX ARTS CENTER—735 Washington St., New York, NY 10014. John Hart, Lit. Mgr. Innovative musicals, to 1 ½ hours; cast to 10. Query only, with synopsis and return postcard. Best submission time: Sept.-Dec.

MUSICAL THEATRE WORKS—440 Lafayette St., New York, NY 10003. Mark Herko, Assoc. Artistic Dir. Full-length musicals, cast to 10; simple sets. Submit manuscript with SASE and cassette score. No payment.

NEW EHRLICH THEATRE—Boston Center for the Arts, 539 Tremont St, Boston, MA 02116. New full-length scripts (no musicals) by Massachusetts playwrights for readings and workshop productions. Include SASE. Address to NEWorks Submissions Program.

NEW TUNERS/PERFORMANCE COMMUNITY—1225 W. Belmont Ave., Chicago, IL 60657. George H. Gorham, Dramaturg. Full-length musicals only, for cast to 15; no wing/fly space. Send manuscript with cassette tape of score, cast list, resumé, and return postcard. Pays on royalty basis.

NEW YORK SHAKESPEARE FESTIVAL/PUBLIC THEATER—425 Lafayette St., New York, NY 10003. Gail Merrifield, Dir. of Plays and Musicals. Plays and musical works for the theater, translations, and adaptations. Submit manuscript, cassette (with musicals) and SASE.

ODYSSEY THEATRE ENSEMBLE—12111 Ohio Ave., Los Angeles, CA 90025. Ron Sossi, Artistic Dir. Full-length comedies, dramas, musicals, and adaptations: provocative subject matter, or plays that stretch and explore the possibilities of theater. Query with synopsis and return postcard. Pays variable rates. Allow 2 to 6 months for reply. Workshops and readings.

OLD GLOBE THEATRE—Simon Edison Center for the Performing Arts, Box 2171, San Diego, CA 92112. Address Robert Berlinger. Full-length comedies and dramas. No unsolicited manuscripts. Submit query with synopsis, or through agent.

OLDCASTLE THEATRE COMPANY—Southern Vermont College, Box 1555, Bennington, VT 05201. Eric Peterson, Dir. Full-length comedies, dramas, and musicals for a small cast (up to 10) and a single stage set. Submit synopsis and cast list in the winter. Reports in 2 months. Offers workshops and readings. Pays expenses for playwright to attend rehearsals. Royalty.

O'NEILL THEATRE CENTER, EUGENE—234 W. 44th St., Suite 901, New York, NY 10036. Annual competition to select new stage and television plays for development at organization's Waterford, CT location. Submission deadline: Dec. 1. Send SASE in the fall for guidelines to National Playwright's Conference, c/o above address. Pays stipend, plus travel/living expenses during conference.

PAPER MILL PLAYHOUSE—Brookside Dr., Millburn, NJ 07041. Maryan F. Stephens, Lit. Advisor. Full-length musicals only. Submit synopsis, tape, and resumé; reporting time, 3 to 4 months.

PENGUIN REPERTORY COMPANY—Box 91, Stony Point, NY 10980. Joe Brancato, Artistic Dir. Full-length comedies and dramas with cast size to six. Submit script, resumé, and SASE. Payment varies.

PENNSYLVANIA STAGE COMPANY—837 Linden St., Allentown, PA 18101. Full-length plays with cast to 8; one set. Send synopsis, cast list, and SASE to Literary Dept. Pays negotiable rates. Allow 6 months for reply. Readings.

PEOPLE'S LIGHT AND THEATRE COMPANY—39 Conestoga Rd., Malvern, PA 19355. Alda Cortese, Lit. Mgr. One-act or full-length comedies, dramas, adaptations. Query with synopsis, resumé, 10 pages of script required. Reports in 6 months. Payment negotiable.

PHILADELPHIA FESTIVAL FOR NEW PLAYS—3900 Chestnut St., Philadelphia, PA 19104. Richard Wolcott, Lit. Mgr. Full-length and one-act comedies, dramas; must be unproduced. Submit script with return postcard, resumé, and SASE. Pays varying rates.

PLAYHOUSE ON THE SQUARE—51 S. Cooper in Overton Sq., Memphis, TN 38104. Jackie Nichols, Artistic Dir. Full-length comedies, dramas; cast to 15. Query. Pays $500.

PLAYWRIGHTS HORIZONS—416 W. 42nd St., New York, NY 10036. Address Literary Dept. Full-length, original comedies, dramas, and musicals by American authors. Send resumé and SASE. Pays varying rates.

PLAYWRIGHTS' PLATFORM—164 Brayton Rd., Boston, MA 02135. B. A. Creasey, Pres. Script development workshops and public readings for New England playwrights only. Full-length and one-act plays of all kinds. Residents of New England send scripts with short synopsis, resumé, return postcard, and SASE.

POPLAR PIKE PLAYHOUSE—7653 Old Poplar Pike, Germantown, TN 38138. Frank Bluestein, Art. Dir. Full-length and one-act comedies, dramas, musicals, and children's plays. Submit synopsis with return postcard and resumé. Pays $300.

PORTLAND STAGE COMPANY—Box 1458, Portland, ME 04104. Richard Hamburger, Artistic Dir. Full-length comedies, dramas, and musicals, for cast to 8. Send synopsis and sample dialogue with return postcard. Pays fee, travel, and living arrangements if play is produced on mainstage, travel and living arrangements only if produced as reading or workshop production.

PRINCETON REPERTORY COMPANY—13 Witherspoon St., Princeton, NJ 08542. Ester Jenkins, Lit. Ed. Full-length comedies and dramas for a cast to 8. One set. Submit synopsis with resumé and cast list, or complete manuscript. Workshops and readings offered.

THE PUERTO RICAN TRAVELING THEATRE—141 W. 94th St., New York, NY 10025. Miriam Colon Valle, Artistic Dir. Full-length and one-act comedies, dramas, and musicals; cast to 8; simple sets. Payment negotiable.

THE REPERTORY THEATRE OF ST. LOUIS—Box 28030, St. Louis, MO 63119. Agent submissions only.

THE ROAD COMPANY—Box 5278 EKS, John City, TN 37603. Robert H. Leonard, Artistic Dir. Full-length and one-act comedies, dramas with social/political relevance to small-town audiences. Send synopsis, cast list, and production history, if any. Pays negotiable rates. Reports in 6 to 12 months.

ROUND HOUSE THEATRE—12210 Bushey Dr., Silver Spring, MD 20902. Address Production Office Mgr. Full-length comedies, dramas, and adaptations; cast to 10; prefer simple set. Send on page synopsis. No unsolicited manuscripts.

SEATTLE GROUP THEATRE—3940 Brooklyn Ave., NE, Seattle, WA 98105. Tim Bond, Lit. Mgr. Full-length satires, dramas, musicals, and translations, cast to 10; simple set. Special interest in plays suitable for multi-ethnic cast; serious plays on social/cultural issues; satires. Query with synopsis, sample dialogue and resumé required. Reporting time: 6 weeks.

SOCIETY HILL PLAYHOUSE—507 S. 8th St., Philadelphia, PA 19147. Walter Vail, Dramaturg. Full-length dramas and comedies; cast to 6; simple set. Submit synopsis and SASE. Reports in 6 months. Nominal payment.

SOHO REPERTORY THEATRE—80 Varick St., New York, NY 10013. Rob Barron, Dir. of Play Development. Full-length dramas, musicals, adaptations, mixed media works, and play readings. No unsolicited manuscripts. Send brief synopsis, cast list, resumé, and up to 10 pages of script. Musicals: tape and lead sheets. Response time: 90 days.

SOUTH COAST REPERTORY—P. O. Box 2197, Costa Mesa, CA 92628. John Glore, Lit. Mgr. Full-length comedies, dramas, musicals, juveniles. Query first with synopsis and resumé. Payment varies.

SPAYTEN DAYVIL THEATRE CO.—c/o Isabel Glasser 16 W. 16th St. #11FN, New York, NY 10011. Full-length comedies and dramas with single set and cast size to 5. SASE required.

STAGE LEFT THEATRE—3244 N. Clark, Chicago, IL 60657. Dennis McCullough, Art. Dir. Full-length comedies, dramas, and adaptations for cast of 10. "We are committed to producing material that is politically and socially conscious." Submit in the spring/summer. Reports in 4 to 6 weeks. Offers workshops and readings. Payment varies.

STAGE ONE: THE LOUISVILLE CHILDREN'S THEATRE—425 W. Market St., Louisville, KY 40202. Dramatized classics, and plays for children ages 4 to 18. Submit script with resumé and SASE. Reports in 4 months.

STAGES REPERTORY THEATRE—3201 Allen Parkway, Suite 101, Houston, TX 77019. Ted Swindley, Artistic Dir. Joe Turner Cantu, Assoc. Art. Dir. Full-length and one-act comedies, dramas, and children's scripts, especially from Texan playwrights; cast to 12; simple set. Submit script, synopsis, resumé, and SASE.

STATE UNIVERSITY OF NEW YORK AT STONY BROOK—Theatre Arts Dept., Stony Brook, NY 11794. John Cameron, Prod. Mgr. One-act and full-length comedies and dramas. Submit synopsis with resumé and SASE. No unsolicited manuscripts. Offers workshops and readings.

STEVE DOBBINS PRODUCTIONS—25 Van Ness Ave., Lower Level, San Francisco, CA 94102. Michael Lojrovic, Lit. Dir. Full-length comedies, dramas, and musicals. Cast to 12. Query with synopsis and resumé. No unsolicited manuscripts. Reports in 6 months. Offers workshops and readings. Pays 6% of gross.

STREET PLAYERS THEATRE—P.O. Box 2687, Norman, OK 73070. Thomas C. Lategola, Art. Dir. Full-length comedies, dramas, and children's plays for four to seven actors, with single sets or open staging. Queries preferred. Reporting time 6 mos. Pays $250, after production.

STUDIO ARENA THEATRE—710 Main St., Buffalo, NY 14202. Comedies, dramas; cast to 12. Particular interest in plays by and about women or minorities. Include synopsis, resumé, cast list.

TAKOMA PLAYERS, INC.—Box 56512, Washington, DC 20012. Andrea Hines, Art. Dir. Realistic, full-length dramas, comedies, and musicals. Special interest in plays suitable to multi-ethinic casts. Submit manuscript with SASE; report in 3 months. Payment negotiable.

TAPER FORUM, MARK—135 N. Grand Ave., Los Angeles, CA 90012. Jessica Teich, Lit. Mgr. Full-length comedies, dramas, musicals, juvenile, adaptations. Query first.

THEATRE AMERICANA—Box 245, Altadena, CA 91001. Full-length comedies and dramas, preferably with American theme. Send manuscript with cast list and SASE. No payment. Allow 3 to 6 months for reply.

THEATRE ARTISTS OF MARIN—Box 473, San Rafael, CA 94915. Charles Brousse, Art. Dir. Full-length comedies, dramas, and musicals for a cast of 2 to 8. Submit synopsis with cast list and return postcard. Reports in 4 to 6 months. Pays $400 before opening.

THEATRE ON THE SQUARE—450 Post St., San Francisco, CA 94105. John Reines, Art. Dir. Full-length comedies, dramas, and musicals for 10-person cast that can be performed on 35 x 55 stage. Submit cast list and script with SASE. Reports in 30 days.

THEATRE THREE REPERTORY COMPANY—1544 Fulton St., Fulton, CA 93721. Gordon Goede, Art. Dir. Comedies, dramas, and children's plays with a one-hour running time. Submit synopsis with return postcard and cast list, fall to January 1. Grant offered as payment.

THEATRE/TEATRO—Bilingual Foundation for the Arts, 421 N. Ave., #19, Los Angeles, CA 90031. Margarita Galban, Art. Dir. Full-length plays about Hispanic experience; small casts. Submit manuscript with return postcard. Pays negotiable rates.

THEATREWORKS/USA—890 Broadway, 7th Fl., New York, NY 10003. Barbara Pasternack, Lit. Man. Small-cast children's musicals only. Playwrights must be within commutable distance to New York City. Submit in spring, summer. Pays royalty.

WALNUT STREET THEATRE COMPANY—9th and Walnut Sts., Philadelphia, PA 19107. Ernest Tremblay, Lit. Mgr. Full-length comedies, dramas, musicals, and adaptations; also, 1- to 5-character plays for 2nd stage. Submit 10 pages sample with return postcard, cast list, and synopsis. Reports in 5 months. Payment varies.

WISDOM BRIDGE THEATRE—1559 W. Howard St., Chicago, IL 60626. Joshua F. Pollack, Acting Lit. Mgr. Plays dealing with contemporary social/political issues; small scale musicals, literary adaptations; cast to 12.

WOOLLY MAMMOTH THEATRE COMPANY—1401 Church St. N.W., Washington, DC 20005. Martin Blank, Lit. Mgr. Looking for off-beat material, unusual writing. Unsolicited scripts accepted. Pay negotiable.

YOUNG MIME THEATRE, GARY—23724 Park Madrid, Casabasas, CA 91302. Gary Young, Art. Dir. Comedy monologues and two-person vignettes, for children and adults, 1 minute to 90 minutes in length; casts of 1 or 2, and portable set. Pays varying rates. Enclose return postcard, resumé, recommendations, cast list and synopsis.

PLAY PUBLISHERS

ART CRAFT PLAY COMPANY—Box 1058, Cedar Rapids, IA 52406. Three-act comedies, mysteries, musicals, and farces, and one-act comedies or dramas, with one set, for production by junior or senior high schools. Pays on royalty basis or by outright purchase.

BAKER'S PLAYS—100 Chauncy St., Boston, MA 02111. Scripts for amateur production: one-act plays for competition, children's plays, musicals, religious drama, full-length plays for high school production. Three- to four-month reading period. Include SASE.

CHILDREN'S PLAYMATE—1100 Waterway Blvd., P. O. Box 567, Indianapolis, IN 46206. Elizabeth A. Rinck, Ed. Plays, 200 to 600 words, for children aged 5 to 7: special emphasis on health, nutrition, exercise, and safety. Pays about 8¢ a word, on publication.

CONTEMPORARY DRAMA SERVICE—Meriwether Publishing Co., Box 7710, 885 Elkton Dr., Colorado Springs, CO 80903. Arthur Zapel, Ed. Books on theatre arts subjects and anthologies. Textbook for speech and drama. Easy-to-stage comedies, skits, one-acts, musicals, puppet scripts, full-length plays for schools and churches. (Jr. High through college level; no elementary level material.) Adaptations of classics and improvised material for classroom use. Comedy monologues and duets. Chancel drama for Christmas and Easter church use. Enclose synopsis. Pays by fee arrangement or on royalty basis.

THE DRAMATIC PUBLISHING CO.—311 Washington St., P. O. Box 109, Woodstock, IL 60098. Full-length and one-act plays, musical comedies for amateur, children, and stock groups. Must run at least thirty minutes. Pays on royalty basis. Address Sally Fyfe. Reports within 10 to 14 weeks.

DRAMATICS—The International Thespian Society, 3368 Central Pkwy., Cincinnati, OH 45225–2392. Don Corathers, Ed. One-act and full-length plays for high school production. Pays $50 to $200, on acceptance.

ELDRIDGE PUBLISHING COMPANY—P. O. Drawer 216, Franklin, OH 45005. Nancy Vorhis, Ed. Dept. One-, two-, and three-act plays and operettas for school, churches, community groups, etc. Special interest in comedies and Christmas plays. Include cassette for operettas. Pays varying rates. Responds in 2 to 3 months.

FRENCH, INC., SAMUEL—45 W. 25th St., New York, NY 10010. Lawrence R. Harbison, Ed. Full-length plays for dinner, community, stock, college, and high school theatres. One-act plays (30 to 45 minutes). Children's plays, 45 to 60 minutes. Pays on royalty basis.

HEUER PUBLISHING COMPANY—Drawer 248, Cedar Rapids, IA 52406. C. Emmett McMullen, Ed. One-act comedies and dramas for contest work; three-act comedies, mysteries, or farces and musicals, with one interior setting, for high school production. Pays royalty or flat fee.

PIONEER DRAMA SERVICE—P. O. Box 22555, Denver, CO 80222. Full-length and one-act plays for young audiences: musicals, melodramas, religious scripts. No unproduced plays, plays with largely male casts or multiple sets. Query. Pays royalty or outright purchase.

PLAYS, THE DRAMA MAGAZINE FOR YOUNG PEOPLE—120 Boylston St., Boston, MA 02116. Elizabeth Preston, Man. Ed. One-act plays, with simple settings, for production by young people, 7 to 17: holiday plays, comedies, dramas, farces, skits, dramatized classics, puppet plays, melodramas, dramatized folktales, and creative dramatics. Maximum lengths: lower grades, 10 double-spaced pages; middle grades, 15 pages; junior and senior high, 20 pages. Casts may be mixed, all-male or all-female; plays with one act preferred. Manuscript specification sheet available on request. Queries suggested for adaptations. Pays good rates, on acceptance. Buys all rights.

SCHOLASTIC SCOPE—730 Broadway, New York, NY 10003. Deborah Sussman, Assoc. Ed. For ages 15 to 18 with 4th- to 5th-grade reading ability. Plays, 1,000 to 6,000 words, on problems of contemporary teenagers, relationships between people in family, job, and school situations. Some mysteries, comedies, and science fiction; plays about minorities. Pays good rates, on acceptance.

SCHOLASTIC VOICE—730 Broadway, New York, NY 10003. Forrest Stone, Ed. For ages 14 to 18 with at least an 8th-grade reading level. Plays, 1,000 to 6,000 words, on any subject. Magazine is distributed though schools. Pays good rates, on acceptence.

THE TELEVISION MARKET

The almost round-the-clock television offerings on commercial, educational, and cable TV stations may lead free-lance writers to believe that opportunities to sell scripts or program ideas are infinite. Unfortunately, this is not true. With few exceptions, producers and programmers do not consider scripts submitted directly to them, no matter how good they are. In general, free lancers can achieve success in this nearly closed field by concentrating on getting their fiction (short and in novel form) and nonfiction published in magazines or books, combed diligently by television producers for possible adaptations. A large percentage of the material offered over all types of networks (in addition to the motion pictures made in Hollywood or especially for TV) is in the form of adaptations of published material.

Writers who want to try their hand at writing directly for this very limited market should be prepared to learn the special techniques and acceptable format of script writing. Also, experience in playwriting and a knowledge of dramatic structure gained through working in amateur, community, or professional theaters can be helpful.

Since virtually all TV producers will read scripts and queries submitted only through recognized agents, we've included a list of agents who have indicated to us that they are willing to read queries for TV scripts. Society of Authors' Representatives (10 Astor Pl., 3rd Floor, New York, NY 10003) will send out a listing of agents upon receipt of an SASE, and *Literary Market Place* (Bowker), available in most libraries, also has list of agents. Before submitting scripts to producers or to agents, authors should query to learn whether they prefer to see the material in script form, or as an outline or summary. A complete list of shows and production companies may be found in *Ross Reports Television,* published monthly by Television Index, Inc., (40–29 27th St., Long Island City, NY 11101).

Writers may wish to register their story, treatment, series format, or script with the Writers Guild of America. This registration does not confer statutory rights, but it does supply evidence of authorship that is effective for ten years (and is renewable after that). For more information, write the Writers Guild of America Registration Service East, Inc., 555 W. 57th St., New York, NY 10019. Dramatic material can also be registered with the U.S. Copyright Office (Register of Copyrights, Library of Congress, Washington, DC 20559). Finally, those interested in writing for television may want to read such daily trade newspapers as *Daily Variety* (1400 N. Cahuenga Blvd., Hollywood, CA 90028) and *Hollywood Reporter* (6715 Sunset Blvd., Hollywood, CA 90028).

TELEVISION SCRIPT AGENTS

MARCIA AMSTERDAM AGENCY—41 W. 82nd St., #9A, New York, NY 10024. Query with SASE.

PEMA BROWNE LTD—185 E. 85th St., New York, NY 10028. No scripts for ongoing shows. Reads queries. Prefer writers with credits.

THE CALDER AGENCY—17420 Ventura Blvd., Suite 4, Encino, CA 91316. Reads queries and synopses for features only; no episode TV material. Movies for TV and long form O.K.

BILL COOPER ASSOCIATES—224 W. 49th St., New York, NY 10019. Will look at developed ideas for comedies, dramas, and motion pictures.

ANN ELMO AGENCY, INC.—60 E. 42nd St., New York, NY 10165. Prefer queries on TV or screen feature material. Writers with screen credits only.

OTTO R. KOZAK LITERARY AGENCY—P.O. Box 152, Long Beach, NY 11561. Query with SASE.

THE LANTZ OFFICE—888 Seventh Ave., New York, NY 10106. Limited market. Query.

L. HARRY LEE LITERARY AGENCY—Box 203, Rocky Point, NY 11778. Reads queries accompanied by SASE only. Episodic and sit-coms, all categories; syndicated programs, such as "Star Trek The Next Generation," movies of the week, mini-series, after school specials. Interested in new sit-com pilots.

LONDON STAR PROMOTIONS—21704 Devonshire St., Suite 200, Chatsworth, CA 91311–2903. Reads queries and synopses.

WILLIAM MORRIS AGENCY—1350 Ave. of the Americas, New York, NY 10019. Reads queries with SASEs.

FLORA ROBERT, INC.—Penthouse A, 157 West 57th St., New York, NY 10019. Query.

ROSENSTONE/WENDER—3 East 48th St., New York, NY 10017. No unsolicited manuscripts. Query.

THE SHUKAT COMPANY, LTD.—340 W. 55th St., #1A, New York, NY 10036. Query.

JACK TANTLEFF—c/o The Tantleff Office, 360 W. 20th St., New York, NY 10011. Reads queries.

DAN WRIGHT—c/o Ann Wright Representatives, Inc., 128 E. 56th St., New York, NY 10022. Reads queries. Specializes in motion pictures and television properties.

WRITERS AND ARTISTS AGENCY—70 West 36th St., #501, New York, NY 10021. Reads queries and treatments, with SASEs. Considers screenplays and plays. Send bio and resumé.

BOOK PUBLISHERS

The following list includes the major publishers of trade books (adult and juvenile fiction and nonfiction) and a representative number of small publishers from across the country. All companies in the list publish both hardcover and paperback books, unless otherwise indicated.

Before sending a complete manuscript to an editor, it is advisable to send a brief query letter describing the proposed book. The letter should also include information about the author's special qualifications for dealing with a particular topic and any previous publication credits. An outline of the book (or a synopsis for fiction) and a sample chapter may also be included.

It is common practice to submit a book manuscript to only one publisher at a time, although it is becoming more and more acceptable for writers, even those without agents, to submit the same query or proposal to more than one editor at the same time.

Book manuscripts may be sent in typing paper boxes (available from a stationer) and sent by first-class mail, or, more common and less expensive, by "Special Fourth Class Rate—Manuscript." For rates, details of insurance, and so forth, inquire at your local post office. With any submission to a publisher, be sure to enclose sufficient postage for the manuscript's return.

Royalty rates for hardcover books usually start at 10% of the retail price of the book and increase after a certain number of copies have been sold. Paperbacks generally have a somewhat lower rate, about 5% to 8%. It is customary for the publishing company to pay the author a cash advance against royalties when the book contract is signed or when the finished manuscript is received. Some publishers pay on a flat fee basis.

ABBEY PRESS—St. Meinrad, IN 47577. Keith McClellan, O.S.B., Pub. Nonfiction books on marriage, parenting, family, and life-challenges with a mainline Judeo-Christian religious slant. Query with table of contents and writing sample.

ABINGDON PRESS—201 Eighth Ave. S., Nashville, TN 37202. Mary Catherine Dean, Ed. Religious books. Query with outline and one or two sample chapters. Guidelines.

ACADEMIC PRESS—Harcourt, Brace, Jovanovich, Inc., 1250 Sixth St., San Diego, CA 92101. Scientific books for professionals; upper level undergraduate and graduate science texts. Query.

ACADEMY CHICAGO, PUBLISHERS—213 West Institute Pl., Chicago, IL 60610. Anita Miller, Ed. General quality adult fiction; classic mysteries with emphasis on character and/or puzzle. History; biographies, travel; books by and about women. Royalty. Also interested in reprinting books dropped by other houses, including academic titles and anthologies. Query with four sample chapters. SASE required.

ACCENT BOOKS—Box 15337, 12100 W. 6th Ave., Denver, CO 80215. Mary Nelson, Exec. Ed. Fiction and nonfiction from evangelical Christian perspective. Query with sample chapters. Royalty. Paperback only. Guidelines.

ACE BOOKS—Imprint of Berkley Publishing Group, 200 Madison Ave., New York, NY 10016. Susan Allison, V.P., Ed.-in-Chief. Science fiction and fantasy. Royalty. Query with first three chapters and outline.

ACROPOLIS BOOKS—2400 17th St. N.W., Washington, DC 20009–9964. A. J. Hackl, Ed. Nonfiction titles. Query with outline and sample chapters. Length varies. Royalty.

ADAMA BOOKS—306 W. 38th St., New York, NY 10018. Bennett Shelkowitz, Man. Dir. Adult nonfiction. Young-adult fiction and nonfiction. Children's picture books. Books with international focus or related to political or social issues. Query with outline and sample chapter.

ADDISON-WESLEY PUBLISHING CO.—Rt. 128, Reading, MA 01867. General Publishing Group: Adult nonfiction on current topics: education, health, psychology, computers, software, business, biography, child care, etc. Royalty.

ALASKA NORTHWEST BOOKS—A Div. of GT/E Discovery Publications. 130 2nd Ave. S., Edmonds, WA 98020. Maureen Zimmerman, Man. Nonfiction, 50,000 to 100,000 words, with an emphasis on natural resources and history of Alaska, Northwestern Canada, and Pacific Northwest: how-to books; biographies; cookbooks; field guides; guidebooks. Send query or sample chapters with outline. Limited market.

THE AMERICAN PSYCHIATRIC PRESS—1400 K St. N.W., Washington, DC 20005. Carol C. Nadelson, M.D., Ed.-in-Chief. Books that interpret scientific and medical aspects of psychiatry for a lay audience and that address specific psychiatric problems. Authors must have appropriate credentials to write on medical topics. Query required. Royalty.

AND BOOKS—702 S. Michigan, South Bend, IN 46618. Janos Szebedinsky, Ed. Adult nonfiction. Topics include computers, fine arts, health, philosophy, sports and recreation, regional subjects, biographies, and religion.

APPLE BOOKS—See Scholastic, Inc.

ARCADE PUBLISHING—Subsidiary of Little, Brown, and Co., 141 Fifth Ave., New York, NY 10010. Richard Seaver, Pub./Ed. Fiction, nonfiction, and children's books. Query first.

ARCHWAY PAPERBACKS—Pocket Books, 1230 Ave. of the Americas, New York, NY 10020. Patricia MacDonald, Sr. Ed. Young-adult contemporary fiction (mystery, suspense thrillers, romance, fantasy, problems) and nonfiction (popular current topics), for ages 11 and up. Query and SASE required; include outline and sample chapter.

ARCO PUBLISHING—Div. of Simon & Schuster, Gulf & Western Bldg., One Gulf & Western Plaza, 16th Fl., New York, NY 10023. Charles Wall, Exec.

Ed. Nonfiction, originals and reprints, from 50,000 words. Career guides, test preparation. Royalty. Query with outline. Return postage required.

ARCSOFT PUBLISHERS—P.O. Box 132, Woodsboro, MD 21798. Anthony Curtis, Pres. Nonfiction hobby books for beginners, personal computing, space science, desktop publishing, journalism, and hobby electronics, for laymen, consumers, beginners and novices. Outright purchase and royalty basis. Query. Paper only.

ATHENEUM PUBLISHERS—Subsidiary of Macmillan Publishing Co., 866 Third Ave., New York, NY 10022. Mr. Lee Goerner, Pub. General nonfiction, biography, history, current affairs, fiction, belles lettres. Query with sample chapters and outline.

THE ATLANTIC MONTHLY PRESS—19 Union Square West, New York, NY 10003. Gary Fisketjon, Ed. Dir. Fiction, general nonfiction. Hardcover and trade paperback. Royalty. SASE required.

AUGSBURG BOOKS—Box 1209, 426 S. Fifth St., Minneapolis, MN 55440. Robert Moluf, Sr. Ed. Religious books for children, youth, or intergenerational family use; devotional, inspirational, and self-help books for Christian market. Query first.

AVERY PUBLISHING GROUP—350 Thorens Ave., Garden City Park, NY 11040. Nonfiction, from 40,000 words, on health, childbirth, child care, health cooking. Query first. Royalty.

AVIATION PUBLISHERS—Ultralight Publications, Inc., One Aviation Way, Lock Box 234, Hummelstown, PA 17036. Michael A. Markowski, Ed. Nonfiction, from 30,000 words, on aviation, cars, model cars and planes, boats, trains, health, and self-help. Query with outline and sample chapters. Royalty.

AVON BOOKS—105 Madison Ave., New York, NY 10016. Susanne Jaffe, Ed. Dir. Modern fiction, general nonfiction, historical romance, 60,000 to 200,000 words. Science fiction, 75,000 to 100,000 words. Query with synopsis and sample chapters. Ellen Edwards, Historical Romance; John Douglas, Science Fiction. Camelot Books: Ellen Krieger, Ed. Fiction and nonfiction for 7- to 10-year-olds. Query. Flare Books: Ellen Krieger, Ed. Fiction and nonfiction for 12-year-olds and up. Query. Royalty. Paperback only.

BACKCOUNTRY PUBLICATIONS—Div. of The Countryman Press, Inc., P. O. Box 175, Woodstock, VT 05091. Carl Taylor, Ed. Regional guidebooks, 150 to 300 pages, on hiking, walking, canoeing, bicycling, mountain biking, cross-country skiing, and fishing. Send outline and sample chapter. Royalty.

BAEN BOOKS—Baen Enterprises, 260 Fifth Ave., New York, NY 10001. Jim Baen, Pres. and Ed.-in-Chief. Strongly plotted science fiction; innovative fantasy. Query with synopsis and manuscript. Royalty.

BAKER BOOK HOUSE—P. O. Box 6287, Grand Rapids, MI 49516–6287. Religious nonfiction. Dan Van't Kerkhoff, Ed. General trade and professional books; Allan Fisher, Ed. Academic and reference books. Royalty.

BALLANTINE BOOKS—201 E. 50th St., New York, NY 10022. Robert Wyatt, Ed.-in-Chief. General fiction and nonfiction. Query.

BALLANTINE/EPIPHANY—201 E. 50th St., New York, NY 10022. Toni Simmons, Ed. Nonfiction (personal growth, self help, decision-making, relationships, biography) with Christian elements or spiritual themes. Will consider fiction with inspirational qualities. Query with outline and sample chapters; manuscripts 60,000 to 75,000 words. SASE. Royalty.

BALSAM PRESS—122 E. 25th St., New York, NY 10010. Barbara Krohn, Exec. Ed. General and illustrated adult nonfiction. Royalty. Query.

BANTAM BOOKS—Div. of Bantam, Doubleday, Dell, 666 Fifth Ave., New York, NY 10103. Linda Grey, Pub., Stephen Rubin, Ed.-in-Chief, Adult Fiction and Nonfiction. General and educational fiction and nonfiction, 75,000 to 100,000 words. Carolyn Nichols, Loveswept. Judy Gitenstein, Ed. Dir., Books for Young Readers; fiction and science fiction, ages 6 to 12. Beverly Horowitz, Ed. Dir., Books for Young Adults; fiction and non-formula romance for teens; Bantam Travel Guides, Dick Scott, Pub. Only agented queries and manuscripts.

BARRON'S—250 Wireless Blvd., Hauppauge, NY 11788. Grace Freedson, Acquisitions Ed. Nonfiction for juveniles (science, nature, history, hobbies, and how-to) and picture books for ages 3 to 6. Nonfiction for adults (business, childcare, sports). Queries required. Guidelines.

BAUHAN, PUBLISHER, WILLIAM L.—Dublin, NH 03444. William L. Bauhan, Ed. Biographies, fine arts, gardening, and history books with an emphasis on New England. Submit query with outline and sample chapter.

BEACON PRESS—25 Beacon St., Boston, MA 02108. Joanne Wyckoff, Exec. Ed. Deborah Johnson, Sr. Ed. General nonfiction: world affairs, sociology, psychology, women's studies, political science, art, anthropology, literature, history, philosophy, religion. Series: Asian Voices (fiction and nonfiction); Barnard New Women Poets; Black Women Writers (fiction); Men and Masculinity (nonfiction); Virago/Beacon Travelers (nonfiction); Night Lights (juveniles). Query first. SASE required.

BEAR & COMPANY, INC.—P.O. Drawer 2860, Santa Fe, NM 87504. Barbara Clow, Ed. Nonfiction "that will help transform our culture philosophically, environmentally, and spiritually." Query with outline and sample chapters. SASE required. Royalty.

BERKLEY PUBLISHING GROUP—200 Madison Ave., New York, NY 10016. Roger Cooper, Pub. Leslie Gelbman, Ed.-in-Chief. General-interest fiction and nonfiction: science fiction, suspense and espionage novels; romance. Submit through agent only. Publishes both reprints and originals. Paper only.

BETHANY HOUSE PUBLISHERS—6820 Auto Club Rd., Minneapolis, MN 55438. Address Editorial Dept. Fiction, nonfiction. Religious. Royalty. Query required.

BETTER HOMES AND GARDENS BOOKS—See Meredith Corporation.

BINFORD & MORT PUBLISHING—1202 N.W. 17th Ave., Portland, OR 97209. J. F. Roberts, Ed. Books on subjects related to the Pacific Coast and the Northwest. Lengths vary. Royalty. Query first.

BLACK LIZARD BOOKS—See Creative Arts Book Co.

BLAIR, PUBLISHERS, JOHN F.—1406 Plaza Dr., Winston-Salem, NC 27103. Stephen D. Kirk, Ed. Dept. Biography, history, fiction, folklore, and guidebooks, with Southeastern tie-in. Length: at least 75,000 words. Royalty. Query.

BONUS BOOKS—160 E. Illinois St., Chicago, IL 60611. Sharon Turner, Ed. Asst. Nonfiction; topics vary widely. Query with sample chapters and SASE. Royalty.

BOOKS FOR PROFESSIONALS—See Harcourt, Brace, Jovanovich.

BOUREGY & CO., INC., THOMAS—Avalon Books, 401 Lafayette St., New York, NY 10003. Barbara J. Brett, Ed. Hardcover library books. Wholesome contemporary romances, and mystery romances about young single (never married) women. Wholesome westerns and contemporary adventure novels. Length: 35,000 to 50,000 words. Query with first chapter and outline. SASE required.

BRADBURY PRESS—866 Third Ave., New York, NY 10022. Barbara Lalicki, Ed. Hardcover: fiction (general, humor, science fiction), grades 4–12; nonfiction (biography, sports, history) up to grade 6; picture books, to age 8. Submit complete manuscript. Royalty.

BRANDEN PRESS—17 Station St., Box 843, Brookline Village, MA 02147. Adolph Caso, Ed. Novels, 250 to 350 pages. Biography and autobiography about or by women. Also considers queries on history, computers, business, performance arts, and translations. Query with SASE. Royalty.

BRETHREN PRESS—1451 Dundee Ave., Elgin, IL 60120. Jeanne Donovan, Book Ed. Quality nonfiction in areas of Bible study and theology, Church history, practical discipleship, and lifestyle issues, social concerns, and devotional life/personal growth. Query with outline and sample chapters for 150- to 250-word manuscripts. Pays royalties or flat fee.

BRICK HOUSE PUBLISHING—Box 134, 11 Thoreau Rd., Acton, MA 01720. Robert Runck, Ed. Books on business, careers, travel, and home design and maintenance. Query with outline and sample chapters. Royalty.

BRIDGE PUBLISHING—2500 Hamilton Blvd., South Plainfield, NJ 07080. Nonfiction manuscripts on biography, autobiography, self-help, psychology, and religion. "Books must be written from an Evangelical Christian perspective, but need not be explicitly religious in nature."

BROADMAN PRESS—127 Ninth Ave. N., Nashville, TN 37234. Harold. S. Smith, Manager. Religious and inspirational fiction and nonfiction. Royalty. Query

BUCKNELL UNIVERSITY PRESS—Bucknell University, Lewisburg, PA 17837. Mills Edgerton, Ed. Scholarly nonfiction. Query. Royalty.

BULFINCH PRESS—(formerly New York Graphic Society Books) Div. of Little, Brown and Co., 34 Beacon St., Boston, MA 02108. Books on fine arts and photography. Query with outline or proposal and vita.

BUSINESS & PROFESSIONAL PUBLISHING DIV.—Div. of Simon & Schuster, Englewood Cliffs, NJ 07632. Ted Nardin, V.P. and Ed.-in-Chief. Nonfiction, how-to, and reference books on business, self-improvement, education, and technical subjects. Hardcover and paperback. Royalty.

CAMELOT BOOKS—See Avon Books.

CAROLRHODA BOOKS—241 First Ave. N., Minneapolis, MN 55401. Rebecca Poole, Ed. Complete manuscripts for ages 7–12: biography, science, nature, history, photo essays; historical fiction for ages 6 to 10; 10 to 15 pages. Guidelines. Outright purchase. Hardcover.

CARROLL AND GRAF PUBLISHERS, INC.—260 Fifth Ave., New York, NY 10001. Kent E. Carroll, Exec. Ed. General fiction and nonfiction. Royalty. Query with SASE.

THE CATHOLIC UNIVERSITY OF AMERICA PRESS—620 Michigan Ave. N.E., Washington, DC 20064. David J. McGonagle, Dir. Scholarly nonfiction. Query with prospectus, annotated table of contents, or introduction and author's curriculum vitae. Royalty.

CBI PUBLISHING—See Van Nostrand Reinhold.

CHARTER BOOKS—Imprint of Berkley Publishing Co., 200 Madison Ave., New York, NY 10012. Roger Cooper, Pub. Adventure, espionage, and suspense fiction, women's contemporary fiction, family sagas, and historical novels. Westerns, male action/adventure, and cartoon books. No unsolicited manuscripts. Royalty or outright purchase. Paperback.

CHATHAM PRESS—P. O. Box A, Old Greenwich, CT 06807. Roger H. Lourie, Man. Dir. Books on the Northeast coast, New England maritime subjects, and the ocean. Royalty. Query with outline, sample chapters, illustrations, and SASE large enough for the return of material.

CHELSEA GREEN PUBLISHING CO.—Route 113, P.O. Box 130, Post Mills, VT 05058–0130. Ian Baldwin, Jr., Ed. Fiction and nonfiction on natural history, biography, history, politics, and travel. Query with outline. Royalty.

CHICAGO REVIEW PRESS—814 N. Franklin St., Chicago, IL 60610. Linda Matthews, Ed. Nonfiction: sports, medicine, anthropology, travel, nature, and regional topics. Query with outline and sample chapters.

CHILTON BOOK CO.—580 Waters Edge, Lombard, IL 60148. Compute! book line as well as Wallace-Homestead books.

CHILTON BOOK CO.—201 King of Prussia Rd., Radnor, PA 19089. Alan F. Turner, Ed. Dir. Computers, antiques and collectables, sewing and crafts, buisness, and automotive. Royalty. Query with outline, sample chapter, and return postage.

CHRONICLE BOOKS—275 Fifth St., San Francisco, CA 94103. Topical nonfiction, history, biography, fiction, art, photography, architecture, nature, food, regional, and children's books. Query with SASE.

CITADEL PRESS—See Lyle Stuart, Inc.

CLARION BOOKS—215 Park Ave. South, New York, NY 10003. Dorothy Briley, Ed. Fiction and picture books. Lively stories, ages 8 to 12 and 10 to 14; short novels (40 to 80 pages), ages 7 to 10. Mysteries, American historical fiction, and humor; picture books for preschool to age 3. Nonfiction: Biography, word play, nature, social studies, and holiday themes. Royalty. Hardcover.

CLIFFHANGER PRESS—P.O. Box 29527, Oakland, CA 94604–9527. Nancy Chirich, Ed. Mystery and suspense. Unagented manuscripts only. Query with first three chapters and outline; SASE. Royalty. Guidelines.

CLOVERDALE PRESS—96 Morton St., New York, NY 10014. Book packager. Contemporary romance, glitz and glamour, generational sagas, historicals, male action adventure, westerns, medical fiction. YA, middle- and lower-grade fiction and nonfiction. New series ideas and individual manuscripts welcome. Query with outline and resumé. Address YA to Marion Vaarn; adult to Lisa Howell.

COLLIER BOOKS—See Macmillan Publishing Co.

COMPCARE PUBLISHERS—18551 Von Karman Ave., Irvine, CA 92715. Bonnie Hesse, Man. Ed. Adult nonfiction; young-adult nonfiction: books on recovery from addictive/compulsive behavior; growth in personal, couple, and family relationships. Submit complete manuscript. Royalty.

COMPUTE! BOOKS—P. O. Box 5406, Greensboro, NC 27403. How-to computer books; specializes in software specific publications. Query preferred. Royalty.

CONCORDIA PUBLISHING HOUSE—3558 S. Jefferson Ave., St. Louis, MO 63118. Practical nonfiction with explicit religious content, conservative Lutheran doctrine. Very little fiction. No poetry. Royalty. Query.

CONSUMER REPORTS BOOKS—51 E. 42nd St., Suite 800, New York, NY 10017. Address Exec. Ed. Nonfiction of interest to consumers. Submit complete manuscript, or send contents, outline, and three chapters, with resumé.

CONTEMPORARY BOOKS, INC.—180 N. Michigan Ave., Chicago, IL 60601. Nancy Crossman, Ed. Dir. Trade nonfiction, 100 to 400 pages, on health, fitness, sports, cooking, humor, business, popular culture, biography, real estate, finance, women's issues. Query with outline and sample chapters. Royalty.

COOK PUBLISHING CO., DAVID C.—850 N. Grove Ave., Elgin, IL 60120. Paul Mouw, Man. Ed., Life Journey, General Titles. Catherine Davis, Man. Ed., Chariot, Children's Books. Fiction that "helps children better understand themselves and their relationship with God"; nonfiction that illuminates the Bible; picture books, ages 1 to 7; fiction for ages 8 to 10, 10 to 12, and 12 to 14. Lengths and payment vary. Query required. Guidelines.

COWARD, MCCANN—Div. of Putnam Publishing Group, 200 Madison Ave., New York, NY 10016. Fiction and nonfiction through agents only.

CRAFTSMAN BOOK COMPANY—6058 Corte del Cedro, P.O. Box 6500, Carlsbad, CA 92008. Laurence D. Jacobs, Ed. How-to construction and estimating manuals for builders, 450 pages. Royalty. Query. Softcover.

CREATIVE ARTS BOOK CO.—833 Bancroft Way, Berkeley, CA 94710. Peg O'Donnell, Ed. Adult nonfiction; no photography, technical books, science fiction, poetry, drama, romance, or art. Black Lizard Books: mystery and suspense fiction. Query with outline and sample chapters. Royalty.

THE CROSSING PRESS—22-D Roache Rd., P.O. Box 1048, Freedom, CA 95019. Elaine Goldman Gill, John Gill, Pubs. Fiction, health, men's studies, feminist studies, science fiction, mysteries, gay topics, cookbooks, health books. Royalty.

CROSSWINDS—300 E. 42nd St., New York, NY 10017. Nancy Jackson, Sr. Ed. Teen romances and stories of the supernatural for foreign markets. Guidelines.

CROWELL, THOMAS Y.—See Harper Junior Books Group.

CROWN PUBLISHERS—225 Park Ave. S., New York, NY 10003. Andrea E. Cascardi, Exec. Ed. Fiction (including humor and mystery), nonfiction (biography, science, sports, nature, music, and history), and picture books for ages 3 and up. Query with outline and sample chapter; send manuscript for picture books. Guidelines.

DAVID PUBLISHERS, INC., JONATHAN—68–22 Eliot Ave., Middle Village, NY 11379. Alfred J. Kolatch, Ed.-in-Chief. General nonfiction (how-to, sports, cooking and food, self-help, etc.) and specializing in Judaica. Royalty or outright purchase. Query with outline, sample chapter, and resumé required. SASE.

DAW BOOKS, INC.—1633 Broadway, New York, NY 10019. Elizabeth R. Wollheim, Ed.-in-Chief. Science fiction and fantasy, 60,000 to 120,000 words. Royalty.

DEL REY BOOKS—201 E. 50th St., New York, NY 10022. Shelly Shapiro, SF Ed. Lester del Rey, V.P. and Fantasy Ed. Science fiction and fantasy; first novelists welcome. Material must be well-paced with logical resolutions. Fantasy with magic basic to plotline. Length, 70,000 to 120,000 words. Complete manuscripts preferred, or outline with 3 sample chapters. Royalty.

DELACORTE PRESS—666 Fifth Ave., New York, NY 10103. Jackie Farber, Robert Miller, Eds. Adult fiction and nonfiction. Juvenile and YA fiction (George Nicholson, Ed.). Accepts fiction (mystery, YA, romance, fantasy, etc.) from agents only.

DELL PUBLISHING—666 Fifth Ave., New York, NY 10103. Dell Books: family sagas, historical romances, war action, general fiction, occult/horror/psychological suspense, true crime, men's adventure. Delta: General-interest nonfiction, psychology, feminism, health, nutrition, child care, science. Delta Trade Paperbacks: nonfiction, self-help, how-to. Laurel: Nonfiction. History, politics, language, reference. Juvenile Books: Yearling (kindergarden through 6th grade; no unsolicited manuscripts); and Laurel-Leaf (grades 7 through 12; no unsolicited manuscripts). Submissions policy for Dell Books: Send four-page narrative synopsis for fiction, or an outline for nonfiction. Enclose SASE. Address submissions to the appropriate Dell division, Editorial Dept., Book Proposal.

DELTA BOOKS—See Dell Publishing Co.

DEMBNER BOOKS—80 Eighth Ave., New York, NY 10011. Therese Eiben, Ed. Popular reference books, popular medicine, mystery fiction. No first-person tragedy, no romance or pornography, no fads. Send synopsis and two sample chapters with SASE. Modest advances against royalties.

DEVIN-ADAIR PUBLISHERS, INC.—6 N. Water St., Greenwich, CT 06830. C. de la Belle Issue, Pub. J. Andrassi, Ed. Books on conservative affairs, Irish topics, Americana, self-help, health, gardening, cooking, and ecology. Royalty. Send outline, sample chapters, and SASE.

DILLON PRESS—242 Portland Ave. S., Minneapolis, MN 55415. Tom Schneider, Nonfiction Ed. Lisa Erskine, Fiction Ed. Juvenile nonfiction: International festivals and holidays, world and U.S. geography, environmental topics, U.S. cities, contemporary and historical biographies for elementary and middle-grade levels, unusual or remarkable animals. Short historical fiction for ages 8 to 12 based on a single event, mystery, adventure, and science fiction. Length, 10 to 90 pages. Royalty and outright purchase. Guidelines.

DOUBLEDAY AND CO.—666 Fifth Ave., New York, NY 10103. Hardcover: mystery/suspense fiction, science fiction, 70,000 to 80,000 words. Send query and outline to appropriate editor: Crime Club or Science Fiction. Wendy Barish, Pub., Books for Young Readers: "Only special books, appropriate for gifts in the bookstore market." Paperback: Martha Levin, Pub., Anchor Press. Adult trade books: general fiction and nonfiction, sociology, psychology, philosophy, women's etc. Herman Gollob, Ed.-in-Chief. Query. SASE required.

DUNNE BOOKS, THOMAS—Imprint of St. Martin's Press, 175 Fifth Ave., New York, NY 10010. Thomas L. Dunne, Ed. Adult fiction (mysteries, trade, SF, etc.) and nonfiction (history, biographies, how-to, etc.). Query with outline and sample chapters and SASE. Royalty.

DUTTON, E. P.—Div. of N.A.L./Penguin, 2 Park Ave., New York, NY 10016. Lucia Monfried, Ed.-in-Chief, Children's Books. Picture books, easy-to-read books; fiction and nonfiction for preschoolers to young adults. Submit outline and sample chapters with query for fiction and nonfiction, complete manuscripts for picture books and easy-to-read books. Manuscripts should be well-written with fresh ideas and child appeal. E.P. Dutton Adult Trade: Richard Marek, Pub., Joyce Engelson, Ed.-in-Chief.

EAST WOODS PRESS—Imprint of The Globe Pequot Press, 429 East Kingston Ave., Charlotte, NC 28203. Sally McMillan, Consulting Ed. Nonfiction on travel, cooking, natural science, regional history, and home improvement. Length requirements and payment rates vary. Query with sample chapter required.

EERDMANS PUBLISHING COMPANY, INC., WM. B—255 Jefferson Ave. S.E., Grand Rapids, MI 49503. Jon Pott, Ed.-in-Chief. Protestant, Roman Catholic, and Orthodox theological nonfiction; American religious history; some fiction. Royalty.

EMC CORP.—300 York Ave., St. Paul, MN 55101. Eileen Slater, Ed. Vocational, career, and consumer education textbooks. Royalty. No unsolicited manuscripts.

ENSLOW PUBLISHERS—Bloy St. & Ramsey Ave., Box 777, Hillside, NJ 07205. R. M. Enslow, Jr., Ed/Pub. Nonfiction for young adults and children on social issues and science topics. Also reference and professional books in science, technology, medicine, and business. Royalty. Query first.

ERIKSSON, PUBLISHER, PAUL S.—208 Battell Bldg., Middlebury, VT 05753. General nonfiction; some fiction. Royalty. Query first.

EVANS & CO., INC., M.—216 E. 49th St., New York, NY 10017. Books on humor, health, self-help, popular psychology, and cookbooks. Western fiction for adults; fiction and nonfiction for young adults. Query with outline, sample chapter, and SASE. Royalty.

FACTS ON FILE PUBLICATIONS—460 Park Ave. S., New York, NY 10016. Gerard Helferich, Ed.-in-Chief. Reference and trade books on business, science, health, language, history, the performing arts, etc. Query with outline and sample chapter. Royalty. Hardcover.

FARRAR, STRAUS & GIROUX—19 Union Sq. West, New York, NY 10003. Fiction, poetry, YA novels, picture books, and nonfiction (history, nature, biography, and science). Query with sample chapter. Address Editorial Dept.

FELL PUBLISHERS, INC.—2131 Hollywood Blvd., Hollywood, FL 33020. Elizabeth Wyatt, Ed. Nonfiction: how-tos, especially business and health. Query with letter or outline and sample chapter, include SASE. Royalty.

THE FEMINIST PRESS AT THE CITY UNIVERSITY OF NEW YORK—311 E. 94th St., New York, NY 10128. Florence Howe, Pub. Reprints of significant "lost" fiction, autobiographies, or other feminist work from the past; biography; original anthologies for classroom adoption; handbooks; bibliographies. Royalty.

FINE, INC., DONALD I.—19 West 21st St., New York, NY 10010. Literary and commercial fiction. General nonfiction. No queries or unsolicited manuscripts. Submit through agent only.

FIREBRAND BOOKS—141 The Commons, Ithaca, NY 14850. Nancy K. Bereano, Ed. Feminist and lesbian fiction and nonfiction. Royalty. Softcover.

FIRESIDE BOOKS—Imprint of Simon & Schuster, 1230 Ave. of the Americas, New York, NY 10020. General nonfiction; cultural and issue-oriented fiction. Royalty basis or outright purchase. Submit outline and one chapter. Trade paperback reprints and originals.

FLARE BOOKS—See Avon Books.

FORTRESS PRESS—426 S. Fifth St., Box 1209, Minneapolis, MN 55440. John Hollar, Dir. Books in the areas of biblical studies, theology, ethics, and church history for academic and professional markets, including libraries. Query first.

FOUR WINDS PRESS—Imprint of Macmillan Publishing Co., 866 Third Ave., New York, NY 10022. Neal Porter, Pub. Cindy Kane, Ed.-in-Chief. Juveniles: picture books, fiction for all ages. Nonfiction for young children. Query with SASE required for nonfiction. No simultaneous submissions. Hardcover only.

THE FREE PRESS—See Macmillan Publishing Co.

FRIENDS UNITED PRESS—101 Quaker Hill Dr., Richmond, IN 47374. Ardith Talbot, Ed. Nonfiction and fiction, 200 pages, on Quaker history, biography, and Quaker faith experience. Royalty. Query with outline and sample chapters.

GARDEN WAY PUBLISHING COMPANY—Storey Communications, Schoolhouse Rd., Pownal, VT 05261. Pamela B. Art, Man. Ed. How-to books on gardening, cooking, building, animals, country living. Royalty or outright purchase. Query with outline and sample chapter.

GINIGER CO. INC., K.S.—1133 Broadway, Suite 1301, New York, NY 10010. General nonfiction; reference and religious. Royalty. Query with SASE; no unsolicited manuscripts.

THE GLOBE PEQUOT PRESS—138 W. Main St., Chester, CT 06412. Laura Strom, Asst. Ed. Nonfiction with national and regional focus; nature and outdoor guides; environment and natural sciences; how tos; gardening; journalism and media; biographies. Travel guidebooks a specialty. Royalty. Query with sample chapter, contents, and one-page synopsis. SASE required.

GOLD EAGLE BOOKS—See Worldwide Library.

GOLDEN PRESS—See Western Publishing Co., Inc.

GRAYWOLF PRESS—Box 75006, St. Paul, MN 55175. Scott M. Walker, Ed. Literary fiction (short story collections and novels), poetry, and essays. Query with sample chapters.

GREENE PRESS, INC., STEPHEN—Div. of Penguin U.S.A., 15 Muzzey St., Lexington, MA 02173. Tom Begner, Pres. General nonfiction; fitness, sports, and nature. Royalty.

GREENWILLOW BOOKS—Imprint of William Morrow and Co., Inc., 105 Madison Ave., New York, NY 10016. Susan Hirschman, Ed.-in-Chief. Children's books for all ages. Picture books.

GROSSET AND DUNLAP, INC.—Div. of Putnam Publishing Group, 200 Madison Ave., New York, NY 10016. Material accepted through agents only.

GROVE WEIDENFELD—841 Broadway, New York, NY 10003–4793. A merger of Grove Press and Weidenfeld & Nicolson. "Looking to publish distinguished fiction and non-fiction." Queries required.

GULLIVER BOOKS—See Harcourt Brace Jovanovich.

HAMMOND INC.—Maplewood, NY 07040. Charles Lees, Ed. Nonfiction: cartographic reference, travel. Payment varies. Query with outline and sample chapters. SASE required.

HANCOCK HOUSE PUBLISHERS—1431 Harrion Ave., Blaine, WA 98230. David Hancock, Ed. Nonfiction: gardening, outdoor guides, Western history, American Indians, real estate, and investing. Royalty.

HARBINGER HOUSE—3131 N. Country Club, Suite 106, Tucson, AZ 85716. Zdenek Gerych, Adult Books Ed. Linnea Gentry, Juvenile Books Ed. Adult fiction and nonfiction, 200 to 300 pages. Picture books, 3 to 30 pages. Juvenile fiction (fairy tales, fantasy adventure) 30 to 50 pages; and nonfiction (natural history, geography, space sciences) of varying lengths. Submit outline and sample chapters for adult books; send complete manuscript for juvenile books. Royalty.

HARCOURT BRACE JOVANOVICH—1250 Sixth Ave., San Diego, CA 92101. Adult trade nonfiction and fiction. Books for Professionals: test preparation guides and other student self-help materials. Miller Accounting Publications, Inc.: professional books for practitioners in accounting and finance; college accounting texts. Juvenile fiction and nonfiction for beginning readers through young adults under imprints: HBJ Children's Books, Gulliver Books, and Voyager Paperbacks. Adult books: no unsolicited manuscripts or queries. Children's books: unsolicited manuscripts accepted by HBJ Children's Books only. Send query or manuscript to Manuscript Submissions, Children's Book Division.

HARLEQUIN BOOKS/CANADA—225 Duncan Mill Rd., Don Mills, Ont., Canada M3B 3K9. Harlequin Romance: Karin Stoecker, Sr. Ed. Contemporary romance novels, 50,000 to 55,000 words, any setting, ranging in plot from the traditional and gentle to the more sophisticated. Query first. Harlequin Regency: Marmie Charndoff, Ed. Short traditional novels set in 19th century Europe, 50,000 to 60,000 words. Harlequin Superromance: Marsha Zinberg, Sr. Ed. Contemporary romance, 85,000 words, with North American or foreign setting. New writers: query first. Published writers: send manuscript, synopsis, and copy of published work. Harlequin Temptation: Lisa Boyes, Sr. Ed. Sensually charged contemporary romantic fantasies, 60,000 to 65,000 words. Query first.

HARLEQUIN BOOKS/U.S.—300 E. 42nd St., 6th Fl., New York, NY 10017. Debra Matteucci, Sr. Ed. Contemporary romances, 70,000 to 75,000 words. Send for tip sheets. Paperback. Harlequin American Romance: Believable situations, set in the U.S. Harlequin Intrigue: Set against backdrop of suspense and adventure. Query.

HARPER & ROW—10 E. 53rd St., New York, NY 10022. Fiction, nonfiction, biography, economics, etc.: Trade Dept.: Agents only, Helen Moore, Man. Ed. College texts: address College Dept. Religion, theology, etc.: address Religious Books Dept., Ice House One, 151 Union St., San Francisco, CA 94111. No unsolicited manuscripts; query only.

HARPER JUNIOR BOOKS GROUP—10 E. 53rd St., New York, NY 10022. K. Magnusson, Admin. Coord. West Coast: P. O. Box 6549, San Pedro, CA 90734. Linda Zuckerman, Exec. Ed. (Query one address only.) Juvenile fiction, nonfiction, and picture books imprints include: Thomas Y. Crowell Co., Publishers; juveniles, etc.; J. B. Lippincott Co.: juveniles, picture books, etc.; Harper & Row: juveniles, picture books, etc.; Trophy Books: paperback juveniles. All published from preschool to young adult titles. Query, send sample chapters, or send complete manuscript. Royalty.

HARVEST HOUSE PUBLISHERS—1075 Arrowsmith, Eugene, OR 97402. Eileen L. Mason, Ed. Nonfiction with evangelical theme: how-tos, educational, health. No biographies, history, or poetry. Query first. SASE required.

HEALTH COMMUNICATIONS, INC.—3201 S.W. 15th St., Deerfield Beach, FL 33442. Marie Stilkind, Ed. Books on self-help and recovery: for adults (250 pages) and juveniles (100 pages). Query with outline and sample chapter, or send manuscript. Royalty.

HEALTH PLUS PUBLISHERS—Box 22001, Phoenix, AZ 85028. Paula E. Clure, Ed. Books on health and fitness. Query with outline and sample chapters.

HEARST BOOKS AND HEARST MARINE BOOKS—See William Morrow and Co.

HEARTLAND PRESS—See Northword Inc.

HEATH & COMPANY, D. C.—125 Spring St., Lexington, MA 02173. Textbooks for schools and colleges. Professional books (Lexington Books Div.). Software and related educational material. Query Barbara Piercecchi, College.

HELDMAN BOOKS, IRMA—275 Central Park W., New York, NY 10024. Irma Heldman, Ed. Mystery and suspense, mainstream fiction, 65,000 words; query for nonfiction. Advance and royalty. Include return postage.

HEMINGWAY WESTERN STUDIES SERIES—Boise State University, 1910 University Dr., Boise, ID 83725. Tom Trusky, Ed. Nonfiction relating to the Inter-Mountain West (Rockies) in areas of history, political science, anthropology, natural sciences, film, fine arts, literary history or criticism. Publishes up to two books annually.

HERALD PRESS—616 Walnut Ave., Scottdale, PA 15683. Christian books for adults and children (age 9 to and up): inspiration, Bible study, self-help, devotionals, current issues, peace studies, church history, missions, and evangelism, family life. Send one-page summary and two sample chapters. Royalty.

HOLIDAY HOUSE, INC.—18 E. 53rd St., New York, NY 10022. Margery S. Cuyler, Vice Pres. General juvenile and young adult fiction and nonfiction. Royalty. Query with outline and sample chapter. Hardcover only.

HOLT AND CO., HENRY—115 W. 18th St., New York, NY 10011. John Macrae, Ed.-in-Chief. Fiction and nonfiction (mysteries, history, autobiographies, natural history, travel, art, and how-to) of highest literary quality. Royalty. Query with SASE required.

HOUGHTON MIFFLIN COMPANY—2 Park St., Boston, MA 02108. Fiction: literary, mainstream, historical, suspense, and science fiction. Nonfiction: history, biography. Query Submissions Dept. with SASE. Children's Book Division, address Mary Lee Donovan: picture books, fiction, and nonfiction for all ages. Query. Royalty.

H. P. BOOKS—Div. of Price Stern Sloan, 360 N. La Cienga Blvd., Los Angeles, CA 90048. Illustrated how-tos on cooking, gardening, photography, health and fitness, automotive, etc. Royalty. Query with SASE.

HUNTER PUBLISHING, INC.—300 Raritan Center Pkwy., Edison, NJ 08818. Michael Hunter, Ed. Travel guides. Query with outline.

INDIANA UNIVERSITY PRESS—10th and Morton Sts., Bloomington, IN 47404. Scholarly nonfiction, especially cultural studies, literary criticism, music, history, women's studies, archaeology, and anthropology, etc. Query with outline and sample chapters. Guideline booklet available. Royalty.

INTIMATE MOMENTS—See Silhouette Books.

JAMESON BOOKS—722 Columbus St., Ottawa, IL 61350. J. G. Campaigne, Ed. American historical fiction for "Frontier Library" series. Some nonfiction. Query with outline and sample chapters. Royalty.

JOHNSON BOOKS, INC.—1880 S. 57th Court, Boulder, CO 80301. Michael McNierney, Ed. Nonfiction: environmental subjects, archaeology, geology, natural history, astronomy, travel guides, outdoor guidebooks, fly fishing, regional. Royalty. Query.

JOVE BOOKS—200 Madison Ave., New York, NY 10016. Fiction and nonfiction. No unsolicited manuscripts.

JOY STREET BOOKS—Imprint of Little, Brown & Co., 34 Beacon St.,

Boston, MA 02108. Melanie Kroupa, Ed.-in-Chief. Juvenile picture books; fiction and nonfiction for middle readers and young adults. Especially interested in fiction for 8 to 12-year-olds and innovative nonfiction. Query with outline and sample chapters for nonfiction; send complete manuscript for fiction. Royalty.

KEATS PUBLISHING, INC.—27 Pine St., Box 876, New Canaan, CT 06840. D.R. Bensen, Ed. Nonfiction: health, inspiration, how-to. Royalty. Query.

KESTRAL BOOKS—See Viking Penguin, Inc.

KNOPF, INC., ALFRED A.—201 E. 50th St., New York, NY 10022. Stephanie Spinner, Assoc. Pub.; Frances Foster and Anne Schwartz, Sr. Eds.; Reg Kahney, Sr. Ed. nonfiction; Sherry Gerstein, Paperback Ed. Distinguished picture books, fiction and nonfiction for middle grades and YAs. Query for nonfiction; send manuscript for fiction. Ashbel Green, V.P. and Sr. Ed.; distinguished fiction and general nonfiction; query. Royalty. Guidelines.

KNOX PRESS, JOHN—See Westminster/John Knox Press.

LAUREL-LEAF BOOKS—See Dell Publishing Co.

LEISURE BOOKS—Div. of Dorchester Publishing Co., 276 Fifth Ave., New York, NY 10001. Audrey LaFehr, Sub. Ed. Historical romance novels, from 90,000 words; horror novels from 80,000 words; men's adventure series, Western series from 50,000 words. Query with synopsis, sample chapters, and SASE. Royalty.

LEONARD BOOKS, HAL—Box 13819, 7777 W. Bluemound Rd., Milwaukee, WI 53213. Glenda Herro, Ed. Prefer subjects related to music and entertainment. Query first. Royalty or flat fee.

LEXINGTON BOOKS—See D.C. Heath & Co.

LIBERTY HOUSE—Imprint of Tab Books, 10 E. 21st St., Suite 1101, New York, NY 10010. David J. Conti, Ed. Dir. Personal finance, investing, real estate, small business books; approach should be practical, realistic, results oriented. Query with outline, sample chapters if available. Royalty.

LION PUBLISHING—1705 Hubbard Ave., Batavia, IL 60510. Fiction and nonfiction written from a Christian viewpoint for a general audience. Juvenile activity books, Bible stories, and fact finder series. Royalty.

LIPPINCOTT COMPANY, J.B.—See Harper Junior Books Group.

LITTLE, BROWN & CO.—34 Beacon St., Boston, MA 02106. Fiction, general nonfiction, sports books; divisions for law and medical texts. Royalty. Submissions only from authors who have previously published in professional or literary journals, newspapers or magazines. Query Ed. Dept., Trade Div. Juvenile fiction (from fantasy and romance to YA and mystery) and nonfiction (science, history, and nature), picture books (ages 3 to 8), and humor/poetry (ages 8 to 10). Prefer manuscripts with SASE. Address Maria Modugno, Ed.-in-Chief. Guidelines.

LODESTAR—Imprint of E.P. Dutton, 2 Park Ave., New York, NY 10016. Virginia Buckley, Ed. Dir. Fiction (YA, mystery, fantasy, science fiction, western) and nonfiction (science, sports, nature, history) considered for ages 9 to 11, 10 to 14, and 12 to up. Also fiction and nonfiction picture books for ages 4–8. Send manuscript for fiction; query for nonfiction.

LONGMAN FINANCIAL SERVICES PUBLISHING—Div. of Longman Group U.S.A., 520 N. Dearborn, Chicago, IL 60610. Books for professionals on financial services, real estate, insurance, securities, banking, etc. Send query with outline and sample chapters to Anita A. Constant, V.P./Publ. Royalty and flat fee.

LOTHROP, LEE & SHEPARD BOOKS—Imprint of William Morrow & Co., Inc., 105 Madison Ave., New York, NY 10016. Juvenile, picture books, fiction, and nonfiction. Royalty. Query.

LOVESWEPT—Imprint of Bantam Books, 666 Fifth Ave., New York, NY 10103. Carolyn Nichols, Assoc. Pub. Highly sensual, adult contemporary romances, approx. 55,000 words. Study field before submitting. Query required. Paperback only.

LOYOLA UNIVERSITY PRESS—3441 N. Ashland Ave., Chicago, IL 60657. George A. Lane, S. J., Ed. Religious material for college-educated Catholic readers. Nonfiction, 200–400 pages. Royalty. Query with outline.

LYNX BOOKS—41 Madison Ave., New York, NY 10010. Judith Stern, Sr. Ed. Manuscripts, 80,000 to 120,000 words, on romance, sagas, men's adventure, horror, science fiction, and thrillers; 70,000 words on self-help, business, and health; 40,000 words, series for boys and girls, 12 yrs. Hardcover and paperback. Query. Royalty.

LYONS & BURFORD, PUBLISHERS—31 W. 21st St., New York, NY 10010. Peter Burford, Ed. Books, 100 to 300 pages, related to the outdoors (camping, history, etc.). Send query with outline. Royalty.

MCELDERRY BOOKS, MARGARET K.—Macmillan Publishers, 866 Third Ave., New York, NY 10022. Margaret K. McElderry, Ed. Picture books; quality fiction, including fantasy, science fiction, humor, and realism; nonfiction. For ages 3 to 5, 6 to 9, 8 to 2, 10 to 14, and 12 and up.

MCKAY COMPANY, DAVID—201 E. 50th St., New York, NY 10022. Nonfiction. Unsolicited manuscripts neither acknowledged nor returned.

MACMILLAN PUBLISHING CO., INC.—866 Third Ave., New York, NY 10022. General Books Division: religious, sports, science and reference books. No fiction. Collier Books: paperbacks. The Free Press: college texts and professional books in social sciences and humanities. Royalty.

MADISON BOOKS—4700 Boston Way, Lanham, MD 20706. Full-length, nonfiction manuscripts on history, biography, popular culture, contemporary affairs, trade reference, and the social sciences. Query required. Royalty.

MAIN STREET PRESS—William Case House, Pittstown, NJ 08867. Martin Greif, Ed. Dir. Illustrated nonfiction: architecture and design, crafts (especially quilting), film, popular culture, and humor. Submit proposal with sample chapters and illustrative material. Royalty or flat fee.

MEADOWBROOK PRESS—18318 Minnetonka Blvd., Deephaven, MN 55391. Ann Nielsen, Submissions Ed. Upbeat, useful books on pregnancy, childbirth, and parenting, travel, humor, children's activities, 60,000 words. Query with outline, sample chapters, and qualifications. Royalty or payment.

MENTOR BOOKS—See New American Library.

MERCURY HOUSE—P. O. Box 640, Forest Knolls, CA 94933. Ms. Alev Lytle, Exec. Ed. Quality fiction and nonfiction, 250 to 350 pages. Query with outline and sample chapters.

MEREDITH CORP. BOOK GROUP—Better Homes and Gardens Books, 1716 Locust St., Des Moines, IA 50336. David A. Kirchner, Man. Ed. Books on gardening, crafts, health, decorating, etc., mostly staff written. Limited market. Query.

MESSNER, JULIAN—Div. of Simon & Schuster, Prentice Hall Bldg., Rt. 9W, Englewood Cliffs, NJ 07632. Jane Steltenpohl, Ed. Dir. Curriculum-oriented nonfiction. General nonfiction, ages 8 to 14, includes science, nature, biography, history, and hobbies. Lengths vary. Royalty.

METAMORPHOUS PRESS—P.O. Box 10616, 3249 N.W. 29th Ave., Portland, OR 97210. Anita Sullivan, Ed. Business, education, health, how-to, humor, performance arts, psychology, sports and recreation, and women's topics. Also children's books that promote self-esteem and self-reliance. "We select books that provide the tools to help people improve their lives and the lives of those around them." Query with sample chapter and outline.

MILLER ACCOUNTING PUBLICATIONS, INC.—See Harcourt, Brace, Jovanovich.

MINSTREL BOOKS—Imprint of Simon & Schuster, 1230 Ave. of the Americas, New York, NY 10020. Patricia MacDonald, Sr. Ed. Fiction for girls and boys ages 7 to 11. Query first with detailed plot outline, sample chapter, and SASE. Royalty.

MORROW AND CO., INC., WILLIAM—105 Madison Ave., New York, NY 10016. James Landis, Pub./Ed.-in-Chief. Adult fiction and nonfiction: no unsolicited manuscripts. Morrow Junior Books: David Reuther, Ed.-in-Chief. Children's books for all ages. Hearst Marine Books: Connie Roosevelt, Ed. Hearst Books: Ann Bramson, Ed. General nonfiction. Submit through agent only.

MORROW QUILL PAPERBACKS—Div. of William Morrow, 105 Madison Ave., New York, NY 10016. Andrew Ambraziejus, Man. Ed. Trade paperbacks. Adult nonfiction. No unsolicited manuscripts.

THE MOUNTAINEERS BOOKS—306 Second Ave. W., Seattle, WA 98119. Stephen Whitney, Ed. Mgr. Nonfiction on mountaineering, backpacking, canoeing, kayaking, bicycling, skiing. Field guides, regional histories, biographies of outdoor people; accounts of expeditions. Nature books. Royalty. Submit sample chapters and outline.

MULTNOMAH PRESS—10209 S.E. Division St., Portland, OR 97266. Conservative, evangelical nonficiton. Send outline and sample chapters. Royalty.

MUSTANG PUBLISHING CO., INC.—Box 9327, New Haven, CT 06533. Rollin A. Riggs, Pres. Nonfiction paperbacks for 18- to 35-year-olds. Send queries for 100- to 300-page books, with outlines and sample chapters. Royalty. SASE required.

THE MYSTERIOUS PRESS—129 W. 56th St., New York, NY 10019. William Malloy, Ed.-in-Chief. Mystery/suspense novels. Agented manuscripts only.

NAIAD PRESS, INC.—Box 10543, Tallahassee, FL 32302. Barbara Grier, Ed. Adult fiction, 60,000 to 70,000 words, with lesbian themes and characters: mysteries, romances, gothics, ghost stories, westerns, regencies, spy novels, etc. Royalty. Query with outline only.

NAL BOOKS—Div. of New American Library, 1633 Broadway, New York, NY 10019. Michaela Hamilton, Exec. Ed. Fiction and nonfiction books. Manuscripts accepted only from agents and upon personal recommendation.

NATUREGRAPH PUBLISHERS—P. O. Box 1075, Happy Camp, CA 96039. Barbara Brown, Ed. Nonfiction: Native American culture, natural history, outdoor living, land and gardening, holistic learning and health, Indian lore, crafts, and how-to. Royalty. Query.

THE NAVAL INSTITUTE PRESS—Annapolis, MD 21402. Nonfiction (60,000 to 100,000 words): How-tos on boating and navigation; battle histories; biography; ship guides. Occasional fiction (75,000 to 110,000 words). Royalty. Query with outline and sample chapters.

NELSON, INC., THOMAS—Nelson Place at Elm Hill Pike, P. O. Box 141000, Nashville, TN 37214–1000. William D. Watkins, Man. Ed. Religious adult nonfiction. Query with outline and sample chapter.

NEW AMERICAN LIBRARY—1633 Broadway, New York, NY 10019. Pat Taylor, Ed. Signet Books: Commercial fiction (historicals, sagas, thrillers, action/adventure novels, westerns, horror, science fiction and fantasy) and nonfiction (self-help, how-to, etc.). Plume Books: hobbies, business, health, cooking, child care, psychology, etc. Mentor Books: Nonfiction originals for the college and high school market. No unsolicited manuscripts.

NEW SOCIETY PUBLISHERS—4527 Springfield Ave., Philadelphia, PA 19143. Books on social change through nonviolent social action. Submit proposals with table of contents and sample chapter. Guidelines.

NEW YORK GRAPHIC SOCIETY BOOKS—See Bulfinch Press.

NEWMARKET PRESS—18 E. 48th St., New York, NY 10017. Theresa Burns, Man. Ed. Nonfiction on health, self-help, child care, parenting, biography, and history. Some fiction. Query first. Royalty.

NITTY GRITTY COOKBOOKS—Bristol Publishing Enterprises, P.O. Box 1737, San Leandro, CA 94577. Patricia J. Hall, Ed. Specialty cookbooks, 120-recipe manuscript pages. Query with outline and sample chapters. Royalty.

NORTHWORD INC.—Box 128, Ashland, WI 54806. Tom Klein, Ed. Natural history and heritage books, 25,000 words; same requirements, with Midwestern approach for Heartland Press. Send outline with sample chapters, or complete manuscript. Royalty or flat fee.

NORTON AND CO., INC., W.W.—500 Fifth Ave., New York, NY 10110. Liz Malcolm, Ed. High quality fiction and nonfiction. No occult, paranormal, religious, genre fiction (formula romance, SF, westerns), cookbooks, arts and crafts, YA or children's books. Royalty. Query with synopsis, 2–3 chapters, and resumé. Return postage and packaging required.

OPEN COURT PUBLISHING COMPANY—Box 599, Peru, IL 61354. Scholarly books on philosophy, psychology, religion, oriental thought, history, public policy, and related topics. Send sample chapters with outline and resumé. Royalty.

ORCHARD BOOKS—Div. of Franklin Watts, 387 Park Ave., New York, NY 10016. Norma Jean Sawicki, Pub. Hardcover picture books and fiction for juveniles; fiction for young adults. Nonfiction and photo essays for young children. Submit complete manuscript. Royalty.

OSBORNE/MCGRAW HILL—2600 Tenth St., Berkeley, CA 94710. Cynthia Hudson, Ed.-in-Chief. Micro computer books for general audience. Query. Royalty.

UNIVERSITY OF NEW MEXICO PRESS—University of New Mexico Press, Albuquerque, NM 87131. Elizabeth C. Hadas, Ed. Dir. David V. Holtby, Claire Sanderson, Dana Asbury, and Barbara Guth, Eds. Scholarly nonfiction on social and cultural anthropology, archaeology, Western history, art, and photography. Royalty. Query.

OXFORD UNIVERSITY PRESS—200 Madison Ave., New York, NY 10016. Authoritative books on literature, history, philosophy, etc.; college textbooks, medical, and reference books. Royalty. Query.

OXMOOR HOUSE, INC.—Box 2262, Birmingham, AL 35201. John Logue, Ed. Nonfiction: art, photography, gardening, decorating, cooking, and crafts. Royalty.

PACER BOOKS FOR YOUNG ADULTS—Imprint Berkley Publishing Group, 200 Madison Ave., New York, NY 10016. Fiction: adventure, fantasy, and role-playing fantasy gamebooks. No unsolicited manuscripts; queries only. Address Melinda Metz. Softcover only.

PANTHEON BOOKS—Div. of Random House, 201 E. 50th St., New York, NY 10022. Nonfiction: academic level for general reader on history, political science, sociology, etc.; picture books; folklore. Some fiction. Royalty. Query; no unsolicited manuscripts.

PARAGON HOUSE—90 Fifth Ave., New York, NY 10011. Ken Stuart, Ed.-in-Chief. Serious nonfiction, including biography, history, reference, and how-to. Query or send or manuscript. Royalty.

PARKER PUBLISHING COMPANY, INC.—West Nyack, NY 10994. James Bradler, Pres. Self-help and how-to books, 65,000 words: health, money opportunities, business, etc. Royalty.

PATH PRESS—53 W. Jackson Blvd., Chicago, IL 60604. Herman C. Gilbert, Ed. Quality books by and about African-Americans and Third-World peoples. Submit outline and sample chapters. Royalty.

PEACHTREE PUBLISHERS, LTD.—494 Armour Circle N.E., Atlanta, GA 30324. Wide variety of fiction and nonfiction. No religious material, SF/fantasy, romance, mystery/detective, historical fiction; no business, scientific, or technical books. Send outline and sample chapters for fiction and nonfiction. SASE required. Royalty.

PEANUT BUTTER PUBLISHING—329 Second Ave. W., Seattle, WA 98119. Elliott Wolf, Ed. Cookbooks as well as regional books and guides. Query with sample chapter and outline. Royalty and flat fee.

PELICAN PUBLISHING CO., INC.—1101 Monroe St., Gretna, LA 70053. James L. Calhoun, Exec. Ed. General nonfiction: Americana, regional, architecture, how-to, travel, cookbooks, inspirational, motivational, music, parenting, etc. Juvenile fiction. Royalty.

PELION PRESS—See The Rosen Publishing Group.

PENGUIN BOOKS—Div. of Viking/Penguin, Inc., 40 W. 23rd St., New York, NY 10010. Adult fiction and nonfiction. Royalty. No unsolicited material.

THE PERMANENT PRESS—R.D. 2, Noyac Rd., Sag Harbor, NY 11963. Judith Shepard, Ed. Seeks original and arresting novels. Trade books, biographies, political commentary. Query. Royalty.

PHAROS BOOKS—200 Park Ave., New York, NY 10166. Hana Umlauf Lane, Ed. Current issues, business and personal finance, food, health, history, how-to, humor, politics, reference, and sports. Nonfiction reference books for children, ages 6 and up. Query with sample chapter and outline. Royalty.

PHILOMEL BOOKS—Div. of The Putnam & Grosset Group, 200 Madison Ave., New York, NY 10016. Patricia Lee Gauch, Ed.-in-Chief. Pamela Wiseman,

Sr. Ed. Fiction, picture books, and some biographies. Fresh, original work with compelling characters and "a truly childlike spirit." Query required.

THE PILGRIM PRESS/UNITED CHURCH PRESS—132 W. 31 St., New York, NY 10001. Larry E. Kalp, Pub. Religious and general-interest nonfiction. Royalty. Query with outline and sample chapters.

PINEAPPLE PRESS—P.O. Drawer 16008, Southside Sta., Sarasota, FL 34239. June Cussen, Ed. Serious fiction and nonfiction, 60,000 to 125,000 words. Query with outline and sample chapters. Royalty.

PIPPIN PRESS—229 E. 85th St., Gracie Sta., Box 92, New York, NY 10028. Barbara Francis, Pub. High-quality picture books for pre-schoolers; middle-group fiction, humor and mysteries; imaginative nonfiction for children of all ages. Royalty. Query with outline.

PLENUM PUBLISHING CORP.—233 Spring St., New York, NY 10013. Linda Greenspan Regan, Sr. Ed. Trade nonfiction, approximately 300 pages, on science, social science, and humanities. Royalty. Query required. Hardcover.

PLUME BOOKS—See New American Library.

POCKET BOOKS—Div. of Simon and Schuster, 1230 Ave. of the Americas, New York, NY 10020. William R. Grose, Ed. Dir. Original fiction and nonfiction. Mystery line: police procedurals, private eye, and amateur sleuth novels; query with outline and sample chapters to Jane Chelius, Sr. Ed. Royalty.

POINT—See Scholastic, Inc.

POPULAR PRESS—Bowling Green State University, Bowling Green, OH 43403. Ms. Pat Browne, Ed. Nonfiction, 250 to 400 pages, examining some aspect of popular culture. Query with outline. Flat fee or royalty.

POSEIDON PRESS—Imprint of Simon & Schuster, 1230 Ave. of the Americas, New York, NY 10020. Ann Patty, V.P./Pub. General fiction and nonfiction. Royalty. No unsolicited material.

PRAEGER PUBLISHERS—Div. of Greenwood Press, 1 Madison Ave., New York, NY 10010. Ron Chambers, Pub. General nonfiction; scholarly and reference books. Royalty. Query with outline.

PRENTICE HALL PRESS—Div. of Simon & Schuster, Gulf & Western Bldg., New York, NY 10023. General nonfiction. No unsolicited manuscripts.

PRESIDIO PRESS—31 Pamaron Way, Novato, CA 94949. Nonfiction: contemporary military history from 50,000 words. Selected military fiction. Royalty. Query.

PRICE STERN SLOAN PUBLISHERS, INC.—360 N. La Cienega Blvd., Los Angeles, CA 90048. Children's books; adult trade nonfiction, including humor.Royalty. Query with SASE required.

PRIMA PUBLISHING AND COMMUNICATIONS—P.O. Box 1260, Rocklin, CA 95677. Ben Dominitz, Pub. Nonfiction on variety of subjects, including fitness and business. "We want books with originality, written by highly qualified individuals." Royalty.

PRUETT PUBLISHING COMPANY—2928 Pearl, Boulder, CO 80301. Jim Pruett, Pres. Gerald Keenan, Sr. Ed. Nonfiction: outdoors and recreation, western U.S. history and travel, adventure travel and railroadiana. Royalty. Query.

PUFFIN BOOKS—See Viking/Penguin.

PUTNAM'S SONS, G.P.—Div. of Putnam Publishing Co., 200 Madison Ave., New York, NY 10016. General fiction and nonfiction. No unsolicited manuscripts or queries.

QUEST BOOKS—Imprint of The Theosophical Publishing House, 306 W. Geneva Rd., P. O. Box 270, Wheaton, IL 60189–0270. Shirley Nicholson, Sr. Ed. Nonfiction books on Eastern and Western religion and philosophy, holism, healing, meditation, yoga, astrology. Royalty. Query.

QUILL—Imprint of William Morrow and Co., Inc., 105 Madison Ave., New York, NY 10016. Doug Stumpf, Andrew Ambraziejus, Eds. Trade paperback nonfiction. Submit through agent only.

RANDOM HOUSE, INC.—201 E. 50th St., New York, NY 10022. Joni Evans, Pub. Jason Epstein, Ed. Dir. J. Shulman, Ed.-in-Chief, Juvenile Books. Stuart Flexner, Ed.-in-Chief, Reference Books. General fiction and nonfiction; reference and college textbooks. Fiction and nonfiction for beginning readers; paperback fiction line for 7- to 9-year-olds; 35 pages max. Royalty. Query with three chapters and outline for nonfiction; complete manuscript for fiction and SASE.

REGNERY GATEWAY—1130 17th St. N.W., Suite 600, Washington, DC 20036. Hardcover and trade paperback nonfiction on public policy. Royalty. Query.

RENAISSANCE HOUSE—541 Oak St., P. O. Box 177, Frederick, CO 80530. Eleanor H. Ayer, Ed. Common country philosophy, Western Americana, World War II, and Rocky Mountain West; biographies and historical books. Submit outline and short bio. Royalty.

REWARD BOOKS—See Business & Professional Publishing Div.

RODALE PRESS—33 E. Minor St., Emmaus, PA 18098. Pat Corpora, Pub. Books on health, gardening, homeowner projects, cookbooks, inspirational topics, pop psychology, woodworking, natural history. Query with outline and sample chapter. Royalty and outright purchase.

RONIN PUBLISHING—P.O. Box 1035, Berkeley, CA 94701. Address the Editors. Accepts proposals for book manuscripts (200 to 300 pages) on career issues and on psychoactive drugs. Royalty.

ROSEN PUBLISHING GROUP—29 E. 21st St., New York, NY 10010. Roger Rosen, Pres. Ruth C. Rosen, Ed. Young adult books, to 40,000 words, on career and personal guidance, journalism, theater, self-help, etc. Pelion Press: music, art, history. Pays varying rates.

ROSSET & CO.—333 Park Ave. S., New York, NY 10010. Barney Rosset, Pub. Fiction and nonfiction on a variety of topics. Send complete manuscript or sample chapters and SASE.

RUTLEDGE HILL PRESS—513 Third Ave. S., Nashville, TN 37210. Ronald E. Pitkin, V.P. Southern interest fiction and nonfiction. Query with outline and sample chapters. Royalty.

ST. ANTHONY MESSENGER PRESS—1615 Republic St., Cincinnati, OH 45210. Lisa Biedenbach, Man. Ed. Inspirational nonfiction for Catholics, supporting a Christian lifestyle in our culture; prayer aids, education, practical spirituality, parish ministry, liturgy resources. Query with 500-word summary. Royalty.

ST. MARTIN'S PRESS—175 Fifth Ave., New York, NY 10010. General adult fiction and nonfiction. Royalty. Query first.

SALEM HOUSE PUBLISHERS—462 Boston St., Topsfield, MA 01983.

Caleb Mason, Assoc. Pub. Adult fiction and nonfiction on variety of subjects. Query first. Royalty.

SANDLAPPER PUBLISHING, INC.—P.O. Box 1932, Orangeburg, SC 29116–1932. Nancy Drake, Book Ed. Books on South Carolina history, culture, cuisine. Submit query with outline and sample chapters.

SCHOLASTIC, INC.—730 Broadway, New York, NY 10003. Point: Regina Griffin, Sr. Ed. Young adult fiction for readers 12 and up. Apple Books: Regina Griffin, Sr. Ed. Fiction for readers ages 8 to 12. Submit complete manuscript with cover letter and SASE. Royalty. Sunfire: Ann Reit, Ed. American historical romances, for girls 12 and up, 55,000 words. Query with outline and three sample chapters. Write for tip sheets.

SCOTT, FORESMAN AND CO.—1900 E. Lake Ave., Glenview, IL 60025. Richard E. Peterson, Pres. Elementary, secondary, and college textbooks and material. Royalty.

SCRIBNER'S SONS, CHARLES—866 Third Ave., New York, NY 10022. Robert Stewart, Ed.-in-Chief. Fiction, general nonfiction, science, history and biography; query first. Clare Costello, Ed., Books for Young Readers: fantasy, mystery, YA, SF, and problem novels, picture books, ages 5 and up, and nonfiction (science and how-tos). Query with outline and sample chapter.

SEVEN SEAS PRESS—International Marine, Box 220, Camden, ME 04843. Jonathan Eaton, VP/Ed. James Babb, Acquisitions Ed. Books on boating (both sailing and power), other marine topics.

SHAPOLSKY PUBLISHERS—136 W. 22nd St., New York, NY 10011. Nonfiction manuscripts on current affairs, Judaica, history, biography, how-to, business, art, and self-help; educational picture books, folk tales for young adults. Payment on royalty and flat fee basis.

SHAW PUBLISHERS, HAROLD—388 Gunderson Dr., Box 567, Wheaton, IL 60189. Ramona Cramer Tucker, Dir. of Ed. Services. Nonfiction, 120 to 220 pages, with an evangelical Christian perspective. Query. Prefers flat fee.

SIERRA CLUB BOOKS—730 Polk St., San Francisco, CA 94109. Nonfiction: environment, natural history, the sciences, outdoors and regional guidebooks; juvenile fiction and nonfiction. Royalty. Query with SASE.

SIFTON BOOKS, ELISABETH/VIKING AND ELISABETH SIFTON BOOKS/PENGUIN—See Viking Penguin Inc.

SIGNET BOOKS—See New American Library.

SILHOUETTE BOOKS—300 E. 42nd St., New York, NY 10017. Karen Solem, Exec. Ed., V.P. Silhouette Romances: Mara Tara Hughes, Sr. Ed. Contemporary romances, 53,000 to 58,000 words. Special Edition: Leslie Kazanjian, Sr. Ed. Sophisticated contemporary romances, 75,000 to 80,000 words. Silhouete Desire: Isabel Swift, Sr. Ed. Sensuous contemporary romances, 53,000 to 60,000 words. Intimate Moments: Leslie Wainger, Sr. Ed. Sensuous, exciting contemporary romances, 80,000 to 85,000 words. Historical romance: 95,000 to 105,000 words, set in England, France, and North America between 1700 and 1900; query with synopsis and three sample chapters to Eliza Shallcross/Tracy Farrell, Eds. Query with synopsis and SASE to appropriate editor. Tipsheets available.

SILVER ARROW BOOKS—Imprint of William Morrow and Co., Inc., 105 Madison Ave., New York, NY 10016. Sherry Arden, Pub. General fiction and nonfiction. Submit through agent.

SIMON & SCHUSTER—1230 Ave. of the Americas, New York, NY 10020. No unsolicited material.

SMITH PUBLISHER, GIBBS/PEREGRINE SMITH BOOKS—P. O. Box 667, Layton, UT 84401. Steve Chapman, Fiction Ed. Madge Baird, Nonfiction Ed. Adult fiction and nonfiction. Query. Royalty.

SOHO PRESS—One Union Sq., New York, NY 10003. Juris Jurjevics, Ed. Adult fiction mysteries, thrillers, and nonfiction, from 75,000 words. Send SASE and complete manuscript. Royalty.

SOUTHERN ILLINOIS UNIVERSITY PRESS—Box 3697, Carbondale, IL 62901. Curtis L. Clark, Ed. Nonfiction in the humanities, 200–400 pages. Royalty. Query with outline and sample chapters.

SOUTHERN METHODIST UNIVERSITY PRESS—Box 415, Dallas, TX 75275. Suzanne Comer, Sr. Ed. Fiction: serious literary fiction, short story collections, set in Texas or the Southwest, 150–400 pages. Nonfiction: scholarly studies in ethics, composition/rhetoric, theater, film, North African archaeology, belles lettres, scholarly writing about Texas or Southwest, 150–400 pages. No juvenile material or poetry. Royalty or flat fee. Query.

SPARKLER BOOKS—See Pharos Books.

SPECTRA BOOKS—Imprint of Bantam Books, 666 Fifth Ave., New York, NY 10103. Lou Aronica, Pub. Science fiction and fantasy, with emphasis on storytelling and characterization. Query; no unsolicited manuscripts. Royalty.

SQUARE ONE PUBLISHERS—501 South Prospect, Madison, WI 53711. Lyn Miller-Lachmann, Ed. Fiction, 45,000 to 60,000 words, for teenagers. No mainstream topics: multi-cultural relations, teens who challenge stereotypes, alternative families, etc. Query with sample chapter.

STANDARD PUBLISHING—8121 Hamilton Ave., Cincinnati, OH 45231. Address Mark Plunkett. Fiction: juveniles, based on Bible or with moral tone. Nonfiction: biblical, Christian education. Conservative evangelical. Query preferred.

STANFORD UNIVERSITY PRESS—Stanford University, Stanford, CA 94305. Norris Pope, Ed. Adult nonfiction. Query with outline and sample chapters. Royalty.

STECK-VAUGHN COMPANY—National Education Corp., 11 Prospect St., Madison, NJ 07940. Walter Kossman, Ed. Nonfiction books for school and library market: biographies for grades 6 and up; and science, social studies, and history books for primary grades through high school. Manuscripts 5,000 to 30,000 words. Query with outline and sample chapters; SASE required. Flat fee and royalty payment.

STEMMER HOUSE PUBLISHERS, INC.—2627 Caves Rd., Owings Mills, MD 21117. Barbara Holdridge, Ed. Juvenile fiction and adult fiction and nonfiction. Royalty. Query with SASE.

STERLING PUBLISHING CO., INC.—387 Park Ave. S., New York, NY 10016. Sheila Anne Barry, Acquisitions Mgr. How-to, hobby, woodworking, health, craft, wine, juvenile and juvenile science, humor, militaria, and sports books. Royalty and outright purchase. Query with outline, sample chapter, and sample illustrations.

STONE WALL PRESS, INC.—1241 30th St. N.W., Washington, D.C.

20007. Nonfiction on natural history, outdoors, conservation, 200 to 300 manuscript pages. Royalty. Query first.

STRAWBERRY HILL PRESS—2594 15th Ave., San Francisco, CA 94127. Carolyn Soto, Ed. Nonfiction: biography, autobiography, history, cooking, health, how-to, philosophy, performance arts, and Third World. Query first with sample chapters, outline, and SASE. Royalty.

STUART, INC., LYLE—120 Enterprise Ave., Secaucus, NJ 07094. Allan J. Wilson, Ed. General fiction and nonfiction. Citadel Press: biography, film, history, limited fiction. Royalty. Query; no unsolicited manuscripts.

SUNFIRE—See Scholastic, Inc.

TAB BOOKS, INC.—Blue Ridge Summit, PA 17294. Ron Powers, Dir. of Acquisitions, Editorial Dept. Nonfiction: electronics, computers, how-to, aviation, business, solar and energy, science and technology, back to basics, automotive, marine and outdoor life, hobby and craft, military history, graphic design, and engineering. Fiction: military. Royalty or outright purchase.

TARCHER, INC., JEREMY P.—9100 Sunset Blvd., Los Angeles, CA 90069. Jeremy P. Tarcher, Ed.-in-Chief. General nonfiction: psychology, spirituality, creativity, personal development, health and fitness, women's concerns, science for the layperson, etc. Royalty. Query with outline, sample chapter, credentials, and SASE.

TAYLOR PUBLISHING CO.—1550 W. Mockingbird Ln., Dallas, TX 75235. Nonfiction: fine arts, biography, cooking, gardening, sports and recreation, true crime, health, self help, humor/trivia, lifestyles. Query with outline and sample chapters. Royalty.

TEMPLE UNIVERSITY PRESS—Broad and Oxford Sts., Philadelphia, PA 19122. Michael Ames, Ed. Adult nonfiction. Query with outline and sample chapters. Royalty.

TEN SPEED PRESS—P.O. Box 7123, Berkeley, CA 94707. Mariah Bear, Ed. Self-help and how-to on careers, recreation, etc.; natural science, history, cookbooks. Query with outline and sample chapters. Royalty. Softcover.

TEXAS MONTHLY PRESS—Box 1569, Austin, TX 78767. Cathy Casey Hale, Dir. Fiction, nonfiction, related to Texas or the Southwest, 60,000 words. Royalty.

TICKNOR & FIELDS—Subsidiary of Houghton Mifflin Company, 52 Vanderbilt Ave., New York, NY 10017. John Herman, Editorial Director. General nonfiction and fiction. Royalty.

TIMES BOOKS—Div. of Random House, Inc., 201 E. 50th St., New York, NY 10022. Hugh O'Neill, Ed. Dir. General nonfiction specializing in business, science, and current affairs. No unsolicited manuscripts or queries accepted.

TOR BOOKS—49 W. 24th St., New York, NY 10010. Beth Meacham, Ed.-in-Chief: Science fiction and fantasy. Exec. Ed.: Thrillers, espionage, and mysteries. Melissa Ann Singer, Ed.: Horror and dark fantasy. Wanda June Alexander, Assoc. Ed.: Historicals. Length: from 60,000 words. Query with outline and sample chapters. Royalty.

TROPHY BOOKS—See Harper Junior Books Group.

TROUBADOR PRESS—360 N. Cienega Blvd., Los Angeles, CA 90048. Juvenile illustrated games, activity, paper doll, coloring, and cut-out books. Royalty or outright purchase. Query with outline and SASE.

TYNDALE HOUSE—336 Gundersen Dr., Box 80, Wheaton, IL 60189. Wendell Hawley, Ed.-in-Chief. Christian. Juvenile and adult fiction and nonfiction on subjects of concern to Christians. Picture books with religious focus for third-grade readers. Submit complete manuscripts. Guidelines.

UNION OF AMERICAN HEBREW CONGREGATIONS—838 Fifth Ave., New York, NY 10021. Sharyn Ruff, Marketing Mgr. Fiction and nonfiction from pre-school to adult. No poetry. Material that deals with traditional and controversial themes in Judaism that appeal to Jewish and non-Jewish readers. Query with detailed table of contents, outline, and sample chapter or complete manuscript.

UNITED RESOURCE PRESS—629 Terminal Way, #10, Costa Mesa, CA 92627. Sally Marshall Corngold, Ed. Well-documented nonfiction books (about 100 pages) on "how-to" personal finance. Query or send complete manuscript. Royalty.

UNIVERSE BOOKS—381 Park Ave. S., New York, NY 10016. Louis Barron, V.P./Ed.-in-Chief. Fine arts and art history, photography, design, social science, contemporary politics, music. Royalty. Query with SASE.

UNIVERSITY OF ALABAMA PRESS—P.O. Box 870380, Tuscaloosa, AL 35487. Nicole Mitchell, Ed. Scholarly and general regional nonfiction. Royalty. Send complete manuscript.

UNIVERSITY OF ARIZONA PRESS—1230 N. Park Ave., Suite 102, Tucson, AZ 85719. Gregory McNamee, Ed.-in-Chief. Barbara Beatty, Acquiring Ed., Sciences. Mark Pry, Acquiring Ed., Humanities. Scholarly nonfiction, to 100,000 words: anthropology, history, the sciences, natural history, American Indian and Latin American studies, regional or national topics, books of personal essays. Query with outline and sample chapters or send complete manuscript. Royalty.

UNIVERSITY OF CALIFORNIA PRESS—2120 Berkeley Way, Berkeley, CA 94720. Address Acquisitions Department. Scholarly nonfiction. Send query, outline, and sample chapters.

UNIVERSITY OF GEORGIA PRESS—University of Georgia, Athens, GA 30602. Karen Orchard, Ed. Short story collections and poetry, scholarly nonfiction and literary criticism, Southern and American history, regional studies. For nonfiction, query with outline and sample chapters. Poetry collections considered in Sept. and Jan. only; short fiction in June and July only. A $10 fee is required for all poetry and fiction submissions. Royalty.

UNIVERSITY OF ILLINOIS PRESS—54 E. Gregory Dr., Champaign, IL 61820. Richard L. Wentworth, Ed.-in-Chief. Short story collections, 140–180 pages; nonfiction; and poetry, 70–100 pages. Rarely considers multiple submissions. Query. Royalty.

UNIVERSITY OF MINNESOTA PRESS—2037 University Ave. S.E., Minneapolis, MN 55414. Terry Cochran, Sr. Ed. Fiction: minority and Third World, 40,000–100,000 words. Nonfiction: literary theory, philosophy, cultural criticism, regional titles, 50,000–225,000 words. Query with detailed prospectus or introduction, table of contents, a sample chapter, and a recent resumé. Royalty.

UNIVERSITY OF NEW MEXICO PRESS—University of New Mexico Press, Albuquerque, NM 87131. Elizabeth C. Hadas, Ed. Dir. David V. Holtby, Claire Sanderson, Dana Asbury, and Barbara Guth, Eds. Scholarly nonfiction on social and cultural anthropology, archaeology, Western history, art, and photography. Royalty. Query.

UNIVERSITY OF NORTH CAROLINA PRESS—P.O. Box 2288, Chapel Hill, NC 27515-2288. David Perry, Ed. General-interest (75,000 to 125,000 words) on the lore, crafts, cooking, gardening, and natural history of the southeast. Royalty. Query preferred.

UNIVERSITY OF TENNESSEE PRESS—293 Communications Bldg., Knoxville, TN 37996–0325. Nonfiction, 200–300 pages. Send query with outline and sample chapters. Royalty.

UNIVERSITY OF UTAH PRESS—101 U.S.B., Salt Lake City, UT 84112. David Catron, Ed. Nonfiction from 200 pages and poetry from 60 pages. (Submit poetry during March only.) Query. Royalty.

UNIVERSITY PRESSES OF FLORIDA—15 N.W. 15th St., Gainesville, FL 32603. Walda Metcalf, Sr. Ed. and Asst. Dir. Nonfiction, 150 to 450 manuscript pages, on regional studies, women's studies, Latin American studies, contemporary literary criticism, sociology, anthropology, archaeology, and history. Royalty.

VAN NOSTRAND REINHOLD—115 Fifth Ave., New York, NY 10003. Chester C. Lucido, Jr., Pres./C.E.O. Business, professional, scientific, and technical publishers of applied reference works. CBI Publishing Co.: Food service and hospitality books. Royalty.

VIKING PENGUIN, INC.—40 W. 23rd St., New York, NY 10010. Kestral Books: Fiction and nonfiction, including biography, history, and sports, for ages 7 to 14; humor; and picture books for ages 2 to 6. Query Children's Books Dept. with outline and sample chapter. SASE required. Adult fiction and nonfiction. Adult hardcovers. Frederick Warne: Children's hardcovers and paperbacks. Penguin Books: Adult fiction and nonfiction paperbacks. Puffin Books: Children's fiction and nonfiction paperbacks. Royalty. No unsolicited material.

VOYAGER PAPERBACKS—See Harcourt Brace Jovanovich.

WALKER AND COMPANY—720 Fifth Ave., New York, NY 10019. Fiction: mysteries, suspense, westerns, regency romance, espionage, and horror. Nonfiction: Americana, biography, history, science, natural history, medicine, psychology, parenting, sports, outdoors, reference, popular science, self-help, business, and music. Juvenile nonfiction, including biography, science, history, music, and nature. Fiction and problem novels for YA. Royalty. Query with synopsis.

WALLACE-HOMESTEAD—See Chilton Book Co.

WARNE, FREDERICK—See Viking Penguin, Inc.

WARNER BOOKS—666 Fifth Ave., New York, NY 10103. Mel Parker, Ed.-in-Chief. Fiction: historical romance, contemporary women's fiction, unusual big-scale horror and suspense. Nonfiction: business books, health and nutrition, self-help. Query with sample chapters. Also publishes trade paperbacks and hardcover titles.

WATTS, INC., FRANKLIN—387 Park Ave. S., New York, NY 10016. Margie Leather, Ed. Nonfiction for grades 3–10, including science, history, and biography. Royalty. Query with SASE required.

WEIDENFELD & NICHOLSON—See Grove Weidenfeld.

WESLEYAN UNIVERSITY PRESS—110 Mt. Vernon St., Middletown, CT 06457–6050. Peter J. Potter, Ed. Three poetry series: Wesleyan new poets, 64 pages; Established poetry series, 64–80 pages; poetry in translation, 64–80 pages. Send complete manuscript. Royalty.

WESTERN PUBLISHING CO., INC.—850 Third Ave., New York, NY 10022. Robin Warner, Pub., Children's Books; Eric Suben, Ed.-in-Chief, Children's

Books. Adult nonfiction: field guides, cookbooks, etc. Children's books, fiction and nonfiction: picture books, storybooks, concept books, novelty books. Royalty and outright purchase. Query required. Same address and requirements for Golden Press.

WESTMINSTER/JOHN KNOX PRESS—100 Witherspoon St., Louisville, KY 30365. Davis Perkins, Ed. Dir. Books that inform, interpret, challenge, and encourage Christian faith and living. Royalty. Send SASE for "Guidelines for a Book Proposal."

WHITMAN, ALBERT—5747 W. Howard St., Niles, IL 60648. Kathleen Tucker, Ed. Picture books; novels, biographies, mysteries, and general nonfiction for middle-grade readers. Submit complete manuscript for picture books, three chapters and outline for longer fiction; query for nonfiction. Royalty.

WILDERNESS PRESS—2440 Bancroft Way, Berkeley, CA 94704. Thomas Winnett, Ed. Nonfiction: sports, recreation, and travel in the western U.S. Royalty.

WILSHIRE BOOK COMPANY—12015 Sherman Rd., North Hollywood, CA 91605. Melvin Powers, Ed. Dir. Psychological, self-help with strong motivational messages. Query or send synopsis. Royalty.

WINDSWEPT HOUSE PUBLISHERS—Mt. Desert, ME 04660. Jane Weinberger, Ed. Children's picture books, 150 words, with black-and-white illustrations. Query first for how-to and teenage novels. Currently overstocked.

WINGBOW PRESS—2929 Fifth St., Berkeley, CA 94710. Randy Fingland, Ed. Nonfiction: women's interests, health, psychology, how-to. Query or sample chapter and outline preferred. Royalty.

WOODBINE HOUSE—10400 Connecticut Ave., Suite 512, Kensington, MD 20895. Susan Stokes, Ed. Nonfiction of all types; especially interested in science, history, special education, travel, military, psychology, natural history, and general reference. Query or submit complete manuscript with SASE. Guidelines. Royalty or outright purchase.

WORD PUBLISHING—5221 O'Connor Blvd., Irving, TX 75039. Al Bryant, Man. Ed. Nonfiction, 65,000 to 85,000 words, dealing with the relationship and/or applications of biblical principles to everyday life. Query with outline and sample chapters. Royalty.

WORKMAN PUBLISHING CO., INC.—708 Broadway, New York, NY 10003. Address the Editors. General nonfiction. Normal contractual terms based on agreement.

WORLDWIDE LIBRARY—Div. of Harlequin Books, 225 Duncan Mill Rd., Don Mills, Ont., Canada M3B 3K9. Randall Toye, Ed. Dir. Action adventure series and future fiction for Gold Eagle imprint; mystery fiction. Query. Paperback only.

YANKEE BOOKS—Main St., Dublin, NH 03444. Sandra Taylor, Sr. Ed. Books relating specifically to New England: cooking, crafts, maritime subjects, travel, gardening, nature, nostalgia, humor, and popular history. No scholarly history, highly technical work, or off-color humor. Royalty. Query or send proposal.

YEARLING BOOKS—See Dell Publishing Co., Inc.

ZEBRA BOOKS—475 Park Ave. S., New York, NY 10016. Ann La Farge, Sr. Ed. Carin Cohen, Fiction Ed. Biography, how-to, humor, self-help. Specializes in popular fiction: horror; historical romance (Heartfire Romances, 107,000 words, and Hologram Romances, 130,000 words); traditional Gothics (first person, 100,000 words); regencies (80,000 to 120,000 words); sagas (150,000 words); glitz (100,000 words); men's adventure; westerns; thrillers, etc. Query with synopsis and sample chapters preferred.

ZOLOTOW BOOKS, CHARLOTTE—Imprint of Harper & Row, 10 E. 53rd St., New York, NY 10022. Address the Editors. Juvenile fiction and nonfiction "with integrity of purpose, beauty of language, and an out-of-ordinary look at ordinary things." Royalty.

ZONDERVAN PUBLISHING HOUSE—1415 Lake Dr. S.E., Grand Rapids, MI 49506. Christian. General fiction and nonfiction; academic and professional books. Address Manuscript Review Ed. Query with outline, sample chapter, and SASE. Royalty. Guidelines.

UNIVERSITY PRESSES

University presses generally publish books of a scholarly nature or of specialized interest by authorities in a given field. A few publish fiction and poetry. Many publish only a handful of titles a year. Always query first. Do not send a manuscript until you have been invited to do so by the editor. Several of the following presses and their detailed editorial submission requirements are included in the *Book Publishers* list.

BRIGHAM YOUNG UNIVERSITY PRESS—209 University Press Bldg., Provo, UT 84602.

BUCKNELL UNIVERSITY PRESS—Bucknell University, Lewisburg, PA 17837.

CAMBRIDGE UNIVERSITY PRESS—40 W. 20th St., New York, NY 10011.

THE CATHOLIC UNIVERSITY OF AMERICA PRESS—620 Michigan Ave. N.E., Washington, DC 20064.

DUKE UNIVERSITY PRESS—Box 6697, College Station, Durham, NC 27708.

DUQUESNE UNIVERSITY PRESS—600 Forbes Ave., Pittsburgh, PA 15282.

GEORGIA STATE UNIVERSITY BUSINESS PRESS—College of Business Administration, University Plaza, Atlanta, GA 30303–3093.

HARVARD UNIVERSITY PRESS—79 Garden St., Cambridge , MA 02138.

INDIANA UNIVERSITY PRESS—10th and Morton Sts., Bloomington, IN 47404.

IOWA STATE UNIVERSITY PRESS—2121 S. State Ave., Ames, IA 50010.

THE JOHNS HOPKINS UNIVERSITY PRESS—701 W. 40th St., Suite 275, Baltimore, MD 21211.

LOUISIANA STATE UNIVERSITY PRESS—LSU, Baton Rouge, LA 70893.

LOYOLA UNIVERSITY PRESS—3441 N. Ashland Ave., Chicago, IL 60657.

MEMPHIS STATE UNIVERSITY PRESS—Memphis State Univ., Memphis, TN 38152.

MICHIGAN STATE UNIVERSITY PRESS—1405 S. Harrison Rd., East Lansing, MI 48823–5202.

THE MIT PRESS—55 Hayward St., Cambridge, MA 02142.

NEW YORK UNIVERSITY PRESS—Washington Sq., New York, NY 10003.

OHIO STATE UNIVERSITY PRESS—180 Pressey Hall, 1070 Carmark Rd., Columbus, OH 43210.

OREGON STATE UNIVERSITY PRESS—101 Waldo Hall, Corvallis, OR 97331. Jo Alexander, Man. Ed.

THE PENNSYLVANIA STATE UNIVERSITY PRESS—215 Wagner Bldg., University Park, PA 16802.

PRINCETON UNIVERSITY PRESS—41 William St., Princeton, NJ 08540.

RUTGERS UNIVERSITY PRESS—109 Church St., New Brunswick, NJ 08901.

SOUTHERN ILLINOIS UNIVERSITY PRESS—Box 3697, Carbondale, IL 62901.

SOUTHERN METHODIST UNIVERSITY PRESS—Box 415, Dallas, TX 75275.

STANFORD UNIVERSITY PRESS—Stanford University, Stanford, CA 94305.

SYRACUSE UNIVERSITY PRESS—1600 Jamesville Ave., Syracuse, NY 13244–5160.

TEMPLE UNIVERSITY PRESS—Broad and Oxford Sts., Philadelphia, PA 19122.

UNIVERSITY OF ALABAMA PRESS—P.O. Box 870380, Tuscaloosa, AL 35487.

UNIVERSITY OF ARIZONA PRESS—1230 N. Park Ave., Suite 102, Tucson, AZ 85719.

UNIVERSITY OF CALIFORNIA PRESS—2120 Berkeley Way, Berkeley, CA 94720.

UNIVERSITY OF CHICAGO PRESS—5801 Ellis Ave., Chicago, IL 60637.

UNIVERSITY OF GEORGIA PRESS—University of Georgia, Athens, GA 30602.

UNIVERSITY OF ILLINOIS PRESS—54 E. Gregory Dr., Champaign, IL 61820.

UNIVERSITY OF MASSACHUSETTS PRESS—Box 429, Amherst, MA 01004.

UNIVERSITY OF MICHIGAN PRESS—P.O. Box 1104, Ann Arbor, MI 48106.

UNIVERSITY OF MINNESOTA PRESS—2037 University Ave. S.E., Minneapolis, MN 55414.

UNIVERSITY OF MISSOURI PRESS—200 Lewis Hall, Columbia, MO 65211.

UNIVERSITY OF NEBRASKA PRESS—901 North 17th St., Lincoln, NE 68588–0520.

UNIVERSITY OF NEW MEXICO PRESS—UNM, Albuquerque, NM 87131.

UNIVERSITY OF NOTRE DAME PRESS—University of Notre Dame, Notre Dame, IN 46556.

UNIVERSITY OF OKLAHOMA PRESS—1005 Asp Ave., Norman, OK 73019–0445.

UNIVERSITY OF PITTSBURGH PRESS—127 North Bellefield Ave., Pittsburgh, PA 15260.

UNIVERSITY OF SOUTH CAROLINA PRESS—1716 College St., Columbia, SC 29208.

UNIVERSITY OF TENNESSEE PRESS—293 Communications Bldg., Knoxville, TN 37996–0325.

UNIVERSITY OF UTAH PRESS—101 U.S.B., Salt Lake City, UT 84112.

UNIVERSITY OF WASHINGTON PRESS—P.O. Box 50096, Seattle, WA 98145–5096.

UNIVERSITY OF WISCONSIN PRESS—114 N. Murray St., Madison, WI 53715–1199.

UNIVERSITY PRESS OF COLORADO—P.O. Box 849, Niwot, CO 80544. Jody Susan Berman, Ed.

UNIVERSITY PRESS OF COLUMBIA—562 West 113th St., New York, NY 10025.

THE UNIVERSITY PRESS OF KENTUCKY—663 S. Limestone St., Lexington, KY 40506–0336.

UNIVERSITY PRESS OF NEW ENGLAND—17 ½ Lebanon St., Hanover, NH 03755.

THE UNIVERSITY PRESS OF VIRGINIA—Box 3608, University Sta., Charlottesville, VA 22903. Nancy C. Essig, Dir.

UNIVERSITY PRESSES OF FLORIDA—15 N.W. 15th St., Gainesville, FL 32603.

WAYNE STATE UNIVERSITY PRESS—5959 Woodward Ave., Detroit, MI 48202.

WESLEYAN UNIVERSITY PRESS—110 Mt.Vernon St., Middletown, CT 06457–6050.

YALE UNIVERSITY PRESS—92A Yale Sta., New Haven, CT 06520.

SYNDICATES

Syndicates are business organizations that buy material from writers and artists to sell to newspapers all over the country and the world. Authors are paid either a percentage of the gross proceeds or an outright fee.

Of course, features by people well known in their fields have the best chance of being syndicated. In general, syndicates want columns that have been popular in a local newspaper, perhaps, or magazine. Since most syndicated fiction has been published previously in magazines or books, beginning fiction writers should try to sell their stories to magazines before submitting them to syndicates.

Always query syndicates before sending manuscripts, since their needs change frequently, and be sure to enclose SASEs with queries and manuscripts.

ARKIN MAGAZINE SYNDICATE—761 N.E. 180th St., N. Miami Beach, FL 33162. Joseph Arkin, Ed. Dir. Articles, 750 to 2,200 words, for trade and professional magazines. Must have small-business slant, written in layman's language, and offer solutions to business problems. Articles should apply to many businesses, not just a specific industry. Pays 3¢ to 10¢ a word, on acceptance. Query preferred.

BUSINESS FEATURES SYNDICATE—P. O. Box 9844, Ft. Lauderdale, FL 33310. Dana K. Cassell, Ed. Articles, 1,500 to 2,000 words, for the independent retailer or small service business owner, on marketing, security, personnel, merchandising, general management. Pays 50% of sales.

CONTEMPORARY FEATURES SYNDICATE—P. O. Box 1258, Jackson, TN 38301. Lloyd Russell, Ed. Articles, 1,000 to 10,000 words: how-to, money savers, business, etc. Self-help pieces for small business. Pays from $25, on acceptance.

FICTION NETWORK—Box 565l, San Francisco, CA 94101. Short stories, one submission per author; submit manuscript unfolded. SASE required. Pays on royalty basis. Allow 15 weeks for reply.

HARRIS & ASSOCIATES FEATURES—12084 Caminito Campana, San Diego, CA 92128. Dick Harris, Ed. Sports and family-oriented features, to 1,200 words; fillers and short humor, 500 to 800 words. Queries preferred. Pays varying rates.

HERITAGE FEATURES SYNDICATE—214 Massachusetts Ave. N.E., Washington, DC 20002. Andy Seamans, Man. Ed. Public policy news features; syndicates weekly bylined columns and editorial cartoons. Query with SASE a must.

THE HOLLYWOOD INSIDE SYNDICATE—Box 49957, Los Angeles, CA 90049. John Austin, Dir. Feature material, 750 to 2,500 words, on TV and film personalities. Story suggestions for 3-part series. Pieces on unusual medical and scientific breakthroughs. Pays on percentage basis for features, negotiated rates for ideas, on acceptance.

KING FEATURES SYNDICATE—235 E. 45th St., New York, NY 10017. Dennis R. Allen, VP/Ed. Dir. Columns, comics; most contributions on contract for regular columns.

LOS ANGELES TIMES SYNDICATE—Times Mirror Sq., Los Angeles, CA 90053. Commentary, features, columns, editorial cartoons, comics, puzzles and games; news services. Query for articles.

NATIONAL NEWS BUREAU—1318 Chancellor St., Philadelphia, PA

19107. Articles, 500 to 800 words, interviews, consumer news, how-tos, travel pieces, reviews, entertainment pieces, features, etc. Pays on publication.

NEW YORK TIMES SYNDICATION SALES—130 Fifth Ave., New York, NY 10011. Paula Reichler, Sr. V.P./Ed. Dir. Previously published articles only, to 2,000 words. Query with published article or tear sheet. Pays varying rates, on publication.

NEWSPAPER ENTERPRISE ASSOCIATION, INC.—200 Park Ave., New York, NY 10166. Gail Robinson, Man. Ed. Ideas for new concepts in syndicated columns. No single stories or stringers. Payment by contractual arrangement.

OCEANIC PRESS SERVICE—P. O. Box 6538, Buena Park, CA 90622–6538. Peter Carbone, General Mgr. Buys reprint rights for foreign markets, on previously published novels, self-help, and how-to books; interviews with celebrities; illustrated features on celebrities, family, health, beauty, personal relations, etc.; cartoons, comic strips. Pays on acceptance or 50:50 syndication. Query.

SELECT FEATURES OF NORTH AMERICA SYNDICATE—235 E. 45th St., New York, NY 10017. Susan Jarzyk, Acquisitions Ed., Select Features. Articles, 1,500 to 2,000 words, and series dealing with lifestyle trends, psychology, health, beauty, fashion, finance, jobs; business personality profiles. Query.

SINGER MEDIA CORP.—3164 W. Tyler Ave., Anaheim, CA 92801. Kurt D. Singer, Ed. U.S. and/or foreign reprint rights to romantic short stories, historical and romantic novels, Gothics, Westerns, and mysteries published during last 25 years; business management titles. Biography, women's-interest material, all lengths. Home repair, real estate, crosswords, psychological quizzes. Interviews with celebrities. Illustrated columns, humor, cartoons, comic strips. Pays on percentage basis or by outright purchase.

TRANSWORLD FEATURE SYNDICATE, INC.—2 Lexington Ave., Suite 1021, New York, NY 10010. Thelma Brown, Syndication Mgr. Feature material for North American and overseas markets. Query required.

TRIBUNE MEDIA SERVICES—64 E. Concord St., Orlando, FL 32801. Michael Argirion, Ed. Continuing columns, comic strips, features, electronic data bases.

UNITED FEATURE SYNDICATE—200 Park Ave., New York, NY 10166. James Robison, Ed. Syndicated columns; no one-shots or series. Payment by contractual arrangement. Send samples with SASE.

UNITED PRESS INTERNATIONAL—1400 Eye St. N.W., Washington, DC 20005. Bill G. Ferguson, Man. Ed. Seldom accepts free-lance material.

LITERARY PRIZE OFFERS

Each year many important literary contests are open to free-lance writers. The short summaries given below are intended merely as guides. Closing dates, requirements, and rules are tentative. Every effort has been made to ensure the accuracy of information provided here. However, due to the ever-changing nature of literary competitions, writers are advised to check the monthly "Prize Offers" column of *The Writer* Magazine (120 Boylston St., Boston, MA 02116) for the most up-to-date contest requirements. No manuscript should be submitted to any competition unless the writer has first checked with the Contest Editor and received complete information about a particular contest.

Send an SASE with all requests for contest rules and application forms.

ACADEMY OF AMERICAN POETS—177 E. 87th St., New York, NY 10128. Offers Walt Whitman Award: Publication and $1,000 cash prize for a book-length poetry manuscript by a poet who has not yet published a volume of poetry. Closes in November.

ACTORS THEATRE OF LOUISVILLE—316 W. Main St., Louisville, KY 40202. Conducts One-Act Play Contest. Offers $1,000 for previously unproduced one-act script. Closes in April.

THE AMERICAN ACADEMY AND INSTITUTE OF ARTS AND LETTERS—633 W. 155th St., New York, NY 10032. Offers Richard Rodgers Production Award, which consists of subsidized production in New York City by a non-profit theater for a musical, play with music, thematic review, or any comparable work other than opera. Closes in November.

AMERICAN HEALTH MAGAZINE—80 Fifth Ave., New York, NY 10011. Offers prize of $2,000 for short story about intense physical experience. Closes in March.

THE ASSOCIATED WRITING PROGRAMS ANNUAL AWARDS SERIES—Old Dominion University, Norfolk, VA 23529–0079. Conducts Annual Awards Series in Poetry, Short Fiction, the Novel, and Nonfiction. In each category the prize is book publication and a $1,000 honorarium. Closes in February. Offers the Edith Shiffert Prize in Poetry: $1,000 cash prize and publication by the University Press of Virginia for an unpublished book-length collection of poetry. Closes in December.

ASSOCIATION OF JEWISH LIBRARIES—15 Goldsmith St., Providence, RI 02906. Address Lillian Schwartz, Secretary. Conducts Sydney Taylor Manuscript Competition for best fiction manuscript for readers ages 8 to 12. Prize is $1,000. Closes in January.

BEVERLY HILLS THEATRE GUILD/JULIE HARRIS PLAYWRIGHT AWARD—2815 N. Beachwood Dr., Los Angeles, CA 90068. Address Marcella Meharg. Offers prize of $5,000, plus possible $2,000 for productions in Los Angeles area, for previously unproduced and unpublished full-length play. A $1,000 second prize and $500 third prize are also offered. Closes in November.

THE CHICAGO TRIBUNE/NELSON ALGREN AWARDS FOR SHORT FICTION—435 N. Michigan Ave., Chicago, IL 60611. Sponsors Nelson Algren Awards for Short Fiction, with a first prize of $5,000 and three prizes of $1,000 for outstanding unpublished short stories of 10,000 words or less, by American writers. Closes in February.

EUGENE V. DEBS FOUNDATION—Dept. Of History, Indiana State Univ., Terre Haute, IN 47809. Offers Bryant Spann Memorial Prize of $1,000 for published or unpublished article or essay on themes relating to social protest or human equality. Closes in April.

DELACORTE PRESS—Dept. BFYR, 1 Dag Hammarskjold Plaza, New York, NY 10017. Sponsors Delacorte Press Prize for outstanding first young adult novel. The prize consists of one Delacorte hardcover and one Dell paperback contract, an advance of $6,000 on royalties, and a $1,500 cash prize. Closes in December.

FICTION NETWORK—P. O. Box 5651, San Francisco, CA 94101. Sponsors Fiction Competition, with a first prize of $500 (or $1,500 if selected by all three judges) for a short story under 5,000 words (no children's or young adult fiction). Closes in September.

HIGHLIGHTS FOR CHILDREN—803 Church St., Honesdale, PA 18431. Conducts Contest for Juvenile Fiction: awards cash prizes and publication of short stories. Closes in February.

HONOLULU MAGAZINE/PARKER PEN—36 Merchant St., Honolulu, HI 96813. Sponsors annual fiction contest, with cash prize of $1,000, plus publication in *Honolulu,* for unpublished short story with Hawaiian theme, setting, and/or characters. Closes in November.

HOUGHTON MIFFLIN COMPANY—2 Park St., Boston, MA 02108. Offers Literary Fellowship for fiction or nonfiction project of exceptional literary merit written by an American author whose work has already been accepted for publication by Houghton Mifflin. Work under consideration must be unpublished and in English. Fellowship consists of $10,000, of which $2,500 is an outright grant and $7,500 is an advance against royalties. There is no deadline. Send SASE for guidelines; unsolicited material will not be read.

HUMBOLDT STATE UNIVERSITY—English Dept., Arcata, CA 95521. Sponsors Raymond Carver Short Story Contest, with a prize of $500, plus publication in the literary journal *Toyon,* and a $250 second prize for an unpublished short story by a writer living in the United States. Closes in November.

INTERNATIONAL SOCIETY OF DRAMATISTS—Fulfillment Center, P. O. Box 1310, Miami, FL 33153. Sponsors Adriatic Award: a prize of $250 for a full-length play. Closes in November.

JEWISH COMMUNITY CENTER THEATRE IN CLEVELAND—3505 Mayfield Rd., Cleveland Heights, OH 44118. Elaine Rembrandt, Dir. of Cultural Arts. Offers cash award of $1,000 and a staged reading for an original, previously unproduced full-length play, on some aspect of the Jewish experience. Closes in December.

CHESTER H. JONES FOUNDATION—P. O. Box 498, Chardon, OH 44024. Conducts the National Poetry Competition, with more than $1,900 in cash prizes (including a $1,000 first prize) for original, unpublished first poems. Closes in March.

LINCOLN COLLEGE—Lincoln, IL 62656. Address Janet Overton. Offers the Billie Murray Denny Poetry Award for original poem by a poet who has not previously published a volume of poetry. First prize of $1,000, 2nd prize of $500, and 3rd prize of $250 are offered. Closes in May.

MADEMOISELLE MAGAZINE—350 Madison Ave., New York, NY 10017. Sponsors Fiction Writers Contest, with first prize of $2,500, plus publication, and second prize of $500, for short fiction by a writer aged 18 to 30. Closes in March.

THE MOUNTAINEERS BOOKS—306 Second Ave. W., Seattle, WA 98119. Address Donna DeShazo, Dir. Offers The Barbara Savage/"Miles From Nowhere" Memorial Award for a book-length, nonfiction personal-adventure narrative. The prize consists of a $3,000 cash award, plus publication and a $12,000 guaranteed advance against royalties. Closes in March of even-numbered years.

717

NATIONAL ENDOWMENT FOR THE ARTS—Washington, DC 20506. Address Director, Literature Program. The National Endowment for the Arts offers fellowships to writers of poetry, fiction, and creative nonfiction. Deadlines vary; write for guidelines.

NATIONAL PLAY AWARD—P. O. Box 71011, Los Angeles, CA 90071. National Play Award consists of $7,500 cash prize, plus $5,000 for production, for an original, previously unproduced play. Sponsored by National Repertory Theatre Foundation. Closes in July of even-numbered years.

THE NATIONAL POETRY SERIES—26 W. 17th St., New York, NY 10001. Sponsors Annual Open Competition for unpublished book-length poetry manuscript. The prize is publication. Closes in February.

THE NEW ENGLAND THEATRE CONFERENCE—50 Exchange St., Waltham, MA 02154. First prize of $500 and second prize of $250 are offered for unpublished and unproduced one-act plays in the John Gassner Memorial Playwriting Award Competition. Closes in April.

NEW VOICES—Boston Center for the Arts, 551 Tremont St., Boston, MA 02116. Conducts Clauder Competition for an unproduced, full-length play by a New England Writer. First prize is $3,000 plus professional production by a New England theater. Runner-up prizes consist of $500 plus staged readings. Closes in June of even-numbered years.

NORTHEASTERN UNIVERSITY PRESS—English Dept., 406 Holmes, Northeastern Univ., Boston, MA 02115. Guy Rotella, Chairman. Offers Samuel French Morse Poetry Prize: publication of full-length poetry manuscript by U.S. poet who has published no more than one book of poems. August is deadline for inquiries; contest closes in September.

O'NEILL THEATER CENTER—234 W. 44th St., Suite 901, New York, NY 10036. Offers stipend, staged readings, and room and board at the National Playwrights Conference, for new stage and television plays. Send SASE for guidelines. Closes in December.

THE PARIS REVIEW—541 E. 72nd St., New York, NY 10021. Sponsors the Aga Khan Prize for Fiction: $1,000, plus publication, for previously unpublished short story. Closes in June. Offers Bernard F. Connors Prize: $1,000, plus publication, for previously unpublished poem. Closes in May. Offers John Train Humor Prize: $1,500, plus publication, for unpublished work of humorous fiction, nonfiction, or poetry. Closes in March.

PEN/JERARD FUND AWARD—468 Broadway, New York, NY 10012. Address John Morrone, Programs & Publications. Offers $3,000 to beginning women writers for a work-in-progress of general nonfiction. Applicants must have published at least one article in a national magazine or major literary magazine, but not more than one book of any kind. Closes in February.

PEN SYNDICATED FICTION PROJECT—P.O. Box 15650, Washington, DC 20003. For short fiction, unpublished or published in literary magazines. Offers $500 for rights to each story selected and $100 each time it is published by a newspaper. Closes in January.

PLAYBOY MAGAZINE COLLEGE FICTION CONTEST—680 N. Lakeshore Dr., Chicago, IL 60611. Sponsors college fiction contest, with first prize of $3,000 and publication in PLAYBOY, for a short story by a college student; second prize is $500. Closes in January.

POETRY SOCIETY OF AMERICA—15 Gramercy Park, New York, NY

718

10003. Conducts annual contests in which cash prizes are offered for unpublished poems: The Celia B. Wagner Memorial Award, the John Masefield Memorial Award, the Elias Lieberman Student Poetry Award, and the Ruth Lake Memorial Award. Closes in December.

PRIVATE EYE WRITERS OF AMERICA—PWA/St. Martin's Press, 175 Fifth Ave., New York, NY 10010. Winner of The Best First Private Eye Novel Contest receives publication with St. Martin's Press plus $10,000 against royalties; open to previously unpublished writers of private eye novels. Closes in August.

REDBOOK MAGAZINE—224 W. 57th St., New York, NY 10019. Conducts Short Story Contest for original fiction. First prize is $2,000, plus publication. Second prize of $1,000 and third prize of $500 are also offered. Closes in May.

FOREST A. ROBERTS-SHIRAS INSTITUTE PLAYWRITING COMPETITION—Forest Roberts Theatre, Northern Michigan Univ., Marquette, MI 49855. Dr. James Panowski, Dir. Conducts annual playwriting competition, with prize of $1,000, plus production, for original, full-length, previously unproduced and unpublished play. Closes in November.

ST. MARTIN'S PRESS/MALICE DOMESTIC CONTEST—Thomas Dunne Books, 175 Fifth Ave., New York, NY 10010. Co-sponsored by Macmillan London, offers publication plus a $10,000 advance against royalties, for Best First Traditional Mystery Novel. Closes in November.

SEVENTEEN—850 Third Ave., New York, NY 10022. Conducts SEVENTEEN/Smith Corona Fiction Contest for original, unpublished short fiction by writers ages 13 to 21. A first prize of $2,000, a word processor, and possible publication is offered. Closes in January.

SIERRA REPERTORY THEATRE—P. O. Box 3030, Sonora, CA 95370. Offers Cummings/Taylor Award of $400, plus production, for original, previously unpublished, unproduced full-length play or musical. Closes in May.

SOCIETY OF AMERICAN TRAVEL WRITERS—1155 Connecticut Ave. N.W., Suite 500, Washington, DC 20036. Sponsors Lowell Thomas Travel Journalism Award for published and broadcast work by U.S. and Canadian travel journalists. Prizes total $8,500. Closes in February.

SUNSET CENTER—P. O. Box 5066, Carmel, CA 93921. Richard Tyler, Dir. Offers prize of up to $2,000 for an original, unproduced full-length play in its annual Festival of Firsts Playwriting Competition. Closes in August.

SUNTORY AWARDS FOR MYSTERY FICTION—c/o Dentsu Inc., 1–11 Tsukiji, Chuo-ku, Tokyo 104, Japan. Co-sponsored by Bungei Shunju publishers and Asahi Broadcasting. Offers 5 million yen (about $35,000) first prize and 1 million yen "Readers Choice" award, plus possible publication and television production for 40,000- to 80,000-word English or Japanese language mystery, suspense, detective, or espionage novel. Closes in January of even-numbered years.

SYRACUSE UNIVERSITY PRESS—1600 Jamesville Ave., Syracuse, NY 13244–5160. Address Director. Sponsors John Ben Snow Prize: $1,500, plus publication, for an unpublished book-length nonfiction manuscript about New York State, especially upstate or central New York. Closes in December.

THEATRE AMERICANA—P.O. Box 245, Altadena, CA 91001. Sponsors the $500 David James Ellis Memorial Award for an original, unproduced full-length play in two or three acts (no musicals or children's plays). Preference is given to American authors and to plays of the American scene. Closes in April.

THEATRE MEMPHIS—630 Perkins Extended, Memphis, TN 38117. Conducts New Play Competition for a full-length play or related one-acts. The prize is $2,500 and production. Closes in October of even-numbered years.

UNITED FOUNDATIONS—Trust for Creators, P.O. Box 4162, Laguna Beach, CA 92652–4162. Awards the Robert Anson Heinlein Memorial Prize of $1,000 plus one- to three-month residency in the United Foundations' Creators Community for unpublished speculative fiction or science fiction in English or French, by writers ages 7 to 35. Closes in September and December. Also, the Karoline Von Dworschak Memorial Prize for English, German, or French language fiction and nonfiction to female authors under 30 years of age; one- to three-month residencies are awarded; closes in March.

THE U.S. NAVAL INSTITUTE—Annapolis, MD 21402. Conducts the Arleigh Burke Essay Contest, with prizes of $2,000, $1,000, and $750, plus publication, for essays on the advancement of professional, literary, or scientific knowledge in the naval or maritime services, and the advancement of the knowledge of sea power. Closes in December.

UNIVERSITY OF ALABAMA AT BIRMINGHAM—Dept. of Theatre and Dance, Univ. Sta., Birmingham, AL 35294. Bob Yowell, Dir. Conducts Ruby Lloyd Apsey Playwriting Competition, with $500 cash prize, plus production and travel expenses, for previously unproduced full-length play. Closes in January.

UNIVERSITY OF GEORGIA PRESS—Athens, GA 30602. Offers Flannery O'Connor Award for Short Fiction: a prize of $500, plus publication, for a book-length collection of short fiction. Closes in July.

UNIVERSITY OF HAWAII—Kennedy Theatre, Univ. of Hawaii, 1770 East-West Rd., Honolulu, HI 96822. Conducts annual Kumu Kahua Playwriting Contest with cash prizes for original plays dealing with some aspect of Hawaiian experience. Write for conditions-of-entry brochure. Closes in January.

UNIVERSITY OF IOWA—Dept. of English, English-Philosophy Bldg., University of Iowa, Iowa City, IA 52242. Conducts John Simmons Short Fiction Award and Iowa Short Fiction Award, each offering $1,000, plus publication, for an unpublished full-length collection of short stories (150 pages or more). Closes in September.

UNIVERSITY OF MASSACHUSETTS PRESS—Juniper Prize, Univ. of Massachusetts Press, c/o Mail Office, Amherst, MA 01003. Offers Juniper Prize of $1,000, plus publication, for a book-length manuscript of poetry. Closes in September.

UNIVERSITY OF PITTSBURGH PRESS—127 N. Bellefield Ave., Pittsburgh, PA 15260. Sponsors Drue Heinz Literature Prize of $5,000, plus publication and royalty contract for unpublished collection of short stories. Closes in August. Also sponsors Agnes Lynch Starrett Poetry Prize of $2,000, plus publication in the Pitt Poetry Series, for book-length collection of poems by poet who has not yet published a volume of poetry. Closes in April.

UNIVERSITY OF WISCONSIN PRESS—Poetry Series, 114 N. Murray St., Madison, WI 53715. Ronald Wallace, Administrator. Offers Brittingham Prize in Poetry: $500, plus publication, for an unpublished book-length poetry manuscript. Closes in September.

WALT WHITMAN CENTER FOR THE ARTS AND HUMANITIES—Second and Cooper Sts., Camden, NJ 08102. Sponsors the annual Camden Poetry

Award: $1,000, plus publication, for an unpublished book-length collection of poetry. Closes in November.

WISCONSIN PUBLIC RADIO DRAMA AWARDS—3319 W. Beltline Hwy., Madison, WI 53713. Norman Michie, Exec. Producer. Competition for original scripts by writers in Illinois, Iowa, Michigan, and Wisconsin. Prizes for thirty-minute radio scripts and professional production and cash awards of $500 (first prize), $300 (second), and $200 (third). Closes in January.

WORD WORKS—P. O. Box 42164, Washington, DC 20015. Offers the Washington Prize of $1,000 plus publication for an unpublished volume of poetry by a living American poet. Closes in March.

YALE UNIVERSITY PRESS—Box 92A, Yale Sta., New Haven, CT 06520. Address Editor, Yale Series of Younger Poets. Conducts Yale Series of Younger Poets Competition, in which the prize is publication of a book-length manuscript of poetry, written by a poet under 40 who has not previously published a volume of poems. Closes in February.

WRITERS COLONIES

Writers colonies offer isolation and freedom from everyday distractions, and a quiet place for writers to concentrate on their work. Though some colonies are quite small, with space for just three or four writers at a time, others can provide accommodations for as many as thirty or forty. The length of a residency may vary, too, from a couple of weeks to five or six months. These programs have strict admissions policies, and writers must submit a formal application or letter of intent, a resumé, writing samples, and letters of recommendation. Write for application information first, enclosing a stamped, self-addressed envelope.

CENTRUM FOUNDATION—The Centrum Foundation sponsors month-long residencies at Fort Worden State Park, a Victorian fort on the Strait of Juan De Fuca in Washington. Nonfiction, fiction, and poetry writers may apply for residency awards, which include housing and a $75 a week stipend. Application deadlines: October 1 and April 1; send letter explaining the project, short biographical note, and sample of published work. Families are welcome, but no separate working space is provided. For details, send SASE to Carol Jane Bangs, Director of Literature Programs, Centrum Foundation, Fort Worden State Park, P.O. Box 1158, Port Townsend, WA 98368.

CUMMINGTON COMMUNITY OF THE ARTS—Residencies for artists of all disciplines. Living/studio space in individual cottages or in two main houses on 100 acres in the Berkshires. Scholarships and work exchange available. During July and August, artists with children are encouraged to apply; there is a children's program with supervised activities. Application deadlines: January 1st for April, May; March 1st for June, July, August; June 1st for September, October, November. Contact Executive Director, Cummington Community of the Arts, RR#1, Box 145, Cummington, MA 01026.

DORLAND MOUNTAIN ARTS COLONY—Novelists, playwrights, poets, nonfiction writers, composers, and visual artists are encouraged to apply for residencies of one to three months. Dorland is a nature preserve located in the Palomar Mountains of Southern California. Fee of $150 a month includes cottage, fuel, and firewood. Application deadlines are March 1 and September 1. Send SASE to Admissions Committee, Dorland Mt. Arts Colony, Box 6, Temecula, CA 92390.

DORSET COLONY HOUSE—Writers and playwrights are offered low-cost room with kitchen facilities at the Colony House in Dorset, Vermont. Periods of residency are 3 to 6 weeks, and are available between October 1 and June 1. Application deadlines are September 15, December 15, and February 15 for the periods immediately following the deadlines. For more information, send SASE to John Nassivera, Director, Dorset Colony House, Dorset, VT 05251.

FINE ARTS WORK CENTER IN PROVINCETOWN—Fellowships, including living and studio space and monthly stipends, are available at the Fine Arts Work Center on Cape Cod, for writers to work independently. Residencies are for 7 months only; apply before February 1 deadline. For details, send SASE to Director, Fine Arts Work Center, P.O. Box 565, 24 Pearl St., Provincetown, MA 02657.

THE HAMBIDGE CENTER—Two-week to two-month residencies are offered to writers, artists, composers, historians, humanists, and scientists at the Hambidge Center for Creative Arts and Sciences located on 600 acres of quiet woods in the north Georgia mountains. Send SASE for application form to Executive Director, The Hambidge Center, P.O. Box 339, Rabun Gap, GA 30568.

THE MACDOWELL COLONY—Studios, room and board at the MacDowell Colony of Peterborough, New Hampshire, for writers to work without interruption in semi-rural woodland setting. Selection is competitive. Apply at least 6 months in advance of season desired; residencies average 6 weeks. For details and admission forms, send SASE to Admissions Coordinator, The MacDowell Colony, 100 High St., Peterborough, NH 03458.

THE MILLAY COLONY FOR THE ARTS—At Steepletop in Austerlitz, New York (former home of Edna St. Vincent Millay) studios, living quarters, and meals are provided to writers at no cost. Residencies are for one month. Application deadlines are February 1, May 1, and September 1. For information and an application form, write to the Millay Colony for the Arts, Inc., Steepletop, Austerlitz, NY 12017.

MONTALVO CENTER FOR THE ARTS—Three-month, low-cost residencies at the Villa Montalvo in the foothills of the Santa Cruz Mountains south of San Francisco, for writers working on specific projects. There are a few small fellowships available to writers with demonstrable financial need. Send self-addressed envelope and 85¢ stamp for application forms to Montalvo Residency Program, P.O. Box 158, Saratoga, CA 95071.

UCROSS FOUNDATION—Residencies, 2 weeks to 4 months, at the Ucross Foundation in the foothills of the Big Horn Mountains in Wyoming, for writers, artists, and scholars to concentrate on their work without interruptions. Two residency sessions are scheduled annually: January-May and August-December. There is no charge for room, board or studio space. Application deadlines are March 1 for fall session and October 1 for spring session. For more information, send SASE to Director, Residency Program, Ucross Foundation, 2836 US Hwy 14–16 East, Clearmont, WY 82835.

VIRGINIA CENTER FOR THE CREATIVE ARTS—Residencies of 1 to 3 months at the Mt. San Angelo Estate in Sweet Briar, Virginia, for writers to work without distraction. Apply at least three months in advance. A limited amount of financial assistance is available. For more information, send SASE to William Smart, Director, Virginia Center for the Creative Arts, Sweet Briar, VA 24595.

HELENE WURLITZER FOUNDATION OF NEW MEXICO—Rent-free and utility-free studios at the Helene Wurlitzer Foundation in Taos, New Mexico, are offered to creative writers and artists in all media. Length of residency varies from 3 to 6 months. The Foundation is closed from October 1 through March 31 annually. For details, write to Henry A. Sauerwein, Jr., Exec. Dir., The Helene Wurlitzer Foundation of New Mexico, Box 545, Taos, NM 87571.

YADDO—Artists, writers, and composers are invited for stays from 2 weeks to 2 months at Yaddo in Saratoga Springs, New York. Voluntary contributions of $20 a day are suggested. No artist deemed worthy of admission by the judging panels will be denied admission on the basis of an inability to contribute. Requests for applications should be sent with SASE before January 15 or August 1 to Myra Sklarew, President, Yaddo, Box 395, Saratoga Springs, NY 12866. An application fee of $20 is required.

WRITERS CONFERENCES

Each year, hundreds of writers conferences are held across the country. The following list, arranged geographically, represents a sampling of conferences; each listing includes the location of the conference, the month during which it is usually held, and the name of the person from whom specific information may be received. Additional conferences are listed annually in the May issue of *The Writer* Magazine.

ALASKA

SITKA SUMMER WRITERS SYMPOSIUM—Sitka, AK. June. Write Box 2420, Sitka, AK 99835.

ANNUAL TRAVEL WRITING CONFERENCE—Juneau, AK. August. Write UAS Cont. Ed., 11120-AA Glacier Hwy., Juneau, AK 99801.

ARKANSAS

ARKANSAS WRITER'S CONFERENCE—Little Rock, AR. June. Write Clovita Rice, 1115 Gillette Dr., Little Rock, AR 72207.

CALIFORNIA

ANNUAL WRITERS CONFERENCE IN CHILDREN'S LITERATURE—Universal City, CA. August. Write Lin Oliver, Dir., SCBW, P.O. Box 296, Mar Vista Station, Los Angeles, CA 90066.

SAN DIEGO STATE UNIVERSITY WRITERS CONFERENCE—San Diego, CA. January. Write SDSU Extended Studies, San Diego, CA 92182.

COLORADO

ASPEN WRITERS CONFERENCE—Aspen, CO. August. Write Karen Chamberlain, Dir., P.O. Drawer 7726D, Aspen, CO 81612.

ANNUAL SCBW CONFERENCE—Denver, CO. September. Write Ann Nagda, Dir., 701 Kalima Ave., CO 80304.

CONNECTICUT

WESLEYAN WRITERS CONFERENCE—Middletown, CT. June. Write Anne Greene, Assoc. Dir., Wesleyan Writers Conf., Wesleyan Univ., Middletown, CT 06457.

WASHINGTON, DC

ANNUAL SPRING WRITERS CONFERENCE—Washington, DC. May. Write Bill Adler, Jr., Pres. WIW, Suite 220, 733 Fifteenth St. NW, Washington, D.C. 20005.

FLORIDA

KEY WEST LITERARY SEMINAR—Key West, FL. January. Write Key West Literary Seminars/New Directions in American Theatre, P.O. Box 391, Sugarloaf Shores, FL 33044.

FLORIDA SPACE COAST WRITERS CONFERENCE—Melbourne, FL. March. Write Dr. Edwin J. Kirschner, F.S.C.W.C., Box 804, Melbourne, FL 32902.

GEORGIA

COUNCIL OF AUTHORS AND JOURNALISTS, INC.—St. Simons Island, GA. June. Write Ann Ritter, Coord., 1214 Laurel Hill Dr., Decatur, GA 30033.

ILLINOIS

ILLINOIS WESLEYAN UNIVERSITY WRITERS' CONFERENCE—Bloomington, IL. July. Write Bettie Wilson Story, Dir., IWUWC, Illinois Wesleyan Univ., P.O. Box 2900, Bloomington, IL 61702.

MISSISSIPPI VALLEY WRITERS CONFERENCE—Rock Island, IL. June. Write David R. Collins, 3403 45th St., Moline, IL 61265.

ANNUAL CHRISTIAN WRITERS INSTITUTE CONFERENCE—Wheaton, IL. May. Write June Eaton, Christian Writers Inst., 388 E. Gundersen Dr., Wheaton, IL 60188.

INDIANA

INDIANA UNIVERSITY WRITERS' CONFERENCE—Bloomington, IN. June. Write Maura Stanton, Dir., IUWC, 464 Ballantine Hall, Bloomington, IN 47405.

IOWA

OUTDOOR WRITERS ASSOC. OF AMERICA CONFERENCE—Des Moines, IA. June. Write Sylvia G. Bashline, Dir., 2017 Cato Ave., Suite 101, State College, PA 16801.

IOWA SUMMER WRITING PROGRAM—Iowa City, IA. July. Write Peggy Houston, Iowa Summer Writing Prog., Div. Cont. Ed., Univ. of Iowa, Iowa City, IA 52242.

KENTUCKY

CREATIVE WRITING CONFERENCE—Richmond, KY. June. Write William Sutton, Dept. of English, Eastern Kentucky Univ., Richmond, KY 40475.

WRITING WORKSHOP FOR PEOPLE OVER 57—Lexington, KY. July. Write Roberta James, Donovan Scholars Program, Ligon House, Univ. of Kentucky, Ligon House, Lexington, KY 40506–0442.

ANNUAL APPALACHIAN WRITERS WORKSHOP—Hindman, KY. July. Write Mike Mullins, Dir., Box 844, Hindman, KY 41822.

LOUISIANA

DEEP SOUTH WRITERS CONFERENCE—Univ. of Southwestern Louisiana, Lafayette, LA. September. Write John Fiero, Dir., USL Box 44691, Univ. of Southwestern Louisiana, Lafayette, LA 70504.

MAINE

STATE OF MAINE WRITERS CONFERENCE—Ocean Park (Old Orchard Beach), ME. August. Write Richard F. Burns, Box 296, Ocean Park, ME 04063.

STONECOAST WRITERS' CONFERENCE—Univ. of Southern Maine, Gorham, ME. August. Write Kenneth Rosen, English Dept., Univ. of Southern Maine, Portland, ME 04103.

ANNUAL MAINE WRITERS WORKSHOP—Oceanville, ME. August. Write George F. Bush, Dir., P.O. Box 905, RD 1, Stonington, ME 04681.

MASSACHUSETTS

EASTERN WRITERS CONFERENCE—Salem, MA. June. Write Rod Kessler, English Dept., Salem State College, Salem, MA 01970.

NEW ENGLAND WRITERS' CONFERENCE AT SIMMONS COLLEGE—Boston, MA. June. Write Theodore Vrettos, Dir., Simmons College, 300 The Fenway, Boston, MA 02115.

HARVARD SUMMER WRITING PROGRAM—Cambridge, MA. Summer. Write Harvard Summer School, Dept. 457, 20 Garden St., Cambridge, MA 02138.

CAPE COD WRITERS' CONFERENCE—West Barnstable, MA. August. Write CCWC c/o Cape Cod Conservatory of Music & Arts, Route 132, West Barnstable MA 02668.

MICHIGAN

CLARION WORKSHOP OF SCIENCE FICTION AND FANTASY WRITING—E. Lansing, MI. Summer. Write Mary Sheridan, E-28 Holmes Hall, Lyman Briggs School, Michigan State Univ., East Lansing, MI 48825.

MINNESOTA

MISSISSIPPI RIVER CREATIVE WRITING WORKSHOP—St. Cloud, MN. June. Write Bill Meissner, Dept. of English, SCSU, St. Cloud, MN 56301.

MISSISSIPPI

MISSISSIPPI WRITERS CONFERENCE—Jackson, MS. July. Send SASE to Lanny McKay, P.O. Box 12346, Jackson, MS 39236.

MISSOURI

MARK TWAIN WRITERS CONFERENCE—Hannibal, MO. June. Write Dr. J. Hefley, Hannibal-LaGrange College, Hannibal, MO 63401.

AVILA COLLEGE WRITER'S CONFERENCE—Kansas City, MO. August. Write David Wissmann, Dir., Avila College, 11901 Wornall Rd., Kansas City, MO 64145.

MONTANA

WESTERN MONTANA WRITERS CONFERENCE—Dillon, MT. July. Write Sally Garrett Dingley, Office of Cont. Ed., WMC, Dillon, MT 59725.

NEVADA

WESTERN MOUNTAIN WRITERS CONFERENCE—Carson City, NV. July. Write John Garmon, Western Nevada Community College, 2201 W. Nye Ln., Carson City, NV 89701.

NEW HAMPSHIRE

ANNUAL SEACOAST WRITERS CONFERENCE—Portsmouth, NH. September. Write Cheryl Kimball, Dir., Seacoast Writers Assn., P.O. Box 6553, Portsmouth, NH 03801.

MILDRED I. REID WRITERS CONFERENCE—Contoocook, NH. July. Write Mildred I. Reid, Writers Colony, Penacook Rd., Contoocook, NH 03229.

NEW JERSEY

ANNUAL NEW JERSEY ROMANCE WRITERS CONFERENCE—Jamesburg, NJ. November. Write Michelle Valigursky, Dir., P.O. Box 646, Oldbridge, NJ 08857.

MAKING A DENT: WRITING TO CHANGE THE WORLD—Morristown, NJ. November. Write Hannelore Hahn, Dir., IWWG, P.O. Box 810, Gracie Station, New York, NY 10028.

726

New Mexico

SOUTHWEST WRITERS CONFERENCE—Albuquerque, NM. September. Write June Gibson, Dir., SWW Conference. P.O. Box 14632, Albuquerque, NM 87191.

New York

TISCH SCHOOL OF THE ARTS—New York Univ., NY. July. Write Roberta Cooper, Tish School of The Arts., NYU, 721 Broadway, 7th Fl., New York, NY 10003.

ANNUAL IWWG WOMEN'S SUMMER WRITING CONFERENCE—Saratoga Springs, NY. July. Write Hannelore Hahn, Exec. Dir., International Women's Writing Guide, P.O. Box 810, Gracie Station, NY 10028.

HOFSTRA'S ANNUAL SUMMER WRITERS' CONFERENCE—Hofstra Univ., NY. July. Write Lewis Sheena, Hofstra Memorial Hall, Rm. 232, Hempstead, NY 11550.

VASSAR INSTITUTE OF PUBLISHING AND WRITING—Vassar College, NY. June. Write Publishing Institute, Vassar College, Box 300, Poughkeepsie, NY 12601.

SOUTHAMPTON WRITERS' CONFERENCE—Southampton, NY. July. Write William Roberson, Dir., Library, Southampton Campus, LIU, Southampton, NY 11968.

CHAUTAUQUA INSTITUTION ANNUAL WRITER'S WORKSHOP—Chautauqua, New York. July and August. Write Christopher McMillan, Dir., Schools Office, Box 1098, Chautauqua Institution, Chautauqua, NY 14722.

North Carolina

BLUE RIDGE CHRISTIAN WRITERS CONFERENCE—Asheville, NC. July. Write Yvonne Lehman, P.O. Box 188, Black Mountain, NC 28711.

DUKE UNIVERSITY WRITERS' CONFERENCE—Durham, NC. June. Write Joe Ashby Porter, Dir., The Bishop's House, Duke Univ., Durham, NC 27708.

Ohio

ANTIOCH WRITERS WORKSHOP—Yellow Springs, OH. July. Write Sandra Love, Dir., 133 N. Walnut St., Yellow Springs, OH 45387.

ANNUAL SKYLINE WRITERS' CONFERENCE AND WORKSHOP—N. Royalton, OH. August. Write Pat Poling, Chmn., 11770 Maple Ridge Dr., North Royalton, OH 44133.

Oklahoma

OKLAHOMA WRITERS FEDERATION, INC.—Oklahoma City, OK. May. Write Linda Steele, Dir., 3617 Meadow Ln., Edmond, OK 73013.

ANNUAL WRITERS OF CHILDREN'S LITERATURE CONFERENCE
—Lawton, OK. June. Write Dr. George E. Stanley, P.O. Box 16355, Cameron Univ. Station, Lawton, OK 73505.

OREGON

HAYSTACK PROGRAM IN THE ARTS—Cannon Beach, OR. Summer. Write David Allen, P.O. Box 1491, Portland State Univ., Portland, OR 97207.

PENNSYLVANIA

PHILADELPHIA WRITERS' CONFERENCE—Philadelphia, PA. June. Send SASE to Hermine Pinto, 830 Montgomery Ave., Apt. 406, Bryn Mawr, PA 19010.

ST. DAVIDS CHRISTIAN WRITERS' CONFERENCE—St. Davids, PA. June. Write S. Eaby, Registrar, 1775 Eden Rd., Lancaster, PA 17601–3523.

RHODE ISLAND

NECON—Bristol, RI. July. Write Robert Plante, Dir., Box 3251, Darlington Branch, Pawtucket, RI 02861.

SOUTH DAKOTA

BLACK HILLS WRITERS CONFERENCE—Hill City, SD. July. Write Paul Lippman, Authors and Artists Agency, 4444 Lakeside Dr., Burbank, CA 91505.

WESTERN WOMEN IN THE ARTS ARTISTS RETREAT—Rapid City, SD. September. Write Katherine P. Murdock, Rt. 1, Box 120, Hot Springs, SD 57747.

TENNESSEE

RANDALL HOUSE WRITERS' CONFERENCE—Nashville, TN. May. Write Harrold D. Harrison, 114 Bush Rd., P.O. Box 17306, Nashville, TN 37217.

TEXAS

ANNUAL WRITERS' CONFERENCE—Dallas, TX. September. Write Janet Harris, P.O. Box 830688, M/S, C.N.1.1., Richardson, TX 75083–0688

UTAH

WRITERS AT WORK—Park City, UT. June. Write Steve Wunderli, P.O. Box 8857, Salt Lake City, UT 84108.

VERMONT

BENNINGTON WRITING WORKSHOPS—Bennington, VT. July. Write Brian Swann, Bennington Writing Workshops, Bennington College, Bennington, VT 05201.

ANNUAL BREAD LOAF WRITERS' CONFERENCE—Ripton, VT. August. Write Bread Loaf Writers' Conference, Middlebury College, W. Middlebury, VT 05753.

VIRGINIA

ANNUAL HIGHLAND SUMMER CONFERENCE—Radford, VA. June. Write Dr. Grace Toney Edwards, Dir., Box 5917, Radford Univ., Radford, VA 24142.

WASHINGTON

PORT TOWNSEND WRITERS' CONFERENCE—Fort Worden State Park, WA. July. Write Carol Jane Bangs, CENTRUM, Box 1158, Port Townsend, WA 98368.

PACIFIC NORTHWEST WRITERS CONFERENCE—Tacoma, WA. July. Write Carol McQuinn, Exec. Sec., PNWC, 17345 Sylvester Rd. S.W., Seattle, WA 98119.

SEATTLE PACIFIC CHRISTIAN WRITERS' CONFERENCE—Seattle, WA. June. Write Rose Reynoldson, Humanities Dept., Seattle, Pacific Univ., Seattle, WA 98119.

WEST VIRGINIA

ANNUAL GOLDEN ROD WRITERS CONFERENCE—Morgantown, WV. October. Write George M. Lies, 525 Grove St., Morgantown, WV 26505.

WISCONSIN

SCHOOL OF ARTS AT RHINELANDER—Rhinelander, WI. July. Write Genevieve Lewis, Admin. Coord., School of Arts at Rhinelander, 610 Langdon St., Rm. 727, Madison, WI 53703.

WYOMING

WYOMING WRITERS CONFERENCE—Powell, WY. June. Write Nancy Ruskowsky, Dir., 331 Road 6 RT, Cody, WY 82414.

CANADA

MARITIME WRITERS' WORKSHOP—Fredericton, New Brunswick. July. Write Steven Peacock, c/o Dept. of Extension, Univ. of New Brunswick, P.O. Box 4400, Fredericton, NB E3B 5A3, Canada.

SASKATCHEWAN SCHOOL OF ARTS—Fort San, Sask. Summer. Write Bonnie Burnard, 2550 Broad St., Regina., Sask., S4P 3V7.Canada

INTERNATIONAL

WRITERS TOUR OF GREECE—Athens, Greece. August to September. Write Richard L. Purthill, Dept. of Philosophy, Western Washington Univ., Bellingham, WA 98225.

STATE ARTS COUNCILS

State arts councils sponsor grants, fellowships, and other programs for writers. To be eligible for funding, a writer *must* be a resident of the state in which he is applying. For more information, write to the addresses below.

ALABAMA STATE COUNCIL ON THE ARTS
Albert B. Head, Executive Director
One Dexter Ave.
Montgomery, AL 36130

ALASKA STATE COUNCIL ON THE ARTS
Christine D'Arcy, Director
619 Warehouse Ave., Suite 220
Anchorage, AK 99501–1682

ARIZONA COMMISSION ON THE ARTS
Shelley Cohn, Executive Director
417 W. Roosevelt
Phoenix, AZ 85003

OFFICE OF ARKANSAS STATE ARTS AND HUMANITIES
Bev Lindsey, Executive Director
The Heritage Center, Suite 200
225 E. Markham
Little Rock, AR 72201

CALIFORNIA ARTS COUNCIL
JoAnn Anglin, Public Information Officer
601 N. 7th St., Suite 100
Sacramento, CA 95814

COLORADO COUNCIL ON THE ARTS AND HUMANITIES
Barbara Neal, Executive Director
750 Pennsylvania St.
Denver, CO 80203–3699

CONNECTICUT COMMISSION ON THE ARTS
John Ostrout, Deputy Director
227 Lawrence St.
Hartford, CT 06106

DELAWARE STATE ARTS COUNCIL
Cecelia Fitzgibbon, Executive Administrator
Carvel State Building
820 N. French St.
Wilmington, DE 19801

FLORIDA ARTS COUNCIL
Ms. Peyton Fearington
Dept. of State
Div. of Cultural Affairs
The Capitol
Tallahassee, FL 32399–0250

GEORGIA COUNCIL FOR THE ARTS
2082 E. Exchange Pl., Suite 100
Tucker, GA 30084

HAWAII STATE FOUNDATION ON CULTURE AND THE ARTS
Sarah M. Richards, Executive Director
335 Merchant St., Room 202
Honolulu, HI 96813

IDAHO COMMISSION ON THE ARTS
304 W. State St.
Boise, ID 83720

ILLINOIS ARTS COUNCIL
Eliud Hernandez, Asst. Deputy Director for Programs
State of Illinois Center
100 W. Randolph, Suite 10–500
Chicago, IL 60601

INDIANA ARTS COMMISSION
47 South Pennsylvania St.
Indianapolis, IN 46204

IOWA STATE ARTS COUNCIL
Julie Baily, Director of Partnership Programs
State Capitol Complex
Des Moines, IA 50319

KANSAS ARTS COMMISSION
700 Jackson, Suite 1004
Topeka, KS 66603–3714

KENTUCKY ARTS COUNCIL
Berry Hill, Louisville Rd.
Frankfort, KY 40601

LOUISIANA COUNCIL FOR MUSIC AND PERFORMING ARTS, INC.
Literature Program Associate
7524 St. Charles Ave.
New Orleans, LA 70118

MAINE ARTS COMMISSION
David Cadigan
State House, Station 25
Augusta, ME 04333

MARYLAND STATE ARTS COUNCIL
Linda Vlasak, Program Director
Artists-in-Education
15 W. Mulberry St.
Baltimore, MD 21201

MASSACHUSETTS COUNCIL ON THE ARTS AND HUMANITIES
Pat Dixon, Literature Coordinator
80 Boylston St., 10th Fl.
Boston, MA 02116

MICHIGAN COUNCIL FOR THE ARTS
Barbara K. Goldman, Executive Director
1200 Sixth Ave.
Detroit, MI 48226–2461

MINNESOTA STATE ARTS BOARD
Karen Mueller
Artist Assistance Program Associate
432 Summit Ave.
St. Paul, MN 55102

COMPAS: WRITERS IN THE SCHOOLS
Molly LaBerge, Executive Director
Randolph Jennings, Director, Arts Education Programs
305 Landmark Center
75 W. 5th St.
St. Paul, MN 55102

MISSISSIPPI ARTS COMMISSION
Jane Crater Hiatt, Executive Director
301 N. Lamar St., Suite 400
Jackson, MS 39201

MISSOURI ARTS COUNCIL
Robin VerHage, Program Administrator for Literature
Wainwright Office Complex
111 N. 7th St., Suite 105
St. Louis, MO 63101–2188

MONTANA ARTS COUNCIL
Julia A. Smith, Director, Artist Services
New York Block
48 North Last Chance Gulch
Helena, MT 59620

NEBRASKA ARTS COUNCIL
Jennifer S. Clark, Executive Director
1313 Farnam On-the-Mall
Omaha, NE 68102–1873

NEVADA STATE COUNCIL ON THE ARTS
William L. Fox, Executive Director
329 Flint St.
Reno, NV 89501

NEW HAMPSHIRE STATE COUNCIL ON THE ARTS
Phenix Hall, 40 N. Main St.
Concord, NH 03301–4974

NEW JERSEY STATE COUNCIL ON THE ARTS
Ronnie B. Weyl, Editor, *Arts New Jersey*
4 North Broad Street CN-306
Trenton, NJ 08625

NEW MEXICO ARTS DIVISION
Artist-in-Residence Program
224 E. Palace Ave.
Santa Fe, NM 87501

NEW YORK STATE COUNCIL ON THE ARTS
Gregory Kolovakos, Director, Literature Program
915 Broadway
New York, NY 10010

NORTH CAROLINA ARTS COUNCIL
Deborah McGill, Literature Director
Dept. of Cultural Resources
Raleigh, NC 27611

NORTH DAKOTA COUNCIL ON THE ARTS
Donna Evenson, Executive Director
Black Building, Suite 606
Fargo, ND 58102

OHIO ARTS COUNCIL
727 E. Main St.
Columbus, OH 43205–1796

STATE ARTS COUNCIL OF OKLAHOMA
Ellen Jonsson, Assistant Director
Jim Thorpe Bldg., Room 640
Oklahoma City, OK 73105

OREGON ARTS COMMISSION
835 Summer St., N.E.
Salem, OR 97301

PENNSYLVANIA COUNCIL ON THE ARTS
Peter Carnahan, Literature and Theatre Programs
David Ball, Artists-in-Education Program
Room 216, Finance Bldg.
Harrisburg, PA 17120

RHODE ISLAND STATE COUNCIL ON THE ARTS
Iona B. Dobbins, Executive Director
95 Cedar St., Suite 103
Providence, RI 02903

SOUTH CAROLINA ARTS COMMISSION
Steve Lewis, Director, Literary Arts Program
1800 Gervais St.
Columbus, SC 29201

SOUTH DAKOTA ARTS COUNCIL
108 W. 11th St.
Sioux Falls, SD 57102

TENNESSEE ARTS COMMISSION
320 Sixth Ave., N., Suite 100
Nashville, TN 37219

TEXAS COMMISSION ON THE ARTS
P.O. Box 13406, Capitol Station
Austin, TX 78711

UTAH ARTS COUNCIL
G. Barnes, Literary Arts Coordinator
617 East South Temple
Salt Lake City, UT 84102

VERMONT COUNCIL ON THE ARTS
Mary Margaret Schoenfeld, Grants Officer
136 State St.
Montpelier, VT 05602

733

VIRGINIA COMMISSION FOR THE ARTS
Peggy J. Baggett, Executive Director
James Monroe Bldg., 17th Fl.
101 N. 14th St.
Richmond, VA 23219

WASHINGTON STATE ARTS COMMISSION
110 9th and Columbia Bldg., MS GH-11
Olympia, WA 98504-4111

WEST VIRGINIA DEPT. OF EDUCATION AND THE ARTS
Culture and History Division
Arts and Humanities Section
The Cultural Center, Capitol Complex
Charleston, WV 25305

WISCONSIN ARTS BOARD
Mr. Arley Curtz, Executive Director
131 W. Wilson St., Suite 301
Madison, WI 53703

WYOMING COUNCIL ON THE ARTS
Joy Thompson, Executive Director
2320 Capitol Ave.
Cheyenne, WY 82002

ORGANIZATIONS FOR WRITERS

THE ACADEMY OF AMERICAN POETS
177 E. 87th St.
New York, NY 10128
Mrs. Edward T. Chase, *President*
Founded in 1934 to "encourage, stimulate, and foster the art of poetry," the AAP sponsors a series of poetry readings in New York City and numerous annual awards. Membership is open to all: $45 annual fee includes subscription to the monthly newsletter and free copies of prize book selections.

AMERICAN MEDICAL WRITERS ASSOCIATION
9650 Rockville Pike
Bethesda, MD 20814
Lillian Sablack, *Executive Director*
Members of this association are engaged in communication about medicine and its allied professions. Any person actively interested in or professionally associated with any medium of medical communication is eligible for membership. The annual dues are $65.

734

AMERICAN SOCIETY OF JOURNALISTS AND AUTHORS, INC.
1501 Broadway, Suite 1907
New York, NY 10036
Alexandra Cantor, *Executive Director*
A nationwide organization dedicated to promoting high standards of non-fiction writing through monthly meetings, annual writers' conferences, etc., ASJA offers extensive benefits and services including referral service, numerous discount services, and the opportunity to explore professional issues and concerns with other writers. Members also receive a monthly newsletter. Membership is open to professional free-lance writers of nonfiction; qualifications are judged by Membership Committee. Call or write for application details. Initiation fee: $50; annual dues $120. Phone number: (212)997–0947; fax number (212) 768–7414.

THE AUTHORS LEAGUE OF AMERICA, INC.
(The Authors Guild and The Dramatists Guild)
234 W. 44th St.
New York, NY 10036
The Authors League of America is a national organization of over 14,000 authors and dramatists, representing them on matters of joint concern, such as copyright, taxes, and freedom of expression. Membership in the league is restricted to authors and dramatists who are members of The Authors Guild and The Dramatists Guild. Matters such as contract terms and subsidiary rights are in the province of the two guilds.

A writer who has published a book in the last seven years with an established publisher, or one who has published several magazine pieces with periodicals of general circulation within the last eighteen months, may be eligible for active voting membership in The Authors Guild. A new writer may be eligible for associate membership on application to the Membership Committee. Dues: $75 a year.

The Dramatists Guild is a professional association of playwrights, composers, and lyricists, established to protect dramatists' rights and to improve working conditions. Services include use of the Guild's contracts, business counseling, publications, and symposia in major cities. All theater writers (produced or not) are eligible for membership.

THE INTERNATIONAL SOCIETY OF DRAMATISTS
Box 1310
Miami, FL 33153
Open to playwrights, agents, producers, screenwriters, and others involved in the theater. Publishes *Dramatist's Bible,* a directory of script opportunities, and *The Globe,* a newsletter with information and news of theaters across the country. Also provides free referral service for playwrights.

MYSTERY WRITERS OF AMERICA, INC.
236 W. 27th St.
New York, NY 10001
Priscilla Ridgway, *Executive Secretary*
The MWA exists for the purpose of raising the prestige of mystery and detective writing, and of defending the rights and increasing the income of all writers in the field of mystery, detection, and fact crime writing. Each year, the MWA presents the Edgar Allan Poe Awards for the best mystery writing in a variety of fields. The four classifications of membership are: *active* (open to any writer who has made a sale in the field of mystery, suspense, or crime

writing); *associate* (for professionals in allied fields/writers in other fields); *corresponding* (writers living outside the U.S.); *affiliate* (for unpublished writers and mystery enthusiasts). Annual dues: $50; $25 for corresponding members.

NATIONAL ASSOCIATION OF SCIENCE WRITERS, INC.
P.O. Box 294
Greenlawn, NY 11740

The NASW promotes the dissemination of accurate information regarding science through all media, and conducts a varied program to increase the flow of news from scientists, to improve the quality of its presentation, and to communicate its meaning to the reading public.

Anyone who has been actively engaged in the dissemination of science information is eligible to apply for membership. Active members must be principally involved in reporting on science through newspapers, magazines, TV, or other media that reach the public directly. Associate members report on science through limited-circulation publications and other media. Annual dues: $45.

THE NATIONAL WRITERS CLUB
1450 S. Havana, Suite 620
Aurora, CO 80012
James Lee Young, *Executive Director*

New and established writers, poets, and playwrights throughout the U.S. and Canada may become members of The National Writers Club, a nonprofit representative organization. Membership includes bimonthly newsletter, *Authorship*. Dues: $60 annually, ($50 Associates), plus a $15 one-time initiation fee. Add $20 outside the USA, Canada, and Mexico for annual membership fee.

NATIONAL WRITERS UNION
13 Astor Pl. 7th Fl.
New York, NY 10003

The National Writers Union, a new labor organization dedicated to bringing about equitable payment and fair treatment of free-lance writers through collective action, has over 2,600 members, including book authors, poets, free-lance journalists, and technical writers in eleven locals nationwide. The NWU offers its members contract and agent information, health insurance plans, press credentials, grievance handling, a union newspaper, and sponsors events across the country. Membership is open to writers who have published a book, play, three articles, five poems, one short story or an equivalent amount of newsletter, publicity, technical, commercial, government or institutional copy, or have written an equivalent amount of unpublished material and are actively seeking publication. Dues range from $50 to $120.

OUTDOOR WRITERS ASSOCIATION OF AMERICA, INC.
2017 Cato Ave., Suite 101
State College, PA 16801
Sylvia G. Bashline, *Executive Director*

The OWAA is a non-profit, international organization representing professional communicators who report and reflect upon America's diverse interests in the outdoors. Membership (by nomination only) includes a monthly publication, *Outdoors Unlimited;* annual conference; annual membership directory; contests. OWAA also provides scholarships to qualified students.

PEN AMERICAN CENTER
568 Broadway
New York, NY 10012
PEN American Center is one of 86 centers that comprise International PEN, a worldwide association of literary writers, offering conferences, writing programs, and financial and educational assistance. Membership is open to writers who have published two books of literary merit, as well as editors, agents, playwrights, and translators who meet specific standards. (Apply to nomination committee.) PEN sponsors annual awards and grants and publishes the quarterly *Pen Newsletter;* and the biennial directory, *Grants and Awards Available to American Writers.*

THE POETRY SOCIETY OF AMERICA
15 Gramercy Park
New York, NY 10003
Elise Paschen, *Administrative Director*
Founded in 1910, The Poetry Society of America seeks through a variety of programs to gain a wider audience for American poetry. The Society offers 19 annual prizes for poetry (with many contests open to non-members as well as members), and sponsors workshops, poetry readings, and publications. Maintains the Van Vooris Library of American Poetry. Dues: $35 annually.

POETS AND WRITERS, INC.
72 Spring St.
New York, NY 10012
Elliot Figman, *Executive Director*
Poets & Writers, Inc. was founded in 1970 to foster the development of poets and fiction writers and to promote communication throughout the literary community. A non-membership organization, it offers a nationwide information center for writers; *Poets & Writers Magazine* and other publications; as well as sponsored readings and workshops.

PRIVATE EYE WRITERS OF AMERICA
Robert J. Randisi, *Executive Director*
1952 Hendrick St.
Brooklyn, NY 11234
Private Eye Writers of America is a national organization that seeks to promote a wider recognition and appreciation of private eye literature. Writers who have published a work of fiction—short story, novel, TV script, or movie screen play—with a private eye as the central character are eligible to join as active members. Serious devotees of the P.I. story may become associate members. Dues: $20 (active), $10 (associate). Annual Shamus Award for the best in P.I. fiction.

ROMANCE WRITERS OF AMERICA
13700 Veterans Memorial Dr., Suite 315
Houston, TX 77014
Bobbi Stinson, *Staff Secretary*
The RWA is an international organization with over 80 local chapters across the U.S. and Canada, open to any writer, published or unpublished, interested in the field of romantic fiction. Annual dues of $45, plus $15 application fee for new members; benefits include annual conference, contest, market information, and bimonthly newsmagazine, *Romance Writers' Report.*

SCIENCE FICTION WRITERS OF AMERICA, INC.

P.O. Box 4236
West Columbia, SC 29171
Peter Dennis Pautz, *Executive Secretary*

The purpose of the SFWA, a professional organization of science fiction and fantasy writers, is to foster and further the interests of writers of fantasy and science fiction. SFWA presents the Nebula Award annually for excellence in the field and publishes the *Bulletin* for its members.

Any writer who has sold a work of science fiction or fantasy is eligible for membership. Dues: $56 per year for active members, $39 for affiliates, plus $10 installation fee; send for application and information. The *Bulletin* is available to nonmembers for $12.50 (four issues) within the U.S.; $16 overseas.

SOCIETY FOR TECHNICAL COMMUNICATION

815 15th St., N.W.
Washington, D.C. 20005
William C. Stolgitis, *Executive Director*

The Society for Technical Communication is a professional organization dedicated to the advancement of the theory and practice of technical communication in all media. The 14,000+ members in the U.S. and other countries include technical writers and editors, publishers, artists and draftsmen, researchers, educators, and audiovisual specialists.

SOCIETY OF AMERICAN TRAVEL WRITERS

1155 Connecticut Ave., Suite 500
Washington, D.C. 20036
Ken Fischer, *Administrative Coordinator*

The Society of American Travel Writers represents writers and other professionals who strive to provide travelers with accurate reports on destinations, facilities, and services.

Membership is by invitation. Active membership is limited to salaried travel writers and others employed as freelancers, who have a steady volume of published or distributed work about travel. Initiation fee for active members is $200, for associate members $400. Annual dues: $100 (active); $200 (associate).

SOCIETY OF CHILDREN'S BOOK WRITERS

P.O. Box 296
Mar Vista Station ⚡
Los Angeles, CA 90066
Lin Oliver, *Executive Director*

This national organization of authors, editors, publishers, illustrators, filmmakers, librarians, and educators offers a variety of services to people who write, illustrate for or share an interest in children's literature. Full memberships are open to those who have had at least one children's book or story published. Associate memberships are open to all those with an interest in children's literature. Yearly dues are $35.

WESTERN WRITERS OF AMERICA

1753 Victoria
Sheridan, WY 82801
Barbara Ketcham, *Secretary/Treasurer*

Published writers of fiction, nonfiction, and poetry pertaining to the traditions, legends, development, and history of the American West may join the nonprofit Western Writers of America. Its chief purpose is to promote a more widespread distribution, readership, and appreciation of the West and its literature. Dues are $60 a year. Sponsors annual Spur Awards, Saddleman Award, and Medicine Pipe Bearer's Award for Published Work.

WRITERS GUILD OF AMERICA, EAST, INC.
555 W. 57th St.
New York, NY 10019
Mona Mangan, *Executive Director*

WRITERS GUILD OF AMERICA, WEST, INC.
8955 Beverly Blvd.
West Hollywood, CA 90048
Brian Walton, *Executive Director*

The Writers Guild of America (East and West) represents writers in the fields of radio, television, and motion pictures in both news and entertainment.

In order to qualify for membership, a writer must fulfill current requirements for employment or sale of material in one of these three fields.

The basic dues are $25 a quarter for the Writers Guild West and $12.50 a quarter in the case of Writers Guild East. In addition, there are quarterly dues based on percentage of the member's earnings in any one of the fields over which the Guild has jurisdiction. The initiation fee is $1,000 for Writers Guild East and $1,500 for Writers Guild West. (Writers living east of the Mississippi join Writers Guild East, and those living west of the Mississippi, Writers Guild West.)

AMERICAN LITERARY AGENTS

Most literary agents do not usually accept new writers as clients. Since the agent's income is a percentage (10% to 20%) of the amount he receives from the sales he makes for his clients, he must have as clients writers who are selling fairly regularly to good markets. Always query an agent first. Do not send any manuscripts until the agent has asked you to do so. The following list is only a partial selection of representative agents. Addresses that include zip codes in parentheses are located in New York City (the majority of agents in this list are in New York). More extensive lists of agents can be obtained by sending a self-addressed, stamped envelope to Society of Authors' Representatives, 10 Astor Pl., 3rd Floor, New York, NY 10003 or Independent Literary Agents Assn., Inc., c/o Sanford J. Greenburger Associates, 55 Fifth Ave., New York, NY 10003.

BRET ADAMS, LTD. 448 W. 44th St. (10036)

JULIAN BACH LITERARY AGENCY, INC. 747 Third Ave. (10017)

LOIS BERMAN The Little Theatre Bldg., 240 W. 44th St. (10036)

GEORGES BORCHARDT, INC. 136 E. 57th St. (10022)

BRANDT & BRANDT LITERARY AGENTS, INC. 1501 Broadway (10036)

THE HELEN BRANN AGENCY, INC. 94 Curtis Rd., Bridgewater, CT 06752

BROADWAY PLAY PUBLISHING 357 W. 20th St. (10011)

CURTIS BROWN, LTD. 10 Astor Pl. (10003)

COLLIER ASSOCIATES 2000 Flat Run Rd., Seaman, OH 45679

FRANCES COLLIN LITERARY AGENCY 110 W. 40th St., Suite 1403 (10018)

DON CONGDON ASSOCIATES, INC. 156 Fifth Ave., Suite 625 (10010)

WILLIAM CRAVER WRITERS AND ARTISTS AGENCY 70 W. 36th St., Suite 501 (10018)

JOAN DAVES 21 W. 26th St. (10010–1083)

ANITA DIAMANT 310 Madison Ave., #1508 (10017)

CANDIDA DONADIO & ASSOCIATES, INC. 231 W. 22nd St. (10011)

ANN ELMO AGENCY, INC. 60 E. 42nd St. (10165)

JOHN FARQUHARSON, LTD. 250 W. 57th St., Suite 1914 (10107)

THE FOX CHASE AGENCY, INC. Public Ledger Bldg. #930, Independence Square, Philadelphia, PA 19106

ROBERT A. FREEDMAN DRAMATIC AGENCY, INC. 1501 Broadway, #2310 (10036)

SAMUEL FRENCH, INC. 45 W. 25th St. (10010)

GRAHAM AGENCY 311 W. 43rd St. (10036)

BLANCHE C. GREGORY, INC. 2 Tudor City Place (10017)

HELEN HARVEY 410 W. 24th St., (10011)

JOHN W. HAWKINS & ASSOCIATES, INC. (formerly Paul R. Reynolds, Inc.) 71 W. 23rd St., Suite 1600 (10010)

INTERNATIONAL CREATIVE MANAGEMENT, INC. 40 W. 57th St. (10019)

JCA LITERARY AGENCY, INC. 242 W. 27th St., #4A (10001)

KIDDE, HOYT & PICARD 335 E. 51st St. (10022)

KNOX BURGER ASSOCIATES, LTD. 39 1/2 Washington Square S. (10012)

LUCY KROLL AGENCY 390 West End Ave. (10024)

THE LANTZ OFFICE 888 Seventh Ave. (10106)

LESCHER & LESCHER, LTD. 67 Irving Pl. (10003)

ELLEN LEVINE LITERARY AGENCY 432 Park Ave. S., #1205 (10016)

STERLING LORD LITERISTIC, INC. 1 Madison Ave. (10010)

GERARD MCCAULEY AGENCY, INC. P.O. Box AE, Katonah, NY 10536

MCINTOSH & OTIS, INC. 310 Madison Ave. (10017)

ELISABETH MARTON 96 Fifth Ave. (10011)

HAROLD MATSON COMPANY, INC. 276 Fifth Ave. (10001)

JED MATTES, INC. 175 W. 73rd St. (10023)

MARY MEAGHER The Gersh Agency N.Y., 130 W. 42nd St., 24th Floor (10036)

HELEN MERRILL, LTD. 435 W. 23rd St., #1A (10011)

WILLIAM MORRIS AGENCY, INC. 1350 Ave. of the Americas (10019)

JEAN V. NAGGAR LITERARY AGENCY 336 E. 73rd St. (10021)

HAROLD OBER ASSOCIATES, INC. 40 E. 49th St. (10017)

FIFI OSCARD ASSOCIATES, INC. 19 W. 44th St. (10036)

PINDER LANE PRODUCTIONS, LTD. 159 W. 53rd St. (10019)

RAINES & RAINES 71 Park Ave. (10016)

FLORA ROBERTS, INC. Penthouse A, 157 W. 57th St. (10019)

ROSENSTONE/WENDER 3 E. 48th St. (10017)

RUSSELL & VOLKENING, INC. 50 W. 29th St. (10001)

JOHN SCHAFFNER ASSOCIATES, INC. 264 Fifth Ave. (10001)

SUSAN SCHULMAN AGENCY 454 W. 44th St. (10036)

THE SHUKAT COMPANY, LTD. 340 W. 55th St., #1A (10019)

PHILIP G. SPITZER LITERARY AGENCY 788 Ninth Ave. (10019)

ROSLYN TARG LITERARY AGENCY, INC. 105 W. 13th St., #15E (10011)

WALLACE AGENCY, INC. 177 E. 70th St. (10021)

THE WENDY WEIL AGENCY, INC. 747 Third Ave. (10017)

MARY YOST ASSOCIATES, INC. 59 E. 54th St., #52 (10022)

INDEX TO MARKETS

743

123916